# Paris

written and researched by

## Ruth Blackmore, James McConnachie, Kate Baillie and Tim Salmon

**ROUGH GUIDES**

NEW YORK • LONDON • DELHI

www.roughguides.com

## Introduction to

# Paris

**Long considered the paragon of style, Paris is the most glamorous city in Europe. It is at once deeply traditional – a village-like metropolis whose inhabitants continue to be notorious for their hauteur – and famously cosmopolitan. While such contradictions and contrasts may be the reality of any city, they are the makings of Paris: consider the tiny lanes and alleyways of the Quartier Latin or Montmartre against the monumental vistas from the Louvre to La Défense; the multiplicity of street markets and old-fashioned pedestrian arcades against the giant underground commercial complexes of Montparnasse and Les Halles; or the aristocratic wealth of the grand quarters against the vibrant chaos of the poorer districts.**

At times, Paris can feel inhumanly magnificent, the arrogance of its monuments encompassing the chilly pomp of the Panthéon, the industrial chic of the Eiffel Tower and the almost spiritual glasswork of the Louvre pyramid. Yet it also operates on a very human scale, with exquisite, secretive little nooks tucked away from the Grands Boulevards and very definite little communities revolving around games of boules and the local boulangerie and café. And even as Paris's culture is transformed by its large immigrant and gay populations, even as extravagant new buildings are commissioned and erected, many of the city's streets, cafés and restaurants remain remarkably, defiantly unchanged.

In the great local tradition of the *flâneur*, or thoughtful boulevard-stroller, Paris is a wonderful city for aimless wandering. Relaxed quarters such as the vibrant Marais, elegant St-Germain and romantic Montmartre are ideal for street-browsing, shopping and café-sitting, and the city's lack of open space is redeemed by beautiful formal gardens, by the pathways and pavements that run beside the River Seine, and by endless hidden or unexpected havens. And everywhere you go, historic landmark buildings and contemporary architectural wonders remind you of the city's pride and grandeur – and stop you getting lost.

There are over 150 **art galleries** and **museums** in the city – few of them duds – and an uncounted number of **cafés**, **brasseries** and **restaurants** lining every street and boulevard. The variety of style and decor is hard to beat, ranging from ultra-modern fashion temples to traditional, mirrored palaces, and from tiny *bistrots* where the emphasis is all on the cooking to bustling Vietnamese diners. After dark, the city's theatres and concert halls host inventive and world-leading productions of **theatre** and **dance**, while many classical **concerts** take place in fine architectural settings, particularly chapels and churches. Above all, Paris is a real **cinema** capital, and the city's vibrant cultural mix puts it at the forefront of the **world music** scene.

> Paris is a wonderful city for aimless wandering

# What to see

Paris has a remarkably coherent and intelligible structure. The city lies in a basin surrounded by hills. It is very nearly circular, confined within limits of the **boulevard périphérique**, which follows the line of the nineteenth-century city boundary. At its widest point, Paris is only about 12km across, which, at a brisk pace, is not much more than two hours' **walk** – by far the best way to discover the life of the city. Through its middle, the **River Seine** flows east to west in a satisfying arc. At the hub of the circle, in the middle of the river, anchors the island from which all the rest grew: the **Île de la Cité** (Chapter 1). Here, the city's oldest religious and secular institutions – the cathedral and the royal palace – overlook the river, which was itself both the city's raison d'être and its lifeline.

The city is divided into twenty **arrondissements**, whose spiral arrangement provides a fairly accurate guide to its historical growth. Centred on the Louvre, they wind outwards in a clockwise direction. The inner hub

## The Métro

Physically, the métro just isn't like other subways, starting with the rubber wheels that make central journeys so smooth and quiet. Then there's the way that stations are sometimes so close that you can see people waiting at the next platform down the line, the anti-social spacing of the platform seating, and the mania for double- or treble-barrelled station names like "Maubert-Mutualité" or "Maisons-Alfort-Les-Juillottes". The best stations have distinct characters: check out the funky multi-coloured lamps at Bonnes Nouvelles station, or the cabinets of treasures in Palais Royal-Musée du Louvre.

The métro even has its own style and courtesy culture. You're just supposed to know instinctively when it gets too crowded to remain seated in the wonderfully named strapontins, the folding seats by the doors. It takes a little longer to learn the effortlessly Parisian flick of the wrist that lifts that little steel lever and opens the doors.

Travelling by métro puts you into closer contact with Parisians than you're likely to get anywhere else. As soon as you set foot below ground, greater Paris's true ethnic and social mix is instantly apparent – the old working-class men, the women in West African dress and the kids from the *banlieue*, so conspicuously absent from the posh boulevards. And every new immigrant group fleeing the latest conflict zone sends a wave of buskers down the tunnels. For tourists, the best things about the métro are its reliability – most of the four and a half million journeys a day pass without event, except when there's a strike – and its cost: roughly two thirds of the ticket price is subsidized by the French taxpayer.

of the city comprises arrondissements 1ᵉʳ to 6ᵉ, and it's here that most of the major sights and museums are to be found. The royal palace and museum of the **Louvre** (Chapter 2) lies on the north or **Right Bank** (*rive droite*) of the Seine, which is the more bustling and urban of the city's two sides. To the west of the Louvre runs the longest and grandest vista of the city – **La Voie Triomphale** (covered in Chapter 3) – comprising the Tuileries gardens, the **Champs-Élysées**, the Arc de Triomphe, and the Grande Arche de la Défense, each an expression of royal or state power across the centuries. North of the Louvre is the commercial and financial quarter, where you can shop in the department stores on the broad **Grands Boulevards** (Chapter 4), in the little boutiques of the glazed-over **passages**, or in the giant, underground mall of **Les Halles**. To the east of the Louvre, the **Marais** (Chapter 5) was *the* prestige address in the seventeenth century; along with the **Bastille** next door, it's now one of the most exciting areas of the city, alive with trendy shops, cafés and nightlife.

The south bank of the river or **Left Bank** (Chapter 6), has a quite different feel, quieter and more village-like. The **Quartier Latin** is the traditional domain of the intelligentsia – of academics, writers, artists and the liberal professions – along with **St-Germain**, which becomes progressively snootier as you travel west towards the haughty **Septième**

(Chapter 7), home of ministries, embassies, museums and the Eiffel Tower. Once you move beyond glitzy **Montparnasse**, the southern swathe of the Left Bank (Chapter 8) alternates high-rise flats with charming bourgeois neighbourhoods, with two relatively new commercial developments lining the riverbanks at the limits of the city.

Back on the Right Bank, many of the outer or higher-number arrondissements were once outlying villages, and were gradually absorbed by the expanding city in the nineteenth century – some, such as **Montmartre** (Chapter 9), **Belleville** (Chapter 10) and **Passy** (Chapter 11), have succeeded in retaining something of their separate village identity. The areas to the east were traditionally poor and working-class, while those to the west held the aristocracy and the newly rich – divisions which to some extent hold true today. One thing Paris is not particularly well endowed with is **parks**. The best are on the fringes of the city, notably the **Bois de Vincennes** (Chapter 10) and the **Bois de Boulogne** (Chapter 11), at the eastern and western edges respectively.

The region surrounding the capital, the **Île-de-France**, is dotted with cathedrals and châteaux. Suburban sights such as the Gothic cathedral at **St-Denis** and the royal palace at **Versailles** are covered in Chapter 12, while day-trip destinations a little further afield,

## The Seine

Referred to by some as Paris's main avenue or the city's 21st arrondissement – and by others as a murky, polluted waterway – the Seine is integral to Paris, sashaying through its centre in a broad arc, taking in the capital's grandest monuments on its way. It even makes its way into the city's coat of arms, which depicts a ship sailing on choppy waters accompanied by the words "sec fluctuat nec mergitur" – "it is tossed about but does not sink", a singularly apt motto for a city that has weathered events as turbulent as the French Revolution and the Commune.

The Seine brought the city into being and was for centuries its lifeblood, a major conduit of trade and commerce. Floods however have always been a regular hazard, sometimes sweeping away bridges, houses and lives. One of the worst recorded was in 1176, when the city was almost completely engulfed. The construction of the quais in the nineteenth century helped to alleviate the problem and these tree-lined walkways have today become one of Paris's major assets – attractive and leafy havens from the city's bustle. Traffic is banned from a large section of the Right Bank quai on Sundays, making way for cyclists, rollerbladers and strollers, and in the summer of 2002 tonnes of sand were imported to create a kind of Paris-sur-Mer on the quais, complete with palm trees and deckchairs – an initiative so popular that it's set to become a regular summer fixture.

including the cathedral town of **Chartres** and Monet's garden at **Giverny**, are described in Chapter 13. An equally accessible outing from the capital is that most un-French of attractions, **Disneyland Paris** (Chapter 14).

# When to go

aris's **climate** is fairly stable, with longish stretches of sun (or rain) year round. Summers are generally hot and quite humid, winters cold and windy and spring and autumn mild. It can rain at any time of year, however: summer sees fewer, heavier showers, while at other times of year there's a tendency to drizzle. Spring is deservedly the classic time to visit, with bright days balanced by rain showers. Autumn and winter can be very rewarding, but on overcast days – all-too-common – the city can feel very melancholy. Winter

> **Spring is deservedly the classic time to visit**

sun, on the other hand, is the city's most flattering light, and hotels and restaurants are relatively uncrowded in this season. By contrast, Paris in high summer can be choking, both with fellow visitors and with the fumes of congested traffic. Between July 15 and the end of August, the balance of Parisian and tourist life can become distorted as large numbers of Parisians desert the city for the coast or mountains. There is, too, the **commercial calendar** to consider – fashion shows, trade fairs and the like. Paris hoteliers warn against September and October, and **finding a room** even at the best of times can be problematic. Early spring, autumn if you book ahead, or the midwinter months will be most rewarding.

Average Paris monthly temperatures and rainfall

|  | Jan | Feb | Mar | Apr | May | Jun | Jul | Aug | Sep | Oct | Nov | Dec |
|---|---|---|---|---|---|---|---|---|---|---|---|---|
| max. temp. (°F) | 43 | 45 | 54 | 61 | 68 | 72 | 77 | 75 | 70 | 61 | 50 | 45 |
| min. temp. (°F) | 34 | 34 | 40 | 43 | 50 | 55 | 59 | 57 | 54 | 46 | 41 | 36 |
| max. temp. (°C) | 6 | 7 | 12 | 16 | 20 | 23 | 25 | 24 | 21 | 16 | 10 | 7 |
| min. temp. (°C) | 1 | 1 | 4 | 6 | 10 | 13 | 15 | 14 | 12 | 8 | 5 | 2 |
| rainfall (inches) | 2.2 | 1.8 | 1.4 | 1.7 | 2.2 | 2.1 | 2.3 | 2.5 | 2.2 | 2.0 | 2.0 | 2.0 |
| rainfall (mm) | 56 | 46 | 35 | 42 | 57 | 54 | 59 | 64 | 55 | 50 | 51 | 50 |

## things not to miss

*It's not possible to see everything Paris has to offer on a short trip – and we don't suggest you try. What follows is a subjective selection of the city highlights, ranging from art-house cinemas to Versailles, all arranged in colour-coded categories to help you find the very best things to see, do and experience. All entries have a page reference to take you straight into the guide, where you can find out more.*

**01 Place des Vosges** Page **107** • A superb architectural ensemble, the elegant Place des Vosges is lined with arcaded seventeenth-century buildings and has an attractive and popular garden at its centre.

## 02 The Lady and the Unicorn Page 122 •

Mysterious, allegorical and utterly compelling, the tapestry known as the Lady and the Unicorn is the glowing highlight of the Musée National du Moyen Âge.

| ACTIVITIES | CONSUME | EVENTS | NATURE | SIGHTS |

## 04 Musée Rodin Page 143
• Elegance matched with passion: Rodin's powerful works are shown off to their best advantage in the sculptor's beautiful eighteenth-century mansion.

## 03 Art-house cinemas Page 321 •
With screenings ranging from old Hollywood classics to avant-garde international cinema, Paris is one of the world's best cities to watch the big screen.

## 05 Musée d'Orsay
Page 144 • This converted railway station makes a stylish setting for the Musée d'Orsay's scintillating collection of Impressionist paintings.

**06 Giverny** Page **240** • Monet's serene Japanese garden makes the perfect escape from the hard city streets.

**07 The Louvre** Page **62** • If the brilliance of the Louvre's art collection doesn't bring you to your knees, the awe-inspiring scale of the place will.

**08 Bastille Day** Page **42** • After the military parades down the Champs-Élysées, the capital turns into one big street party.

**09 Palais Royal** Page **90** • Daniel Buren's black-and-white striped column stumps add a splash of folly to this otherwise stately ensemble of enchanting arcades and restful gardens, a perfect retreat from the bustle of the city.

**10 Markets** Page **345** • Paris has long drawn hunters of antiques and bric-a-brac to its flea markets, but it also has fantastic local food markets, which range from the upmarket and organic to the raucous and exotic.

**11** **Musée Jacquemart-André** Page **79** • This sumptuous Second Empire residence, built for the art-loving Jacquemart-André couple, is preserved more or less intact, complete with its fabulous collection of Italian, Dutch and French masters.

**13** **Musée Picasso** Page **105** • The largest collection of Picassos anywhere, superbly displayed in a beautiful Renaissance mansion.

**12** **The Catacombs** Page **154** • The bones that line the passages of the catacombs belong to around six million skeletons – more than twice the population of the living city above.

**14** **Sainte Chapelle**
Page **55** • The glorious interior of the Sainte Chapelle, with its almost entirely stained-glass walls, ranks among the finest achievements of French High Gothic.

**19 Jardin du Luxembourg**

Page **132** • The oasis of the Left Bank: students hang out on the lawns, old men play chess under the trees and children sail toy yachts around the pond.

**20 Disneyland Paris** Page **242** • Kids love it. And who are you to disagree?

**21 Marais bars** Page **287** • Chill out in the trendy, relaxed bars of the Marais quarter.

**22 Versailles** Page **217** • Very slowly, the exquisite furnishings that filled Versailles before the Revolution are being restored to it, giving a melancholy feel to this behemoth of a royal palace.

## 23 Père-Lachaise Page 195 •
Pay homage to Chopin, Oscar Wilde or Jim Morrison – just some of the countless notables buried in what is arguably the world's most famous cemetery.

## 24 Renting blades Page 356 •
On Friday nights, rollerblade fever overtakes the city streets, but it's a cool way to travel at any time.

## 25 Clothes shopping Page 334 •
Add a dash of Parisian chic to your wardrobe.

## 26 Brasseries Page 276 •
Exquisite belle époque interiors, enormous platters of seafood, steak and choucroute, and bustling white-aproned waiters: the city's traditional brasseries offer an authentic slice of Parisian life.

## 27 Pompidou Centre
Page 96 • The Pompidou's radical "inside-out" architecture still draws the crowds, but don't miss its fine modern art museum inside, with significant holdings of works by Matisse, Kandinsky and Picasso.

# Contents

# Using this Rough Guide

We've tried to make this Rough Guide a good read and easy to use. The book is divided into eight main sections, and you should be able to find whatever you want in one of them.

## Front section

The front **colour section** offers a quick tour of Paris. The **introduction** aims to give you a feel for the place and tells you the best times to go. Next, the authors round up their favourite aspects of Paris in the **things not to miss** section – whether it's great cafés, fantastic day-trips or a special museum. Right after this comes the Rough Guide's full **contents** list.

## Basics

The basics section covers all the **pre-departure** nitty-gritty to help you plan your trip, and the practicalities you'll want to know once you're there. This is where to find out how to get there, what paperwork you'll need, what to do about money and insurance, how to get around – in fact just about every piece of **general practical information** you might need.

## The City

This is the heart of the Rough Guide, divided into user-friendly chapters, each of which covers a city district or nearby day-trip destinations. Every chapter starts with an **introduction** that helps you to decide where to go, and a **map** of the area locating all the sights, hotels and restaurants recommended in the guide.

## Listings

Listings contains all the consumer information you need to make the most of your stay, with chapters on **accommodation**, places to **eat and drink, nightlife** and **culture** spots, **shopping** and **sports**.

## Contexts

Read Contexts to get a deeper understanding of what makes Paris tick. We include a brief **history**, and a further reading section that reviews dozens of **books** relating to the city.

## Language

The **language** section offers useful guidance for speaking French and includes a comprehensive **menu reader**. Here you'll also find a **glossary** of French and architectural terms.

## Index + small print

Apart from a **full index**, which includes maps as well as places, this section covers publishing information, credits and acknowledgements, and also has our contact details in case you want to send in updates, corrections or suggestions for improving the book.

## Colour maps

The back section contains five **maps and plans** to give you an overview of the city and help you explore.

# Map and chapter list

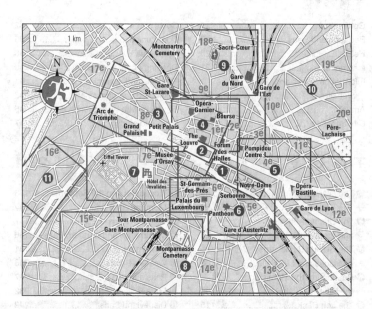

# Contents

# Listings

# Contexts

# Language

# Index + small print

# Colour maps

# Map symbols

Maps are listed in the full index using coloured text.

| | | | |
|---|---|---|---|
| Autoroute | | ◉ | Accommodation |
| Main road | | ▣ | Restaurant |
| Minor road | | ✡ | Synagogue |
| Steps | | 🅿 | Parking |
| Tunnel | | 🆃 | Toilets |
| Railway | | Ⓜ | Metro station |
| TGV | | Ⓡ | RER station |
| Footpath | | Ⓣ | Tram stop |
| Wall | | | Building |
| River | | Church |
| Place of interest | | Park |
| Information office | | Cemetery |

# Basics

# Basics

# Getting there

The quickest way of reaching Paris from most parts of the United Kingdom and Ireland is by air, though from southeast England this is now closely rivalled by the Eurostar rail link, which makes the journey from London to Paris in under three hours. From the US and Canada a number of airlines fly direct to Paris, while from Australia or New Zealand, although you can fly direct to Paris, in general the cheapest airfares are via Asia.

Airfares usually depend on the **season**, with the highest being around early June to the end of August; fares drop during the "shoulder" seasons – roughly September through October and April to May – and you'll get the best prices during the low season, November to March (excluding Christmas and New Year when prices are hiked up and seats are at a premium) and if you book well in advance. Note also that flying on weekends is generally more expensive; price ranges quoted below assume midweek travel.

You can often get cheap flights by going through a **specialist flight agent** – either a consolidator, who buys up blocks of tickets from the airlines and sells them at a discount, or a **discount agent**, who in addition to dealing with discounted flights may also offer special student and youth fares and a range of other travel-related services such as travel insurance, rail passes, car rentals, tours and the like. Some agents specialize in **charter flights**, which may be cheaper than anything available on a scheduled flight, but departure dates are fixed and withdrawal penalties are high. Another possibility is to see if you can arrange a **courier flight**, although you'll need a flexible schedule, and preferably be travelling alone with very little luggage. In return for shepherding a parcel through customs, you can expect to get a deeply discounted ticket. You'll probably also be restricted in the duration of your stay. If you travel a lot, **discount travel clubs** are another option – the annual membership fee may be worth it for benefits such as cut-price air tickets and car rental.

If Paris is only one stop on a longer journey, you might want to consider buying a **Round-the-World** (RTW) ticket. Some travel agents can sell you an "off-the-shelf" RTW ticket that will have you touching down in about half a dozen cities (Paris is on many itineraries); others will have to assemble one for you, which can be tailored to your needs but is apt to be more expensive. Figure on at least $3400 for a RTW including Paris, excluding taxes.

It's also worth noting that an **InterRail Pass** (see p.12) may be useful if you're visiting Paris as part of a longer European trip, since, depending on the number of zones you choose, the pass covers train travel from many parts of Europe to France, and vice versa.

## Booking flights online

Many airlines and discount travel websites offer you the opportunity to book your tickets online, cutting out the costs of agents and middlemen. Good deals can often be found through discount or auction sites, as well as through the airlines' own websites.

### Online booking agents and general travel sites

ⓦtravel.yahoo.com Incorporates a lot of Rough Guide material in its coverage of destination countries and cities across the world, with information about places to eat, sleep etc.
ⓦwww.cheapflights.com Bookings from the UK and Ireland only (for US, ⓦwww.cheapflights.com; for Canada, ⓦwww.cheapflights.ca; for Australia, ⓦwww.cheapflights.com.au). Flight deals, travel agents, plus links to other travel sites.
ⓦwww.cheaptickets.com Discount flight specialists (US only).
ⓦwww.etn.nl/discount.htm A hub of consolidator and discount agent Web links,

maintained by the nonprofit European Travel Network.

@**www.expedia.com** Discount airfares, all-airline search engine and daily deals (US only; for the UK, @www.expedia.co.uk; for Canada, @www.expedia.ca).

@**www.flyaow.com** Online air travel info and reservations site.

@**www.gaytravel.com** Gay online travel agent, offering accommodation, cruises, tours and more.

@**www.geocities.com/thavery2000** Has an extensive list of airline toll-free numbers (from the US) and websites.

@**www.hotwire.com** Bookings from the US only. Last-minute savings of up to forty percent on regular published fares. Travellers must be at least 18 and there are no refunds, transfers or changes allowed. Log-in required.

@**www.lastminute.com** Offers good last-minute holiday package and flight-only deals (UK only; for Australia, @www.lastminute.com.au).

@**www.priceline.com** Name-your-own-price website that has deals at around forty percent off standard fares. You cannot specify flight times (although you do specify dates) and the tickets are non-refundable, non-transferable and non-changeable (US only; for the UK, @www .priceline.co.uk).

@**www.skyauction.com** Bookings from the US only. Auctions tickets and travel packages using a "second bid" scheme. The best strategy is to bid the maximum you're willing to pay, since if you win you'll pay just enough to beat the runner-up regardless of your maximum bid.

@**www.smilinjack.com/airlines.htm** Lists an up-to-date compilation of airline website addresses.

@**www.travel.com.au** Australia ☎1300/130 482 or 02/9249 5444, ☎02/9262 3525; New Zealand ☎0800/468 332, @www.travel.co.nz. Comprehensive online travel company.

@**www.travelocity.com** Destination guides, hot Web fares and best deals for car rental, accommodation and lodging as well as fares. Provides access to the travel agent system SABRE, the most comprehensive central reservations system in the US.

@**www.travelshop.com.au** Australian website offering discounted flights, packages, insurance, and online bookings.

## From the UK and Ireland

The quickest way of reaching Paris from Britain is **by plane** (flying time from London is one hour ten minutes), though the London–Paris **Eurostar** is an attractive alter-native – especially if you live in the southeast – taking you from London Waterloo to the heart of Paris in under three hours, and it's competitively priced. The standard rail- or road-and-sea routes usually cost less, but can be uncomfortable, and if you're going for just a short break, the added journey time could drastically eat into your holiday.

### By plane

The most competitive air fares from the UK and Ireland are with the budget, **no-frills airlines**: EasyJet, Ryanair and bmibaby. Tickets can be purchased by phone or slightly cheaper over the Internet. At the time of writing, **EasyJet** was offering fares from London Luton, Liverpool and Newcastle to Paris Charles de Gaulle (Paris CDG) for around £75. For a similar price, **Ryanair** flies from Glasgow Prestwick, Dublin and Shannon to Paris Beauvais, 65km northwest of the city, while British Midland's low-cost subsidiary, **bmibaby**, was flying from East Midlands airport and Cardiff to Paris CDG for around £60. All fares are inclusive of airport tax. Sometimes you can pick up tickets for even less – as little as £45 – if you book well in advance and travel at off-peak times. A newcomer on the scene, the airline **MyTravelLite**, part of the My Travel group, has started operating flights from Birmingham to Paris Beauvais, and although their standard tickets aren't cheap – £198, excluding tax – it's worth watching out for their frequent sales, which can offer deals such as free flights with only tax to pay, making a total fare of £26.25 return.

The national carriers are rarely cheaper than the low-cost airlines, though they do sometimes have special offers and promotions. Standard fares start at around £80 from London, Birmingham, Manchester and Belfast, £110 from Glasgow and €100 from Dublin, with airport tax extra. **Air France** flies to Paris CDG from Heathrow and London City Airport, as well as from Manchester, Birmingham, Aberdeen, Bristol, Southampton, Newcastle, Edinburgh and Glasgow (via Birmingham), while **British Airways** flies from both Gatwick and Heathrow, and direct from Birmingham, Manchester, Glasgow and Edinburgh. BA also operates flights from Belfast, Newcastle and Aberdeen via London, Edinburgh, Birmingham or Manchester. **British Midland** flies to Paris CDG from Heathrow, and via London from Manchester, Teeside and Belfast. In Ireland, **Aer Lingus** operates daily flights from Dublin and Cork to Paris CDG.

Finding the best deal involves ringing round or checking the websites of the various airlines or specialist agents (see below) and comparing prices and timings. **Students** and those under 26 should enquire about discounts on scheduled flights or contact STA Travel or usit NOW (see below).

### Airlines in the UK and Ireland

**Aer Lingus** UK ☎0845/084 4444, Republic of Ireland ☎0818/365 000, @www.aerlingus.ie.
**Air France** UK ☎0845/084 5111, @www.airfrance.co.uk; Republic of Ireland ☎01/605 0383, @www.airfrance.com/ie.
**bmibaby** ☎0870/264 2229, @www.bmibaby.com.
**British Airways** UK ☎0845/773 3377, Republic of Ireland ☎1800/626 747, @www.ba.com.
**British Midland** UK ☎0870/607 0555, Republic of Ireland ☎01/407 3036, @www.flybmi.com.
**EasyJet** UK ☎0870/600 0000, @www.easyjet.com.
**MyTravelLite** ☎08701/564 564, @www.mytravellite.com.
**Ryanair** UK ☎0871/246 0000, Republic of Ireland ☎0818/303 030, @www.ryanair.com.

### Flight and travel agents

**Co-op Travel Care** UK ☎0870/112 0099, @www.travelcareonline.com. Flights and holidays around the world.
**Destination Group** ☎020/7400 7045, @www.destination-group.com. Portal site for discount airfares.
**Flightbookers** UK ☎0870/010 7000, @www.ebookers.com. Low fares on an extensive selection of scheduled flights.
**Joe Walsh Tours** Republic of Ireland ☎01/676 0991, @www.joewalshtours.ie. General budget fares agent.
**Neenan Travel** Republic of Ireland ☎01/607 9900, @www.neenantrav.ie. Specialists in European city breaks.
**North South Travel** UK ☎ & ☎01245/608 291, @www.northsouthtravel.co.uk. Friendly, competitive travel agency, offering discounted fares worldwide – profits are used to support projects in the developing

world, especially the promotion of sustainable tourism.
**Premier Travel** Northern Ireland ☎028/7126 3333, @www.premiertravel.uk.com. Discount flight specialists.
**Rosetta Travel** Northern Ireland ☎028/9064 4996, @www.rosettatravel.com. Flight and holiday agent.
**STA Travel** UK ☎0870/1600 599, @www.statravel.co.uk. Worldwide specialists in low-cost flights and tours for students and under-26s, though other customers welcome.
**Top Deck** UK ☎020/7244 8000, @www.topdecktravel.co.uk. Long-established agent dealing in discount flights.
**Trailfinders** UK ☎020/7628 7628, @www.trailfinders.co.uk; Republic of Ireland ☎01/677 7888, @www.trailfinders.ie. One of the best-informed and most efficient agents for independent travellers.
**Travel Cuts** ☎020/7255 2082 or 7255 1944, @www.travelcuts.co.uk. Canadian company specializing in budget, student and youth travel.
**usit NOW** Republic of Ireland ☎01/602 1600, Northern Ireland ☎028/9032 7111, @www.usitnow.ie. Student and youth specialists for flights and trains.

## By train

The Channel Tunnel has slashed travelling time **by train** from London to Paris and has also led to a multitude of cut-rate deals on regular train and ferry fares. **Eurostar** operates high-speed passenger trains daily from London Waterloo **to Paris Gare du Nord** via Ashford in Kent and the Channel Tunnel in two hours forty minutes. There are at least thirteen trains daily to Paris Gare du Nord, though only around half stop at Ashford. A once-daily separate, direct train **to Disneyland Paris** leaves at around 9.30am, returning from Paris at around 7.30pm; journey time is under three hours.

The cheapest **standard class return fare** with Eurostar from London to Paris is a weekend day return (also available for travel on bank holidays); this costs £59 and can be purchased up to thirty minutes before departure, but cannot be changed or refunded. For longer trips, there's the "Leisure Apex 14" (£79), which must be bought at least fourteen days in advance and must include a Saturday night, with fixed outward and return dates and no refunds. Sold subject to the same terms, the "Leisure 7" (£99) must be bought at least seven days in advance, while the "Leisure" (£120) is the same ticket but can be purchased up to thirty minutes before departure, providing there are seats available. All these deals have limited availability, so it pays to plan ahead; tickets go on sale three months before the date of travel. Otherwise, for a high-season ticket with changeable departure and return times, bought close to your leaving date, you're looking at £298. **First-class** fares, which include meals, start from £109 for a weekend day return. Standard return fares to **Disneyland Paris** start at £99; these must include an overnight stay and are non-exchangeable and non-refundable. More flexible tickets are available from £149 upwards. The fare for a child aged 4–11 is £50.

There are also special youth and senior tickets available to under-26s and over-60s: these cost £59 and are fully flexible and exchangeable but non-refundable. They're subject to availability, so obviously the sooner you book the better. Tickets for Disneyland, subject to the same conditions, cost £99.

**All tickets** can be bought directly by phone or Internet from Eurostar (see below), from most travel agents, from all mainline rail stations in Britain or through Rail Europe (see below). You can get **through-ticketing** from other mainline stations in Britain. Typical add-on prices for a return ticket to Paris are: £30 from Edinburgh or Glasgow; £20 from Manchester; £13.50 from Birmingham.

### Rail and sea

Crossing the Channel **by sea** works out slightly cheaper than using the Channel Tunnel, but takes considerably longer and is obviously less convenient unless you live in the southeast. You can catch one of the many trains from London Victoria to connect with cross-Channel ferries or hovercrafts, with an onward train service on the other side. However, the **Hoverspeed SeaTrain Express** is now the only combined train/sea ticket package to Paris available. Trains depart from London Charing Cross or Victoria for Dover, connecting with a high-

speed Seacat to Calais, with another train connection to Paris Gare du Nord. **Tickets** cost £44 one way or £56 for a five-day return, £67 for a standard return (no youth price available). Tickets are available from Hoverspeed (see p.14).

### Rail passes

If you plan to use the rail network to visit other regions of France, you might consider buying a **rail pass**. The **Eurodomino Freedom pass**, available from Rail Europe (SNCF) or STA, offers unlimited rail travel through France for between three (£127) and eight (£239) days within a calendar month; passengers **under 26** pay £91 and £179 respectively.

**InterRail** passes cover eight European "zones" and are available for either 12- or 22-day or one-month periods; you must have been resident in Europe for at least six months before you can buy the pass. Two types of passes are available – one for people under 26 and a more expensive one for the over-26s. France is in the zone including Belgium, the Netherlands and Luxembourg. A 12-day pass to travel in this area is £125/182 (under/over 26), a 22-day pass £149/219; a two-zone pass valid for a month is £195/275; a three-zone, £225/320 and an all-zones £265/379. The pass is available from the same outlets as the Eurodomino (see above). InterRail passes do not include travel between Britain and the Continent, although InterRail pass holders are eligible for discounts on rail travel in Britain and Northern Ireland. The InterRail pass and the Eurodomino Freedom pass both give a discount on the London–Paris Eurostar service.

### Rail contacts

**Eurostar** ☎0870/160 6600, ⓦwww.eurostar.com.
**Northern Ireland Railways** ☎028/9089 9411, ⓦwww.nirailways.co.uk. Also sells InterRail passes.
**Rail Europe** ☎0870/584 8848, ⓦwww.raileurope.co.uk. SNCF French Railways.

### By bus

**Eurolines** runs regular bus/ferry services from Victoria coach station in London to Paris, taking around eight hours. Prices are much lower than for the same journey by train, with adult return fares in July and August and around Christmas currently at £50; off-peak fares are currently as low as £32, as long as you book at least thirty days in advance. Regional return fares from England and Wales are available, as are student and youth discounts. If you're visiting other parts of Europe as well, it's worth considering the **Eurolines pass**, covering all the major cities in Europe (including Paris) and valid for either fifteen days (£135; under 26s or over 60s £113), thirty days (£189/153) or sixty days (£239/189); add on around £40 for high-season prices (June to mid-Sept). **Tickets** are available from the company direct (see below), from National Express agents and from most high-street travel agents.

From mid-April to mid-October **Busabout** operates a hop-on, hop-off service, which calls off at Paris, as well as numerous other cities in Europe. There's a link from London to Paris and through tickets from elsewhere in Britain and Ireland. Two types of **pass** are available online or from STA and other affiliated tour agents (as listed on the website). The Consecutive Pass is available for periods of two weeks (£209/189, over 26/under 26) up to three months (£589/529). The Flexi Pass allows anything from seven days' travel within a month (£209/189) to twenty-four days in five months (£549/489).

### Bus contacts

Busabout UK ☎020/7950 1661,
⊛www.busabout.com.
Eurolines UK ☎0870/514 3219, Republic of Ireland ☎01/836 6111, ⊛www.eurolines.co.uk. Tickets can also be purchased from any Eurolines or National Express agent (☎0870/580 8080, ⊛www .nationalexpress.co.uk or ⊛www.gobycoach.com).

### By car

The most convenient way of taking your **car** across to France is to drive down to the **Channel Tunnel**, load it on the train shuttle, and be whisked under the Channel in 35 minutes to Sangatte on the French side, just outside Calais. From there, it's little more than three hours' drive to Paris on the fast autoroutes A26 and A1 (tolls payable).

The Channel Tunnel entrance is off the M20 at junction 11A, just outside Folkestone. The sole operator, **Eurotunnel**, offers a continuous service, with up to four departures per hour (only one per hour midnight–6am). You must arrive at least thirty minutes before departure.

**Tickets** are available through Eurotunnel's Call Centre (see overleaf), over the Internet or from your local travel agent. Fares are calculated per car, not passenger. Tickets are subject to availability, so it pays to plan ahead. Short-stay (two- to five-days) fares have to be bought at least seven days in advance and start at £123, while for longer periods tickets cost upwards of £223 and have to be booked at least fourteen days in advance. It's also worth looking out for special offers: for example, from September to December cheaper tickets are usually offered for the following January to December.

### By car and ferry

The cheapest and quickest cross-Channel options for most car travellers are the **ferry or high-speed catamaran** links between **Dover and Calais**. Crossings from the other south-coast ports to Normandy and Brittany take much longer and are probably only worth considering if Paris is part of a bigger tour of northwest France. The options are Newhaven to Dieppe, Portsmouth to Cherbourg/Le Havre/Caen/St Malo, Poole to Cherbourg and Plymouth to Roscoff. If you're coming from the north of England or Scotland, opting for the Hull–Zeebrugge (Belgium) crossing overnight with P&O North Sea Ferries makes economic sense. From **Ireland**, putting the car on the ferry from Cork or Rosslare outside Wexford to Cherbourg or to Roscoff in Brittany cuts out a lot of driving time.

**Ferry prices** vary according to the season and, for motorists, the size of car. The popular Dover–Calais routeing costs from £120 one-way for a car and two adults in low season, but cheaper deals are regularly available. Return prices are substantially cheaper than one-way fares, but generally need to be booked in advance. Cheap-day return tickets are available from £35; a five-day return starts at £99. Fares from Ireland

(Cork to Roscoff) start at around €200. **Foot passengers** can expect to pay around £20 for a return ticket.

You can either contact the companies direct or go through a travel agent to reserve space in advance (essential during peak season); alternatively, you can browse the Ferrysavers website @www.ferrysavers .co.uk for a list of cheap crossings and book online. The ferry companies will also often offer **special deals** on three-, five- and ten-day returns, or discounts for regular users who own a property abroad. The tour operator **Eurodrive** (☎020/8324 4009, @www .eurodrive.co.uk) can also arrange discounts on ferry crossings and the Eurotunnel for people taking their cars to France, and can book accommodation en route to Paris at competitive rates.

### Ferry contacts

**Brittany Ferries** UK ☎0870/901 2400, Republic of Ireland ☎021/4277 801, @www.brittanyferries .co.uk. Poole to Cherbourg; Portsmouth to Caen and St Malo; Plymouth to Roscoff (March–Nov/Dec); Cork to Roscoff (March–Oct only).

**Eurotunnel** UK ☎0870/535 3535, @www.eurotunnel.com.

**Hoverspeed** UK ☎0870/240 8070, @www.hoverspeed.co.uk. Twenty-four daily departures. Dover to Calais and Ostend; Newhaven to Dieppe.

**Irish Ferries** UK ☎0870/517 1717, Northern Ireland ☎0800/0182 211, Republic of Ireland ☎1890/313 131, @www.irishferries.com. Rosslare to Cherbourg and Roscoff. March to end Sept.

**P&O North Sea Ferries** UK ☎0870/129 6002, @www.ponorthseaferries.com. Hull to Rotterdam and Zeebrugge.

**P&O Portsmouth** UK ☎0870/242 4999, @www.poportsmouth.com. Portsmouth to Cherbourg and Le Havre

**P&O Stena Line** UK ☎0870/600 0600 or 01304/864 003, @www.posl.com. Dover to Calais.

**Sea France** UK ☎0870/571 1711, @www.seafrance.com. Dover to Calais.

### Lift-shares

To arrange a **lift-share**, consult the notice boards of specialist **travellers' bookshops** or put up your own notice. Nomad Books at 781 Fulham Rd, London SW6 (☎020/7736

4000), has a particularly good noticeboard downstairs. The travel magazine **Wanderlust** has a useful "Connections" page and a similar page online worth consulting for possible lift-shares/travel companions; you can also advertise (£5 for up to fifty words; £7 extra for a box number if you don't want your address or phone number published). Address mail to: Connections, *Wanderlust*, PO Box 1832, Windsor, Berks SL4 1YT or log onto their site @www .wanderlust.co.uk.

**Coming back**, contact the French **ride-share organization** Allostop Provoya, based at 1 rue Condorcet, 75009 Paris (Mon–Fri 10am–1pm & 2–6.30pm, Sat 10am–1pm & 2–5pm; M° Cadet/Poissonnière; ☎01.53.20 .42.42, ℻01.53.20.42.44, @allostop @ecritel.fr). You'll be asked to pay a registration fee (from €7 to €10 depending on the distance you want to travel), plus you'll have to give €0.34 per km to the driver. Alternatively, you can buy a €36 membership card good for eight trips over two years.

### Package tours and specialist operators

Any travel agent will be able to provide details of the many operators running **package tours** to Paris, which can work out to be a competitively priced way of travelling, especially if you're flying from a regional airport. Some are straightforward travel-plus-hotel affairs, whereas others are city breaks that include meals and set itineraries. Packages can also be a good idea if you're on a tight schedule – they'll often include transfers to and from your hotel and sometimes guided tours or theatre tickets, which can leave you more time to enjoy your stay. In addition to the addresses below, bear in mind that most of the ferry companies (see above) also offer their own travel and accommodation deals. Maison de la France, the French Government Tourist Office (see p.22), can provide a list of package operators. You'll also find operators listed on the Holiday France website (@www.holidayfrance.org.uk), run by the Association of British Tour Operators to France.

**Bridge Travel** ☎0870/1917 270, @www.bridgetravel.co.uk. Short breaks to Paris and Disneyland; two nights' accommodation plus Eurostars starts from £135.

**British Airways Holidays** ☎0870/442 3820, 🌐www.baholidays.co.uk. Good for Paris accommodation and flight packages from regional airports; prices from £170 for two nights.

**Ebookers** 🌐www.ebookers.com Website with a wide range of discounted package deals, as well as flights only.

**French Travel Service** ☎0870/241 5415, 🌐www.raileurope.co.uk. Two-night city breaks from £148, including Eurostar.

**Go Holidays** ☎01/874 4126, 🌐www.goholidays.ie. Dublin-based French holiday specialists offering breaks to Paris, Disneyland Paris, fly-drive packages, and charter flights in high season (May–Sept) from Shannon and Cork to Paris.

**Kirker Europe** ☎020/7231 3333, 🌐www.kirkerholidays.com. Specialists in quality short breaks in characterful hotels within walking distance of major sights. Departures from most regional airports, with arrival transfers included. Two-night packages in Paris from £239 to £756, depending on accommodation and mode of transport.

**ShortBreaks Ltd** ☎020/8402 0007, 🌐www.short-breaks.com. Specialists in European city breaks. Travelling on Eurostar and spending two nights in Paris in a three-star hotel costs £142.

**Thomas Cook** ☎0870/7500 512, 🌐www.thomascook.co.uk. Long established 24-hour travel agency for package holidays or scheduled flights, with bureau de change issuing Thomas Cook travellers' cheques, travel insurance and car rental.

**Time Off** ☎0845/733 6622. Short breaks to Paris by air or Eurostar (and Orient Express packages) in comfortable central accommodation. Two nights in a one-star hotel, travelling by Eurostar, from £150. Also flights from regional airports; a two-night package flying from Belfast via London for example will cost £217.

**Travelscene Ltd** ☎0870/7779 987, 🌐www.travelscene.co.uk. Short breaks in all grades of accommodation, by air, Eurostar or car/shuttle or car/ferry. Two nights in a two-star hotel by Eurostar from £145; by air from £155.

**VFB Holidays** ☎01242/240336, 🌐www.vfbholidays.co.uk. Flights from regional destinations including Newcastle, Glasgow and Bristol. A four-night break in a three-star hotel travelling with Eurostar starts at £195.

## From the USA and Canada

The most comprehensive range of **flights** from the USA is offered by Air France, the French national carrier, which flies non-stop to Paris Charles de Gaulle airport from selected cities, including New York, Boston and Los Angeles, in most instances daily. However, Air France does tend to be expensive. The **major American competitors** are usually cheaper, but offer fewer non-stop routes. Of those offering non-stop routes, American, Delta and United have the biggest range. American flies to Paris non-stop from Dallas, Miami, Chicago and JFK and has good connections from cities all over the country. Delta flies non-stop from Atlanta, New York and Cincinnati; and United flies non-stop from San Francisco, Chicago, Miami and Washington DC. In addition, Northwest flies direct from Detroit. You could also travel with one of the **European** carriers, such as British Airways or KLM, from the US or Canada to Paris via their home base: London and Amsterdam respectively.

The **lowest discounted scheduled fares** you're likely to get in low/high season flying midweek to Paris are US$448/966 from Chicago, $470/1000 from Houston, $500/1050 from Los Angeles, $430/960 from New York and US$408/635 from Washington DC.

The strong links between France and Québec's Francophone community ensure regular air services **from Canada to Paris**. Air France and Air Canada offer **non-stop services** to Paris from the major Canadian cities. The lowest discounted scheduled fares for midweek travel to Paris will be around CDN$975 (low season) and CDN$1600 (high season) from Montréal and Toronto, and CDN$1400/1900 from Vancouver. **Travel Cuts** and **New Frontiers** are the most likely sources of good-value discounted seats.

### Airlines in North America

The following either fly direct to Paris or via a gateway city.

**Air Canada** ☎1-888/247-2262, 🌐www.aircanada.ca.

**Air France** US ☎1-800/237-2747, 🌐www.airfrance.com; Canada ☎1-800/667-2747, 🌐www.airfrance.ca.

**American Airlines** ☎1-800/433-7300, 🌐www.aa.com.

**British Airways** ☎1-800/247-9297, 🌐www.british-airways.com.

Continental Airlines domestic ☎1-800/523-3273, international ☎1-800/231-0856, ⓦwww.continental.com.
Delta Air Lines ☎1-800/241-4141, ⓦwww.delta.com.
Icelandair ☎1-800/223-5500, ⓦwww.icelandair.com.
Northwest/KLM Airlines domestic ☎1-800/225-2525, international ☎1-800/447-4747; ⓦwww.nwa.com, ⓦwww.klm.com.
United Airlines domestic ☎1-800/241-6522, international ☎1-800/538-2929; ⓦwww.ual.com.
US Airways domestic ☎1-800/428-4322, international ☎1-800/622-1015; ⓦwww.usair.com.
Virgin Atlantic Airways ☎1-800/862-8621, ⓦwww.virgin-atlantic.com.

## Courier flights

Air Courier Association ☎1-800/282-1202, ⓦwww.aircourier.org or ⓦwww.cheaptrips.com. Courier flight broker. Membership (1yr/$29, 3yr/$58, 5yr/$87) also entitles you to ten percent discount on travel insurance and name-your-own-price non-courier flights.
International Association of Air Travel Couriers ☎308/632-3273, ⓦwww.courier.org. Courier flight broker with membership fee of $45/yr.

## Discount agents, consolidators and travel clubs in North America

Air Brokers International ☎1-800/883-3273, ⓦwww.airbrokers.com. Consolidator and specialist in round-the-world and Circle Pacific tickets.
Airtech ☎212/219-7000, ⓦwww.airtech.com. Standby seat broker; also deals in consolidator fares and courier flights.
Airtreks.com ☎1-877-AIRTREKS or 415/912-5600, ⓦwww.airtreks.com. Round-the-world and Circle Pacific tickets. The website features an interactive database that lets you build and price your own round-the-world itinerary.
Council Travel ☎1-800/2COUNCIL, ⓦwww.counciltravel.com. Nationwide organization that mostly specializes in student/budget travel. Flights from the US only. Owned by STA Travel.
Educational Travel Center ☎1-800/747-5551 or 608/256-5551, ⓦwww.edtrav.com. Student/youth discount agent.
New Frontiers ☎1-800/677-0720 or 310/670-7318, ⓦwww.newfrontiers.com. French discount-travel firm based in Los Angeles.
SkyLink US ☎1-800/AIR-ONLY or 212/573-8980,

Canada ☎1-800/SKY-LINK, ⓦwww.skylinkus.com. Consolidator.
STA Travel US ☎1-800/781-4040, Canada ☎1-888/427-5639, ⓦwww.sta-travel.com. World-wide specialists in independent travel; also student IDs, travel insurance, car rental, rail passes, etc.
Student Flights ☎1-800/255-8000 or 480/951-1177, ⓦwww.isecard.com. Student/youth fares, student IDs.
Travac ☎1-800/TRAV-800, ⓦwww.thetravelsite.com. Consolidator and charter broker with offices in New York City and Orlando.
Travelers Advantage ☎1-877/259-2691, ⓦwww.travelersadvantage.com. Discount travel club; annual membership fee required (currently $1 for 3 months' trial).
Travel Cuts Canada ☎1-800/667-2887, US ☎1-866/246-9762, ⓦwww.travelcuts.com. Canadian student-travel organization.
Worldtek Travel ☎1-800/243-1723, ⓦwww.worldtek.com. Discount travel agency for worldwide travel.

## Package tours

Dozens of tour operators offer reasonably priced packages to Paris and the surrounding countryside. Many can put together very **flexible deals**, sometimes amounting to no more than a flight and accommodation; if you're planning to travel in moderate or luxurious style, and especially if your trip is geared around special interests, such packages can work out cheaper than the same arrangements made on arrival. A **tour** is inevitably more confining than independent travel, but it can help you make the most of your time if you're on a tight schedule; and if Paris is your first stop on a longer trip, a tour can ensure a worry-free first few days while you're finding your feet. In addition to the agencies listed below bear in mind that the airlines offer reasonably priced packages including round-trip airfare, hotel, some sightseeing tours and, in the case of fly-drive packages, a rental car.

### Tour operators in North America
**Abercrombie & Kent** ☎1-800/323-7308 or 630/954-2944, ⓦwww.abercrombiekent.com. An upmarket travel agency, which runs a variety of guided tours to France, many including a number of days in Paris. A nine-day tour of Paris, the Loire and Normandy for example starts at $4980.

**AESU Travel** ☎1-800/638-7640, 1-800/695-AESU, or 410/366-5494, ✪www.aesu.com. Tours, independent city stays and discount airfares for under-35s.

**American Airlines Fly Away Vacations** ☎1-800/321 2121, ✪www.aavacations.com. Package tours, fly-drive programmes; a two-night all-in package to Paris costs around $1000.

**CBT Tours** ☎1-800/736-2453 or 312/475-0625, ✪www.cbttours.com. Bike tours throughout France from US$120 per day, some starting or ending in Paris.

**Contiki** ☎1-888/CONTIKI, ✪www.contiki.com. Budget tours to Europe for under-35s. A twelve-day "Best of France" tour, with three days in Paris, starts from around $900, not including airfare.

**Cosmos** ☎1-800/276-1241, ✪www.cosmosvacations.com. Group tours and city breaks with an independent focus. The fifteen-day "Grand Tour of France", including a couple of days in Paris, starts from US$1400 with airfare included.

**Cross-Culture** ☎1-800/491-1148 or 413/256-6303, ✪www.crosscultureinc.com. Billed as tours for travellers rather than "tourists", itineraries include a week in Paris with excursions to Chartres and Giverny.

**Delta Vacations** ☎1-800/654-6559, ✪www.deltavacations.com. Packages, escorted tours and fly-drive programmes.

**EC Tours** ☎1-800/388-0877, ✪www.ectours.com. City tours and individually planned tours of regions like Normandy, the Loire and the French Riviera.

**Europe Train Tours** ☎1-800/551 2085, ✪www.ettours.com. Independent train and escorted motorcoach tours. A three-night London–Paris deal, including travel on Eurostar, starts at $315.

**Europe Through the Back Door** ☎425/771-8303 ext. 298, ✪www.ricksteves.com. Off-the-beaten-track, small-group tours to Europe. The fourteen-day Paris and the Heart of France tour starts from $2350, excluding airfares.

**The French Experience** ☎1-800/283-7262 or 212/986 3800, ✪www.frenchexperience.com. Self-drive tours, apartment rentals, airfare arrangements. A three-night city break starts from $388, excluding airfares.

**Insight International Tours** ☎1-800/582-8380, ✪www.inusa.insightvacations.com. Runs a variety of tours to Europe. Their thirteen-night Jewels of Europe package costs $1125, not including flights.

**Mountain Travel Sobek** ☎1-888/MTSOBEK or 510/527-8100, ✪www.mtsobek.com. Chiefly an adventure-tour company, but also offers a Paris tour for budding photographers.

**New Frontiers** ☎1-800/677-0720 or 310/670-7318, ✪www.newfrontiers.com. Charter airline tickets, city packages and *à la carte* accommodation.

At the time of writing they were offering a five-night special in Paris and Rome from $899, flights included, from Los Angeles.

**Rail Europe US** ☎1-877/257-2887, Canada ☎1-800/361-RAIL, ✪www.raileurope.com. Rail, air, hotel and car reservations.

# From Australia and New Zealand

Most people travelling to Paris from Australia and New Zealand will choose to travel via London, although there are scheduled flights to Paris from Sydney, Melbourne, Brisbane, Cairns, Perth and Auckland. Most airlines can add-on a Paris leg to any Australia/New Zealand–Europe ticket. Flights via Asia, with a transfer or overnight stop in the airlines' home ports, are generally the cheapest option, while those routed through the US tend to be slightly pricier.

Fares vary according to the **season**, and seasons vary slightly depending on the airline, but in general, low season lasts from mid-January to the end of February, and from 1 October to the end of November; high season is from mid-May to the end of August, and from the beginning of December to mid-January. Typical economy fares from Australia in low season start at around A$2000, in high season at A$2500. Fares from Perth or Darwin cost around A$200 less via Asia, or A$400 more via the US. Low-season scheduled fares from Auckland start at around NZ$2200, rising to NZ$2800 upwards in the high season.

## Airlines in Australia and New Zealand

**Air France** Australia ☎02/9244 2100, New Zealand ☎09/308 3352, ✪www.airfrance.com.au.

**British Airways** Australia ☎1300/767 177, New Zealand ☎0800/274 847 or 09/356 8690, ✪www.britishairways.com

**Cathay Pacific** Australia ☎13 17 47, ✪www.cathaypacific.com/au; New Zealand ☎09/379 0861 or 0508/800 454, ✪www.cathaypacific.com/nz.

**Garuda** Australia ☎02/9334 9970, New Zealand ☎09/366 1862, ✪www.garuda-indonesia.com.

**Japan Airlines** Australia ☎02/9272 1111, New Zealand ☎09/379 9906, ✪www.japanair.com.

**KLM/Northwest Airlines** Australia ☎1300/303 747, ✪www.klm.com/au_en; New Zealand ☎09/309 1782, ✪www.klm.com/nz_en.

**Lauda Air** Australia ☎1800/642 438 or 02/9251 6155; New Zealand ☎09/522 5948, ⊛www.aua.com.

**Lufthansa** Australia ☎1300/655 727, ⊛www.lufthansa-australia.com; New Zealand ☎09/303 1529, ⊛www.lufthansa .com/index_en.html.

**Malaysian Airlines** Australia ☎13 26 27, New Zealand ☎0800/777 747, ⊛www .malaysiaairlines.com.my.

**Qantas** Australia ☎13 13 13, ⊛www.qantas .com.au; New Zealand ☎0800/808 767, ⊛www.qantas.co.nz.

**Singapore Airlines** Australia ☎13 10 11, New Zealand ☎0800/808 909, ⊛www .singaporeair.com.

**Sri Lankan Airlines** Australia ☎02/9244 2234, New Zealand ☎09/308 3353, ⊛www.srilankan.lk

**Thai Airways** Australia ☎1300/651 960, New Zealand ☎09/377 0268, ⊛www.thaiair.com.

**United Airlines** Australia ☎13 17 77, ⊛www.unitedairlines.com.au; New Zealand ☎09/379 3800 or 0800/508 648, ⊛www.unitedairlines.co.nz.

## Package tours

A number of **tour operators** organize trips to Paris. As well as flights and accommodation, most companies also offer a range of itineraries that take in the major sights and activities. Bookings are usually made through travel agents who carry a wide selection of brochures for you to choose from. An organized tour is worth considering if you have ambitious sightseeing plans and limited time, are uneasy with the language and customs or just don't like travelling alone.

**Explore Holidays** Australia ☎02/9857 6200 or 1300/731 000, ⊛www.exploreholidays.com.au. Wide variety of accommodation and package tours throughout France, including hotel and apartment stays in Paris.

**Flight Centre** Australia ☎13 31 33 or 02/9235 3522, ⊛www.flightcentre.com.au; New Zealand ☎0800/243 544 or 09/358 4310, ⊛www .flightcentre.co.nz.

**France Unlimited** Australia ☎03/9531 8787. All French travel arrangements, including chateaux stays, Alpine hiking and cycling tours.

**French Travel Connection** Australia ☎02/9966 1177, ⊛www.frenchtravel.com.au. Everything to do with travel to and around France.

**Holiday Shoppe** New Zealand ☎0800/808 480, ⊛www.holidayshoppe.co.nz. Good deals on flights, hotels and packages.

**Silke's Travel** Australia ☎1800/807 860 or 02/8347 2000, ⊛www.silkes.com.au. Gay and lesbian specialist travel agent.

**STA Travel** Australia ☎1300/733 035, ⊛www.statravel.com.au; New Zealand ☎0508/782 872, ⊛www.statravel.co.nz. Fare discounts for students and those under 26, as well as visas, student cards and travel insurance.

**Student Uni Travel** Australia ☎02/9232 8444, ⊛www.sut.com.au; New Zealand ☎09/379 4224, ⊛www.sut.co.nz. Student/youth discounts and travel advice.

**Tempo Holidays** Australia ☎1300/362 844 or 03/9646 0277, ⊛www.yallatours.com.au. Mediterranean specialists offering a variety of package options, including Paris breaks.

**Viatour** Australia ☎02/8219 5400, ⊛www.viator.com. Bookings for hundreds of travel suppliers worldwide, covering all regions of France.

# Red tape and visas

Citizens of EU (European Union) countries, and thirty-one other countries, including Canada, the United States, Australia, New Zealand and Norway, do not need any sort of visa to enter France, and can stay for up to ninety days. All other passport holders must obtain a visa before arrival.

**Visa application** procedures vary from embassy to embassy, so it's best to phone or consult their website first; with the French embassy in London, for example, you have to make an appointment.

Three **types of visa** are currently issued: a transit visa, valid for two months; a short-stay (*court séjour*) visa, valid for ninety days after the date of issue and good for multiple entries; and a long-stay (*long séjour*) visa, which allows for multiple stays of ninety days over three years, but which is issued only after an examination of an individual's circumstances. EU citizens (or other non-visa citizens) who **stay longer than three months** are officially supposed to apply for a **Carte de Séjour**, for which you'll have to show proof of adequate funds to support a long stay in France. However, EU passports are rarely stamped, so there is no evidence of how long you've been in the country. If your passport does get stamped, you can cross the border – to Belgium or Germany, for example – and re-enter for another ninety days legitimately.

## French embassies and consulates overseas

**Australia** Embassy: 6 Perth Ave, Yarralumla ACT 2600 ☎02/6216 0100, ⊛www.ambafrance-au.org. Consulate: 31 Market St, Sydney, NSW 2000 ☎02/9261 5779, ⊛www.consulfrance-sydney.org.

**Britain** Embassy: 58 Knightsbridge, London SW1X 7JT ☎020/7201 1004, ⊛www.ambafrance-uk.org. Consulates: 21 Cromwell Rd, London SW7 2EN ☎020/7073 1201, ⊛www.ambafrance-uk.org; 21 Randolph Crescent, Edinburgh EH3 7TT ☎0131/225 7954, ⊛www.consulfrance-edimbourg.org.

**Canada** Embassy: 42 Promenade Sussex, Ottawa, ON K1M 2C9 ☎613/789 1795, ⊛www .ambafrance-ca.org. Consulates: 1 place Ville Marie Bureau 2601, Montréal, Québec H3B 4S3 ☎514/878 4385, ⊛www.consulfrance-montreal.org; 25 rue St-Louis, Québec QC G1R 3Y8 ☎418/694 2294, ⊛www.consulfrance-quebec.org; 130 Bloor St West, Suite 400, Toronto, ON M5S 1N5 ☎416/925 8041, ⊛www.consulfrance-toronto.org; 1130 West Pender St, Suite 1100, Vancouver BC V6E 4A4 ☎604/681 4345, ⊛www.consulfrance-vancouver.org; 777 Main St, Suite 800, Moncton, New Brunswick E1C 1E9 ☎506/857 4191, ⊛www.consulfrance-moncton.org.

**Ireland** 36 Ailesbury Rd, Dublin 4 ☎01/260 1666, ⊛www.ambafrance.ie.

**New Zealand** 34–42 Nanners St, Wellington ☎04/384 2555, ⊛www.ambafrance-nz.org.

**USA** Embassy: 4101 Reservoir Rd NW, Washington DC 20007 ☎202/944 6195, ⊛www.info-france-usa.org. Consulates: Prominence in Buckhead, Suite 1840, 3475 Piedmont Rd, NE, Atlanta, GA 30305 ☎404/495 1660, ⊛www.consulatfranceatlanta.org; Park Square Building, Suite 750, 31 St James Ave, Boston, MA 02116 ☎617/542 7374, ⊛www.consulfrance-boston.org; 737 North Michigan Ave, Suite 2020, Chicago, IL 60611 ☎312/787 5360, ⊛www.consulfrance-chicago.org; 777 Post Oak Boulevard, Suite 600, Houston, Texas 77056 ☎713/572 2799, ⊛www.consulfrance-houston.org; 10990 Wilshire Blvd, Suite 300, Los Angeles, CA 90024 ☎310/235 3200, ⊛www.consulfrance-losangeles.org; 934 Fifth Ave, New York, NY 10021 ☎212/606 3689, ⊛www.consulfrance-newyork.org; One Biscayne Tower, Suite 1710, 2 South Biscayne Blvd, Miami, Florida 33131 ☎305/372 9799, ⊛www.consulfrance-miami.org; 1340 Poydras St, Amoco Building, Suite 1710, New Orleans, Louisiana 70112 ☎504/523 5772, ⊛www.consulfrance-nouvelleorleans.org; 540 Bush St, San Francisco CA 94108 ☎ 415/397 4330, ⊛www.consulfrance-sanfrancisco.org.

# Health

Citizens of all EU countries are entitled to take advantage of French health services under the same terms as residents, if they have the correct documentation. British citizens need form E111, available from post offices. Non-EU citizens have to pay for most medical attention and are strongly advised to take out some form of travel insurance (see opposite).

Under the French Social Security system, every hospital visit, doctor's consultation and prescribed medicine incurs a charge, which you have to pay upfront. Although all EU citizens with the correct documents are entitled to a refund of 70–75 percent of the standard fee for medical and dental expenses, providing the doctor is government registered (a *médecin conventionné*), this can still leave a hefty shortfall, especially after a stay in hospital.

## Doctors and pharmacies

To find a **doctor**, ask at any *pharmacie*, local police station, tourist office or your hotel. Alternatively, look under "Médecins" in the Yellow Pages of the phone directory. An average consultation fee should be between €20 and €25. You will be given a *Feuille de Soins* (statement of treatment) for later insurance claims. Prescriptions should be taken to a *pharmacie* and must be paid for; the medicines will have little stickers (*vignettes*) attached to them, which you should remove and stick to your *Feuille de Soins*, together with the prescription itself.

In serious emergencies you will always be admitted to the nearest hospital (*hôpital*), either under your own power or by ambulance, which even French citizens must pay for; many people call the fire brigade (*pompiers*) instead, who are equipped to deal with medical emergencies and are the fastest and most reliable emergency service. For a list of phone numbers to call in a medical emergency, consult the "Directory", p.375.

**Pharmacies**, signalled by an illuminated green cross, can give advice on minor complaints and prescribe appropriate medicines. They're also equipped to provide first-aid help on request (for a fee). They keep normal shop hours (roughly 9am–7pm), and a number stay open all night: details of the nearest one open are posted in all pharmacies. Pharmacies open at night include Dérhy/Pharmacie des Champs-Élysées, 84 av des Champs-Élysées, 8e (☎01.45.62.02.41; 24hr; Mº George-V); Pharmacie Européenne, 6 place de Clichy, 9e (☎01.48.74.65.18; 24hr; Mº Place-de-Clichy); Pharmacie des Halles, 10 bd Sébastopol, 4e (☎01.42.72.03.23; Mon–Sat 9am–midnight, Sun noon–midnight; Mº Châtelet); Pharmacie Matignon, 2 rue Jean-Mermoz, 8e (☎01.43.59.86.55; daily 8.30am–2am; Mº Franklin-D.Roosevelt); Pharmacie Internationale de Paris, 5 pl Pigalle, 9e (☎01.48.78.38.12; daily to 1am; Mº Pigalle); Grande Pharmacie de la Nation, 13 place de la Nation, 11e (☎01.43.73.24.03; Mon noon–midnight, Tues–Sat 8am–midnight, Sun 8pm–midnight; Mº Nation).

# Insurance

Even though EU health care privileges apply in France, you'd do well to take out an insurance policy before travelling to cover against theft, loss and illness or injury. Before paying for a new policy, however, it's worth checking whether you are already covered: some all-risks home insurance policies may cover your possessions when overseas, and many private medical schemes include cover when abroad. In Canada, provincial health plans usually provide partial cover for medical mishaps overseas, while holders of official student/teacher/youth cards in Canada and the US are entitled to meagre accident coverage and hospital in-patient benefits. Students will often find that their student health coverage extends during the vacations and for one term beyond the date of last enrolment.

After exhausting the possibilities above, you might want to contact a specialist travel insurance company, or consider the travel insurance deal we offer (see box). A typical travel insurance policy usually provides cover for the loss of baggage, tickets and – up to a certain limit – cash or cheques, as well as cancellation or curtailment of your journey. Many policies can be chopped and changed to exclude coverage you don't need – for example, sickness and accident benefits can often be excluded or included at will. If you do take medical coverage, ascertain whether benefits will be paid as treatment proceeds or only after return home, and whether there is a 24-hour medical emergency number. When securing baggage cover, make sure that the per-article limit – typically under £500 – will cover your most valuable possession. If you need to make a claim, you should keep receipts for medicines and medical treatment (see Health, opposite), and in the event you have anything stolen, you must obtain an official statement from the police (called a *constat de vol*).

## Rough Guides travel insurance

**Rough Guide** offers its own low-cost travel insurance, especially customized for our statistically low-risk readers by a leading British broker, provided by the American International Group (AIG) and registered with the British regulatory body, GISC (the General Insurance Standards Council).

There are five main Rough Guides insurance plans: **No Frills** for the bare minimum for secure travel; **Essential**, which provides decent all-round cover; **Premier** for comprehensive cover with a wide range of benefits; Extended Stay for cover lasting two months to a year; and **Annual multi-trip**, a cost-effective way of getting Premier cover if you travel more than once a year. Premier, Annual Multi-Trip and Extended Stay policies can be supplemented by a **"Hazardous Pursuits Extension"** if you plan to indulge in sports considered dangerous, such as scuba-diving or trekking.

For a **policy quote**, call the Rough Guide Insurance Line: toll-free in the UK ☎0800/015 09 06 or ☎+44 1392 314 665 from elsewhere. Alternatively, get an online quote at www.roughguides.com/insurance

# Information, maps and websites

## Information

The main Paris **tourist office** is at 127 av des Champs-Élysées, 8ᵉ (daily 9am–8pm, except Oct–March Sun 11am–7pm; ☎08.92 .68.31.12, ⓦwww.paris-touristoffice.com; Mᵒ Georges V). There are branch offices at the Gare de Lyon (Mon–Sat 8am–8pm) and the Eiffel Tower (May–Sept daily 11am–6.40pm). They give out information on Paris and the suburbs, can book hotel accommodation for you, and they also sell the Carte Musées et Monuments (see p.33), travel passes and phone cards.

It's also worth picking up the free *Paris Map* – this might be behind the counter, so you'll need to ask. Within the new Carrousel du Louvre, underground below the triumphal arch at the east end of the Tuileries, is the **Espace du Tourisme d'Île de France** (daily except Tues 10am–7pm; ☎01.44.50.19.98), which has stylishly presented information on attractions and activities in Paris and the surrounding area.

Alternative sources of information are the **Hôtel de Ville information office** – Bureau d'Accueil – at 29 rue de Rivoli, 4ᵉ (Mon–Sat 9am–6pm; ☎01.42.76.43.43, ⓦwww.paris-france.org; Mᵒ Hôtel-de-Ville). For detailed what's-on information it's worth buying one of Paris's **listings magazines**, *L'Officiel des Spectacles* (€0.35), *Pariscope* (€0.40) or *Zurban* (€0.80), available from all newsagents and kiosks. *Pariscope*, in particular, has a huge and comprehensive section on films and a small English section with weekly entertainment highlights, restaurant reviews and a special interest page put together by *Time Out*. On a Wednesday, both *Le Monde* and *Le Figaro* bring out free listings supplements, offering a more discerning selection of events for the week. You could also keep a look out for the free weekly listings newspaper, *A nous Paris*, which comes out every Monday and is available from métro stations.

## French Government Tourist Offices Abroad (Maisons de la France)

The general website ⓦwww.franceguide .com has email addresses for all tourist offices below.

**Australia** Level 20, 25, Bligh St, Sydney, NSW 2000 ☎02/9231 5244, ℻02/9221 8682.

**Canada** 1981 av McGill College, Suite 490, Montréal, QC H3A 2W9 ☎514/288 4264, ℻514/845 4868.

**Ireland** 30 Merrion St Upper, Dublin 2 ☎1560/235 235.

**UK** 178 Piccadilly, London W1V 0AL ☎09068/244 123 (60p/min), ℻020/7493 6594.

**USA** 444, Madison Avenue, New York, NY 10022 ☎410/286 8310, ℻212/838 7855; John Hancock Center, Suite 3214, 875 North Michigan Avenue, Chicago, IL 60611 ☎312/751 7800, ℻312/337 6339; 9454 Wilshire Blvd, Suite 715, Beverly Hills, CA 90212 ☎310/271 6665, ℻310/276 2835.

*Note that New Zealand does not have a French Government Tourist Office.*

## Maps

The maps in this guide and the free *Paris Map* (see above) should be adequate for a short sightseeing stay, but for a more detailed map your best bet is the pocket-sized *L'indispensable Plan de Paris* 1:15,000, published by Atlas Indispensable (€6); it comes in a robust plastic cover, and gives two double pages to most arrondissements, plus métro, bus and suburban maps, and full A-Z street listings. Also very detailed, but rather more unwieldy is the Michelin no. 10, the 1:10,000 *Plan de Paris*. More conveniently sized are the *Rough Guide Map: Paris*, produced on waterproof paper, and the *Falkplan*, which folds out only as you need it. If you're staying any length of time you might want to go for one of the various bound, book-form street plans (such as the Michelin *Paris Plan*, or the smaller L'indispensable *Paris Pratique*), which have a street index, bus-route diagrams, useful addresses, and show car parks and one-way streets.

## Map outlets

### In the UK and Ireland

**Blackwell's Map and Travel Shop** 50 Broad St, Oxford OX1 3BQ ☎01865/793550, ⊚http://maps.blackwell.co.uk/index.html.
**Easons Bookshop** 40 O'Connell St, Dublin 1 ☎01/873 3811, ⊚www.eason.ie.
**Heffers Map and Travel** 20 Trinity St, Cambridge CB2 1TJ ☎01865/333536, ⊚www.heffers.co.uk.
**Hodges Figgis Bookshop** 56–58 Dawson St, Dublin 2 ☎01/677 4754, ⊚www.hodgesfiggis.com.
**James Thin Booksellers** 53–59 South Bridge, Edinburgh EH1 1YS ☎0131/622 8222, ⊚www.jthin.co.uk.
**The Map Shop** 30a Belvoir St, Leicester LE1 6QH ☎0116/247 1400, ⊚www.mapshopleicester.co.uk.
**National Map Centre** 22–24 Caxton St, London SW1H 0QU ☎020/7222 2466, ⊚www.mapsnmc.co.uk, ⊜info@mapsnmc.co.uk.
**Newcastle Map Centre** 55 Grey St, Newcastle-upon-Tyne, NE1 6EF ☎0191/261 5622.
**Ordnance Survey Ireland** Phoenix Park, Dublin 8 ☎01/8025 349, ⊚www.irlgov.ie/osi, ⊜osni@osni.gov.uk.
**Ordnance Survey of Northern Ireland** Colby House, Stranmillis Ct, Belfast BT9 5BJ ☎028/9025 5755, ⊚www.osni.gov.uk.
**Stanfords** 12–14 Long Acre, WC2E 9LP ☎020/7836 1321, ⊚www.stanfords.co.uk, ⊜sales@stanfords.co.uk. Maps available by mail, phone order, or email. Other branches within British Airways offices at 156 Regent St, London W1R 5TA ☎020/7434 4744, and 29 Corn St, Bristol BS1 1HT ☎0117/929 9966.
**The Travel Bookshop** 13–15 Blenheim Crescent, W11 2EE ☎020/7229 5260, ⊚www.thetravelbookshop.co.uk.

### In the US and Canada

**Adventurous Traveler.com** US ☎1-800/282-3963, ⊚adventuroustraveler.com.
**Book Passage** 51 Tamal Vista Blvd, Corte Madera, CA 94925 ☎1-800/999-7909, ⊚www.bookpassage.com.
**Distant Lands** 56 S Raymond Ave, Pasadena, CA 91105 ☎1-800/310-3220, ⊚www.distantlands.com.
**Elliot Bay Book Company** 101 S Main St,

Seattle, WA 98104 ☎1-800/962-5311, ⊚www.elliotbaybook.com.
**Globe Corner Bookstore** 28 Church St, Cambridge, MA 02138 ☎1-800/358-6013, ⊚www.globercorner.com.
**Map Link** 30 S La Patera Lane, Unit 5, Santa Barbara, CA 93117 ☎1-800/962-1394, ⊚www.maplink.com.
**Rand McNally** US ☎1-800/333-0136, ⊚www.randmcnally.com. Around thirty stores across the US; dial ext 2111 or check the website for the nearest location.
**The Travel Bug Bookstore** 2667 W Broadway, Vancouver V6K 2G2 ☎604/737-1122, ⊚www.swifty.com/tbug.
**World of Maps** 1235 Wellington St, Ottawa, Ontario K1Y 3A3 ☎1-800/214-8524, ⊚www.worldofmaps.com.

### In Australia and New Zealand

**The Map Shop** 6–10 Peel St, Adelaide, SA 5000 ☎08/8231 2033, ⊚www.mapshop.net.au.
**MapWorld** 173 Gloucester St, Christchurch ☎0800/627 967 or 03/374 5399, ⊚www.mapworld.co.nz.
**Mapland** 372 Little Bourke St, Melbourne, Victoria 3000 ☎03/9670 4383, ⊚www.mapland.com.au.
**Perth Map Centre** 900 Hay St, Perth, WA 6000 ☎08/9322 5733, ⊚www.perthmap.com.au.
**Specialty Maps** 46 Albert St, Auckland 1001 ☎09/307 2217, ⊚www.specialtymaps.co.nz.

## Useful websites

Many useful **websites** are listed throughout "Basics", especially for tour operators. Below are some more general, useful or interesting sites (most offer a choice between English or French).

⊚**www.insee.fr** The website of the National Institute of Statistics and Economical Studies – France in facts and figures.
⊚**www.pagesjaunes.fr** French yellow pages online.
⊚**www.paris.fr** The Paris mairie (town hall) website for information on the day-to-day running of Paris, events and visiting Paris.
⊚**www.parisbalades.com** Well-orchestrated site that zooms in on Parisian localities with in-depth historical and architectural detail.
⊚**www.zingueurs.com** All you need to know about Parisian *bistrot* life, with concerts, exhibitions and shows listings.
⊚**www.galerieslafayette.com** One of Paris's largest department stores online for an insight into the latest fashions in Paris – you can even create

your own three-dimensional model to try on the new collections.

ⓦ**www.parissi.com** A listings website that has its finger on the pulse and can keep you up-to-date on events in Paris. Particularly good for nightlife.

ⓦ**www.culture.fr** The Ministry of Culture and Communication's site, with press releases and links to various cultural organizations in France.

ⓦ**www.jazzfrance.com** Brilliant bilingual site for jazz fans, covering everything from venues and festivals, and an up-to-date diary. Links to music stores.

ⓦ**www.zurban.com** An online rendering (in French only) of the weekly listings mag.

ⓦ**www.paris-touristoffice.com** The website of the Paris tourist office, with impressive detail on Paris and France – though unfortunately not all as up-to-date as it could be. Links to other sites including universities and a national ballet diary.

ⓦ**www.lemonde.fr** In French only; a version of the highbrow daily newspaper.

ⓦ**www.webbar.fr** The website of Paris's best cybercafé, with details of the events it hosts – from art exhibitions to DJ-nights, and even cyber exhibitions on the site itself.

ⓦ**www.parisvoice.com** The online version of the anglophone expat magazine (see p.38), with reviews of restaurants and shops, as well as current shows and exhibitions.

# Arrival

Many British travellers to Paris arrive by Eurostar at the central Gare du Nord train station, while more far-flung visitors are likely to land at one of Paris's two main airports: Charles de Gaulle and Orly, both well connected to the city centre by public transport.

Trains from other parts of France or continental Europe draw in at one of the six central mainline stations. Almost all the **buses** coming into Paris – whether international or domestic – arrive at the main **gare routière** at 28 av du Général-de-Gaulle, Bagnolet, at the eastern edge of the city; métro Gallieni (line 3) links it to the centre. If you're **driving** in yourself, don't try to go straight across the city to your destination. Use the ring road – the **boulevard périphérique** – to get around to the nearest *porte*: it's much quicker, except at rush hour, and far easier to navigate.

**Disneyland Paris** is linked by bus to both Charles de Gaulle and Orly airports: for details of these services, plus train links from the centre to the purpose-built Marne La Vallée TGV, see p.243.

## By air

The two main Paris **airports** that deal with international flights are Roissy-Charles de Gaulle and Orly, both well connected to the centre. Information on them can be found on ⓦwww.adp.fr. A third airport, Beauvais, is used by some of the low-cost airlines.

### Roissy-Charles de Gaulle Airport

**Roissy-Charles de Gaulle Airport** (24hr information in English ☏01.48.62.22.80), usually referred to as Charles de Gaulle and abbreviated to CDG or Paris CDG, is 23km northeast of the city. The airport has two main terminals, CDG 1 and CDG 2. Make sure you know which terminal your flight is departing from when it's time to leave Paris, so you take the correct bus or get off at the right train station. A TGV station links the airport (CDG 2) with Bordeaux, Brussels, Lille, Lyon, Nantes, Marseille and Rennes.

There are various ways of getting to the centre of Paris: the cheapest and probably the quickest is the **Roissyrail** train link which runs on RER line B (every fifteen minutes from 5am until midnight; 30min; €7.70 one-way). You can pick it up direct at CDG 2, but from CDG 1 you have to get a shuttle bus (*navette*) to the RER station. The train stops at Gare du Nord, Châtelet-Les Halles, St-Michel and Denfert-Rochereau, all of which have métro stations for onward travel. On the way back to the airport, if you're picking up the RER from the Gare du Nord, note that all but the first train of the day depart from platform 43, where there's an English-speaking **information desk** indicated by a large question mark (daily 8am–8pm); confirm here which station you should get off at by checking the airline code on your ticket against the information board, or ask the staff to help you. A number of RER stopping trains also serve the airports; these only take about five minutes more than the Roissyrail to get to the centre, though they aren't designed to accommodate luggage.

An alternative to the RER, and costing only a little more, is the **Roissybus** which connects CDG 1 and CDG 2 with the Opéra-Garnier (corner of rues Auber and Scribe; RER Auber/métro Opéra); it runs every fifteen minutes from 5.45am to 11pm, costs €8 one-way and takes around 45 minutes. **Air France** also operates two bus services (information in English ☎01.41.56.89.00, ⊛www.cars-airfrance.com). The green-coded line 2 (€10 one way, €17 return) leaves from CDG 1 and CDG 2 every fifteen minutes from 5.45am to 11pm stopping at avenue Carnot, outside Charles-de-Gaulle-Étoile RER/métro between the Arc de Triomphe and rue Tilsitt before terminating at Porte Maillot (métro) on the northwest edge of the city. The yellow-coded line 4 (€11.50 one way, €19.55 return) departs from CDG 1 and CDG 2 every thirty minutes from 7am to 9.30pm, terminating near Gare Montparnasse and stopping at Gare de Lyon; journey times vary from forty minutes to over an hour depending on traffic. Leaving Paris, the green-coded line 2 (for CDG 2) departs from 1 av Carnot, right outside the RER exit of Charles-de-Gaulle-Étoile, and from Porte Maillot on Boulevard Gouvion St-Cyr. The yellow-coded line 4 for both CDG 1 and CDG 2 leaves from 20 bis bd Diderot outside Gare de Lyon and near Gare Montparnasse at rue du Commandant

René-Mouchotte in front of the *Méridien Hotel*.

A further option worth considering if you don't want the hassle of public transport and are reluctant to pay out for a taxi is a **minibus** door-to-door service, called Blue Vans (€14.50 per head if there are two or more people, €22 for a single person; no extra charge for luggage; 6am–7.30pm). Bookings must be made at least 48 hours in advance on ☎01.30.11.13.00, by fax (℻01.30.11.13.09) or via their website ⊛www.airportshuttle.fr. **Taxis** into central Paris from CDG cost around €36, plus a small luggage supplement (€0.90 per piece of luggage), and should take between fifty minutes and one hour. Note that if your flight gets in after midnight your only means of transport is a taxi.

## Orly Airport

**Orly Airport** (information in English daily 6am–11.30pm ☎01.49.75.15.15), 14km south of Paris, has two terminals, Orly Sud (south; for international flights) and Orly Ouest (west; for domestic flights), linked by shuttle bus but easily walkable. One of the easiest ways into the centre is the **Orlyval**, a fast train shuttle link to RER line B station Antony, followed by métro connection stops at Denfert-Rochereau, St-Michel and Châtelet-Les Halles; it runs every four to eight minutes Monday to Saturday from 6.30am to 11pm, from 7am Sundays and holidays (€8.65 one-way; 35min to Châtelet). Another service connecting with the RER is the **Orlyrail** bus–rail link: a shuttle bus takes you to RER line C station Pont de Rungis, from where the Orlyrail train leaves every twenty minutes from 5.50am to 10.50pm for the Gare d'Austerlitz and other métro connection stops (€5.15 one-way; train 35min, total journey around 50min). Leaving Paris, the train runs from Gare d'Austerlitz from 5.50am to 11.50pm.

Two fast bus services are also worth considering: the **Orlybus**, which runs to Denfert-Rochereau RER/métro station in the 14e (every 15min, 6am–11.30pm; €5.50 one way; around 30min); and the **Jetbus**, which runs to métro Villejuif-Louis-Aragon (métro line 7) every fifteen minutes between 6.15am and 10.15pm (€4.80; 15min). Finally, an **Air France bus** (information in English ☎01.41.56.89.00, ⓦwww.cars-airfrance .com) runs to the Invalides Air France Terminal on rue Esnault Peletrie, close to Les Invalides itself, via Montparnasse (stopping at Porte d'Orléans and Duroc if requested in advance) every fifteen minutes from 6am to 11.30pm (€7.50 one-way, €12.75 return; about 35min). Leaving Paris, the bus can be caught from the Invalides Air France Terminal and from Montparnasse on rue du Commandant-René-Mouchotte in front of the *Méridien Hotel*.

**Taxis** take about 35 minutes to reach the centre of Paris and cost at least €20.

## Beauvais Airport

**Beauvais airport** (☎08.92.68.20.66, ⓦwww.airportbeauvais.com), 65km north-west of Paris, is served by Ryanair from Dublin, Shannon and Glasgow and My TravelLite from Birmingham. Coaches (€20 return) shuttle between the airport and Porte Maillot in the 17e arrondissement, connected by métro line 1 with the centre, and take about an hour. The coach leaves between fifteen and thirty minutes after the flight has arrived and about three hours before the flight departs on the way back. Tickets can be bought at Arrivals or from the Beauvais shop at 1 boulevard Pershing, near the Porte Maillot terminal.

## By train

Paris has six mainline train stations. **Eurostar** (☎08.36.35.35.39, ⓦwww .eurostar.com) terminates at **Gare du Nord**, rue Dunkerque, in the northeast of the city – a bustling convergence of international, long-distance and suburban trains, the métro and several bus routes. Coming off the train, turn left for the métro and the RER, right for taxis (a sample price would be €9 to a hotel in the 4e) and the secure **left luggage** (Mon–Fri 6.15am–11pm, Sat & Sun 6.45am–11pm; €0.7–5.31 depending on the locker size), both down the escalators opposite the Avis car rental desk. You can get a shower (€7 for 20min) in the public toilets (daily 6am–midnight; toilets €1) at the bottom of the métro escalators, and change money at two **bureaux de change** at the station (daily 6.15am–11.25pm). The Gare du Nord is also the arrival point for trains from Calais and other north-European countries.

Nearby, the **Gare de l'Est** (place du 11-Novembre-1918, 10e) serves eastern France and central and eastern Europe. The **Gare St-Lazare** (place du Havre, 8e), serving the Normandy coast and Dieppe, is the most central, close to the Madeleine and the Opéra-Garnier. Still on the Right Bank but towards the southeast corner is the **Gare de Lyon** (place Louis-Armand, 12e), for trains to Italy and Switzerland and TGV lines to southeast France. South of the river, **Gare Montparnasse** (bd de Vaugirard, 15e) is the terminus for Chartres, Brittany, the Atlantic coast and TGV lines to southwest France. **Gare d'Austerlitz** (bd de l'Hôpital, 13e) serves the Loire Valley and the Dordogne. The motorail station, **Gare de Paris-Bercy**, is down the tracks from the Gare de Lyon on boulevard de Bercy, 12e.

All the stations are equipped with cafés, restaurants, *tabacs*, ATMs and bureaux de change (long waits in season), and all are connected with the métro system; Gare du Nord and Gare de Lyon also have **tourist offices** which book same-day accommodation. **Left-luggage** facilities are available at all train stations under heavy security, but are limited.

For **information** on national train services and reservations phone ☎08.36.35.35.39 (if you dial extension 2 you should go through to an English-speaking operator) or consult the website ⓦwww.sncf.fr. For information on suburban lines call ☎01.53.90.20.20. You can buy **tickets** at any SNCF station and at travel agents.

# City transport

While walking is undoubtedly the best way to discover Paris, the city's integrated public transport system of bus, métro and trains – the RATP (Régie Autonome des Transports Parisiens) – is cheap, fast and meticulously signposted. For details on tickets and the various passes available see overleaf.

## The métro and RER

The **métro**, combined with the **RER** (Réseau Express Régional) suburban express lines, is the simplest way of moving around the city and also one of the cheapest – €1.30 for a single journey anywhere in the centre. Many of the métro lines follow the streets above; line 1 for example shadows the Champs-Élysées and rue de Rivoli. The métro runs from 5.30am to around 12.30am, RER trains from 5am to 12.30am. Stations (abbreviated: M° Concorde, RER Luxembourg, etc) are evenly spaced and you'll rarely find yourself more than 500m from one in the centre, though the interchanges can involve a lot of legwork, including many stairs. You'll find a métro map in the colour section at the back of this book; alternatively, free **maps** of varying sizes and detail are available at most stations (in descending scale, ask for either a *Grand Plan de Paris*, a *Petit Plan de Paris* or a *Paris Plan de Poche*). The lines are **colour-coded** and designated by numbers for the métro and by letters for the RER. You also need to know the direction of travel – signposted using the names of the terminus: for example, travelling from Montparnasse to Châtelet, you follow the sign "Direction Porte-de-Clignancourt"; from Gare d'Austerlitz to Grenelle on line 10 you follow "Direction Boulogne–Pont-de-St-Cloud". The numerous interchanges (*correspondances*) make it possible to cover most of the city in a more or less straight line. For RER journeys beyond the city, make sure that the station you want is illuminated on the platform display board. For more on métro life and etiquette see the box on p.v.

## Buses

**Buses** are often rather neglected in favour of the métro, but can be very useful where the métro journey doesn't quite work. They aren't difficult to use and naturally you see much more, plus journeys are getting quicker with the introduction of bus lanes. Free **route maps** are available at métro stations, bus terminals and the tourist office; the best, showing the métro and RER as well, is the *Grand Plan de Paris*. Every bus stop displays the numbers of the buses that stop there, a map showing all the stops on the route, and the times of the first and last buses. Generally speaking, buses run from 6.30am to 8.30pm with some services continuing to 1.30am. Around half the lines don't operate on Sundays and holidays – the *Grand Plan de Paris* (see above) lists those that do. You can buy a single **ticket** (€1.30 from the driver), or use a pre-purchased *carnet* ticket or pass (see overleaf). Press the red button to request a stop – the *arrêt demandé* sign will then light up. A number of bus routes (see p.46) are designed to be easily accessible for wheelchairs and prams.

From mid-April to mid-September, a special orange-and-white **Balabus** service (not to be confused with Batobus, see p.29) passes all the major tourist sights between Grande Arche de la Défense and Gare de Lyon. They run on Sundays and holidays every fifteen to twenty minutes from noon to 9pm. Bus stops are marked "Balabus", and you'll need one to three bus tickets, depending on the length of your journey: check the information at the bus stop or ask the driver. The Paris Visites, Mobilis and Carte Orange passes (see overleaf) are all valid too. **Night buses** (Noctambus) run on eighteen routes every hour (extra services on weekends) from 1am to 5.30am between place du Châtelet, west of the Hôtel de Ville, and the suburbs. Details of the routes are available on ⊕ www.citefutee.com/orienter/ noctambus.php.

## Touring Paris by public transport

A good way to take in the city sights is to hop on a bus. **Bus #20** (wheelchair accessible) from Gare de Lyon follows the Grands Boulevards and does a loop through the 1er and 2e arrondissements. **Bus #24** between Porte de Bercy and Gare St-Lazare follows the left bank of the Seine. **Bus #29** has an open platform at the back, which makes it fun for sightseeing – it runs from Gare St Lazare past the Opéra Garnier, the Pompidou Centre, through the Marais and past the Bastille to the Gare de Lyon. For La Voie Triomphale, take a trip on **bus #73** between La Défense and the Musée d'Orsay. Many more bus journeys – outside rush hours – are worthwhile trips in themselves: you can get hold of the Grand Plan de Paris from a métro station and check out the routes of buses #38, #48, #64, #67, #68, #69, #82, #87 and #95.

The métro, surprisingly, can also provide some scenery: the overground line on the southern route between Charles-de-Gaulle/Étoile and Nation (line 6) gives you views of the Eiffel Tower, the Île des Cygnes, the Invalides, the new Bibliothèque Nationale and the Finance Ministry.

## Tickets and passes

For a short stay in the city, it's worth buying **carnets** of ten tickets, available from any station or *tabac* (€9.60, as opposed to €1.30 for an individual ticket). The city's integrated transport system is divided into five **zones**; the métro system more or less fits into zones 1 and 2. The same **tickets** are valid for bus, métro and, within the city limits and immediate suburbs (zones 1 and 2), the RER express rail lines, which also extend far out into the Île de France. Only one ticket is ever needed on the métro system, and within zones 1 and 2 for any RER or bus journey, but you can't switch between buses or between bus and métro/RER on the same ticket. **Night buses** (Noctambus) require separate tickets costing €2.44 each (buy these on board), unless you have a weekly or monthly travel pass (see below). For **RER journeys** beyond zones 1 and 2 you must buy an RER ticket; visitors often get caught out, for instance, when they take the RER to La Défense instead of the métro. **Children** under 4 travel free and from ages 4 to 10 at half price. Don't buy from the touts who hang round the main stations – you'll pay well over the odds, quite often for a used ticket – and be sure to keep your ticket until the end of the journey as you'll be fined on the spot if you can't produce one. If you're doing a number of journeys in one day, it might be worth getting a *mobilis* **day pass** (from €5 for the city to €11.70 to include the outer suburbs, though not the airports), which offers unlimited access to the métro, buses and, depending on which zones you choose, the RER.

If you've arrived early in the week and are staying more than three days, it's more economical to buy a **Carte Orange** with a weekly coupon (*coupon hebdomadaire*). It costs €13.75 for zones 1 and 2, is valid for an unlimited number of journeys from Monday morning to Sunday evening, and is on sale at all métro stations and *tabacs* (you'll need a passport photo). You can only buy a coupon for the current week until Wednesday; from Thursday you can buy a coupon to begin the following Monday. There's also a monthly coupon (*mensuel*) for €46.05 for zones 1 and 2. You need to write your Carte Orange number on the coupon.

Also available are the **Paris Visites**, one-, two-, three- and five-day visitors' passes at €8.35/13.70/18.25/26.65 for Paris and close suburbs, or €16.75/26.65/37.35/45.70 to include the airports, Versailles and Disneyland Paris (make sure you buy this one when you arrive at Roissy-Charles de Gaulle or Orly to get maximum value). A half-price child's version is also available. They're less good value than the Carte Orange and *mobilis* passes, but they do give reductions on certain tourist attractions. You can buy them from métro and RER stations, tourist offices and online at ⊛ www.parisvisite.tm.fr. If you're going to Paris by Eurostar, you could save yourself time by buying the passes at Waterloo International – either from the information point or the souvenir shop underneath the escalator that heads up to platform entrances 21A/22A. You can get the Carte Musées et Monuments (see p.33) and Disneyland tickets here, too.

Both the Carte Orange and the Paris Visites entitle you to **unlimited travel** (in the zones you have chosen) on bus, métro, RER, SNCF and the Montmartre funicular. On the métro you put the Carte Orange coupon through the turnstile slot (make sure you retrieve it afterwards); on a bus you show the whole *carte* to the driver as you board – don't put it into the punching machine.

The RATP also runs numerous **excursions**, some to quite far-flung places, which are far less expensive than those offered by commercial operators. Details are available from the RATP's Bureau de Tourisme, place de la Madeleine, 1$^{er}$ (℡01.40.06.71.45; M° Madeleine). For 24-hour recorded **information in English** on all RATP services call ℡08.92.68.41.14 (premium rate) or visit online at ✆www.ratp.fr.

## Taxis

The best place to get a taxi is at a **taxi rank** (*arrêt taxi* – there are around 470 of them) – usually more effective than hailing from the street. The large white light signals the taxi is free; the orange light means it's in use. You can also call a taxi out: **phone numbers** are shown at the taxi ranks, or try Taxis Bleus (℡08.91.70.10.10, ✆www.taxis-bleus.com), Alpha Taxis (℡01.45.85.85.85) or Artaxi (℡01.42.03.50.50). That said, finding a taxi at lunchtime and any time after 7pm can be almost impossible: the powerfully unionized and heavily regulated system is stacked against the user, and there simply aren't enough cabs, or drivers willing to work the graveyard shifts.

Taxi **charges** are fairly reasonable: between €6.50 and €11 for a central daytime journey, though considerably more if you call one out. Before you get into the taxi, you can tell which of the three **rates** is operating from the three small indicator lights on its roof: "A" (passenger side; white) indicates the daytime rate (7am–7pm) for Paris within the *boulevard*

*périphérique* (around €0.60 per km); "B" (orange) is the rate for Paris at night, on Sunday and on public holidays, and for the suburbs during the day (€1 per km); "C" (blue) is the night rate for the suburbs (€1.20 per km). In addition there's a minimum charge of €5, a time charge of around €20 an hour for when the car is stationary, an extra charge of €0.75 if you're picked up from a mainline train station, and a €0.90 charge for each piece of luggage carried. **Tipping** is not mandatory, but ten percent will be expected. Taxi drivers do not have to take more than **three passengers** (they don't like people sitting in the front); if a fourth passenger is accepted, an extra charge of €2.50 will be added.

## Boats

There remains one final mode of public transport, **Batobus** (✆www.batobus.com), which operates from April to October, stopping at eight points along the Seine in the following order: Port de la Bourdonnais (M° Eiffel Tower/Trocadéro), quai de Solférino (M° Assemblée Nationale), quai Malaquais (M° St-Germain-des-Prés), quai de Montebello (M° Notre-Dame), quai St Bernard (Jardin des Plantes), quai de l'Hôtel de Ville (M° Hôtel-de-Ville/Centre-Pompidou), quai du Louvre (M° Musée du Louvre) and Port des Champs-Élysées (M° Champs-Élysées). Boats run every twenty-five minutes from 10am to 9pm from June to September and from 10am to 7pm in April, May and October. The total journey time is around thirty minutes, and tickets cost €3.50 for the first stop, €2 for subsequent stops, or €10 for a day pass.

## Driving and parking

Travelling around by **car** – in the daytime at least – is hardly worth it because of the difficulty of finding parking spaces. You're better off finding a motel-style place on the edge of the city and using public transport. But if you're determined to use the **pay-and-display parking system** you must first buy a Paris Carte from a *tabac*, then look for the blue "P" signs alongside grey parking meters. Introduce the card into the meter – it costs €1.60 an hour, for a maximum of

two hours. Covered car parks cost up to €2.30 per hour. Whatever you do, don't park in a bus lane or the Axe Rouge **express routes** (marked with a red square). Should you be towed away, you'll find your car in the pound (*fourrière*) belonging to that particular arrondissement – check with the local *mairie* for the address.

The French **drive on the right** and if your car is right-hand drive, you must have your headlight dip adjusted to the right before you go – it's a legal requirement – and as a courtesy, change or paint them to yellow or stick on black glare deflectors. Remember also that you have to be 18 years of age to drive in France, regardless of whether you hold a licence in your own country.

In the event of a **breakdown**, call SOS Dépannage (℡01.47.07.99.99) for round-the-clock assistance. Alternatively, ask the police.

## Car rental

The big international **car rental** companies have offices at the airports and at several locations in the city. Avis (℡01.46.10.60.60, ⓦwww.avis.com), located at Gare du Nord, do good weekend prices: their "Parisien weekend" car rental extends from noon on Thursday to noon on Tuesday, with two days working out at around €60 per day, to five days at about €45 per day. Other big names are listed in the "Directory" of the guide, p.375.

North Americans and Australians in particular should be forewarned that it's difficult to rent a car with automatic transmission in France; if you can't drive a manual, try and book an automatic well in advance, possibly before you leave home, and be prepared to pay a much higher price for it.

## Cycling

Since 1996, the Mairie de Paris has made great efforts to introduce dedicated **cycle lanes** in Paris. You can pick up a free leaflet, *Paris à Vélo*, outlining the routes, from town halls, the tourist office or bike rental outlets. Unfortunately, very few stretches are separate from the roads and, given the way Parisians park and drive, the new lanes are very much a token gesture. The best **road-free cycle routes** are the promenade plantée (see p.199) along the old railway line from Vincennes into the 12ᵉ arrondissement (though the viaduct section between the Jardin de Reuilly and the Bastille is for pedestrians only), rue Vercingétorix from place de Catalogne to Porte de Vanves in the 14ᵉ, and the quais of Canal St-Martin, the Bassin de la Villette and the Canal de l'Ourcq. The new bridge across the Seine, Pont Charles-de-Gaulle between the Gare de Lyon and Gare d'Austerlitz, has separate lanes, as do boulevard d'Auriol, rue Albert-Bayer, avenue Edison, and rues Baudricourt, Château-des-Rentiers and Nationale in the 13ᵉ. The Seine is a favourite spot with cyclists on Sundays: cars are banned from the central quais, as well as the quais along the Canal St-Martin, between 10am and 4pm. If you prefer cycling in a more natural environment, you'll find extensive cycle tracks in the Bois de Boulogne and the Bois de Vincennes. Cycle tracks are also widely used by rollerbladers.

For details of bike rental and guided cycling tours, see p.357 of "Activities and sports ".

# Costs and money

Like all European capital cities, Paris has the potential to be very expensive, certainly more so than the rest of France, but it compares favourably to the standards set by other North European cities because of the relatively low cost of accommodation and eating out.

If you are one of two people sharing a comfortable central hotel room, you can manage a reasonably snug existence, including restaurant lunch and dinner, getting around, museum and café stops, on €100 per person per day (around £70/US$100). At the bottom line, by watching the pennies, staying at a hostel (€20 for B&B), being strong-willed about cups of coffee and drinks, and admiring monuments and museums from the outside (or on free entry days, see below), you could survive on as little as €40 (around £28/US$40) a day, including a cheap restaurant meal – less if you limit eating to street snacks or market food.

For two or more people, hotel **accommodation** can be almost as cheap as hostels, but a sensible average estimate for a comfortable double room would start from €55 (though perfectly adequate but simple doubles can be had from €24). Single-rated and -sized rooms are often available, starting at €17 in a cheap hotel. Breakfast at most hotels is an extra €4.50–7 and usually consists of coffee, croissant, bread and orange juice; it's about the same as you'd pay in a bar (where the coffee and ambience are generally more agreeable).

As for other food, you can spend as much or as little as you like. There are large numbers of reasonable, if not very exciting, **restaurants** with three- or four-course menus for between €12 and €22; the lunchtime *menu* is nearly always cheaper and you can get a filling midday *plat du jour* (dish of the day) of hot food for under €10. **Picnic fare**, obviously, is much less costly, especially when you buy in the markets and cheap supermarket chains; generous takeaway baguette sandwiches from cafés and *boulangeries* range from €2–4.60).

**Wine** and **beer** are both very cheap in supermarkets. The mark-up on wine in restaurants is high, though the house wine, served by the carafe, in cheaper establishments is still very good value. **Drinks in cafés** and bars are what really makes a hole in your pocket; remember that it's cheaper to be at the bar than at a table in cafés and most expensive to sit outside on the terrace. A black espresso coffee (*un café*) is the cheapest drink (around €1 if drunk at the bar). A café crème ranges from €1.40 at the bar to €3.50 on the outside terrace. Wine and draught lager are also reasonably priced: *un demi*, around a half pint, costs from around €1.60 at the bar to €3.50 on the terrace outside. Mixed drinks or cocktails cost from €6.50. Glasses of tap water are free.

**Transport** within the city is inexpensive. The Carte Orange, for example, with a €13.75 weekly ticket (see p.28 for more details), gives you a week's unlimited travel on buses and métro/RER in central Paris.

## Reductions

**Museums and monuments** are likely to prove one of the biggest wallet-eroders, though some state-run museums are free (see opposite) or have free admission on Sundays. For **children and teenagers**, the range of reductions can be quite bewildering, as each institution has its own policy. In many museums under-18s are free; all monuments are free for under-12s. Universally, however, under-4s are usually free, less often under-8s. Half-price or reduced admission is normally available for 5- to 18-year-olds. Some more **commercial attractions**, however, begin to charge adult rates at 12.

If you are a full-time student, it's worthwhile carrying the **ISIC Card** (International Student

# Paris for free

The permanent collections at all **municipal museums** are free all year round. The museums are: Musée d'Art Moderne de la Ville de Paris, Maison de Balzac, Musée Carnavalet, Musée Cognac Jay, Musée de la Vie Romantique, Musée Zadkine, Maison de Victor Hugo, and Musée Jean Moulin. All **national museums** are free the first Sunday of the month, including the Louvre, Pompidou Centre, and the Picasso and Rodin museums; see ⊛www.rmn.fr for a full list.

Churches, cemeteries and, of course, **markets** are free (except for some specialist annual antique and book markets). Most **parks** are free but some gardens within have small entry charges, usually around €1.50. **Libraries** and the cultural centres of different countries put on films, shows and exhibitions for next to nothing (details in the listings mags, see p.22); most libraries themselves are free, but some have entry charges – in such cases a day-pass might cost around €4. Other free **cultural offerings** appear regularly, from bands in the streets to firework shows, courtesy of the Mairie de Paris (publicized on the electronic billboards around Paris).

Identity Card; ⊛www.isiccard.com) to gain entrance **reductions** (usually about a third off). The card is universally accepted as ID, while the student card from your home institution is not. The card costs £6/US$22/Can$16/AUS$16.50/NZ$21/€12.70 in the Republic of Ireland. You have to be 26 or younger to qualify for the **International Youth Travel Card**, which costs £7/US$22/AUS$16.50/NZ$20/€12.70 in the Republic of Ireland and carries the same benefits. Teachers qualify for the **International Teacher Card**, offering similar discounts and costing £7/US$22/Can$16/AUS$16.50/NZ$21. All these cards are available in the US from Council Travel, STA, Travel CUTS and, in Canada, Hostelling International; in Australia and New Zealand from STA; and in the UK from STA or CTS Travel (⊛www.ctstravel.co.uk). See "Getting there", pp.9–18, for addresses.

For those **over 60 or 65**, depending on the institution (regardless of whether you are still working or not), reductions are available, though not as widely as they were a few years ago. You will need to carry your passport around with you as proof of age.

Whatever your age, if you are going to do a lot of museum duty, it's worth considering buying the **Carte Musées et Monuments** (€15 one-day, €30 three-day, €45 five-day). Available from the tourist office, RER/métro stations and museums, as well as the Eurostar terminal at London Waterloo,

they're valid for seventy museums and monuments (though not special exhibitions) in and around Paris, and allow you to bypass ticket queues (though not the security checkpoints).

## Money

The easiest way to access your funds while away is with a debit or credit card that can be used abroad. You might also want to bring some travellers' cheques as a back-up, and it's always a good idea to have some euros on you when you arrive.

### Currency and the exchange rate

On January 1, 2002, France was one of twelve European Union countries to change over to a single currency, the **euro** (EU$). The euro is split into 100 cents. There are seven euro **notes** – in denominations of 500, 200, 100, 50, 20, 10, and 5 euros, each a different colour and size – and eight different **coin** denominations, including 2 and 1 euros, then 50, 20, 10, 5, 2, and 1 cents. Euro coins feature a common EU design on one face, but different country-specific designs on the other. No matter what the design, all euro coins and notes can be used in any of the twelve member states (Austria, Belgium, Finland, France, Germany, Greece, Ireland, Italy, Luxembourg, Portugal, Spain and The Netherlands).

At the time of writing, the exchange rate hovered around €1.60 to the pound, €1 to the US dollar, €0.66 to the Canadian dollar, €0.57 to the Australian dollar, and €0.50 to the New Zealand dollar. For the most up-to-date exchange rates, consult the Currency Converter website ⓦwww.oanda.com.

## Travellers' cheques

**Travellers' cheques** are one of the safest ways of carrying your money, as they're insured. Worldwide, travellers' cheques are available from almost any major bank (whether you have an account there or not), and from special American Express or Thomas Cook offices, usually for a service charge of one to two percent. Check with your own bank first, as they may offer cheques free of charge provided you meet certain conditions. It pays to get a selection of denominations. Make sure to keep the purchase agreement and a record of the cheque serial numbers safe and separate from the cheques themselves. In the event that cheques are lost or stolen, the issuing company will expect you to report the loss immediately; most companies claim to replace lost or stolen cheques within 24 hours.

The most widely recognized brands are **Visa** and **American Express**, which most banks and bureaux de change will change. American Express travellers' cheques can also be cashed at post offices.

You might consider getting **euro traveller cheques** rather than your own national currency: they're increasingly accepted as cash in larger establishments and you should get the face value of the cheques when you change them, so commission is only paid on purchase. Banks being banks, however, this is not always the case.

## Credit and debit cards

**Credit cards** are widely accepted and one of the most convenient ways of paying for things whilst abroad. They also tend to offer the most competitive exchange and commission rates. Visa – often referred to as Carte Bleue in France – is almost uni-versally recognized; Access, MasterCard – sometimes called EuroCard – and American Express rank a bit lower. It's always worth checking first, however, that restaurants and hotels will accept your card; some smaller ones won't, despite the sign. Be aware, also, that French cards have a smart chip and machines may reject the magnetic strip of British, American or Australasian cards, even if they are valid. If your card is refused because of this, you might try explaining that your card is not a *carte à puces*, like the French ones, but a *carte à piste magnétique*.

You can also use credit cards for **cash advances** at banks and in ATMs. The PIN number should be the same as the one you use at home, but check with your credit-card company before you leave. Also, because French credit cards are smart cards, some ATMs baulk at foreign plastic and tell you that your request for money has been denied. If that happens, just try another machine. All ATMs give you the choice of instructions in French or English. Remember that all cash advances are treated as loans, with interest accruing daily from the date of withdrawal; there may be a transaction fee on top of this, so withdrawing lots of small amounts can work out expensive.

It's better, if possible, to make withdrawals from ATMs using your **debit card**, for which the flat transaction fee is usually quite small – your bank will able to advise on this. Make sure you have a PIN that's designed to work overseas. However, it's unwise to rely on ATMs as your sole source of money, as a lost, stolen or malfunctioning card would leave you with nothing – always have some spare currency or travellers' cheques as a back-up.

To cancel **lost** or **stolen cards**, call the following 24-hour numbers: American Express ☏01.47.77.72.00; Diners' Club ☏08.10.31.41.59; MasterCard ☏08.00.90.13.87; Visa ☏08.00.90.11.79.

## Changing money and banking hours

Exchange rates and commission fees charged by banks and bureaux de change vary considerably. On the whole, the best exchange rates are offered by **banks**, though there's always a commission charge on top (1–2 percent commission on travellers' cheques, and a 2–4 percent commission on cash). It pays to be very wary of **bureaux de change** as they can really rip you off. Check their rates carefully: some outfits are known to post, somewhat misleadingly, the rate at which they sell rather than buy, so you think you're getting a good rate of exchange when you're not. The exchange bureaux on the Champs-Elysées, near *McDonald's*, are usually pretty reputable, but check the rates carefully all the same.

Standard **banking hours** are Monday to Friday from 9am to 4 or 5pm. Some banks close at midday (noon/12.30pm–2/2.30pm); some are open on Saturday 9am to noon. All are closed on Sunday and public holidays. They will have a notice on the door if they do currency exchange. Money-exchange bureaux stay open longer (until 6 or 7pm), tend not to close for lunch and may even open on Sundays in the more touristy areas.

Rue de la Paix and other streets around the Opéra-Garnier in the 1er arrondissement are full of **banks**, and there are plenty of money-exchange bureaux on the rue de Rivoli, the Champs-Élysées and in the train stations. There are also **automatic exchange machines** at the airports and train stations and outside many money-exchange bureaux. They accept £10 and £20 notes as well as dollars and other European currency notes, but offer a very poor rate of exchange.

## Wiring money

Having **money wired** from home using one of the companies listed below is never convenient or cheap, and should be considered a last resort. It's also possible to have money wired directly from a bank in your home country, although this is somewhat less reliable because it involves two separate institutions. If you go this route, your home bank will need the address of the branch bank where you want to pick up the money and the address and telex number of its head office, which will act as the clearing house; money wired this way normally takes two working days to arrive, and costs around £25/$40 per transaction.

### Money-wiring companies

**Thomas Cook** US ☎1-800/287-7362, Canada ☎1-888/823-4732, UK ☎01733/318 922, Ireland ☎01/677 1721, ⊛www.us.thomascook.com.
**Travelers Express Moneygram** US ☎1-800/926-3947, Canada ☎1-800/933-3278, ⊛www.moneygram.com.
**Western Union** US and Canada ☎1-800/325-6000, Australia ☎1800/501 500, New Zealand ☎09/270 0050, UK ☎0800/833 833, Ireland ☎1800/395 395, ⊛www.westernunion.com.

# Communications

## Post offices

French **post offices** (*bureaux de poste* or *PTT*s) – look for bright yellow-and-blue La Poste signs – are generally open from 8am to 7pm Monday to Friday, and 8am to noon on Saturday. However, Paris's **main office**, at 52 rue du Louvre, 1er (M° Étienne-Marcel), is open 24 hours (for all postal services, but not banking and money changing). It's the best place to have your mail sent, unless you have a particular branch office in mind.

**Poste restante** letters should be addressed (preferably with the surname first, underlined and in capitals) to Poste Restante, 52 rue du Louvre, 75001 Paris (☎01.40.28.76.00). To **collect your mail**, you need a passport or other convincing ID, and there'll be a charge of around €0.46 for every letter. You should ask for all your names to be checked, as filing systems are not brilliant.

Most post offices now have yellow-coloured *guichet automatiques* – automatic machines that weigh your letter or package and give you the correct stamps (*timbres*), as well as sticky labels and tape, saving you a lot of time queuing for counter service. Instructions are in English and French. You'll need small change; there should be a machine that can change notes. Standard letters (20g or less) and postcards within France and to European Union countries cost €0.46, to North America €0.67 and to Australia and New Zealand €0.79. For sending letters, remember that you can also buy stamps from **tabacs**. For further information on postal rates, among other things, log on to the post office website ⓦwww.laposte.fr.

You can send **faxes** from post offices: the official French word is *télécopie*, but "fax" is commonplace. You can also use the Internet at post offices, change money, and make photocopies and phone calls. To post your letter on the street, look for the bright yellow post boxes.

## Phones

You can make **international phone calls** from any telephone box (*cabine*) and receive calls where there's a blue logo of a ringing bell. You'll need to buy a **phone card** (*télé-carte*; 50-unit card for €7.40 or 120-units for €14.75) as coin boxes have been almost phased out (but see below). You can also buy a card with a PIN number (*une carte à code*), available for €7.50 or €15 from

tabacs or newsagents, which can be used with a public or private telephone; just dial the toll-free number provided, followed by your PIN number (given on the card) and then the subscriber number. Credit cards can also be used in many call boxes. **Coin-only boxes** do still exist in cafés, bars, hotel foyers and rural areas; they take 10, 20 and 50 cents and €1; put the money in after lifting up the receiver and before dialling. You can keep adding more coins once you are connected. The major **international calling codes** are given opposite; remember to omit the initial 0 of the local area code from the subscriber's number.

For **calls within France** – local or long-distance – dial all ten digits of the number. Paris and Île-de-France numbers start with ☎01. Numbers beginning with ☎08.00 are free numbers; those beginning with ☎08.36 are premium-rate (from €0.34 per minute), and those beginning with 06 are mobile and therefore also expensive to call. Local calls are timed in France.

Off-peak **charges** (for local, long-distance and international calls) apply on weekdays between 7pm and 8am, and all day Saturday and Sunday, as well as holidays.

A convenient way of phoning home from abroad is via a **telephone charge card** from your phone company back home. Using a PIN number, you can make calls from most hotel, public and private phones that will be charged to your account. Since most major charge cards are free to obtain, it's certainly worth getting one at least for emergencies; enquire first though whether France is covered, and bear in mind that rates aren't necessarily cheaper than calling from a public phone.

To avoid payment altogether, you can, of course, make a reverse charge or **collect call** – known in French as *téléphoner en PCV*. This can be done through the operator in the UK, by dialling the Home Direct number ☎08.00.99.00.44 and asking for a "reverse charge call"; to get an English-speaking operator for North America, dial ☎08.00.99.00.11.

---

### Paris addresses

The **postcode** in Paris addresses consists of the generic 750 plus the number of the arrondissement: so, for example, the 14ᵉ becomes 75014 Paris.

*Bis* and *ter* (as in 4 bis rue de la Fontaine) are the equivalent of "a" and "b".

---

### Mobile phones

If you want to use your **mobile phone**, you'll

## International dialling codes & useful numbers

France is one hour ahead of Britain, six hours ahead of Eastern Standard Time (eg New York), and nine hours ahead of Pacific Standard Time (eg Los Angeles). Australia is eight to ten hours ahead of Paris, depending on which part of the continent you're in.

### Phoning abroad from France
Dial ☎00 + IDD code + area code minus first 0 + subscriber number

**IDD codes:**

Britain ☎44
Ireland ☎353
USA and Canada ☎1

Australia ☎61
New Zealand ☎64

### From abroad to Paris
**From Britain**: dial ☎00 33 + nine-digit number (leaving out the first 0).
**From the USA and Canada**: dial ☎011 33 + nine-digit number (leaving out the first 0).
**From Australia**: dial ☎011 33 + nine-digit number (leaving out the first 0).
**From New Zealand**: dial ☎044 33 + nine-digit number (leaving out the first 0).

### Useful numbers within France
**International directory enquiries** ☎32.12, followed by the country code (€3 per call)
**French directory enquiries, operator assistance** ☎12
**Telegrams** By phone: internal ☎36.55; external ☎08.00.33.44.11 (all languages)
**Time** ☎36.99
**Weather** ☎08.92.68.02.75 for Paris (€0.46 per minute)

need to check with your phone provider whether it will work in France, and what the call charges are. **In the UK**, for all but the very top-of-the-range packages, you'll have to inform your phone provider before going abroad to get international access switched on. You may get charged extra for this depending on your existing package and where you are travelling to. You are also likely to be charged extra for incoming calls when abroad, as the people calling you will be paying the usual rate. If you want to retrieve messages while you're away, you'll have to ask your provider for a new access code, as your home one is unlikely to work abroad. Most UK mobiles use GSM, which gives access to most places worldwide, except the US. For further information about using your phone abroad, check out ☞www.telecomsadvice.org.uk/features/using_your_mobile_abroad.htm.

Unless you have a tri-band phone, it's unlikely that a mobile bought for use in the **US** will work outside the States, with many only working within the region designated by the area code in the phone number, ie 212, 415 etc. They tend to be very expensive to own in the US, too, as users are billed for both incoming and outgoing calls. Calling a US mobile, however, costs no more than making a call to a landline in that area code. For details of which mobiles will work outside the US, contact your mobile service provider. Most mobiles in **Australia and New Zealand** use GSM, which works well in Europe.

## Email and the Internet

France was initially rather slow to take up the **Internet** owing in part to its familiarity with Minitel (see overleaf) and the dominance of the English language on the Net. Recently, however, Internet use has soared, and most museums and institutions have sites on the World Wide Web. You can get into a list of all French servers via the Centre National de Recherche Scientifique on ☞www.urec.fr or visit the Ministry of Culture's site on ☞www.culture.fr.

One of the best ways to keep in touch while travelling is to sign up for a free **Internet email address** that can be accessed from anywhere, for example YahooMail or Hotmail – accessible through ⓦwww.yahoo.com and ⓦwww.hotmail.com. Once you've set up an account, you can use these sites to pick up and send mail from any Internet café, or hotel with Internet access.

For those travelling with a **laptop**, ⓦwww.kropla.com is a useful website giving information on how to plug it in when abroad, phone country codes around the world, and electrical systems in different countries.

### Internet Access

You can stay online while in Paris at the handful of **cybercafés**, as well as several shops and libraries that offer Internet access.

**Accessnet Cybercafé 37 rue la Lappe, 11ᵉ.** Friendly Internet café with fifteen terminals. Mᵒ Bastille. Daily 10am–7pm.

**Cyber Cube 5 rue Mignon, 6ᵉ (Mᵒ Odéon/St-Michel) & 12 rue Daval, 11ᵉ (Mᵒ Bastille).** Internet access along with all kinds of other computer-linked services. Mon–Sat 10am–10pm.

**Cybercafé de Paris 15 rue des Halles, 1ᵉʳ.** Cybercafé with sixty machines in the region of Les Halles. Mᵒ Beaubourg/Châtelet-Les Halles. Mon–Sat 9am–midnight.

**Easyeverything 6 rue de la Harpe, 5ᵉ (Mᵒ St-Michel; Mon–Sat 7am–8pm, Sun 9am–8pm).** One of the city's largest Internet places with over 250 machines; not much ambience, but "easy" and

practical. Other branches at 31/37 bd de Sebastopol, 2ᵉ, and 15 rue de Rome, 8ᵉ.

**Forum des Images 2 Grande Galerie, Forum des Halles, 1ᵉʳ (see "Activities and sports" p.358).**

**La Poste** Most post offices now have a computer geared up for public Internet access. You need to buy a card first (€7, including 1hr connection), which can be recharged at €4 for a further hour's connection.

**Web 46 46 rue de Roi-de-Sicile, 4ᵉ.** Principally an Internet access zone, although there is a vending machine for snacks and drinks. Mᵒ St-Paul. Mon–Fri 9.30am–midnight, Sat 9.30–9pm, Sun 1.30pm–midnight.

**Web Bar 32 rue de Picardie, 3ᵉ (see "Eating & Drinking" p.290).**

## Minitel

Although it's been virtually superseded by the Internet, you'll still come across **Minitel**, a dinosaurial online computer found in post offices and elsewhere, allowing access through the phone lines to directories, databases, chat lines, etc. Most organizations, from sports federations to government institutions to gay groups, have a code consisting of numbers and letters to call up information, leave messages, make reservations and so on. You dial the number on the phone, wait for a fax-type tone, then type the letters on the keyboard. Lastly, press *Connexion Fin* (the same key also ends the connection). If you're computer-literate and can understand basic keyboard terms in French (*retour* – return, *envoi* – enter, etc), you shouldn't find them hard to use. Be warned though that most services cost more than phone rates.

# The media

## Newspapers and magazines

British **newspapers**, the *Washington Post*, *New York Times* and the *International Herald Tribune*, are widely on sale on the same day.

The free monthly *Paris Voice* magazine (ⓦwww.parisvoice.com), produced by the American Church at 65 quai d'Orsay, 7ᵉ, has good listings, ads for flats and courses, and interesting articles on current events. It's available from the church and from English-language bookshops (see p.332). *FUSAC* (*France USA Contacts*; ☻www.fusac.fr), a free American fortnightly available in various cafés, restaurants, shops and colleges, is also useful for flats, jobs, travel, alternative medicine, therapy and the like.

Of the **French daily papers**, the centre-left *Le Monde* is the most intellectual; it is widely respected, though somewhat austere and has only recently introduced colour photographs. *Libération*, founded by Jean-Paul Sartre in the 1960s, is moderately left-wing, and more colloquial, with good, if choosy, coverage, while rigorous left-wing criticism of the French government comes from *L'Humanité*, the Communist Party paper, currently fighting for survival. *Le Figaro* is the most respected right-wing national. The best-selling tabloid is *Le Parisien* (known as *Aujourd'hui* outside Paris), good on local news and events, followed by the downmarket *France-Soir*, and *L'Équipe*, dedicated to sports coverage.

**Weeklies** of the *Newsweek/Time* model include the wide-ranging and socialist-inclined *Le Nouvel Observateur* and the centrist *L'Express*. The best investigative journalism is to be found in the weekly satirical paper *Le Canard Enchaîné*, while *Charlie Hebdo* is a sort of *Private Eye* or *Spy Magazine* equivalent. International viewpoints are aired in the *Courrier International* which collates and translates into French a selection of articles from the worldwide press. *Paris-Match* provides gossip about stars and the royal families.

**Monthlies** include the young and trendy – and cheap – *Nova*, with excellent listings of cultural events, and its more expensive competitor *Technikart,* good on clubbing. There are, of course, the French *Vogue, Marie-Claire* and *Elle*, and the more challenging and modern *Jalouse*, for women's fashion

and lifestyle. Men's lifestyle magazines have recently made an appearance in France – *Men's Health* is one of the most popular.

"Moral" **censorship** of the press is rare. On the newsstands you'll find pornography of every shade, as well as covers featuring drugs, sex, blasphemy and bizarre forms of grossness. You'll also find French **comics** (*bandes dessinées*) that often indulge such adult interests: wildly and wonderfully illustrated, they are considered to be quite an art form with whole shops devoted to them (see p.333 of the "Shopping" chapter).

## TV and radio

**French TV** has six terrestrial channels: three public (France 2, Arte/France 5 and France 3); one subscription (Canal Plus); and two commercial open broadcasts (TF1 and M6). In addition, there are numerous **cable** networks, including LCI (French news), CNN, the BBC World Service, BBC Prime (*Eastenders*, etc), Planète, which specializes in documentaries, Paris Première (lots of VO – *version originale* – films), and Canal Jimmy (*Friends* and the like in VO). The main French **news broadcasts** are at 8pm on F2 and TF1.

With a **radio**, you can tune into various English-language broadcasts. BBC (☻www.bbc.co.uk/worldservice), Radio Canada (☻www.rcinet.ca), and Voice of America (☻www.voa.gov) list all the world service frequencies around the globe. You can also listen to the news in English on Radio France International (RFI; ☻www.rfi.fr) at 7am, 2pm and 4.30pm on 738kHz AM. For radio news in French, there's the state-run France Inter (87.8FM), Europe 1 (104.7FM), or round-the-clock news on France Info (105.5FM).

For more on Parisian television and film, see Chapter 15.

# Opening hours and holidays

## Opening hours

Most shops, businesses, information services, museums and banks in Paris stay open all day. The exceptions are the smaller shops and enterprises, which may close for lunch sometime between 12.30pm and 2pm. Basic hours of business are from 8 or 9am to 6.30 or 7.30pm Monday to Saturday for the big shops and Tuesday to Saturday for smaller shops (some of the smaller shops may open on Monday afternoon). You can always find boulangeries and food shops that do stay open, however, on days when others close – on Sunday normally until noon. See p.35 for standard banking hours.

**Restaurants, bars and cafés** often close on Sunday or Monday. It's common for bars and cafés to stay open to 2am, and even extend hours on a Friday and Saturday night, closing earlier on Sunday. Restaurants won't usually serve after 10pm, though some brasseries cater for night owls and serve meals till the early hours. Most small businesses, including some hotels, take a **holiday** between the middle of July and the end of August.

**Museums** open between 9 and 10am and close between 5 and 6pm. Summer times may differ from winter times; if they do, both are indicated in the listings of the Guide. Summer hours usually extend from mid-May or early June to mid-September, but sometimes they apply only during July and August, occasionally even from Palm Sunday to All Saints' Day. Don't be caught out by museum **closing days** – usually Monday or Tuesday and sometimes both. **Churches** and **cathedrals** are almost always open all day, with charges only for the crypt, treasuries or cloister.

## Public holidays

France has thirteen **national holidays** (*jours fériés*) when most shops and businesses, though not necessarily museums or restaurants, are closed. **May** in particular is a big month for holidays, when Ascension Day normally falls, as sometimes does Pentecost, added to May Day and Victory Day. It makes a peaceful time to visit, as people clear out of town over several weekends, but many businesses will have erratic opening hours. Just about everywhere, including museums, is closed on May 1. July 14 heralds the beginning of the French holiday season and people leave town en masse between then and the end of August.

### National holiday dates

**January 1** New Year's Day
**Easter Sunday**
**Easter Monday**
**Ascension Day** (forty days after Easter)
**Pentecost or Whitsun** (seventh Sunday after Easter, plus the Monday)
**May 1** May Day/Labour Day
**May 8** Victory in Europe Day
**July 14** Bastille Day
**August 15** Assumption of the Virgin Mary
**November 1** All Saints' Day
**November 11** 1918 Armistice Day
**December 25** Christmas Day

# Festivals and events

With all that's going on in Paris, festivals – in the traditional "popular" sense – are no big deal. But there is an impressive array of arts events and an inspired inter-nationalist jamboree at the Fête de l'Humanité. The tourist office produces a biannual *Saisons de Paris – Calendrier des Manifestations*, which gives details of all the mainstream events; otherwise, check the listings and other Paris maga-zines (see p.22). Many Parisian quartiers like Belleville, Ménilmontant and Montmartre have *portes ouvertes* (open doors) weeks when artists' studios are open to the public and some festivities are laid on – keep an eye open for posters and flyers.

## January

**La Grande Parade (January 1)** New Year's Day parade, with floats, dancers and bands, from Porte St-Martin to Madeleine (ⓦ www.parisparade.com).

## February

**Salon de l'Agriculture (end of February to beginning of March)** The biggest agricultural show in the world at the Parc des Expositions, Porte de Versailles (ⓦ www.salon-agriculture.com).
**Chinese New Year** Paris's Chinese community bring in the New Year in the 13ᵉ around av d'Ivry.

## March

**Banlieues Bleues (early March to early April)** International jazz festival in the towns of Seine-Saint-Denis (Blanc-Mesnil, Drancy, Aubervilliers, Pantin, St-Ouen, Bobigny); info on ☎01.49.22.10.10, ⓦ www.banlieuesbleues.org.
**Festival Exit** International festival of contemporary dance, performance and theatre at Créteil; information from Maison des Arts, place Salvador-Allende, 94000 Créteil (☎01.45.13.19.19, ⓦ www.maccreteil.com).
**Festival de Films des Femmes (end of March/beginning of April)** Women's film festival at Créteil; information from Maison des Arts, place Salvador-Allende, 94000 Créteil (☎01.49.80.38.98, ⓦ www.filmsdefemmes.com).
**Festival du Film de Paris (end of March to beginning of April)** Mostly mainstream films on preview at the Cinéma Gaumont Marignan, 27–33 av des Champs-Élysées, 8e (☎08.36.68.75.55, ⓦ www.festivaldufilmdeparis.com).

## April

**Poisson d'Avril (April 1)** April Fools' Day with spoofs in the media and kids sticking paper fishes on the backs of the unsuspecting.
**Foire du Trône (April to May)** Funfair located in the 12e, Pelouse de Reuilly and Bois de Vincennes (ⓦ www.foiredutrone.com).
**Marathon International de Paris** The Paris Marathon departs from Place de la Concorde and arrives at the Hippodrome de Vincennes 42km later. There's also a half-marathon in March (ⓦ www.parismarathon.com).
**Foire de Paris (end April/beginning of May)** Food, wine, house and home fair at the Parc des Expositions, Porte de Versailles (ⓦ www.foiredeparis.fr).

## May

**Fête du Travail (May 1)** May Day. Everything closes and there are marches and festivities in eastern Paris and around place de la Bastille. Lilies of the valley are sold everywhere.
**Finale de la Coupe de France** French football championships final at the Stade de France (☎01.55.93.00.00).
**Internationaux de France de Tennis (last week of May and first week of June)** The French Open tennis championships at Roland Garros (ⓦ www.rolandgarros.org).
**Jazz in the Parc Floral (May to July)** Big jazz names give free concerts in the Parc Floral at the Bois de Vincennes (entrance to park €1.50; ☎01.55.94.20.20, ⓦ www.parcfloraldeparis.com).
**Printemps des Rues (end of May)** Free street performances in the areas of La Villette, Gambetta,

Nation and République (📶www
.leprintempsdesrues.com).

## June

**Journées de la maison Contemporaine** More
than 350 houses designed by modern architects are
opened up to the public (📶www
.maisonscontemporaines.com).
**Festival Agora** Contemporary theatre/dance/music
festival organized by IRCAM and the Pompidou
Centre (☎01.44.78.48.16, 📶www.ircam.fr).
**Festival de St-Denis** (last two weeks in June)
Classical and world music festival with
opportunities to hear music in the Gothic St-Denis
Basilica (☎01.48.13.06.07, 📶www.festival-
saint-denis.fr).
**Fête de la Musique** (June 21) Live bands and
free concerts throughout the city (☎01.40.03.94.70,
📶www.fetedelamusique.culture.fr).
**Feux de la Saint-Jean** (around June 21)
Fireworks for St-Jean's Day at the Parc de la Villette
and quai St-Bernard.
**Marche des Fiertés LGBT** Lesbian and Gay Pride
march ☎01.53.01.47.01, 📶www.inter-lgbt.org.
**Foire St-Germain** (June to July) Concerts, antique
fairs, poetry and exhibitions in the 6e
(☎01.40.46.75.12, 📶www.foiresaintgermain.org).
**Festival de Chopin** (mid-June to July) Chopin
recitals by candlelight, held in the Orangerie de
Bagatelle, in the Bois de Boulogne (📶www.frederic-
chopin.com).

## July

**La Goutte d'Or en Fête** (first week) Music festival
of rap, reggae, raï with local and international
performers (☎01.46.07.61.64, 📶www
.gouttedorenfete.org).
**Bastille Day** (July 14 and evening before) The
1789 surrender of the Bastille is celebrated in official
pomp, with parades of tanks down the Champs-
Élysées, firework displays and concerts. At night
there is dancing in the streets around place de la
Bastille to good French bands.
**Arrivée du Tour de France Cycliste** (third or
fourth Sunday) The Tour de France cyclists cross the
finishing line in the avenue des Champs-Élysées
(📶www.letour.fr).
**Paris Quartier d'Été** Music, cinema, dance and
theatre events around the city (☎01.44.94.98.00,
📶www.quartierdete.com).
**Festival de Cinéma en Plein Air** (mid-July to
end Aug) Open-air cinema for free at Parc de la
Villette (☎01.40.03.75.75, 📶www
.la-villette.com).

**Paris-Plage** (mid July to mid-Aug) A popular
initiative launched by the mayor, Bertrand Delanoë, in
which the *quais* of the Seine are closed to traffic and
transformed into mini-beaches, complete with
imported sand and palm trees.

## August

**Cinéma au clair de lune** Open-air screenings of
films shot in Paris and shown near the location
where they were filmed (☎01.44.76.62.00,
📶www.forumdesimages.net).
**Fête de l'Assomption** (Aug 15) A procession from
Notre-Dame around the Ile de la Cité.

## September

**Fête de l'Humanité** (second weekend)
Sponsored by the French Communist Party and
*L'Humanité* newspaper, this annual three-day event
just north of Paris at La Courneuve attracts people
in their tens of thousands and of every political
persuasion. Food and drink (all very cheap), and
music and crafts from every corner of the globe,
are the predominant features, rather than political
platforms. Each French regional CP has a vast
restaurant tent with its specialities; French and
foreign bands play on an open-air stage; and the
event ends on Sunday night with an impressive
firework display. (M° La Courneuve, then bus #177
or special shuttle from RER). Info on
☎01.49.22.72.72, 📶www.humanite.presse.fr.
**Villette Jazz Festival** (mid-Sept) One of the city's
best jazz festivals, held in the park and Grande Halle
at la Villette (☎08.03.30.63.06, 📶www
.la-villette.com).
**Journées du Patrimoine** (third weekend) A
France-wide event where normally off-limits
buildings – like the Palais de l'Elysée where the
President resides – are opened to a curious public.
Details in local press and on 📶www.jp.culture.fr.
**Festival d'Automne** (end of September to end of
December) Theatre and music festival including
companies from Eastern Europe, America and Japan;
multilingual productions; lots of avant-garde and
multimedia stuff, most of it very exciting
(☎01.53.45.17.17, 📶www.festival-automne.com).
**Techno Parade** (mid September) One of the
highlights of the Rendez-vous Electroniques
festival. Floats with sound systems parade from
Place de la République to Pelouse de Reuilly,
where a big party is held (☎01.42.47.84.76,
📶www.technopol.net).
**Rendez-vous Electroniques** (mid-Sept) A
celebration of electronic music in the city's clubs and
other venues (📶www.tecnopol.net).

## October

**Fêtes des Vendanges (first or second Saturday)**
The grape harvest festival in the Montmartre
vineyard, at the corner of rue des Saules and rue St-
Vincent (☎01.46.06.00.32, ✆www.comite-des-
fetes-18.com).
**Nuit Blanche (early Oct)** All-night cultural events
at unusual venues (☎08.20.00.75.75,
✆www.paris.fr).
**Foire Internationale d'Art Contemporain
(FIAC)** International contemporary art fair held at
Paris Expo, Porte de Versailles (☎08.36.68.00.51,
✆www.fiaconline.com).
**Prix de l'Arc de Triomphe** Horse flat racing with
high stakes at Longchamp (☎08.21.21.32.13,
✆www.france-galop.com).
**Salon du Chocolat (Oct to Nov)** Chocolatiers
come to the Carrousel du Louvre from all over to
show off their chocolate-making skills
(✆www.chocoland.com).

## November

**Festival d'Art Sacré de la Ville de Paris (end
of November to mid-December)** Concerts and
recitals of church music in Paris's churches and
concert halls (☎01.44.70.64.10).
**Mois de la Photo (biennial – even years)**
Photographic exhibitions held in museums, galleries
and cultural centres throughout the city
(☎01.44.78.75.00).
**Festival FNAC-Inrockuptibles (early Nov)**
Dubbed *Les Inrocks*, a rock festival featuring lots of
new names at various venues around town, put on
by the book and record chain-store FNAC
(✆www.fnac.fr).
**Le Beaujolais Nouveau (third Thurs in Nov)**
Cafés and wine bars celebrate the new vintage.
**Lancement des Illuminations des Champs-
Élysées (end of November)** Jazz bands, the
Republican Guard and an international star turning
on the Christmas lights down the Champs-Élysées.

## December

**Le Nouvel An (December 31)** New Year's Eve
means fireworks, drinking and kissing, notably on the
Champs-Élysées.
**Patinoire de l'Hôtel de Ville (mid-December to
end of February)** Ice-skating rink in front of the town
hall. Free entry but you pay for rental of ice-skates
(✆www.paris.fr).

# Crime and personal safety

Petty theft is bad in the crowded hang-outs of the capital, as in most major cities;
the métro, train stations and Les Halles are notorious pickpocket grounds. It
makes sense to take the normal precautions: not flashing wads of notes or travellers' cheques around; carrying your bag or wallet securely; and never letting
cameras and other valuables out of your sight. But the best security is having a
good insurance policy, keeping a separate record of cheque numbers, credit
card numbers and the phone numbers for cancelling them, and the relevant
details of all your valuables.

**Cars** with foreign number plates are standard
prey. Vehicles are rarely stolen, but tape-
decks and luggage left in cars make tempting
targets. Good insurance is the only answer,
but even so, try not to leave any valuables in
plain view. If you have an **accident** while driving, officially you have to fill in and sign a **con-**
**stat à l'amiable** (jointly agreed statement);
car insurers are supposed to give you this
with the policy, though in practice few seem
to have heard of it. For **non-criminal driving
offences** such as speeding, the police can
impose an on-the-spot fine. **Drink-driving** is
heavily penalized.

43

If you need to **report a theft**, go along to the commissariat de police of the arrondissement in which the theft took place, where they will fill out a *constat de vol*. The first thing they'll ask for is your passport, and vehicle documents if relevant. Although the police are not always as co-operative as they might be, it is their duty to assist you if you've lost your passport or all your money.

Should you be **arrested** on any charge, you have the right to contact your consulate (see below). People caught **smuggling or possessing drugs**, even a small amount of marijuana, are liable to find themselves in jail, and consulates will not be sympathetic. This is not to say that hard-drug consumption isn't a visible activity: there are scores of kids dealing in *poudre* (heroin) in Paris, and the authorities are unable to do much about it.

**Free legal advice** over the phone (in French) is available from SOS Avocats (☎08.03.39.33.00; Mon–Fri 7–11.30pm; closed July & Aug).

### Foreign embassies and consulates in Paris

**Australia** 4 rue Jean-Rey, 15e; M° Bir-Hakeim ☎01.40.59.33.00, ⊛www.austgov.fr.
**Canada** 35 av Montaigne, 8e; M° Franklin-D.Roosevelt ☎01.44.43.29.00, ⊛www.amb-canada.fr.
**Ireland** 4 rue Rude, 16e; M° Charles-de-Gaulle-Étoile ☎01.44.17.67.00.
**New Zealand** 7 rue Léonard-de-Vinci, 16e; M° Victor-Hugo ☎01.45.00.24.11.
**South Africa** 59 quai d'Orsay, 7e; M° Invalides ☎01.53.59.23.23.
**UK** 35 rue du Faubourg-St-Honoré, 8e; M° Concorde ☎01.44.51.31.00, ⊛www.amb-grandebretagne.fr.
**US** 2 rue St-Florentin, 1er; M° Concorde ☎01.43.12.22.22, ⊛www.amb-usa.fr.

## The police

French **police** (in popular argot, *les flics*) are barely polite at the best of times, and can be extremely unpleasant if you get on the wrong side of them. In Paris, the city police force

Emergency number to call for police ☎17.

has an ugly history of cock-ups, including sporadic shootings of innocent people and brutality against "suspects" – often just ordinary teenagers and black people. You can be stopped at any time and asked to produce ID. If that does happen to you, it's highly inadvisable to be difficult or facetious.

The **two main types** of police – the Police Nationale and the Gendarmerie Nationale – are for all practical purposes indistinguishable. The **CRS** (Compagnies Républicaines de Sécurité), on the other hand, are an entirely different proposition. They are a mobile force of paramilitary heavies, used to guard sensitive embassies, "control" demonstrations, and generally intimidate the populace on those occasions when the public authorities judge that it is stepping out of line.

## Racism

France has a bad reputation for **racist attitudes** and behaviour. This is in part due to the country's infamous **Front National party**, an openly racist, far-right party, whose leader, Jean-Marie Le Pen, sent shockwaves round the country when he won over 17 percent of the vote in the first round of the presidential elections in May 2002. Though partly a protest vote against the mainstream parties, the result reflected a significant swing to the right fuelled by fears of crime, immigration and unemployment. On the positive side, around a million people took to the streets of Paris after the first round of the elections to protest at Le Pen's anti-immigration policies, and the Front National failed to secure any seats in the subsequent parliamentary elections in June. The presidential elections also saw Christiane Taubira become France's first black presidential candidate, receiving 2.3 percent of the vote.

France however has a long way to go before it becomes a racially tolerant nation. **Discrimination** in employment is common, and for the moment, if you are black or Arab, or look as if you might be, you're likely to come up against some form of unpleasantness: hotels claiming to be booked up, nightclubs pretending to be members only (that said, at some nightclubs, being black carries cachet and earns immediate entrance) and police demanding your papers are depressingly frequent occurrences. In addition, being black, of whatever ethnic origin, can make entering the country difficult. Changes in passport regulations have put an end to outright refusal to let some holidaymakers in, but customs and immigration officers can still be obstructive and malicious. In North African-dominated areas of Paris such as the Goutte d'Or, identity checks by the police are common. The clampdown on illegal immigration (and much tougher laws) has resulted in a significant increase in police stop-and-search operations. Carrying your passport at all times is a good idea (you are legally required to have some identification on you in any case).

There are many **antiracist organizations** including SOS Racisme, 28 rue des Petits-Écuries, 10ᵉ (☎01.53.24.67.67, ⓦwww .sos-racisme.org; Mᵒ Château-d'Eau). Though it doesn't represent the majority of immigrants and their descendants in France (for rioting kids in Paris's suburbs, it's an irrelevant middle-class outfit), SOS Racisme has done a great deal over the last few years to raise consciousness amongst young white French people. If you speak French, they will give you support should you be the victim of a racist assault (phone first, as opening times vary), or you can ring ☎114, a free national helpline for victims of discrimination. The police are unlikely to be sympathetic – your consulate may be more helpful.

# Travellers with disabilities

Paris has no special reputation for providing ease of access or facilities for disabled travellers. The way cars park on pavements makes wheelchair travel a nightmare, and the métro system has endless flights of steps. Museums, however, are getting much better; the Cité des Sciences has won European awards for its accessibility to those with sight, hearing and mobility disabilities. The Louvre has similarly good access. In a number of theatres the text is displayed for the deaf and hard-of-hearing during some performances.

Up-to-date **information** is best obtained from organizations at home before you leave, such as the French tourist board (ⓦwww.franceguide.com) or from the French disability organizations (see below). Another useful source of information is *Access in Paris* by Gordon Couch and Ben Roberts, published in Britain by Quiller Press (£6.95), a thorough **guide** to accommodation, monuments, museums, restaurants and travel to the city, though bear in mind that it was published in 1993, so some of the information will be out of date. Holiday Care has an information sheet on accessible **accommodation** in France.

**Eurostar** offers an excellent deal for wheelchair-users. There are two spaces in

the first-class carriages for wheelchairs, each with an accompanying seat for a companion. **Fares** are a flat rate of £59 return for both passengers from Paris and London (with fully flexible dates) and though it's not absolutely guaranteed, you will normally get the first-class meal as well. No advance bookings are necessary, though the limited spaces make it wise to reserve ahead and arrange the special assistance which Eurostar offers at either end. Most of the cross-Channel **ferry companies** offer good facilities, though up-to-date information about access is difficult to obtain. As for **airlines**, British Airways has a better-than-average record for treatment of disabled passengers, and from North America, Virgin and Air Canada come out tops in terms of disability awareness (and seating arrangements) and might be worth contacting first for any information they can provide.

The French Government Tourist Office in London distributes a **booklet on hotels**, called *Paris, Île de France: Hôtels et Residences de Tourisme* which details those with disabled access. For more information contact the organizations below.

## Getting around

If you are physically handicapped, **taxis** are obliged by law to carry you and to help you into the vehicle, also to carry your guide dog if you are blind. The suburban agency **GiHP** (Mon–Fri 6.30am–6.30pm; ☎01.41.83 .15.15, ✉www.gihpidf.asso.fr) has taxicabs and minibuses fully adapted to wheelchairs; at least 24-hour advance notice is needed. Aihrop (Mon–Fri 8am–noon & 1.30–6pm, ☎01.41.29.01.29) arranges transport to and from the airports and within the city.

For travel on the **buses**, **métro** or **RER**, the RATP offers accompanied journeys for disabled people not in wheelchairs – *Les compagnons du voyage* – which costs €14 an hour and is available daily 6.30am–8pm. You have to book on ☎01.45.83.67.77 (Mon–Fri 6am–7pm, Sat & Sun 9am–6pm) at least a day in advance. As long as they are registered with the organization, blind passengers can request a free companion from the volunteer organization Auxiliaires des Aveugles (☎01.43.06.39.68).

For **wheelchair-users**, some RER stations are accessible, though only very few, like Vincennes and Marne-la-Vallée (for Disneyland), can be used autonomously, while others, including Châtelet-les-Halles, Denfert-Rochereau, Gare de Lyon and Grande Arche de la Défense, require an official to work the lift for you. The new **Météor métro line** (14) and the RER line E are designed to be easily accessible by all. A number of bus lines, including #20, linking Gare de Lyon and Gare St-Lazare, via Opéra, and PC which plies the periphery boulevards, have specially designed, lower floors for wheelchair-users; you can find a full list on the Paris transport site ✉www.citefutee.com – click on the wheelchair sign. You can also

download a transport map of Paris showing exactly which stops are wheelchair accessible. A Braille métro **map** costing €1.80 and a separate bus map are obtainable from L'Association Valentin Haüy (AVH), 5 rue Duroc, 7e (☎01.44.49.27.27, ✉www.avh .asso.fr). **Cars** with hand controls (category O) can be rented from Hertz, usually with 48 hours' advance notice (in France call ☎01.39.38 .38.38).

## Useful contacts for travellers with a disability

### Paris

**APF (Association des Paralysés de France)** 17 bd Auguste-Blanqui, 13e ☎01.40.78.69.00, ✉www.apf.asso.fr. A national organization providing useful information including guides on Paris (in French only) for disabled visitors. Their guide, *Paris comme sur des Roulettes* (Paris on Wheels), costing €7.47 and detailing how to get about on wheels (not cars) in Paris, is available from their office or can be downloaded from ✉www.coliac.cnt.fr, the site for the Comité de liaison pour l'accessibilite, which promotes the rights of the disabled in France. To download the guide look up *informations locales* and click on Paris.
**✉www.jaccede.com** A handy website (in French only) giving a list of museums, monuments and other public places in Paris that are accessible with a wheelchair.

### UK and Ireland

**Holiday Care** 2nd Floor, Imperial Building, Victoria Rd, Horley, Surrey RH6 7PZ ☎01293/774535, Minicom ☎01293/776943,
**✉www.holidaycare.org.uk.** Information on all aspects of travel, including free lists of accessible accommodation in France, and an information pack about financial help for holidays.
**Irish Wheelchair Association** Blackheath Drive, Clontarf, Dublin 3 ☎01/833 8241, ☎833 3873, ✉iwa@iol.ie. Useful information provided about travelling abroad with a wheelchair.
**RADAR (Royal Association for Disability and Rehabilitation)** 12 City Forum, 250 City Rd, London EC1V 8AF ☎020/7250 3222, Minicom ☎020/7250 4119, ✉www.radar.org.uk. They publish a guide on travel in Europe (£11 inc. p&p) and are a good source of advice.
**Tripscope** Alexandra House, Albany Rd, Brentford, Middlesex TW8 0NE ☎0845/7585 641, ✉www.justmobility.co.uk/tripscope,

@tripscope@cableinet.co.uk. Phone-in travel information and advice service for those with mobility difficulties.

## North America

**Access-Able** @www.access-able.com. Online resource for travellers with disabilities.
**Directions Unlimited** 123 Green Lane, Bedford Hills, NY 10507 ⊕1-800/533-5343 or 914/241-1700. Tour operator specializing in custom tours for people with disabilities.
**Mobility International USA** 451 Broadway, Eugene, OR 97401, voice and TDD ⊕541/343-1284, @www.miusa.org. Information and referral services, access guides, tours and exchange programmes. Annual membership $35 (includes quarterly newsletter).
**Society for the Advancement of Travelers with Handicaps (SATH)** 347 Fifth Ave, Suite 610 New York, NY 10016 ⊕212/447 7284, @www.sath.org. Non-profit, educational organization that has actively represented travellers with disabilities since 1976.
**Travel Information Service** ⊕215/456 9600. Telephone-only information and referral service for disabled travellers.

**Twin Peaks Press** Box 129, Vancouver, WA 98666 ⊕360/694 2462 or 1-800/637 2256, @www.twinpeak.virtualave.net. Publisher of the *Directory of Travel Agencies for the Disabled* ($19.95), listing more than 370 agencies worldwide; *Travel for the Disabled* ($19.95); *Directory of Accessible Van Rentals* ($12.95) and *Wheelchair Vagabond* ($19.95), loaded with personal tips.
**Wheels Up!** ⊕1-888/389-4335, @www .wheelsup.com. Provides discounted airfare and tour prices for disabled travellers, also publishes a free monthly newsletter and has a comprehensive website.

## Australia and New Zealand

**ACROD** (Australian Council for Rehabilitation of the Disabled), PO Box 60, Curtin ACT 2605 ⊕02/6282 4333; Suite 103, 1st floor, 1–5 Commercial Rd, Kings Grove 2208 ⊕02/9554 3666. Provides lists of travel agencies and tour operators for people with disabilities.
**Disabled Persons Assembly** 4/173–175 Victoria St, Wellington ⊕04/801 9100. Resource centre with lists of travel agencies and tour operators for people with disabilities.

# Work and study

## Work

EU nationals can legally **work in France**, while most North Americans and Australasians (specialists aside) who manage to work and live in Paris do so on luck, brazenness and willingness to live in pretty grotty conditions. An exhausting combination of bar and club work, freelance translating, data processing, typing, busking, providing novel services like home-delivery fish'n'chips, teaching English or computer programming, dancing or modelling are some of the ways people get by. Great if you're into self-promotion and living hand-to-mouth, but if you're not, it might be wise to think twice – and remember that unemployment in France is high.

Anyone staying in France for more than three months must have a **carte de séjour**, or residency permit – citizens of the EU are entitled to one automatically. France has a **minimum wage** (the SMIC – *Salaire Minimum Interprofessionnel de Croissance*); indexed to the cost of living, it's currently around €6.80 an hour (for a maximum 169-hr month). By law, all EU nationals are entitled to exactly the same pay, conditions and trade union rights as French nationals. Employers, however, are likely to pay lower wages to temporary foreign workers who don't have easy legal resources, and make them work longer hours. It's also worth noting that if you're a full-time non-EU student in France (see p.49), you can get a

## French bureaucracy: a warning

**French officialdom and bureaucracy** can damage your health. That Gallic shrug and *"Ce n'est pas possible"* is not the result of training programmes in making life difficult for foreigners: they drive most French citizens mad as well. Sorting out social security, long-stay visas, job contracts, bank accounts, tenancy agreements, university enrolment or any other financial, legal or state matter, requires serious commitment. Your reserves of patience, diligence, energy (both physical and mental) and equanimity in the face of bloody-mindedness and Catch-22s will be tested to the full. Expect to spend days repeatedly visiting the same office and considerable sums on official translations of every imaginable document. Before you throw yourself into the Seine in despair, remember that others are going through it, too, and sharing the frustration may well help: the American Church (see below) is the place for such contacts.

non-EU **work permit** for the following summer as long as your visa is still valid.

If you're looking for secure employment, it's important to begin planning before you leave home. A few **books** that might be worth consulting are *Work Your Way Around the World* by Susan Griffith, *Live and Work in France* by Victoria Pybus and *Summer Jobs Abroad*, all published by Vacation Work (9 Park End St, Oxford OX1 1HJ; ☎01865/241 978, ⊛www.vacationwork.co.uk).

Finding a job in a **French language school** is best done in advance. In Britain, jobs are often advertised in the *Guardian*'s "Education" section (every Tues) and in the weekly *Times Educational Supplement*. Late summer is usually the best time. You don't need fluent French to get a post, but a degree and a TEFL (Teaching English as a Foreign Language) qualification are usually required. A useful resource is *Teaching English Abroad* (£12.95 plus postage) published by Vacation Work (see above), while the British Council's website, ⊛www .britishcouncil.org/work/jobs.htm, has a list of English-teaching vacancies. If you apply for jobs from home, most schools will fix up the necessary papers for you. EU nationals don't need a work permit, but getting a *carte de séjour* and social security can still be tricky should employers refuse to help. It's quite feasible to find a teaching job once you're already in France, but you may have to accept semi-official status and no job security. For addresses of schools, look under *"Écoles de Langues"* in the *Professions* directory of the phone book. Offering **private lessons** (via university

notice boards or classified ads), you'll have lots of competition.

For **temporary work** check the ads in *Paris Voice* and *FUSAC* (see p.38) and keep an eye on the notice boards at the Anglophone churches: the American Church in Paris (65 quai d'Orsay, 7e; Mo Invalides); St George's English Church (7 rue Auguste-Vacquerie, 16e; Mo Charles-de-Gaulle/ Étoile); St Michael's Anglican Church (5 rue d'Aguesseau, 8e; Mo Madeleine); and the American Cathedral (23 av George V, 8e; Mo Alma-Marceau). You could also try the notice boards located in the offices of CIDJ at 101 quai Branly, 15e (Mon–Sat 10am–6pm; Mo Bir-Hakeim), and CROUS, 39 av Georges Bernanos, 5e (RER Port-Royal), both youth information agencies which advertise a number of temporary jobs for foreigners.

The **national employment agency**, ANPE (Agence Nationale pour l'Emploi; ⊛www .anpe.fr), advertises temporary jobs in all fields and, in theory, offers a whole range of services to job-seekers; though it's open to all EU citizens, it is not renowned for its help-fulness to foreigners. Non-EU citizens will have to show a work permit to apply for any of their jobs. It's worth getting in touch with **CIEE (Council on International Educational Exchange)**, which can arrange three-month work programmes for US, Canadian and Australasian students and recent graduates, as well as help Britons find work. Although they do have an office in Paris, at 1 place de l'Odéon, 6e (☎01.44.41.74.99; Mo Odéon), it's better to arrange things in advance: in Britain, they're based at 52 Poland St, London W1V 4JQ

(☏020/7478 2000; ✆www.ciee.org), and have offices in North America and Australia. Other possible sources include the "Offres d'Emploi" (Job Offers) in *Le Monde*, *Le Figaro* and the *International Herald Tribune*, and noticeboards at English bookshops.

Some people have found jobs **selling magazines** on the street and **leafleting** just by asking people already doing it for the agency address. The American/Irish/British **bars and restaurants** sometimes have vacancies. You'll need to speak French, look smart and be prepared to work very long hours. Obviously, the better your French, the better your chances are of finding work.

Although **working as an au pair** is easily set up through any number of agencies (lists are available from French embassies or consulates, and there are lots of ads in *The Lady* in the UK), this sort of work can be total misery if you end up with an unpleasant employer, with conditions, pay and treatment the next worst thing to slavery. If you're determined to try – and it can be a very good way of learning the language – it's better to apply once in France, where you can at least meet the family first and check things out. If you want to arrange it first through an agency try Avalon Au Pairs, in Britain (☏01344/778246), in the US the American Institute for Foreign Study (☏1-800/727-2437, ✆www.aifs.com), or in Paris itself Accueil Familial des Jeunes Étrangers (☏01.42.22.50.34). These have positions for female au pairs only and will fill you in on the general terms and conditions (never very generous); you shouldn't get paid less than €260 a month (on top of board and lodging and some sort of travel pass).

## Claiming benefit in Paris

Any EU citizen who has been signing on for **unemployment benefit** for a minimum period of four to six weeks at home, and intends to continue doing so in Paris, needs a letter of introduction from their own social security office, plus an E303 certificate of authorization (be sure to give them plenty of warning to prepare this). You must register within seven days with the Agence Nationale pour l'Emploi (ANPE), whose offices are listed under *Administration du Travail et de l'Emploi* in the Yellow Pages or ANPE in the White Pages.

It's possible to claim benefit for up to three months while you look for work, but it can often take that amount of time for the paperwork to be processed (also see warning on p.48). Pensioners can arrange for their **pensions** to be paid in France, but cannot receive French state pensions.

## Study

It's relatively easy to be a student in Paris. Foreigners pay no more than French nationals to enrol on a course, and the only problem then is to support yourself. Your *carte de séjour* and – for EU nationals – social security will be assured, and you'll be eligible for subsidized accommodation, meals and all the student reductions. Few people want to do undergraduate degrees abroad, but for higher degrees or other diplomas, the range of options is enormous. Strict entry requirements, including an exam in French, apply only for undergraduate degrees.

Generally, French universities are much less formal than British ones, and many people perfect their fluency in the language while studying. For full details and prospectuses, go to the Cultural Service of any French embassy or consulate (see p.19 for the addresses).

Embassies and consulates can also give details of **language courses**, which often combine with lectures on French "civilization" and are usually very costly. In Britain, the **French Institute**, 17 Queensbury Place, London SW7 2DT (☏020/7073 1350, ✆www.ambafrance.org.uk/institut), can provide a list of language courses in France. Courses at the non-profit making **Alliance Française** (101 bd Raspail, 6e; ☏01.42.84.90.00, ✆www.alliancefr.org; Mº St-Placide) are reasonably priced and well regarded, while the **Sorbonne** (47 rue des Écoles, 5e; ☏01.40.46.22.11) has special six-month courses aimed at foreigners. Saying you studied French at the latter may impress your friends, but there are no prerequisites and the courses are very old-fashioned and grammar-based.

# The City

# The City

# The Islands

A t the very heart of Paris, in the middle of the Seine, lie two enticing river islands: the Île de la Cité and the Île St-Louis. The former is the ancient core of the city, harbouring Paris's most venerable monuments – the Gothic cathedral of Notre-Dame and the stunning Sainte Chapelle. Amid the grandeur you'll also find some unexpected leafy havens, like the square du Vert-Galant, an ideal retreat from the bustle of the city. Linked to the Île de la Cité by a footbridge, the smaller Ile St-Louis may not have any sights to speak of, but possesses a charm all of its own, with its handsome ensemble of seventeenth-century houses, villagey streets and tree-lined quais.

## Île de la Cité

The **Île de la Cité** is where Paris began. It was settled in around 300 BC by a Celtic tribe, the Parisii, and the town that grew up was known as Lutetia. In 52 BC, it was overrun by Julius Caesar's troops. A natural defensive site commanding a major east–west river trade route, it was an obvious candidate for a bright future – the Romans garrisoned it and laid out one of their standard military town plans. While they never attached any great political importance to the town, they endowed it with an administrative centre, constructing a palace-fortress that became the stronghold of the Merovingian kings in 508, then of the counts of Paris, who in 987 became kings of France.

The Frankish kings set about transforming the old Gallo-Roman fortress into a splendid palace, of which the **Sainte Chapelle** and the **Conciergerie** prison survive today. At the other end of the island, they erected their most famous monument, the great cathedral of **Notre-Dame**. By the early thirteenth century the small Île de la Cité teemed with life, somehow managing to accommodate twelve parishes, not to mention numerous chapels and monasteries.  Such was the level of activity that monks at one of the monasteries, the Saint-Magloire, found the island too noisy, moving out in 1138 to quieter premises on the right bank.

It takes some stretch of the imagination today to picture what this medieval city must have looked like, for nearly all of it was erased in the nineteenth century by Baron Haussmann, Napoléon III's Préfet de la Seine (a post equivalent to mayor of Paris) – some 25,000 people were displaced and ninety streets destroyed. In their place were raised four vast edifices in bland Baronial-Bureaucratik, largely given over to housing the law. Haussmann is also to thank for the windswept plaza, known as the *parvis*, in front of Notre-Dame, which

| RESTAURANTS, BARS & CAFÉS | | ACCOMMODATION | |
|---|---|---|---|
| Berthillon | C | Henri IV | 1 |
| Taverne Henri IV | A | Hôtel de Lutèce | 2 |
| Les Fous de l'île | B | | |
| Nos Ancêtres les Gaulois | E | | |
| Le Relais de l'île | D | | |

at least has the virtue of allowing an uncluttered view of the facade. The few corners of the island that remain untouched by Haussmann include the **square du Vert-Galant** and **place Dauphine**, both delightful havens of calm.

The cathedral, Conciergerie and Sainte Chapelle inevitably attract large **crowds** and it's not unusual to have to queue for entry. Things are generally a bit quieter if you visit early in the morning or late afternoon.

## Pont-Neuf and the square du Vert-Galant

A pleasant approach to the Île de la Cité is via the **Pont-Neuf**, a rather misleading name given that it's the city's oldest surviving bridge, built in 1607 by Henri IV. One of the city's first great town planners, Henri would sometimes come to inspect the bridge's progress, delighting the workmen on one occasion by taking a flying leap over a half-built arch. On completion the Pont-Neuf became a popular spot with street entertainers and actors, who played to the crowds milling around the stalls and booths installed in the bridge's bays, these days occupied by stone seats.

A stone construction with twelve arches, the bridge links the western tip of the island with both banks of the river, and was the first in Paris not to have houses built on it and to have a proper pavement – usually pedestrians were expected to share the mud-filled road with horse traffic. Henri is commemorated with an equestrian statue halfway across and also lends his nickname to the **square du Vert-Galant**, enclosed within the triangular stern of the island, reached via steps leading down behind the statue. "Vert-Galant", meaning a "green" or "lusty" gentleman, is a reference to Henri's legendary amorous exploits, and he would no doubt have approved of this tranquil, tree-lined garden, a popular haunt of lovers – the prime spot to occupy is the knoll dotted with trees at the extreme point of the island. If being this close to the river gives you the urge to get out onto it, you could hop onto one of the river boats, the Bateaux-Vedettes du Pont-Neuf, that

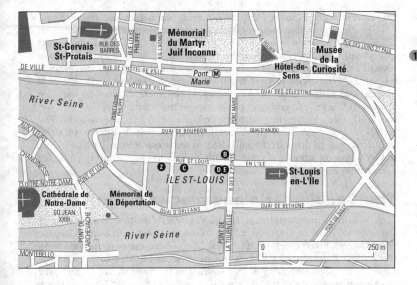

dock here on the north side of the *square* (for details of these and other river boats see p.349).

# Place Dauphine and the Sainte Chapelle

On the eastern side of the bridge, across the street from the statue of Henri IV, red-brick seventeenth-century houses flank the entrance to **place Dauphine**, one of the city's most secluded and attractive squares. The noise of traffic recedes here to be replaced by nothing more intrusive than the gentle tap of boules being played in the shade of the chestnuts. The further end is blocked by the hulking facade of the **Palais de Justice**, which swallowed up the palace that was home to the French kings until Étienne Marcel's bloody revolt in 1358 frightened them off to the greater security of the Louvre.

The only part of the old palace that remains in its entirety is the **Sainte Chapelle** (daily: April–Sept 9.30am–6.30pm; Oct–March 10am–5pm; €5.50, combined admission to the Conciergerie €8; M° Cité), its fragile-looking spire soaring high above the Palais buildings and its excessive height in relation to its length giving it the appearance of a lopped-off cathedral choir. Though damaged in the Revolution, during which it was used as a flour warehouse, it was sensitively restored in the mid-nineteenth century, and remains one of the finest achievements of French High Gothic, renowned for its exquisite stained-glass windows. It was built by Louis IX in 1242–48 to house a collection of holy relics he had bought at an extortionate price – far more than it cost to build the Sainte Chapelle – from the bankrupt empire of Byzantium. The relics – supposedly Christ's crown of thorns and sections of the True Cross – are now kept in Notre-Dame's treasury and displayed every Good Friday.

The Sainte Chapelle actually consists of two chapels: the rather dark **lower chapel**, with its star-painted ceiling, was intended for the servants, while the upper chapel, reached via a spiral staircase, was reserved for the court. The **upper chapel** is a truly dazzling sight, its walls made almost entirely of magnificent stained glass held up by powerful supports, which the medieval builders cleverly crafted to appear delicate and fragile by dividing them into clusters of pencil-thin columns. The glowing blues and reds of the stained glass dapple the interior giving the impression of being surrounded by a myriad brilliant butterflies. The windows, two-thirds of which are original, tell virtually the entire story of the Bible, beginning on the north side with Genesis and various other books of the Old Testament, continuing with the Passion of Christ (east end) and the history of the Sainte Chapelle relics (on the south side), and ending with the Apocalypse in the rose window. The chapel is frequently used for classical **concerts**, which offer a pleasant, unhurried way to drink in the splendour of the surroundings. It's best to buy tickets a little in advance if you can, otherwise you can end up queuing for a long time on the door.

## The Conciergerie and place Lépine

Nearby in the same complex, at 1 boulevard du Palais, is the **Conciergerie** (same hours as Sainte Chapelle; €5.50, combined ticket with Sainte Chapelle €8; M° Cité), Paris's oldest prison, where Marie-Antoinette and, in their turn, the leading figures of the Revolution, were incarcerated before execution. Entering the Conciergerie, you find yourself in the vaulted, late-Gothic Salle des Gens d'armes, one of the few remaining vestiges of the old Capetian kings' palace and the oldest surviving medieval hall in Europe. This splendid and impressive space, consisting of three rows of columns and four naves, was, before its transformation into a prison, the canteen and recreation room of the royal household staff. The far end is separated off by an iron grille; during the Revolution this area was reserved for prisoners who couldn't afford to bribe a guard for their own cell and were known as the *pailleux* because all they had to sleep on was hay (*paille*).

Beyond is a corridor where prisoners were allowed to wander freely – there's a number of reconstructed rooms here, like the euphemistically named "salle de toilette", where the condemned had their hair cropped and shirt collars ripped in preparation for the guillotine. On the upper storey is a reconstruction of **Marie-Antoinette's cell**. Pains have been taken to make it as authentic as possible, using evidence from contemporary accounts: watched over by a guard, a wax figure in black sits reading with her back to us; in front of her a crucifix hangs against torn and peeling fleur-de-lys wallpaper.

Outside the Conciergerie stands the **Tour de l'Horloge**, built around 1350, and so called because it displayed Paris's first public clock. The original was replaced in 1585 and survives to this day – an ornate affair flanked with classical figures representing Law and Justice. East from here **place Lépine** was named after the police boss who gave Paris's coppers their white truncheons and whistles. The police headquarters in fact stands on one side of the square; more popularly known as the Quai des Orfèvres, it will be familiar to readers of Georges Simenon's Maigret novels. Livening up the square on the other side is an exuberant **flower market**, held daily and augmented by a chirruping bird market on Sundays.

## Cathédrale de Notre-Dame

One of the masterpieces of the Gothic age, the **Cathédrale de Notre-Dame** (Mon–Fri & Sun 8am–7pm, Sat 8am–12.30pm & 2–7pm; free; M° St-Michel/Cité) rears up from the Île de la Cité like a great ship moored by huge

△ Cathédrale de Notre-Dame

flying buttresses. You'd never guess their existence, though, if you approach from the H-shaped west front – the exterior's most impressive feature with its strong vertical divisions counterbalanced by the horizontal emphasis of gallery and frieze, all centred on a rose window. It's a solid, no-nonsense design, confessing its Romanesque ancestry.

Built on the site of the Merovingian cathedral of Saint-Étienne, itself sited on the old Roman temple to Jupiter, Notre-Dame was begun in 1160 under the auspices of Bishop de Sully and completed around 1345. The cathedral's seminaries became an ecclesiastical powerhouse, churning out six popes in the course of the thirteenth and fourteenth centuries, though it subsequently lost some of its pre-eminence to other sees, such as Rheims and St-Denis. The building fell into decline over the centuries, suffering its worst depredations during the Revolution when the frieze of Old Testament kings on the facade was damaged by enthusiasts who mistook them for the kings of France. Napoleon restored some of the cathedral's prestige by crowning himself emperor here in 1804, though the walls were so dilapidated they had to be covered with drapes to provide a sufficiently grand backdrop.

It was only in the 1820s that the cathedral was at last given a much-needed **restoration** – largely thanks to a petition drawn up by Victor Hugo, who had also stirred public interest through his novel *The Hunchback of Notre-Dame*, in which he lamented the sorry state of the cathedral (Gothic architecture was particularly favoured by Romantic novelists like Hugo, who deemed the soaring naves of the great cathedrals singularly suited to sheltering "tormented souls"). The task of restoration was entrusted to Viollet-le-Duc, who carried out an extensive and thorough renovation – some would say too thorough – remaking much of the statuary on the facade (the originals can be seen in the Musée National du Moyen-Âge, see p.121) and adding the steeple and baleful-looking gargoyles, which you can see close up if you brave the ascent of the **towers** (daily: April–Sept Mon–Thurs 9am–7.30pm, Fri–Sun 9am–9pm; Oct–March 10am–5pm; €5.50).

The facade was given a thorough clean in the run-up to the millennium, removing years of accumulated grime and allowing the magnificent **carvings over the portals** to make their full impact. Perhaps the most arresting is the scene over the central portal, showing the *Day of Judgement*: the lower frieze is a whirl of movement as the dead rise up from their graves, while above Christ presides, sending those on his right to heaven and those on his left to grisly torments in hell – the condemned include a fair number of what look like bishops and kings, suggesting that the craftsmen of the day were not without freedom to criticize the authorities. They weren't lacking in a sense of humour either: all around this arch peer out alert and mischievous-looking angels, said to be modelled on the cathedral choirboys of the time. The left portal shows Mary being crowned by Christ, with scenes of her life in the lower friezes, while the right portal depicts the Virgin enthroned, and below, episodes from the life of Saint Anne (Mary's mother) and the life of Christ. These are masterfully put together, using visual devices and symbols to communicate more than just the bare-bones story – in the nativity scene, for example, the infant Christ is placed above Mary to show his elevated status and lies on an altar rather than in a crib, symbolizing his future sacrifice.

**Inside**, you're struck immediately by the dramatic contrast between the darkness of the nave and the light falling on the first great clustered pillars of the choir, emphasizing the sacred nature of the sanctuary. It is the end walls of the transepts that admit all this light, nearly two-thirds glass, including two

## Peter Abélard

On rue Chanoinesse, the cathedral school of Notre-Dame, forerunner of the Sorbonne, once flourished. Around the year 1200, one of the teachers was **Peter Abélard**. A philosophical whizz kid and cocker of snooks at the establishment intellectuals of his time, he was very popular with his students and not at all with the authorities, who thought they caught a distinct whiff of heresy. Forced to leave the cathedral school, he set up shop on the Left Bank with his disciples and, in effect, founded the University of Paris. Less successful, though much better known, is the story of his love life. While living near the rue Chanoinesse, behind the cathedral, he fell passionately in love with his landlord's niece, Héloïse, and she with him. She had a baby, her uncle had him castrated, and the story ended in convents, lifelong separation and lengthy correspondence. They were reunited in death and lie side by side in Père-Lachaise cemetery (see p.195).

magnificent rose windows coloured in imperial purple. These, the vaulting and the soaring shafts reaching to the springs of the vaults, are all definite Gothic elements, while there remains a strong sense of Romanesque in the stout round pillars of the nave and the general sense of four-squareness. The **trésor** (daily 9.30am–6pm; €2.50) contains mostly ornate nineteenth-century monstrances and chalices and isn't really worth the entry fee.

Free guided **tours** (1hr–1hr 30min) take place in French every weekday at noon and on Saturday at 2pm, and in English on Wednesday at noon; gather at the welcome desk near the entrance. A leisurely way to take in the interior are the free **organ recitals**, held every Sunday at around 4 or 5pm. The instrument, by the great nineteenth-century organ-maker Aristide Cavaillé-Coll, is one of France's finest, with over six thousand pipes.

Before you leave, walk round to the public garden at the east end for a view of the **flying buttresses** supporting the choir, and then along the riverside under the south transept, where you can sit – in springtime with the cherry blossom drifting down. On the other side of the cathedral, to the north, lie **rues Chanoinesse, des Ursins and de la Colombe**, three of the few streets on the island to have survived Haussmann's attentions. There's nothing particularly special about them, but the old houses here give some flavour of the more atmospheric pre-Haussmann Île de la Cité.

## The kilomètre zéro and crypte archéologique

Notre-Dame isn't only at the heart of Paris, it's also the symbolic heart of the country – outside on the pavement by the west door is a spot, marked by a bronze star, known as **kilomètre zéro**, from which all main-road distances in France are calculated.

Opposite Notre-Dame, at the far end of the square, steps lead down to the atmospherically lit **crypte archéologique** (Tues–Sun 10am–6pm; €3.30), worth visiting if you want to know more about the history of the island. This large excavated area under the *parvis* reveals remains of the original cathedral, as well as vestiges of the streets and houses that once clustered around Notre-Dame: most are medieval, but some date as far back as Gallo-Roman times and include parts of a Roman hypocaust (heating system).

## Le Mémorial de la Déportation

At the eastern tip of the island is the symbolic tomb of the 200,000 French who died in Nazi concentration camps during World War II – Resistance fighters, Jews and forced labourers among them. The **Mémorial de la Déportation** is scarcely visible above ground; stairs hardly shoulder-wide descend into a space like a prison yard and then into the stifling crypt (gates to crypt open daily 10am–noon & 2–5pm; free), where thousands of points of light represent the dead. Floor and ceiling are black, and it ends in a black, raw hole, with a single naked bulb hanging in the middle. On either side are empty barred cells. Above the exit are the words "Forgive. Do not forget." In contrast, the little green park surrounding the memorial is more of a celebration of life and a popular hang-out on a fine evening.

# The Île St-Louis

Often considered the most romantic part of Paris, the **Île St-Louis** is prime strolling territory. Unlike its larger neighbour, the Île de la Cité, it has no monuments or sights as such, save for a small **museum** at 6 quai d'Orléans devoted to the Romantic Polish poet Adam Mickiewicz (Thurs 2–6pm or by appointment on T01.43.54.35.61; free). Instead, you'll find tall houses on single-lane streets, tree-lined *quais*, a school, a church, assorted restaurants and cafés, and interesting shops. The island feels somewhat removed from the rest of Paris, with its own distinct charm, an oasis little touched by the city's turbulent years of revolution and upheaval. Inhabitants of the island even have their own name – "Louisiens". It's also one of the city's most covetable addresses – the Pretender to the French throne and Baron Guy de Rothschild have their residences here.

For centuries the Île St-Louis was nothing but swampy pastureland, a haunt of lovers, duellists and miscreants on the run, until in the seventeenth century the real-estate developer, Christophe Marie, had the bright idea of filling it with elegant mansions, so that by 1660 the island was quite transformed. In the 1840s the Île gained popularity as a Bohemian hangout, much like the Île de Louviers (see p.113) a decade earlier. The Haschischins club met every month on the ground floor of the **Hôtel Lauzun**, 17 quai d'Anjou. As the name suggests, hashish was handed round – apparently in the form of a green jelly – at these gatherings, attended by Manet, Balzac, Nerval and Baudelaire, among others. Baudelaire in fact lived in the building for a while in a small apartment on the second floor, where he wrote much of *Les Fleurs du Mal* and ran up large debts furnishing his rooms with antiques. The hôtel, built in 1657, has an intact interior, complete with splendid trompe l'oeil decorations, and is often used for government receptions (pre-arranged group visits are sometimes possible; call T01.42.76.57.99).

A **popular approach** to the island is via Pont Louis-Phillipe just east of the Hôtel de Ville. It's a good spot to start a wander down rue St-Louis-en-l'Île, where you could follow in the footsteps of most visitors and stop at *M. Berthillon* (no.31; see p.278), for one of their exquisite sorbets or ice creams. If you're looking for absolute seclusion, head for the **southern quais**, or climb over the low gate on the right of the garden across boulevard Henri-

IV to reach the best sunbathing spot in Paris. The island is best avoided on weekend afternoons, when the narrow streets get uncomfortably crowded. It's particularly atmospheric in the evening, and dinner here (see p.278 for restaurant recommendations), followed by an arm-in-arm wander along the *quais*, is a must in any lovers' itinerary.

2

# The Louvre

The **Louvre** – catch-all term for the palace and the museum it houses – cuts a grand Classical swathe right through the centre of the city, its stately ranks of carved pilasters, arches and pediments stretching west along the right bank of the Seine from the Île de la Cité towards the Voie Triomphale. So, when François Mitterrand added a futuristic steel-and-glass pyramid bang in the middle of its courtyard in the late 1980s, he was making a statement: the Louvre was to be transformed from a dusty dinosaur into a modern, inspiring and accessible wonder of the world.

A cultural edifice as monumental and venerable as the Louvre no doubt needed a big broom to sweep away the cobwebs, but in opening up new wings to the public and expanding the amount of the collection on show, the state was only continuing a tradition started two hundred years earlier when the French revolution threw open the doors of the royal palace to the citizens of the new republic. And as architectural patron, Mitterrand was simply following in the footsteps of François I, Catherine de Médicis, Louis XIV, Napoleon, and all the other French rulers who have knocked down, rebuilt, extended or altered the palace. Even if you don't venture inside, the sheer bravado of the architectural ensemble is thrilling.

The palace is now almost entirely given over to the **Musée du Louvre**, one of the world's great museums, covering the finest European painting, sculpture and objets d'art from the Middle Ages to the beginnings of Impressionism, plus an unrivalled collection of antiquities from Egypt, the Middle East, Greece and Rome. Giant in scale and stature, the French collection is nothing less than the gold standard of the nation's artistic tradition.

Quite separate from the Louvre proper, but still within the palace, are three museums under the aegis of the **Union Centrale des Arts Décoratifs**, dedicated to fashion and textiles, decorative arts and advertising.

## The Palais du Louvre

The original **Palais du Louvre** was little more than a feudal fortress, begun by Philippe-Auguste in 1200 to store his scrolls, jewels and swords, while he himself lived on the Île de la Cité. Charles V was the first French king to make the castle his residence – the ground plan of his palace can be seen traced on the pavement of the Cour Carré – but not until 1546, the year before the death of François I, were the first stones of the Louvre we see today laid, by the architect Pierre Lescot. During the ensuing reign of Henri II, he demolished the old fortress and built the two wings that now form the southwestern corner of the

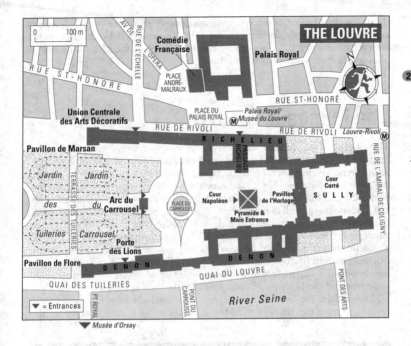

**Cour Carré** (to the left of the clock tower). It's just possible to imagine how extraordinary and how graceful the building would have looked, a gleaming example of the new Renaissance style surrounded by the late Gothic of Charles V's day.

Such a radical break with tradition was anathema to the architects working under Louis XIII and Louis XIV, who completed the Cour Carré by copying Lescot's original façade – Louis XIV himself was far more interested in over-seeing the construction of his new palace at Versailles. The only hint of novelty lies in the four central *pavillons*, designed under the quirky, troubled influence of Mannerism. Distinct in design, but no more architecturally innovative is Claude Perrault's academically Classical colonnade facing rue de l'Admiral de Coligny, which somehow beat Bernini's design for the same contract. Napoléon III's main contributions – the courtyard façades of the nineteenth-century Richelieu and Denon wings – conservatively repeat the theme of the Cour Carré.

But for all its many additions and alterations, the palace long remained a sur-prisingly harmonious building with a grandeur, symmetry, and Frenchness entirely suited to this most historic of Parisian landmarks. That is, until 1989, when, following a century of stagnation, I.M. Pei's controversial **Pyramide** erupted from the centre of the Cour Napoléon like a visitor from another architectural planet. As part of the same Mitterand makeover, the Finance Ministry moved out of the northern Richelieu wing, whose two main court-yards were then dramatically roofed over in glass. The **Passage Richelieu**, linking the Cour Napoleon with rue de Rivoli, now offers a better view of the sculptures in these courtyards than that from inside the museum.

Napoleon's pink marble **Arc du Carrousel**, just east of place du Carrousel, originally formed a gateway for the Palais des Tuileries (see box on p.64). It has always looked a bit out of place, despite sitting precisely on the Voie Triomphale axis. The arch is now definitively and forlornly upstaged by the Pyramide, which has outlasted its critics' spleen and found a place for itself in the hearts of even the most conservative Parisians.

# The Musée du Louvre

The origins of the **Musée du Louvre** lie in the personal art collection of François I, who summoned Leonardo da Vinci from Milan to add some prestige to the French Renaissance. Leonardo brought his greatest works with him across the Alps, including the *Mona Lisa*, which remains the museum's most famous possession and the *idée fixe* of an unhealthy number of visitors. Although artists and academics – as well as prostitutes – lived in the palace under Louis XIV, and the French Academy ran salons as early as 1725, the Louvre was only opened as an art gallery in 1793, the year of Louis XVI's execution. Turning the palace into a museum wasn't quite the pure Revolutionary gesture it seems, however, as the original plan had been conceived under Louis XV. Within a decade of its opening, Napoleon's wagonloads of war booty – not all of which has been returned – transformed the Louvre's art collection into the world's largest.

Though there are too many masterpieces to highlight here, few visitors will be able to resist the allure of the *Mona Lisa* (see p.68), if only to see what the

## The lost Palais des Tuileries

For much of its life, the Palais du Louvre was twinned with the **Palais des Tuileries**, which stood some 500m to the west. Built in 1559 for **Catherine de Médicis** shortly after the accidental death of her husband, Henri II, it was a place where she could maintain her political independence while wielding power on behalf of her sickly son, François II. It was apparently Catherine herself who conceived the idea of linking the two palaces by a *grande galerie* running along the right bank of the Seine, but in 1572 she abandoned the entire project. Tradition has it that she was warned by a soothsayer to "beware of St-Germain" if she wanted to live into old age – the Tuileries lay in the parish of St-Germain l'Auxerrois. It's more likely that the palace's situation just outside the protection of the city walls was the problem, as 1572 was a dangerous year. On 24 August, the bells of St-Germain l'Auxerrois rang out according to a pre-arranged signal, whereupon radical Catholics set about the murder of some 3000 Parisian Protestants, possibly under the secret orders of Catherine herself.

It wasn't until forty years after the St Bartholomew's Day Massacre, under Henri IV, that the two palaces were finally linked, and thereafter the Tuileries superseded the Louvre as a principal home of the royal family. It was here that Louis XVI was kept under virtual house arrest by the revolutionary mob until the *sans-culottes* finally lost patience on 20 June 1792, breaking in and forcing the king to don the revolutionary red bonnet. The Tuileries was revived under Napoleon, who built the Arc du Carrousel facing its central pavilion, and its status grew still greater under his nephew, Napoléon III, who finally enclosed both royal palaces around a single gigantic courtyard, the whole complex being dubbed the Cité Impérial. This glorious perfection didn't last long: the Tuileries was completely burnt during the Paris Commune of 1871. Today, the Louvre faces only gardens (see p.81), though they still bear the illustrious Tuileries name.

fuss is all about. If you're planning on making a short visit, you might consider confining yourself to this, the Denon section of the museum, which also houses the rest of the Italian paintings and the great French nineteenth century canvases, as well as the great Italian and Classical sculptures. A relatively peaceful alternative would be to focus on the grand chronologies of French painting and sculpture.

## Orientation

At first overwhelming, the supremely rational layout of the museum can actually be quite fun to master. Core to the plan are the three wings: Denon (south), Richelieu (north) and Sully (east, around the giant quadrangle of the Cour Carré). Within these wings, each floor falls into one of seven sections: Antiquities (Oriental, Egyptian and Classical); Sculpture; Painting; the Medieval Louvre; and Objets d'art. Some sections spread across two wings, or two floors of the same wing. The system's only drawback is that it doesn't spotlight the palace's magnificently decorated suites and rooms that give such a strong identity to certain sections.

### Louvre practicalities and survival

Tales of queues outside the Pyramide, miles of energy-sapping corridors and paparazzi-style jostles in front of the *Mona Lisa* can leave you feeling somewhat intimidated by the Louvre before you've even set foot in the place. The following practical information and survival tips should help to make the most of a visit.

On fine days, queueing for the **main entrance** at the Pyramide at least gives you time to appreciate the geometric pyramids and fountains of the Cour Napoléon. If it's raining or the queues look too long it's worth making for the **alternative entrances**: via the Porte des Lions, just east of the Pont Royal, or directly under the Arc du Carrousel; the latter can also be accessed from 99 rue de Rivoli and from the line #1 platform of the Palais Royal-Musée du Louvre métro stop. If you've already got a ticket or a museum pass (see p.33) you can also enter from the Passage Richelieu. Disabled access is via the futuristic rising and sinking column in the middle of the Pyramide.

**Opening hours** for the permanent collection are 9am to 9.45pm Mondays and Wednesdays, 9am to 6pm Thursday to Sunday. They're closed on Tuesday. Parts of the museum are closed one day a week on a rotating basis, so if you're interested in a particular section it's worth checking the schedule on the museum noticeboards or online at ⓦwww.louvre.fr, though the most popular rooms are always open.

The usual **entry fee** is €7.50 but after 3pm and on Sunday this is reduced to €5. Under-18s get in free at all times, and on the first Sunday of each month admission is free for everyone, unless it's a public holiday. **Tickets** can be bought in advance by calling ☏0892.68.36.22; from branches of FNAC (see pp.332 & 343) and Virgin Megastore (conveniently, there's one right outside the entrance under the Arc du Carrousel); or online at ⓦwww.louvre.fr.

Your ticket allows you to step outside for a break, though the museum itself has three good, only moderately overpriced, **cafés** – the relatively quiet *Café Richelieu* (first floor, Richelieu), the cosy *Café Denon* (lower ground floor, Denon), and the busier *Café Mollien* (first floor, Denon), which also has a summer terrace. The various cafés and restaurants under the Pyramide are mostly noisy and unpleasant.

Don't attempt to see too much – even if you spent the entire day here you'd only see a fraction of the collection. If you want to explore the Louvre in **peace**, stay away from the Denon wing, or time your visit to coincide with the evening openings on Mondays and Wednesdays.

From the Hall Napoleon, under the Pyramide, stairs lead south into the **Denon wing**, by far the most popular area of the museum, with the must-see Italian masterpieces of the Grande Galerie, the famous nineteenth-century French large-format paintings and the *Mona Lisa*, all on the first floor. Denon also houses Classical and Italian sculpture on its two lower floors.

Serious lovers of French art will head north to the **Richelieu wing** for the French sculpture collection; the grand chronology of French painting, which begins on the second floor; and the superb objets d'art collection on the first floor, which includes everything French that's not painting or sculpture – furniture, tapestries, crystal, jewels. Richelieu also houses Middle-Eastern antiquities and Islamic art (ground and lower ground floors), and northern European painting (second floor).

Rather fewer visitors begin with the **Sully wing**, although it's here that the story begins, with the foundations of Philippe-Auguste's twelfth-century fortress on the lower ground floor. The floors above mostly continue chronologies begun in other wings, with antiquities from Greece and the Levant (ground floor), and the seventeenth- and eighteenth-century periods from the Objets d'art (first floor) and French painting (second floor) sections. The complete Pharaonic Egypt collection is here too.

The Porte des Lions, on the Quai des Tuileries, provides one of the quickest ways into the museum, via the **Pavillon des Sessions**. Until the new museum on Quai Branly is finished, probably in 2006 (see p.140), the pavillon's half dozen rooms will house statuary from **Africa**, **Asia**, **Oceania and the Americas**. From the *pavillon*, a staircase leads up into Spanish and Italian paintings, just a few steps from the Grande Galerie.

It's well worth picking up a **floor plan** from the information booth in the Hall Napoleon, or at one of the alternative gates. This makes sense of it all by colour-coding the various sections, as well as highlighting a few of the best-known masterpieces.

# Painting

The largest section by far is **Painting**, divided into two areas on opposite sides of the museum, one devoted to French and Northern European painting, the other to Italian, Spanish and large-scale nineteenth-century French works. Interspersed throughout are rooms dedicated to the Louvre's impressive collection of **Prints and Drawings**, including prized sketches and preliminary drawings by Ingres and Rubens and some attributed to Leonardo da Vinci. Because of their susceptibility to the light, the drawings are exhibited in rotation.

## French painting

The main chronological circuit of **French painting** begins on the second floor of the Richelieu wing, and continues right round the Cour Carré in the Sully wing. It traces the extraordinary development of French painting from its edgy beginnings through Classical bombast and on to ardent Romanticism, ending with Corot, whose airy landscapes anticipate the Impressionists. Surprisingly few works predate the Renaissance, and the preliminary Richelieu section is chiefly of interest for the portraits of French kings, from the Sienese-style *Portrait of John the Good* to Jean Fouquet's pinched-looking *Charles VII* and Jean Clouet's noble *François I*, who attracted numerous Italian artists to his court. Look out too for the strange atmosphere of the two Schools of Fontainebleau (rooms 9 and 10), which were heavily influenced by Italian

Mannerist painting. Two portraits of royal mistresses are provocatively erotic: from the First School of Fontainebleau, Henri II's mistress, Diane de Poitiers, is depicted semi-nude as the huntress Diana, while in a Second School piece, Gabrielle d'Estrées, the favourite of Henri IV, is shown sharing a bath with her sister, pinching her nipple as if plucking a cherry.

It's not until Poussin breaks onto the scene, in room 13, that a definitively French style emerges. As the undisputed master of **French classicism**, his profound themes, taken from antiquity, the bible and mythology, were to influence generations of artists to come. The Arcadian Shepherds, showing four shepherds interpreting the inscription "et in arcadia ego" (I, too, in Arcadia), has been taken to mean that death exists even in pastoral paradise. You'll need a healthy appetite for Classicism in the next suite of rooms, but there are some arresting portraits by Hyacinthe Rigaud, whose Louis XIV shows all the terrifying power of the king, and Philippe de Champaigne, whose portrait of his patron Cardinal Richelieu is even more imposing. The paintings of Georges de la Tour are more idiosyncratic. Card Sharp is compelling for its uneasy poise and strange lack of depth, though his Christ with Joseph in the Carpenter's Shop is a more typical work, mystically lit by a single candle.

Moving into the rather less severe **eighteenth century**, the more intimate paintings of Watteau come as a relief, as do Chardin's intense still lifes – notably The Skate – and the inspired rococo sketches by Fragonard known as the Figures of Fantasy, traditionally thought to have been completed in just one hour. From the southern wing of Sully to the end of this section, the chilly wind of Neoclassicism blows through the paintings of Gros, Gérard, Prud'hon, David and Ingres, contrasting with the more sentimental style that begins with Greuze and continues into the Romanticism of Géricault and Delacroix. Ingres' exquisite portraits were understandably much in demand in his day, but his true predilection was for historical subject matter and the female form, the latter appearing throughout the whole of his career, in his bathers from 1808 and 1828 and in his Turkish Bath, at once sensuous and abstracted. The final set of rooms takes in Milet, Corot and the **Barbizon school** of painting, the precursor of Impressionism. For anything later you'll have to head over to the Musée d'Orsay (see p.144).

## Northern European painting

The western end of Richelieu's second floor is given over to a relatively selective collection of **German**, **Flemish** and **Dutch** paintings, though the seventeenth century Dutch suite is strong, with no less than twelve paintings by Rembrandt – look out for Bathsheba and The Supper at Emmaus – and two serene canvases from Vermeer, The Astronomer and The Lacemaker. A brilliant set of works by Rubens can be found in the Médicis gallery (room 18), a whole room dedicated to the glory of Queen Marie de Médicis as commissioned by herself. The swirling colours and swaths of flapping cloth were to influence French painters from Fragonard to Delacroix.

## Italian and Spanish painting

Over in the Denon wing, on the first floor, the second area of the Louvre devoted to painting is dominated by the staggering **Italian collection**. The first two rooms house frescoes including two exquisite Botticelli allegories painted for the Villa Lemmi near Florence. Next, the high-ceilinged **Salon Carré** (room 3), used to exhibit paintings since the first "salon" of the Royal Academy in 1725, displays the so-called Primitives, with works by Giotto, Cimabue and Fra Angelico, as well as one of Uccello's bizarrely theoretical

## The Mona Lisa

Though the **Mona Lisa** is undoubtedly a very fine painting, its unparalleled celebrity demands an explanation. The picture's fame seems to rest not on its qualities but on the mysteries and controversies that have long surrounded it, as well as its apparently seductive attraction to male admirers – Napoleon had the picture removed from the Louvre and hung in his bedroom in the Tuileries palace.

"Mona Lisa" is, in fact, an English corruption of Monna Lisa – the historian Giorgio Vasari's polite way of referring to *madonna* (my lady) Lisa Gherardini, whose portrait he describes in his sixteenth-century *Lives of the Most Excellent Italian Architects, Painters and Sculptors*. She was married to one Francesco del Giocondo, from whose surname the Italians get their name for the painting, *la Gioconda*, and the French their *la Joconde*. However, it's not certain that the *Mona Lisa* depicts Monna Lisa. The portrait Vasari described, having never seen it himself, had eyebrows where the hair "grows thickly in one place" (the *Mona Lisa* has none) and "parting lips" (she smiles, but her mouth is closed). The only other contemporary description is by the secretary to Cardinal Louis of Aragon, who visited Leonardo at Amboise, where the painter was living out his last years at the court of François I. Leonardo apparently showed the cardinal three pictures that he had brought with him to France, including "one of a certain Florentine lady, done from life". And that's about it for identification, which has left the field wide open to conspiracy theorists, amateur speculators and owners of questionable copies or rival Leonardo works.

What is certain is that the *Mona Lisa* turned up in the bathroom of Fontainebleau, which Henri IV decided to restore in the 1590s. It remained largely neglected by public and art historians alike until, after it had been hanging in the Louvre for almost seventy years, the poet and novelist Théophile Gautier turned his hand to a guide-book to the Louvre. He singled out the "adorable Joconde" for praise: "She is always there smiling with sensuality, mocking her numerous lovers. She has the serene countenance of a woman sure that she will remain beautiful forever". A few years later, Gautier's erotic obsession seemed to have deepened, and the myth of the smile was given its finest articulation: "the sinuous, serpentine mouth, turned up at the corners in a violet penumbra, mocks the viewer with such sweetness, grace and superiority that we feel timid, like schoolboys in the presence of a duchess."

In England, the Mona Lisa was made famous by the prose stylist, Walter Pater, in 1869. According to him: "The presence that rose thus so strangely beside the waters, is expressive of what in the ways of a thousand years men had come to desire... She is older than the rocks among which she sits; like the vampire, she has been dead many times, and learned the secrets of the grave; and has been a diver in deep seas, and keeps their fallen day about her; and trafficked for strange webs with Eastern merchants; and, as Leda, was the mother of Helen of Troy, and, as Saint Anne, the mother of Mary; and all this has been to her but as the sound of lyres and flutes, and lives only in the delicacy with which it has moulded the changing lineaments, and tinged the eyelids and hands." So when the picture was stolen by an Italian security guard on 21 August 1911, and only recovered in December 1913, the stage was set for the *prima donna* of the Renaissance.

panels of the *Battle of San Romano*. To the west of the Salon, the famous **Grande Galerie**, originally built under Catherine de Médici's orders to link the Louvre and Tuileries palaces, stretches into the distance, parading all the great names of the Italian Renaissance – Mantegna, Filippo Lippi, Raphael, Coreggio, Titian. Leonardo da Vinci's *Virgin of the Rocks* and *Virgin and Child with St Anne* are on display here, untroubled by crowds, while his *Mona Lisa* (see box above) is expected to return to the **Salle des États** (room 6), on the right, late in 2003, along with Paolo Veronese's huge *Marriage at Cana*. If you want to catch *La Jioconde* – as she's known to the French – without the usual swarm of snap-happy admirers for company, go first or last thing in the day. The Mannerists kick in about halfway along the Grande Galerie, with a wonderfully weird *St Anne with Four Saints* by Il Pontormo and a *Pietà* by Rosso Fiorentino; the later part of the Galerie dwindles in quality and breadth as it moves towards the eighteenth century.

Venetian painting is largely relegated to the far end of Denon, with Piazzetta's large *Assumption* of 1735 and twelve Guardi scenes of festivities celebrating the accession of Doge Alvise Mocenigo IV. Adjacent, the relatively small but worthwhile **Spanish collection** has a few gems, notably Murillo's tender *Beggar Boy*, and the *Marquise de Santa Cruz* amongst the Goya portraits. From room 32, stairs lead down to the ground floor and the temporary section on the art of Africa, Asia Oceania and the Americas.

### French Nationalism and Romanticism

Running parallel to the Grande Galerie are two giant rooms dedicated to **French Nationalism** and Romanticism. The plan labels this section "large format French paintings", and it features some of the best-known French works. The Salle Mollien (room 75) boasts David's epic *Coronation of Napoleon I*, in which Napoleon is shown crowning himself with a rather crestfallen clergy in the background; almost unbelievably, David conceived this work as part of a much larger composition. Nearby are some fine portraits of women, including Prud'hon's Leonardo-like *Josephine in the Park at Malmaison*, some compellingly perfect canvases by Ingres and a self-portrait (with her daughter) by Elisabeth-Louise Vigée Lebrun, the court artist to Marie-Antoinette.

In the Salle Daru (room 77), **Romanticism** is heralded by Géricault's dramatic *Raft of the Medusa*, based on a notorious incident off the coast of Senegal in 1816. The survivors are seen despairing as a ship disappears over the horizon – as a survivor described it, "from the delirium of joy we fell into profound despondency and grief". The fifteen shown here were the last of 150 shipwrecked sailors who had escaped on the raft – thirst, murder and cannibalism having carried off the rest. The dead figure lying face down with his arm extended was modelled by Delacroix, whose *Liberty Leading the People* also hangs in this room. Delacroix's work is a famous icon of revolution, though you can tell by the hats that it depicts the 1830 revolution, which brought in the "bourgeois king" Louis-Philippe, rather than that of 1789. On seeing the painting, Louis-Philippe promptly ordered it kept out of sight so as not to give anyone dangerous ideas.

## Sculpture

The museum's extensive collection of **French Sculpture** is arranged on the lowest two levels of the Richelieu wing, with the more monumental pieces housed in two grand, glass-roofed courtyards. Many sculptures removed from the park at Marly (see p.223) grace the Cour Marly, notably the four triumphal equestrian statues known as the *Marly Horses*, two by Coysevox for Louis XIV, at the top of the stairs, and two by Costou for Louis XV, on the tall plinths to the side of the courtyard. Cour Puget has Pierre Puget's dynamic *Milon de Crotone* as its centrepiece, the lion's claws tearing into Milon's apparently soft flesh and the entire piece writhing around its skilfully diffused axis.

The surrounding rooms trace the development of sculpture in France from painful Romanesque Crucifixions through to the nineteenth century and the lofty public works of David d'Angers. Among the startlingly realistic Gothic pieces, you can't miss the Burgundian *Tomb of Philippe Pot*, borne by hooded mourners known as *pleurants*. The Italian influence is strongly felt in Michel Colombe's relief of *St George Slaying the Dragon*, but there is something distinctively French in the strangely liquid bas reliefs sculpted by Jean Goujon in the 1540s, at around the same time as he was working on Lescot's facade for the Cour Carré. Towards the end of the course you may find yourself crying out for an end to all the gracefully perfect nudes and grandiose busts of noblemen. The charming vignette of François Rude's *Neapolitan Fisherboy* provides some respite, but the only real antidote is Rodin and you'll have to leave the Louvre to see any of his works.

Alternatively, make for the smaller, more intense **Italian sculpture** section in the long Galerie Mollien (room 4), on the ground floor of Denon. Here you'll find such bold masterpieces as two of Michelangelo's writhing *Slaves*, the anonymous *Veiled Woman* and Canova's irresistible *Cupid and Psyche*. Immediately below, in the old stables on the lower ground floor (room 1), are the earlier Italians, notably Duccio's virtuoso *Virgin and Child Surrounded by Angels*. Adjacent are some severely Gothic Virgins from Flanders and Germany (rooms A–C) and the **Tactile Gallery**, where you can run your hands over copies of some of the most important sculptures from the collection.

## Objets d'art

The vast **Objets d'art** section, on the first floor of the Richelieu wing, presents the finest tapestries, ceramics, jewellery and furniture commissioned by France's most wealthy and influential patrons, beginning with an exquisite little equestrian sculpture of Charlemagne (or possibly it's Charles the Bald) and continuing through eighty-one relentlessly superb rooms to a salon decorated in the style of Louis-Philippe, the last king of France. Walking through the entire chronology is an enlightening experience, giving a powerful sense of the evolution of aesthetic taste at its most refined and opulent. The exception is the Middle Ages section, of a more pious nature, which includes carved ivories, Limoges enamels, and three precious vases commissioned by Abbot Suger, the mastermind of the Gothic basilica at St-Denis.

Numerous rooms have been partially recreated in the style of a particular epoch, and in these surroundings it's not hard to imagine yourself strutting through a Renaissance chamber or gracing an eighteenth century salon, especially as whole suites are often devoid of other visitors. The apotheosis of the whole experience comes towards the end, as the circuit passes through the breathtaking apartments of Napoléon III's Minister of State, full of plush upholstery, immense chandeliers, gilded putti, caryatids and dramatic ceiling frescoes, in true Second Empire style.

An astounding outpost of the Objets d'Art collection awaits in the **Apollo Gallery** (Denon wing, first floor, room 66), though restoration works will keep the room closed for 2003 and much of 2004. Set amid a glorious golden decor symbolizing Louis XIV (the Sun King) as Apollo (the sun god), are the crown jewels of France, including the mammoth Regent diamond sported by Louis XV, Louis XVI, Charles X and Napoleon I. The central ceiling painting, by Delacroix, depicts *Apollo Defeating the Python*.

## Antiquities

The enormous **Antiquities** collection practically forms a parallel museum of its own, taking up most of the Sully wing, other than the top floor, and creeping into Denon and Richelieu on the lower levels. The embarrassment of riches, a perennial problem for visitors to the Louvre, is at its most intractable here. The superb Egyptian collection reflects the longstanding French fascination with Egyptology, while the outstanding Greek and Roman collections date back to the eager acquisitions of François I, Richelieu and Mazarin. The so-called Oriental section, which presents a major collection of artefacts from the Near and Middle East, is relatively manageable in size.

## Oriental Antiquities

**Oriental Antiquities** (Richelieu wing, ground floor) covers the sculptures, stone-carved writings, pottery and other relics of the ancient Middle and Near East, including the Mesopotamian, Sumerian, Babylonian, Assyrian and Phoenician civilizations, plus the art of ancient Persia. The highlight of this section is the boldly sculpted stonework, much of it in relief. Watch out for the statues and busts depicting the young Sumerian prince Gudea, and the black, two-metre-high Code of Hammurabi, which dates from around 1800 BC, during the Mesapotamian civilization. Standing erect like a warning finger, a series of royal precepts (the "code") is crowned with a stern depiction of the king meeting the sun god Shamash, dispenser of justice. The Cour Khorsabad, adjacent, is dominated by two giant, Assyrian winged bulls (one is a reproduction) that once acted as guardians to the palace of Sargon II, from which many treasures were brought to the Louvre. The utterly refined **Arts of Islam** collection lies below, on the lower ground floor. Bizarrely, the so-called *Baptistery of St Louis*, an exquisite fourteenth-century Syrian brass bowl, was used for numerous royal christenings in the nineteenth century.

## Egyptian Antiquities

Jean-François Champollion, who translated the hieroglyphics of the Rosetta Stone, was the first curator of the collection of **Egyptian Antiquities** – now the biggest and most important in the world after the Egyptian Museum in Cairo. Starting on the ground floor of the Sully wing, the thematic circuit leads up from the atmospheric crypt of the Sphinx (room 1) to the Nile, source of all life in Egypt, and takes the visitor through the everyday life of pharaonic Egypt by way of cooking utensils, jewellery, the principles of hieroglyphics, musical instruments, sarcophagi, a host of mummified cats and dozens of examples of the delicate naturalism of Egyptian decorative technique, such as the wall tiles depicting a piebald calf galloping through fields of papyrus, and a duck taking off from a marsh.

Upstairs, on the first floor, the chronological circuit keeps the masterpieces on the right-hand side, while numerous pots and statuettes of more specialist interest are displayed to the left. Among the major exhibits are the *Great Sphinx*, carved from a single block of pink granite, the polychrome *Seated Scribe* statue, the striking, life-size, wooden statue of Chancellor Nakhti, a bust of Amenophis IV and a low-relief sculpture of Sethi I and the goddess Hathor. Post-pharaonic Egypt is exhibited on the lower ground floor level of the Denon wing. The legacy of the pharaohs is easily discernible in the funerary trappings of Roman Egypt, though a new and startling naturalism stares out of the faces of the mummy portraits.

## Greek and Roman Antiquities

The collection of **Greek and Roman Antiquities**, mostly statues, is one of the finest in the world. The biggest crowd-pullers in the museum, after the

*Mona Lisa*, are here: the *Winged Victory of Samothrace*, at the top of Denon's great staircase, and the *Venus de Milo* (room 12). Venus is surrounded by hordes of less familiar Aphrodites, from the graceful marble head known as the "Kaufmann Head" and the delightful Venus of Arles – both early copies of the work of the great sculptor Praxiteles – to the strange *Dame d'Auxerre*.

This section of the museum is housed in Lescot's original wing. In the **Salle des Caryatides** (room 17), which houses Roman copies of Greek works, the musicians' balcony is supported by four giant caryatids, sculpted in 1550 by Jean Goujon. Just beyond, the Henri II staircase is carved with the initials H and D for Henri and his mistress Diane de Poitiers, along with symbols of the hunt recalling the Roman goddess Diana.

In the Roman section a sterner style takes over, but there are some very attractive mosaics from Asia Minor and luminous frescoes from Pompeii and Herculaneum. At the time of writing, work was in progress to turn the Cour Visconti (Denon's mirror image of the Cour Puget) into a courtyard for works of late antiquity. Works on the two lower levels are complemented by smaller groupings by medium on the first floor including a daunting assemblage of Greek pottery and a section on Greek and Roman glass and precious objects, room 33 of which has a heart-stirring ceiling decoration of blue and white birds painted by Georges Braque in 1953.

## The Medieval Louvre

For a complete change of scene, you can always descend to the strange **Medieval Louvre** section, on the lower ground floor of Sully. The stump of Philippe-Auguste's keep soars up dramatically towards the enormous concrete ceiling like a pillar holding up the entire modern edifice, while vestiges of Charles V's medieval palace walls buttress the edges of the vast chamber. A similar but more intimate effect can be felt in the adjacent Salle St-Louis, with its carved pillars and vaults cut short by the modern roof.

To see how Charles V's Louvre used to look, check out the postcards (on sale everywhere) of the October scene from *Les Très Riches Heures du Duc de Berry*, a mid-fifteenth century prayer book that depicted some of the great châteaux of the realm. Seen rising behind the high city walls that run along the Seine, the Louvre seems impossibly remote, a strange blend of fairy-tale castle and imposing fortress. In the foreground, peasants are shown ploughing and sowing in the green fields of St-Germain-des-Prés.

# Union Centrale des Arts Décoratifs

The other museums housed in the Palais du Louvre come under the umbrella organization **Union Centrale des Arts Décoratifs**. Often unjustly overlooked, their exhibitions can be among the city's most innovative, run by professionals from within the fashion and advertising industries rather than state museum administrators. The entrance for all three museums is at 107 rue de Rivoli (Tues–Fri 11am–6pm, Sat & Sun 10am–6pm; €7; Ⓦ www.ucad.fr).

The **Musée de la Mode et du Textile** holds high-quality temporary exhibitions drawn from the large permanent collection aimed at demonstrating the most brilliant and cutting-edge of Paris fashions from all eras. Recent exhibitions have included Jackie Kennedy's famous 1960s dresses and a look at the work of the couturier.

On the top floor, the **Musée de la Publicité** shows off its collection of advertising posters through cleverly themed, temporary exhibitions. The space is appropriately trendy – half-exposed brickwork and steel panelling, and half-crumbling Louvre finery – and there's a bar as well as a dozen computers where you can access the archive.

Until the modern collections reopen (2004 or 2005), the restrained, traditional **Musée des Arts Décoratifs**, seems something of the odd man out, though its eclectic collection of art and superbly crafted furnishing fits the Union Centrale's "design" theme. The work may seem humble in comparison with the Louvre's airy *Objets d'art* section, but most were made to be lived with or actually used, and the museum is a less daunting prospect as a result. At the time of writing, only the medieval and Renaissance rooms were open, showing off curiously shaped and beautifully carved chairs, dressers and tables, religious paintings, Venetian glass, some wonderful tapestries – including the delightful late-fifteenth-century *Le Berger*, depicting a shepherd surrounded by a very woolly flock – and a room entirely decorated and furnished as a late-medieval bedroom. The fascinating contemporary collections will display works by French, Italian and Japanese designers, including some great examples of the work of Philippe Starck.

# The Champs-Élysées and Tuileries

T he nine-kilometre axis that extends from the Louvre at the heart of the city to the Défense business district in the west is often referred to as the **Voie Triomphale**, or Triumphal Way. Offering impressive vistas along the entire length, it also incorporates some of the city's most famous landmarks – the **avenue des Champs-Élysées**, **place de la Concorde**, **Tuileries gardens** and the **Arc de Triomphe**. The whole ensemble is so regular and geometrical it looks as though it might have been laid out by a single town planner rather than successive kings, emperors and presidents, all keen to add their stamp and promote French power and prestige. Last to join the list was President Mitterrand (whose *grands projets* for the city outdid even Napoleon's) – his glass pyramid entrance to the Louvre (see Chapter 2) and immense marble-clad cubic arch at La Défense (see Chapter 11) effectively marking each end of the historic axis. The two great constructions echo each other in scale and geometry, with both aligned at the same slight angle away from the axis – a detail that, given the distance involved, has to be appreciated conceptually rather than visually.

## The Arc de Triomphe

The best view of the Voie Triomphale is from the top of the **Arc de Triomphe** (daily: April–Sept 9.30am–11pm; Oct–March 10am–10.30pm; €7; Mº Charles-de-Gaulle-Étoile), towering above the traffic in the middle of place Charles-de-Gaulle, better known as **place de l'Étoile**. The arch was begun by Napoleon in 1806 in homage to the armies of France and himself, but it wasn't actually finished until 1836 by Louis Philippe, who dedicated it to the French army in general. Later, victorious invading armies would use the arch to humiliate the French. After the Prussians' triumphal march in 1871, Parisians lit bonfires beneath the arch and down the Champs-Élysées to eradicate the "stain" of German boots. Still a potent symbol of the country's military might, the arch is the starting point for the annual Bastille Day procession, a bombastic march-past of tanks, guns and flags. A more poignant ceremony is conducted every evening at 6.30pm at the foot of the monument, when war veterans stoke up the flame at the **tomb of an unknown soldier**, killed in the Great War.

Access to the arch is via underground stairs on the north corner of the Champs-Élysées. The names of 660 generals and numerous French battles are engraved on its inside, while reliefs adorn the exterior: be sure to see François Rude's extraordinarily dramatic *Marseillaise*, in which an Amazon-type figure personifying the Revolution charges forward with a sword, her face contorted in a fierce rallying cry. If you're up for climbing the 280 steps to the top, you'll be amply rewarded with panoramic views, at their best towards dusk on a sunny day when the marble of the Grande Arche de la Défense sparkles in the setting sun and the Louvre is bathed in warm light. While you're up there take a look at the small **museum**, a collection of prints and photos of the Arc de Triomphe's history, including the alternative proposals for a triumphal monument before the arch was settled on; if things had gone differently you might have been climbing up steps into the belly of a giant elephant with a fountain gushing out of its trunk.

# The Champs-Élysées and around

Twelve avenues radiate out from the place de l'Étoile, of which the best known is the **Champs-Élysées**, a popular rallying point at times of national crisis as well as celebration: crowds thronged here to greet Général de Gaulle as he walked down the avenue just after the Liberation in May 1944, and many turned out to support him again in 1968 in the wake of the student riots; more recently, thousands congregated in 1998 to party all night after France won the World Cup. It's also the scene of annual processions on November 11 and Bastille Day, while the Tour de France ends here in July with a final flourish.

Broad and tree-lined, the gently sloping avenue looks at its most impressive from a distance, especially from place de la Concorde. Close up, it's a little disappointing, with its constant stream of traffic and preponderance of fast-food outlets, airline offices and chain stores – a far cry from its heyday during the Second Empire when members of the *haute bourgeoisie* built themselves splendid mansions along its length and fashionable society would come to stroll and frequent the cafés and theatres. Although most of the mansions subsequently gave way to office blocks and the *beau monde* moved elsewhere, some of the avenue's former glitz lives on at the *Lido* cabaret, *Fouquet's* high-class restaurant-bar (which hosts the César film awards each year), the perfumier Guerlain's shop at no. 68 and the former belle époque *Claridges* hotel at no. 74, now a swanky shopping arcade. There are signs that the avenue's prospects are looking up again: a number of designer shops have recently moved in, a branch of the sumptuous *Ladurée* tea room has appeared, and new, fashionable restaurants and bars in the streets around are injecting a fresh buzz and glamour.

One of the streets to the south that has long had fashionable status is the **avenue Montaigne**, a catwalk of designer shops such as Dior, Prada and Chanel. Right at the bottom is the **Théâtre des Champs-Élysées**, built in 1913 and one of the first buildings in Paris to be made of reinforced concrete, its exterior softened with marble reliefs by Bourdelle. The architect, Auguste Perret, went on to rebuild much of Le Havre in the aftermath of World War II. The theatre has seen a number of notable premieres and debuts including that of Josephine Baker in 1925, who created a sensation with her sensual, abandoned dancing. It's perhaps best known though for being the scene of a riot

RESTAURANTS

| L'Appart' | H |
| Dragons Élysées | F |
| La Fermette Marbeuf 1900 | L |
| Lasserre | M |
| Le Relais de l'Entrecôte | N |
| Rue Balzac | E |
| Spoon, Food and Wine | K |
| Le Tillsit | D |
| Yvan | G |

on May 29, 1913, on the occasion of the world premiere of Stravinsky's *Rite of Spring*. The music's unprecedented rhythmic and harmonic ferocity provoked violent reactions among the audience. The whole performance was punctuated with catcalls so loud the dancers could barely hear the orchestra, objects were thrown at the conductor and fist-fights broke out in the stalls.

On the lower stretch of the avenue des Champs-Élysées, beyond the Rond-Point des Champs-Élysées, shops give way to flowerbeds and lawns. The gigantic building with grandiose Neoclassical exteriors, glass roofs and exuberant flying statuary rising above the greenery to the south is the **Grand Palais**, created with its neighbour, the **Petit Palais**, for the 1900 **Exposition Universelle**. Today, both contain permanent museums and also host good temporary exhibitions. Between the two lies the **place Clemenceau**, presided over by statues of Georges Clemenceau, French prime minister at the end of World War I, and a recently-added bronze of General de Gaulle in mid-stride. From here the **avenue Winston-Churchill** leads down towards the Seine,

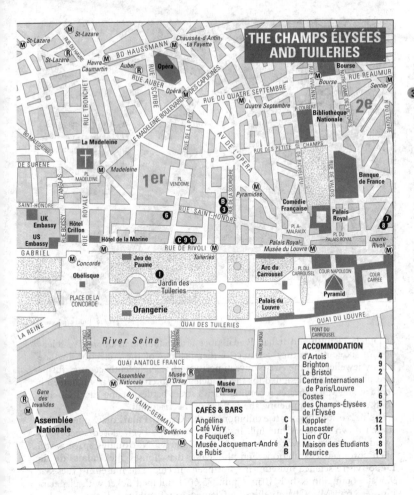

THE CHAMPS ÉLYSÉES
AND TUILERIES

**ACCOMMODATION**

| | |
|---|---|
| d'Artois | 4 |
| Brighton | 9 |
| Le Bristol | 2 |
| Centre International de Paris/Louvre | 7 |
| Costes | 6 |
| des Champs-Élysées | 5 |
| de l'Élysée | 1 |
| Keppler | 12 |
| Lancaster | 11 |
| Lion d'Or | 3 |
| Maison des Étudiants | 8 |
| Meurice | 10 |

**CAFÉS & BARS**

| | |
|---|---|
| Angélina | C |
| Café Véry | I |
| Le Fouquet's | J |
| Musée Jacquemart-André | A |
| Le Rubis | B |

culminating with a statue of the man himself. To the north of Place Clemenceau, combat police guard the high walls round the presidential **Palais de l'Élysée** and the line of ministries and embassies ending with the US in prime position on the corner of place de la Concorde. On Thursdays and at weekends there's a **postage-stamp market** at the corner of avenues Gabriel and Marigny.

## The Petit Palais and Grand Palais

The **Petit Palais** (closed for renovation until the autumn of 2005) is normally the site of major, changing exhibitions and the **Musée des Beaux-Arts**, which at first sight seems to house a collection of leftovers, encompassing every period from the Renaissance to the 1920s, after the other main galleries have taken their pick. It does, however, hold some real gems: Monet's *Sunset at Lavacourt* and Boudin's *Gust of Wind at Le Havre* stand out against some rather uninspiring Renoirs, Morisots, Cézannes and Manets. There's a small collection

77

△ Statue, Jardin des Tuileries

of Dutch, Flemish and Italian Renaissance art, including an impressive selection of sixteenth-century ceramics. Other features of the collection include fantasy jewellery of the Art Nouveau period, effete eighteenth-century furniture, plaster models designed for the Madeleine church in the early nineteenth century, and vast canvases recording Paris's street battles during the 1830 and 1848 revolutions, trumpeting the victory of the Tricolour.

The best of the major art exhibitions at the **Grand Palais** draw queues that stretch down avenue Churchill. Inside, the nave has been closed since 1993 awaiting restoration work but part of the **Galeries Nationales** space is still open for major exhibitions and the wing that houses the **Palais de la Découverte** science museum has not been affected. The museum (Tues–Sat 9.30am–6pm, Sun & hols 10am–7pm; €5.60, combined ticket with planetarium €8.65; M° Champs-Élysées-Clemenceau/Franklin-D.Roosevelt) has brightened itself up considerably since the Cité des Sciences arrived on the scene. It can't really compete, but it does have plenty of interactive exhibits, some very good temporary shows and an excellent planetarium.

# North of the Arc de Triomphe and Champs-Élysées

North of the Arc de Triomphe, the 16e and 17e arrondissements are for the most part cold and soulless, their huge fortified apartments empty much of the time while their owners – royal, exiled royal, ex-royal or just extremely rich – jet between their other residences dotted about the globe. The eighth arrondissement north of the Champs-Élysées, however, has more to offer commercially and culturally with some of the *hôtels particuliers* (mansions) housing select museums. One such building, the Hôtel André, offers the highlight of the area, the magnificent art collection of the **Musée Jacquemart-André** (see below).

The best avenue to start wandering down from place de l'Étoile – apart from the Champs-Élysées – is the northerly **avenue de Wagram**. Devotees of Art Nouveau can stop in front of no. 34 and contemplate Jules Lavirotte's design of 1904, which won best Parisian facade in 1905. Less taxing aesthetic judgements are called for in front of the flower market and cafés of **place des Ternes**, the first big junction on avenue de Wagram, where rue du Faubourg-St-Honoré begins, heading southeast. You can take this street and then the second left to admire the five gold onion domes of the Russian Orthodox Cathédrale Alexandre-Nevski, at 6 rue Daru, witness to Picasso's marriage to Olga Khoklova in 1918. Continuing further down rue du Faubourg-St-Honoré brings you to rue Berryer (third on the right) and the superb, classical Hôtel Salomon de Rothschild at no. 9–11, where the **Centre National de la Photographie** (daily except Tues noon–7pm, Mon till 9pm; ⓦ www.cnp-photographie.com; €4.60; M° George-V & M° St-Philippe-du-Roule) hosts excellent temporary photographic exhibitions. The most exotic building in the area can be seen by turning left on rue de Monceau – the **Chinese pagoda**, on the junction with rue de Courcelles, built by C T Loo in 1926 as a private art gallery and still in the hands of the same family.

Heading north up rue de Courcelles brings you past the enormous gilded gates of the avenue Hoche entrance to **Parc de Monceau** (M° Monceau). The park has a roller-skating rink and kids' play facilities but otherwise it's a rather formal affair with replica antique colonnades and artificial grottoes. Half the people who command the heights of the French economy spent their infancy there, promenaded in prams by their nannies.

On avenue Vélasquez, by the east gate of Parc de Monceau, at no. 7, the **Musée Cernuschi** (currently closed for renovation until sometime in 2004) houses a small collection of far-eastern art, mainly ancient Chinese, bequeathed to the state by the banker Cernuschi, who nearly lost his life for giving money to the Commune. The first floor alternates between contemporary Chinese painting and temporary exhibitions, whilst the ground floor hosts the permanent collection. There are some exquisite pieces here, including a selection of ceremonial jade objects from the Shang era (1550–1050bc), and some unique ceramics detailing everyday life in ancient China, but on the whole the collection is of fairly specialized interest. Right beside the Cernuschi, with its entrance at no. 63 rue de Monceau, is the **Musée Nissim de Camondo** (Wed–Sun 10am–5pm; €4.60; M° Monceau & M° Villiers), named after both Count Moïse Camondo's father and his son, who was killed while flying missions for France in World War I. The count's taste for late eighteenth-century French aristocratic luxuries led him to commission this new residence in the style of the Petit Trianon at Versailles for himself and his collection. The eighteenth-century tapestries, paintings, gilded furniture, and tableware of the porcelain and solid silver variety have been impeccably assembled, with only a few of the anachronistic mod cons of an early twentieth-century aristocratic home surfacing.

# Musée Jacquemart-André

Just a few blocks to the south of the Parc de Monceau, at 158 boulevard Haussmann, stands the lavishly ornamented palace of the nineteenth-century banker and art-lover Édouard André and his wife, former society portraitist Nélie Jacquemart. Built in 1870 to grace Baron Haussmann's grand new boulevard, the Hôtel André is now the **Musée Jacquemart-André** (daily 10am–6pm; ⓦ www.musee-jacquemart-andre.com; €8; M° Miromesnil/St-Philippe-du-Roule), housing the couple's impressive private art collection and a fabulous *salon de thé* (see p.279 for review) – the meeting place of the elegant and discreet. Bequeathed to the Institut de France by Édouard's widow, the Hôtel André deploys the couple's collection exactly as they ordained. Nélie painted Édouard's portrait in 1872 – on display in what were their private apartments on the ground floor – and nine years later they were married, after which Nélie gave up her painting career and the pair devoted their spare time to collecting art, travelling around Europe for six months of the year searching for pieces. Their preference for **Italian art** is evident in the stunning collection of fifteenth- and sixteenth-century genius, including the works of Tiepolo, Botticelli, Donatello, Mantegna and Uccello, which forms the core of the collection. Almost as compelling as the splendid interior and art collection is the insight gleaned into an extraordinary marriage and grand nineteenth-century lifestyle, brought to life by the fascinating narration on the free audio-guide (available in English).

In Room 1, mostly eighteenth-century French paintings are displayed, including several portraits by **Boucher**, in addition to two lively paintings of Venice by Canaletto. Room 2, the reception area, has specially constructed folding doors which, when opened, transformed the space into a ballroom large enough to contain a thousand guests. Room 3 contains three huge tapestries depicting Russian scenes that capture the fashion for Slav exoticism of the mid-eighteenth century. Room 6, formerly the library, focuses on Dutch and Flemish paintings, including three by **Van Dyck** and two by **Rembrandt** – *The Portrait of Dr A. Tholinx* and an early work, *The Pilgrims of Emmaus*, showing remarkable use of chiaroscuro. Room 7 is the Salon de Musique (and the other half of the ballroom), whose dramatic high ceiling is decorated with a mural by Pierre Victor Galant; the musicians would play from the gallery, and you're treated to a mini-concert on the audioguide as you gaze at the ceiling. In Room 8, a huge, animated fresco by **Tiepolo** depicting the French king Henri III being received by Frederigo Contarini in Venice, graces the extraordinary marble, bronze and wrought-iron double spiral staircase that leads from an interior garden of palm trees up to the musician's gallery. Room 9, once the smoking room, where the men would retreat after dinner, is hung with the work of eighteenth-century English portraitists, among them a painting by **Joshua Reynolds**.

Leading off the music gallery are the intimate rooms in which the couple displayed their **early Renaissance Italian collection**. The first was intended as Nélie's studio, but she instead decorated it as a sculpture gallery – including three bronzes by **Donatello** – its walls covered in low-relief sculpture. The dimly-lit Florentine room next door includes a wonderful, brightly coloured *Saint George Slaying the Dragon* (1440) by **Paolo Uccello**, a **Botticelli** *Virgin and Child* (1470) depicted with touching beauty and fragility, and an exquisite sixteenth-century inlaid choir stall. Adjacent is the Venetian room, with paintings by **Bellini** and **Mantegna** among others.

# Place de la Concorde

At the eastern end of the Champs-Élysées, the grand-scale **place de la Concorde** is much less peaceful than its name suggests. Between 1793 and 1795, some 1300 people died here beneath the Revolutionary guillotine: Louis XVI, Marie-Antoinette, Danton and Robespierre among them. Today, constantly circumnavigated by traffic, the centrepiece of the *place* is a gold-tipped obelisk from the temple of Ramses at Luxor, offered as a favour-currying gesture by the viceroy of Egypt in 1829. From the centre of the square you can admire the alignment of the French parliament, the Assemblée Nationale, on the far side of the Seine, with the church of the Madeleine at the end of rue Royale, to the north. The Neoclassical *Hôtel Crillon* – the ultimate luxury address for visitors to Paris – and its twin, the Hôtel de la Marine, housing the Ministry of the Navy, flank the entrance to rue Royale, which, needless to say, meets the Voie Triomphale at a precise right angle.

# The Tuileries Gardens

Extending for around 1km from the place de la Concorde to the Louvre, the **Jardin des Tuileries** is the formal French garden par excellence, forming the splendid backdrop to many a Parisian Sunday promenade. The grand central alley is lined with shady, clipped chestnuts and manicured lawns, and framed at each end by ornamental pools, surrounded by an impressive gallery of statues (by the likes of Rodin, Coustou and Coysevox) brought here from Versailles and Marly (Louis XIV's retreat from Versailles, no longer in existence), though many are copies, the originals having been transferred to the Louvre. The much sought-after chairs strewn around the ponds are a good spot from which to admire the statues, watch children chase boats around the pond and observe promenading Parisians. There are also a number of cafés nestling among the trees, ideal retreats on sunny days when the glare of the sun on the gravel of the central alley can be quite dazzling.

The garden's **history** actually goes back to the 1570s when Catherine de Médicis had the site cleared of the medieval warren of tilemakers (*tuileries*) that stood here to make way for a palace and grounds (see box on p.64). The Palais des Tuileries, as it became known, was surrounded with formal vegetable gardens, a labyrinth and a chequerboard of flowerbeds. The present layout however is largely the work of the landscape architect Le Nôtre, who was commissioned by Louis XIV a hundred years later to redesign the gardens on a grander scale. Employing techniques perfected at Versailles, Le Nôtre took the opportunity to further indulge his passion for symmetry, straight avenues, formal flowerbeds and splendid vistas. During the eighteenth century, the gardens were where flash Parisians came to preen and party, and in 1783 the Montgolfier brothers, Joseph and Etienne, launched the first successful hot air balloon here. The first serious replanting was carried out after the Revolution, and in the nineteenth century, rare species were added to the garden, by this time dominated by chestnut trees. Sadly, some of the oldest specimens were lost in the December 1999 storms: the centennial chestnuts around the two central oval ponds are now the most senior.

At the eastern end of the gardens in front of the Louvre is the **Jardin du Carrousel**, a raised terrace where the Palais des Tuileries, burnt down by the Communards in 1871, was sited. It's now planted with trim yew hedges, between which stand oddly static bronzes of buxom female nudes by Maillol (for more on Maillol, see p.143).

The two buildings flanking the garden at the western, Concorde end, are the Orangerie, by the river, and the **Jeu de Paume**, by rue de Rivoli (Tues noon–9.30pm, Wed–Fri noon–7pm, Sat & Sun 10am–7pm; €6; M° Concorde), once a royal tennis court and the place where French Impressionist paintings were displayed before being transferred to the Musée d'Orsay. In a subsequent renovation, huge windows were cut into the Jeu de Paume's classical temple walls, allowing light to flood in, and it's now one of the city's best exhibition spaces for contemporary art – usually major retrospectives of established artists.

The **Orangerie**, a private art collection including many of Monet's large waterlily paintings, is currently closed for renovation and due to reopen in the summer of 2004. Work is underway to convert many of the existing exterior walls to glass, in line with Monet's request that as much natural light as possible reach his masterpieces. The rest of the collection, featuring works by Renoir, Sisley, Matisse, Cézanne, Utrillo, Modigliani and Soutine, will be rearranged and possibly added to from the collection's reserves.

# The Grands Boulevards, passages and Les Halles

B uilt on the site of the city's old ramparts, the **Grands Boulevards** extend in a long arc from the **Église de la Madeleine** in the west to the Bastille in the east. Once highly fashionable thoroughfares where *le tout Paris* would come to promenade and seek entertainment, they're still a vibrant and colourful part of the city, with their brasseries, theatres and cinemas.

The streets off the Grands Boulevards constitute the city's main **commercial and financial district**. Right at the heart of the area stand the solid institutions of the **Banque de France** and the **Bourse**, while just to the north, beyond the glittering **Opéra Garnier**, are the large department stores **Galeries Lafayette** and **Printemps**. Rather more well-heeled shopping is concentrated on the rue St-Honoré in the west and the streets around elegant **place Vendôme**, lined with top couturiers, jewellers and art dealers. Scattered around the whole of the Grands Boulevards area are the delightful **passages** – nineteenth-century arcades with glass roofs and tiled floors that hark back to shopping from a different era.

In the south, the **Palais Royal** arcades and gardens provide a perfect retreat from the traffic and make a handy shortcut through to the **Bibliothèque Nationale**. Further east, the **Sentier** district is the centre of the rag trade, while nearby **rue St-Denis** sees trade of a seedier kind. Just south of here is **Les Halles**, once the food market of Paris, though no former trader would recognize it as such. Of all the changes to the city in the last 25 years, the transformation of Les Halles into an underground RER/métro station and shopping centre is the least inspired – though overground it does provide some much-needed greenery.

## The Grands Boulevards

The **Grands Boulevards** is the collective name given to the eight streets that form one long, wide thoroughfare running from the Madeleine to

République, then down to the Bastille. The western section, from the Madeleine to Porte St-Denis, follows the rampart built by Charles V. When its defensive purpose became redundant with the offensive foreign policy of Louis XIV, the walls were pulled down and the ditches filled in, leaving a wide promenade (given the name *boulevard* after the military term for the level part of a rampart). In the mid-eighteenth century, the boulevard became a fashionable place to be seen on horseback or in one's carriage. At the same time, the eastern section developed a more colourful reputation, derived from its association with street theatre, mime, juggling, puppets, waxworks and cafés of ill repute, earning itself the nickname the *boulevard du Crime*. Much of this was swept away, however, in the latter half of the nineteenth century by Baron Haussmann when he created the huge place de la République.

In the nineteenth century, the café clientele of the west-end **boulevard des Italiens** set the trends for all of Paris, in terms of manners, dress and conversation. The Grands Boulevards were cobbled, and Paris's first horse-drawn omnibus rattled from the Madeleine to the Bastille. From the bourgeois intellectuals in the west to the artisan fun-lovers in the east, this thoroughfare had its finger on the city's pulse. As recently as the 1950s, a visitor to Paris would, as a matter of course, have gone for a stroll along the Grands Boulevards to see "*Paris vivant*". And today, in amongst the burger bars, there are still theatres and cinemas (including the Max Linder and the Grand Rex – the latter an extraordinary building inside and out, see p.322), and numerous brasseries and cafés, which, though not the most fashionable or innovative, still belong to the tradition of the Grands Boulevards, immortalized in the film *Les Enfants du Paradis*. It was at 14 **boulevard des Capucines**, in 1895, that Paris saw its first film, or animated photography, as the Lumière brothers' invention was called. Some years earlier, in 1874, another artistic revolution had taken place at no. 35 in the former studio of photographer Félix Nadar – the first **Impressionist exhibition**. It was greeted with outrage by the art world; as one critic said of Monet's *Impression, Soleil Levant* ("Impression: sunrise"), "it was worse than anyone had hitherto dared to paint".

A remnant from the fun-loving times on the Grands Boulevards are the waxworks in the **Musée Grévin** (daily 10am–6pm; €15, children €9; M° Rue Montmartre), on boulevard Montmartre. The collection has recently been overhauled and expanded, with the addition of 80 new figures – mainly French literary, media and political personalities and the usual bunch of Hollywood actors. The revamp doesn't really warrant the increased entry fee, but still, it's quite a fun outing – you can prop up the bar with Ernest Hemingway or have your photo taken next to Isabelle Adjani. Many of the displays illustrate scenes from French history, especially the more grisly episodes such as the St Bartholomew massacre. Perhaps the best thing about the museum, though, is the original rooms: the magical Palais des Mirages (Hall of Mirrors), built for the Exposition Universelle in 1900; the theatre with its sculptures by Bourdelle; and the 1882 Baroque-style Hall of Columns, where among other unlikely juxtapositions, Lara Croft stands a few feet away from Charles de Gaulle and Voltaire smiles across at Marilyn Monroe.

# Opéra Garnier and around

Set back from the boulevard des Capucines is the dazzling Opéra de Paris – usually referred to as the **Opéra Garnier** (ⓦ www.opera-de-paris.fr; M° Opéra) to distinguish it from the new opera house at the Bastille. Constructed

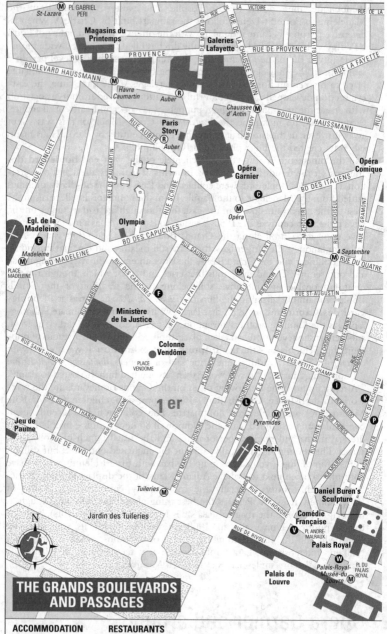

THE GRANDS BOULEVARDS
AND PASSAGES

| ACCOMMODATION | | RESTAURANTS | | | | | |
|---|---|---|---|---|---|---|---|
| Chopin | 1 | Baan Boran | P | Dilan | O | Le Grand Véfour | Q |
| de Noailles | 3 | Chartier | B | Foujita | L | Higuma | I |
| Vivienne | 2 | Au Petit Riche | A | Le Grand Café Capucines | C | Le Vaudeville | J |
| | | Le Dauphin | V | Le Grand Colbert | G | | |

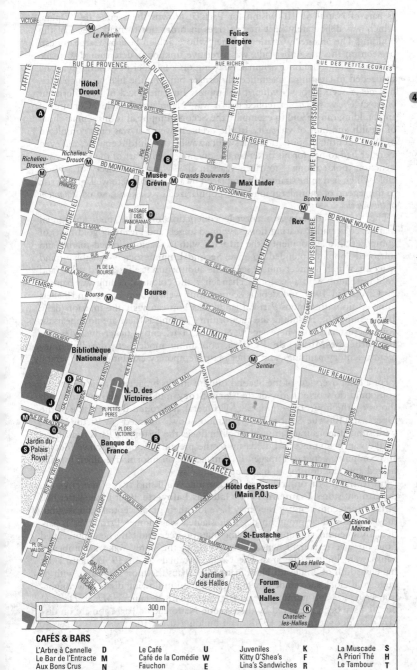

**CAFÉS & BARS**

| | | | | | | | |
|---|---|---|---|---|---|---|---|
| L'Arbre à Cannelle | D | Le Café | U | Juveniles | K | La Muscade | S |
| Le Bar de l'Entracte | M | Café de la Comédie | W | Kitty O'Shea's | F | A Priori Thé | H |
| Aux Bons Crus | N | Fauchon | E | Lina's Sandwiches | R | Le Tambour | T |

as part of Napoléon III's vision for Paris, it crowns the avenue de l'Opéra, which was deliberately kept free of trees in order not to mask views of the building. The architect, Charles Garnier, whose golden bust by Carpeaux can be seen on the rue Auber side, was a relative unknown, determined to make his mark with something original. Drawing on a number of existing styles, he succeeded in creating a magnificently ornate building the like of which Paris had never seen before – when the Empress Eugénie asked in bewilderment what style it was, Garnier replied that it was "Napoléon III style". Certainly, if any building can be said to exemplify the Second Empire, it is this – in its show of wealth and hint of vulgarity. In the event, however, it was only completed in 1875 after the Empire had been swept away by the Third Republic, and even Garnier had to pay for his ticket on the opening night. Part of the reason construction took so long – fourteen years in all – was the discovery of a water table which had to be drained and replaced by a huge concrete well, giving rise to the legend of an underground lake, popularized by Gaston Leroux's *Phantom of the Opera*.

The theatre's **facade** is a fairytale concoction of white, pink and green marble, colonnades, rearing horses, winged angels and gleaming gold busts of composers. No less opulent is the **interior** with its spacious, gilded-marble and mirrored lobbies, intended to give Second-Empire society suitably grand spaces in which to meet and be seen. The auditorium itself is all red velvet and gold leaf, hung with a six-tonne chandelier; the colourful ceiling was painted by Chagall in 1964 and depicts scenes from well-known operas and ballets jumbled up with famous Parisian landmarks. You can **visit** the interior (daily 10am–5pm; €6), including the auditorium – as long as there are no rehearsals; your best chance is between 1 & 2pm. The entry ticket includes the **Bibliothèque-Musée de l'Opéra**, containing model sets, dreadful nineteenth-century paintings, and rather better temporary exhibitions on operatic themes.

For a brief overview of the Second Empire and its broader historical context, you could do worse than visit the **Paris-Story** multimedia show (daily with shows on the hour 9am–7pm; €8; Mº Opéra), just round the west side of the Opéra, at 11bis rue Scribe. The 45-minute show, "narrated" by Victor Hugo, with simultaneous translation in English, traces the history of Paris right from its Roman beginnings as Lutetia up to the present day, using archive footage and computer-generated images. It all makes for an informative, albeit romanticized, introduction to the make-up of the city.

Just to the north, on boulevard Haussmann, you'll find two of the city's big department stores, **Printemps** and **Galeries Lafayette**. Built in the latter half of the nineteenth century, they may have lost their grand central staircases, but they still sport their proud fin-de-siècle stained-glass domes. Printemps' is particularly splendid, coloured in glowing hues of green and blue, best appreciated from the café-restaurant beneath. Following in the stores' wake, a number of banks were built in the area. The Crédit Lyonnais at no. 19 Boulevard des Italiens, south of boulevard Haussmann, is perhaps the most imposing, with its huge gold clock surrounded by gigantic women in flowing disarray. Wrought-iron balconies and hunting friezes from the 1840s restaurant *Maison Dorée*, at no. 20, have been preserved by the Banque Nationale de Paris, and are on display next door to its sleek 1930s main building at no. 16.

# The Église de la Madeleine

South of boulevard Haussmann, almost filling the whole of the place de la Madeleine, looms the somewhat ungainly, oversized edifice of the **Église de la Madeleine** (M° Madeleine), the parish church of the cream of Parisian high society. Modelled on a Greek classical temple, the church is surrounded by 52 Corinthian columns and fronted by a huge pediment depicting *The Last Judgement*; its facade is a near mirror image in fact of the Assemblée Nationale, directly opposite, on the far side of the place de la Concorde – a fine vista best appreciated from the top of the Madeleine steps. Originally intended as a monument to Napoleon's army – a plan abandoned after the French were defeated by the Russians in 1812 – the building narrowly escaped being turned into a railway station before finally being consecrated to Mary Magdalene in 1845. Inside, a theatrical stone sculpture of the Magdalene being swept up to heaven by two angels, executed by Charles Marochetti (1805–67), draws your eye to the high altar. The half-dome above is decorated with a fresco by Jules-Claude Ziegler (1804–1856), a student of Ingres; entitled *The History of Christianity*, it commemorates the concordat signed between the church and state after the end of the Revolution, and shows all the key figures in Christendom, with Napoleon, where else, but centre-stage. The church's interior is otherwise rather dull and gloomy, heavy with gilt-edged marble. If you're lucky, the sombre atmosphere may be broken by the sound of the organ, reckoned to be one of Paris's best – the church is in fact a regular venue for recitals and choral concerts. Illustrious past organists include Saint-Saëns and Fauré, whose famous *Requiem* was premiered at the Madeleine in 1888 – to be heard here again at the composer's own funeral 36 years later.

The rest of the square is given over to nourishment of a rather less spiritual nature in the form of Paris's top **gourmet food stores** Fauchon and Hédiard. Their remarkable displays are a feast for the eyes, and both have *salon de thés* where you can sample some of their epicurean treats. On the east side of the Madeleine church is one of the city's oldest flower markets dating back to 1832, open every day except Monday, while nearby are what must be Paris's most luxurious public toilets, preserving their original 1905 Art Nouveau décor.

# Place Vendôme

A short walk east of place de la Madeleine lies **place Vendôme**, one of the city's most impressive set pieces, built by Versailles architect Hardouin-Mansart during the final years of Louis XIV's reign. It's a pleasingly symmetrical, eight-sided *place*, enclosed by a harmonious ensemble of elegant mansions, graced with Corinthian pilasters, mascarons and steeply pitched roofs. Once the grand residences of tax collectors and financiers, they now house such luxury establishments as the *Ritz* hotel, Cartier, Bulgari and other top-flight jewellers, lending the square a decidedly exclusive air. The Ministry of Justice is also sited here, on the west side; its façade still has the marble plaque showing a standard metre put here in 1795 in order to familiarize Parisians with the new unit of measure. No. 12, on the opposite side, now occupied by Chaumet jewellers, is where Chopin died, in 1849. Somewhat out of proportion with the rest of the square, the centrepiece is a towering triumphal **column**, modelled on Trajan's column in Rome, and surmounted by a statue of Napoleon dressed as Caesar. It was raised in 1806 to celebrate the Battle of Austerlitz – bronze reliefs of scenes of the battle, cast from 1200 recycled Austro-Russian cannons, spiral their way up the column. The column that stands here today is actually a replica of the original, brought crashing down during the Commune in 1871.

A healthy bank balance comes in handy if you intend to do more than window-shop in the streets around here, especially ancient **rue St-Honoré** and its faubourg extension west, a preserve of top fashion designers and art galleries. East of place Vendôme, on rues **St-Roch** and **Ste-Anne** in particular, the Japanese community has established a mini enclave, with a number of shops and restaurants (see "Listings" on pp.282–283 for recommendations).

# The Palais Royal

Following rue St-Honoré west you come to the **Palais Royal** (M° Palais-Royal-Musée-du-Louvre), built for Cardinal Richelieu in 1624, though little now remains of the original palace. The current building houses various governmental bodies and the **Comédie Française**, longstanding venue for the classics of French theatre. Hidden away behind lie sedate **gardens** lined with stately eighteenth-century three-storey buildings built over arcades housing mainly antique and designer shops. One of them, Guillaumot, selling antique books and manuscripts (153 **Galerie de Valois**), was founded in 1785. Further down, at no. 142, is an exquisite purple-panelled *parfumerie*, Les Salons du Palais Royal Shiseido.

Past residents of the desirable flats above the arcades include Cocteau and Colette – the latter lived here until her death in 1954 and enjoyed looking out over the gardens when she was too crippled with arthritis to walk. It's certainly an attractive and peaceful oasis, with avenues of clipped limes, fountains and flowerbeds, and popular on weekends with newlyweds who come here to be photographed, though surprisingly unfrequented at other times. You'd hardly guess that for a time this was a site of gambling dens, brothels and funfair attractions – there was even a *café mécanique*, where you sat at a table, sent your order down one of its legs, and were served via the other. The prohibition on public gambling in 1838 put an end to the fun and the Grands Boulevards took up the baton. Folly, some might say, has returned – in the form of Daniel Buren's black-and-white striped pillars, rather like sticks of Brighton rock, all of varying heights, dotted about the main courtyard in front of the palace. Installed in 1986 after the space was cleared of cars, they're a rather disconcerting sight, but are certainly popular with children and rollerbladers, who treat them as an adventure playground and obstacle course respectively.

# The passages, Bibliothèque Nationale and Bourse

Conceived by town planners in the nineteenth century to protect pedestrians from mud and horse-drawn vehicles, the **passages**, or shopping arcades, are now enjoying a new lease of life as havens from traffic. By around 1840 there were over one hundred of them, but a number were later destroyed to make way for Haussmann's boulevards and only twenty remain. For decades they were left to crumble and decay, but many have recently been renovated and restored to something approaching their former glory and are being colonized by chic boutiques. Their entrances are easy to miss and where you emerge at the other end can be quite a surprise. Most are closed at night and on Sundays.

The most homogeneous and aristocratic of the *passages*, with painted ceilings and panelled shop fronts divided by faux marble columns, is **Galerie Véro-Dodat** (between rue Croix-des-Petits-Champs and rue Jean-Jacques Rousseau; M° Palais-Royal-Musée-du-Louvre), named after the two pork butchers who set it up in 1824. It's recently been spruced up, and fashionable new shops have begun to open up in place of the older businesses. Retaining the old style at no. 26, Monsieur Capia still keeps a collection of antique dolls in a shop piled high with miscellaneous curios.

The **Banque de France** lies a short way northwest of Galerie Véro-Dodat. Rather than negotiating its massive bulk to reach the *passages* further north, it's more pleasant to walk through the garden of the Palais Royal via place de Valois. Rue de Montpensier, running alongside the gardens to the west, is connected to rue de Richelieu by several tiny *passages*, of which Hulot brings you out at the statue of Molière on the junction of rues Richelieu and Molière. A certain charm also lingers about rue de Beaujolais, bordering the northern end of the gardens, with its corner café looking out on the Théâtre du Palais-Royal, and with glimpses into the venerable *Grand Véfour* restaurant (see p.282), plus more short arcades leading up to rue des Petits-Champs.

On the other side of rue des Petits-Champs, just to the left as you come from rue de Beaujolais, looms the forbidding wall of the **Bibliothèque Nationale Richelieu**, part of whose enormous collection has been transferred to the new François Mitterrand site in the 13e (see p.165). The library's origins go back to the 1660s, when Louis XIV's finance minister Colbert deposited a collection of royal manuscripts here, and it was first opened to the public in 1692. Visiting its temporary exhibitions (closed Sun) will give you access to some of the more beautiful parts of the building – the **Galerie Mazarine** in particular, with its panelled ceilings painted by Romanelli. You can also see a display of coins and ancient treasures in the **Cabinet des Monnaies, Médailles et Antiques** (Mon–Fri 9am–6pm, Sat 9am–5pm; free). There's no restriction on entering the library, nor on peering into the atmospheric reading rooms. Researchers take their cigarette and sandwich breaks in a courtyard on rue Vivienne, in a corner of which stands a pensive statue of Jean-Paul Sartre.

**Galerie Colbert**, one of two *passages* linking rue Vivienne with rue des Petits-Champs is currently closed and is due to be incorporated into a new national institute of art history, under the umbrella of the Bibliothèque Nationale, though you can still access the 1830s-style brasserie, *Le Grand Colbert* (see "Listings" on p.282), to which senior librarians and academics retire for lunch. The flamboyant decor of Grecian and marine motifs in the larger **Galerie Vivienne** establishes the perfect ambience in which to buy Jean-Paul Gaultier gear, or you can browse in the antiquarian bookshop, Librairie Jousseaume, which dates back to the *passage*'s earliest days.

From here you can detour three blocks west past the Bibliothèque Nationale to see a more workaday *passage*. The **passage Choiseul**, between rue des Petits-Champs and rue St-Augustin, has takeaway food, cheap clothes shops, stationers and bars, plus a few arty outlets along its tiled length of almost 200m. It was here that the author Louis-Ferdinand Céline lived as a boy, a period and location vividly recounted in his novel *Death on Credit* (see "Books" on p.404).

Back at Galerie Vivienne, you can exit onto rue Vivienne and head north for further *passages*. En route you'll pass the **Bourse**, the Paris stock exchange (€8.50), an imposing Neoclassical edifice built under Napoleon in 1808 and enlarged in 1903 with the addition of two side wings. To visit you'll need to book in advance on ☎01.49.27.55.55. Guided tours around the eerily quiet building (most of the action takes place on-line these days) last about an hour and include a presentation on how *Parisbourse* works. Overshadowing the Bourse from the south is the antennae-topped building of AFP, the French news agency. Rue Réaumur, running east from here, used to be the Fleet Street of Paris, but now only *Le Figaro*'s central offices remain, on the junction of rue Montmartre and rue du Louvre, alongside a mural of tulips laid across newspaper cuttings.

The grid of arcades north of the Bourse, just off rue Vivienne, is known as the **passage des Panoramas**. In need of a little repair and not as elegant as some of the other *passages*, it combines old-fashioned chic and workaday atmosphere. Most of the eateries make no pretence at style, but one old brasserie, *L'Arbre à Cannelle* (see "Listings" on p.280), has fantastic carved wood panelling, and there are still bric-a-brac shops, stamp and secondhand postcard dealers and a printshop with its original 1867 fittings. It was around the Panoramas, in 1817, that the first Parisian gas lamps were tried out.

In **passage Jouffroy**, across boulevard Montmartre, a M. Segas sells walking canes and theatrical antiques opposite a shop displaying every conceivable fitting and furnishing for a doll's house. Near the romantic *Hôtel Chopin* (reviewed on p.257), Paul Vulin spreads his secondhand books along the passageway, and Ciné-Doc serves cinephiles. Crossing rue de la Grange-Batelière, you enter **passage Verdeau**, where a few of the old postcard and camera dealers still trade alongside smart new art galleries and a designer Italian delicatessen.

At the top of rue Richelieu, the tiny **passage des Princes**, with its beautiful glass ceiling, stained-glass decoration and twirly lamps, was due at the time of writing to be taken over by the toy emporium JouéClub and set to become one of the largest toy stores in Paris. Its erstwhile neighbour, the passage de l'Opéra, described in surreal detail by Louis Aragon in *Paris Peasant*, was eaten up with the completion of Haussmann's boulevards.

While in this area, you could also take a look at what's up for auction at the Paris equivalent of Christie's and Sotheby's, the **Hôtel Drouot** (9 rue Drouot; M° Le Peletier & M° Richelieu-Drouot). To spare any fear of unintended hand movements landing you in the bankruptcy courts, you can simply wander round looking at the goods before the action starts (11am–6pm on the eve of the sale, 11am–noon on the day itself). Auctions are announced in the press, under "Ventes aux Enchères"; you'll find details, including photos of pieces, in the widely available weekly *Gazette de l'Hôtel Drouot* or on their website ⓦwww.drouot.fr.

# Sentier and St Denis

At the heart of the 2[e] arrondissement lies the **Sentier** district, largely given over to the rag trade. The frenetic trading and deliveries of cloth, the food market on rue des Petits-Carreaux, and the general to-ing and fro-ing make a lively change from the office-bound quartiers further west. On **place du**

**Caire**, beneath an extraordinary pseudo-Egyptian facade of grotesque Pharaonic heads (a celebration of Napoleon's conquest of Egypt), an archway opens onto a series of arcades, the **passage du Caire**. This, contrary to any visible evidence, is the oldest of all the *passages* and entirely monopolized by wholesale clothes shops.

The garment business gets progressively more upmarket as you head west from the trade area. Louis XIV's attractive **place des Victoires**, adjoined to the north by the appealingly asymmetrical place des Petits-Pères, is full of designer clothes shops, with extravagant window displays and matching price tags. The trend continues on the upper stretch of rue Étienne Marcel, with young, hip fashion boutiques taking over at the lower end. Just north of Mº Étienne-Marcel, between rue St-Denis and rue Dessoubs, arches the three-storey **Grand-Cerf**, stylistically the best of all the *passages*. The wrought-iron work, glass roof and plain-wood shop fronts have all been cleaned, attracting stylish arts, crafts and contemporary design shops.

Running north from here, **rue St-Denis** is the city's centuries-old red-light area. Attempts by the 2ᵉ arrondissement *mairie* to rid the street of its pimps and prostitutes have been to no avail; despite pedestrianizing the area between rues Étienne-Marcel and Réaumur (to stop kerb-crawling) and encouraging cafés like the *English Frog and Rosbif* to move in among the porn outlets, there are still weary women waiting in doorways between peepshows, striptease joints and sex-video shops.

The emphasis on rues Montmartre, Montorgueil and Turbigo, leading south from rue Réaumur, turns towards food as they approach Les Halles. Worth lingering over in particular is pedestrianized **rue Montorgueil**, where traditional grocery stalls, butchers and *patissiers* of longstanding (one, Stohrer's, has been here since 1730) ply their trade alongside newer arrivals.

# Les Halles

Described by Zola as "*le ventre* (stomach) *de Paris*", **Les Halles** was Paris's main food market for over eight hundred years until it was moved out to the suburbs in 1969 and replaced by a large shopping and leisure complex, much of it underground. There was widespread opposition to the destruction of Victor Baltard's nineteenth-century pavilions, and considerable disquiet at the changes renovation of the area might bring but the authorities' excuse to proceed was the RER and métro interchange they had to have below. Much of the area above ground was landscaped with gardens – a haunt largely of drunks and the homeless these days – and hardly any trace remains of the working-class quarter, with its night bars and bistros for the market traders. Nowadays, rents rival the 16ᵉ, and the all-night places serve and profit from a markedly different clientèle, such that Les Halles is constantly promoted as the hotspot of Paris, where the cool and famous congregate. In fact, anyone with any sense and money hangs out in the traditional bourgeois quartiers to the west, or the fashionable eastern arrondissements – many of the people milling about here are up from the suburbs. The area has also become a target of pickpockets, and the law, plus canine arm, are often in evidence.

From Châtelet-Les Halles RER, you surface only after ascending from levels -4 to 0 of the **Forum des Halles** centre, which stretches underground from the Bourse du Commerce rotunda to rue Pierre-Lescot. The overground

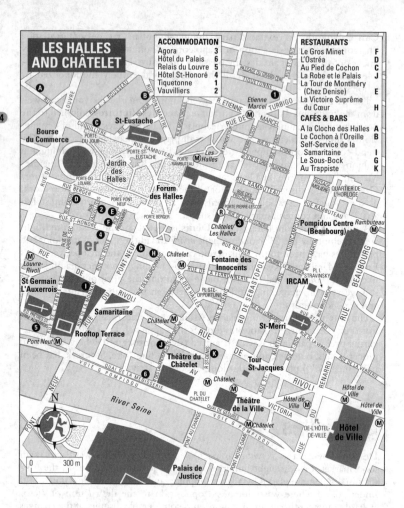

**LES HALLES AND CHÂTELET**

**ACCOMMODATION**
| | |
|---|---|
| Agora | 3 |
| Hôtel du Palais | 6 |
| Relais du Louvre | 5 |
| Hôtel St-Honoré | 4 |
| Tiquetonne | 1 |
| Vauvilliers | 2 |

**RESTAURANTS**
| | |
|---|---|
| Le Gros Minet | F |
| L'Ostréa | D |
| Au Pied de Cochon | C |
| La Robe et le Palais | J |
| La Tour de Montlhéry (Chez Denise) | E |
| La Victoire Suprême du Cœur | H |

**CAFÉS & BARS**
| | |
|---|---|
| A la Cloche des Halles | A |
| Le Cochon à l'Oreille | B |
| Self-Service de la Samaritaine | I |
| Le Sous-Bock | G |
| Au Trappiste | K |

section comprises aquarium-like arcades of shops, arranged around a sunken patio. The shops are mostly devoted to high-street fashion, though there's also a large FNAC bookshop and the Forum des Créateurs, an outlet for young fashion designers. It's not all commerce, however: there's scope for various diversions including swimming, billiards and movie-going. You could also check out the **Pavillon des Arts** (daily except Mon 11.30am–6.30pm; €5.50), a temporary art exhibition space.

For an antidote to steel and glass troglodytism head for the soaring vaults of the church of **St-Eustache**, on the north side of the gardens. This beautiful church, built between 1532 and 1637, is Gothic in structure, with lofty naves and graceful flying buttresses, and Renaissance in decoration – all Corinthian columns and rounded arcades. From the church's pulpit, during the Commune, a woman "preached" the abolition of marriage; Molière was baptized here, Rameau and Marivaux were buried here. The side chapels contain some significant works of art, including, in the tenth chapel in the ambulatory, an early

Rubens (*The Pilgrims at Emmaus*), and in the sixth chapel on the north side, Coysevox's marble sculpture over the tomb of Colbert, Louis XIV's finance minister. In the Chapelle St-Joseph, a naïve relief by British artist Raymond Mason, entitled *The Departure of Fruit and Vegetables from the Heart of Paris, 28 February 1969*, portrays the area's more recent history. Nearby is a bronze triptych, *La Vie de Christ*, one of Keith Haring's last works. The church has a long musical tradition, and is a popular venue for concerts and organ recitals.

On the other side of Les Halles, you can join the throng around the **Fontaine des Innocents** to admire the water cascading down its perfect Renaissance proportions. The fountain takes its name from the cemetery that used to occupy this site, the Cimetière des Innocents. Full to overflowing, the cemetery was closed down in 1786 and its contents transferred to the catacombs in Denfert-Rochereau (see p.154).

# Châtelet

There's a labyrinth of tiny streets to explore between the Fontaine des Innocents and place du Châtelet, once the site of a notorious fortress prison, now a maelstrom of traffic overlooked by two grand theatres, the **Théâtre Musical de Paris** and the **Théâtre de la Ville**. On the quayside, whose name (*Mégisserie*) refers to the treatment of animal skins in medieval times when this was an area of abattoirs, there are now plants and pets for sale. Further along the riverfront, towards the Louvre, the three blocks of **La Samaritaine** (Mon–Sat 9.30am–7pm, Thurs till 10pm) recall the days when aesthetics, not marketing psychology, determined the decoration of a department store. The building, now completely restored, was built in 1903 in pure Art Nouveau style, with gold, green, and glass exteriors, and, inside, brightly painted wrought-iron staircases and balconies against huge backdrops of ceramic floral patterns, though best of all are the excellent views of the Seine and Paris skyline from the tenth-floor terrace café (take the lift to floor nine in the Magasin Principal and then walk up two flights).

# 5

# Beaubourg, the Marais and the Bastille

The **Pompidou Centre**, or Beaubourg, as it's known locally, lies a few blocks away from Les Halles across boulevard Sébastopol. Built in the 1970s and hailed for its groundbreaking architecture, the Pompidou remains an enduring, popular focus for the surrounding quartier **Beaubourg**, with its art galleries, cafés and crowded pavements.

To the east lies the **Marais**, one of the loveliest areas of central Paris and perfect for wandering; no major thoroughfares disturb the aristocratic mansions (many now housing museums and galleries), medieval lanes, Jewish quarter and plethora of small, appealing restaurants, shops, cafés and bars.

The **Bastille** used to belong in spirit and in style to the working-class districts of eastern Paris. Since the construction of the new opera house, however, it has become a magnet for artists and young people who have brought with them an energetic nightlife, making this very much one of Paris's central hotspots.

## The Pompidou Centre

The **Pompidou Centre** (Ⓦ www.centrepompidou.fr; M° Rambuteau/Hôtel-de-Ville), one of the twentieth century's most radical buildings, provoked very mixed reactions on its opening in 1977. Since then, it has won over the critics and public alike, and become one of the city's most recognizable and popular landmarks, drawing large numbers to its excellent modern art museum and high-profile exhibitions.

The architects, Renzo Piano and Richard Rogers, turned common assumptions about what an art gallery should be on their head. Wanting to move away from the idea of galleries as closed treasure chests to create something more open and accessible, they stripped the skin off the building and made all the "bones" visible. The infrastructure was put on the outside: escalator tubes and utility pipes, colour-coded according to their function, climb around the exterior, giving the building its crazy snakes-and-ladder appearance. A recent extensive renovation has given the centre more gallery space and a general sprucing up, with slick lighting and a stylish café and rooftop restaurant. Unfortunately, the escalator on the outside of the building, affording wonderful **views over the city**, is no longer free – access is with the museum ticket only.

There's no monumental entrance to the centre – just a large, sloping piazza, popular with buskers, magicians, mime artists and portrait painters, not to mention a small encampment of homeless people. Inside, Levels One, Two and Three are devoted to the BPI or **Bibliothèque Publique** (Mon–Fri noon–10pm, Sat & Sun 11am–10pm; free), which has an impressive collection of 2500 periodicals including international press, 10,000 CDs to listen to and 2200 documentary films to ponder from the relative solitude of one of its 2000 seats. The **Musée National d'Art Moderne** presides over the fourth and fifth floors, with the sixth floor reserved for special exhibitions.

## Musée National d'Art Moderne

The **Musée National d'Art Moderne** (daily except Tues 11am–9pm; €5.49; audio-guide in English €4.57) is reached via the escalator. Your ticket is only valid for a single visit, so you can't, for example, pop out for a break in one of the centre's cafés and re-enter. The museum's collection offers a near-complete visual essay on the history of twentieth-century art, with the fifth floor covering the period 1905 to 1960, and the fourth 1960 to the present day. The fourth floor also displays a number of architectural models and furniture by contemporary designers. The collection is densely and efficiently organized, so, unlike many of the more unwieldy museums in Paris, half a day is probably enough for a comfortable, rewarding visit. It's worth noting that the collection is frequently rehung, so the account below may not be entirely accurate at the time of your visit.

### Fauvism, Cubism and Dada

The collection kicks off on the fifth floor with the **Fauvists**, a group of painters including André Derain, Maurice de Vlaminck and Georges Braque, who gathered around Henri Matisse at the beginning of the twentieth century, and whose paintings are characterized by vivid colours that often bear no relation to the reality of the object depicted. In Georges Braque's *L'Estaque* (1906) in **room 2**, colour instead becomes a way of composing and structuring a picture, with trees and sky broken down into blocks of vibrant reds and greens; Matisse's *Luxe 1* is another fine example, the colourful nudes recalling the primitive figures of Gauguin.

"Primitive man" – in harmony with nature and uncorrupted by civilization – was a popular subject with contemporary artists, and one that influenced Picasso. Inspired by African masks and sculpture, **Picasso** began organizing form into geometrical shapes and pioneered **Cubism**. In his *Femme assise dans un fauteuil* (1910) in **room 3**, different angles of the subject are shown all at once, giving rise to complex patterns and creating the effect of movement. Hung alongside Picasso's works, and almost indistinguishable from them, are **Braque**'s *Nature morte au violon* (1911), *Femme à la guitare* (1913) and others. The juxtaposition of these paintings illustrates the intellectual and artistic dialogue that went on between the two artists, who lived next door to each other at the Bateau Lavoir (see p.168) in Montmartre.

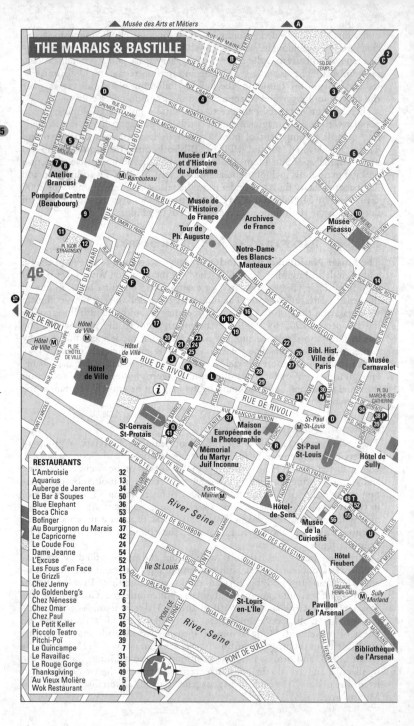

THE MARAIS & BASTILLE

Musée des Arts et Métiers

RUE AU MAIRE

RUE DES VERTUS

RUE DES GRAVILLIERS

RUE CHAPON

RUE DE PICARDIE

SQ. DU TEMPLE

RUE DE BRETAGNE

RUE DE BEAUCE

RUE DU GRENIER-ST-LAZARE

RUE DE MONTMORENCY

RUE MICHEL LE COMTE

RUE CHARLOT

RUE DE SAINTONGE

RUE DE POITOU

RUE DE TURENNE

RUE VIEILLE DU TEMPLE

RUE DE THORIGNY

Musée d'Art et d'Histoire du Judaisme

RUE DES 4 FILS

RUE DE LA PERLE

Musée Picasso

RUE RAMBUTEAU

Rambuteau

Atelier Brancusi

Pompidou Centre (Beaubourg)

RUE SIMON LE FRANC

Musée de l'Histoire de France

Archives de France

Tour de Ph. Auguste

Notre-Dame des Blancs-Manteaux

PL. IGOR STRAVINSKY

RUE ST MERRI

RUE DES BLANCS MANTEAUX

4e

RUE STE CROIX DE LA BRETONNERIE

RUE DES FRANCS BOURGEOIS

RUE PARC ROYAL

RUE DE LA VERRERIE

RUE PAYENNE

RUE DE SÉVIGNÉ

RUE DE RIVOLI

Hôtel de Ville

Hôtel de Ville

Bibl. Hist. Ville de Paris

Musée Carnavalet

Hôtel de Ville

RUE DE RIVOLI

PL. DU MARCHE-STE-CATHERINE

St-Gervais St-Protais

Maison Européenne de la Photographie

RUE FRANÇOIS MIRON

St-Paul St-Louis

Hôtel de Sully

Mémorial du Martyr Juif Inconnu

St-Paul St-Louis

RUE CHARLEMAGNE

PONT D'ARCOLE

QUAI DE L'HÔTEL DE VILLE

Hôtel de Ville

Hôtel-de-Sens

Musée de la Curiosité

Pont Marie

River Seine

QUAI DE BOURBON

QUAI DES CÉLESTINS

Hôtel Fieubert

Île St Louis

QUAI D'ANJOU

QUAI DES ORLÉANS

St-Louis en-L'Île

SQUARE HENRI-GALLI

Sully Morland

Pavillon de l'Arsenal

QUAI DE BÉTHUNE

River Seine

PONT DE SULLY

PONT DE LA TOURNELLE

QUAI HENRY IV

Bibliothèque de l'Arsenal

N

RESTAURANTS
L'Ambroisie                   32
Aquarius                      13
Auberge de Jarente            34
Le Bar à Soupes               50
Blue Elephant                 36
Boca Chica                    53
Bofinger                      46
Au Bourgignon du Marais       37
Le Capricorne                 42
Le Coude Fou                  24
Dame Jeanne                   54
L'Excuse                      52
Les Fous d'en Face            21
Le Grizzli                    15
Chez Jenny                     1
Jo Goldenberg's               27
Chez Nénesse                   6
Chez Omar                      3
Chez Paul                     57
Le Petit Keller               45
Piccolo Teatro                28
Pitchi-Poï                    39
Le Quincampe                   7
Le Ravaillac                  31
Le Rouge Gorge                56
Thanksgiving                  49
Au Vieux Molière               5
Wok Restaurant                40

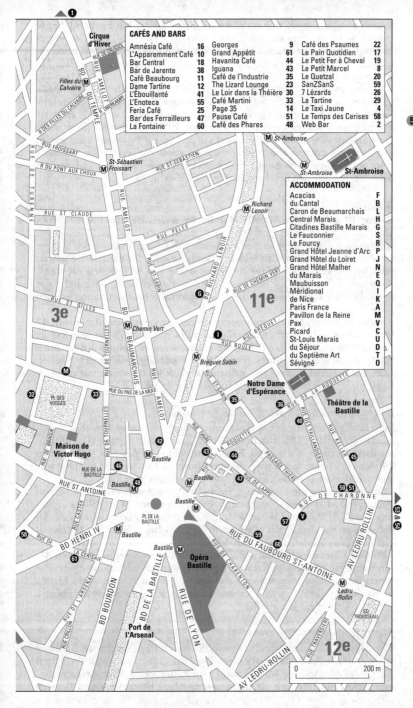

**CAFÉS AND BARS**

| | | | | | |
|---|---|---|---|---|---|
| Amnésia Café | 16 | Georges | 9 | Café des Psaumes | 22 |
| L'Apparement Café | 10 | Grand Appétit | 61 | Le Pain Quotidien | 17 |
| Bar Central | 18 | Havanita Café | 44 | Le Petit Fer à Cheval | 19 |
| Bar de Jarente | 38 | Iguana | 43 | Le Petit Marcel | 8 |
| Café Beaubourg | 11 | Café de l'Industrie | 35 | Le Quetzal | 20 |
| Dame Tartine | 12 | The Lizard Lounge | 23 | SanZSanS | 59 |
| L'Ébouillanté | 41 | Le Loir dans la Théière | 30 | 7 Lézards | 26 |
| L'Enoteca | 55 | Café Martini | 33 | La Tartine | 29 |
| Feria Café | 25 | Page 35 | 14 | Le Taxi Jaune | 4 |
| Bar des Ferrailleurs | 47 | Pause Café | 51 | Le Temps des Cerises | 58 |
| La Fontaine | 60 | Café des Phares | 48 | Web Bar | 2 |

**BEAUBOURG, THE MARAIS AND THE BASTILLE**

**ACCOMMODATION**

| | |
|---|---|
| Acacias | F |
| du Cantal | B |
| Caron de Beaumarchais | L |
| Central Marais | H |
| Citadines Bastille Marais | G |
| Le Fauconnier | S |
| Le Fourcy | R |
| Grand Hôtel Jeanne d'Arc | P |
| Grand Hôtel du Loiret | J |
| Grand Hôtel Malher | N |
| du Marais | E |
| Maubuisson | Q |
| Méridional | I |
| de Nice | K |
| Paris France | A |
| Pavillon de la Reine | M |
| Pax | V |
| Picard | C |
| St-Louis Marais | U |
| du Séjour | D |
| du Septième Art | T |
| Sévigné | O |

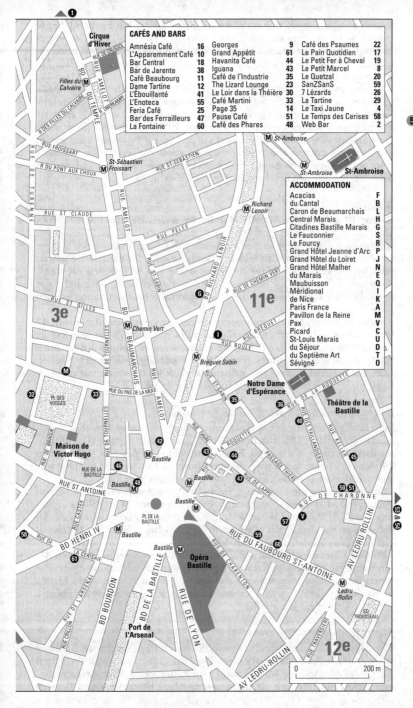

99

Another artist heavily influenced by the new Cubism was **Fernand Léger** (**room 4**). In paintings such as *Femme en rouge et vert* (1914) and *Contraste de Formes* (1913), Léger creates his own distinctive form of Cubism based on tubular shapes, said to be inspired by the modern machinery of World War I in which he fought.

Another product of the horror of the 1914–18 war was the nihilistic **Dada** movement, a revolt against petty bourgeois values. **Room 7** displays work by leading members, including **Marcel Duchamp**, who selected everyday objects ("ready-mades") such as the *Hat Rack* (1917), and elevated them, without modification, to the rank of works of art, simply by taking them out of their ordinary context and putting them on display. As well as the *Hat Rack*, you can also inspect Duchamp's most notorious ready-made – a urinal – which he called *Fontaine* and first exhibited in New York in 1917.

## Abstract Art

**Room 10** is devoted to **Wassily Kandinsky**, widely hailed as the founder of **abstract art**. His series entitled *Impressions*, *Improvisations* and *Compositions* consists of non-figurative shapes and swathes of colour, and heralded a move away from an obsession with subject towards a passion for the creative process itself. The lyrical quality of the series, not unlike that of a musical riff, introduced the art world to the importance of the existence of the artist and, more precisely, the guiding force of the artist's spirituality in the creation of each piece.

**Sonia Delaunay**, another pioneer of abstract art, is represented in **room 12** by a number of her characteristically colourful paintings. In the wonderfully vibrant *Marché de Minho* (1916), the juxtaposition of colours makes some appear to recede and others come forward, creating a shimmering effect; Delaunay believed that colours influence each other and create vibrations by being placed side by side, bringing the painting to life.

## Surrealism and abstract expressionism

Surrealism, an offshoot of the Dada movement, dominates in later rooms with works by Magritte, Dali and Ernst. Typical of the movement's exploration of the darker recesses of the mind, **Ernst**'s disturbing *Ubu Imperator* (1923; **room 20**) depicts a figure that is part man, part Tower of Pisa and part spinning top, and would seem to symbolize the perversion of male authority.

Shying away from the figurative, American **abstract expressionists** Jackson Pollock and Mark Rothko make an appearance in **room 34**. In Pollock's splattery *No 26A, Black and White* (1948), the two colours seem to struggle for domination; the dark bands of colour in Rothko's large canvas *No. 14 (Browns over Dark)*, in contrast, draw the viewer in.

**Matisse**'s later experiments with form and colour are on show in **room 41**. His technique of *découpage* (creating a picture from cut-out coloured pieces of paper) freed colour from drawing and line, and is perfected in works like *La Tristesse du Roi* (1952), in which a woman dances while an elderly king plays a guitar, mourning his lost youth.

## From Pop Art to the present

The collection continues on the fourth floor with **Pop Art** (**room 3**). Easily recognizable is **Andy Warhol**'s piece *Ten Lizes* (1963), in which the actress Elizabeth Taylor sports a Mona Lisa-like smile. In room 4 **Yves Klein** prefigures performance art with his *Grande anthropophagie bleue; Hommage a Tennessee*

*Williams* (1960), one in a series of "body prints" in which the artist turned female models into human paintbrushes, covering them in paint to create his artworks. Most of the prints are executed in International Klein Blue, a beautiful deep and luminous blue which the artist patented himself.

Displays of more recent works are subject to change, but established artists you're likely to come across include Claes Oldenburg, Christian Boltanski and Daniel Buren. **Christian Boltanski** is known for his large *mise-en-scène* installations, often containing veiled allusions to the Holocaust. His *Réserve* (1990–99), currently on display, is a room hung with lots of musty-smelling secondhand clothes; the effect is oddly oppressive, the absence of the original wearers suggesting death and anonymity. **Daniel Buren**'s works are easy to spot: they all bear his trademark stripes, exactly 8.7cm in width. He caused a furore in 1986 with his installation of black-and-white, vertically striped columns in the courtyard of the Palais Royal (see p.90), and his work was widely criticized and vilified by the press. Now, however, in his sixties, the one-time enfant terrible of the art world has become one of France's most respected living artists – a status confirmed by a one-man show at the Pompidou Centre in 2002.

Up-and-coming names you might come across are **Pierre Huyghe**, who uses video to explore the relationships between reality and fiction, history and memory, often taking film clips as his source material; and **Annette Messager**, whose large-scale installations use everyday objects to create unsettling works, often challenging perceptions of women.

## Atelier Brancusi

On the northern edge of the Pompidou Centre, down some steps off the piazza, in a small separate one-level building, is the **Atelier Brancusi** (daily except Tues 2–6pm; combined ticket with the Musée National d'Art Moderne). Upon his death in 1956, the sculptor **Constantin Brancusi** bequeathed the contents of his 15ᵉ arrondissement studio to the state, on the condition that it be reconstructed exactly as it was found. The artist became obsessed with the spatial relationship of the sculptures in his studio, going so far as to supplant each sold work with a plaster copy, and the four interconnected rooms of the studio faithfully adhere to his arrangements. Studios one and two are crowded with fluid sculptures of highly polished brass and marble, his trademark abstract bird and column shapes, stylized busts and objects poised as though they're about to take flight. Unfortunately, the rooms are behind glass, adding a feeling of sterility and distance. Perhaps the most satisfying rooms are ateliers three and four, his private quarters, where his tools are displayed on one wall almost like works of art themselves.

# Quartier Beaubourg and the Hôtel de Ville

The lively quartier around the Pompidou Centre, known as **Beaubourg**, also offers much in the way of visual art. The colourful, moving sculptures and fountains in the pool in front of Église St-Merri on **place Igor Stravinsky**, on the south side of the Pompidou Centre, were created by Jean Tinguely and Niki de St-Phalle; this squirting waterworks pays homage to Stravinsky – each fountain corresponds to one of his compositions (*The Firebird*, *The Rite of Spring*, etc) – but shows scant respect for passers-by. Stravinsky's music in many ways paved the way for the pioneering work of **IRCAM** (Institut de la Recherche et de la Coordination Acoustique/Musique), whose entrance is on the west side of the square. Founded by the composer Pierre Boulez, it's a research centre for contemporary music and a venue for concerts; much of it is underground, with an overground extension by Renzo Piano. For more on IRCAM's activities see p.316.

To the north of the Pompidou Centre numerous commercial art galleries and the odd bookshop and *salon de thé* occupy the attractive *hôtels particuliers* of narrow, pedestrianized **rue Quincampoix**. Halfway down the street on the right is the delightful, cobbled **passage Molière**, with its quirky shops, such as Des Mains et des Pieds, where you can get a plaster cast made of your hand or foot.

A little further east of here, hidden on impasse Berthaud, off rue Beaubourg, is the **Musée de la Poupée** (daily except Mon 10am–6pm; €6; M° Rambuteau), a doll museum certain to appeal to small children. In addition to the impressive collection of antique dolls, there are displays of finely detailed tiny irons and sewing machines, furniture and pots and pans and other minuscule accessories.

South of the Pompidou Centre, rue Renard runs down to the **Hôtel de Ville**, the seat of the city's government and a mansion of gargantuan proportions in florid neo-Renaissance style, modelled pretty much on the previous building burned down in the Commune. An illustrated history of this edifice, always a prime target in riots and revolutions, is displayed along the platform of M° Châtelet on the Neuilly–Vincennes line. Those opposed to the establishments of kings and emperors created their alternative municipal governments in this building: the Revolutionaries installed themselves here in 1789, the poet Lamartine proclaimed the Second Republic here in 1848, and Gambetta the Third Republic in 1870. But, with the defeat of the Commune in 1871, the conservatives, in control once again, concluded that the Parisian municipal authority had to go if order was to be maintained and the people kept in their place. Thereafter Paris was ruled directly by the ministry of the interior until eventually, in 1977, the city was allowed to run its own affairs and Jacques Chirac was elected mayor.

# The Marais

The **Marais** today comprises most of the 3$^e$ and 4$^e$ arrondissements. Yet until the thirteenth century, when the Knights Templar (see box on p.109) set up house in its northern section, now known as the **quartier du Temple**, and began to drain the land, it was an uninhabitable riverside swamp (*marais*). The grand and aristocratic character that has become its hallmark was not acquired until around 1600, when the area became the object of royal patronage, especially after the construction of the **place des Vosges** – or place Royale, as it was then known – by Henri IV in 1605.

Its apogee was relatively short-lived, for the aristocracy began to move away after the king took his court to Versailles in the latter part of the seventeenth century, leaving their mansions to the trading classes, who were in turn displaced during the Revolution. Thereafter, the masses moved in and the mansions became multi-occupied slum tenements. Their grandeur decayed and the streets degenerated into unserviced squalor – and stayed that way until the 1960s.

Since then, however, gentrification has proceeded apace, and the quarter has become known for its exclusivity, sophistication and artsy leanings and for being the neighbourhood of choice for gay Parisians, who are to be credited with bringing both business and style to the area. Renovated mansions, with their intimate courtyards and sumptuous architectural detail, have become museums, libraries, offices and chic flats, flanked by designer clothes stores, art galleries and interior design shops. Having largely escaped the depredations of modern development, as well as the heavy-handed attentions of Baron Haussmann, the Marais is one of the most seductive districts of Paris – old, secluded, as lively and lighthearted by night as it is by day, and with as many alluring shops, bars and places to eat as you could wish for.

Through the middle, dividing it roughly north and south, runs the busy **rue de Rivoli** and its continuation to the Bastille, rue St-Antoine. South of this line is the quartier St-Paul-St-Gervais, the riverside and the Arsenal. To the north, more heterogeneous as well as more fun to walk around, are most of the shops and museums, place des Vosges, the **Jewish quarter** and the quartier du Temple. Every street boasts an abundance of colour and detail: magnificent *portes cochères* (huge double carriage gates) with elaborate handles and knockers, stone and iron bollards that protected pedestrians from ruthless carriage drivers, cobbled courtyards, elegant iron railings and gates, sculpted house fronts, chichi boutiques, ethnic grocers – a wealth of interest.

# Rue des Francs-Bourgeois

The main lateral street of the northern part of the Marais, which also forms the boundary between the 3e and 4e arrondissements, is the **rue des Francs-Bourgeois**. Beatnik Jack Kerouac translated it as "the street of the outspoken middle classes", which is a fair description of the contemporary residents, though the name in fact means "people exempt from tax", in reference to the penurious inmates of a medieval almshouse that once stood on the site of no. 34.

At the western end of the street at no. 60, the magnificent eighteenth-century Palais Soubise, fronted by an impressive colonnaded courtyard, houses the **Archives Nationales de France** and the **Musée de l'Histoire de France** (Mon & Wed–Fri 10am–12.30pm & 2–5.30pm, Sat & Sun 2.30–5.30pm; €3.50; M° Rambuteau & M° St-Paul), the latter of which hosts permanent and temporary exhibits of documents from the archives. Among the authentic bits of paper that fill the archive's vaults are a medieval English monarch's challenge to his French counterpart to stake his kingdom on a duel, and Joan of Arc's trial proceedings with a doodled impression of her in the margin. A section on the Revolution includes the book of samples from which Marie-Antoinette chose her dress each morning, and a Republican children's alphabet where "J" stands for Jean-Jacques Rousseau and "L" for labourer. The museum also provides an opportunity to enter perhaps the Marais' most splendid mansion, with some fine Rococo interiors and paintings by the likes of Boucher.

Opposite the Palais Soubise, at the back of a driveway for the Crédit Municipal bank, stands a pepperpot tower that formed part of the **city walls**; these were built by King Philippe-Auguste early in the thirteenth century to link up with his new fortress, the Louvre. Further along, past several more imposing facades and the peculiarly public lycée classrooms at no. 28, you can enter the courtyard of the **Hôtel d'Albret** (no. 31). This eighteenth-century mansion is home to the cultural department of the mayor of Paris, its dignified facade enhanced or marred, depending on your point of view, by a concrete and steel column, a 1989 Bicentennial work by Bernard Pagès, in which red and blue "ribbons" hang down over thorns.

The next landmarks on the street, at the junction with rues Payenne and Pavée, are two of the Marais' grandest **hôtels**, the sixteenth-century Carnavalet and Lamoignon, housing, respectively, the Musée Carnavalet (see below) and the **Bibliothèque Historique de la Ville de Paris**, the latter housing centuries' worth of texts and picture books about the city (see p.352 for opening times). Next to the Lamoignon, on rue Pavée – so called because it was among the first Paris streets to be paved, in 1450 – was the site of **La Force prison**, where many of the Revolution's victims were incarcerated, including the Princesse de Lamballe, who was lynched in the massacres of September 1792. Her head was presented on a stake to her friend Marie-Antoinette.

## Musée Carnavalet

The **Musée Carnavalet** (daily except Mon 10am–6pm; free; M° St-Paul), its entrance at 23 rue de Sévigné, off rue des Francs-Bourgeois, is a fascinating museum that charts the history of Paris from its origins up to the belle époque through an extraordinary collection of paintings, sculptures, decorative arts and archeological finds. The museum's setting in two beautiful Renaissance mansions, Hôtel Carnavalet and Hôtel Le Peletier, surrounded by attractive gardens, makes a visit worthwhile in itself. There are 140 rooms in all, impossible to visit in one go, so it's best to pick up a floor plan and decide which areas you'd like to concentrate on.

The **ground floor** displays nineteenth- and early twentieth-century shop and inn signs and engrossing models of Paris through the ages, along with maps and plans, showing how much Haussmann's grand boulevards changed the face of the city. The recently renovated **orangerie** houses a significant collection of Neolithic finds, including a number of wooden pirogues unearthed during the redevelopment of the Bercy riverside area in the 1990s.

On the **first floor**, decorative arts feature strongly, with numerous recreated salons and boudoirs full of richly sculpted wood panelling and tapestries from the time of Louis XII to Louis XVI, rescued from buildings that had to be destroyed for Haussmann's boulevards. Room 21 is devoted to the famous letter-writer **Madame de Sévigné**, who lived in the Carnavalet mansion and wrote a series of letters to her daughter, which vividly portray her privileged lifestyle under the reign of Louis XIV. You can see her Chinese lacquered writing desk, as well as portraits of her and various contemporaries, such as Molière and Corneille. Rooms 128 to 148 are largely devoted to the **Belle Epoque**, evoked through numerous paintings of the period and some wonderful **Art Nouveau** interiors, most stunning of which is a jewellery shop, with its peacock-green décor and swirly motifs, designed by Alphonse Mucha and reassembled here in its entirety. Also well preserved is José-Maria Sert's **Art Deco** ballroom, with its extravagant gold-leaf décor and grand-scale paintings, including one of the Queen of Sheba with a train of elephants. Nearby is a section on literary life at the beginning of the twentieth century, including a reconstruction of **Proust's cork-lined bedroom** (room 147).

The **second floor** has rooms full of mementos of the **French Revolution**: models of the Bastille, original declarations of the Rights of Man and the Citizen, sculpted allegories of Reason, crockery with revolutionary slogans, glorious models of the guillotine and execution orders to make you shed a tear for the royalists as well. The post-Revolution and **Napoleonic period** is covered on the ground floor, in rooms 115–121; look out for Napoleon's favourite canteen, which accompanied him on his military exploits and consists of 110 pieces ingeniously contained within a case no bigger than a picnic hamper. Among the items is a full set of gold cutlery, a gold-handled toothbrush, two candelabras and a dinky geometry set – everything an emperor could possibly need while on campaign.

## More Marais mansions

West of the Musée Carnavalet, three other Marais mansions also house museums. In a parallel street, rue Elzévir, one block west of rue Payenne, the **Musée Cognacq-Jay** (daily except Mon 10am–5.40pm; free; M° St-Paul & M° Chemin-Vert) occupies the fine Hôtel Donon at no. 8. The Cognacq-Jay family built up the Samaritaine department store – you can see a history of the family and their charitable works in a series of dioramas on the tenth-floor terrace of the store (see p.338 of "Shops and markets"). As well as being noted philanthropists, they were lovers of European art. Their collection of eighteenth-century pieces on show includes works by Canaletto, Fragonard, Rubens and Rembrandt, as well as an exquisite still life by Chardin, displayed in beautifully carved wood-panelled rooms filled with Sèvres porcelain and Louis XV furniture.

The remaining two museums are decidedly quirky in nature, unlikely to divert you unless you happen to have an interest in security or taxidermy. Locks rule the day in the **Musée de la Serrure-Bricard** (Mon–Fri 2–5pm; closed Aug; €4.57; M° Chemin-Vert & M° St Paul) in the cellars of the Hôtel Libéral-Bruand at 1 rue de la Perle. The collection includes the fittings for Napoléon III's palace doors (the one for the Tuileries bashed in by revolutionaries), locks that trapped your hand or shot your head off if you tried a false key, and a seventeenth-century wonder made by a craftsman kept under lock and key for four years. The rest of the exhibits are pretty boring, though the *hôtel* setting is some compensation.

Rue de la Perle's continuation, across rue Vieille du Temple, is rue des Quatre Fils. On its corner, at 60 rue des Archives, is the equally specialized **Musée de la Chasse et de la Nature** (Tues–Sun 11am–6pm; €4.60; M° Rambuteau), housed in the beautiful Hôtel Guénégaud. Devoted mainly to hunting, the museum's collections include a formidable array of stuffed animals and trophies of the hunt. Weapons range from prehistoric stone arrow-heads to highly decorative crossbows and guns, and there are many paintings by French artists romanticizing the chase.

## Musée Picasso

On the northern side of rue des Francs-Bourgeois, rue Payenne leads up to the lovely gardens and houses of **rue du Parc-Royal** and on to **rue de Thorigny**. Here, at no. 5, the magnificent classical facade of the seventeenth-century **Hôtel Salé**, built for a rich salt-tax collector, conceals the **Musée Picasso** (daily except Tues 9.30am–5.30pm; 8pm on Thurs; March & April until 5.30pm; €5.50, Sun €4; M° Chemin Vert or St-Paul). It's the largest collection of Picassos anywhere, representing almost all the major periods of the artist's life from 1905 onwards. Many of the works were owned by Picasso and on his death in 1973 were seized by the state in lieu

△ Musée Picasso

of taxes owed. The result is an unedited body of work, which, although not among the most recognizable of Picasso's masterpieces, nevertheless provides a sense of the artist's development and an insight into the person behind the myth. In addition, the collection includes paintings Picasso bought or was given by contemporaries such as Matisse and Cézanne; his African masks and sculptures; his Communist party membership cards and sketches of Stalin; and photographs of him in his studio taken by Brassaï.

The **exhibition** unfolds chronologically, starting with the artist's blue period, studies for the *Demoiselles d'Avignon*, and his experiments with Cubism and Surrealism. It then moves on to his larger-scale works on themes of war and peace (eg, *Massacre in Korea*, 1951) and his later preoccupations with love and death, reflected in his Minotaur and bullfighting paintings. Perhaps some of the most engaging works, though, are his more personal ones – those of his children, wives and lovers – such as *Olga pensive* (1923), in which his first wife is shown lost in thought, the deep blue of her dress reflecting her mood. The breakdown of their marriage was probably behind the Surrealist-influenced *Femme dans le Fauteuil Rouge* (room 7): the violent clash of colours and the woman's grotesquely deformed body tell of acute distress. Two portraits of later lovers, Dora Maar and Marie-Thérèse (both painted in 1937), exhibited side by side in room 13, show how the two women inspired Picasso in very different ways: they strike the same pose, but Dora Maar is painted with strong lines and vibrant colours, suggesting a passionate, vivacious personality, while Marie-Thérèse's muted colours and soft contours convey serenity and peace.

The museum also holds a substantial number of Picasso's **engravings**, **ceramics** and **sculpture**, reflecting the remarkable ease with which the artist moved from one medium to another. Some of the most arresting sculptures (room 17) are those he created from recycled household objects, such as the endearing *La Chèvre* (Goat), whose stomach is made from a basket, and the *Tête de taureau*, an ingenious pairing of a bicycle seat and handlebars. Another striking work is the huge bronze *L'Homme au mouton* (1943), showing a man carrying a struggling sheep, as though offering it for sacrifice.

# Place des Vosges and around

Continuing along rue des Francs-Bourgeois east of the Musée Carnavalet, you can't miss the beautiful **place des Vosges**, a masterpiece of aristocratic elegance and the first example of planned development in the history of Paris. It's a vast square of symmetrical pink brick and stone mansions built over arcades. Undertaken in 1605 at the inspiration of Henri IV, it was inaugurated in 1612 for the wedding of Louis XIII and Anne of Austria; it is Louis's statue – or, rather, a replica of it – that stands hidden by chestnut trees in the middle of the grass and gravel gardens. Originally called place Royale, it was renamed Vosges in 1800 in honour of the *département*, which was the first to pay its share of the expenses of the revolutionary wars.

Royal patronage of the area goes back to the days when a royal palace, the Hôtel des Tournelles, stood on the north side of what is now the place des Vosges. It remained in use until 1559, having served also as the residence of the Duke of Bedford when he governed northern France in the name of England in the 1420s. Catherine de Médicis had the Hôtel des Tournelles demolished after the death of her husband Henri II in 1559 and the vacant space became a huge horse market, trading between one and two thousand horses every Saturday. So it remained until Henri IV decided on the construction of his place Royale.

Through all the vicissitudes of history, the *place* has never lost its cachet as a smart address. Today, well-heeled Parisians pause in the arcades at art, antique and fashion shops, and lunch alfresco at the restaurants while buskers play classical music. In the garden, toddlers, octogenarians, workers and schoolchildren on lunch breaks sit or play in the only green space of any size in the locality – unusually for Paris, you're allowed to sprawl on the grass.

Among the many celebrities who made their homes here was Victor Hugo; his house, at no. 6, where he wrote much of *Les Misérables*, is now a museum, the **Maison de Victor Hugo** (Tues–Sun 10am–6pm; closed hols; free; M° Chemin-Vert/Bastille), in which a whole room is devoted to posters of its various stage adaptations. Hugo was extraordinarily multi-talented: as well as writing, he drew – many of his ink drawings are exhibited – and designed his own furniture; he even put together the extraordinary Chinese-style dining room on display here. That apart, the usual portraits, manuscripts and memorabilia shed sparse light on the man and his work, particularly if you don't read French.

From the southwest corner of the *place*, a door leads through to the formal château garden, orangerie and exquisite Renaissance facade of the **Hôtel de Sully**. The garden, with its park benches, makes for a peaceful rest-stop, or you can pass through the building, nodding at the sphinxes on the stairs, as a pleasing short cut to rue St-Antoine. Temporary photographic exhibitions, usually with social, historical or anthropological themes, are mounted in the *hôtel* by the **Mission du Patrimoine Photographique** (Tues–Sun 10am–6.30pm; €4). You can also browse in the bookshop with its extensive collection of books on Paris, some in English (Tues–Sun 10am–7pm).

A short distance back to the west along rue St-Antoine, almost opposite the sixteenth-century **church of St-Paul**, which was inaugurated by Cardinal Richelieu, you'll find another square. A complete contrast to the imposing formality of the place des Vosges, the tiny **place du Marché-Ste-Catherine** is a perfect example of that other great French architectural talent: an unerring eye for the intimate, the small-scale, the apparently accidental, and the irresistibly charming.

## The Jewish quarter: rue des Rosiers

One block south of the rue des Francs-Bourgeois, the area around narrow **rue des Rosiers** has traditionally been the **Jewish quarter** of the city ever since the twelfth century, and remains so, despite incursions by trendy bars and clothes shops. Although the *hammam* is now a designer store, and many of the little grocers, bakers, bookshops and original cafés are under pressure to follow suit (for a long time local flats were kept empty, not for property speculation but to try to stem the middle-class invasion), the area manages to retain its Jewish identity. There's also a distinctly Mediterranean flavour to the *quartier*, testimony to the influence of the **North African Sephardim**, who, since the end of World War II, have sought refuge here from the uncertainties of life in the French ex-colonies. They have replenished Paris's Jewish population, depleted when its Ashkenazim, having escaped the pogroms of Eastern Europe, were rounded up by the Nazis and the French police and transported back east to concentration camps.

Don't leave the area without wandering the surrounding streets: rue du Roi-de-Sicile, the minute **place Bourg-Tibourg** off rue de Rivoli, **rue des Écouffes**, **rue Ste-Croix-de-la-Bretonnerie** (with its lively gay bars), buzzing **rue Vieille-du-Temple**, and **rue des Archives**, where a medieval cloister, the Cloître des Billettes, at nos. 22–26, hosts free exhibitions of art and crafts (daily 11am–7pm). On the other side of rue de Rivoli, at 17 rue Geoffroy l'Asnier, the **Centre de Documentation Juive Contemporaine** (Mon–Fri 10am–1pm & 2–5pm; €2.30; ⓦwww.memorial-cdjc.org; M° St-Paul & M° Pont-Marie) mounts exhibitions concerned with genocides and oppression of peoples, and guards the sombre **Mémorial du Martyr Juif Inconnu** (Memorial to the Unknown Jewish Martyr).

# The Quartier du Temple

The northern part of the Marais is ethnic, local, old-fashioned and working-class. As you get beyond the cluster of art galleries and brasseries that have sprung up around the Picasso museum, or, over to the west, across rue Michel-le-Comte, the aristocratic stone facades of the southern Marais give way to the more humble, though no less attractive, stucco, paint and thick-slatted shutters of seventeenth- and eighteenth-century streets. Some bear the names of old rural French provinces: **Beauce**, **Perche**, **Saintonge**, **Picardie**. Ordinary cafés and shops occupy the ground floors, while rag-trade leather workshops and printers – though these are getting fewer – operate in the interior of the cobbled courtyards.

Robespierre lived in the **rue de Saintonge**, at no. 64, demolished in 1834. In the adjacent **rue Charlot**, at no. 9, yet another Marais mansion, the Hôtel de Retz, has been colonized by artists. It now houses the **Passage de Retz** (daily except Mon 10am–7pm; €6; M° Filles-du-Calvaire), with changing exhibitions of fine art and design from young artists; there's also a bookshop and café. Opposite, in the dead-end **ruelle de Sourdis**, one section of street has remained unchanged since its construction in 1626. Further along, on the corner of **rue du Perche**, a little classical facade on a leafy courtyard hides the **Armenian church of Ste-Croix**, testimony to the many Armenians who sought refuge here from the Turkish pogroms of World War I. Further still, on the left and almost to the busy rue de Bretagne, is the easily missed entrance

## The Knights Templar

The military order of the **Knights Templar** was established in Jerusalem at the time of the Crusades to protect pilgrims to the Holy Land. Its members quickly became exceedingly rich and powerful, with some nine thousand commands spread across Europe. They acquired land in the *marais* in Paris around 1140, and began to build. After the loss of Palestine in 1291, this fortress property, which covered the area now bounded by rues du Temple, Bretagne, Picardie and Béranger and constituted a separate town without the city walls, became their international headquarters, as the seat of their Grand Master.

They came to a sticky end, however, early in the fourteenth century, when King Philippe le Bel, alarmed at their power and in alliance with Pope Clement V, had them tried for sacrilege, blasphemy and sodomy. Fifty-four of them were burnt, including, in 1314, the Grand Master himself, in the presence of the king. Thereafter the order was abolished.

The Temple buildings continued to exist until the Revolution, with about four thousand inhabitants: a mixed population, consisting of artisans not subject to the city's trade regulations, debtors seeking freedom from prosecution, and some rich residents of private *hôtels*. Louis XVI and the royal family were imprisoned in the keep in 1792 (see box overleaf). It was finally demolished in 1808 by Napoleon, determined to eradicate any possible focus for royalist nostalgia.

to the **Marché des Enfants-Rouges**, one of the smallest and least-known food markets in Paris. Across rue de Bretagne, rue de Picardie leads up to the **Carreau du Temple**.

Nothing remains of the **Knights Templar**'s installations beyond the name of "Temple". The **Carreau** itself, which is a fine *halles*-like structure, shelters a clothes market (Tues–Sun mornings) with a heavy preponderance of leather gear. **Rue de la Corderie**, a pretty little street on the north side, opening into an otherworldly *place*, has a couple of pleasant cafés under the trees.

These streets have a genteel and somewhat provincial air about them, but a couple of blocks to the west it's a different story. **Rue du Temple**, itself lined with many beautiful houses dating back to the seventeenth century (no. 41, for instance, the Hôtel Aigle d'Or, is the last surviving coaching inn of the period), is the dividing line, full of fascinating little businesses trading in fashion accessories: chains, bangles, beads – everything you can think of. Further along is the Musée d'Art et d'Histoire du Judaïsme.

## Musée d'Art et d'Histoire du Judaïsme

At no. 71 rue du Temple, the attractively restored Hôtel de Saint-Aignan is now home to the **Musée d'Art et d'Histoire du Judaïsme** (Mon–Fri 11am–6pm, Sun 10am–6pm; €6.10; Ⓦwww.mahj.org; M° Rambuteau). Opened in 1998, it's a combination of the collections of the now closed Musée d'Art Juif in Montmartre, Isaac Strauss, conductor of the Paris Opera orchestra, and the Dreyfus archives, a gift to the museum from his grandchildren. The museum traces the culture, history and artistic endeavours mainly of the **Jews in France**, though there are also many artefacts from the rest of Europe and North Africa. The result is a very comprehensive collection, as educational as

### The Temple and Louis XVI

Louis XVI, Marie-Antoinette, their two children and immediate family were imprisoned in the keep of the Knights Templar's ancient fortress in August 1792 by the revolutionary government. By the end of 1794, when all the adults had been executed, the two children – a teenage girl and the 9- or 10-year-old dauphin, now, in the eyes of royalists, Louis XVII – remained there alone, in the charge of a family called Simon. Louis XVII was literally walled up, allowed no communication with other human beings, not even his sister, who was living on the floor above. He died of tuberculosis in 1795, a half-crazed imbecile, and was buried in a public grave.

At least that is what appeared to be his fate. A number of clues, however, point to hocus-pocus. The doctor who certified the child's death kept a lock of his hair, but it was later found not to correspond with the colour of the young Louis XVII's hair, as remembered by his sister. Mme Simon confessed on her deathbed that she had substituted another child for Louis XVII. And a sympathetic sexton admitted that he had exhumed the body of this imbecile child and reburied it in the cloister of the Église Ste-Marguerite in the Faubourg St-Antoine (see p.198), but when this body was dug up it was found to be that of an 18-year-old.

A plausible theory is that the real Louis XVII died early in 1794. But since Robespierre needed the heir to the throne as a hostage with which to menace internal and foreign royalist enemies, he had Louis disposed of in secret and substituted the idiot. Taking advantage of this atmosphere of uncertainty, 43 different people subsequently claimed to be Louis XVII. After centuries of speculation, all rumours were put to rest in the spring of 2000 when DNA from the child who died of TB was found to match samples obtained from locks of Marie-Antoinette's hair, and also that of several other maternal relatives.

it is beautiful. Free audioguides in English are available and well worth picking up if you want to get the most out of the museum.

It's spread out over three floors with the collection housed on the upper two in a series of smallish rooms, each packed with pieces from the Middle Ages to the twentieth century. Highlights include a Gothic-style hannukkah lamp, one of the very few French Jewish artefacts to survive from the period before the expulsion of the Jews from France in 1394; an Italian gilded circumcision chair from the seventeenth century; and a completely intact late-nineteenth-century Austrian *sukkah*, decorated with paintings of Jerusalem and the Mount of Olives and built as a temporary dwelling for the celebration of the Harvest. Other artefacts include Moroccan wedding garments, highly decorated marriage contracts from eighteenth-century Modena and gorgeous, almost whimsical, spice containers.

Appropriately enough, one room is devoted to the notorious **Dreyfus affair**, documented with letters, photographs and press clippings; you can read Émile Zola's famous letter *"J'accuse"* in which the novelist defends Dreyfus's innocence, and the letters that Dreyfus sent to his wife from prison on Devil's Island in which he talks of *épouvantable* ("terrible") suffering and loneliness. There's also a significant collection of paintings and sculpture by **Jewish artists** – Marc Chagall, Samuel Hirszenberg, Chaïm Soutine and Jacques Lipchitz – who came to live in Paris at the beginning of the twentieth century. Though it may seem an odd omission, there's nothing about the Holocaust. The only reference is an installation by contemporary artist Christian Boltanski: one of the exterior walls of a small courtyard is covered with black-bordered death announcements printed with the names of the Jewish artisans who once lived in the building, a number of whom were deported. Its very understatement has a powerful impact and is perhaps all that's needed to evoke recent Jewish history.

## Chinatown and the Musée des Arts et Métiers

The streets to the west of rue du Temple are narrow, dark, and riddled with passages, the houses half-timbered and bulging with age. Practically every house is a Chinese wholesale business, many of them trading leather – and, on the face of it at least, not very friendly. This was Paris's **original Chinatown**, fed by thousands of immigrant workers brought in to fill the factories while French men were being sent off to the trenches of World War I.

West of rue Volta is the **Musée des Arts et Métiers** (daily except Mon 10am–6pm, Thurs until 9.30pm; €5.50; Ⓦ www.arts-et-metiers.net; M° Arts et Métiers), at 60 rue de Réaumur. This fascinating museum of technological innovation is part of the Conservatoire des Arts et Métiers and incorporates the former Benedictine priory of St-Martin-des-Champs, its original chapel dating from the fourth century. Extensively revamped a few years ago, the museum happily combines creaky old floors and spacious rooms with high-tech, twenty-first-century touches. Its most important exhibit is Foucault's pendulum, which had been on loan in recent years to the Panthéon, where Foucault's successful experiment to prove the rotation of the earth was first conducted in 1851 (see p.124). The famous orb now resides under glass in the chapel, surrounded by all manner of planes and automobiles.

Other exhibits include the laboratory of Lavoisier, the French chemist who first showed that water is a combination of oxygen and hydrogen and, hanging as if in mid-flight above the grand staircase is the elegant "Avion 3", a flying machine complete with feathered propellers, which was donated to the Conservatoire after several ill-fated attempts to fly it.

# South: the Quartier St-Paul-St-Gervais and the Pavillon de l'Arsenal

In the southern section of the Marais, below rues de Rivoli and St-Antoine, the crooked steps and lanterns of rue Cloche-Perce, the tottering timbered houses of rue François-Miron, the medieval buildings behind the church of St-Gervais-St-Protais, and the scent of roses are Paris at its most atmospheric. The late Gothic **St-Gervais-St-Protais**, somewhat battered on the outside owing to a direct hit from a shell fired from Big Bertha in 1918, is more pleasing inside, with some lovely stained glass, carved misericords and a seventeenth-century organ, Paris's oldest. Between rues Fourcy and François-Miron (entrance at 4 rue de Fourcy), a gorgeous Marais mansion, the early eighteenth-century Hôtel Hénault de Cantobre, has been turned into a vast and serene space dedicated to the art of contemporary photography, the **Maison Européenne de la Photographie** (Wed–Sun 11am–8pm; €5, free Wed after 5pm; M° St-Paul/Pont-Marie). Temporary shows combine with a revolving exhibition of the Maison's permanent collection; young photographers and news photographers get a look in, as well as artists using photography in multi-media creations or installation art. A library and *videothèque* can be freely consulted, and there's a stylish café designed by architect Nestor Perkal.

Shift eastwards to the next tangle of streets and you'll find chic, modern flats in the "**Village St-Paul**", with clusters of antique shops in the courtyards. This part of the Marais suffered a postwar hatchet job, and, although seventeenth- and eighteenth-century magnificence is still in evidence (there's even a stretch of the city's defensive wall dating from the early thirteenth century in the lycée playground on rue des Jardins St-Paul), it lacks the architectural cohesion of the Marais to the north. The fifteenth-century **Hôtel de Sens**, on the rue du Figuier, looks bizarre in its isolation. The public library it now houses, the **Bibliothèque Forney**, filled with volumes on fine and applied arts, makes a good excuse to explore this outstanding medieval building. See p.352 for the library's opening hours.

Amid the antique shops on nearby rue St-Paul is the **Musée de la Curiosité et de la Magie** (Wed, Sat & Sun 2–7pm; €7; M° St-Paul/Sully-Morland) at no. 11, a delightful museum of magic and illusion. A few tricks are explained, but don't expect to glean all the answers. Automatas, distorting mirrors and optical illusions, things that float on thin air, a box for sawing people in half – they're all on view with examples from the eighteenth and nineteenth centuries, as well as contemporary magicians' tools. The best fun is a live demonstration of the art (every 30min from 2.30–6pm) by a skilled magician. The museum shop sells books on conjuring and magic cards, wands, boxes, scarves and the like. Groups of schoolchildren tend to visit on Wednesday, so it's better to visit at weekends.

On rue du Petit-Musc, there's an entertaining combination of 1930s' Modernism and nineteenth-century exuberance in the Hôtel Fieubert (now a school). Diagonally opposite, at 21 bd Morland, the **Pavillon de l'Arsenal** (Tues–Sat 10.30am–6.30pm, Sun 11am–7pm; free; M° Sully-Morland) is an excellent addition to the city's art of self-promotion. The aim of the pavilion is to present the city's current **architectural projects** to the public and show how past and present developments have evolved as part and parcel of Parisian history. To this end they have a permanent exhibition of photographs, plans and models, including one of the whole city, with a spotlight to highlight a touch-screen choice of 30,000 images.

The **southeast corner of the 4ᵉ arrondissement**, jutting out into the Seine, has its own distinct character. It's been taken up since the nineteenth century by the Célestins barracks and was previously the site of the Arsenal, which used to overlook a third island in the Seine. Boulevard Morland was built in 1843, covering over the arm of the river that formed the Île de Louviers. The deranged poet Gérard de Nerval escaped here as a boy and lived for days in a log cabin he made with wood scavenged from the island's timberyards. In the 1830s, his more extrovert contemporaries –Victor Hugo, Liszt, Delacroix, Alexandre Dumas and co – were using the library of the former residence of Louis XlV's artillery chief as a meeting place. While the literati discussed turning art into a revolutionary form, the locals were on the streets giving the authorities reason to build more barracks.

# The Bastille

The column surmounted by the gilded "Spirit of Liberty" on **place de la Bastille** was erected to commemorate not the surrender of the **prison** – whose only visible remains have been transported to square Henri-Galli at the end of boulevard Henri-IV – in 1789, but the July Revolution of 1830, that replaced the autocratic Charles X with the "Citizen King" Louis-Philippe. When Louis-Philippe fled in the more significant 1848 Revolution, his throne was burnt beside the column and a new inscription added. Four months later, the workers again took to the streets. All of eastern Paris was barricaded, with the fiercest fighting on rue du Faubourg-St-Antoine, until the rebellion was quelled with the usual massacres and deportation of survivors. However, it is the events of July 14, 1789, symbol of the end of feudalism in Europe, that France celebrates every year on Bastille Day, and the square remains an important rallying point for political protest, as seen in the huge anti-Le Pen demonstrations in 2002.

The Bicentennial of the French Revolution in 1989 was marked by the inauguration of a new opera house on place de la Bastille, the **Opéra Bastille** (for information on performances see p.318), one of François Mitterrand's pet projects. Filling almost the entire block between rues de Lyon, Charenton and Moreau, it has shifted the focus of place de la Bastille, so that the column is no longer the pivotal point; in fact, it's easy to miss it altogether when dazzled by the night-time glare of lights emanating from the Opéra. One critic described it as a "hippopotamus in a bathtub", and you can see his point. The architect, Uruguyan Carlos Ott, was concerned that his design should not bring an overbearing monumentalism to place de la Bastille. The different depths and layers of the semicircular facade do give a certain sense of the building stepping back, but self-effacing it is not. Time, use and familiarity have more or less reconciled it to its surroundings, and people happily sit on its steps, wander into its shops and libraries, and camp out all night for the free performance on July 14.

The opera's construction destroyed no small amount of low-rent housing, but as with most speculative developments, the pace of change is uneven: old tool shops and ironmongers still survive alongside cocktail haunts and sushi bars; and laundries and cobblers flank electronic notebook outlets. On **rue de Lappe**, *Balajo* is one remnant of a very Parisian tradition: the *bals musettes*, or music halls of 1930s *gai Paris*, frequented between the wars by Piaf, Jean Gabin and Rita Hayworth. It was founded by one Jo de France, who introduced glitter and spectacle into what were then seedy gangster dives, enticing Parisians from the other side of the city to savour the rue de Lappe lowlife. Today, the rue de Lappe is one of the liveliest night-time spots in Paris, crammed with animated, young bars, full to bursting on the weekends. Hip bars and cafés have also sprung up in the surrounding streets, especially on **rue de Charonne**, also home to fashion boutiques and wacky interior designers, while alternative, hippy outfits cluster on **rues Keller** and **de la Roquette**.

# The Left Bank

The **Left Bank** (*rive gauche*) has become synonymous with all things dissident and intellectual, especially radical student types. Although, topographically speaking, all Paris south of the river is the Left Bank, the name refers particularly to the traditionally Bohemian haunts around the **boulevard St-Michel**. To the east of the boulevard, the medieval **Quartier Latin** clings to its student traditions, while **St-Germain** gets more and more chi-chi the further west from St-Michel you go.

In modern times the Left Bank's reputation for turbulence and innovation has been renewed by the activities of painters and writers like Picasso, Apollinaire, Breton, Henry Miller, Anaïs Nin and Hemingway after World War I; Camus, Sartre, Juliette Greco and the Existentialists after World War II; and the political turmoil of 1968, which escalated from student demonstrations and barricades to factory occupations, massive strikes and the near-overthrow of de Gaulle's presidency. Nowadays, the streets from which such revolution sprang house expensive flats, art galleries and high-end fashion boutiques, and the cafés once frequented by penniless intellectuals and struggling artists are filled with the well-educated bourgeois. Over the years, those who question authority and the status quo have decamped to other parts of the city and those who define it – politicians, designers, photographers and journalists – have taken their place. Despite this transformation, the small streets, busy shops and lively neighbourhood feel make this the perfect place to stroll or people-watch over a late-afternoon coffee or an after-dinner drink.

## Quartier Latin

Taking its name from the language spoken by university scholars in medieval times, the **Quartier Latin** is a loosely defined area. The traditional heartland of the quarter lies between the river and the medieval colleges which once huddled on the slopes of the Montagne-Ste-Geneviève, a hill now crowned by the proud **Panthéon**; these days the "Latin quarter" is shorthand for most of the 5$^e$ arrondissement, east of the boulevard St-Michel. Students at the many universities and colleges maintain the area's scholarly and rowdy traditions (politics coming a distant third these days) in the cheaper bars, cafés and *bistrots*, decamping to the Luxembourg gardens (see p.132) on sunny days. The quarter's medieval heritage is superbly displayed in the Roman and sixteenth-century buildings housing the **Musée National du Moyen Âge**, worth visiting just for the stunning tapestry series, the *Lady with the Unicorn*. Out towards the eastern end of the 5$^e$, the theme is more Arabic than Latin in the brilliantly

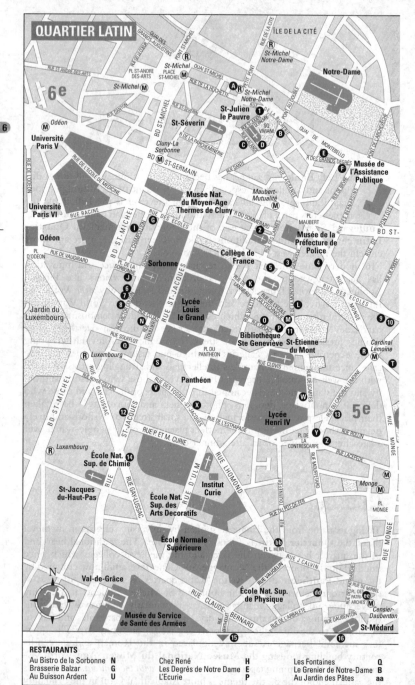

# QUARTIER LATIN

ÎLE DE LA CITÉ

Notre-Dame

St-Michel
Notre-Dame

6e

St-Michel

Université
Paris V

Odéon

St-Julien
le Pauvre

St-Séverin

Cluny-La
Sorbonne

Musée de
l'Assistance
Publique

Musée Nat.
du Moyen-Age
Thermes de Cluny

Université
Paris VI

Odéon

Collège de
France

Musée de la
Préfecture de
Police

Sorbonne

Jardin du
Luxembourg

Lycée
Louis
le Grand

Cardinal
Lemoine

Luxembourg

Bibliothèque
Ste Geneviève

St-Étienne
du Mont

PL DU
PANTHÉON

Panthéon

Luxembourg

Lycée
Henri IV

5e

École Nat.
Sup. de Chimie

St-Jacques
du-Haut-Pas

Institut
Curie

École Nat.
Sup. des
Arts Decoratifs

Monge

École Normale
Supérieure

Val-de-Grâce

École Nat. Sup.
de Physique

Musée du Service
de Santé des Armées

Censier-
Daubenton

St-Médard

N

6

THE LEFT BANK

116

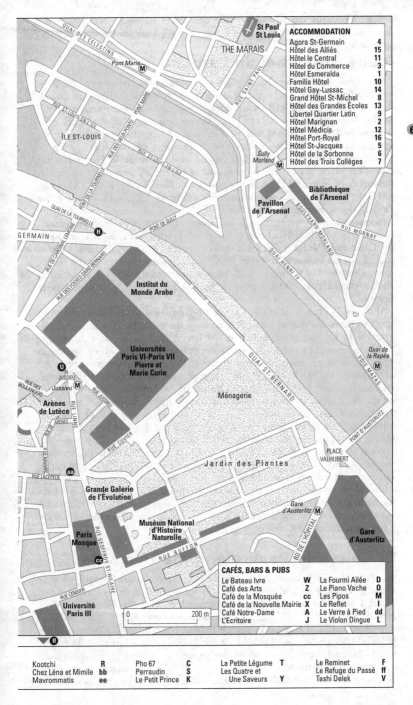

**ACCOMMODATION**

| | |
|---|---|
| Agora St-Germain | 4 |
| Hôtel des Alliés | 15 |
| Hôtel le Central | 11 |
| Hôtel du Commerce | 3 |
| Hôtel Esmeralda | 1 |
| Familia Hôtel | 10 |
| Hôtel Gay-Lussac | 14 |
| Grand Hôtel St-Michel | 8 |
| Hôtel des Grandes Écoles | 13 |
| Libertel Quartier Latin | 9 |
| Hôtel Marignan | 2 |
| Hôtel Médicis | 12 |
| Hôtel Port-Royal | 16 |
| Hôtel St-Jacques | 5 |
| Hôtel de la Sorbonne | 6 |
| Hôtel des Trois Collèges | 7 |

**CAFÉS, BARS & PUBS**

| | | | |
|---|---|---|---|
| Le Bateau Ivre | W | La Fourmi Ailée | D |
| Café des Arts | Z | Le Piano Vache | O |
| Café de la Mosquée | cc | Les Pipos | M |
| Café de la Nouvelle Mairie | X | Le Reflet | I |
| Café Notre-Dame | A | Le Verre à Pied | dd |
| L'Ecritoire | J | Le Violon Dingue | L |

| | | | | | |
|---|---|---|---|---|---|
| Kootchi | R | Pho 67 | C | La Petite Légume | T | Le Reminet | F |
| Chez Léna et Mimile | bb | Perraudin | S | Les Quatre et | | Le Refuge du Passé | ff |
| Mavrommatis | ee | Le Petit Prince | K | Une Saveurs | Y | Tashi Delek | V |

designed **Institut du Monde Arabe** and **Paris mosque**. Nearby are the flowerbeds, zoo and natural history museum of the leafy **Jardin des Plantes**.

## Place St-Michel and around

The pivotal point of the Quartier Latin is **place St-Michel**, where the tree-lined boulevard St-Michel begins. The name is redolent of student chic, though these days dull commercial outlets have largely taken over the famous "boul' Mich". Nevertheless, the cafés and shops around place St-Michel and place St-André-des-Arts are jammed with people, mainly young and, in summer, largely foreign, while the fountain on the *place* is a favourite meeting spot.

The touristy scrum is at its ugliest on and around **rue de la Huchette**, just east of the place St-Michel. The only sign of the street's former incarnation as the mecca of beats and bums in the post-World War II years is the Théâtre de la Huchette, which still shows Ionesco's *Cantatrice Chauve* (*The Bald Prima Donna*) almost fifty years on; the rest is given over to cheap bars and Greek seafood-and-disco tavernas of indifferent quality and inflated prices. Connecting rue de la Huchette to the riverside is the evocatively named **rue du Chat-qui-Pêche** (Fishing Cat Street), a narrow slice of medieval Paris as it used to look before Haussmann set to work clearing the way for the boulevards. One word of warning: watch your wallet amid the bustling crowds; this area, particularly around the *place*, is known for its pickpockets and petty thieves.

At the end of rue de la Huchette, **rue St-Jacques** is aligned along the main street of Roman Paris, its name derived from the vastly popular medieval pilgrimage to the shrine of St Jacques (St James) in Santiago de Compostela, northern Spain. For the millions who set out from the church of St-Jacques (only the tower remains), just across the river, this bit of hill was their first taste of the road. One block south of rue de la Huchette, and west of rue St-Jacques, stands the mainly fifteenth-century **church of St-Séverin**, with its entrance on rue des Prêtres St-Séverin (Mon–Sat 11am–7.15pm, Sun 9am–8.30pm; M° St-Michel/Cluny-La Sorbonne). It's one of the city's most elegant churches, with splendidly virtuoso chiselwork in the pillars of the Flamboyant choir, as well as stained glass by the modern French painter Jean Bazaine. The flame-like carving that gave the *flamboyant* (blazing) style its name flickers in the window arch above the entrance, while inside, the first three pillars of the nave betray the earlier, thirteenth-century origins of the church.

One block to the south of the church, **rue de la Parcheminerie** is where medieval scribes and parchment sellers used to congregate. It's worth cricking your neck to look at the decorations on the facades, including that of no. 29, where you'll find the Canadian-run Abbey Bookshop.

## St-Julien-le-Pauvre and the riverside

Just east of rue St-Jacques, and back towards the river, **square Viviani** – a welcome patch of grass and trees – provides the most flattering of all views of Notre-Dame. The ancient, listing tree propped on a couple of concrete pillars is reputed to be Paris's oldest, a false acacia brought over from Guyana in 1680. The mutilated and disfigured church behind is **St-Julien-le-Pauvre** (daily 9.30am–12.30pm & 3–6.30pm; M° St-Michel/Maubert Mutualité). The same age as Notre-Dame, it used to be the venue for university assemblies until rumbustious students tore it apart in 1524. For the last hundred years it has belonged to a Greek Catholic sect, hence the unexpected iconostasis screening the sanctuary. The hefty slabs of stone by the well at the entrance are all that remain of the Roman thoroughfare now overlain by rue St-Jacques. It's a quiet and intimate place, ideal for a moment's pause.

A few yards from square Viviani, on the river bank, rue de la Bûcherie is the home of the American-run English-language bookshop **Shakespeare and Co.** (see p.332), haunted by the ghosts of James Joyce and other expatriate literati – though the original Shakespeare and Co, owned by the American Sylvia Beach, the long-suffering publisher of Joyce's *Ulysses*, was in fact on rue de l'Odéon. These days the shop is staffed by young Hemingways who sleep upstairs and pay their rent to George Whitman – the current owner and grandson of Walt – by manning the tills. More books, postcards, prints and assorted goods are on sale from the **bouquinistes**, who display their wares in green padlocked boxes hooked onto the parapet of the **riverside quais** – which, in spite of their romantic reputation, are not much fun to walk along because of the ceaseless road traffic.

Continuing upstream to quai de la Tournelle, you can stop en-route at the Hôtel de Miramion (at no. 47), where the **Musée de l'Assistance Publique-Hôpitaux de Paris** (Tues–Sun 10am–6pm; €4; M° Maubert-Mutualité) recounts the history of Paris's hospitals through paintings, sculptures, pharmaceutical containers, surgical instruments and so on. Though there are some beautiful old ceramic jars for recherché medicaments such as *sang de dragon* (dragon's blood), and a number of curious sentimental paintings among the portraits of medical worthies, it's better to press on as far as the tip of the Île St-Louis and the **Pont de Sully** for a dramatic view of the apse and steeple of Notre-Dame. From here, a riverside garden stretches to the east, dotted with modern sculpture.

## Institut du Monde Arabe

Looming over the Pont de Sully is the bold glass and aluminium mass of the **Institut du Monde Arabe** (Tues–Sun 10am–6pm; Ⓦ www.imarabe.org; M° Jussieu/Cardinal-Lemoine) – a stunning and radical piece of architectural engineering. Designed by the architect of the moment, Jean Nouvel – who went on to design the ambitious Fondation Cartier (see p.153) and the brand new Musée du Quai Branly (see p.140) – its broad southern facade comprises thousands of tiny light-sensitive shutters which modulate the light levels inside while simultaneously mimicking a *moucharabiyah*, the traditional Arab latticework balcony. Unfortunately, the computer system operating the little steel diaphragms has a habit of crashing so you may not get to see the full effect.

The institute inside is relatively tame, though a few hit exhibitions and concerts pull in the curious, open-minded visitors sought by its creators – the Mitterrand government in collaboration with the Arab League. A sleek permanent **museum** (€4) begins on the seventh floor, using an array of exquisite artefacts to trace the evolution of the arts and sciences in the Islamic world. The topmost level, dedicated to pre-Islamic finds, is somewhat surprising, as the Carthaginian sculptures and pottery display a distinctively Roman influence, while a beautiful seventh-century Tunisian mosaic hails from an early church. One floor down, brass celestial globes, astrolabes, compasses and sundials illustrate the cutting-edge Arab research that so influenced the West in the Middle Ages, along with illustrated manuscripts, weights and measures, and the grinding and mixing implements for medicines. But the museum's treasures are kept on the lowest floor, with exquisitely crafted ceramics, metalwork and carpets from all over the Muslim world – from Spain to Central Asia.

△ Institut du Monde Arabe

On other levels there are a library and multimedia centre for scholars, a space for temporary exhibitions, a specialist bookshop that sells good Arab music CDs, and an auditorium for regular films and concerts, often featuring leading performers from the Arab world. Up on the ninth floor, the terrace offers brilliant **views over the Seine** towards the apse of Notre-Dame. At the adjacent café-restaurant you can drink mint tea and nibble on cakes; for something more substantial there's the self-service restaurant *Moucharabiyah* where you can tuck into a plate of couscous while marvelling at the aperture action of the windows.

Walking back west along boulevard St-Germain towards boulevard St-Michel, you pass rue de Pontoise with its Art-Deco swimming pool and primary school, and **place Maubert**, which has a good food market on Tuesday, Thursday and Saturday mornings.

Just past place Maubert, the ugly modern police building houses the **Musée de la Préfecture de Police**, at 1bis rue des Carmes. The history of the Paris police force, as presented in this collection of uniforms, arms and papers, is dry stuff, but the murder weapons used by legendary criminals may titillate, and voluntarily walking into a working Paris police station has its own peculiar frisson.

Further south, the Paris mosque (see p.125) makes an obvious next destination.

# The Musée National du Moyen Âge (Hôtel de Cluny)

Five minutes' walk south of Place St-Michel, up boulevard St-Michel, the walls of the third-century **Roman baths** are visible in the garden of the **Hôtel de Cluny**, a sixteenth-century mansion built by the abbots of the powerful Cluny monastery as their Paris pied-à-terre. The *hôtel* now houses the richly rewarding **Musée National du Moyen Âge**, with its entrance at 6 place Paul-Painlevé, off rue des Écoles (daily except Tues 9.15am–5.45pm; €5.50, €4 on Sun; Ⓦ www.musee-moyenage.fr; M° Cluny-La Sorbonne). The two-level museum is a treasure house of medieval art and tapestries, its masterpiece being the wonderful tapestry series of *La Dame à la licorne* (*The Lady with the Unicorn*). The building provides a perfect setting for the art – from the huge carved-stone medieval fireplaces and perfect little chapel, to the cool, intricately bricked Gallo-Roman baths filled with sculptural fragments. A pamphlet in English provides a plan of the museum, and while you're wandering around look out for the laminated information sheets in English provided in some rooms.

There's no charge for entry to the beautiful, shady courtyard or to the grounds running along boulevard St-Germain, the latter of which harbour lawns, benches and a children's playground. Excellent **concerts** of medieval music, often featuring vocal groups backed by outlandish-sounding instruments, are usually held inside the museum on Friday lunchtime (12.30pm) and Saturday afternoon (4pm). Call ☎01.53.73.78.00 for programme information.

## Ground floor

Seemingly the backdrop to the artefacts on display, the **tapestries** that hang in most rooms are in fact the highlight of the collection. In room 3, there's an exquisite Resurrection scene embroidered in gold and silver thread, with sleeping guards in medieval armour, and a fourteenth-century embroidery of two leopards in red and gold. Scenes of manorial life are hung in room 4: these sixteenth-century Dutch tapestries are full of flowers and birds, and include scenes such as a woman spinning while her servant patiently holds the threads for her, a lover making advances, a woman in her bath which is overflowing into a duck pond, and a hunting party leaving for the chase.

Room 5 holds attractively naïve wood and alabaster altarpiece plaques found in homes and churches all over Europe and produced in England by the **Nottingham workshops**. Adjacent (room 6) are some wonderful backlit fragments of stained glass from the **Sainte Chapelle** (see p.55), removed here during the chapel's mid-nineteenth-century renovation. It's fascinating to see the workmanship close up, particularly in bizarre little scenes such as one of a martyr having his eyes gouged out.

Down the steps and inside the modern building built around the old baths, room 8 houses the twenty-one thirteenth-century heads of the **Kings of Judea** from the west front of Notre-Dame, lopped off during the French Revolution in the general iconoclastic frenzy, and only discovered in a 1977 excavation near the Opéra Garnier. The blurred, eroded faces and damaged crowns of the Old Testament kings are lined up in a melancholy row of fallen nobility, next to a stage of headless robed figures. Arching over the *frigidarium* (room 9), the cold room of the **Gallo-Roman baths**, the vaults are preserved intact – though temporarily protected by corrugated sheets pending funds for restoration. They shelter two beautifully carved first- and second-century capitals, the so-called *Seine Boatmen's Pillar* and the *Pillar of St-Landry*, which has animated-looking gods and musicians adorning three of its faces. From the Roman baths it's a smooth transition to room 10, with its (modern) vaulting and mainly Romanesque works, notably two harrowing wooden *Crucifixions*. Three alarmingly fish-eyed heads, detached from the portals of the royal basilica at St-Denis, guard the entrance to room 11, with its Gothic sculptures.

## First floor

Undisputed star of the collection is the exquisitely executed **Lady with the Unicorn**, displayed in a specially darkened, chapel-like chamber (**room 13**) on the first floor. Even if you don't like tapestries, it's quite simply superb. The richly coloured, detailed and highly allegorical series depicts the five senses, each tapestry featuring a beautiful woman flanked by a lion and a unicorn. Dating from the late fifteenth century, the tapestries were probably made in Brussels for the Le Viste family, merchants from Lyon, perhaps to celebrate the family acquiring its own coat of arms – three crescents on a diagonal blue stripe, as shown on the flags floating in various scenes. Each tapestry has a delicate red background worked with a myriad of tiny flowers, birds, plants and animals. In the centre, the richly dressed young woman takes a sweet from a proffered goblet (taste); plays a portable organ (hearing); makes a necklace of carnations (smell); holds a mirror up to the unicorn who whimsically admires his own reflection (sight); and strokes the unicorn's horn with one hand (touch). The final panel, entitled *A Mon Seul Désir* ("To My Only Desire") and depicting the woman putting away her necklace into a jewellery box held out by her servant remains ambiguous. Some authorities think it represents the dangerous passions engendered by sensuality – the open tent behind is certainly suggestive – others that it shows the sixth "moral sense" that guards against such sinfulness.

The rest of the first floor is an amazing ragbag of carved choir stalls, altarpieces, ivories, stained glass, illuminated Books of Hours, games, brassware and all manner of precious objets d'art. Ecclesiastical gold and enamels fill room 16, notably some seventh-century Visigothic votive crowns and the delicate, long-stemmed **Golden Rose of Basel**, a papal gift dating from 1330. From room 17 onwards you're back in the Hôtel de Cluny section. The bright tapestries, beams and carved fireplaces make it possible to forget you're in a museum, especially in the *hôtel's* original Flamboyant **chapel** (room 20), which preserves its remarkable vault splaying out from a central pillar.

## The Sorbonne and around

"Making it" in France has always meant going to Paris, and it's as true for students as for social climbers. In the heart of the Quartier Latin, on the south side of rue des Écoles, lie a cluster of grim-looking buildings that constitute the major components of the brilliant and mandarin world of French intellectual activity: the Sorbonne, Collège de France and Lycée Louis-le-Grand. From rue des Écoles, **Rue Champollion**, with its huddle of arty cinemas and cinema café, *Le Reflet* (see p.293), leads to the traffic-free **place de la Sorbonne**. It's a lovely place to sit, with its lime trees, fountains, cafés and book-toting students. The main front is dominated by the **Chapelle Ste-Ursule**, built in the 1640s by the great Cardinal Richelieu, whose tomb it contains. A building of enormous influence in its unabashed emulation of the Roman Counter-Reformation style, it helped establish a trend for domes, which mushroomed over the city's skyline in the latter part of the century.

You can usually put your nose into the main courtyard of the **Sorbonne** without anyone objecting. Once the most important of the medieval colleges huddled on the top of the Montagne-Ste-Geneviève, it attracted the finest scholars from all over Europe to debate theology, as well as political questions such as relations between the king and the Pope. On 3 May 1968, the Sorbonne became a flashpoint in the student-led rebellion against institutional stagnation when a riot broke out after police attempted to break up a political meeting in the courtyard. The faculty buildings were occupied by radicals and the college briefly became a vibrant commune before it was finally stormed by the police on 16 June. The shake-up in the higher education system that followed transformed the Sorbonne into the more prosaic "Paris IV"; it's now largely attended by arts and social science students.

The foundation of the **Collège de France**, alongside, was first mooted by the Renaissance king François I, in order to establish the study of Greek and Hebrew in France. It's now a leading research institution, attracting the giants of the intellectual world – Barthes, Foucault, Lévy-Strauss. Behind it, on rue St-Jacques, the **Lycée Louis-le-Grand** numbers Molière, Robespierre, Sartre and Victor Hugo among its former pupils. In some ways it's an ordinary *lycée*, or secondary school, but it's also a portal to academic and political success, hot-housing some of France's brightest students for their entry exams to the *grandes écoles*, a kind of elite university. The study programme is renowned for reducing the most brilliant pupils to stressed-out wrecks; just one in ten get through.

## The Panthéon and St-Étienne-du-Mont

The most visible of Paris's many domes graces the hulk of the **Panthéon** (daily: April–Sept 10am–6.30pm; Oct–March 10am–6pm; €7; RER Luxembourg/M° Cardinal-Lemoine), which tops the Montagne Ste-Geneviève. The present structure was built by Louis XV, ostensibly as thanks to Ste Geneviève, the patron saint of Paris, for curing him of illness, but also as part of a grand plan to emphasize the unity of the church and state, troubled at the time by growing divisions between Jesuits and Jansenists: not only did the original church at this spot entomb Geneviève, it had been founded by Clovis, France's first Christian king. The building was only completed in 1789, whereupon the Revolution promptly transformed it into a mausoleum, adding the words *"Aux grands hommes la patrie reconnaissante"* ("The nation honours its great men") underneath the pediment of the giant portico. The remains of French cultural giants such as Voltaire, Rousseau, Hugo and Zola are now entombed in the vast, barrel-vaulted crypt below, along with more recent arrivals: Marie Curie (the only woman) and Alexandre Dumas, the last to be "panthéonized" here, in 2002, with much fanfare.

The Panthéon's interior is well worth a visit for its oddly secular frescoes and sculptures, and monumental design, originally conceived as a combination of the virtues of Classical Greek and Gothic construction. You can also see a working model of **Foucault's Pendulum** swinging from the dome (the original is under glass at the Musée des Arts et Métiers – see p.111). The French physicist Léon Foucault devised the experiment, conducted at the Panthéon in 1851, to demonstrate vividly the rotation of the earth. While the pendulum appeared to rotate over a 24-hour period, it was in fact the earth beneath it turning. The demonstration wowed the scientific establishment and the public alike, with huge crowds turning up to watch the ground move beneath their feet.

Sloping gently downhill from the main portico of the Panthéon, broad rue Soufflot entices you west towards the Luxembourg gardens (see p.132). On the east side of the Panthéon, however, peeping over the walls of the Lycée Henri IV, look out for the lone Gothic tower which is all that remains of the earlier church of Ste-Geneviève. Ste-Geneviève's remains, and those of two seventeenth-century literary giants who didn't make the Panthéon, Pascal and Racine, lie close at hand in the church of **St-Étienne-du-Mont**, on the corner of rue Clovis. The church's facade is a bit of a hotch-potch, but it conceals a stunning and highly unexpected interior. The transition from Flamboyant Gothic choir to sixteenth-century nave would be startling if the eye wasn't distracted by a strange high-level catwalk which springs from pillar to pillar before transforming itself into a rood screen which arches across the width of the nave. This last feature is highly unusual in itself; most French rood screens fell victim to Protestant iconoclasts, reformers or revolutionaries. Exceptionally tall windows flood the church with light, and the cloister has some good seventeenth-century stained glass.

Further down rue Clovis, a huge piece of Philippe-Auguste's twelfth-century **city walls** emerges from among the houses.

## Val-de-Grâce

Heading south from the Panthéon, you quickly leave other tourists behind as you penetrate the academic heart of the Quartier Latin, lorded over by the Curie and oceanographic institutes and the elite **École Normale Supérieure**, on rue d'Ulm. Definitely more *supérieure* than *normale*, its students – dubbed *normaliens* – are France's academic elite, bred for top arts jobs in universities and lycées. It's a closed world to outsiders, and there's not much point in coming this far south unless it's to see the magnificent Baroque church of **Val-de-Grâce** (Sat & Sun 2–5pm), set just back from rue St-Jacques. Built by Anne of Austria as an act of pious gratitude following the birth of her first son in 1638, the church is a suitably awesome monument to the young prince who went on to reign as Louis XIV, with its dome and double-pedimented facade thrusting skywards. The old Benedictine convent adjoining the church to the south was turned into a military teaching hospital after the Revolution, and it remains one of Paris's main hospitals. The first floor of the cloister is now home to the **Musée du Service de Santé des Armées** (Sat & Sun 1.30–5pm; €4.50), an extraordinarily thorough history of military medicine. The mock-ups of field hospitals and gory details of prosthetic limbs and reconstructive plastic surgery aren't for the faint-hearted.

Around the corner from the hospital, the busy **boulevard de Port-Royal** forms the boundary with the 13e arrondissement; from here it's just a short step west to the bright lights and brasseries of Montparnasse (see p.147).

## Contrescarpe and rue Mouffetard

East of the Panthéon, the villagey **rue de la Montagne-Ste-Geneviève** descends towards place Maubert, passing the pleasant cafés and restaurants around rue de l'École-Polytechnique. The road takes its name from one of the grandest and most notorious of the *grandes écoles* that used to be based here – a quasi-military college that prepares its students, known as "*les X*", for top jobs in research and administration and requires them to wear khaki suits in class. It has since decamped to the suburbs of Palaiseau leaving its old buildings to the Ministry of Research and Technology – a trip down memory lane for many of its staff no doubt.

Heading uphill, rue Descartes runs into the tiny and attractive **place de la Contrescarpe**. Once an arty hangout where Hemingway wrote – in the café *La Chope* – and Georges Brassens sang, it's now a tourist hotspot. Just to the east, on rue Lacépède, is a municipal crèche whose lovely curved frontage was inspired by the shape of a pregnant woman's belly.

The ancient **rue Mouffetard** begins just off place de la Contrescarpe, winding downhill to the **church of St-Médard**, once a country parish church beside the now-covered River Bièvre. The street's origins may be Roman, but most of the upper half is tackily modern, given over to touristy eating places. On the facade of no. 12 is a curious painted-glass sign from a different era, depicting a black man in striped trousers waiting on his mistress, with the unconvincing legend, "*Au Nègre Joyeux*". The bottom half of the street, with its sumptuous fruit and vegetable stalls – among lots of clothes and shoe shops and cafés – still maintains an authentic neighbour-hood air, particularly in the mornings when the market is in full swing. Continuing south, Avenue des Gobelins leads into the 13e arrondissement, passing the Gobelins tapestry workshops (see p.163) on the way up to busy place de l'Italie.

## The Paris mosque and Jardin des Plantes

A little further east from rue Mouffetard, across rue Monge, lie some of the city's most agreeable surprises. Just beyond Place du Puits de l'Ermite stand the gate and crenellated walls of the **Paris mosque** (daily except Fri & Muslim holidays 9am–noon & 2–6pm; €3). You can walk in the sunken garden and patios with their polychrome tiles and carved ceilings, but non-Muslims are asked not to enter the prayer room – though no-one seems to mind if you watch from a discreet distance during prayers. The gate on the southeast corner of the complex, on rue Daubenton, leads into a lovely **tearoom** with a garden (see p.292), and an atmospheric **hammam** (see p.355).

Behind the mosque, the **Jardin des Plantes** (daily: summer 7.30am–8pm; winter 8am–dusk; free; ⓦ www.mnhn.fr; Mº Austerlitz/Jussieu/Monge) was founded as a medicinal herb garden in 1626. It gradually evolved as Paris's botanical gardens and with hothouses, shady avenues of trees, lawns to sprawl on, museums and a zoo, it's a pleasant oasis in which to while away a few hours. There's an entrance at the corner of rues Geoffroy-St-Hilaire and Buffon, alongside the museum shop selling wonderful books and postcards; other entrances are further north on the corner with rue Cuvier, the main gate on rue Cuvier itself, and on quai St-Bernard. If you enter by the rue Cuvier entrance, you'll get to see a fine cedar of Lebanon planted in 1734, raised from seed sent over from the Oxford Botanical Gardens, and a slice of an American sequoia more than 2000 years old. In the nearby physics labs, Henri Becquerel discovered radioactivity in 1896, and two years later the Curies discovered radium (Pierre ended his days under the wheels of a brewer's dray on rue Dauphine).

Magnificent, varied floral beds make a fine approach to the collection of buildings that form the **Muséum National d'Histoire Naturelle**. Skip the musty museums of paleontology, anatomy, mineralogy, entomology and paleobotany in favour of the **Grande Galerie de l'Évolution**, (daily except Tues 10am–6pm, Thurs till 10pm; €6.10), housed in a dramatically restored nineteenth-century glass-domed building (the entrance is off rue Buffon). You can't fail to be wowed by the sheer scale of the interior, where the story of evolution and the relations between human beings and nature is told with the aid of stuffed animals (rescued from the dusty old zoology museum and restored to such spruceness that they look alive) and a combination of clever lighting effects, ambient music and birdsong, videos and touch-screen data-bases. If you really want to do something as old-fashioned as reading, there are wooden lecture boards in English to accompany the aurals and visuals. On the lower level, submarine light suffuses the space where the murkiest deep-ocean creatures are displayed. Above, glass lifts rise silently from the savannah, where a closely packed line of huge African animals, headed by an elephant, look as if they're stepping onto Noah's ark. It's all great fun for children, and there's even a small interactive centre for kids on the first floor (see p.368).

Live animals can be seen in the small **ménagerie** across the park to the northeast near rue Cuvier (summer Mon–Sat 9.30am–6pm, Sun 9.30am–6.30pm; winter daily 9.30am–5pm; €6). Founded here just after the Revolution, it is France's oldest zoo – and looks it. The old-fashioned iron cages of the big cats' *fauverie*, the stinky vivarium and the unkempt, glazed-in primate house are frankly depressing, though these animals will at least be spared the fate of their predecessors during the starvation months of the 1870 Prussian siege. Thankfully, most of the rest of the zoo is pleasantly park-like and given over to deer, antelope, goats, buffaloes and other marvellous beasts that seem happy enough in their outdoor enclosures. In the **Microzoo** you can inspect headlice and other minuscule wonders through a microscope.

A short distance away to the northwest, with entrances in rue de Navarre, rue des Arènes and another through a passage on rue Monge, is the **Arènes de Lutèce**. It's an unexpected backwater hidden from the street, and, along with the Roman baths (see p.121), Paris's only Roman remains. A few ghostly rows of stone seats are all that's left of an amphitheatre that once sat ten thousand; the entertainment now provided by the old men playing boules in the sand below. Benches, gardens and a kids' playground stand behind.

# St-Germain

The northern half of the 6ᵉ arrondissement, asymmetrically centred on **place St-Germain-des-Prés**, is one of the most picturesque, lively and wealthy square kilometres in the city. It's got the money, elegance and sophistication, but also an easy-going tolerance and simplicity that comes from a long association with mould-breakers and trendsetters in the arts, philosophy, politics and sciences. Increasingly, the high-end fashion business is taking over – the streets around the Carrefour de la Croix-Rouge and Place St-Sulpice swarm with internationally known boutiques. Around rue Jacob, on the north side of boulevard St-Germain, it's antique shops and art dealers that dominate. After **shopping**, nightlife is the main attraction, though it's pretty conservative these days, a far cry from the postwar era when Sartre and de Beauvoir were leading lights in the intellectual set, and Juliette Gréco and Léo Ferré sang in the cellar jazz bars.

There are plenty of churches, markets and cafés to take in as you shop or stroll, and you can always rest up in the delightful **Jardin du Luxembourg**, bordering the Quartier Latin towards the southern end of the 6ᵉ. Notoriously romantic, and packed with students, it is one of the largest and loveliest green spaces in the city.

## The Pont des Arts and Institut de France

The most dramatic approach to St-Germain is to cross the river from the Louvre by the elegant footbridge, the **Pont des Arts**, taking in the classic upstream view of the Île de la Cité, with barges moored at the quai de Conti, and the Tour St-Jacques and Hôtel de Ville breaking the skyline of the Right Bank.

The graceful dome and pediment at the end of the bridge belong to the **Collège des Quatre-Nations**, seat of the **Institut de France**. Of the Institut's five academies of arts and sciences, the most famous is the **Académie Française**, an august body of writers and scholars whose mission is to award literary prizes and safeguard the purity of the French language. Recent creations include the excellent word *baladeur* for "Walkman", but rearguard actions against Anglo-Saxon terms in science, management and webspeak have been hopelessly ineffective. Becoming an *Académicien* is the ultimate accolade, and the chosen few are known as *Immortels* – though ironically, by the time they have accumulated enough prestige to be elected, most are not long for this world. The list of *immortels* is hardly avant garde: among the forty-strong group at the time of writing, one was a cardinal and just two were women. Public lectures are given by the Academies of Philosophy (Mon 2.45pm), Science (Tues 3pm) and Belles Lettres (Fri 3.30pm); casual visitors are also welcome to look around the courtyard. If you ask politely at the gate you will be given a visitor's pass for the exquisite **Bibliothèque Mazarine** (Mon–Fri 10am–6pm; free), where scholars of religious history sit in hushed contemplation of some of the 200,000 sixteenth- and seventeenth-century volumes, surrounded by *rocaille* chandeliers, marble busts and Corinthian columns.

Next door to the Institut, at 11 quai de Conti, is the **Hôtel des Monnaies**, redesigned as the Mint in the late eighteenth century and now reduced to housing the **Musée de la Monnaie** (Tues–Fri 11am–5.30pm, Sat & Sun noon–5.30pm; €6). Its dry collection of coins and coin-making tools might, at a pinch, appeal to those deeply nostalgic for the franc, or Balzac lovers curious

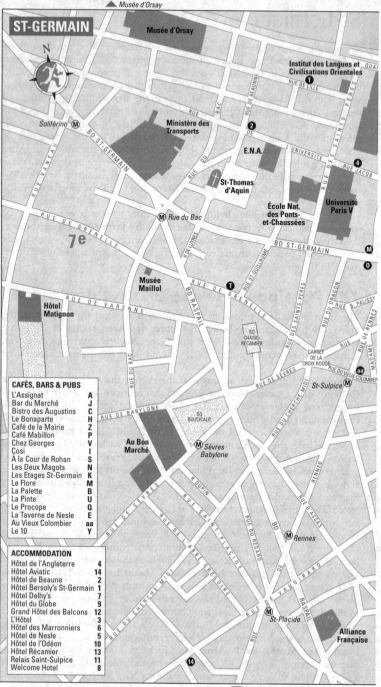

ST-GERMAIN

Musée d'Orsay

Musée d'Orsay

Institut des Langues et
Civilisations Orientales ❶

RUE DE LILLE

N

Soliférino Ⓜ

Ministère des
Transports ❷

BD ST-GERMAIN

RUE DE BEAUNE

RUE DE LILLE

QUAI

RUE DU BAC

DE

L'UNIVERSITÉ

RUE DES SAINTS-PÈRES

E.N.A.

RUE DE

RUE JACOB ❹

St-Thomas
d'Aquin

École Nat.
des Ponts-
et-Chaussées

Université
Paris V

RUE VANEAU

Ⓜ Rue du Bac

RUE DU BAC

RUE DE GRENELLE

7e

RUE LUYNES

BD ST-GERMAIN Ⓜ

Ⓞ

Musée
Maillol

RUE DE GRENELLE Ⓣ

RUE ST-GUILLAUME

BD RASPAIL

RUE DU DRAGON

RUE B. PALISSY

Hôtel
Matignon

RUE DE VARENNE

RUE DE VARENNE

RUE DES SAINTS-PÈRES

RUE DE RENNES

RUE MADAME

SQ
CHAISE-
RÉCAMIER

CARREF
DE LA
CROIX ROUGE

RUE DU VIEUX-COLOMBIER

RUE DE SÈVRES

St-Sulpice Ⓜ

aa

**CAFÉS, BARS & PUBS**
L'Assignat                          **A**
Bar du Marché                   **J**
Bistro des Augustins         **C**
Le Bonaparte                     **H**
Café de la Mairie               **Z**
Café Mabillon                    **P**
Chez Georges                     **V**
Cosi                                    **I**
À la Cour de Rohan            **S**
Les Deux Magots              **N**
Les Etages St-Germain      **K**
Le Flore                             **M**
La Palette                           **B**
La Pinte                             **U**
Le Procope                         **Q**
La Taverne de Nesle          **E**
Au Vieux Colombier           **aa**
Le 10                                  **Y**

RUE DU BAC

RUE DE BABYLONE

SQ
BOUCICAUT

Au Bon
Marché

Ⓜ Sèvres
Babylone

RUE DE SÈVRES

RUE DUPIN

RUE DU CHERCHE-MIDI

RENNES

RUE D'ASSAS

**ACCOMMODATION**
Hôtel de l'Angleterre              4
Hôtel Aviatic                          14
Hôtel de Beaune                     2
Hôtel Bersoly's St-Germain    1
Hôtel Delhy's                          7
Hôtel du Globe                        9
Grand Hôtel des Balcons       12
L'Hôtel                                    3
Hôtel des Marronniers           6
Hôtel de Nesle                        5
Hôtel de l'Odéon                   10
Hôtel Récamier                     13
Relais Saint-Sulpice             11
Welcome Hotel                       8

RUE DE L'ABBÉ GRÉGOIRE

RUE SAINT-PLACIDE

RUE DU REGARD

BD RASPAIL

BD DE VAUGIRARD

Ⓜ Rennes

RUE DU CHERCHE-MIDI

Ⓜ
St-Placide

Alliance
Française

❶❹

128

Gare Montparnasse

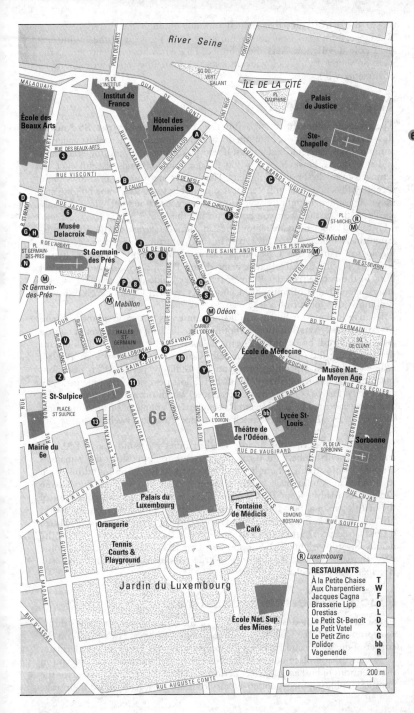

River Seine

ÎLE DE LA CITÉ

PONT DES ARTS

MALAQUAIS

PL DE L'INSTITUT

QUAI DE CONTI

PONT NEUF

SQ DU VERT GALANT

PL DAUPHINE

Institut de France

Palais de Justice

Hôtel des Monnaies

Ste-Chapelle

École des Beaux Arts

RUE BONAPARTE

RUE DES BEAUX-ARTS

**3**

RUE MAZARINE

RUE QUENEBAUD

RUE DE NEVERS

RUE VISCONTI

R CALLOT

**B**

R DE NESLE

**A**

QUAI DES GRANDS-AUGUSTINS

**C**

R DE SEINE

RUE JACOB

**6**

RUE MAZARINE

**5**

RUE CHRISTINE

**D**

R. ST-BENOÎT

RUE DE L'ECHAUDE

**E**

RUE DES GRANDS-AUGUSTINS

RUE GIT LE COEUR

PL ST-MICHEL

**R**

**M**

Musée Delacroix

**G H**

R DE L'ABBAYE

RUE DE BUCI

**I J**

**F**

RUE SAINT ANDRE DES ARTS

St-Michel

PL ST-GERMAIN-DES-PRES

St Germain-des Prés

**K L**

RUE MAZET

RUE DE L'ANCIENNE COMEDIE

COUR DU COMMERCE

PL ST ANDRE DES ARTS

**M**

**7**

RUE ST-SEVERIN

**N**

St Germain-des-Prés

**M**

**P 8**

BD ST-GERMAIN

**R**

RUE DE SEINE

RUE GREGOIRE DE TOURS

**Q**

RUE DE L'EPERON

DANTON

RUE HAUTEFEUILLE

BD ST-MICHEL

BD ST GERMAIN

**M** Mabillon

**S**

RUE

GERMAIN

FOUR

RUE MABILLON

RUE PRINCESSE

HALLES ST-GERMAIN

**M** Odéon

CARREF DE L'ODEON

RUE DE L'ECOLE

SQ DE CLUNY

DU

RUE DES CANETTES

**V W**

RUE LOBINEAU

R DES 4 VENTS

**9**

École de Médecine

RUE DE MEDECINE

**Z**

**X**

RUE SAINT-SULPICE

**10**

**Y**

RUE MONSIEUR-LE-PRINCE

Musée Nat. du Moyen Age

RUE DES ECOLES

St-Sulpice

**11**

RUE TOURNON

**12**

RUE RACINE

PL DE LA SORBONNE

Sorbonne

**13**

PLACE ST SULPICE

RUE GARANCIERE

RUE DE CONDE

PL DE L'ODEON

**bb**

Lycée St-Louis

BD ST-MICHEL

RUE DE LA SORBONNE

Mairie du 6e

RUE FEROU

RUE SERVANDONI

6e

Théâtre de de l'Odéon

RUE DE VAUGIRARD

RUE CUJAS

RUE BONAPARTE

RUE DE VAUGIRARD

Palais du Luxembourg

RUE DE MEDICIS

LE PRINCE

PL EDMOND ROSTAND

RUE SOUFFLOT

RUE GUYNEMER

Orangerie

Fontaine de Médicis

Café

**R** Luxembourg

Tennis Courts & Playground

RUE MADAME

RUE D'ASSAS

Jardin du Luxembourg

École Nat. Sup. des Mines

**RESTAURANTS**

| | |
|---|---|
| À la Petite Chaise | T |
| Aux Charpentiers | W |
| Jacques Cagna | F |
| Brasserie Lipp | O |
| Orestias | L |
| Le Petit St-Benoît | D |
| Le Petit Vatel | X |
| Le Petit Zinc | G |
| Polidor | bb |
| Vagenende | R |

RUE AUGUSTE COMTE

0          200 m

to see the actual coins that slipped so easily through the fingers of young Rastignac, from gold *Louis* to the humble *sou*. To the west of the Institut lies the **École des Beaux-Arts**, the School of Fine Art, whose students throng the *quais* on sunny days, sketch pads on knee; it's sometimes open for exhibitions of students' work.

## The riverside

The riverside chunk of the 6$^e$ arrondissement is defined by **rue St-André-des-Arts** and **rue Jacob**, both lined with bookshops, commercial art galleries, antique shops, cafés and restaurants. If you poke your nose into the courtyards and side streets, however, you'll find foliage, fountains and peaceful enclaves removed from the bustle of the city. The houses are four to six storeys high, seventeenth- and eighteenth-century, some noble, some stiff, some bulging and skew, all painted in infinite gradations of grey, pearl and off-white. Broadly speaking, the further west you go the posher the houses.

Historical associations are legion: Picasso painted *Guernica* in rue des Grands-Augustins; Molière started his career in rue Mazarine; Robespierre et al. split ideological hairs at the *Café Procope* in rue de l'Ancienne-Comédie. In rue Visconti, Racine died, Delacroix painted, and Balzac's printing business went bust. In the parallel rue des Beaux-Arts, Oscar Wilde died (see p.261), Corot and Ampère (father of amps) lived, and the crazy poet Gérard de Nerval went walking with a lobster on a lead.

If you're looking for lunch, you'll find numerous places on **place** and **rue St-André-des-Arts**, but more tempting is the brilliant food market in **rue de Buci**, up towards boulevard St-Germain. Just before you get to it, look out for the intriguing little passage on the left, **Cour du Commerce St André**, where Marat had a printing press and Dr Guillotin perfected his notorious machine by lopping off sheep's heads in the loft next door. Backing onto the street is *Le Procope* – Paris's first coffeehouse, which opened its doors in 1686 and was frequented by Voltaire and Robespierre. A couple of smaller courtyards open off it, revealing another stretch of Philippe-Auguste's twelfth-century city wall.

An alternative corner for midday food or quiet is around rue de l'Abbaye and rue du Furstemberg. At 6 rue du Furstemburg, opposite a tiny square, is Delacroix's old studio, where he lived and worked from 1857 until his death in 1863. The studio backs onto a secret garden and is now the **Musée Delacroix** (daily except Tues 9.30am–5pm; €5), with a small collection of the artist's personal belongings as well as temporary exhibitions of his work. His major work is exhibited permanently at the Louvre and the Musée d'Orsay (see pp.67 and 145), and you can see the murals he painted at the nearby St-Sulpice church (see opposite). This is also the beginning of some very upmarket shopping territory – rue Jacob, rue de Seine and rue Bonaparte in particular.

## Place St-Germain-des-Prés

**Place St-Germain-des-Prés**, the hub of the *quartier*, is only a stone's throw away from the Musée Delacroix, with the *Deux Magots* café (see p.295) on the corner of the square and *Flore* (see p.296) just down the boulevard St-Germain. Be warned that a place on the *terrasse* of either will inevitably involve you in the attentions of buskers and street performers. Both cafés are renowned for the number of philosophico-politico-literary backsides that have shined their seats, although nowadays they've almostly entirely fallen victim to their fame. The snootier *Brasserie Lipp*, across the boulevard, is a longtime haunt of the more successful practitioners of these trades.

The robust, eleventh-century tower opposite the *Deux Magots* belongs to the **church of St-Germain-des-Prés**, all that remains of an enormous Benedictine monastery. Inside, the transformation from Romanesque nave to early Gothic choir is visible even under the heavy greens and golds of nine-teenth-century paintwork. In the choir, the marble columns of the middle tri-forium level date from an even earlier church on this site, which was erected in the sixth century and housed the remains of the Merovingian kings. The last chapel on the south side houses the tomb of the philosopher René Descartes. In the corner of the churchyard, by rue Bonaparte, a little Picasso head of a woman is dedicated to the memory of the poet Apollinaire.

## St-Sulpice to the Odéon

**South of boulevard St-Germain**, the streets around the church of St-Sulpice (see below) are calm and classy. **Rue Mabillon** is pretty, with a row of old houses set back below the level of the modern street. On the left stand the **halles St-Germain**, incorporating a swimming pool, gym, audi-torium and commercial complex, built on the site of a fifteenth-century market. Rue Mabillon leads through to the front of the enormous **church of St-Sulpice** (daily 7.30am–7.30pm), an austerely classical edifice, erected either side of 1700, with a Doric colonnade surmounted by an Ionic, and Corinthian pilasters in the towers. Uncut masonry blocks still protrude from the south tower, awaiting the sculptor's chisel. The gloomy interior, con-taining three Delacroix murals in the first chapel on the right, including one of St-Michael slaying a dragon, is not to everyone's taste. But, softened by the chestnut trees and fountain of the square, the ensemble is peaceful and harmonious.

On the sunny north side of **place St-Sulpice**, the outside tables at the *Café de la Mairie* hum with trendy chatter on fine days, but the main attractions here are the fashion boutiques, like the very elegant **Yves Saint Laurent Rive Gauche**, on the corner of the ancient **rue des Canettes** – though Yves himself has finally quit (see p.334). Further along the same side of the *place*, there's Saint Laurent for men, and from there on it's spend, spend, spend down rues Bonaparte, Madame, de Sèvres, de Grenelle, du Four, des Saints-Pères . . .

Hard to believe now, but smack in the middle of all this, at the carrefour de la Croix Rouge, there was a major barricade in 1871, fiercely defended by Eugène Varlin, one of the leading lights of the **Commune** (see p.170). He was later betrayed by a priest, half-beaten to death and shot by government troops on Montmartre hill. These days you're more likely to be suffering from till-shock than shell-shock. You may feel safer in rue Princesse at the small, friendly and well-stocked American bookshop, The Village Voice (see p.332), where you can browse through the latest literature and journals. Or you could retreat to the less stylish eastern edge of the quartier, around boulevard St-Michel, where the university is firmly implanted, its attendant bookshops displaying scientific and medical tomes, as well as skeletons and instruments of medical torture. Rue Monsieur le Prince is lined with inexpensive restaurants, many of them Japanese, as well as the classic bistro, *Polidor* (see p.297). Heading south along rue de l'Odéon, towards the Luxembourg gardens, you can take in the Doric portico of the **Théâtre de l'Odéon** en route.

# Jardin du Luxembourg

Fronting onto **rue de Vaugirard**, Paris's longest street, the **Palais du Luxembourg** was constructed for Marie de Médicis, Henri IV's widow, to remind her of the Palazzo Pitti and Giardino di Boboli of her native Florence. Today it is the seat of the French Senate and its lovely **gardens** (open roughly dawn to dusk) are the chief lung of the Left Bank, with formal lawns and floral parterres dotted with trees – some of which are kept in giant pots, and taken inside in winter. The gardens get fantastically crowded on summer days, when the most contested spot is the shady **Fontaine de Médicis** in the northeast corner. Most of the **lawns** are out-of-bounds but metal chairs are liberally distributed around the gravel paths, and if you can find a clearing among the hundreds of young bodies you can lie out on the grass of the southernmost strip. Alternatively, there's a delightful tree-shaded **café** roughly 100m northeast of the pond.

Children rent toy yachts to sail on the central round pond, but the western side is the more active area, with **tennis courts** (see p.358), donkey rides, a large children's playground and the inevitable sandy area for boules. Sculptural works are scattered around the park, including an 1890 monument to the painter Delacroix by Jules Dalou and a suitably bizarre homage to the Surrealist poet Paul Eluard by the sculptor Ossip Zadkine, more of whose works can be seen in the nearby Musée Zadkine (see p.153). The quieter, wooded southwest corner ends in a miniature orchard of elaborately espaliered pear trees whose fruits grace the tables of senators or, if surplus to requirements, are given to associations for the homeless. Temporary art exhibitions take place in the **Orangerie** (entrance from 19 rue de Vaugirard, opposite rue Férou), as does the "Expo-Automne", held annually in the last week of September to show off fruits and floral decorations, many grown in the Luxembourg's own gardens and hothouses.

# Trocadéro and the Septième

From the terrace of the **Palais de Chaillot** on place du Trocadéro, as you look out across the river to the **Eiffel Tower** and **École Militaire**, or let your gaze run from the ornate 1900 Pont Alexandre III along the grassy Esplanade to the **Hôtel des Invalides**, the vistas are splendid. This is town planning on a grand scale, upstaging the minor interests and details of everyday lives. In the shadow of this giant riverside landscape, the **Septième arrondissement** (7e) runs east along the Left Bank towards St-Germain, populated with endless ministries, embassies and luxurious official residences.

But for all the pomp, corners of more amenable life do exist – in **rue de Babylone**, and in the streets between the Invalides and the Champ de Mars – and there's a host of excellent **museums**, particularly for nineteenth and twentieth-century art. First among them is the unmissable **Musée d'Orsay** with its unrivalled collection of Impressionist paintings. Elsewhere you'll find museums devoted to modern and contemporary art, sewers, anthropology, war, Asian art, the sculptors Rodin and Maillol and, in the near future, architecture and primitive art. But of all the mega-monuments in the area, the best is undoubtedly the **Eiffel Tower**. No matter how many pictures, photos, models or glimpses from elsewhere in the city you may have seen, it is still, when you get up close, an amazing structure.

## Trocadéro

Between place du Trocadéro and the place de l'Alma two rather ugly 1930s "palaces" are each home to a couple of museums. The **Palais de Chaillot**, which faces the Eiffel Tower across the river, houses museums of naval history and anthropology, and will soon add the state-of-the-art Cité de l'Architecture et du Patrimoine to the collection. Just to the east, the **Palais de Tokyo** houses the even more cutting-edge Site de Création Contemporaine, an exhibition space for contemporary art, as well as the Musée d'Art Moderne de la Ville de Paris, the city's own museum of modern art. Between the two palaces, the superbly revamped **Musée Guimet** boasts a stunning display of Oriental and especially Buddhist art.

△ The Eiffel Tower & the Champ de Mars

# The Palais de Chaillot

The **Palais de Chaillot** was built in 1937 for the Exposition Universelle on a site that has been a ruler's favourite since Catherine de Médicis constructed one of her playpens there in the early sixteenth century. A bastardized modernist-Classical monster, it has acquired a forlorn air since the fire of 1996 and the decision to move the Cinemathèque (see p.323) to rue de Bercy. To add further insult, almost all of the **Musée de l'Homme**'s (daily except Tues 9.45am–5.15pm; closed public hols; €5; M° Trocadéro) ethnographical collection has been moved across the river to Chirac's folly on quai Branly (see p.140), leaving behind a depleted, old-fashioned version in the southern wing, which uses its dusty collection of tribal costumes, musical instruments and traditional tools and artwork to explain non-Western cultures. On the ground floor of the same wing, the **Musée de la Marine** (daily except Tues 10am–6pm; €7) traces French naval history using models of ships and their accoutrements. It's also home to the original Jules Verne trophy – awarded for non-stop round-the-world sailing – a hull-shaped streak of glass invisibly suspended by magnets within its cabinet.

The northern wing of the palace is occupied by the **Théâtre National de Chaillot**, which stages diverse but usually radical productions under the central terrace. Planned for the same wing is the **Cité de l'Architecture et du Patrimoine**, a combined institute, library and **museum of architecture** due to open in 2004. On the ground floor, giant plaster casts of sections of great French buildings will tell the story of French architecture from the Middle Ages through to the nineteenth century; upstairs will be the nineteenth- and twentieth-century galleries, with photographs, designs and original architectural models. The *terrasse* extending between the two wings is a popular hangout for in-line skaters and souvenir vendors – and the place to plant yourself for the view across to the Eiffel Tower and the École Militaire.

# Musée Guimet and Musée de la Mode

As you head east and downhill from Trocadéro, a couple of excellent, rather specialized museums stand within a stone's throw of each other. The first, on place d'Iéna, is the wonderful **Musée National des Arts Asiatiques – Guimet** (daily except Tues 10am–6pm; €5.50; M° Iéna; Ⓦwww.museeguimet.fr), whose breathtaking roofed-in courtyard provides an airy, modern space in which to show off the museum's world-renowned collection of **Khmer sculpture** – from the civilization that produced Cambodia's Angkor Wat. The museum winds round four floors groaning under the weight of statues of Buddhas and gods, some fierce, some meditative, all of them dramatically lit and imaginatively displayed on plinths or in sometimes surprising niches and cabinets. Each room is devoted to a different country of origin, stretching from Afghanistan to China. The Buddhist statues of the **Gandhara civilization**, on the first floor, betray a fascinating debt to Greek sculpture, while the fierce demons from Nepal, the many-armed gold gods of South India or the pot-bellied Chinese Buddhas are stunningly exotic. Ceramics, paintings and other objets d'art are scattered among the statuary, and on the third floor is a rotunda used by the collection's founder, **Émile Guimet**, for the first Buddhist ceremony ever held in France. A great collector and patron of the arts, Guimet came from a family of enormously wealthy industrialists and espoused the Christian-socialist-egalitarian theories about society, class and government proposed by Fournier, Saint-Simon and, in Britain, Robert Owen.

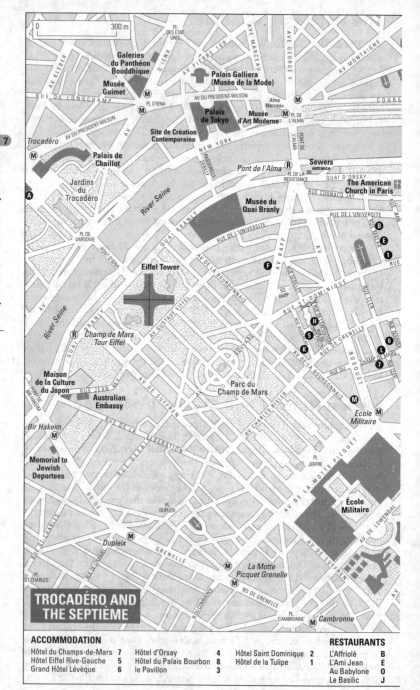

TROCADÉRO AND
THE SEPTIÈME

## ACCOMMODATION

| | | | |
|---|---|---|---|
| Hôtel du Champs-de-Mars | 7 | Hôtel d'Orsay | 4 |
| Hôtel Eiffel Rive-Gauche | 5 | Hôtel du Palais Bourbon | 8 |
| Grand Hôtel Lévèque | 6 | le Pavillon | 3 |

| | |
|---|---|
| Hôtel Saint Dominique | 2 |
| Hôtel de la Tulipe | 1 |

## RESTAURANTS

| | |
|---|---|
| L'Affriolé | B |
| L'Ami Jean | E |
| Au Babylone | O |
| Le Basilic | J |

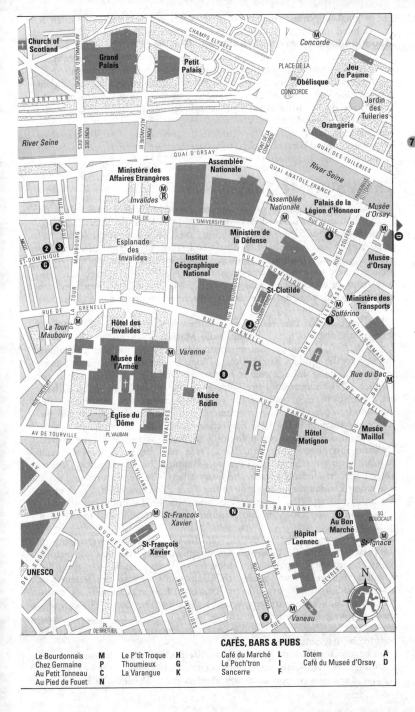

**CAFÉS, BARS & PUBS**

| | | | | | |
|---|---|---|---|---|---|
| Le Bourdonnais | **M** | Le P'tit Troque | **H** | Café du Marché | **L** | Totem | **A** |
| Chez Germaine | **P** | Thoumieux | **G** | Le Poch'tron | **I** | Café du Museé d'Orsay | **D** |
| Au Petit Tonneau | **C** | La Varangue | **K** | Sancerre | **F** | | |
| Au Pied de Fouet | **N** | | | | | | |

His original collection, which he brought back from his travels in Asia in 1876, is exhibited nearby in the small and attractive **Galeries du Panthéon Bouddhique**, at 19 avenue d'Iéna. Above the rotunda, two beautiful Chinese lacquer screens crown the topmost floor, while at the back of the museum is a small Japanese garden, complete with bamboo, pussy willow and water.

A little further to the east, opposite the Palais de Tokyo, set in small gardens at 10 avenue Pierre 1er de Serbie, stands the grandiose Palais Galliera, home to the **Musée de la Mode et du Costume** (daily except Monday 10am–6pm; €7; M° Iéna/Alma-Marceau). The museum's collection of clothes and fashion accessories from the eighteenth century to the present day is exhibited in temporary, themed shows of which there are two or three a year – during changeovers the museum is closed.

# The Palais de Tokyo

Nearby, with its entrance on avenue du Président-Wilson, the **Palais de Tokyo** houses the **Musée d'Art Moderne de la Ville de Paris** (Tues–Fri 10am–5.45pm, Sat & Sun 10am–6.45pm; closed Mon & public hols; free; M° Iéna/Alma-Marceau). The museum's collection can't rival that of the Pompidou Centre, but the environment is perhaps more contemplative – and architecturally more fitting when it comes to works by early-twentieth-century artists, of which there's a major collection. In general, the lower floors are dedicated to the museum's permanent collection; the upper floors given over to temporary exhibitions.

The museum has two enormous and marvellous centrepieces. Facing the stairs as you descend, the chapel-like **salle Matisse** is devoted to Matisse's *La Danse de Paris*, beginning with an incomplete early version and progressing through to the finished work, displayed high on the wall, its sinuous figures seemingly leaping through colour. Further on, Dufy's enormous mural *La Fée Électricité* ("The Electricity Fairy") fills an entire, curved room with 250 lyrical, colourful panels recounting the story of electricity from Aristotle to the then-modern power station – a reminder of the building's beginnings as the Electricity Pavilion in the 1937 Exposition Universelle.

The main collection is chronologically themed, starting with Fauvism and Cubism, and progressing through to Dada and the École de Paris, and beyond. Most artists working in France – Braque, Chagall, Delaunay, Derain, Dufy, Léger, Modigliani, Picasso and many others – are represented and there is a strong Parisian theme to many of the works. The collection is kept up to the minute by an active buying policy, and some bold acquisitions of sculpture, painting and video by contemporary artists are displayed in the final suite of rooms.

Squatting – with official approval – in the semi-derelict western wing of the palace, the **Site de Création Contemporaine** (Tues–Sun noon–midnight; cost of entry depends on exhibitions; Ⓦwww.palaisdetokyo.com) has staged a number of avant-garde exhibitions and events since it opened in 2002, including a show of works by Paris-born Louise Bourgeois, a temporary occupation by squatter-artists and a skateboarding demo. The constant flow of young French artists installing, working on or taking down their works, and hanging out in the bar-restaurant, bookshop and library further adds to the arty ambiance.

Just beyond the Palais de Tokyo, in **place de l'Alma**, the replica of the flame from the Statue of Liberty was given to France in 1987 as a symbol of Franco-American relations; it's now an unofficial memorial to **Princess Diana**, whose car crashed in the adjacent underpass, with the odd bunch of flowers and graffiti messages along the lines of "Mexico love you Diana". From here, if you head back downstream, you can reach the Eiffel Tower via the Passerelle Debilly footbridge (in front of the Palais de Tokyo).

# The Septième

Across the river from Trocadéro, the **Eiffel Tower** offers the most impressive vista of all, while the area at its feet to the east, the **Septième arrondissment** (7ᵉ), is worth exploring for the classy shops and restaurants around **rue Cler**. Much of the rest of this quarter is dominated by monumental government buildings and the military edifices of the **École Militaire** and **Hôtel des Invalides**, the latter housing the impressive war museum and, appropriately enough, the **tomb of Napoleon**. Tucked away in the streets towards St-Germain, the **Musée Rodin** and **Musée Maillol** show off the two sculptors' works in the intimate surroundings of handsome *hôtels*.

## The Eiffel Tower

It's hard to believe that the **Eiffel Tower**, the quintessential symbol both of Paris and the brilliance of industrial engineering, was designed to be a temporary structure for a fair. Late-nineteenth-century Europe had a taste for giant-scale, colonialist–capitalist extravaganzas, but Paris's 1889 Exposition Universelle was particularly ambitious: when completed, the tower, at 300m, was the tallest building in the world. Reactions were violent. Outraged critics protested against this "grimy factory chimney". "Is Paris", they asked, "going to be associated with the grotesque, mercantile imaginings of a constructor of machines?" Eiffel himself thought it was beautiful. "The first principle of architectural aesthetics," he said, "prescribes that the basic lines of a structure must correspond precisely to its specified use . . . To a certain extent the tower was formed by the wind itself."

Curiously, this most celebrated of landmarks was only saved from demolition by the sudden need for "wireless telegraphy" aerials in the first decade of the twentieth century. The tower's role in telecommunications – its only function apart from tourism – has only become more important, and the original crown is now masked by an efflorescence of antennae. Over the last century, the structure has needed few adjustments, but it has seen some surprising cosmetic changes: the original deep red paint-scheme has been covered up with a sober, dusty-chocolate brown since the late 1960s – at least the city is spared the canary yellow that covered the tower for most of its first decade. At night, the tower is illuminated from within, its sweeping searchlight giving it the appearance of a huge urban lighthouse.

**Going up** (daily: mid-June to Aug 9am–midnight; Sept to mid-June 9.30am–11pm) costs €9.90 (for the top; access closes at 10.30pm), €6.90 (second level) or €3.70 (first level); you can also climb the stairs as far as the second level for a mere €3 (access to the stairs closes at 6pm from Sept to mid-June). Paris looks surreally microscopic from the top and though the views are arguably better from the second level, especially on hazier days, there's something irresistible about taking the lift all the way. The view is, of course, the main attraction, but you can also peer through a window into Eiffel's airy little show-off study, at the very top, while at the second level is the hyper-gastro-nomic restaurant, *Jules Verne*.

# The École Militaire and around

Stretching back from the legs of the Eiffel Tower, the long rectangular gardens of the **Champs de Mars** lead to the eighteenth-century buildings of the **École Militaire**, originally founded in 1751 by Louis XV for the training of aristocratic army officers. The most famous graduate is Napoleon, but a less illustrious, better-loved French soldier, Cambronne, has his name remembered in a neighbouring street and square. He commanded the last surviving unit of Napoleon's Imperial Guard at Waterloo. Surrounded and reduced to a bare handful of men, Cambronne was called on to surrender by the English. He shouted back into the darkness one word – *"Merde"* – the most common French swear word, known euphemistically ever since as *le mot de Cambronne*.

The surrounding quartier may be expensive and sought after as an address, but physically it's uninspiring – a case in point is the exterior of the **UNESCO building** at the back of the École Militaire. Controversial at the time of its construction in 1958, these days it looks somewhat pedestrian, and badly weathered. It can be visited (Mon–Fri 9.30am–noon & 2.30–5pm; free), and there are a number of artworks inside, of which the most noticeable is an enor-mous mobile by Alexander Calder. The finest feature is a quiet Japanese garden, to which you can repair on a summer's day to read a paper bought from the well-stocked kiosk in the foyer.

# Musée du Quai Branly

A short distance upstream of the Eiffel Tower, on quai Branly, work continues on the new **Musée du Quai Branly** (or possibly the Musée des Arts Premiers; ⓦ www.quaibranly.fr), which will bring together the Musée des Arts d'Afrique et d'Océanie and the ethnography department from the Musée de l'Homme, along with space for temporary exhibitions, plays and contemporary non-European dance. One of Jacques Chirac's pet projects (the president has a passion for non-European art), the need for such a museum has been the sub-ject of much controversy and debate, with ethnographers, on one side, reluc-tant to witness the separation of existing collections, notably that of the Musée de l'Homme (see p.135), and art-lovers, on the other, decrying the whole quasi-colonial enterprise of ethnography. Architect Jean Nouvel's design is for a curving, futuristic edifice on stilts with a garden behind a giant glass curtain – rather like his Fondation Cartier in the 14ᵉ (see p.153). The museum is unlikely to be completed before the end of 2005 at the earliest; in the mean-time a small selection is being showcased in the Louvre's Pavillon des Sessions (see p.66).

# The sewers

A little way east of the quai Branly site, on the northeast side of the busy junc-tion of place de la Résistance, is the entrance to the **sewers** (les égouts; May–Sept Mon–Wed, Sat & Sun 11am–5pm; rest of year Mon–Wed, Sat & Sun 11am–4pm; €4). It's dark, damp and noisy with gushing water, but sur-prisingly not all that smelly, though there's little doubt that you're in a sewer given the cadaverous pallor of the superannuated sewermen who wait on you. The main part of the visit runs along a gantry walk poised alarmingly above a main sewer, where bilingual displays of photographs, engravings, dredging tools, lamps and other flotsam and jetsam turn the history of the city's water supply and waste management into a surprisingly fascinating topic. Interested parties may find Victor Hugo's description in *Les Misérables* even more satisfying: twenty pages on the value of human excrement as manure (25 million francs' worth down the plughole in the 1860s), and the history of the sewer system, including the sewage flood of 1802 and the first perilous survey of the system in 1805, whose findings included a piece of Marat's winding sheet and the skeleton of an orang-utan.

The visit is more than half a publicity exercise by the sewage board, showing the natural water cycle becoming disrupted by the city's over-dense population, then slowly controlled by increasingly good management. What it doesn't tell you is that the work isn't quite finished. Almost all the effluent from the sewers goes to the Achèves treatment plant, northwest of Paris, but around thirty times a year parts of the system get overloaded with rainwater, and the sewer workers have to empty the excess – waste and all – straight into the Seine.

## Quai d'Orsay and rue Cler

A little further upstream still, the **American Church** on quai d'Orsay, together with the American College nearby at 31 av Bosquet, is a nodal point in the well-organized life of Paris's large American community; its noticeboard usually plastered with job and accommodation offers and demands.

Newspapers reporting on French foreign policy use "the quai d'Orsay" to refer to the Ministère des Affaires Étrangères (Ministry of Foreign Affairs), which sits next to the Esplanade des Invalides and the Palais Bourbon, home of the **Assemblée Nationale**. Napoleon, never a great one for democracy, had the riverfront facade of the Palais Bourbon done to match the pseudo-Greek of the Madeleine. The result is an entrance that sheds little light on what's happening within.

Just to the southwest, and in stark contrast to the austerity of much of the rest of the quartier, is the attractive, villagey wedge of early nineteenth-century streets between avenue Bosquet and the Invalides. Chief among them is the lively market street **rue Cler**, whose cross-streets, rue de Grenelle and rue St-Dominique, are full of neighbourhood shops, posh *bistrots* and little hotels.

## Les Invalides and the Église du Dôme

The **Esplanade des Invalides**, striking due south from **Pont Alexandre III**, is a more attractive and uncluttered vista than the one from the Palais de

---

**Notable buildings in the Septième**

**29 avenue Rapp** (RER Pont de l'Alma). Art Nouveau to the extreme with bulls' heads, turbaned women and unusual colour changes. Designed by Lavirotte, 1901.

**Square Rapp**, off avenue Rapp (RER Pont de l'Alma). A bizarre ensemble: more Lavirotte at no. 43, a trellis trompe l'oeil and the Société Théosophique de France.

**12 rue Sédillot** (RER Pont de l'Alma). Art Nouveau and Art Deco elements in superb dormers and wrought-iron grills and balconies, again by Lavirotte, 1899.

**Conservatoire de Musique**, 7 rue Jean-Nicot (M° Invalides). Christian Portzamparc playing with a half-peeled tube of a tower.

Chaillot to the École Militaire. Looming at the Esplanade's southern end, with its resplendently gilded dome and heavy facade, is the **Hôtel des Invalides**, built as a home for invalided soldiers on the orders of Louis XIV. Under the dome are two churches, one for the soldiers, the other intended as a mausoleum for the king but now containing the mortal remains of Napoleon.

Les Invalides today houses the vast **Musée de l'Armée** (daily: April–Sept 10am–6pm; Oct–March 10am–5pm; €6 ticket also valid for Napoleon's tomb, see below; Ⓦ www.invalides.org), the national war museum, whose most interesting wing, reached via the south entrance beside the Église du Dôme, is devoted to Général de Gaulle and World War II. The battles, the resistance and the slow liberation are documented through imaginatively displayed war memorabilia combined with gripping reels of contemporary footage, many of which have an English-language option. You leave shocked, stirred, and with the distinct impression that de Gaulle was personally responsible for the liberation of France.

By comparison, the vast collection of armour, uniforms and weapons that makes up the main part of the museum, on either side of the front court, is probably best left to tin-soldier fanatics or military history buffs. The **east wing** is given over to a stuffy history of the French armed forces from Louis XIV to Napoleon III, including a large section devoted to Napoleon's armies with some of Napoleon's personal effects including his horse, campaign tent and trademark hat and coat. The theme over in the **west wing** is much the same, if rather shinier, the old arsenal having been filled with medieval and Renaissance weaponry and armour, most of it laid out as if ready for use. Highlights include the extraordinary mail made for François I, a big man for his time, and a dimly lit chamber of beautifully worked Oriental weaponry. Upstairs, the 1914–18 gallery manages to reduce the epic tragedy of that conflict to some quibbles over helmet design.

Up under the roof of the east wing, the super-scale models of French ports and fortified cities in the **Musée des Plans–Reliefs** (same hours and ticket as Musée de l'Armée above) are crying out for a few miniature armies. Essentially giant three-dimensional maps, they were created to plan defences or plot potential artillery positions. The collection was begun in 1668 by Louvois, Louis XIV's war minister, and was classed a historic monument in 1927 – their usefulness superseded by technical advances. With the eerie green glow of their landscapes only just illuminating the long, tunnel-like attic, the effect is rather chilling.

## Église du Dôme

Both of the Invalides churches are cold and dreary inside. The **Soldier's Church** is reached from the main courtyard, while the **Église du Dôme** (both churches same hours and ticket as Musée de l'Armée above) has a separate entrance on the south side of the complex. The latter is a supreme example of architectural pomposity, with Corinthian columns and pilasters, and grandiose frescoes in abundance. Napoleon lies in a hole in the floor in a sarcophagus of red porphyry, enclosed within a gallery decorated with friezes of execrable taste and grovelling piety, captioned with quotations of awesome conceit from the great man such as "By its simplicity my code of law has done more good in France than all the laws which have preceded me"; and "Wherever the shadow of my rule has fallen, it has left lasting traces of its value". Napoleon's shadow still fell heavily on Paris on 14th December 1840, the day on which his ashes, freshly returned from St. Helena, were carried through the streets from the newly completed Arc de Triomphe to the

## Bonaparte's bones

In 2002 a French historian asked for Napoleon's ashes to be exhumed for DNA testing, claiming that the remains had been swapped for those of his maître d'hôtel on St.Helena, one Jean-Baptiste Cipriani. Apparently, a witness at the original 1821 burial observed that the great man's teeth were "most villainous", whereas at the exhumation it was reported that they were "exceptionally white". There is some reason for suspicion, as the last round of tests – on a lock of the emperor's hair – suggested he had died of arsenic poisoning, not cancer, as the British claimed. The mystery remains unresolved, as the French defence ministry refused to give up the ashes for testing.

Invalides. Even though Louis-Philippe, a Bourbon, was on the throne, and the emperor's nephew, Louis-Napoléon, had been imprisoned for attempting a coup four months earlier, the Bonapartists came out in force – half a million of them – to watch the Emperor's last journey. Victor Hugo commented that "it felt as if the whole of Paris had been poured to one side of the city, like liquid in a vase which has been tilted".

Far more affecting than Napoleon's tomb is the simple memorial to **Maréchal Foch**, commander-in-chief of the allied forces at the end of World War I, which stands in the side chapel by the stairs leading down to the crypt. The marshal's effigy is borne by a phalanx of bronze infantrymen displaying a soldierly grief, the whole chamber flooded by blue light from the stained-glass windows.

## The Musée Rodin and Musée Maillol

Immediately east of Les Invalides is the **Musée Rodin**, on the corner of rue de Varenne, at no. 77 (daily except Mon: April–Sept 9.30am–5.45pm, garden closes at 6.45pm; Oct–March 9.30am–4.45pm, garden closes at 5pm; €5, garden only €1; Mᵒ Varenne). The museum's setting is superbly elegant, a beautiful eighteenth-century mansion which the sculptor leased from the state in return for the gift of all his work upon his death. Bronze versions of major projects like *The Burghers of Calais, The Thinker, The Gate of Hell* and *Ugolino and His Sons* are exhibited in the garden – the latter forming the centrepiece of the ornamental pond.

Things get even better inside – the vigorous energy of the sculptures contrasting with the worn wooden panelling of the *boiseries* and the tarnished mirrors and chandeliers. It's usually very crowded with visitors eager to see much-loved works like *The Hand of God* and *The Kiss* – originally designed to portray Paolo and Francesca da Rimini, from Dante's *Divine Comedy* – but it's well worth lingering by the vibrant, impressionistic clay works, small studies that Rodin took from life. In fact, most of the works here are in clay or plaster, as these are considered to be Rodin's finest achievements – after completing his apprenticeship, he rarely picked up a chisel, in line with the common nineteenth century practice of delegating the task of working up stone and bronze versions to assistants. Instead, he would return to his plaster casts again and again, modifying and refining them and sometimes leaving them deliberately "unfinished". On the ground floor, there's a room devoted to Camille Claudel, Rodin's pupil, model and lover. Among her works is *The Age of Maturity*, symbolising her ultimate rejection by Rodin, and a bust of the artist himself. Claudel's perception of her teacher was so akin to Rodin's own that he considered it as his self-portrait.

The rest of rue de Varenne and the parallel rue de Grenelle is full of aristocratic mansions, including the **Hôtel Matignon**, the prime minister's residence. At 61 rue de Grenelle, a handsome eighteenth-century house has been
turned into the **Musée Maillol** (daily except Tues 11am–6pm; €7; M° Rue-
du-Bac), overstuffed with sculptor Aristide Maillol's endlessly buxom female
nudes, copies of which stand in the Louvre's Jardin du Carrousel. His most
famous work, the seated *Mediterranean* with its simple, smooth curves, can be
found on the first floor at the top of the stairs. The exhibits belong to Dina
Vierny, Maillol's former model and inspiration, and works by other contemporaries are also collected here, including drawings by Matisse, Dufy and
Bonnard, for whom Dina also modelled; humorously erotic paintings by
Bombois; and the odd Picasso, Degas, Gauguin and Kandinsky. The museum
also organizes excellent exhibitions of twentieth-century art among which
have been Frida Kahlo and Diego Rivera.

From the Musée Maillol, rue du Bac leads south into rue de Sèvres, cutting
across **rue de Babylone**, another of the Septième's livelier streets, which
begins with the city's oldest department store, **Au Bon Marché**, renowned for
its food halls (see p.338), and ends with the crazy, rich man's folly **La Pagode**,
at no. 57bis. The building was brought over from Japan at the turn of the century and for a long time was used as an arts cinema; it has recently been renovated, with a café in the Japanese garden inside.

# The Musée d'Orsay

Facing the Tuileries across the river, on the eastern side of the Septième, the
elegant but formal stone facade of the **Musée d'Orsay** barely hints at the all-
pervasive light that illuminates its cathedral-like interior (daily except Mon
9am–6pm, Thurs till 9.15pm; mid-Sept to mid-June opens at 10am; €8.50,
€6.50 after 4.15pm & Thurs after 8pm, free to under-18s and on first Sun of
the month; M° Solférino/RER Musée-d'Orsay; ⓦ www.musee-orsay.fr).
Housing painting and sculpture from the period 1848 to 1914, and thus bridging the gap between the Louvre and Beaubourg, its highlights are the electri-
fying works of the **Impressionists** and **Post-Impressionists**. (The entrance
is on the west side, on rue de la Légion de l'Honneur.)

The building was inaugurated as a **railway station** for the 1900 World Fair
and continued to serve the stations of southwest France until 1939. Orson
Welles used it as the setting for his film of Kafka's *The Trial*, filling the high,
narrow corridors with filing cabinets to create a nightmarishly claustrophobic
setting. De Gaulle used it to announce his coup d'état of May 19, 1958 – his
messianic return to power to save the *patrie* from disintegration over the
Algerian liberation war. Notwithstanding this illustrious history, it was only
saved from a hotel developer's bulldozer by the colossal wave of public indig-
nation and remorse at the destruction of Les Halles.

The job of redesigning the interior as a museum was given, in 1986, to the
Milanese Gae Aulenti, the fashionable architect who had transformed Venice's
flashy Palazzo Grassi two years earlier. Her design is as considered as it is beautiful, though the crowds of visitors streaming from one room to the next can
provoke the uncomfortable feeling that you're late for a train. Taken at an easy
pace, you could easily spend half a day, if not a whole one, meandering
through the rooms in their numbered, chronological order, but the **layout**
makes it easy to confine your visit to a specific section, each of which has a
very distinctive atmosphere. The collection begins on the ground floor, under
the huge vault of steel and glass, then continues up to the attics of the upper

level, before ending with the terraces of the middle level, overlooking the main chamber.

The **café** on the upper level of the museum, and the gilded restaurant and tearoom on the middle level, are wonderful spots to recuperate.

## Ground floor

The **ground floor**, under the great glass arch, is devoted to pre-1870 work, with a double row of sculptures running down the central aisle like railway tracks, and paintings in the odd little bunkers on either side. Chief among the **mid-nineteenth-century sculptors** in the central aisle is Carpeaux, whose *Ugolin* shows the damned Count Ugolino, from Dante's *Divine Comedy*, gnawing at his fingers with pain and hunger as he contemplates consuming the bodies of his dying children. The original plaster of the *Four Quarters of the World Bearing the Celestial Sphere*, the bronze version of which stands at the foot of the Jardin du Luxembourg, is also his. Nearby, Charles Cordier's polychrome busts of black Africans, in bronze and coloured stone, seem strangely explicit to modern eyes.

On the south side of this level, towards rue de Lille, the first set of rooms (1–3) is dedicated to **Ingres**, **Delacroix** – the bulk of whose work is in the Louvre – and the serious-minded works of the painters acceptable to the mid-nineteenth century salons; just beyond (rooms 11–13) are the relatively wacky works of Puvis de Chavannes, Gustave Moreau and the younger Degas.

The influential **Barbizon school** and the **Realists** are showcased on the Seine side (rooms 4–7), with canvases by Daumier, Corot, Millet and Courbet which depart from the accepted norms of moralism and idealization of the past. The soft-toned landscapes by Millet and Corot, and quickly executed scenes by Daubigny, such as his *La Neige*, were influential on later, avowed Impressionists. In room 7, Courbet's *L'Origine du Monde* has the power to shock even contemporary audiences. The explicit, nude female torso was acquired from psychoanalyst Jacques Lacan, who had had it screened behind a decorative panel. Just a few steps away, room 14 explodes with the early controversies of **Monet**'s violently light-filled *Femmes au Jardin* (1867) and **Manet**'s provocative *Olympia* (1863), which heralded the arrival of Impressionism. The latter was as controversial in its day for its colour contrasts and sensual surfaces as for the portrayal of Olympia as a high-class whore who returns the stares of her audience with a look of insolent defiance.

## Upper level: Impressionism and Post-Impressionism

To continue chronologically, proceed straight to the **upper level**, whose rooms have a more intimate feel, done up almost like a suite of attic studios. You'll first pass through the private collection donated by assiduous collector and art historian Moreau-Nélaton (room 29), featuring some of the most famous **Impressionist** images like Monet's *Poppies* and Manet's *Déjeuner sur l'Herbe*, which sent the critics into apoplexies of rage and disgust when it appeared in 1863, and was refused for that year's Salon.

From this point on, you'll have to fight off the persistent sense of familiarity or recognition – Degas' *L'Absinthe*, Renoir's *Bal du Moulin de la Galette*, Monet's *Femme a l'Ombrelle* – in order to appreciate Impressionism's vibrant, experimental vigour. There's a host of small-scale landscapes and outdoor scenes by Renoir, Sisley, Pissarro and Monet in rooms 30–32, paintings which owed much of their brilliance to the novel practice of setting up easels in the open – often as not on the banks of the Seine. Less typical works include

Degas' ballet-dancers, which demonstrate his principal interest in movement and line as opposed to the more common Impressionist concern with light, and *Le Berceau* (1872), by Berthe Morisot, the first woman to join the early Impressionists. More heavyweight masterpieces can be found in rooms 34 and 39, devoted to **Monet** and **Renoir** in their middle and late periods. The development of Monet's obsessions is shown with five of his Rouen cathedral series, each painted in different light conditions. Room 35 is full of the fervid colours and disturbing rhythms of **Van Gogh**, while **Cézanne**, another step removed from the preoccupations of the mainstream Impressionists, is wonderfully represented in room 36. One of the canvases most revealing of his art is *Pommes et Oranges* (1895–1900), with its multiple viewpoints.

Passing the **café** – with its summer terrace and wonderful view of Montmartre through the giant railway clock – and the little rooms (37 and 38) housing **Degas'** atmospheric pastels, you arrive at a dimly lit, melancholy chamber (40) devoted to more **pastels**, by Redon, Manet, Mondrian and others. The next and final suite of rooms on this level is given over to the various offspring of Impressionism, and has an edgier, more modern feel, with a much greater emphasis on psychology. It begins with Rousseau's dreamlike *La Charmeuse de Serpent* (1907) and continues past **Gauguin'**s ambivalent Tahitian paintings to **Pointillist** works by Seurat (the famous *Cirque*), Signac and others, ending with **Toulouse-Lautrec** at his caricaturial nightclubbing best – one large canvas including a rear view of Oscar Wilde at his grossest.

## Middle level

Don't miss the covetable little Kaganovitch collection (rooms 49 & 50) on your way down to the middle level, where the flow of the painting section continues with **Vuillard** and **Bonnard** (rooms 71 & 72), tucked away behind Pompon's irresistible sculpture of a polar bear, on the rue de Lille side of the railway chamber. Vuillard and Bonnard began their careers as part of an Art Nouveau group known as the **Nabis**, and strong Japanese influences can be seen in Vuillard's decorative screen, *Jardins Publics* (1894) and Bonnard's *La Partie de Croquet* (1892). The Impressionist interest in light is still evident, but it seems subservient to a highly distinctive palette, with colours that are at once muted and intense.

On the far side of this level, overlooking the Seine (rooms 55–58), you can see a less familiar side of late-nineteenth-century painting, with large-scale, epic, naturalist works such as Detaille's stirring *Le Rêve* (1888) and Cormon's *Caïn* (1880), as well as the famously effete *Portrait of Marcel Proust* by Jacques-Emile Blanche. The painting collection ends with a troubling handful of international **Symbolist** paintings: room 60, overlooking the Seine, is dominated by the almost formless wash of leaves and petals that constitutes Klimt's *Rosiers sous les Arbres*, along with some of Munch's lesser-known works.

On the parallel sculpture terraces, nineteenth-century marbles on the Seine side face early twentieth-century pieces across the divide, but the **Rodin terrace** bridging the two puts almost everything else to shame. Rodin's *Ugolin* is even grimmer than Carpeaux's, immediately below, while his *Fugit Amor*, a response to his pupil and lover Camille Claudel's *L'Age Mûr*, adjacent, is a powerful image of the end of their liaison. It's a pity, but few visitors will have energy left for the half-dozen rooms of superb **Art Nouveau** furniture and *objets*.

# 8

# Montparnasse and southern Paris

The swathe of cafés, brasseries and cinemas that runs through the heart of modern **Montparnasse** has long been a honeypot for pleasure-seekers, a kind of border town dividing the lands of the well-heeled opinion-formers and power-brokers of St-Germain and the 7e from the amorphous populations of the three arrondissements of **southern Paris**, the **13e**, **14e** and **15e**. Overscale developments from the 1950s to the present day have scarred parts of this southern side of the city, but there are three great parks, **Georges–Brassens**, **Montsouris** and **André Citroën**, and some enticing pockets of Paris that have been allowed to evolve in a happily patchy way. Lively areas such as **Pernety** and **Plaisance** in the 14e, the **quartier du Commerce** in the 15e, and the **Butte-aux-Cailles** quartier in the 13e are pleasant places to explore, and well off the tourist track.

For **transport** through the outer 15e, 14e and 13e arrondissements, bus #62 plies a useful route along rues de la Convention, Alésia and Tolbiac.

## Montparnasse and the 14e

The story goes that students used to drink and declaim poetry from the top of a pile of spoil deposited from the Denfert-Rochereau quarries, on what is now place Pablo Picasso, calling the mound Mount Parnassus after the legendary home of the muses of poetry and song, and of drunken Bacchus. This may or may not be how the area got its name but the reputation of **Montparnasse** for carousing persists to this day, though its status as a nightspot really stems from the construction of the Mur des Fermiers Généraux in 1784, or "Customs Wall", which split the high-taxed city from the poorer, less regulated township areas beyond. Bohemians and left-leaning intellectuals gravitated from the staid city centre to Montparnasse's inexpensive cafés and nightspots; among them Verlaine and Baudelaire in the nineteenth century, Trotsky, Hemingway, Sartre and de Beauvoir in the twentieth. Montparnasse's lasting fame, however, rests on the patronage of artists, especially during the 1920s, following the exodus from Montmartre. Picasso, Matisse, Kandinsky, Man Ray, Modigliani, Giacometti and Chagall were all habitués of the celebrated cafés around Place Vavin, and many were buried in

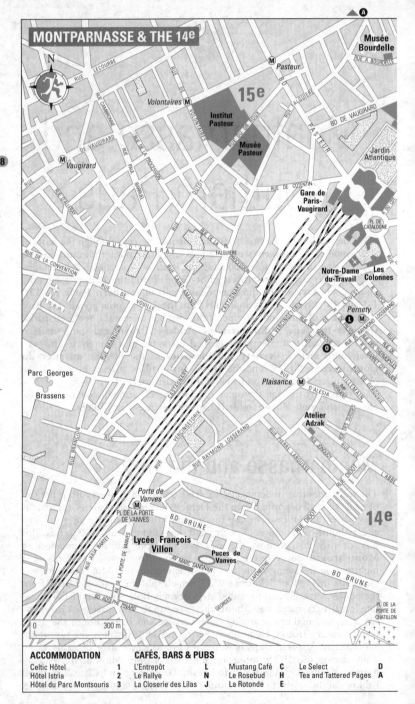

# MONTPARNASSE & THE 14e

N

15e

Musée
Bourdelle

RUE A. BOURDELLE

Ⓜ Pasteur

Volontaires Ⓜ

Institut
Pasteur

Jardin
Atlantique

Ⓜ Vaugirard

Musée
Pasteur

RUE DE COTENTIN

Gare de
Paris-
Vaugirard

PL DE
CATALOGNE

PL
FALGUIÈRE

Notre-Dame
du-Travail

Les
Colonnes

Pernety
Ⓛ Ⓜ

Parc Georges

Brassens

Plaisance Ⓜ
D'ALESIA

Atelier
Adzak

Porte de
Vanves
Ⓜ
PL DE LA PORTE
DE VANVES

BD BRUNE

14e

Lycée François
Villon

Puces de
Vanves

AV MARC SANGNIER

BD BRUNE

PL DE LA
PORTE DE
CHATILLON

0                300 m

8

148

## ACCOMMODATION

Celtic Hôtel              1
Hôtel Istria              2
Hôtel du Parc Montsouris  3

## CAFÉS, BARS & PUBS

L'Entrepôt                L
Le Rallye                 N
La Closerie des Lilas     J

Mustang Café    C
Le Rosebud      H
La Rotonde      E

Le Select                 D
Tea and Tattered Pages    A

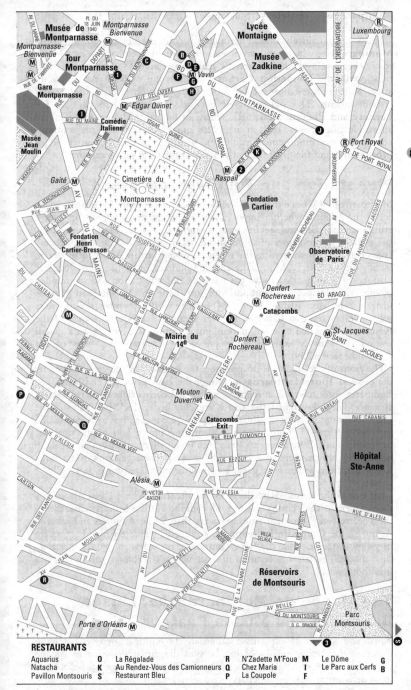

Musée de Montparnasse
PL DU 18 JUIN 1940
Montparnasse Bienvenue
Montparnasse-Bienvenüe
Tour Montparnasse
Gare Montparnasse
Musée Jean Moulin
Comédie Italienn
Gaité
Edgar Quinet
Cimetière du Montparnasse
Fondation Henri Cartier-Bresson
Lycée Montaigne
Musée Zadkine
Vavin
Raspail
Fondation Cartier
Luxembourg
Port Royal
Observatoire de Paris
Denfert Rochereau
BD ARAGO
Catacombs
Denfert Rochereau
St-Jacques
Mairie du 14e
Mouton Duvernet
Catacombs Exit
Alésia
PL VICTOR BASCH
Hôpital Ste-Anne
Réservoirs de Montsouris
Porte d'Orléans
Parc Montsouris

## RESTAURANTS

| | | | | | |
|---|---|---|---|---|---|
| Aquarius | O | La Régalade | R | N'Zadette M'Foua | M |
| Natacha | K | Au Rendez-Vous des Camionneurs | Q | Chez Maria | I |
| Pavillon Montsouris | S | Restaurant Bleu | P | La Coupole | F |

| | |
|---|---|
| Le Dôme | G |
| Le Parc aux Cerfs | B |

**Montparnasse cemetery**. Still more bones lie nearby in the grim **catacombs**.

The area immediately around the station is dominated by the gigantic **Tour Montparnasse**, which you can ascend for a superb view of the city. In the tower's shadow, a handful of **artist's museums** recall Montparnasse's traditions, while the **Fondation Cartier** showcases the work of contemporary artists. South of the station, the **14ᵉ** is one of the most characterful of the outer arrondissements. The old-fashioned networks of streets still exist in the **Pernety** and **Plaisance** quartiers, where many artists chose to live in the affordable *villas* (mews) built in the 1920s and 1930s. Down in the southeast corner of the arrondissement you'll find plenty of green space in the **Parc Montsouris** and the giant student campus of the **Cité Universitaire**.

## The station and Tour Montparnasse

Montparnasse was once the great arrival and departure point for boat travellers across the Atlantic, whether impoverished emigrants or passengers on luxury cruises, and for Bretons seeking work in the capital. The Breton influence is still evident in the names of some of the nearby restaurants, and the Atlantic connection is remembered in the recently created **Jardin Atlantique** (access by lifts on rue Cdt. R. Mouchotte and bd Vaugirard, or by the stairs alongside platform #1), suspended above the tracks behind the station and surrounded by high-rise blocks. Facing out onto the garden, the tiny **Musée Jean Moulin** (daily except Mon 10am–5.40pm; €4) may be worth stopping in at if you're waiting for a train to Chartres. It gives a rather dry potted history of the Resistance illustrated by a few photos, posters and newspapers, with a special section on Jean Moulin, wartime prefect of Chartres and hero of the Resistance (see p.239).

The front of the station is unappealing, the prospect of the city blocked by the colossal **Tour Montparnasse**, one of the city's principal and least-liked landmarks, most tolerable at night, when the red corner lights give it a certain elegance. The **view from the top** is arguably better than the one from the Eiffel Tower in that it has the Eiffel Tower in it, plus it costs less to ascend (daily: summer 9.30am–11.30pm; winter 9.30am–10.30pm; €7.60 to the open-air tower-top on the 59th floor, €6.40 to 56th floor gallery room; entrance on the north side). Alternatively, you could indulge in an expensive drink in the 56th-storey bar, from where you get a tremendous view westwards, especially at sunset.

Just east of the station, **Rue de la Gaité**, the street where Trotsky lived, is a slice of turn-of-the-century theatreland, with the Théâtre Montparnasse facing the Théâtre Gaité-Montparnasse, and a fair share of porn outlets and junkies. At no. 17, the **Comédie Italienne** has commedia dell'arte painted scenes on its yellow exterior, while the **Rive Gauche**, at no. 6, has an equally spectacular frontage. The street is featured in a mural that's visible as you look south from boulevard Edgar-Quinet.

## The Musée de Montparnasse, Musée Bourdelle and Musée Pasteur

North and west of Montparnasse station are three little-visited yet beguiling museums. At 21 avenue du Maine, beyond the raised slip-road of rue de l'Arrivée, a piece of Montparnasse's illustrious artistic heritage has been saved from demolition. A half-hidden, ivy-clad alley leads to what was once Marie

△ Montparnasse cemetery

Vassilieff's studio, now converted into the **Musée de Montparnasse** (Tues–Sun 10am–6pm; €4; M° Montparnasse-Bienvenüe & M° Falguière), hosting temporary exhibitions based on Montparnasse artists past and present. Vassilieff lived here between 1912 and 1929, during which time many leading contemporary artists (Picasso, Léger, Modigliani, Chagall, Braque, among others) visited to wine, dine and dance with her. Architect's offices now occupy many of the studios nearby, but there's also a private art gallery and a flower shop whose beautiful blooms spill out into the alley.

On rue Antoine-Bourdelle, opposite the Musée de Montparnasse, a garden of sculptures invites you into the **Musée Bourdelle** (Tues–Sun 10am–5.40pm; free). As Rodin's pupil and Giacometti's teacher, Bourdelle's work bridges the period between naturalism and a more geometrically conceived style. His monumental sculptures get pride of place in the chapel-like, modernist grand hall, but other, more intimate areas of the museum are as rewarding. The sculptor's atmospheric old **studio**, musty with the smells of its ageing parquet floor and greying plaster, is littered with half-complete works that face a chilly northern light. Elsewhere, there's a wonderful series of Beethoven busts and masks, sculpted between 1887 and 1929, and a basement extension in which you can see studies for the sculptor's greatest works, the *Monument à Mickiewicz* and the *Monument au Général Alvear*. On the far side of the garden, Bourdelle's living quarters have been preserved complete with shabby bed, stove and some sombre paintings from his private collection.

Just around the corner to the right, on rue Falguière, the bold facade of the Île-de-France urban-planning department veers up and away from the line of the street in the smoothest of curves, like the hull of a fantasy spaceship.

Between rue du Docteur-Roux and rue Falguière, the **Institut Pasteur** is renowned for its research into AIDS, a specialism that grew out of the work of its founder Louis Pasteur, who discovered vaccination. For the last few years of his life, after he had finally won the recognition and the laboratory he deserved, Pasteur lived and worked in the house at 25 rue du Docteur-Roux, now the **Musée Pasteur** (guided tours in French and English daily 2–5.30pm, closed Aug; €3; Ⓦwww.pasteur.fr; M° Pasteur). The tour takes you through the Pasteurs' private apartment, with its perfectly preserved nineteenth-century interior, and on through Pasteur's original laboratory, almost untouched, and finally to his Byzantine-style mausoleum.

## Boulevard du Montparnasse

Most of the life of the Montparnasse quartier is concentrated on **boulevard du Montparnasse**, from the station as far as Vavin métro. Like other Left Bank quartiers, Montparnasse still trades on its association with the wild characters of the interwar artistic and literary boom. Many were habitués of the cafés *Select*, *Coupole*, *Dôme*, *Rotonde* and *Closerie des Lilas*, all of which are still going strong on the boulevard – though the prices have gone up since Hemingway noted that "all had good beer and the aperitifs cost reasonable prices that were clearly marked on the saucers". Even by the 1930s, Montparnasse's heyday was passing as the fashionable intelligentsia moved on to St-Germain, but the brasseries remain proudly Parisian classics and this stretch of the boulevard still stays up late. The numerous **cinemas** here – six on the boulevard alone – are almost all of the multi-screen variety, specializing in mass-market French and US films.

The animated part of the boulevard ends at **boulevard Raspail**, where Rodin's **Balzac** broods over the traffic, though literary curiosity might take

**26 rue Vavin**, 6ᵉ. Mᵒ Vavin. A block of flats decked in white and blue tiles, with terraced balconies filled with exuberant gardens in the air. Built by Henri Sauvage in 1912.

**Rue Schoelcher and rue Froidevaux**, 14ᵉ. Mᵒ Raspail & Mᵒ Denfert-Rochereau. An excellent selection of nineteenth- and twentieth-century styles, of particular note being 5, 5bis and 11 rue Schoelcher, 11 and 23 rue Froidevaux, this last a 1930s block of artists' studios, with huge windows for northern light and fabulous ceramic mosaics.

**266 boulevard Raspail**, 14ᵉ. Mᵒ Raspail & Mᵒ Denfert-Rochereau. An interior design school with a marked Beaubourg influence: external stairs and blue pipe columns in front, plus the 1990s delight of glass and metal shuttering.

**31 rue Campagne-Première**, 14ᵉ. Mᵒ Raspail. A myriad of earthenware tiles cover the concrete structure of these desirable 1912 *appartements* with huge windows.

you down as far as the rather swanky brasserie **Closerie des Lilas**, on the corner of the tree-lined avenue connecting the Observatory and Luxembourg Gardens in a classic grand Parisian vista. Hemingway used to come here to write, and Marshal Ney, one of Napoleon's most glamorous generals, was killed by a royalist firing squad on the pavement outside in 1815. He's still there, waving his sword, immortalized in stone.

# The Musée Zadkine and Fondation Cartier

Just north of the boulevard du Montparnasse, and within a few minutes' walk of the Jardin du Luxembourg (see p.132), is the tiny **Musée Zadkine**, at 100 bis rue d'Assas (Tues–Sun 10am–6pm; €4; Mᵒ Vavin & RER Port-Royal). The museum occupies the Russian-born sculptor **Ossip Zadkine**'s studio-house, where he lived and worked from 1928 – after a spell at La Ruche (see p.160) – until his death in 1967. In the garden, enclosed by ivy-covered studios and dwarfed by tall buildings, his angular Cubist bronzes seem to struggle for light – one of the most compelling, *Orphée*, is half buried among the bushes. Inside, is a collection of his gentler wooden torsos, along with smaller-scale bronze and stone works, notably *Femme à l'Éventail*. Studies for the renowned *La Ville Détruite*, whose twisted, agonised torso was intended to express the horror of aerial bombing, can be seen inside and in the garden.

Taking a shortcut down rue Campagne-Première leads through to boulevard Raspail and the **Fondation Cartier pour l'Art Contemporain**, at no. 261 (Tues–Sun noon–8pm; €5; Mᵒ Raspail); it's no more than ten minutes' walk. The foundation is housed in a stunning glass and steel construction designed in 1994 by Jean Nouvel, architect of the Institut du Monde Arabe (see p.119). A glass wall follows the line of the street like a false start to the building proper, leaving space for the Tree of Liberty planted by Chateaubriand during the Revolution to grow in the garden behind. All kinds of contemporary art – installations, videos, multi-media – often by foreign artists little known in France, are shown in temporary exhibitions that use the light and very generous spaces to maximum advantage.

# Montparnasse cemetery and the catacombs

To the east of the station, the daily food **market** on boulevard Edgar-Quinet provides the cafés in the surrounding streets with their down-to-earth clientele, in marked contrast to the renowned establishments a stone's throw away on boulevard du Montparnasse. On Sundays (10am–dusk), over a hundred craftworkers take over the market; photographers jostle with potters, clothes designers with painters, and it's a great place to browse away the day.

Just to the south is the main entrance to **Montparnasse cemetery** (mid-March to Oct Mon–Fri 8am–6pm, Sat 8.30am–6pm, Sun 9am–6pm; Nov–mid-March closes 5.30pm; M° Raspail/Gaîté/Edgar Quinet), a gloomy city of the dead with ranks of miniature temples, dreary and bizarre, and plenty of illustrious names, from Baudelaire to Beckett, Gainsbourg to Saint-Saëns – you can pick up a leaflet and map from the guardhouse by each entrance. The joint grave of Jean-Paul Sartre and Simone de Beauvoir lies immediately right of the entrance on boulevard Edgar-Quinet. Sartre lived out the last few decades of his life just a few metres away on boulevard Raspail. Down avenue de l'Ouest, which follows the western wall of the cemetery, you'll find the tombs of Baudelaire (who has a more impressive cenotaph by rue Émile-Richard, on avenue Transversale); the sculptor Zadkine (see p.153); and the Fascist Pierre Laval, a member of Pétain's government, who, after the war, was executed for treason, not long after an unsuccessful suicide attempt. As an antidote, you can pay homage to Proudhon, the anarchist who coined the phrase "Property is theft!"; he lies in Division 1, by the Carrefour du Rond-Point. In the southwest corner of the cemetery is an old windmill, one of the seventeenth-century taverns frequented by the carousing, versifying students who are supposed to have given the Montparnasse district its name. Right in the northern corner is a tomb with a sculpture by Brancusi – *The Kiss* – which makes a far sadder statement than the dramatic and passionate scenes of grief adorning so many of the graves here. And, for seekers of the bizarre, by the wall along avenue du Boulevard (parallel to boulevard Raspail) you can see the inventor of a safe gas lamp, Charles Pigeon, in bed next to his sleeping wife, reading a book by the light of his invention.

If you want to spend more time among the dead, you can also descend into the **catacombs** (Tues 11am–4pm, Wed–Sun 9am–4pm; €5; M° Denfert-Rochereau) in nearby **place Denfert-Rochereau**, formerly place d'Enfer, or "Hell Square". Originally quarries, they were stacked with millions of bones cleared from the old charnel houses and cemeteries between 1785 and 1871, a municipal solution to the lack of space in the city's graveyards. It's estimated that the remains of six million Parisians are interred here – more than double the population of the modern city not counting the suburbs. Lining the passageway, the long thigh bones are stacked end-on, forming a wall to keep in the smaller bones, which can just be seen heaped higgledy-piggledy behind. These high femoral walls are further inset with skulls and plaques carrying macabre quotations such as "happy is he who always has the hour of his death in front of his eyes, and readies himself every day to die". Older children often love the whole experience, though there are a good couple of kilometres to walk, and it can quickly become claustrophobic in the extreme, not to mention cold and gungy underfoot. Spare a thought for the uniformed guardians, placed here to obstruct trophy-hunters and to prevent local youths of a Gothic bent slyly losing themselves and regrouping for midnight parties.

As well as interesting architecture around the cemetery (see box on p.153), there are quiet little streets to the south, between avenue du Maine and place Denfert-Rochereau, plus clothes and craft shops and a busy food market on rue Daguerre. Before and during the war, Sartre and Simone de Beauvoir kept separate rooms in the hotel at no. 24 rue Cels; a plaque gives a quote from each on the subject of their togetherness.

## Observatoire de Paris

About 500m to the northeast of the catacombs, on avenue de l'Observatoire, the classical **Observatoire de Paris** sat on France's zero meridian line from the 1660s, when it was constructed, until 1884. After that date, they reluctantly agreed that 0° longitude should pass through a small village in Normandy that happened to be due south of Greenwich. Visiting the Observatoire is a complicated procedure and all you'll see are old maps and instruments, but the original line is visible in the garden behind on boulevard Arago, marked by a medallion set in the pavement. In 1986, 200th anniversary of the astronomer François Arago's birth, 135 of these medallions were set along the Arago line in Paris. Many have since been uprooted but a few can still be spotted in various locations. On the other side of the boulevard de Port-Royal, the green avenue de l'Observatoire stretches north into the Jardin du Luxembourg (see p.132).

## Pernety, Plaisance and the Puces de Vanves

Just south of Montparnasse station, the gargantuan Ricardo Bofill housing development around **place de Catalogne** gives way to a walkway along the old rue Vercingétorix and to the changing but still cosy atmosphere, long lived in by artists, of **Pernety**. It's an appropriate location for the brand-new steel-and-glass **Fondation Cartier-Bresson**, Impasse Lebouis (Tues, Thurs & Fri 1–6.30pm, Wed 1–9pm, Sat 11am–6.45pm; €2; ⓦwww.henricartierbresson .org; M° Gaîté), which exhibits photos, negatives, drawings and even films by the grand old photographer of Paris, as well as showcasing the work of younger photographers through temporary exhibitions. Over on rue Vercingétorix, the **church of Notre-Dame du Travail** was built at the end of the nineteenth century to cater for a congregation swollen by the men employed in building the Eiffel Tower and the surrounding exhibition palaces for the Exposition Universelle. The stone came from the Cloth Pavilion and the slender metal columns of the interior from the Palace of Industry.

A short step to the south, wandering around Cité Bauer, rue des Thermopyles and rue Didot reveals adorable houses, secluded courtyards and quiet mews, and on the corner of rue du Moulin Vert and rue Hippolyte-Maindron you'll find Giacometti's old ramshackle studio and home. Cinema has one of its best Parisian venues at **L'Entrepôt**, 7–9 rue Francis-de-Pressensé, with spaces for talks, meals and drinks, and even a garden where they sometimes light incense in the trees on summer nights (see p.321). South again, **rue d'Alésia**, the main east–west route through the 14ᵉ, has a small **food market** every Thursday and Sunday between the Plaisance métro and rue Didot, but is best known for its **clothes shops** (see p.335), many selling discounted couturier creations. These congregate towards place Victor & Hélène Basch, where there's another delightful example of an old-style mews, the **Villa d'Alésia**.

Just south of rue d'Alésia, at 3 rue Jonquoy, the **Atelier Adzak** (usually open Sat & Sun 3–7pm during exhibitions; ring in advance for information or to visit at other times ☎01.45.43.06.98; free; M° Plaisance) is a showcase for the work of British sculptor Roy Adzak, as well as a living and working space for artists from around the world. Adzak, who is best known for his comment "good art is not what it looks like, but what it does to us", built the studio with his own hands in the 1980s, along with the permanent sculpture garden, and there are frequent temporary exhibitions of painting, drawing and sculpture by associated artists.

At the weekend it's worth heading out to the southern edge of the arrondissement for one of the city's best **flea markets**, known as the **Puces de Vanves**. Starting at daybreak (see p.345), it spreads along the pavements of avenues Marc-Sangnier and Georges-Lafenestre, petering out at its western end in place de la Porte-de-Vanves, where the city fortifications used to run until the 1920s.

## Parc Montsouris and the Cité Universitaire

In the southeastern corner of the arrondissement, there are still more artistic associations: Dalí, Lurcat, Miller and Durrell lived in the tiny cobbled street of **Villa Seurat** off rue de la Tombe-Issoire; Lenin and his wife, Krupskaya, lodged across the street at 4 rue Marie-Rose; Le Corbusier built the studio at 53 av Reille, close to the secretive and verdant square du Montsouris which links with rue Nansouty; and Georges Braque's home was in the cul-de-sac now named after him off this street. All these characters would have taken strolls in the nearby **Parc Montsouris** (RER Cité-Universitaire). It's a pleasant place to wander, with its unlikely contours, winding paths and waterfall above the lake – even the RER tracks cutting right through it fail to dent its charm. More surprising features include a meteorological office, a marker of the old meridian line, near boulevard Jourdan, and, by the southwest entrance, a kiosk run by the French Astronomy Association.

On the other side of boulevard Jourdan, several thousand students from more than one hundred different countries live in the curious array of buildings of the **Cité Universitaire**. The central Maison Internationale resembles a traditional French château, while the diverse styles of the others reflect the variety of nations and peoples who study here: Cambodia is guarded by startling stone creatures, while the red brick of the Collège Franco-Britannique all too accurately recalls Britain's institutional buildings. Switzerland (designed by Le Corbusier) and the USA are the most popular for their relatively luxurious rooms. The Cité puts on films, shows and other events (check the notice boards in the Maison Internationale or online at ⓦwww.ciup.fr), and you can eat cheaply in the cafeterias if you have a student card.

# The 15ᵉ

Though it's the largest and most populous of them all, the **15ᵉ arrondissement** falls off the agenda for most visitors as it lacks even a single important building or monument. In the southern corners, however, are two modern and attractive **parks** that are especially good for kids: the **Parc André-Citroën**, built over the old Citroën works, and the **Parc Georges-Brassens**, on the site of a former abattoir. Elsewhere in the 15ᵉ there are some pleasant areas to wander around, many with offbeat associations, such as the island **Allée des Cygnes**, and the artist colony known as **La Ruche**.

# The riverbank

The western edge of the 15$^e$ arrondissement fronts the Seine from the Eiffel Tower to beyond Pont du Garigliano, bristling with office blocks and miniature skyscrapers. The most recent addition to the river-front skyline is the glass **Maison de la Culture du Japon à Paris**, at 101 quai Branly (Tues–Sat noon–7pm; Thurs till 8pm; Ⓦ www.mcjp.asso.fr; M° Bir-Hakeim), a symbol of prosperous Franco–Japanese relations which contains a cinema, library, exhibition-space and opportunity to take part in a Japanese tea ceremony (Wed 3pm & 4pm; book two weeks in advance on ☎01.44.37.95.00; €7). Just off Pont de Bir-Hakeim, at the beginning of boulevard de Grenelle, in a rather undignified enclosure sandwiched by high-rise buildings, a plaque commemorates the notorious **rafle du Vel d'Hiv**, the Nazi and French-aided round-up of 13,152 Parisian Jews in July 1942. Nine thousand of them, including four thousand children, were interned here at the now-vanished cycle track for a week before being carted off to Auschwitz. Only thirty adults survived.

The quaysides are pretty inaccessible, but one place to walk is the **Allée des Cygnes**, a narrow island in midstream joining the Pont de Grenelle and the double-decker road and rail bridge, Pont de Bir-Hakeim. It's a strange place – one of Samuel Beckett's favourites – with just birds, trees and a path to walk along, and, at the downstream end, a scaled-down version of the **Statue of Liberty**. This was one of the four preliminary models constructed between 1874 and 1884 by sculptor Auguste Bartholdi, with the help of Gustave Eiffel, before the finished article (originally intended for Alexandria in Egypt) was presented to New York. Contemporary photos show the final version, assembled in Bartholdi's rue de Chazelles workshop, towering over the houses of the 17$^e$ like a bizarre female King Kong.

# Parc André-Citroën

The **Parc André-Citroën** (mid-May to Aug Mon–Fri 7.30am–10pm, Sat & Sun 9am–10pm; Sept to mid-May Mon–Fri 7.30am–7pm, Sat & Sun 9am–7pm; M° Javel & M° Balard), on the banks of the Seine, between Pont du Garigliano and Pont Mirabeau, is not a park for traditionalists. The central grassy area is a straightforward enough place to lounge or kick a football, but around it you'll find concrete terraces and walled gardens with abstract themes: the sound garden has bubbling water on one side and a gushing cascade on the other, while the blue, pink and black gardens each present a colourful display with every season. You can visit the hothouses with mimosa, fish-tailed palms and other sweet-smelling shrubbery, but on warm days the most tempting feature is the large platform sprouting a capricious set of automated fountain jets, luring children and occasionally adults to dodge the sudden spurts of water. Best of all, perhaps, is the **tethered balloon**, which rises and sinks regularly on calm days, taking small groups up for great views of the city (daily 9am–5pm; call to check weather conditions on the day ☎01.44.26.20.00; €10, under-12s €5).

Across rue Balard, which runs down the eastern side of the park, is the totally new **quartier du Citroën-Cévennes**, with pedestrianized streets, sports centres, youth clubs and the **Bibliothèque St-Charles**, a children's library on rue de la Montagne-d'Aulas. The peculiar black building, with slanting metallic bands, was built in 1990 and designed by Franck Hammoutene.

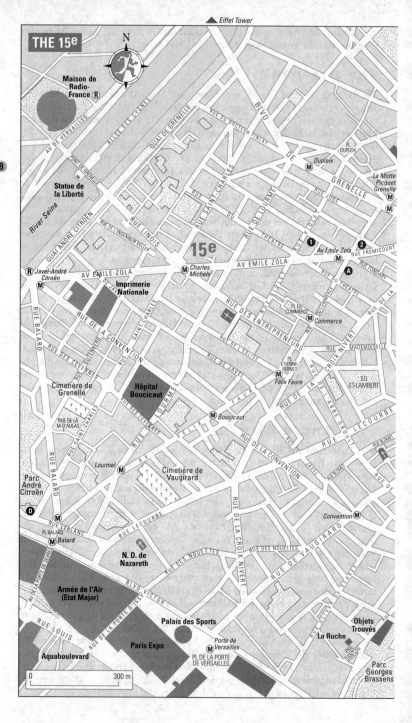

▲ Eiffel Tower

THE 15e

N

Maison de Radio-France ®

AV DE VERSAILLES

ALLÉE DES CYGNES

QUAI DE GRENELLE

RUE DU DOCTEUR FINLAY

BLVD

PL DUPLEIX

Dupleix Ⓜ

DE

GRENELLE

La Motte Picquet Grenelle Ⓜ

PONT DE GRENELLE

Statue de la Liberté

River Seine

QUAI ANDRÉ CITROËN

RUE DE L'INGÉNIEUR KELLER

RUE LINOIS

RUE SAINT-CHARLES

RUE DU THÉATRE

RUE DE LOURMEL

RUE JUGE

15e

AV EMILE ZOLA

Ⓜ Charles Michels

Ⓜ Javel-André Citroën ®

AV EMILE ZOLA

Imprimerie Nationale

RUE DE JAVEL

RUE SAINT-CHARLES

RUE DES CÉVENNES

RUE GUTENBERG

RUE DE LA CONVENTION

RUE BALARD

Cimetière de Grenelle

Hôpital Boucicaut

RUE SAINT-CHARLES

RUE DES CÉVENNES

RUE DE LA M-D'AULAS

① Av Emile Zola ②

Ⓐ

RUE FREMICOURT

RUE FONDARY

RUE DU THÉATRE

PL DU COMMERCE

Ⓜ Commerce

RUE DE LA CROIX NIVERT

RUE DES ENTREPRENEURS

RUE DE L'ÉGLISE

RUE DE JAVEL

PL ETIENNE-PERNET

Félix Faure

RUE FÉLIX FAURE

Ⓜ Boucicaut

RUE LOURMEL

RUE DE LA CONVENTION

RUE DE LA CROIX NIVERT

RUE BLOMET

RUE DE L'ABBÉ GROULT

RUE LECOURBE

RUE BLOMET

MADEMOISELLE

SQ ST-LAMBERT

✝

RUE BALARD

Parc André Citroën

Ⓓ

RUE LEBLANC

PL BALARD

Ⓜ Balard

Lourmel Ⓜ

Cimetière de Vaugirard

✝ ✝ ✝
✝ ✝

RUE LECOURBE

RUE DES NOUETTES

RUE DE LA CONVENTION

RUE DE VAUGIRARD

Convention Ⓜ

RUE OLIVIER DE SERRES

N. D. de Nazareth ✝

BLVD VICTOR

RUE DES NOUETTES

RUE DE VAUGIRARD

Objets Trouvés

La Ruche

AV DE LA PORTE DE SÈVRES

Armée de l'Air (Etat Major)

RUE LOUIS

RUE DE LA PORTE D'ISSY

Paris Expo

Palais des Sports

Porte de Versailles

PL DE LA PORTE DE VERSAILLES

POR DANTZIG

Parc Georges Brassens

Aquaboulevard

0 _____ 300 m

8

MONTPARNASSE AND SOUTHERN PARIS

158

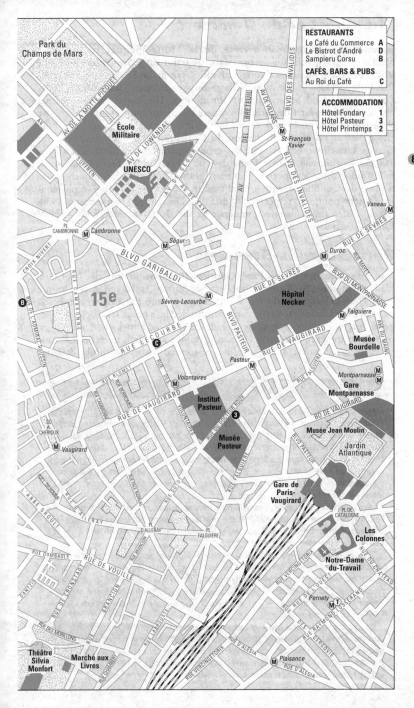

Park du
Champs de Mars

École
Militaire

UNESCO

St-François
Xavier

Vaneau

PL
CAMBRONNE · Cambronne

Ségur

Duroc

RUE DE SEVRES

RUE DE SEVRES

BLVD GARIBALDI

BLVD DU MONTPARNASSE

15e

Sèvres-Lecourbe

Hôpital
Necker

Falguière

Musée
Bourdelle

RUE LECOURBE

Pasteur

Montparnasse

Volontaires

Gare
Montparnasse

RUE DE VAUGIRARD

Institut
Pasteur

Vaugirard

Musée
Pasteur

Musée Jean Moulin

Jardin
Atlantique

Gare de
Paris-
Vaugirard

PL
D'ALLERAY

PL
FALGUIÈRE

PL DE
CATALOGNE

Les
Colonnes

RUE DE VOUILLÉ

Notre-Dame
du-Travail

RUE VERCINGÉTORIX

Pernety

RUE D'ALÉSIA

Théâtre
Silvia
Monfort

Marché aux
Livres

Plaisance

RUE D'ALÉSIA

RESTAURANTS
Le Café du Commerce    A
Le Bistrot d'André      D
Sampieru Corsu          B

CAFÉS, BARS & PUBS
Au Roi du Café          C

ACCOMMODATION
Hôtel Fondary           1
Hôtel Pasteur           3
Hôtel Printemps         2

# The quartier du Commerce

If you start walking down **avenue de la Motte-Picquet**, by the École Militaire, you'll get the full flavour of the **quartier du Commerce**. That's the staid end, where brasseries throng with officers from the École, and 150 expensive antique shops in the stuffy **Village Suisse** (all open Thurs–Mon) display Louis Quinze and Second Empire furnishings. The nature of the quartier changes at **boulevard de Grenelle**, where the métro runs on iron piers above the street. Seedy hotels rent rooms by the month, and the corner cafés offer cheap *plats du jour*. It was in the **rue du Commerce**, which begins here, that George Orwell worked as a dishwasher, an experience described in his *Down and Out in Paris and London*. These days it's a lively, old-fashioned high street full of small shops and peeling, shuttered houses. Towards the end of the street is place du Commerce, with a bandstand in the middle, a model of old-fashioned petit-bourgeois respectability that could be a frozen frame from a 1930s movie. Cafés and pâtisseries proliferate as rue du Commerce ends at place Étienne-Pernet.

# Parc Georges-Brassens

The main entrance of the **Parc Georges-Brassens**, on rue des Morillons (daily dawn–dusk; M° Convention/Porte-de-Vanves), is flanked by two bronze bulls. The old Vaugirard abattoir was transformed into this park in the 1980s, and the original clock tower remains, surrounded by a pond. It's a delight, especially for children – attractions include puppets and rocks and merry-go-rounds for the kids, a mountain stream with pine and birch trees, beehives and a tiny terraced vineyard, and a garden of scented herbs and shrubs designed

## La Ruche

After the World Fair ended, Eiffel's iron-and-glass wine pavilion was bought by Alfred Boucher, sculptor of public monuments and friend of Rodin, and re-erected in passage Dantzig in an altruistic gesture of help for struggling artists. Very soon **La Ruche**, or the Beehive, became home to Fernand Léger, Modigliani (briefly), Chagall, Soutine, Ossip Zadkine and many others, mainly Jewish refugees from pogroms in Poland and Russia. Boucher, somewhat overwhelmed by the unconventional work and behaviour of his protégés, commented good-naturedly: "I'm like a hen who finds she has laid ducks' eggs."

Léger, evoking the poverty, recalls how he was invited to lunch one day by four Russian residents who had just made a few francs selling cat pelts. The meal was the cats, dismembered and fricasséed in vodka. "It burnt your mouth and it stank," he noted, "but it was better than nothing."

The writer Blaise Centrars was a regular visitor, as were Apollinaire and Max Jacob, who provided a link with the Picasso gang across the river in Montmartre, and there was much cross-fertilization going on in the cafés, too, especially *La Rotonde*, at 105 boulevard du Montparnasse (see p.299). But at La Ruche itself, the French were in a minority – you were much more likely to hear Yiddish, Polish, Russian or Italian spoken.

It's still something of a Tower of Babel these days, with Irish, American, Italian and Japanese artists in residence, although, as an Italian mosaicist who has been there since the 1950s said, there's no longer the Bohemian camaraderie and festivity of the old days. The buildings were saved from the bulldozers in 1970 by a campaign led by Marc Chagall, since which time physical conditions have improved.

principally for the blind (best in late spring). The corrugated pyramid with a helter-skelter-like spiral is a theatre, the Silvia-Montfort.

On Saturdays and Sundays, take a look in the sheds of the old horse market between the park and **rue Brancion**, to the east, where dozens of **book dealers** set out their stock. On the west side of the park, in a secluded garden in passage Dantzig, off rue Dantzig, stands an unusual polygonal building known as **La Ruche**. It was designed by Eiffel and started life as the wine pavilion for the 1900 trade fair (see box opposite).

# The 13e

To the tight-knit community who lived in the crowded, rat-ridden and ramshackle slums around **rue Nationale** in the postwar years, Paris was another place, rarely ventured into. Come the 1950s and 1960s, however, the city planners, here as elsewhere, came up with their usual solution to the housing problem – getting rid of the slums to make way for tower blocks. The architectural gloom of the southeastern half of the arrondissement is only alleviated by the culinary delights of the **Chinese quarter** and one or two clever new buildings. West of avenue d'Italie and avenue des Gobelins – site of the famous tapestry works – there remains the almost untouched quartier of the **Butte-aux-Cailles**, and little streets and cul-de-sacs of prewar houses and studios. The eastern edge of the 13e, meanwhile, along the riverfront, is in the throes of mammoth development centred around the new **Bibliothèque Nationale**.

## The Butte-aux-Cailles

Between boulevard Auguste-Blanqui and rue Bobillot is the **Butte-aux-Cailles**, whose name can be translated picturesquely as the hill (*butte*) of the quails (*cailles*), although there is talk of a more prosaic Monsieur Cailles.
It's a pleasantly animated quarter, the main rue de la Butte-aux-Cailles cobbled and furnished with attractive lampposts, as well as one of the green Art Nouveau municipal drinking fountains donated to the city by the nineteenth-century British art collector Sir Richard Wallace. Alongside the old establishments – the bar *La Folie en Tête* at no. 33 and the restaurant *Le Temps des Cerises* at nos. 18–20 – are plenty of new and trendy places to eat and drink, most of which stay open till the small hours.

South of rue de Tolbiac, small houses with fancy brickwork, decorative tiles and timbers, crazy-paving walls and near-vertical roofs have remained intact: especially between rues Boussingault and Brillat-Savarin, near place de Rungis, and on place de l'Abbé-G-Henocque, rue Dieulafoy and rue Henri-Pape.

## Gobelins

**Place d'Italie**, the central junction of the 13e, is one of those Parisian roundabouts that takes half an hour to cross. On its north side is the ornate mairie of the arrondissement, while to the south is a new Gaumont cinema whose curving glass frontage cleverly advertises the giant screen within – the two are roughly the same size. In the 1848 Revolution, the *place* was barricaded and the scene of one short-lived victory of the Left. A government general and his officers were allowed through the barricades, only to be surrounded and dragged

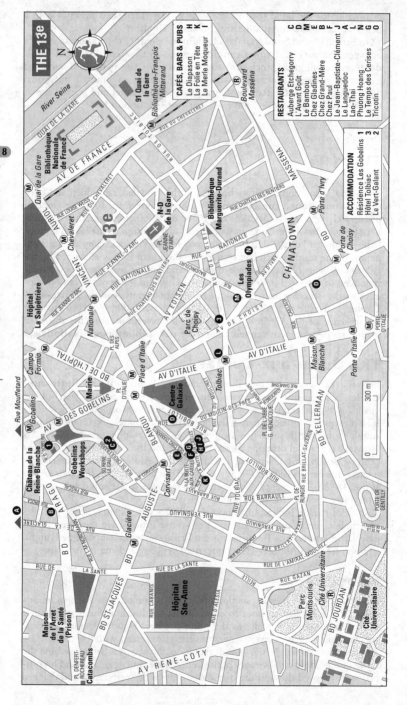

THE 13e

N

River Seine

Bibliothèque-François
Mitterand

91 Quai de
la Gare

Bibliothèque
Nationale
de France

CAFÉS, BARS & PUBS    H
Le Diapason                    H
La Folie en Tête              K
Le Merle Moqueur           I

RESTAURANTS
Auberge Etchegorry          C
L'Avant Goût                    D
Le Bambou                      M
Chez Gladines                  E
Chez Grand-Mère             B
Chez Paul                        F
Le Jean-Baptiste-Clément  J
Le Languedoc                   A
Lao-Thai                         L
Phuong Hoang                 N
Le Temps des Cerises       G
Tricotin                          O

ACCOMMODATION
Résidence Les Gobelins     1
Hôtel Tolbiac                   3
Le Vert-Galant                 2

Hôpital
La Salpêtrière

N-D
de la Gare

Bibliothèque
Marguerite-Durand

Les
Olympiades

CHINATOWN

Parc de
Choisy

Centre
Galaxie

Château de la
Reine Blanche

Gobelins
Workshops

Maison
de l'Arret
de la Santé
(Prison)

Hôpital
Ste-Anne

Parc
Montsouris

Cité
Universitaire

Catacombs

0      300 m

off to the police station, where the commander was persuaded to write an order of retreat and a letter promising three million francs for the poor of Paris. Needless to say, neither was honoured and reprisals were heavy.

Many of those involved in the uprising were tanners, laundry-workers or dye-makers, with their workplace the banks of the River Bièvre. This area was deemed a health hazard and covered over in 1910 (creating rues Berbier-du-Mets and Croulebarbe) – the main source of pollution being the dyes from the **Gobelins tapestry workshops**, at 42 avenue des Gobelins, which had operated here for some four hundred years. On the guided tour (in French only; Tues–Thurs 2pm & 2.45pm; €8; M° Gobelins), you can watch tapestries being made by painfully slow traditional methods: each weaver completes between one and four square metres a year. The designs are now exactingly specified by contemporary artists, and almost all of the dozen or so works completed each year are destined for French government offices. An on-site museum is planned to open in 2005, displaying both old and contemporary tapestries.

Hidden just north of Gobelins is an exquisite fairy-tale tower and gateway hemmed in by workshops and lockups. This is all that remains of the **Château de la Reine Blanche**, where the young Charles VI of France supposedly went mad after a riotous party in 1393 when he was nearly burnt alive. The tower and gate date from when the château was rebuilt in the sixteenth century, and it is all currently being converted into luxury apartments. You can take a look through the courtyard at 4 rue Gustave-Geffroy. A stone's throw away, between rues Berbier and Corvisart, is a big public garden – although nothing very special, it's handy for a snooze or picnic if you're out this way.

The ornate, bourgeois buildings between boulevards St-Marcel and Vincent-Auriol are dominated by the immense **Hôpital de la Salpêtrière**, built under Louis XIV to dispose of the dispossessed, and later used as a psychiatric hospital – today it's a general hospital. Jean Charcot, who believed that susceptibility to hypnosis proved hysteria, staged his theatrical demonstrations here, with Freud as one of his fascinated witnesses.

# Chinatown and Tolbiac

The area between rue de Tolbiac, avenue de Choisy and boulevard Masséna is what is known as the **Chinatown** of Paris, despite the presence of several other east Asian communities. Avenues de Choisy and d'Ivry are full of Vietnamese, Thai, Cambodian and Laotian restaurants and food shops, as is **Les Olympiades**, an extraordinary semi-derelict pedestrian area seemingly suspended between giant tower blocks. One escalator leads up to it from 66 av d'Ivry, next door to a sliproad leading down to an underground car park; halfway down this access road lurks a tiny **Buddhist temple** and community centre, advertised by a pair of red Chinese lanterns dimly visible in the gloom. On Monday, Wednesday and Friday afternoons, from around 2.30pm, there are informal **concerts** of Chinese music; the rest of the time you'll find elderly Chinese people playing games and dozing on rickety sofas. As you step out into avenue d'Ivry, you'll find the huge Tang-Frères **Chinese supermarket** (see p.343), stacked with mind- and stomach-boggling goods.

On the north side of rue de Tolbiac, the **parc de Choisy** offers outdoor ping-pong tables with concrete nets and shady trees. There are some good modern buildings near here: Christian de Portzamparc's public housing estate on rue des Hautes-Formes, and, at 106 rue du Château-des-Rentiers, a ten-storey block of public flats whose facade, on rue Jean-Colly, has a map of the quartier in coloured tiles, with pipes to show the métro lines. Serious Le

△ Paris métro

Corbusier fans could make the long slog down rue Cantagrel, where his Salvation Army building, blackened by traffic fumes, stands at no. 12.

# The Bibliothèque Nationale

Following rue Tolbiac or boulevard Vincent-Auriol to the river, you reach a vast building site which, the French economy permitting, is slowly being transformed into an entirely new district called **Paris Rive Gauche**, stretching from the Gare d'Austerlitz to the perimeter. Its star attraction, which Mitterrand managed to inaugurate though not open just before his death, is the **Bibliothèque Nationale de France**, accessible from the métro stations at quai de la Gare or the spanking new Bibliothèque-François Mitterrand station. There are occasional small-scale exhibitions, and the **reading rooms** on the "haut-jardin" level – along with their unrivalled collection of foreign newspapers – are open to everyone over 16 (Tues–Sat 10am–8pm, Sun noon–7pm; €3 for a day pass; Ⓦwww.bnf.fr). The garden level, below, is reserved for accredited researchers only, while the garden itself is completely out of bounds.

The four enormous L-shaped towers at the corners of the site were intended to look like open books, but attracted widespread derision after shutters had to be added behind the glazing in order to protect the collections from sunlight. Once you mount the wooden steps surrounding the library, however, the perspective changes utterly. Now you're looking down into a huge sunken pine wood, with glass walls that filter light into the floors below your feet; it's like standing at the edge of a secret ravine. The concept is startlingly original, and almost fulfils architect Dominique Perault's intention to seek "a kind of sensibility capable of combining rigour and emotion, which will generate a sense of dignity, a well-tempered soul for the buildings of the French Republic."

Independently of the official plans, interesting cultural events are springing up in their own right. There are several **barges** – an ex-lighthouse boat and a Chinese barge amongst them – moored along the quay in front of the library that make excellent places for a drink and live music (see p.310), and cutting-edge art galleries have sprung up on rue Louise Weiss, behind the library. It's not all new, though: the gigantic old **mills** and warehouses just south of Pont de Tolbiac, occupied by musicians, anarchists, oddballs and artists, are, thankfully, set to stay, but have a fight on their hands to keep the space around them free.

# 9

# Montmartre and northern Paris

**M**ontmartre lies in the middle of the largely petit-bourgeois and working-class 18ᵉ arrondissement, respectable round the slopes of the hill (or Butte Montmartre), distinctly less so around **Pigalle** on the northern edge of the 9ᵉ arrondissement and towards the **Gare du Nord** and **Gare de l'Est** into the 10ᵉ arrondissement, where the colourful bazaar-like shops and depressing slums of the **Goutte d'Or** crowd along the rail lines. On its northern edge, across the so-called "plain of Montmartre", lies the extensive **St-Ouen flea market**. To the west, between avenue de **Clichy** and the St-Lazare train lines, is the little-explored **Batignolles** quartier.

## Montmartre

At 130m, the **Butte Montmartre** is the highest point in Paris. The various theories as to the origin of its name all have a Roman connection: it could be a corruption of *Mons Martyrum* – "the Martyrs' hill" – the martyrs being St Denis and his companions; on the other hand, it might have been named *Mons Mercurii*, in honour of a Roman shrine to Mercury; or possibly *Mons Martis*, after a shrine to Mars.

In spite of being one of the city's chief tourist attractions, the Butte manages to retain the quiet, almost secretive, air of its rural origins. Incorporated into the city only in the mid-nineteenth century, it received its first major influx of population from the poor displaced by Haussmann's rebuilding programme. Its heyday was from the last years of the century to World War I, when its rustic charms and low rents attracted crowds of artists. Although that traditional community of workers and artists has largely been supplanted by a more chic and prosperous class of Bohemians, the quartier's physical appearance has changed little, thanks largely to the warren of **plaster-of-Paris quarries** that perforate its bowels and render the ground too unstable for new building.

The most popular **access** route is via the rue de Steinkerque and the steps below the **Sacré-Cœur**, Montmartre's hilltop church and most famous landmark (the funicular railway from place Suzanne-Valadon is covered by ordinary métro tickets). But for a quieter approach, head up via place des Abbesses or rue Lepic, where you'll have the streets to yourself.

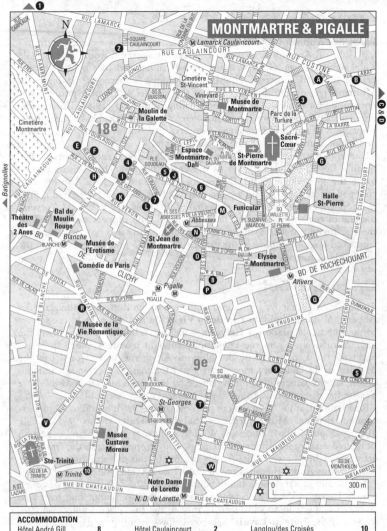

# MONTMARTRE & PIGALLE

## ACCOMMODATION

| | | | | | |
|---|---|---|---|---|---|
| Hôtel André Gill | 8 | Hôtel Caulaincourt | 2 | Langlou/des Croisés | 10 |
| Hôtel Bonséjour | 4 | Hôtel du Commerce | 6 | Perfect Hotel | 9 |
| Hôtel le Bouquet de Montmartre | 7 | Hôtel du Puy de Dôme | 1 | Timhotel Montmartre | 5 |
| | | Ermitage | 3 | | |

## RESTAURANTS

| | | | | | |
|---|---|---|---|---|---|
| L'Alsaco | S | L'Homme Tranquille | O | Le Rendez-vous des Chauffeurs | D |
| L'Assiette | A | Le Moulin à Vins | K | Le Restaurant | K |
| La Casserole | C | A la Pomponnette | F | La Table d'Anvers | Q |
| Aux Deux-Théâtres | V | Le Relais Gascon | N | Velly | W |
| Au Grain de Folie | M | Le Relais Savoyard | U | Au Virage Lepic | E |
| Haynes | T | | | | |

## CAFÉS, BARS AND PUBS

| | | | | | |
|---|---|---|---|---|---|
| Le Bar du Relais | J | La Fourmi Café | P | Au Petit Café de Montmartre | H |
| Le Dépanneur | R | Aux Négociants | B | Le Sancerre | L |
| L'Été en Pente Douce | G | | | | |

# Around Place des Abbesses

**Place des Abbesses** is postcard-pretty, with one of the few complete surviving Guimard Art Nouveau métro entrances (transferred from the Hôtel de Ville), with glass porch as well as original railings and the slightly obscene orange-tongued lanterns. The bizarre-looking church of **St-Jean de Montmartre**, on the downhill side of the *place*, is well worth putting your nose inside for its radical construction, dating to the early 1900s. The incredibly slender pillars and broad vaulting were only made possible by the experimental use of reinforced concrete, a material that was, as its architect Anatole de Baudot claimed, both the bones and the skin.

East from the *place*, at the Chapelle des Auxiliatrices in rue Yvonne-Le-Tac, Ignatius Loyola founded the **Jesuit** movement in 1534. This is also supposed to be the spot where **Saint Denis**, the first Bishop of Paris, had his head chopped off by the Romans around 250 AD. He's said to have carried it until he dropped, on the site of the cathedral of St-Denis (see p.229). Just beyond the end of rue Yvonne-Le-Tac, in the beautiful little **place Charles-Dullin**, the Théâtre de l'Atelier is still going strong after nearly two centuries. Heading west from place des Abbesses, the café *Le Sancerre* is a popular sun-trap on the south side of rue des Abbesses.

# Up to the Butte

Two quiet and attractive routes lead to the top of the Butte from the place des Abbesses. You can climb up **rue de la Vieuville** and the stairs in rue Drevet to the minuscule **place du Calvaire**, which has a lovely view back over the city; alternatively, go up rue Durantin, then right on rue Tholozé and right again on rue Lepic into rue des Norvins. Along rue Lepic, you'll pass the **Moulin de la Galette**, a lone survivor of Montmartre's forty-odd windmills whose famous dances were immortalized by Renoir in his *Bal du Moulin de la Galette*; the painting now hangs in the Musée d'Orsay (see p.145).

Rue Poulbot, at the beginning of rue des Norvins, leads round to the underground **Espace Montmartre – Salvador Dalí**, at no. 9–11 (daily 10am–6.30pm; €7; M° Abbesses). With its giant souvenir shop and collection of limited-edition sculptures and etchings, many created towards the end of the artist's life when he was quite frankly cashing in, this museum lives up to the anagram that André Breton made of Dalí's name: Avida Dollars.

Artistic and literary associations abound hereabouts. Zola, Berlioz, Turgenev, Seurat, Degas and Van Gogh lived in the area. Picasso, Braque and Juan Gris invented Cubism in an old piano factory in the tiny place Émile-Goudeau, known as the **Bateau-Lavoir** (see box below); it still provides studio space

## Picasso at the Bateau-Lavoir

**Picasso** came to the **Bateau-Lavoir** in 1904 and stayed for the best part of a decade working (he painted *Les Demoiselles d'Avignon* here) and sharing loves, quarrels, febrile discussions, opium trips and diverse escapades with Braque, Juan Gris, Modigliani, Max Jacob, Apollinaire and others both famous and obscure. It was on the place Émile-Goudeau that he had his first encounter with the beautiful Fernande Olivier, thrusting a kitten into her hand as she passed by. "I laughed," she said, "and he took me to see his studio." Fernande became his model and lover.

Although what you see today is a reconstruction, it still has the same aspect on the street side, and little has changed in the square itself.

△ Sacré Cœur

for artists, though the original building burnt down some years ago. At the foot of the Butte, on place Blanche, Toulouse-Lautrec's inspiration, the **Moulin Rouge**, still survives, albeit a mere shadow of its former self. **Rue Lepic** begins here, its winding contours recalling the lane that once served the plaster quarry wagons. A busy market occupies the lower part of the street, but once above rue des Abbesses it reverts to a mixture of tranquil and furtive elegance. Round the corner above rue Tourlaque, a flight of steps and a muddy path sneak between gardens to **avenue Junot**, where the actress Anouk Aimée has her home. Off to the left is the secluded and exclusive cul-de-sac **Villa Léandre**, while to the right, the Cubist house of Dadaist poet Tristan Tzara stands on the corner of another exclusive enclave of houses and gardens, the **Hameau des Artistes**. Higher up the street the **square Suzanne–Buisson** provides a gentle haven, with a sunken boules pitch overlooked by a statue of St Denis clutching his head to his breast.

# Place du Tertre, St-Pierre and the Sacré-Cœur

The heart of Montmartre, the **place du Tertre**, photogenic but totally bogus,

## The Paris Commune

On March 18, 1871, in the **place du Tertre**, Montmartre's most illustrious mayor and future prime minister of France, **Georges Clemenceau**, flapped about trying to prevent the bloodshed that gave birth to the **Paris Commune** and the ensuing battle with the national government.

Paris had finally fallen to the Prussian army on 28 January, after four months' siege, with peace terms agreed by the end of February, but the future of the newly declared Third Republic was still uncertain. Adolphe Thiers' conservative government dispatched a body of troops under General Lecomte to take possession of 170 guns, which the National Guard, most of them workers, controlled on the high ground of **Montmartre**. Although the troops seized the guns easily in the dark before dawn, they had failed to bring any horses to tow them away. That gave Louise Michel, the great woman revolutionary, time to raise the alarm.

A large and angry crowd gathered, fearing another restoration of empire or monarchy, such as had happened after the 1848 Revolution. They persuaded the troops to take no action and arrested General Lecomte, along with another general, Clément Thomas, whose part in the brutal repression of the 1848 republican uprising had won him no friends among the people. The two generals were shot and mutilated in the garden of **no. 36 rue du Chevalier-de-la-Barre**, behind the Sacré-Cœur. By the following morning, the government had decamped to Versailles, leaving the Hôtel de Ville and the whole of the city in the hands of the National Guard, who then proclaimed the Commune.

Divided among themselves and isolated from the rest of France, the Communards finally succumbed to government assault after a week's bloody street-fighting, the *semaine sanglante*, between May 21 and 28. No-one knows how many of them died – certainly no fewer than 20,000, with another 10,000 executed or deported. By way of government revenge, Eugène Varlin, one of the founder-members of the First International and a leading light in the Commune, was shot on the selfsame spot where the two generals had been killed just a few weeks before.

It was a working-class revolt, as the particulars of those involved clearly demonstrate, but it hardly had time to be as socialist as subsequent mythologizing would have it. The terrible cost of repression had long-term effects on the French left wing: thereafter, not to be revolutionary seemed like a betrayal of the dead.

is jammed with tourists, overpriced restaurants and "artists" knocking up lurid oils of Paris landmarks from memory. Its trees, once under threat of destruction for safety reasons by overzealous officialdom, have been saved by the well-orchestrated protests of its influential residents.

Similar protests early in the twentieth century saved the **church of St-Pierre**, between place du Tertre and the Sacré-Coeur, which was due to be replaced by St-Jean de Montmartre (see p.168). St-Pierre, which rivals St-Germain-des-Prés for the title of oldest church in Paris, is all that remains of a Benedictine convent that occupied the Butte Montmartre from the twelfth century onwards. Though much altered, with modern stained glass throughout, it still retains its Romanesque and early Gothic feel. The four ancient columns inside the church, two by the door and two in the choir, are probably leftovers from the Roman shrine that stood on the hill, and their capitals date from Merovingian times, as does the cemetery outside.

Crowning the Butte is the **Sacré-Cœur** (daily 6am–10.30pm; M° Abbesses & M° Anvers), a weird pastiche of a Byzantine style whose pimply tower and white ice-cream-dome has somehow become an essential part of the Paris skyline. Construction was started in the 1870s on the initiative of the Catholic Church to atone for the "crimes" of the Commune (see box opposite). The thwarted opposition, which included Clemenceau, eventually got its revenge by naming the space at the foot of the monumental staircase **square Willette**, after the local artist who turned out on inauguration day to shout "Long live the devil!" The interior is more neo-Byzantine nonsense, and the best thing about the Sacré-Cœur is the **view from the top** (daily 8am–6.30pm; €5). It's almost as high as the Eiffel Tower, and you can see the layout of the whole city – a wide, flat basin ringed by low hills, with stands of high-rise blocks in the southeastern corner, on the heights of Belleville, and at La Défense in the west. The tall tower-block in the middle of the city is the Tour Montparnasse and beyond, in the hazy distance, are the high flat faces of southern suburban *cités*.

## The northern side of the Butte

**Rue des Saules** tips steeply down the north side of the Butte past the terraces of the tiny **Montmartre vineyard**. Its annual harvest in mid-September yields an extraordinary 1500kg of grapes, producing in the region of 1500 bottles of pretty foul wine. A small festival celebrates the harvest on the first weekend of October. To the right, **rue Cortot** cuts through to the water tower, whose distinctive form, together with that of the Sacré-Cœur, is one of the landmarks of the city's skyline.

At 12 rue Cortot, a pretty old house with a grassy courtyard was occupied at different times by Renoir, Dufy, Suzanne Valadon and her mad son, Utrillo. It's now the **Musée de Montmartre** (daily except Mon 10am–12.30pm & 1.30–6pm; €4; M° Lamarck-Caulaincourt), whose mainly disappointing exhibits attempt to recreate the atmosphere of Montmartre's pioneering heyday, via a selection of Toulouse-Lautrec posters, mock-ups of various period rooms – including a bar complete with original *zinc*, or pewter top – and various painted impressions of how the Butte once looked. The museum does, however, offer a magnificent view from the back over the hilly northern reaches of the city and the vineyard, and the shop usually has a few bottles of Montmartre wine.

Berlioz lived with his English wife in the corner house on the steps of rue du Mont-Cenis, from where there's a breathtaking view northwards along the canyon of the steps, as well as back up towards place du Calvaire. The steps are perfect sepia-romantic Montmartre – a double handrail runs down the centre, with the lampposts between – and the streets below are among the quietest and least touristy in Montmartre.

## The Halle St-Pierre

To the south and east of the Sacré-Cœur, the slopes of the Butte drop steeply down towards boulevard Barbès and the Goutte d'Or (see p.174). Directly below are the gardens of square Willette, milling with tourists. To avoid the crowds, make instead for the quiet gardens to the north of the Sacré-Cœur, the **Parc de la Turlure**, or head down the steeply stepped rue Utrillo, turning right at the pleasant café, *L'Eté en Pente Douce* (see p.302), which has outdoor tables on the corner of rue Paul Albert. From here, more steps lead down along the edge of the gardens to rue Ronsard, where overhanging greenery masks the now-sealed entrances to the quarries. The original plaster of Paris was extracted from here, and the revolutionaries of 1848 used the caverns as a refuge. The circular **Halle St-Pierre** (daily 10am–6pm; admission fee to temporary shows varies; M° Anvers), at the bottom of rue Ronsard, hosts excellent changing exhibitions of folk art, art brut and art naïf; recent shows have included some alternative-minded French and American painters and an exhibition of giant movie posters from Ghana. Each artist exhibiting here leaves a work behind to swell the permanent collection, works from which are shown on the ground floor in the **Musée d'Art Naïf Max-Fourny**. There's also an auditorium for film, theatre, music and dance, a bookshop and a cheap cafeteria with the day's papers to read.

## Montmartre cemetery

West of the Butte, near the beginning of rue Caulaincourt in place Clichy, lies the **Montmartre cemetery** (March 16–Nov 5 Mon–Fri 8am–6pm, Sat from 8.30am, Sun from 9am; Nov 6–March 15 closes 5.30pm; M° Blanche & M° Place-de-Clichy). Tucked down below street level in the hollow of an old quarry, it's a tangle of trees and funerary pomposity, more intimate and less melancholy than Père-Lachaise or Montparnasse (see pp.195 and 154).

The illustrious dead at rest here include Stendhal, Berlioz, Degas, Feydeau, Offenbach, Nijinsky and François Truffaut, as well La Goulue, the dancer at the Moulin Rouge immortalized by Toulouse-Lautrec. Zola's grave is here too, though his remains have been transferred to the Panthéon (see p.123). There's also a large Jewish section by the east wall. The entrance is on avenue Rachel under rue Caulaincourt, next to an antique cast-iron poor-box (*Tronc pour les Pauvres*).

# Pigalle

From place Clichy in the west to Barbès-Rochechouart in the east, the hill of Montmartre is underlined by the sleazy **boulevards de Clichy** and **de Rochechouart**, the centre of the roadway often occupied by bumper-car pistes and other funfair sideshows. At the eastern **Barbès** end, where the métro clatters by on iron trestles, the crowds teem round the Tati department store, the cheapest in the city, while the pavements are thick with Arab and African street vendors offering watches, trinkets and textiles.

For many foreigners, entertainment in Paris is still synonymous with those mythical names the Moulin Rouge, Folies Bergères and Lido. These **cabarets** flash their presence from the Champs-Élysées to boulevard Montmartre but bear little resemblance to their bygone artistic patina. The evening (a very expensive one at around €90 and up) is comprised of dinner and a glitzy show full of special effects and bare-breasted women sporting large coloured feathers, and the audience is mainly made up of package-tourists whose holiday deal includes an evening at the cabaret.

The **Lido** (116bis av des Champs-Elysées, 8ᵉ, ☎01.40.76.56.10, ⓦwww.lido.fr) intersperses multi-coloured plumage and illuminated distant flesh with conjurors playing tricks with the clothes and possessions of the audience. Then back come the computer-choreographed "Bluebell Girls", in a technical tour de force of light show, music and a moving stage transporting the thighs and breasts to more far-away exotica – the sea, a volcano, arctic plain or Pacific island. Ever since the eponymous film came out, they've been taking bookings two months in advance at the **Moulin Rouge** (82 bd de Clichy, 18ᵉ ☎01.53.09.82.82, ⓦwww.moulinrouge.fr) – of the same ilk with its "Doriss Girls", and still trading on its Toulouse-Lautrec painted fame as the place for "the most celebrated can-can in the world". The oldest cabaret, the **Folies Bergères**, reopened in 1993 after a brief closure, and is now trying its hand as a night-club, while at the **Crazy Horse** (12 av George V, 8ᵉ, ☎01.47.23.32.32, ⓦwww.crazyhorseparis.com), the theatrical experience convinces the audience that they are watching art as well as the prettiest girls in Paris.

Although the whole spectacle of the cabaret is considered respectable, all things considered, it is related to the other "Live Shows" touted along the boulevard de Clichy. Moving from the glamour cabarets to the "Live Sex" venues is to leave the world of gloss and exportable Frenchness for a world of sealed-cover porn without cultural borders.

At the **place Clichy** end, tour buses from all over Europe feed their contents into massive hotels. In the middle, between **place Blanche** and **place Pigalle**, sex shows, sex shops and prostitutes, both male and female, vie for the custom of *solitaires* and couples alike. It's an area in which respectability and sleaze rub very close shoulders. One of the city's most elegant private *villas*, **avenue Frochot** leads off **place Pigalle** itself. In the adjacent streets – **rues de Douai**, **Victor-Massé** and **Houdon** – specialist music shops (this is *the* area for instruments and sound systems) and grey house facades are interspersed with tiny ill-lit bars where "hostesses" lurk in complicated tackle.

Perfectly placed amongst all the sex shops and shows is the **Musée de l'Erotisme** (daily 10am–2am; €7), testament to its owner's fascination with sex as expressed in folk art. The ground floor and first floor are awash with model phalluses, fertility symbols and intertwined figurines from all over Asia, Africa and pre-Colombian Latin America. The European pieces tend to the satirical or plain smutty, with lots of naughty nuns and priests caught in compromising situations. The rest of the floors upstairs are devoted to temporary exhibitions.

# South of Pigalle

The rest of the 9ᵉ arrondissement, which stretches south of Pigalle, is a relatively quiet quarter and a tad dull, with the exception of some blocks of streets round **place St-Georges**, where Thiers, president of the Third Republic, lived in a house that's now a library (rebuilt after being burnt by the Commune). In the centre of the *place* stands a statue of the nineteenth-century cartoonist Gavarni, who made a speciality of lampooning the mistresses that were de rigueur for bourgeois males of the time. This was the mistresses' quartier – they were known as *lorettes*, after the nearby church of Notre-Dame-de-Lorette.

The cheap rents hereabouts also attracted musicians, painters and writers in the nineteenth century – Chopin, Dumas, Delacroix and George Sand all lived in the area. The **Musée de la Vie Romantique** at 16 rue Chaptal (daily except Mon 10am–6pm, closed public hols; €4.50 during exhibitions, otherwise free; M° St-Georges, M° Blanche & M° Pigalle), sets out to evoke the Romantic period in what was once the painter Ary Scheffer's abode. The shuttered house itself is a delightful surprise, facing onto a cobbled courtyard at the end of a private alley, while the interior preserves the rich colours of a typical bourgeois home of the nineteenth century. George Sand used to visit here, and the ground floor consists mainly of bits and pieces associated with her, including jewels, locks of hair and a cast of her lover Chopin's surprisingly small hand. Scheffer was art tutor to Louis-Philippe's children, and upstairs are a number of his hideously sentimental aristocratic portraits.

Further east, **place Toudouze** and **rues Clauzel**, **Milton** and **Rodier** are worth a look. Renovation has revealed some beautiful and elegantly ornamented façades. **Rue St-Lazare**, between the St-Lazare station and the hideous church of Ste-Trinité, is a welcome swath of activity amid the residential calm. Opposite rue de la Tour-des-Dames, where two or three gracious mansions and gardens recall the days when this was the very edge of the city, you'll find the bizarre and little-visited **museum** dedicated to the fantastical, Symbolist works of **Gustave Moreau** (daily except Tues 10am–12.45pm & 2–5.15pm; €3.40; M° St-Georges, M° Blanche & M° Pigalle). The museum's design was conceived by Moreau himself, to be carved out of the house he shared with his parents for many years; you can visit their tiny, stuffy apartments crammed with furniture and trinkets. The paintings get more room – two huge, studio-like spaces connected by a beautiful spiral staircase – but the effect is no less cluttered. Moreau's canvases hang cheek-by-jowl, every surface crawling with figures and decorative swirls – literally crawling in the case of *The Daughters of Thespius* – or alive with deep colours and provocative symbolism, as in the museum's pièce de résistance, *Jupiter and Sémélé*. For all the rampantly decadent symbolism, many viewers haven't been quite convinced. Degas, for one, commented that Moreau was "a hermit who knows the train timetable".

# The Goutte d'Or and the northern stations

Continuing east from Pigalle, boulevard Rochechouart becomes boulevard de la Chapelle, along the north side of which, between **boulevard Barbès** and the **Gare du Nord** rail lines, stretches the poetically named, crumbling and squalid quartier of the **Goutte d'Or**. Its name – the "Drop of Gold" – derives from the vineyard that occupied this site in medieval times. Since World War I, however, when large numbers of North Africans were imported to replenish the ranks of Frenchmen dying in the trenches, it has gradually become an immigrant ghetto.

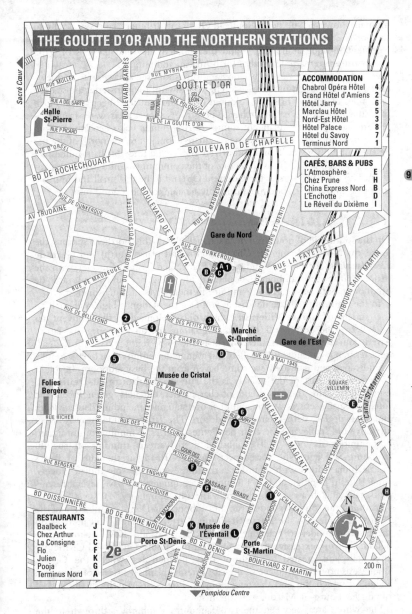

THE GOUTTE D'OR AND THE NORTHERN STATIONS

**ACCOMMODATION**
| | |
|---|---|
| Chabrol Opéra Hôtel | 4 |
| Grand Hôtel d'Amiens | 2 |
| Hôtel Jarry | 6 |
| Marclau Hôtel | 5 |
| Nord-Est Hôtel | 3 |
| Hôtel Palace | 8 |
| Hôtel du Savoy | 7 |
| Terminus Nord | 1 |

**CAFÉS, BARS & PUBS**
| | |
|---|---|
| L'Atmosphère | E |
| Chez Prune | H |
| China Express Nord | B |
| L'Enchotte | D |
| Le Réveil du Dixième | I |

**RESTAURANTS**
| | |
|---|---|
| Baalbeck | J |
| Chez Arthur | L |
| La Consigne | C |
| Flo | F |
| Julien | K |
| Pooja | G |
| Terminus Nord | A |

Sacré Cœur

GOUTTE D'OR

Halle St-Pierre

Gare du Nord

10e

Marché St-Quentin

Gare de l'Est

Musée de Cristal

Folies Bergère

SQUARE VILLEMIN

Canal St-Martin

Porte St-Denis

Musée de l'Éventail

Porte St-Martin

2e

Pompidou Centre

Many of the buildings in the area remain in a lamentable state of decay. While artists, writers and others have moved in, attracted by the only affordable property left in the city, a major programme of pulling down, rebuilding and cleaning up is underway. As the physical backdrop changes, so inevitably does the character of the *quartier*. Much of **rue de la Goutte-d'Or** itself is new, including a lovely nursery school on the corner with rue Islettes. For the moment, however, rue de la Goutte-d'Or and its tributary lanes, especially to the north – rue Myrha, rue Léon, the Marché Dejean, rue Polonceau (with its basement mosque at no. 55) – and the cobbled alley and gardens of **Villa Poissonnière** remain distinctly North African and poor.

Washing hangs from every balcony and tiny shops sell snazzy cloth and jewellery as well as traditional *djellabas*. The windows of the pâtisseries are stacked with trays of equally brightly coloured cakes and pastries. Sheeps' heads grin from the slabs of the halal butchers. The grocers shovel their wares from barrels and sacks, and the plangent sounds of Arab music echo evocatively from the record shops. In the playground of square Léon, just to the north of the rue de la Goutte d'Or, you'll find authorized graffiti and three brilliant murals. It's an interesting place to sit, as all sectors of the community come here for recreation. The cafés and bars of the Goutte d'Or tend to be too small and intimate to appeal to outsiders, but you'd certainly be able to find a good mint tea.

## The stations and faubourgs

On the south side of boulevard de la Chapelle lie the big northern stations, the **Gare du Nord** (serving the Channel ports and places north) and **Gare de l'Est** (serving northeastern and eastern France and Eastern Europe), with the major traffic thoroughfares, boulevard de Magenta and boulevard de Strasbourg, both bustling, noisy and not in themselves of much interest.

To the right of the Gare de l'Est as you face the station, a high wall encloses the gardens of **square Villemin**, which once belonged to the Couvent des Récollets – the near wreck of a building along rue du Faubourg-St-Martin. Saved from the bulldozers, the convent is due to be renovated whilst the gardens (entrance on rue des Récollets and avenue de Verdun) have been carefully relandscaped and provide a welcome haven from the busy faubourgs beyond.

The liveliest part of the quarter is the **rue du Faubourg-St-Denis**, full, especially towards the lower end, of charcuteries, butchers, greengrocers and foreign delicatessens, as well as a number of restaurants, including *Brasserie Julien* and *Brasserie Flo*, with their superb decors. The latter is hidden away in an attractive old stableyard, the cour des Petites-Écuries. A number of immigrant communities are now well established in the streets running off rue du Faubourg-St-Denis. The glazed-over **Passage Brady** is the hub of Paris's "Little India", lined with identikit curry houses and one sole Indian grocers' shop. Rues d'Enghien and de l'Échiquier are quieter but have several restaurants, cafés and shops serving the area's Turkish community.

Spanning the southern end of rue du Faubourg-St-Denis, on the edge of the $2^e$ arrondissement, is the **Porte St-Denis**, a triumphal arch built in 1672 on the Roman model to celebrate the victories of Louis XIV. Feeling secure behind Vauban's extensive frontier fortifications, Louis demolished Charles V's city walls and created a swath of leafy promenades, where the Grands Boulevards now run. In place of the city gates he planned a series of triumphal arches, of which this and the neighbouring **Porte St-Martin**, at the end of rue du Faubourg-St-Martin, were the first.

The whole area between the two faubourgs ("suburbs") through to the provincial **rue du Faubourg-Poissonnière** is honeycombed with passages and courtyards. China and glass enthusiasts should take a walk along **rue de Paradis**, whose shops specialize in such wares, with the Baccarat firm's collection of exquisite crystal, the **Musée du Cristal** at no. 30 (open Mon–Sat 10am–6pm; €3; M° Poissonnière & M° Gare-de-l'Est), tucked away with the shop behind the classical facade bearing the names of the Baccarat and St Louis cristallerie. Close by, at no. 18, is the magnificent mosaic and tiled facade of Monsieur Boulanger's Choisy-le-Roi **tileworks** shop, now closed to the general public, but you can peer through the gate and admire more exuberant ceramics featuring peacock tails and flamingos on the stairs and floors.

Another stop for curio-seekers is the **Musée de l'Éventail**, or Fan Museum, at 2 bd de Strasbourg (Mon–Wed 2–6pm; closed Aug; €5; M° Strasbourg-St-Denis). In a workshop and showroom dating from the end of the nineteenth century, Anne Hoguet continues the family tradition of fan-making. The workshop takes up the first two rooms and displays a small collection of utensils and materials. In the showroom, walnut drawers and cabinets contain the 900-strong collection of fans which are exhibited by rotation. These days, customers are almost exclusively from the world of haute couture or theatre.

Across boulevard Bonne-Nouvelle, the southern limit of the 10$^e$ arrondissement, are the *passages* of place du Caire and rue St-Denis leading down to Les Halles.

# Batignolles to Clichy

West of Montmartre cemetery, in a district bounded by the St-Lazare train lines, marshalling yards and avenue de Clichy, lies the "village" of **Batignolles** – sufficiently conscious of its uniqueness to have formed an association for the preservation of its *caractère villageois*. Its heart is rue des Batignolles. The poet Verlaine was brought up here, while Stéphane Mallarmé lived on boulevard des Batignolles, at the end of rue des Batignolles. At the northern end of the street, the attractive semicircular **place du Dr F. Lobligeois** frames the colonnaded church of **Ste-Marie-des-Batignolles**, its entrance modelled on the Madeleine; behind the church, the tired and trampled greenery of **square Batignolles** stretches back to the big rail marshalling yards. On the corner of the *place*, the modern bar *L'Endroit* attracts the bourgeois youth of the neighbourhood.

From rue des Batignolles, rue Legendre and rue des Dames lead southeast across the train lines to **rue de Lévis** and one of the city's most flamboyant and appetizing food and clothes markets, held every day except Monday. To the northeast, the long **rue des Moines** leads towards Guy-Môquet, with a covered market on the corner of rue Lemercier. This is the working-class Paris of the movies: all small, animated, friendly shops, four- or five-storey houses in shades of peeling grey, and brown-stained bars, where locals stand and drink at the *zinc*. Across avenue de Clichy, round **rue de la Jonquière**, the quiet streets are redolent of petit-bourgeois North African respectability, interspersed with decidedly upper-crust enclaves. The latter are typified by the film-set perfection of the **Cité des Fleurs**, a residential lane of magnificent private houses and gardens.

## The Batignolles Cemetery and the Dog Cemetery

Right at the frontier of the 17$^e$ and Clichy, under the périphérique, lies the little-visited **Cimetière des Batignolles**, with the graves of André Breton, Verlaine and Blaise Cendrars (M° Porte-de-Clichy). A great deal more

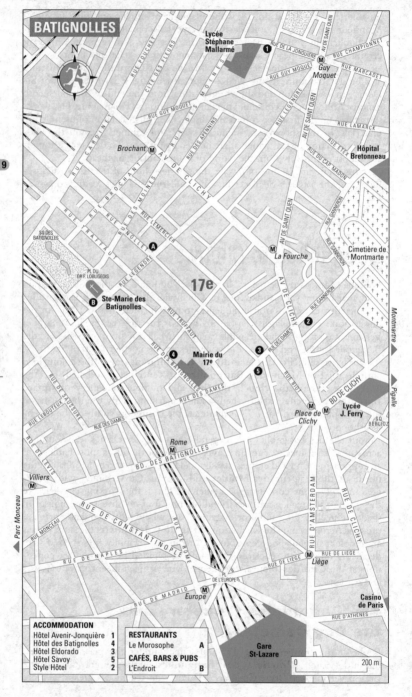

# BATIGNOLLES

N

Lycée Stéphane Mallarmé

Guy Moquet

Brochant

Hôpital Bretonneau

Cimetière de Montmartre

La Fourche

17e

Ste-Marie des Batignolles

Mairie du 17e

Place de Clichy

Lycée J. Ferry

SQ. BERLIOZ

Rome

BD. DES BATIGNOLLES

Villiers

Parc Monceau

Europe

Liège

Casino de Paris

Gare St-Lazare

Montmartre ▶

Pigalle ▶

SQ. DES BATIGNOLLES

PL. DU DR F. LOBLIGEOIS

PL. DE L'EUROPE

ACCOMMODATION
Hôtel Avenir-Jonquière     1
Hôtel des Batignolles      4
Hôtel Eldorado             3
Hôtel Savoy                5
Style Hôtel                2

RESTAURANTS
Le Morosophe               A

CAFÉS, BARS & PUBS
L'Endroit                  B

0          200 m

curious, and more lugubrious, is the **dog cemetery** (daily except Tues: mid-March to mid-Oct 10am–7pm, mid-Oct to mid-March 10am–5pm; €3; M°
Mairie-de-Clichy), on the banks of the Seine at Asnières, one métro stop
beyond Porte de Clichy. It's outside the city proper but accessible on the métro
line 13, about fifteen minutes' walk from M° Mairie-de-Clichy along rue
Martre, then left at the far end of Pont de Clichy. Privately owned, this
Cimetière des Chiens occupies a tree-shaded ridgelet that was once an island
in the river. Most of its tiny graves decked with plastic flowers, some going
back as far as 1900, belong to dogs and cats, many with epigraphs of the kind:
"To Fifi, the only consolation of my wretched existence". Among the more
exotic cadavers are a Muscovite bear, a wolf, a lioness, the 1920 Grand National
winner, and the French Rintintin, vintage 1933.

# St-Ouen market

The market is located on the northern edge of the 18e arrondissement in what
is the suburb of St-Ouen. It spreads between the **Porte de St-Ouen** and the
**Porte de Clignancourt**, with the bulk of the licensed markets closer to the
latter. The best métro stop is Porte-de-Clignancourt (métro line 4).

Officially open on Saturday, Sunday and Monday from 9am to 6.30pm –
although this can vary depending on the weather, and many stands are closed
on a Monday – the **puces de St-Ouen** claims to be the largest flea market in
the world, the name "flea" deriving from the state of the secondhand mattresses, clothes and other junk sold here when the market first operated in the
free-for-all zone outside the city walls. Nowadays, however, it's predominantly
a proper – and very expensive – **antiques** market, selling mainly furniture but
also such trendy "junk" as old café counters, telephones, traffic lights, posters,
juke-boxes and petrol pumps.

First impressions as you walk up the busy Porte de Clignancourt from the
métro stop are that there's nothing for sale but cheap jeans, leather jackets and
African souvenirs, whilst the Porte-de-St-Ouen métro approach brings you
past the dregs of secondhand merchandise. Between the two, along **rue Jean-
Henri-Fabre** and its continuation **rue du Dr Babinski**, just on the north
side of the périphérique, something of the old rag-and-bone element survives
alongside grey- and black-market imports, the modern-day equivalent. To the
tune of stall-holders' music systems, constant traffic noise and multinational
conversations, job-lots of batteries jostle with rip-off DVDs, household cleaning products with African labels, and endless stalls of shoddy clothing.

There are, however, twelve official markets within the complex. Marché
**Biron** – the poshest – Marché **Cambo**, Marché **Antica** and Marché **Malassis**
all sell serious and expensive antique furniture. Marché **Vernaison** – the oldest
– has the most diverse collection of old and new furniture and knick-knacks,
while Marché **Serpette** and Marché **des Rosiers** concentrate on twentieth-
century decorative pieces. The relatively new and swish Marché **Dauphine** has
mostly rather expensive furniture and furnishings, while Marché **Paul-Bert**,
offers all kinds of furniture, china, and the like. The shops in Marché **Malik**
stock mostly discount and vintage clothes, as well as some high-class couturier
stuff. Finally, there's Marché **Jules-Vallès** and Marché **Lécuyer-Vallès**, which
are the cheapest, most junk-like ... and most likely to throw up an unexpected
treasure.

It can be fun to wander around, but it's foolish to expect any bargains. In some ways the streets of St-Ouen beyond the market are just as interesting for the glimpse they give of a tempo of living long vanished from the city itself. Should hunger overtake you, there's a touristy *restaurant-buvette* in the centre of Marché Vernaison, *Chez Louisette*, where the great gypsy jazz guitarist, Django Reinhardt, sometimes played. There's also plenty of opportunity for snacks on rue Paul Bert and a good brasserie which serves huge salads.

# Eastern Paris

The **Canal St-Martin**, running from the Bastille in the south to the place de la Bataille de Stalingrad in the north, can be seen as marking the boundary between central and eastern Paris. The area east of the canal has traditionally been the home of the working classes, dating back to the establishment of the **Faubourg St-Antoine** as the workshop of the city in the fifteenth century. Later, during the Industrial Revolution in the mid-nineteenth century, the old villages of **Belleville**, **Ménilmontant** and **Charonne** were colonized by the French rural poor. These populations supplied the people-power for the insurrections of 1830, 1832, 1848 and 1851, and the short-lived Commune of 1871, which divided the city in two, with the centre and west battling to preserve the status quo against the oppressed and radical east. Indeed, for much of the nineteenth century, the establishment feared nothing more than the "descente de Belleville" – the descent from the heights of Belleville of the revolutionary mob. It was in order to contain this threat that so much of the Canal St-Martin, a natural line of defence, was covered over by **Baron Haussmann** in 1860.

Today, only a few reminders of these turbulent times survive, such as the *Mur des Fédérés* in **Père-Lachaise cemetery** recording the death of 147 Communards, the Bastille column, and a few streets bearing the names of popular leaders. Some of the old working-class character of the district lives on in places: narrow streets and artisans' houses survive in Belleville, Ménilmontant and off the Canal St-Martin, while rue du Faubourg-St-Antoine is still full of cabinet-makers and joiners. Much of the area, however, has undergone redevelopment over the last few decades. Crumbling, dank and insanitary houses were replaced by shelving-unit apartment blocks in the 60s and 70s, giving way in recent years to more imaginative and attractive constructions. In places, redevelopment has inevitably shifted older populations further out into the suburbs; the Canal St-Martin for example has now been colonized by the new arty and media intelligentsia. Elsewhere, particularly in Ménilmontant and the Oberkampf area, rents remain relatively low, attracting significant numbers of students and artists who have created a thriving, alternative bar scene. Further east, Belleville has been settled by sizeable **ethnic populations**, especially North Africans, Malians, Turks and Chinese, making it one of the most diverse areas of the city and an excellent place for sampling exotic cuisine.

As well as new housing development, Eastern Paris has also been the site of some of the city's most ambitious large-scale projects. North of Belleville, the old meat market area of **La Villette** is now a futuristic science museum and park, while down in the 12e much of the **Bercy** riverside area has been landscaped with a huge new park, and the old wine warehouses have been converted into shops and restaurants.

# The Canal St-Martin and around

Completed in 1825, the **Canal St-Martin** was built so that river traffic could shortcut the great western loop of the Seine around Paris. As it happened, it also turned out to be a splendid natural defence for the rebellious quarters of eastern Paris: the canal was spanned by six swing-bridges, which could easily be drawn up to halt the advance of government troops. Napoléon III's solution was simply to cover over the lower stretch in the latter half of the nineteenth century; the canal now runs underground at the Bastille, emerging after a mile and a half near the rue du Faubourg-du-Temple, and continuing up to the **place de la Bataille de Stalingrad**.

The northern reaches of the exposed canal still have a slightly industrial feel, but the southern part, along the **quai de Jemmapes** and **quai de Valmy** (M° Jacques-Bonsergent), has a great deal of charm, with plane trees lining the cobbled *quais,* and elegant high-arched footbridges punctuating the spaces between the locks, from where you can still watch the odd barge slowly rising or sinking to the next level. The bars, cafés and boutiques lining this stretch and the streets running off it have an alternative, bohemian feel, frequented by media types in black polo-necks. Inevitably, having acquired a certain cachet, the district has attracted property developers, and bland apartment blocks have elbowed in among the traditional, solid, mid-nineteenth-century residences. One of the older buildings, at 102 quai de Jemmapes, is the **Hôtel du Nord**, so named because the barges that once plied the canal came from the north, and made famous by Marcel Carné's film, starring Arletty and Jean Gabin. Its facade has been restored and it now thrives as a bar and bistrot. On the other side of the canal, in the **rue de la Grange-aux-Belles** (see box below), the name of *Le Pont-Tournant* (The Swing-Bridge) café recalls the canal's more vigorous youth. It's a lively area – on Sundays the *quais* are closed to traffic and given over to strollers, rollerbladers and cyclists, and in summer people hang out along the canal's edge and on the café terraces. There's a strong sense of community in the area too and local residents are very active in the preservation of their neighbourhood, the **square Villemin** gardens abutting the canal just above rue des Récollets being one successful instance.

Some of the side streets off this stretch of the canal are worth exploring, such as **rue des Vinaigriers**, a little south of the gardens, where a Second Empire shopfront bears fluted wooden pilasters crowned with capitals of grapes and a gilded Bacchus. Across the street, the surely geriatric Cercle National des Garibaldiens still has a meeting place, and at no. 35, Poursin has been making brass buckles since 1830.

## The Montfaucon gallows

Long ago, **rue de la Grange-aux-Belles**, on the north side of the Hôpital St-Louis, was a dusty track leading uphill, past fields, en route to Germany. Where no. 53 now stands, a path led to the top of a small hillock. Here, in 1325, on the king's orders, an enormous **gallows** was built, consisting of a plinth 6m high, on which stood sixteen stone pillars each 10m high. These were joined by chains, from which malefactors were hanged in clusters. They were left there until they disintegrated, by way of example, and they stank so badly that when the wind blew from the northeast they infected the nostrils of the still far-off city. The practice continued until the seventeenth century. Bones and other remains from the pit into which they were thrown were found during the building of a garage in 1954.

## Canal boat trips

A leisurely way of seeing the Canal St-Martin is the **boat trips** run by Canauxrama (reservations ℡01.42.39.15.00) between the Port de l'Arsenal, opposite 50 bd de la Bastille, 12ᵉ (M° Bastille), and the Bassin de la Villette, 13 quai de la Loire, 19ᵉ (M° Jaurès), north of the Canal St-Martin. Departing daily at 9.45am and 2.30pm from the Bastille and at 9.45am and 2.45pm from Bassin de la Villette, the ride lasts nearly three hours and costs €13. The more stylish **catamaran** of Paris-Canal also runs three-hour trips between the Musée d'Orsay, quai Anatole-France, 7ᵉ (RER Musée d'Orsay), and the Parc de la Villette (La Folie des Visites du Parc; M° Porte-de-Pantin); boats operate in both directions daily from the end of March to mid-November, leaving the museum at 9.30am, and the park at 2.30pm (reservations ℡01.42.40.96.97; €16, children €9). More information is available on ⓦwww.pariscanal.com. Both trips involve a rather spooky mile-and-a-half stretch underground along the covered-over part of the canal.

Just across the canal from here is one of the finest buildings in Paris, the early seventeenth-century **Hôpital St-Louis**, built in the same style as the **place des Vosges** (see p.107). Although it still functions as a hospital, you can walk into its quiet central courtyard and admire the elegant brick and stone facades and steep-pitched roofs that once sheltered Paris's plague victims – the original purpose for which it was built.

South of here, the wide boulevard built over the covered section of the canal, **Richard Lenoir**, has recently been attractively landscaped all along its centre, with arched footbridges dotted along, reminding you of the water flowing underground. It's worth a wander on Thursday and Saturday mornings in particular, when a traditional **food market**, known for its choice range of regional produce, sets up on the lower stretch, near the Bastille.

# Place de la Bataille de Stalingrad and Bassin de la Villette

The Canal St-Martin goes underground again at the **place de la Bataille de Stalingrad**, dominated by the Neoclassical **Rotonde de la Villette**, with portico and pediments surmounted by a rotunda. This was one of the toll houses designed by the architect Ledoux as part of Louis XVI's scheme to tax all goods entering the city. At that time, every road out of the city had a customs post, or *barrière*, linked by a six-metre-high wall, known as "Le Mur des Fermiers-Généraux" – a major irritant in the run-up to the French Revolution. Backing the toll house is an elegant aerial stretch of métro, supported by Neoclassical iron and stone pillars.

Beyond here the canal widens out into the **Bassin de la Villette**, built in 1808. The recobbled docks area today bears few traces of its days as France's premier port, its dockside buildings now offering **canal boat trips** (see p.350), and boasting a multiplex cinema, MK2 (see p.323), with a popular waterfront brasserie, *Le Rendez-Vous des Quais* (see p.305). On Sundays and holidays people stroll along the *quais*, play *boules*, fish or take a rowing boat out in the dock, but despite the clean-up, the area retains a slightly industrial and seedy feel.

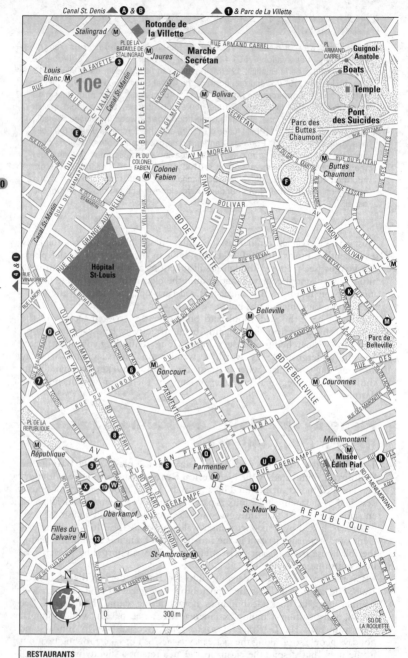

Canal St. Denis ▲ Ⓐ & Ⓑ   ▲ ❶ & Parc de La Villette

Rotonde de
la Villette

Stalingrad Ⓜ
PL DE LA
BATAILLE DE
STALINGRAD
RUE ARMAND CARREL

PL
ARMAND
CARREL

Guignol-
Anatole

Marché
Secrétan

❸ Jaures

● Boats

■ Temple

Louis
Blanc Ⓜ

10e

Ⓜ Bolivar

Parc des
Buttes
Chaumont

Pont
des Suicides

Ⓔ

PL DU
COLONEL
FABIEN

Colonel
Fabien
Ⓜ

Ⓕ

Buttes
Chaumont

BOLIVAR

Hôpital
St-Louis

BD DE LA VILLETTE

Belleville

Ⓜ

Ⓝ

RUE DE BELLEVILLE

Ⓚ

Ⓜ

Ⓞ

Ⓜ
Goncourt

❻

11e

Parc de
Belleville

❼

Ⓜ Couronnes

Ⓜ
République

PL DE LA
RÉPUBLIQUE

❽

Ménilmontant

Ⓡ

Ⓠ
Ⓢ

Parmentier
Ⓜ

Ⓥ

Ⓤ

Musée
Édith Piaf

❾

RUE OBERKAMPF

Ⓧ  Ⓦ
❿

❶❶

Ⓨ

Oberkampf
Ⓜ

St-Maur Ⓜ

RÉPUBLIQUE

Filles du
Calvaire
❸

St-Ambroise Ⓜ

N

0        300 m

SQ DE
LA ROQUETTE

## RESTAURANTS

| | | | | | | | |
|---|---|---|---|---|---|---|---|
| Astier | **S** | L'Homme Bleu | **Q** | Le Pacifique | **G** | Chez Prune | **O** |
| Restaurant de Bourgogne | **I** | Chez Jean | **P** | Au Pavillon Puebla | **F** | Aux Rendez-Vous des Amis | **Z** |
| Le Clown Bar | **Y** | Lao Siam | **H** | Pho-Dong-Huong | **N** | Au Rendez-Vous de la Marine | **A** |

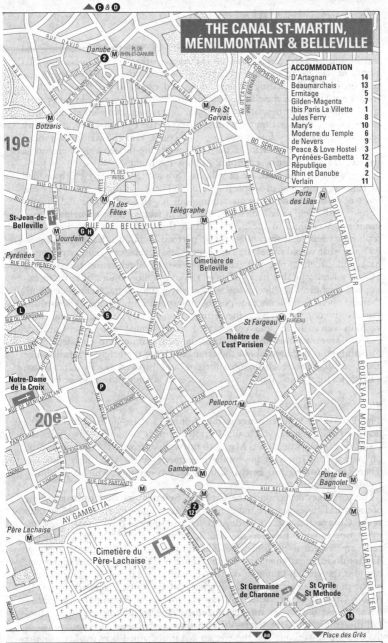

**ACCOMMODATION**

| | |
|---|---|
| D'Artagnan | 14 |
| Beaumarchais | 13 |
| Ermitage | 5 |
| Gilden-Magenta | 7 |
| Ibis Paris La Villette | 1 |
| Jules Ferry | 8 |
| Mary's | 10 |
| Moderne du Temple de Nevers | 6 |
| Peace & Love Hostel | 3 |
| Pyrénées-Gambetta | 12 |
| République | 4 |
| Rhin et Danube | 2 |
| Verlain | 11 |

Danube
PL DE RHIN-ET-DANUBE
Botzaris
19e
Pré St Gervais
Porte des Lilas
St-Jean-de-Belleville
Pl des Fêtes
Télégraphe
Pyrénées
Jourdain
Cimetière de Belleville
St Fargeau
PL ST FARGEAU
Théâtre de L'est Parisien
Notre-Dame de la Croix
20e
Pelleport
Gambetta
Porte de Bagnolet
Père Lachaise
Cimetière du Père-Lachaise
St Germaine de Charonne
St Cyrile St Methode
Place des Grès

**CAFÉS AND BARS**

| | | | | |
|---|---|---|---|---|
| Le Rendez-Vous des Quais | **B** | Aux Saveurs du Liban | **D** | Le Baratin | **K** | Cithéa | **U** | Lou Pascalou | **R** | L'Opus | **E** |
| Rital & Courts | **M** | Au Trou Normand | **X** | Le Blue Billard | **V** | La Flèche d'Or | **aa** | Café de la Musique | **C** | Le Vieux Belleville | **L** |
| | | Le Zéphyr | **J** | Café Charbon | **T** | Chez Imogène | **W** | | | |

# Parc de la Villette

All the meat for Paris used to come from **La Villette**. Slaughtering and butchering, and industries based on the meat markets' by-products, provided plenty of jobs for its dense population, whose recreation time was spent betting on cockfights, skating or swimming, and eating in the numerous local restaurants famed for their fresh meat. In the 1960s, vast sums of money were spent building a vast new abattoir. Yet, just as it neared completion, the emergence of new refrigeration techniques rendered the centralized meat industry redundant. The only solution was to switch course entirely: billions continued to be poured into La Villette in the 1980s, with the revised aim of creating a **music, art and science complex** to blow the mind.

The end result, the **Parc de la Villette** (ⓦ www.lavillette.fr), which opened in 1986, is enormous in scope and volume. There's so much going on here, most of it stimulating and entertaining, but it's all so disparate and disconnected, with such a clash of styles, that it can feel more overwhelming than inspiring. According to the park's creators, this is all intentional, and philosophically justified. It was conceived by Bernard Tschumi as a futuristic "activity" park that would dispel the eighteenth- and nineteenth-century notion of parks and gardens as places of gentle and well-ordered relaxation. Instead, we're offered a landscape that backs off from the old-fashioned idea of unity, meaning and purpose, that "deconstructs" the whole into its fragmented elements, thereby opening up numerous possible interpretations. Yet there's something vaguely disconcerting about the setting. The 900-metre straight **walkway**, with its wavy shelter and complicated metal bridge across the Canal de l'Ourcq, seems to insist that you cover the park from end to end, and there's something too dogmatic about the arrangement of the bright red **follies** like chopped-off cranes, each slightly different but all spaced exactly 120m apart. The park's focal point, the Cité des Sciences, is alarming for its sheer bulk.

## Visiting the park

The Parc de la Villette is **accessible** from M° Porte-de-la-Villette, at the northern end by avenue Corentin-Cariou and the Cité des Sciences; from the Canal de l'Ourcq's quai de la Marne to the west; or from M° Porte-de-Pantin, on avenue Jean-Jaurès, at the southern entrance by the Cité de la Musique. There's an **information centre** at the southern entrance, which should help you get your bearings.

The park's key attraction is the **Cité des Sciences et de l'Industrie**, one of the world's finest science museums. High-tech film experiences are on offer at the **Cinaxe** and at the **Géode**, and you can squeeze through the *Argonaute* submarine beached between the Cité and the Canal de l'Ourcq. Rock concerts are staged at the inflatable **Zénith** venue, and there's live music at **Trabendo** in one of the park's bright red follies. On sticky summer nights you can join the crowds lounging on the acres of grass known as "prairies" for a movie in the open air (part of the Festival du Cinéma en Plein Air; see p.324). At the **Cité de la Musique** you can hear the latest experimental compositions, or visit the superb **music museum**. Plays are performed in the nineteenth-century **Théâtre Paris-Villette**, dwarfed between the western half of the Cité de la Musique and the elegant old iron-framed beef market hall, the **Grande Halle**, venue for large-scale art and trade shows. You'll find all the park's films, exhibitions, concerts and plays detailed in *Pariscope* (see p.22). Additional draws for children include the **dragon slide** of recycled drums and pipes; **gardens** of "mirrors", "mists", "winds and dunes" and "islands"; other areas with trampolines, sounds, bamboos and vines; and a "prairie" where a giant bicycle appears half buried in the ground. See p.363 of "Kids' Paris" for more information.

# The Cité des Sciences et de l'Industrie

The park's dominant building is the enormous **Cité des Sciences et de l'Industrie** (Tues–Sat 10am–6pm, Sun 10am–7pm; €7.50 includes admission to Explora, temporary exhibitions and the Louis-Lumière 3D Cinema; ⓦwww.cite-sciences.fr; M° Porte-de-la-Villette), an abandoned abattoir redesigned by architect Adrien Fainsilber and transformed into a high-tech museum. Four times the size of the Pompidou Centre, from the outside it appears fortress-like, despite the transparency of its giant glass walls beneath a dark blue lattice of steel, reinforced by walkways that accelerate out towards the Géode across a moat level with the underground floors. Once you are inside, however, the solidity of first impressions is totally reversed by the **three themes** of water (around the building), vegetation (in three greenhouses) and light – with which the building is flooded, from vast skylights as well as the glass facade.

This is the science museum to end all science museums, and worth visiting for the interior of the building alone: all glass and stainless steel, crow's-nests and cantilevered platforms, bridges and suspended walkways, the different levels linked by lifts and escalators around a huge central space open to the full 40m height of the roof. It may be colossal, but you are more likely to lose yourself mentally rather than physically, and come out after several hours reeling with images and ideas about DNA, quasars, bacteria reproduction, curved space or rocket launching. Entry to the building itself is free, as are some of the facilities within – the cafés, aquarium, médiathèques, and viewing of documentaries (in French) in the Salle Jean-Bertin and the Salle Jean-Painlevé. The ticket for Explora (the permanent exhibition) is valid all day, but for four entries only.

An **audioguide in English** is available at the counter in the main hall (€3.80), and includes details about the architecture, explanations for Explora and the soundtrack for some of the planetarium shows (2pm, 3pm, 4pm & 5pm). It's recommended if you want to make the most of the museum, unless your French is very good. For details of the **Cité des Enfants** and temporary exhibitions geared to kids (for which you have to be accompanied by a child), see p.363.

The exhibition space, **Explora**, is ranged across the top two floors (pick up a detailed plan in English from the welcome desk on *niveau* 1) and includes both temporary shows and a permanent exhibition divided into twenty units. These cover a variety of subjects, among them sound, robots, computer science, expression and behaviour, oceans, energy, light, the environment, mathematics, medicine, space and language. As the name suggests, the emphasis is on exploring, and the means used are interactive computers, multi-media displays, videos, holograms, animated models and games.

On **level 1**, a classic example of chaos theory introduces the **maths section**: La Fontaine Turbulente is a wheel of glasses rotating below a stream of water in which the switch between clockwise and anticlockwise motion is unpredictable beyond two minutes. An "inertial carousel" – a revolving drum (2–6pm only) – provides a four-minute insight into the strange transformations of objects in motion. In **Les Sons** (sounds), you can watch a video of an

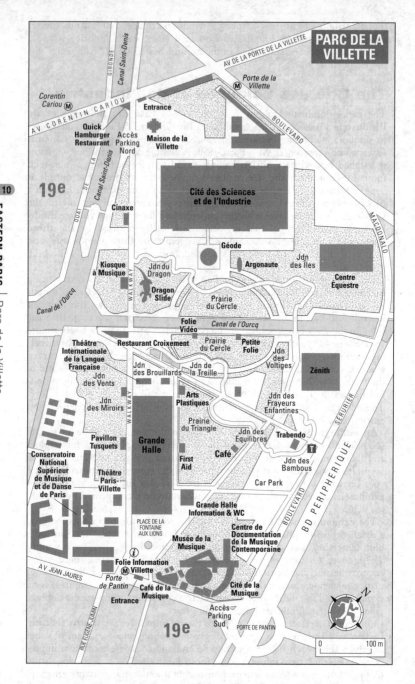

# PARC DE LA VILLETTE

AV DE LA PORTE DE LA VILLETTE

Canal Saint-Denis

GIRONDE

Porte de la Villette Ⓜ

BOULEVARD

Corentin Cariou Ⓜ

AV CORENTIN CARIOU

Entrance

Quick Hamburger Restaurant

Accès Parking Nord

Maison de la Villette

Canal Saint-Denis

QUAI DE LA

19e

Cité des Sciences et de l'Industrie

Cinaxe

MACDONALD

Géode

Kiosque à Musique

Jdn du Dragon

Argonaute

Jdn des Îles

Centre Équestre

WALKWAY

Dragon Slide

Prairie du Cercle

Canal de l'Ourcq

Folie Vidéo

Canal de l'Ourcq

Théâtre Internationale de la Langue Française

Restaurant Croixement

Prairie du Cercle

Petite Folie

Jdn des Voltiges

Zénith

Jdn des Vents

Jdn des Brouillards

Jdn de la Treille

Jdn des Miroirs

Arts Plastiques

Jdn des Frayeurs Enfantines

WALKWAY

Prairie du Triangle

Jdn des Équilibres

Trabendo

T

Pavillon Tusquets

Grande Halle

First Aid

Café

Jdn des Bambous

Conservatoire National Supérieur de Musique et de Danse de Paris

Théâtre Paris-Villette

Car Park

SÉRURIER

BOULEVARD PERIPHERIQUE

BD PERIPHERIQUE

PLACE DE LA FONTAINE AUX LIONS

Grande Halle Information & WC

Centre de Documentation de la Musique Contemporaine

Musée de la Musique

ⓘ Folie Information

Ⓜ Villette

AV JEAN JAURES

Porte de Pantin

Café de la Musique

Cité de la Musique

Entrance

19e

Accès Parking Sud

PORTE DE PANTIN

RUE EUGENE-JUMIN

N

0        100 m

x-rayed jaw and throat talking or sit in a cubicle and feel your body tingle with physical sensations as a rainstorm crashes around you. In **Expressions et Comportements**, you can take part in interactive videos, changing the behaviour of the characters to engineer a different outcome, and you can watch an "Odorama" video. In **Computers**, you can steer robots through mazes, make music by your own movements, try out a flight simulation, or watch computer-guided puppet shows and holograms of different eras' visions of the universe.

On **level 2**, in the **biology section**, you can examine microbes magnified millions of times. In the **medicine section**, smell the herbs used by different cultures as alternative remedies. In **Etoiles et Galaxies**, explore large-scale models of space rockets and space stations and a real Mirage jet fighter. The **Jeux de Lumière** is a whole series of experiments to do with colour, optical illusions, refraction and the like. You can have your head spun further by a session in the **planetarium** (shows 11am, noon, 2pm, 3pm, 4pm & 5pm; 35min; €2.50).

Back on the ground floor, the **Cinéma Louis-Lumière** shows short stereoscopic (3D) films every half hour or so, for which you'll have to queue. General documentaries in French only are shown in the **Salle Jean-Bertin** (programmes at 10.15am, 2.15pm & 4.15pm; free), and more serious scientific documentaries in the **Salle Jean-Painlevé** (*niveau* S1; Sat & Sun 4pm & 5.30pm; free). In the **Médiathèque** (S1 & S2; noon–6.45pm; free), a multimedia library, you can select from over 4000 films at individual consoles, as well as consult educational software, books and magazines. Information on current French and international scientific research is displayed in the **Salle Science Actualités** (S1), next door to the **Cité des Métiers** (noon–6pm; free), the latter of which provides free access to information on finding work, changing careers, training, creating your own employment, and working conditions in different countries. It even offers an on-the-spot consultancy with a careers advisor. Finally, on the lowest floor (S2), you can eat and drink beside an **aquarium** filled with Mediterranean sea life.

## The Géode, the Cinaxe and the Argonaute

In front of the museum complex floats the **Géode** (hourly shows 10.30am–9.30pm, till 7.30pm on Sun, closed Mon; €8.75; Ⓦwww.lageode.fr), a bubble of reflecting steel dropped from an intergalactic boules game into a pool of water that ripples with the mirrored image of the Cité. Inside, the sphere holds a screen for Omnimax 180° films, not noted for their plots but a great visual experience. Or there's the **Cinaxe**, between the Cité and the Canal St-Denis (screenings every 15min 11am–1pm & 2–5pm, closed Mon; €5.20 or €4.50 with Explora ticket) combining 70mm film shot at thirty frames a second with seats that move, so that a bobsleigh ride down the Cresta Run, for example, not only looks unbelievably real, but feels it, too. You can clamber around a real 1957 French military **submarine** beside the Géode, the *Argonaute* (Mon–Fri 10.30am–5.30pm, Sat & Sun 11am–6pm; €3), and view the park through its periscope.

## The Cité de la Musique

Crossing the Canal de L'Ourcq south of the Géode, a walkway leads past the Grande Salle to the **Cité de la Musique** (Ⓦwww.cite-musique.fr), in two complexes either side of the Porte-de-Pantin entrance. To the west the waves and funnels, irregular polygons and non-parallel lines of the Conservatoire de Paris, the city's music school, make abstract sense: windows in sequences like musical notation; the wavy roof, which, according to the architect, **Christian de Portzamparc**, is like a Gregorian chant, but could equally suggest the movement of a dancer or a conductor's baton; and the crescendo of the rising curves of the facade.

The wedge-shaped complex to the east contains the public spaces, which include the excellent Musée de la Musique, the chic *Café de la Musique* (see review on p.306), a music and dance information centre, and a concert hall whose ovoid dome rises like a perfect soufflé from the roof line. The harsh semi-exterior element of a girdered "arrow" pointing down to the entrance arch pretending to be another red folly hides an unexpectedly sensual interior. A glass-roofed arcade spirals round the auditorium, the combination of pale-blue walls, a subtly sloping floor and the height to the ceiling creating a sense of calm and uplift.

### The Musée de la Musique

The **Musée de la Musique** (Tues–Sat noon–6pm, Sun 10am–6pm; €6.10; M° Porte-de-Pantin) presents the history of music from the end of the Renaissance to the present day, both visually, exhibiting some 4500 instruments, and aurally, via headsets (available in English; free) and interactive displays. Glass case after glass case hold gleaming, beautiful instruments – jewel-inlaid, crystal flutes and a fabulous lyre-guitar, all made in Paris in the early 1800s, are some impressive examples. The instruments are presented in the context of a key work in the history of Western music: as you step past each case, the headphones are programmed to emit a short scholarly narration, followed by a delightful concert. It's a truly transporting – and educational – experience to gaze at the grouping of harps, made in Paris between 1760 and 1900, and hear an excerpt of music as heavenly as the instruments you're looking at.

The museum also includes an **auditorium**, where regular concerts are held, in addition to a huge archive of documents and sound recordings, and spaces for workshops, films and audiovisuals.

# Belleville, Ménilmontant and Charonne

The old villages of **Belleville**, **Ménilmontant** and **Charonne**, only incorporated into the city in 1860, are strung out along the western slopes of a ridge that rises steadily from the Seine at Bercy to an altitude of 128m near Belleville's place des Fêtes, the highest point in Paris after Montmartre. The area is fairly run-down and even a bit dodgy in places, but there are pockets of charm here and it's home to what is probably one of the most diverse populations in the city: a mix of traditional working class, various ethnic communities, and a good number of students and artists – Ménilmontant in particular hosts quite an alternative scene with some good bars. The quickest and easiest way to get out here is to take a trip on the #26 **bus** from the Gare du Nord, getting on and off at strategic points along the **avenue de Simon–Bolivar** and **rue des Pyrénées**, which between them run the whole length of the ridge to Porte de Vincennes.

A good place to start a tour of the area is the **Parc des Buttes-Chaumont**, north of the Belleville heights. It was constructed under Haussmann in the

## Claude Chappe and the rue du Télégraphe

The rue du Télégraphe, running south off the eastern end of rue de Belleville along-side the Cimetière de Belleville, is named in memory of Claude Chappe's invention of the **optical telegraph**. Chappe first tested his device here in September 1792, in a corner of the cemetery. When word of his activities got out, he was nearly lynched by a mob that assumed he was trying to signal to the king, who was at that time imprisoned in the Temple (see p.110). Eventually, two lines were set up, from Belleville to Strasbourg and the east, and from Montmartre to Lille and the north. By 1840, it was possible to send a message to Calais in three minutes, via 27 relays, and to Strasbourg in seven minutes, using 46 relays. Chappe himself did not live to see the fruits of his invention: his patent was contested in 1805, and distraught, he threw himself into a sewer (his grave is in nearby Père-Lachaise).

1860s to camouflage what until then had been a desolate warren of disused quarries, rubbish dumps and shacks. Out of this rather unlikely setting, a fairy-tale-like park was created – there's a grotto with a cascade and artificial stalactites, and a picturesque lake from which a huge rock rises up, topped with a delicate Corinthian temple. You can cross the lake via a suspension bridge, or take the shorter **Pont des Suicides**. This, according to Louis Aragon, the literary grand old man of the French Communist Party, "before metal grills were erected along its sides, claimed victims even from passers-by who had had no intention whatsoever of killing themselves but were suddenly tempted by the abyss . . ." (*Le Paysan de Paris*). From the temple you get fine views of the Sacré-Cœur and beyond, and you can also go boating on the lake. The park stays open all night and, equally rarely for Paris, you're not cautioned off the grass.

# Belleville

East of the parc des Buttes-Chaumont, between rue de Crimée and **place de Rhin-et-Danube**, dozens of cobbled and gardened *villas* lead off from rue Miguel-Hidalgo, rue du Général-Brunet, rue de la Liberté, rue de l'Égalité and rue de Mouzaïa. It is so light and airy here, you wonder why places like Auteuil and Passy should ever have seemed so much more desirable. Heading south, you meet the main street **rue de Belleville**. Close to its highest point is the **place des Fêtes**, still with a market, though no longer so festive. Once the village green, it's now surrounded by concrete tower blocks and shopping parades, a terrible monument to the unimaginative redevelopment of the 1960s and 1970s. The little *place* is green nonetheless, containing a small park with a rotunda, lawns and trees, its benches filled with locals on a pleasant day. As you descend the steepening gradient of rue Belleville, round the church of St-Jean-Baptiste-de-Belleville, among the boulangeries and charcuteries, you could be in the busy main street of any French provincial town. Continuing down rue de Belleville past rue des Pyrénées, at the corner of **rue Julien-Lacroix**, you come to a square that has been created from an empty lot. On the side of one of the exposed apartment building walls, there's a large mural of a detective and nearby the neo-realist artist Ben has sculpted a trompe-l'œil sculpture of a sign being erected which says "*Il faut se méfier des mots*" ("Words must be mistrusted").

Below rue des Pyrénées, bits of old Belleville remain – dilapidated – alongside the new. On the wall of no. 72 rue de Belleville, a plaque commemorates the birth of the legendary chanteuse, **Édith Piaf**, although she was in fact found abandoned as a baby on the steps here.

## La descente de la Courtille

The name *Courtille* comes from *courti*, "garden" in the Picard dialect. The heights of Belleville were known as **La Haute Courtille** in the nineteenth century, while the lower part around rue du Faubourg-du-Temple and rue de la Fontaine-au-Roi was **La Basse Courtille**. Both were full of boozers and dance halls, where people flocked from the city on high days and holidays.

The wildest revels of the year took place on the night of Mardi Gras, when thousands of masked people turned out to celebrate the end of the *carnaval*. Next morning – Ash Wednesday – they descended in drunken procession from Belleville to the city, in up to a thousand horse-drawn vehicles: *la descente de la Courtille*.

A little lower off rue de Belleville, the cobbled **rue Piat** climbs past the beautiful wrought-iron gate of the jungly **Villa Otoz** to the **Parc de Belleville**, created in the mid-1990s. From the terrace at the junction with rue des Envierges, there's a fantastic view across the city, especially at sunset. At your feet, the small park descends in a series of more terraces and waterfalls – a total success compared to the nondescript development of the previous decade. Inevitably, this has not been lost on restaurateurs and several upscale eateries have opened their doors in the area, a possible sign of change to come.

Continuing straight ahead, a path crosses the top of the park past a minuscule vineyard and turns into steps that drop down to **rue des Couronnes**. Some of the adjacent streets are worth a wander for a feel of the changing times – rue de la Mare, rue des Envierges, rue des Cascades – with two or three beautiful old houses in overgrown gardens, alongside new housing that follows the height and curves of the streets and *passages* between them.

Between the bottom of the park and boulevard de Belleville, original housing and a teeming street life have been all but erased, despite the concerted efforts of the local organization for the preservation of Belleville, who fought hard for restoration rather than demolition and for saving the little cafés, restaurants and shops that gave the quartier its life. Rue Ramponeau, running west from the Parc de Belleville, has a historic record of resistance: at the junction with rue de Tourtille, the very last barricade of the Commune was defended single-handedly for fifteen minutes by the last fighting Communard, before he melted away – to write a book about it all (see p.398).

It's also in these streets and on the boulevard that the strong **ethnic diversity** of Belleville becomes apparent. Rue Ramponeau, for example, is still full of kosher shops, belonging to Sephardic Jews from Tunisia. Around the crossroads of rue du Faubourg-du-Temple and boulevard de Belleville, there are dozens of Chinese restaurants and a scattering of restaurants owned by Turks, Greeks and East Europeans. On the boulevard, especially during the Tuesday and Friday morning market, you see women from Mali, Gambia and Zaire, often wearing local dress, and men in burnouses. All this diversity is reflected in the produce on sale.

The boulevard is lined with dramatic new architecture, employing jutting triangles, curves, and the occasional reference to the roof lines of nineteenth-century Parisian blocks. The combination of old and new continues in **Basse Belleville**, in the large triangle of streets below boulevard de Belleville, bounded by rue du Faubourg-du-Temple (the most lively) and avenue de la République. The area retains a blend of French and immigrant workshops, small businesses, and traditional houses built with *passages* burrowing into courtyards. Here, *La Java*, at 105 rue du Faubourg-du-Temple, was a favourite hangout of Piaf's in its *bal musette* days; the original dance hall interior is still intact, but the dancing and music are now distinctly Latino. Zany high-tech metal and glass at no. 117 on the same street co-exists with small, unchanged business premises in the Cour des Bretons. Goods still cost around half the price as those in shops in the centre of the city, despite a number of increasingly fashionable restaurants.

## Ménilmontant

Like Belleville, **Ménilmontant** aligns itself along one straight, steep, long street, the **rue de Ménilmontant** and its lower extension **rue Oberkampf**. Although seedy and dilapidated in parts, its popularity with students and artists has brought a cutting-edge vitality to the area. Alternative shops and trendy bars and restaurants have sprung up among the grocers and cheap hardware stores, especially along rue Oberkampf, which now hosts a vibrant bar scene: some of the most popular hangouts are *Café Charbon* (see p.306), a renovated dance hall, the nearby *Cithéa* club (see p.306) and *Le Mécano*. The upper reaches of rue de Ménilmontant, above rue Sorbier, are quieter, and looking back, you find yourself dead in line with the rooftop of the Pompidou Centre, a measure of how high you are above the rest of the city.

Like Belleville itself, the area closest to boulevard Belleville has been almost completely demolished and rebuilt – on a small scale, around courtyards with open spaces for kids to play. Centred on rue des Amandiers, this part of Ménilmontant suffers the very odd fate of being a bit too squeaky-clean and unweathered as yet, and the café count has dropped to near zero. **Rue Elisa-Borey** turns into steps alongside the extraordinary France Telecom building, topped with great bunches of masts, which faces a lovely small park on rue Sorbier.

Cross the park, take a right, then a left into rue Boyer, and you'll find the splendid mosaic and sculpted constructivist facade of **La Bellevilloise** at no. 25,

### The bygone eastern villages

Before redevelopment, the superb hillside location combined with cobbled lanes, individual gardens, numerous stairways, and local shops and cafés perfectly integrated with human-scale housing, gave the area around Belleville and Ménilmontant a unique charm – quite the equal of Montmartre, but without the touristy commercialism.

For a picture of what it was like, there's no more evocative record than Willy Ronis's atmospheric photographs in *Belleville Ménilmontant* (see p.401). But there's still on-the-ground evidence, in addition to the little cul-de-sacs of terraced houses and gardens east of rue des Pyrénées. There are alleys so narrow that nothing but the knife-grinder's tricycle could fit down them, like **passage de la Duée**, 17 rue de la Duée, and little detached houses, like 97 rue Villiers-de-l'Isle-Adam. You can also see the less romantic side of life in the grim neo-Gothic fortress housing estates of 140 rue de Ménilmontant, built in 1925 for the influx of rural populations after World War I, and the 1913 Villa Stendhal, off rue Stendhal, east of the southern section of rue des Pyrénées, in the Charonne area. In marked contrast is the housing right over to the east, near the Porte de Bagnolet, provided for workers in 1908 and almost unmatched in the city. From place Octave-Chanute, wide stone steps bordered by lanterns lead up to a miraculous little sequence of streets of terraced houses and gardens, some with Art Nouveau glass porches, fancy brickwork and the shade of lilac and cherry trees.

built for the PCF in 1925 to celebrate fifty years of work and science. Saved from demolition by a preservation order, it is now home to a theatre school.

A short way before it, a delightful lane of village houses and gardens, **rue Laurence-Savart**, climbs up to rue du Retrait. The latter street ends on rue des Pyrénées opposite the poetically named alley of sighs, the "*passage des Soupirs*". **Rue des Pyrénées**, the main cross-route through this *quartier*, is itself redolent of the provinces, getting busier as it approaches place Gambetta. The post office at no. 248 has a big ceramic wall-piece by the sculptor Zadkine. Close by place Gambetta, on rue Malte-Brun, is the glass frontage of the **Théâtre National de la Colline**, built in 1987 to replace the dingy old cinema that used to house the theatre. You can snack in its **cafeteria** and pick up brochures on current productions.

Just 200m west of the place Gambetta is the Père-Lachaise cemetery (see opposite). There's more melancholy to be found near the northwest corner of the cemetery, where the **street names** echo the long-vanished orchards and rustic pursuits of the villagers: Amandiers (almond trees), Pruniers (plum trees), Mûriers (mulberry trees), Pressoir (wine press). Further west, across boulevard de Ménilmontant, another era is captured in the **Musée Édith Piaf**, at 5 rue Crespin-du-Gast (Mon–Thurs 1–6pm; closed Sept; admission by appointment only on ☎01.43.55.52.72; donation; M° Ménilmontant & M° St-Maur). Piaf was not an acquisitive person: the few clothes (yes, a little black dress), letters, toys, paintings and photographs that she left are almost all here, along with every one of her recordings. The venue is a small flat lived in by her devoted friend Bernard Marchois, and the "Amis d'Édith Piaf" will show you around and tell you stories about her life.

# Charonne

With its perfect little Romanesque church, St-Germain-de-Charonne, and the cobbled street of rue St-Blaise, Charonne retains its village-like atmosphere. To get to this unexpected and little-visited corner of the city, take the southwest radial, avenue du Père-Lachaise from place Gambetta, and then turn left along rue des Rondeaux, the street that follows the Père-Lachaise cemetery wall, past some very desirable residences. Cross rue des Pyrénées by the bridge in rue Renouvier, turn right on rue Stendhal (Villa Stendhal is opposite – see box on p.193) past the underground reservoir that serves as a gigantic header tank for the stopcocks that wash the city's gutters, and go down the steps at the end to rue de Bagnolet. Alternatively, take rue Lisfranc off rue Stendhal and right on rue des Prairies then straight on to rue de Bagnolet. It's a longer way round, but **rue des Prairies** has excellent examples of sensitive and imaginative housing developments. The new buildings have a pleasing variety of designs and colours, with bright tiling and ochre shades of cladding.

In place St-Blaise stands **St-Germain-de-Charonne** (M° Porte de Bagnolet & M° Gambetta), which has changed little, and its Romanesque belfry not at all, since the thirteenth century. It's one of only two Paris churches to have its own graveyard (the other is St-Pierre in Montmartre) – several hundred Communards were buried after being accidentally disinterred during the construction of a reservoir in 1897. Elsewhere in Paris, charnel houses were the norm, with the bones emptied into the catacombs as more space was required. It was not until the nineteenth century that public cemeteries appeared on the scene, the most famous being **Père-Lachaise** (see opposite).

Opposite the church, the old cobbled village high street, **rue St-Blaise**, pedestrianized to place des Grés, was one of the most picturesque in Paris, until it was prettified further, the face-lift removing much of its charm. Beyond place des Grés, everything has been rebuilt, and though an avenue of green trees has softened the hard new edges of the modern housing development, the line of shops (including a supermarket) are characterless as are the few cafés. Rue de Vitruve, however, which crosses rue St-Blaise at place des Grés, has a great modern swimming pool and the colourful *D'Artagnan* youth hostel just to the north (see p.268 for details); and to the south, at no. 39, a school, built in 1982. Designed by Jacques Bardet, the school's rectangular mass is broken up by open-air segments, enclosed only by the structural steel lattice of the building over which plants spread. But the best thing is hidden round the corner, visible as you approach from rue des Pyrénées – a huge sculptured **salamander** and its footprints mounted on the windowless side of a building on rue R.A. Marquet. Engraved above the street sign are the words: "A legend is told that a salamander, after passing by the square where it would have left a long trail, set off towards rue R.A. Marquet and stopped to rest on a corner of rue Vitruve."

# Père-Lachaise cemetery

Final resting place of a host of French notables, as well as a fair few foreigners, **Père-Lachaise** (Mon–Fri 8am–5.30pm, Sat 8.30am–5.30pm, Sun 9am–5.30pm; free; M° Père-Lachaise/Phillipe-Auguste) is sited on a hill commanding grand views of Paris and sprawls across some 116 acres, making it one of the world's largest cemeteries. In fact, it's a bit like a miniature town in itself with its grid-like layout, signposts and neat cobbled lanes – a veritable "city of the dead". Size aside, it's surely also one of the most atmospheric cemeteries – an eerily beautiful haven, with terraced slopes and magnificent old trees that spread their branches over the moss-grown tombs as though shading them from the outside world.

Finding individual graves can be a tricky business. The **map** below and the free plans given out at the entrance will point you in the right direction, but it's worth buying a slightly more detailed map as it's easy to get lost; the best one is published by Éditions Métropolitain Paris (around €2) and should be available in the newsagents and florists near the **main entrance** on boulevard de Ménilmontant.

Père-Lachaise was opened in 1804 and turned out to be an incredibly successful piece of land speculation. Nicolas Frochot, the urban planner who bought the land, persuaded the civil authorities to have **Molière**, **La Fontaine**, **Abélard** and **Héloïse** reburied in his new cemetery, and to be interred in Père-Lachaise quickly became the ultimate status symbol for the rich and successful. Ironically, Frochot even sold a plot to the original owner for considerably more money than the price he had paid for the entire site. Even today, the rates are extremely high.

Among the most visited graves is that of **Chopin** (Division 11), who has a willowy muse mourning his loss and is often attended by groups of Poles laying wreaths and flowers in the red and white colours of the Polish flag. Many other musicians repose nearby, among them Bellini, Cherubini, the violinist Kreutzer, whose commemorative column leans precariously to one side, and the more recently deceased French jazz pianist, Michel Petrucciani. **Rossini** is honoured with a spot on the avenue principale, though in fact his remains have been transferred to his native Italy. Swarms also flock to the grave of ex-Doors

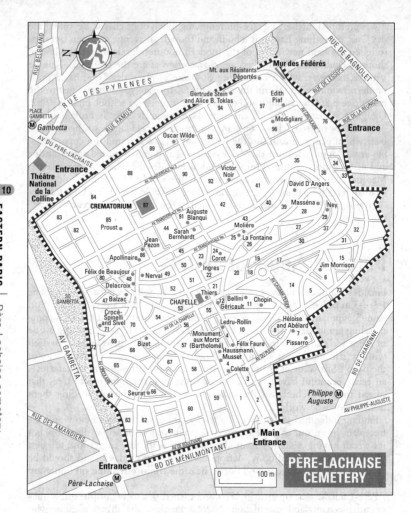

PÈRE-LACHAISE CEMETERY

lead singer **Jim Morrison** (Division 6), who died in Paris at the age of 28. Once graffiti-covered and wreathed in marijuana fumes, it has been cleaned up and put under police guard to ensure it stays that way, though this hasn't stopped fans scribbling messages in praise of love and drugs on other tombs, and trees, nearby.

Some of the most celebrated dead have unremarkable tombs, while those whose fame died with them have the most expressive monuments. Femme fatale **Colette**'s tomb, close to the main entrance in Division 4, for example, is very plain, though always covered in flowers. The same holds true for the divine **Sarah Bernhardt**'s (Division 44) and the great chanteuse **Édith Piaf**'s (Division 97). **Marcel Proust** lies in his family's black-marble, conventional tomb (Division 85). Just across the way is the rather incongruous-looking **Crematorium** (Division 87), crudely modelled on the Aghia Sophia in Istanbul, with domes and minarets. Here among others of equal or lesser renown lie the ashes of Max Ernst, Georges Pérec and American dancer Isadora Duncan, who was strangled when her scarf got tangled in the rear axle of her open-top car.

In contrast to these modest monuments, in Division 48 a now-forgotten French diplomat, Félix de Beaujour, is marked with an enormous tower, around 140 feet high (opinions differ on whether the sculptor's intention was a lighthouse, a giant phallus or a contemporary take on an Etruscan obelisk). To the north in Division 86, one **Jean Pezon**, a lion-tamer, is shown riding the pet lion that ate him. In Division 71, two men lie together hand in hand – Crocé-Spinelli and Sivel, a pair of balloonists who went so high they died from lack of oxygen. In Division 92, journalist **Victor Noir** – shot at the age of 22 in 1870 by Prince Napoleon for daring to criticize him – is portrayed at the moment of death, flat on his back, fully clothed, his top hat fallen by his feet. However it's not as a magnet for anti-censorship campaigners that his tomb has become famous, but as a lucky charm – a prominent part of his anatomy has been worn shiny by the touch of infertile women, hoping for a cure.

Other bed scenes include **Félix Faure** (Division 4), French president, who died in the arms of his mistress in the Élysée palace in 1899; draped in a French flag, his head to one side, he cuts rather a romantic figure. **Géricault** reclines on cushions of stone (Division 12), paint palette in hand, his face taut with concentration; below is a sculpted relief of part of his best-known painting *The Raft of the Medusa*. Close by is the relaxed figure of **Jean Carriès**, a model-maker, in felt hat and overalls, holding a self-portrait in the palm of his hand. For a more fearsome view of death, there's the tomb of a French judge, **Raphaël Roger**, in Division 94, where a figure, cowled from head to foot, stands sentinel beneath a pointed arch; or the poet in Division 6, bursting out of his granite block.

Painter **Corot** (Division 24) and novelist **Balzac** (Division 48) both have fine busts; Balzac set the final tragic scene of his novel *Père Goriot* in Père Lachaise. One of the most impressive of the individual tombs, the base of which is usually covered in lipstick kisses, is **Oscar Wilde's** (Division 89), topped with a sculpture by Jacob Epstein of a mysterious Pharaonic winged messenger (sadly vandalized of its once prominent member, which was last seen being used as a paper weight by the director of the cemetery). The inscription behind is a grim verse from *The Ballad of Reading Gaol*.

Approaching Oscar Wilde's grave from the centre of the cemetery, you pass the tomb of **Auguste Blanqui** (Division 91), after whom so many French streets are named. Described by Karl Marx as the nineteenth century's greatest revolutionary, he served his time in jail – 33 years in all – for political activities that spanned the 1830 Revolution to the Paris Commune.

South from Blanqui's and Wilde's graves, in Division 96, you'll find the grave of **Modigliani** and his lover **Jeanne Herbuterne**, who killed herself in crazed grief a few days after he died in agony from meningitis. **Laura Marx**, Karl's daughter, and her husband **Paul Lafargue**, who committed suicide together in 1911, also lie in this southeast corner of the cemetery (Division 76).

It is the monuments to the collective, violent deaths, however, that have the power to change a sunny outing to Père-Lachaise into a much more sombre experience. In Division 97, you'll find the memorials to the **victims of the Nazi concentration camps**, to executed **Resistance fighters** and to those who were never accounted for in the genocide of World War II. The sculptures are relentless in their images of inhumanity, of people forced to collaborate in their own degradation and death.

Finally, marking one of the bloodiest episodes in French history, there is the **Mur des Fédérés** (Division 76), the wall where the last troops of the Paris Commune were lined up and shot in the final days of the battle in 1871. The man who ordered their execution, **Adolphe Thiers**, lies in the centre of the cemetery in Division 55.

# Down to the Faubourg St-Antoine

The principal thoroughfares running from Père–Lachaise back to the Bastille are **rue de la Roquette** and **rue de Charonne**. There's nothing particularly special about the numerous *passages* and ragged streets that lead off these into the lower 11<sup>e</sup> arrondissement, except that they are utterly Parisian, with the odd detail of a building, the obscurity of a shop's speciality, the display of vegetables in a greengrocer's, or the graffiti on a Second Empire street fountain to charm an aimless wanderer. Plus the occasional reminder of the sheer political toughness of French working-class tradition, as in the plaque on some flats in **rue de la Folie-Regnault** commemorating the first FTP (Francs-Tireurs Partisans) Resistance group, which used to meet here until it was betrayed and its members executed in 1941. Further north, **square de la Roquette** was the site of an old prison, where 4000 members of the Resistance were incarcerated in 1944. The low, forbidding gateway on rue de la Roquette has been preserved in their memory.

South of rue de Charonne, between rue St-Bernard and impasse Charrière, stands the rustic-looking **church of Ste-Marguerite** (Mon–Sat 8am–noon & 3–7.30pm, Sun 8.30am–noon & 5–7.30pm; M° Charonne), with a garden beside it dedicated to the memory of Raoul Nordling, the Swedish consul who persuaded the retreating Germans not to blow up Paris in 1944. The church itself was built in 1624 to accommodate the growing population of the faubourg, which was about 40,000 in 1710 and 100,000 in 1900. The sculptures on the transept pediments were made by its first full-blown parish priest. The inside of the church is wide-bodied, low and quiet, with a distinctly rural feel. The stained-glass windows record a very local history: the visit in 1802 of Pope Pius VII, who was in Paris for Napoleon's coronation; the miraculous cure of a Madame Delafosse in the rue de Charonne on May 31, 1725; the fatal wounding of Monseigneur Affre, the archbishop of Paris, in the course of a street battle in the faubourg on June 25, 1848; the murder of sixteen Carmelite nuns at the Barrière du Trône in 1794; and the quartier's dead of World War I. In the now disused cemetery of Ste-Marguerite, lies the body of Louis XVII, the 10-year-old heir of the guillotined Louis XVI, who died in the Temple prison (see box on p.110). The cemetery also received the dead from the Bastille prison.

From square R. Nordling, rue de la Forge-Royale – with the *Casbah* nightclub magnificently decorated in North African style at no. 18 – takes you down to rue du Faubourg-St-Antoine. After Louis XI licensed the establishment of craftsmen in the fifteenth century, the faubourg became the principal working-class quartier of Paris, cradle of revolutions and mother of street-fighters. From its beginnings, the principal trade associated with it has been **furniture-making**, and this was where the classic styles of French furniture – Louis Quatorze, Louis Quinze, Second Empire – were developed. Many furniture workshops, as well as related trades such as inlayers, stainers and polishers, still inhabit the maze of interconnecting yards and *passages* that run off the faubourg, especially at the western end. One of the most attractive courtyards is at no. 56, with its lemon trees, and ivy- and rose-covered buildings.

To the east, rue du Faubourg-St-Antoine ends at **place de la Nation**. The *place* is adorned with the "Triumph of the Republic" bronze, and, at the start of the Cours de Vincennes, the bizarre ensemble of two medieval monarchs, looking very small and sheepish in pens on the top of two high columns. During the Revolution, when the old name of place du Trône became place du Trône-Renversé ("the overturned throne"), more people were guillotined here than on the more notorious execution site of place de la Concorde.

# The 12ᵉ

The **12ᵉ** arrondissement has been the focus of a number of ambitious urban regeneration programmes in recent years. The rundown **Bercy** riverside district in particular has undergone extensive redevelopment, with the creation of a large park and the conversion of the area's old wine warehouses into attractive cafés and shops. One of the most imaginative developments has been the creation of the **Promenade Plantée**, the landscaping of a stretch of old railway line, running from the Bastille right across the 12ᵉ to the green expanse of the **Bois de Vincennes**. Other parts of the 12ᵉ remain resolutely unchanged, such as the traditional **place d'Aligre market**.

## Place d'Aligre market

The **place d'Aligre market** (Mº Ledru-Rollin), between avenue Daumesnil and rue du Faubourg St-Antoine, is a lively, raucous affair, held every morning except Monday, and particularly animated on Saturdays and Sundays. The square itself is given over to clothes and bric-a-brac stalls, selling anything from old gramophone players to odd bits of crockery. There's also a covered food market with the usual line-up of *fromageries* and *charcuteries*, plus more unusual stalls like the one selling numerous varieties of olive oil. It's along the adjoining rue d'Aligre, however, where the market really comes to life, the vendors, many of Algerian origin, doing a frenetic trade in fruit and veg. As the market winds down, you could follow the locals to the old-fashioned *Baron Rouge* wine bar (see p.308) for a glass of wine and *saucisson*, or drink in the North African atmosphere at the *Ruche à Miel* café at 19 rue d'Aligre and order some mint tea with sticky cakes. Before leaving the area it's also worth taking a look at the old-style *boulangerie* on the corner of rues Charenton and Emilio-Castelar, with its beautiful painted glass panels, the queue of shoppers outside testifying to the excellence of its bread and pâtisseries.

## The Promenade Plantée and around

The **Promenade Plantée** (Mº Bastille/Ledru-Rollin), also known as the Coulée Verte, is an excellent way to see a little-visited part of the city – and from an unusual angle. This stretch of disused railway line, much of it along a viaduct, has been ingeniously converted into an elevated walkway and planted with a profusion of trees and flowers – cherry trees, maples, limes, roses and lavender. The walkway starts near the beginning of **avenue Daumesnil**, just

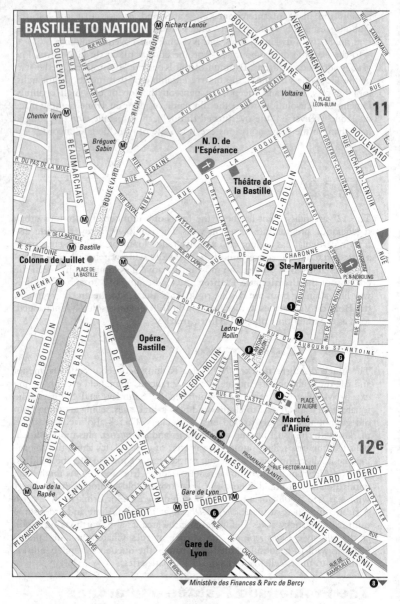

BASTILLE TO NATION

N. D. de l'Espérance

Théâtre de la Bastille

Ste-Marguerite

Colonne de Juillet

Opéra-Bastille

Ledru-Rollin

Marché d'Aligre

12e

Gare de Lyon

Gare de Lyon

▼ Ministère des Finances & Parc de Bercy

south of the Bastille opera house, and is reached via a flight of stone steps – or lifts – with a number of similar access points all the way along. It takes you to the Parc de Reuilly, then descends to ground level and continues nearly as far as the périphérique, from where you can follow signs to the Bois de Vincennes. The whole walk is around 4.5km long, but if you don't feel like doing the entire thing you could just walk the first part – along the viaduct – which also

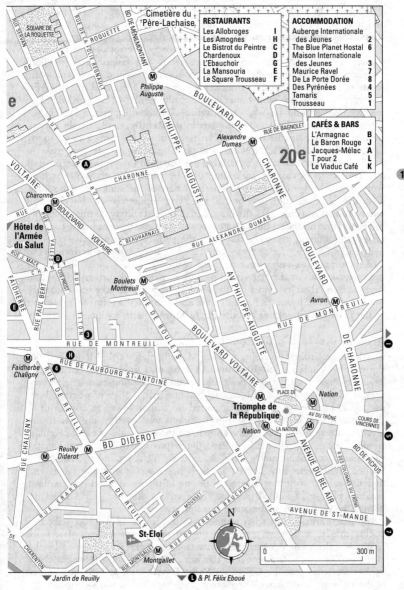

RESTAURANTS
| Les Allobroges | I |
| Les Amognes | H |
| Le Bistrot du Peintre | C |
| Chardenoux | D |
| L'Ebauchoir | G |
| La Mansouria | E |
| Le Square Trousseau | F |

ACCOMMODATION
| Auberge Internationale des Jeunes | 2 |
| The Blue Planet Hostal | 6 |
| Maison Internationale des Jeunes | 3 |
| Maurice Ravel | 7 |
| De La Porte Dorée | 8 |
| Des Pyrénées | 4 |
| Tamaris | 5 |
| Trousseau | 1 |

CAFÉS & BARS
| L'Armagnac | B |
| Le Baron Rouge | J |
| Jacques-Mélac | A |
| T pour 2 | L |
| Le Viaduc Café | K |

happens to be the most attractive stretch, running past venerable old mansion blocks and giving you a bird's eye view of the street below. Small architectural details such as decorative mouldings and elaborate wrought-iron balconies that you wouldn't normally notice at street level come to light – the oddest sight are the caryatids adorning the police station at the end of the avenue Daumesnil stretch of the walkway.

The arches of the viaduct itself have had their red brickwork scrubbed clean and have been converted into attractive spaces for artisans' studios and craftshops, collectively known as the **Viaduc des Arts**. The workshops house a wealth of creativity: furniture and tapestry restorers, interior designers, cabinet makers, violin- and flute-makers, embroiderers and fashion and jewellery designers; a full list and map is available from no. 23 avenue Daumesnil – the location of SEMA (Société d'Encouragement aux Métiers d'Art; Tues–Fri 1–5pm, plus weekends same hours during exhibitions; ☎01.55.78.85.85). The viaduct ends around halfway down avenue Daumesnil, but the Promenade Plantée continues, taking you to the **Jardin de Reuilly**, an old freight station, now an inviting, circular expanse of lawn, popular with picnickers on sunny days, and bordered by terraces and arbours. The open-air café here makes a good refreshment halt if you're walking the length of the promenade. You can also choose to bypass the park altogether by taking the gracefully arching wooden footbridge that spans it. The next part of the walkway – the **allée Vivaldi** – is a rather nondescript road lined with modern blocks, but then you enter a tunnel and emerge at the other end in the old railway cutting, a delightful stretch that meanders through a canopy of trees and flowers, below the level of the surrounding streets. At this point the path divides into two – one for pedestrians, the other for cyclists – landscaped all along, taking you through the odd ivy-draped, ex-railway tunnel, until you come to a wrought-iron spiral staircase; take this or the right-hand path up to road level, turn right onto the ring road, and then left under the flyover. A right-turn will take you onto busy boulevard de la Guyane, and a short walk along here will eventually bring you to the **Bois de Vincennes** and the **Porte Dorée** metro station.

### Around the Jardin de Reuilly

North of the Jardin de Reuilly, on place M. de Fontenay (M° Montgâllet), lies the peculiar church of **St-Éloi**, built in 1968 to a ground-plan of a right-angled triangle with the altar positioned at one of the non-right-angled corners. It all feels more like an industrial building than a place of worship: both outside and inside are clad with lacquered aluminium leaves, in honour of St Éloi, patron saint of jewellers and iron-workers who lived in this area in the seventeenth century. Close by the church, on the other side of rue de Reuilly, is one of the most perfect *villas* in Paris, the **impasse Mousset**. Roses, clematis, wisteria and honeysuckle wind across telegraph lines and up the white-washed walls of its tiny houses; a rusted hotel sign advertising wines and liqueurs, as well as beds, still hangs from one of the houses; and you can hear children playing in hidden gardens. There are no designer offices here, just homes, the odd artist's studio and a small printworks.

Another unusual church lies southeast of the Jardin de Reuilly – about a twenty-minute walk down avenue Daumesnil, on the other side of place Félix Eboué, on the right. An extremely narrow brickwork facade, topped by the tallest bell tower in Paris, conceals the vast cupola – filling the whole block behind the street – of the **Église du Saint-Esprit**, built in 1931 in memory of the colonial missionaries. The Roman Catholic Church was worried by the possible reaction of the anticlerical, communist sympathies of the local residents, hence the disguise of its enormous dimensions.

# Bercy

Over the last decade or so, the former warehouse district of **Bercy**, along the Seine just east of the Gare de Lyon, has been transformed by a series of ambitious, ultra-modern developments designed to complement the grand-scale "Seine Rive Gauche" project (see p.165) on the opposite bank. As you emerge from Bercy metro station one of the first things you notice is the **Ministère des Finances**, a monster of a building, constructed in 1990 to house the treasury staff after they had finally agreed to move out of the Richelieu wing of the Louvre. Housing some 4700 employees, it stretches like a giant loading bridge from above the river (where higher bureaucrats and ministers arrive by boat) to rue de Bercy, a distance of some 400m.

A little east of here squats the charmless **Palais Omnisports de Bercy**. Built in 1983, its concrete bunker frame clad with grass covers a vast arena used for sporting and cultural events (see p.319 for more details). Beyond it, the area that used to house the old Bercy warehouses, where for centuries the capital's wine supplies were unloaded from river barges, is now the extensive **Parc de Bercy**. Here, the French formal garden has been given a modern twist, with geometric lines and grid-like flowerbeds, but it also cleverly incorporates elements of the old warehouse site such as disused railway tracks and cobbled lanes. The western section of the park is a fairly unexciting expanse of grass with a huge stepped fountain (popular with children) set into one of the grassy banks, but the area east has arbours, rose gardens, lily ponds, an *orangerie*, a "Pavillon" for contemporary art exhibitions (Wed–Sun noon–6pm; free) and a **Maison du Jardinage**, which provides information on all aspects of gardening.

Of the new buildings surrounding the park, the most striking, on rue Paul-Belmondo, on the north side, is the ex-American Centre, designed by the architect Frank O. Gehry. Constructed from zinc, glass and limestone, it resembles a falling pack of cards – according to Gehry, the inspiration was Matisse's collages, done "with a simple pair of scissors". Less simple has been the transferral here of the **Cinématèque** from the Palais de Chaillot (see p.135). After a few setbacks, it seems work is now under way to construct a museum of the history of the cinema, four cinema screens, shops, a library and restaurant. Work should be complete by 2005; in the meantime, you can follow its progress online at Ⓦ www.51ruedebercy.com.

A little east of here, arched footbridges take you over the busy rue Kessel into the eastern extension of the park and the adjoining **Bercy Village** (M° Cour Saint-Émilion), the hub of which is the **Cour Saint Émilion**, a pedestrianized, cobbled street lined with former wine warehouses that have been stylishly converted into smart cafés, wine bars and shops. Another set of old stone wine warehouses at no. 53 avenue des-Terroirs-de-France now house the privately owned funfair museum, the **Musée des Arts Forains**, with its collection of funfair rides, fairground music and Venetian carnival rooms. At the time of writing, it offered tours to groups only (Ⓣ 01.43.40.16.15), though this may change, and at any rate, there's no stopping you peeking in the entrance to see the traditional architecture.

# Vincennes

Beyond the 12$^e$ arrondissement, across the boulevard périphérique, lies the **Bois de Vincennes**. Besides the Bois de Boulogne, this is the largest green space that the city has to offer, and hence a favourite family Sunday retreat. The best places to head for are the Parc Floral, the Château de Vincennes on the northern edge, the arboretum, the two lakes and the zoo. Note that sights are

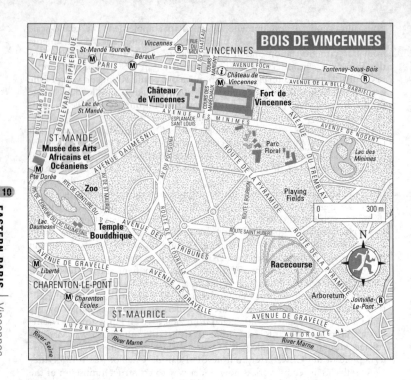

quite a long distance from each other, so to avoid a lot of footslogging you may want to just target one or two, or you could rent a bike from the outlet on the Esplanade St-Louis (weekends and holidays; €3 per hour), near the Château de Vincennes. The three main metro stops giving access to the park are M° Porte-Dorée, M° Porte-de-Charenton and M° Château-de-Vincennes, and it's also served by buses #46 and #86.

If you've only got a limited amount of time, you should make for the **Parc Floral** (daily: summer 9.30am–8pm; winter 9.30am–dusk; €1.50; Ⓦwww .parcfloraldeparis.com; M° Château de Vincennes, then bus #112 or a short walk), just behind the Fort de Vincennes. This is one of the best gardens in Paris – flowers are always in bloom in the Jardin des Quatres Saisons, you can picnic beneath pines, then wander through concentrations of camellias, rhododendrons, cacti, ferns, irises and bonsai trees. Between April and September, there are art and horticultural exhibitions in several pavilions, free jazz and classical music concerts, and numerous activities for children including a mini-golf of Parisian monuments (see p.361 for more information on activities for children). A brasserie, *Les Magnolias*, with pleasant outdoor seating, in the centre of the park, does a decent two-course set menu for €14.50.

To the east of the Parc Floral is the **Cartoucherie de Vincennes**, an old ammunitions factory, now home to four theatre companies, including the radical Théâtre du Soleil (see p.324). On the northern edge of the *bois*, the **Château de Vincennes** (daily 10am–noon & 1.15–6pm) – erstwhile royal medieval residence, then state prison, porcelain factory, weapons dump and military training school – is still undergoing restoration work started by

Napoléon III. Guided tours on a choice of two different circuits are available (1hr 15min guided tours at 11am, 2.15pm, 3pm & 4.30pm, €5.50; 40min tours at 10.15am, 11.45am, 1.30pm & 5.15pm, €4). The fourteenth-century keep is currently closed for repairs but both circuits stop by another highlight – the Flamboyant-Gothic **Chapelle Royale**, completed in the mid-sixteenth century and decorated with superb Renaissance stained-glass windows.

If you're after a lazy afternoon in the park, you could go boating on the **Lac Daumesnil**, near the Porte Dorée entrance, or feed the ducks on the **Lac des Minimes** (bus #112 from Vincennes métro), on the other side of the wood. In the southeast corner off route de la Pyramide you can wander among 2000 trees of over 800 different species that have been cultivated in the **Arboretum** (Mon–Fri 9.30am–6.30pm; free).

North of the Lac Daumesnil, at 53 avenue de St-Maurice, is the city's largest **zoo** (April–Sept Mon–Sat 9am–6pm, Sun 9am– 6.30pm; Oct–March closes one hour earlier; €8, children €5; M° Porte-Dorée or #46 bus), one of the first to replace cages with trenches and use landscaping to give the animals room to exercise. More information is given in "Kids' Paris", p.362.

The fenced enclave on the southern side of Lac Daumesnil harbours a **Buddhist centre**, with Tibetan temple, Vietnamese chapel and international pagoda; all occasionally visitable (information on ☎01.43.41.54.48). As far as real woods go, the *bois* comes into its own once you're east of avenue de St-Maurice. Boules competitions are popular – there's usually a collection of devotees between route de la Tourelle and avenue du Polygone.

Just outside the Bois de Vincennes, across the way from the Porte Dorée entrance, all is currently in a state of flux in the building that used to house the Musée des Arts Africains et Océaniens. The museum's rich collection of masks, jewellery, head-dresses and other artefacts was removed at the beginning of 2003 and is due to be transferred to the new Quai Branly museum (see p.140). There is talk of transforming the site into a new museum of Decorative Arts, though this has yet to be confirmed. You can still visit the Art Deco building (daily except Tues 10am–5.30pm; €5.60; M° Porte-Dorée), constructed for the 1931 Colonial Exhibition, though all you'll see at present is the occasional temporary exhibition and the museum's popular **aquarium** with its large collection of tropical fish and crocodile pit.

# Western Paris

Western Paris consists of the well-manicured 16ᵉ and 17ᵉ arrondissements, often referred to as the **Beaux Quartiers**. The 16ᵉ is aristocratic and rich; the 17ᵉ, or at least the southern part of it, bourgeois and rich, embodying the staid, cautious values of the nineteenth-century manufacturing and trading classes. The area is mainly residential with few specific sights as such, the chief exception being the **Musée Marmottan**, known for its impressive collection of Monets. The northern half of the 16ᵉ, towards place Victor-Hugo and place de **l'Étoile**, is leafy though still distinctly metropolitan in feel. The southern part, round the old villages of **Auteuil** and **Passy** is particularly pleasant for strolling. It has an almost provincial air, with its tight knot of streets and charming *villas* – leafy lanes of attractive old houses, fronted with English-style gardens, full of roses, ivy and wisteria. Although they're often closed off to non-residents, should you find the access gate open, no one seems to mind if you wander in. Owing to the relatively late incorporation of the villages into the city in 1860 and amenability to new construction, the 16ᵉ boasts a number of interesting examples of turn-of-the-century and early **twentieth-century architecture**, notably pieces by Hector Guimard, designer of the swirly green Art Nouveau métro stations, and Le Corbusier and Mallet-Stevens, architects of the first "Cubist" buildings.

## Auteuil

The ideal place to start an architectural exploration of the Beaux Quartiers is the **Église d'Auteuil** métro station. Around this area are several of Hector Guimard's **Art Nouveau** buildings: at 34 rue Boileau, 8 av de la Villa-de-la-Réunion, 41 rue Chardon-Lagache, 142 av de Versailles, and 39 bd Exelmans.

The house at no. 34 **rue Boileau** was one of Guimard's first commissions, in 1891. To reach it from Église d'Auteuil métro, head directly west along rue d'Auteuil for 200m, then turn left (south) into Boileau. A high fence and wisteria obscure much of the view, but you can see some of the decorative tilework under the eaves and around the doors and windows. Further down the street, just before you reach boulevard Exelmans, the Vietnamese embassy at no. 62 successfully combines 1970s Western architecture with the traditional Vietnamese elements of a pagoda roof and earthenware tiles. Continue south for half a kilometre along rue Boileau beyond boulevard Exelmans, turn right onto rue Parent de Rosan and you'll find a series of enchanting *villas* off to the right, backing onto the Auteuil cemetery.

Handy bus routes for exploring Auteuil are the #52 and the #72. The #52 runs between M° Opéra in the centre and M° Boulogne-Pont-de-St-Cloud near the Parc des Princes, stopping at rue Poisson en route, while the #72's route extends between métro Hôtel-de-Ville in the Marais and M° Boulogne-Pont-de-St-Cloud, stopping en route by the Exelmans crossroads near some of Guimard's buildings on avenue de Versailles.

Rue Boileau terminates on avenue de Versailles, where you can turn left and head back to the Église d'Auteuil métro via the Guimard apartment block at 142 av de Versailles (1905), with its characteristic Art Nouveau flower motifs and sinuous, curling lines. It's just by the Exelmans crossroads (on bus #72's route). You can then cut across the **Jardin de Ste–Périne**, once the rural residence of the monks of Ste Geneviève's abbey, established here in 1109, to get back to the métro. The entrances to the garden are opposite 135 av de Versailles and alongside the hospital on rue Mirabeau, just north of the rue Chardon-Lagache junction.

For more of the life of the quartier, follow the old village high street, **rue d'Auteuil**, west from the métro exit to **place Lorrain**, which hosts a Saturday market. From here you could take rue de la Fontaine for some more Guimard buildings and the Maison de Radio France, or if the bulgy curves of Art Nouveau make you feel queasy, head up rue du Dr-Blanche for the cool, rectilinear lines of Cubist architects Le Corbusier and Mallet-Stevens (see below).

# Rue de la Fontaine and the Maison de Radio-France

**Rue de la Fontaine** runs northeast from place Lorrain to the Radio-France building and has Guimard buildings at nos. 14, 17, 19, 21 and 60. Among these, no. 14 is the most famous: the "Castel Béranger" (1898), with exuberant Art Nouveau decoration and shapes in the bay windows, the roofline and the chimney. At no. 65 there's a huge block of artists' studios by Henri Sauvage (1926) with a fascinating colour scheme, bearing signs of a Cubist influence. The **Maison de Radio France**, its entrance at 116 av du Président Kennedy, is the national radio headquarters; you can visit here for free concerts (see p.317) or take a guided tour through the **Musée de Radio France** (Mon–Fri 10.30–11.30am & 2.30–4.30pm; €5; RER Av-du-Prés-Kennedy–Maison-de-Radio-France & M° Ranelagh), which illustrates the history of broadcasting through a wide collection of equipment including some early Marconi radios.

# From place Lorrain to the Musée Marmottan

Just off place Lorrain, in rue Poussin (on bus #52's route), carriage gates open onto **Villa Montmorency**, one of the grander *villas* – more like an exclusive estate (with a security guard on the gate). The writer André Gide, and the Goncourt brothers of Prix Goncourt fame, lived in this one. Behind it, in a cul-de-sac off rue du Dr-Blanche, are **Le Corbusier**'s first private houses (1923), the Villa Jeanneret and the Villa La Roche, now in the care of

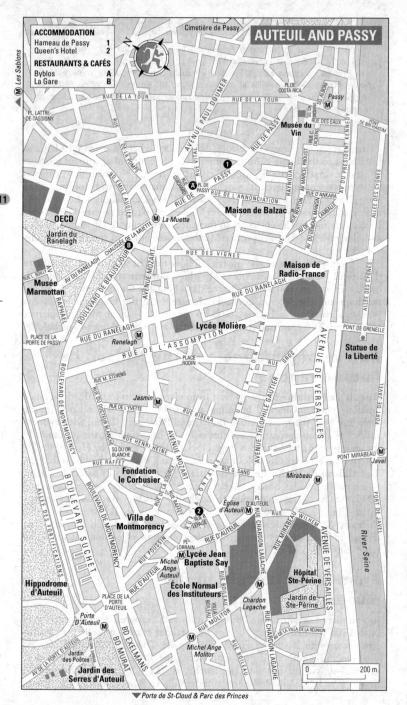

AUTEUIL AND PASSY

ACCOMMODATION
Hameau de Passy          1
Queen's Hotel            2
RESTAURANTS & CAFÉS
Byblos                   A
La Gare                  B

Cimetière de Passy

Les Sablons

PL. LATTRE-
DE-TASSIGNY

RUE DE LA TOUR

RUE DE LA TOUR

PL DE
COSTA RICA

Passy

RUE DES EAUX

Musée du
Vin

AVENUE PAUL DOUMER

RUE DE PASSY

RUE DE LA POMPE

BD. ÉMILE AUGIER

RUE VITAL

RUE GUICHARD

PL. DE
PASSY

RUE DE L'ANNONCIATION

Maison de Balzac

OECD

Jardin du
Ranelagh

La Muette

CHAUSSÉE DE LA MUETTE

RUE DES VIGNES

Maison de
Radio-France

Musée
Marmottan

BOULEVARD DE BEAUSÉJOUR

AVENUE MOZART

RUE DU RANELAGH

RUE DU RANELAGH

PLACE DE LA
PORTE DE PASSY

Ranelagh

Lycée Molière

RUE DE L'ASSOMPTION

Statue de
la Liberté

PLACE
RODIN

PONT DE GRENELLE

RUE M. STEVENS

AVENUE DE VERSAILLES

Jasmin

RUE DE L'YVETTE

RUE RIBERA

AVENUE MOZART

RUE HENRI HEINE

RUE G. SAND

PONT MIRABEAU

Javel

BOULEVARD DE MONTMORENCY

RUE RAFFET

Fondation
le Corbusier

Mirabeau

RUE DE LA SOURCE

Villa de
Montmorency

Église
d'Auteuil

PL
D'AUTEUIL

River Seine

RUE D'AUTEUIL

RUE CHARDON LAGACHE

Hippodrome
d'Auteuil

Lycée Jean
Baptiste Say

Michel
Ange
Auteuil

École Normal
des Instituteurs

Hôpital
Ste-Périne

PLACE DE LA
PORTE
D'AUTEUIL

Chardon
Lagache

Jardin de
Ste-Périne

Porte
D'Auteuil

RUE MOLITOR

Michel Ange
Molitor

BD EXELMANS

BD MURAT

Jardin
des Poètes

Jardin des
Serres d'Auteuil

0          200 m

Porte de St-Cloud & Parc des Princes

the Fondation Le Corbusier. You can visit one of the houses, the **Villa La Roche** (Mon–Thurs 10am–12.30pm & 1.30–6pm, Fri 10am–12.30pm & 1.30–5pm, closed Aug; €2.40; M° Jasmin), built in strictly Cubist style, very plain, with windows in bands, the only extravagance a curved frontage. They look commonplace enough now from the outside, but were a great contrast with anything that had gone before, and once you're inside, the spatial play still seems groundbreaking. The interior is appropriately decorated with Cubist paintings.

Further north along rue du Dr-Blanche and off to the right, the tiny **rue Mallet-Stevens** was built entirely by the architect of the same name, also in Cubist style. No. 12, where Robert Mallet-Stevens had his offices, has been altered, along with other houses in the street, but you can still see the architectural intention of sculpting the entire street space as a cohesive unit.

Continue to the end of rue du Dr-Blanche, turn left and then right onto boulevard Beauséjour; a shortcut immediately opposite rue du Ranelagh across the disused Petite Ceinture rail line takes you to shady avenue Raphaël, which runs alongside the pretty **Jardin du Ranelagh** (with a rather engaging sculpture of the fabulist La Fontaine with an eagle and fox) and on to the Musée Marmottan.

## The Musée Marmottan

The **Musée Marmottan** (daily 10am–6pm; €6.50; ⓦ www.marmottan.com; M° Muette), 2 rue Louis-Boilly, is best known for its excellent collection of **Monet paintings**, bequeathed to the museum by the artist's son. Among them is *Impression, soleil levant*, a canvas from 1872 of a misty Le Havre morning, and whose title the critics usurped to give the Impressionist movement its name. The painting was stolen from the gallery in October 1985, along with eight other paintings. After a police operation lasting five years, which extended as far afield as Japan, the paintings were discovered in a villa in southern Corsica – they're back on show with greatly tightened security. There's also a dazzling selection of works from Monet's last years at Giverny; these paintings show the increasingly abstract quality of the artist's later work and include several *Nymphéas* (Waterlilies), *Le Pont Japonais*, *L'Allée des Rosiers* and *La Saule Pleureur*, where rich colours are laid on in thick, excited whorls and lines. The collection also features some of Monet's contemporaries – Manet, Renoir and **Berthe Morisot**. The last is particularly well represented, with two rooms devoted to her wonderfully delicate, summery canvases.

In addition, the museum displays some splendid examples of First Empire pomposity: chairs with golden sphinxes for armrests, candelabra of complicated headdresses and twining serpents, and a small and beautiful collection of thirteenth- to sixteenth-century **manuscript illuminations** – look out for the decorated capital R framing an exquisitely drawn portrait of Saint Catherine of Alexandria.

# West of Auteuil

West of place de la Porte d'Auteuil are two gardens: the **Jardin des Poètes** (daily 9am–6pm; free), with its entrance on avenue du Général Sarrail, and the **Jardin des Serres d'Auteuil** (daily 10am–5pm, closes 4pm in winter; €0.75; M° Porte-d'Auteuil), its main entrance at 3 av de la Porte d'Auteuil (or you can enter from the Jardin des Poètes). You can't escape the traffic noise completely, but the Jardin des Poètes is extremely tranquil. Famous French poets are each remembered by a verse (of a mostly pastoral nature) engraved on small stones surrounded by little flowerbeds. A statue of Victor Hugo by Rodin, almost obscured by a laurel bush, stands in the middle of this very informal garden. Approaching the Auteuil garden and the greenhouses (*serres*) from the Jardin des Poètes, you pass the delightful potting sheds with rickety wooden blinds. Then you're into a formal garden, beautifully laid out around the big old-fashioned metal-frame greenhouses. There may be a special exhibition on – azaleas in April, for example – in which case there'll be an extra entrance fee for the greenhouses.

Directly beyond the Jardin des Serres d'Auteuil is the **Stade Roland Garros**, venue for the French tennis championships (see p.359 for information about watching a tournament). To the south is the main rugby and domestic football stadium, the **Parc des Princes**, at 24 rue du Commandant-Guilbaud, where apart from seeing a match (for more on which see p.358), you can visit the **Musée du Sport Français** (daily except Wed & Fri 9.30am–12.30pm & 2–5pm; €3; M° Porte-de-St-Cloud). Here, books, posters, paintings and sculptures tell the history of French sport, along with trophies and boots, caps and gloves worn by the famous.

The **Jardins Albert Kahn** (Tues–Sun 11am–6pm; garden & museum entry €3.30; M° Boulogne-Pont-de-St-Cloud & M° Marcel-Semblat) at 14 rue du Port, to the south in the neighbouring suburb of Boulogne-Billancourt, consists of a very pretty garden and a small museum dedicated to temporary exhibitions of "*Les Archives de la Planète*" – photographs and films collected by banker and philanthropist Albert Kahn between 1909 and 1931 to record human activities and ways of life that he knew would soon disappear for ever. His aim in the design of the garden was to combine English, French, Japanese and other styles to demonstrate the possibility of a harmonious, peaceful world. It's an enchanting place, with rhododendrons and camellias under blue cedars, a rose garden and an espaliered orchard, a forest of Moroccan pines and streams with Japanese bridges beside pagoda teahouses, Buddhas and pyramids of pebbles. A palm hothouse has been turned into a very chic *salon de thé*, serving such delights as pear liqueur and *marrons glacés* sorbet.

# Passy

Northeast of Auteuil, the area around the old village of **Passy**, too, offers scope for a good meandering walk, from La Muette métro, through old characterful streets like rue de l'Annonciation, to Balzac's house, and through more cobbled streets to the Seine and Pont de Bir-Hakeim near Passy métro.

## From La Muette to the Maison de Balzac

From La Muette métro, head east along the old high street, **rue de Passy**, past an eye-catching parade of boutiques, until you reach **place de Passy** and the crowded but leisurely terrace of *Le Paris Passy* café. From the *place*, stroll southeast along cobbled, pedestrianized **rue de l'Annonciation**, a pleasant blend of down-to-earth and genteel well-heeled which gives more of the flavour of old Passy. You may no longer be able to have your Bechstein repaired here or your furniture lacquered, but the food shops that now dominate the street have delectable displays guaranteed to make your mouth water.

When you hit rue Raynouard, cross the road and veer to your right, where at no. 47 you'll discover the **Maison de Balzac** (Tues–Sun 10am–5.40pm; €3.35; M° Av-du-Prés-Kennedy–Maison-de-Radio-France & M° Passy), a delightful, summery little house with pale-green shutters and a decorative iron entrance porch, tucked away down some steps among a tree-filled garden. Balzac moved to this secluded spot in 1840 in the hope of evading his creditors. He lived under a pseudonym, and visitors had to give a special password before being admitted. Should any unwelcome callers manage to get past the door, Balzac would escape via a backdoor and down to the river via a network of underground cellars. It was here that he wrote some of his best-known works, including *La Cousine Bette* and *Le Cousin Pons*. The museum preserves his study, simple writing desk and monogrammed cafetière – frequent doses of caffeine must have been essential during his long writing stints, which could extend up to 16 to 18 hours a day for weeks on end. One room is devoted to the development of ideas for the creation of a monument to Balzac, resulting in the famously blobby Rodin sculpture of the writer: caricatures of the sculpture by cartoonists of the time are on display here. Other exhibits include letters to Mme Hanska, whom he eventually married after an eighteen-year courtship, and a highly complex family tree of around a thousand of the four thousand-plus characters that feature in his *Comédie Humaine*. Outside, the shady, rose-filled garden is a delightful place to dally on wrought-iron seats, surrounded by busts of the writer.

Behind Balzac's house, and reached via some steps descending from rue Raynouard, **rue Berton** is a cobbled path with gas lights still in place, blocked off by the heavy security of the Turkish embassy. The building, an eighteenth-century château shrouded by greenery and screened by a high wall and guards, was once a clinic where the pioneering Dr Blanche tried to treat the mad Maupassant and Gérard de Nerval, among others; before that it was the home of Marie-Antoinette's friend, the Princesse de Lamballe, who met a grisly fate at the hands of revolutionaries in 1792. You can get a better view of the building from cobbled **rue d'Ankara**, reached by heading down avenue de Lamballe and then right into avenue du Général-Mangin.

## East to the Musée du Vin and Pont de Bir-Hakeim

From rue d'Ankara, head northeast along avenue Marcel-Proust, turn right and then left onto rue Charles Dickens and follow it until it hits rue des Eaux. Rue des Eaux was where fashionable Parisians used to come in the eighteenth century for the therapeutic benefits of the once-famous ferruginous and sulphuric Passy waters. Today, the street is enclosed by a canyon of moneyed apartments, which dwarf the eighteenth-century houses of **square Charles-Dickens**. In one of them, burrowing back into the cellars of a vanished, fourteenth-century monastery, which produced wine until the Revolution, is the **Musée du Vin** (daily except Mon 10am–6pm; €6.50; admission includes a glass of wine; Ⓦ www.museeduvinparis.com). The exhibition itself is rather disappointing – viticultural bits and bobs, such as an array of corkscrews dating back two hundred years, some of them looking more like instruments of torture. It's worth a visit, however, for the extensive stone vaulted cellars and passages that connect to the ancient quarry tunnels – not visitable – from which the stone for

Notre-Dame was hewn. The visit includes a *dégustation* – you might try the museum's own wine, Château Labastidié, a fine, blackcurranty tipple produced in the southwest. The place also has a restaurant, or you can just come in for a glass of wine and some cheese between 3pm and 5pm.

Back on rue Raynouard, head northeast to place du Costa-Rica, take the first right into rue de l'Alboni and go down the steps into square Alboni, a patch of garden enclosed by tall apartment buildings as solid as banks. Here the métro line emerges from what used to be a vine-covered hillside for the Passy stop – more like a country station – before rumbling out across the river by the **Pont de Bir-Hakeim**, the distinctive bridge famously featured in the racy Bertolucci film *Last Tango in Paris*, starring Marlon Brando. From here you're well placed to hop back onto the métro, or cross the bridge and head north along the water to the Eiffel Tower about 500m along.

# Bois de Boulogne

The **Bois de Boulogne**, running all the way down the west side of the 16$^e$, was designed by Baron Haussmann and supposedly modelled on London's Hyde Park – though it's a very French interpretation. The "bois" of the name is somewhat deceptive, though the extensive parklands (just under 900 hectares) do contain some remnants of the once great Forêt de Rouvray. As its location may suggest, the Bois was once the playground of the wealthy, although it also established a reputation as the site of illicit sex romps; it was popularly said that "*Les mariages du bois de Boulogne ne se font pas devant Monsieur le Curé*"– "Unions cemented in the Bois de Boulogne do not take place in the presence of a priest." Today's unions are no less disreputable – the area is a favoured haunt for prostitutes and accompanying kerb-crawlers who, despite an obvious police presence and the night-time closure of certain roads, still do business along its periphery. Accompanying the sex trade is a certain amount of crime; the *bois* is a very unwise choice for a midnight promenade.

While entry to the overall park is free, there are several attractions within it that have entry fees or opening times: the **Jardin d'Acclimatation**, which is aimed at children (see p.363 for more information); the excellent Musée National des Arts et Traditions Populaires; the beautiful floral displays of the Parc de Bagatelle; and the **racecourses** at Longchamp and Auteuil. You can also partake of a wealth of activities: there's a **riding** school, a **bowling** alley, **bike rental** (for which you'll need to leave your passport as security) at the entrance to the Jardin d'Acclimatation and 14km of cycling routes; and **boating** on the Lac Inférieur. The best, and wildest, part for **walking** is towards the southwest corner.

The fascinating **Musée National des Arts et Traditions Populaires** (daily except Tues 9.30am–5.15pm; €3.85; M° Les Sablons & M° Porte-Maillot) lies on the northern edge of the park, at 6 av du Mahatma Gandhi, beside one of the entrances to the Jardin d'Acclimatation and signposted from M° Les Sablons (from where it's about a fifteen-minute walk). It celebrates the highly specialized skills and techniques of the now-endangered crafts of, among others, boat-building, shepherding, weaving, pottery and stone-cutting as they existed before industrialization, standardization and mass production. Downstairs, there's a study section with casefuls of various implements, and

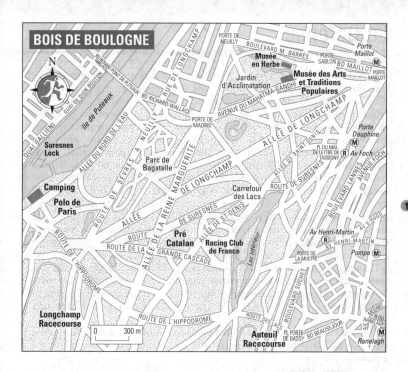

BOIS DE BOULOGNE

cubicles where you can call up explanatory slide shows (explanations in French).

Leaving the museum and following avenue du Mahatma Gandhi to allée de la Reine Marguerite will take you to the **Parc de Bagatelle** (daily 9am–7pm; €0.75; M° Porte-Maillot, then bus #244), spread out to the south and west. Comprising a range of garden styles from French and English to Japanese, its most famous feature is the stunning **rose garden** of the charming Château de Bagatelle. The château was designed and built in just over sixty days in 1775 as a wager between Comte d'Artois, the owner, and his sister-in-law Marie Antoinette, who said it could not be achieved in less than three months. The best time for the roses is June, while in other parts of the garden there are beautiful displays of tulips, hyacinths and daffodils in early April, irises in May, and waterlilies in early August.

Bang in the middle of the Bois de Boulogne, the Pré Catalan park is famous for its huge beech tree and, outside an open-air theatre, its **Jardin Shakespeare**, where you can study the herbs, trees and flowers referred to in the bard's plays.

Exiting the park at Porte Dauphine, Avenue Foch runs northeast from the Bois de Boulogne to Étoile through the 16ᵉ. Two blocks east of here is the beginning of rue de la Faisanderie, where at no.16 you'll find one of Paris's oddest museums, the **Musée de la Contrefaçon** (Tues–Sun 2–5.30pm; €2.30; M° Porte-Dauphin), set up to deliver an anti-counterfeiting message. Examples of imitation products, labels and brand marks trying to pass themselves off as the genuine article are all on display, in most cases alongside the real thing.

# La Défense

**La Défense**, accessible by RER line A and métro line 1, has been elevated to one of the top places of pilgrimage for visitors to Paris by the construction of **La Grande Arche**, built in 1989 to mark the bicentenary of the revolution. This beautiful and astounding structure, a 112-metre hollow cube clad in white marble, is positioned 6km from the Arc de Triomphe at the far end of the Voie Triomphale, completing the western axis of the monumental east–west vista. Suspended within its hollow, large enough to enclose Notre-Dame with ease, is a "cloud" canopy, which looks like the top half of a circus tent.

Designed by the Danish architect Johann Otto von Spreckelsen, who died before its completion, La Grande Arche is a pure and graceful example of design wedded to innovative engineering, on a par with the Eiffel Tower and in marked contrast to other recent Parisian monuments. The arch houses a government ministry, international businesses, an information centre on the European Union ("Sources d'Europe"; Mon–Fri 10am–6pm) and, in the roof section, the Fondation Internationale des Droits de l'Homme, which stages exhibitions and conferences on issues related to human rights.

Transparent lift shafts make for a thrilling ride to the rooftop, from where, as well as having access to the exhibitions, you can admire Jean-Pierre Raynaud's "Map of the Heavens" marble patios. The lift (daily 10am–8pm; closes an hour earlier in winter; €7), however, is pricey, and the views no more impressive than from the series of steps that lead up to the base of the arch, itself a popular meeting and viewing point – on a clear day, you can scan from the marble path on the *parvis* below you to the Arc de Triomphe, and beyond to the Louvre.

The **closest stations** to La Défense are M°/RER Grande-Arche-de-la-Défense, though for the most dramatic approach to the Grande Arche and to see the sculptures (see below) it's worth getting off a stop early, at M° Esplanade-de-la-Défense.

## Around La Grande Arche

Back on the ground, between La Grande Arche and the river extends Paris's prestige **business district**, La Défense, an extraordinary monument to late-twentieth-century capitalism, stretching along the pedestrianized, sculpture- and fountain-strewn Esplanade du Général de Gaulle. In front of you, along the axis of the Voie Triomphale, an assortment of towers – apartment blocks, offices of Elf, Gan, Total, banks and other businesses – compete for size and dazzle of surface. Finance made flesh, they are worth the trip out in themselves. Over a hundred thousand people come here to work during the week, and with cinemas, tourist attractions and a huge shopping centre, it's often a popular and animated place at weekends too, although the bustle of the daytime melts away to leave everywhere rather empty by night.

On the south side of the arch is the shiny globe of the **Dôme-Imax**, which has displaced La Villette's Géode (see p.189) as the world's largest cinema screen. On the other side of the La Grande Arche, the undulating CNIT building was the first intimation of the area's modernist architectural future when it was erected in the 1950s as a trade exhibition centre. The floor of the hangar-like building, all gleaming granite, is softened by slender bamboo trees; the serious activity takes place off in the far corners, where every major computer company has an office. There's also a FNAC store, and a selection of overpriced

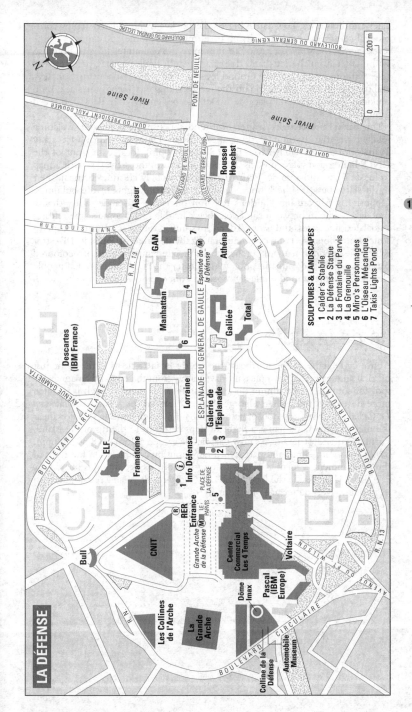

## LA DÉFENSE

**SCULPTURES & LANDSCAPES**
1 Calder's Stabile
2 La Défense Statue
3 La Fontaine du Parvis
4 La Grenouille
5 Miro's Personnages
6 L'Oiseau Mécanique
7 Takis' Lights Pond

200 m

0

N

River Seine
River Seine

BOULEVARD DU GENERAL LECLERC
BOULEVARD DU GENERAL KOENIG
PONT DE NEUILLY
QUAI DU PRESIDENT PAUL DOUMER
QUAI DE DION BOUTON
BOULEVARD DE NEUILLY
BOULEVARD PIERRE GAUDIN

Roussel
Hoechst

Assur

RUE LOUIS BLANC

R.N. 13

GAN

Athéna

7

Esplanade de
la Défense Ⓜ

Manhattan

4

Total

Galilée

Descartes
(IBM France)

6

ESPLANADE DU GENERAL DE GAULLE

Lorraine

AVENUE GAMBETTA

BOULEVARD CIRCULAIRE

Galerie de
l'Esplanade

3

2

ELF

Framatome

Info Défense
1 ⓘ

PLACE DE
LA DÉFENSE

BOULEVARD CIRCULAIRE

R.N. 13

Bull

CNIT

Ⓡ RER
Entrance

Grande Arche
de la Défense Ⓜ

LE
PARIS

5

Centre
Commercial
Les 4 Temps

Voltaire

R.N.

Les Collines
de l'Arche

La Grande
Arche

Dôme
Imax

Pascal (IBM
Europe)

AVENUE DU PRESIDENT WILSON

Colline de la
Défense

BOULEVARD CIRCULAIRE

Automobile
Museum

cafés and brasseries. Less damaging to the pocket is the Quatre-Temps commercial centre, the biggest of its ilk in Europe with some 250 shops on three levels, across the *parvis*, opposite. To minimize the encounter (if you should so wish), enter from the left-hand doors, and you'll find crêperies, pizzerias and cafés without having to leave ground level. In a new wave of construction, several more high-rises have gone up, the most striking of which is the sleek, EDF building, like a tail fin, on place de la Défense, designed by the Pei Cobb Freed group.

The **bizarre artworks** scattered around the Esplanade provide welcome relief from the corporate skyscrapers. **Info Défense** (April–Oct daily 10am–6pm; Nov–March Mon–Fri 9.30am–5.30pm), located in front of the CNIT building, displays models and photographs of the artworks, with a map to locate them and a guide. **Joan Miró**'s giant wobbly creatures bemoan their misfit status beneath the biting edges and curveless heights of the buildings. Opposite is **Alexander Calder**'s red iron offering – a stabile rather than a mobile – while in between the two, a black marble metronome shape releases a goal-less line across the *parvis*. **Torricini**'s huge fat frog screams to escape to a nice quiet pond. A statue commemorating the **defence of Paris** in 1870 (for which the district is named) perches on a concrete plinth in front of a coloured plastic waterfall and fountain pool, while nearer the river, disembodied people clutch each other round endlessly repeated concrete flowerbeds.

# Île de la Jatte

Above La Défense, to the northeast, the **Île de la Jatte** floats in the Seine just off rich and leafy Neuilly, a pleasant haven away from the city and an agreeable spot for some al fresco dining on a hot summer's evening, though it is much more developed than when Georges Seurat captured the scene, *A Sunday on La Grand Jatte*, with tiny dots of paint in 1884. From the Pont de Levallois, near the métro of the same name, a flight of steps descends to the tip of the island. Formerly an industrial site, it's now part public garden (Mon–Fri 8.30am–6pm, Sat & Sun 10am–8pm) and part stylish new housing complex. On the right of the development, a former *manège* (riding-school) has become the smart *Café de la Jatte*, while beside the bridge the old *Guinguette de Neuilly* restaurant, with its pleasant riverside terrace, still flourishes.

# Paris suburbs

The outskirts of Paris have been swallowed up by the capital's expansion, but despite a bland proliferation of industrial buildings and modern flats, many towns, especially to the south and west, retain their identities and links with the past. Royal or noble châteaux dedicated to hunting and other leisured pursuits once studded the region, and it's surprisingly easy to escape the city on a day-trip to take a stroll in the **gardens**, **parks and forests** that surround them. The most renowned château by far is **Versailles**, an overwhelming monument to the reigns of Louis XIV and Louis XVI, which is being slowly restored to its former glory. The much more modest **Malmaison** preserves the exquisite Empire furnishings of Napoleon's wife, Josephine, while all that's left of **Marly-le-Roi** are its gardens. It wasn't just kings and emperors who liked to escape the city: the countryside around Paris is inextricably linked to the **Impressionist** movement. Local museums at **Chatou** and **Auvers-sur-Oise** bear testimony to this artistic connection with their memories of carousing, carefree painters and musicians in the early 1900s, whilst Meudon claims **Rodin**'s final home and resting-place.

The northern and eastern suburbs have more than their fair share of *cités* (high-rise housing estates), but are punctuated by distractions. At **St-Denis**, the impressive Gothic basilica was the wellspring of the Gothic style, and the burial place of almost all the French kings; these days, it stands proudly at the centre of a fascinating multi-ethnic suburb. Whether the various suburban museums deserve your attention will depend on your degree of interest in the subjects they represent: French prehistory at the château of **St-Germain-en-Laye**; air and space travel at **Le Bourget**; and the authoritative collection of china at **Sèvres**.

All of the attractions listed in this section are easily accessible by train, RER, métro and bus. For other attractions in Île-de-France, the tourist office (Espace Tourisme d'Île-de-France, Ⓦ www.paris-ile-de-france.com, see p.22) in Paris is a good source of information.

## Versailles

Twenty kilometres southwest of Paris, the royal town of Versailles is renowned for the **Château de Versailles**, the enormous palace built for Louis XIV which is today one of the most visited monuments in France. It was inspired by the young Louis XIV's envy of his finance minister's château at Vaux-le-Vicomte (see p.234), a construction which he was determined to outdo. He

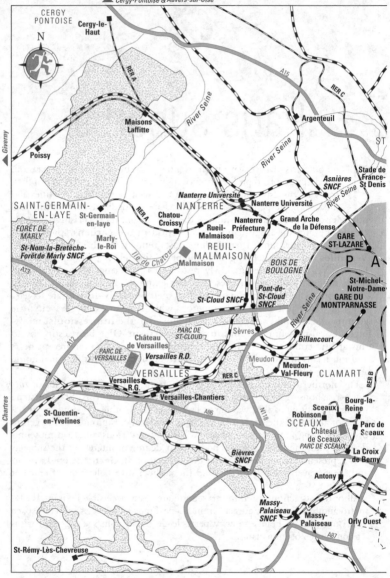

recruited the design team of Vaux-le-Vicomte – architect Le Vau, painter Le Brun and gardener Le Nôtre – and ordered something a hundred times the size. Versailles is the apotheosis of French regal indulgence, and even if the extravagant, self-aggrandizing decor of the "Sun King" is not to your liking, the palace's historical significance and anecdotes will enthral, and its park is a delight.

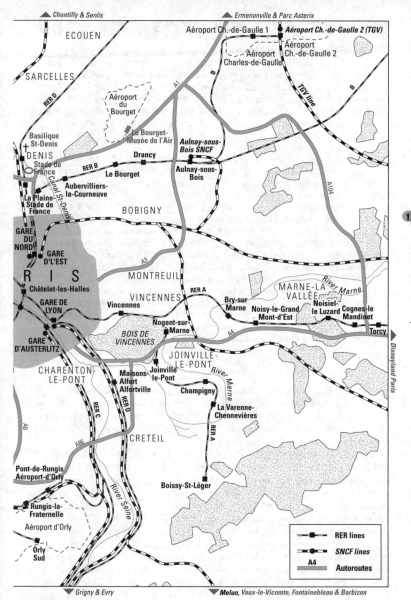

## The château

A great sloping sweep of cobbled courtyard, backed by the old stables, forms a suitably grand prelude to the **château**. It was never meant to be a home. Second only to God, and the head of an immensely powerful state, its master, Louis XIV, was an institution as much as a private individual. His risings and

## Versaille practicalities

To **get to Versailles**, take the RER line C5 to Versailles-Rive Gauche (40min); turn right out of the station and then immediately left to approach the palace – a five-minute walk. The château is **open** throughout the year, except on Mondays, public holidays and during occasional state events (May–Sept 9am–6.30pm; Oct–April 9am–5.30pm; @www.chateauversailles.fr). A "passport" (€20) allows unhindered access throughout, but otherwise the various sections of the palace and its gardens each have a separate entrance fee. If you're coming by public transport, note that RER and train stations sell a combined transport and château entry ticket, which allows you to skip the main queue.

As you approach the château and the central **Cour de Marbre**, the courtyard just beyond the equestrian statue of Louis XIV, various **entry points** are clearly indicated by letters. Entrance A, opposite the chapel on the right, is often signalled by long queues; this door allows access to the main showcase rooms of the palace, the **State Apartments** and **Hall of Mirrors**, which can be visited without a guide (€7.50, or €5.30 after 3.30pm). If you want to see the **King's Bedchamber** without going on a tour, make for Entrance C, in the top left-hand corner of the courtyard; you have to rent an **audioguide** (€4) for the privilege. Entrance D is the place to book yourself on a **guided tour** (€4–8), which take you to wings of the palace that can't otherwise be seen; there are various itineraries throughout the day, including English-language tours, and they can all be booked in the morning (call ☎01.30.83.76.20 to find out what tours will be running). You should turn up reasonably early in the day to make sure of a place. It's well worth taking at least one tour if only for the guides' commentaries, which are usually extremely well-informed – though some anecdotes should be taken with a pinch of salt and one or two guides seem to be outright royalists. Don't set out to see the whole palace in one day – it's not possible.

sittings, comings and goings, were minutely regulated and rigidly encased in ceremony, attendance at which was an honour much sought after by courtiers. Versailles was the headquarters of every arm of the state, and the entire court of around 3500 nobles lived in the palace (in a state of unhygienic squalor according to contemporary accounts).

Construction began in 1664 and lasted virtually until Louis XIV's death in 1715, after which the château was abandoned for a few years before being reoccupied by Louis XV in 1722. It remained a residence of the royal family until the Revolution of 1789, when the furniture was sold and the pictures dispatched to the Louvre. Thereafter Versailles fell into ruin until Louis-Philippe established his giant museum of French Glory here; it still exists, though most is mothballed. In 1871, during the Paris Commune, the château became the seat of the nationalist government, and the French parliament continued to meet in Louis XV's opera building until 1879. Restoration only began in earnest between the two world wars, but today it proceeds apace, the château's management scouring the auction houses of the world in the search for original furnishings from Louis XVI's day. Ironically, they have been helped in the task by the efforts of the revolutionaries, who inventoried all the palace's furnishings before they were auctioned off in 1793–4, a process that took a year.

The rooms you can visit without a guide are known as the **State Apartments**, as they were used for all the king's official business. The route leads past the royal chapel, a grand structure that ranks among France's finest Baroque creations. From there, a procession of gilded drawing rooms leads to

△ Versailles

the king's throne room and the dazzling **Galerie des Glaces** (Hall of Mirrors), where the Treaty of Versailles was signed after World War I. Under the golden barrel ceiling, with its paintings by Charles Le Brun showing the glories of Louis XIV, Georges Clemenceau finally won his notorious "war guilt" clause, which blamed the entire conflict on German aggression. The *galerie* is best viewed at the end of the day, when the crowds have departed and the setting sun floods it from the west, across the park. More fabulously rich rooms, this time belonging to the queen's apartments, line the northern wing, beginning with the queen's bedchamber, which has been restored exactly as it was in its last refit, of 1787, with hardly a surface unadorned with gold leaf. At the end of the visit, the staircase leads down to the **Hall of Battles**, whose oversize canvases unashamedly blow the trumpet for France's historic military victories; be thankful that most of the rest of Louis-Philippe's historical museum is out of bounds.

## The park

You could spend the whole day just exploring the **park** at Versailles (daily 7am–dusk), along with its lesser outcrops of royal mania: the Italianate **Grand Trianon**, designed by Hardouin-Mansart in 1687 as a "country retreat" for Louis XIV; and the more modest **Petit Trianon**, built by Gabriel in the 1760s for Louis XV's mistress, Mme de Pompadour (daily: April–Oct noon–6.30pm; Nov–March noon–5.30pm; combined ticket for both Trianons €5). The interior of the latter is the more appealing, its restrained elegance refreshing after the over-indulgences of the palace – as was intended. Just beyond these is the bizarre **Hameau de la Reine**, a play village and thatch-roofed farm built in 1783 for Marie-Antoinette to indulge the fashionable Rousseau-inspired fantasy of returning to the natural life. It's quintessentially picturesque, but you can't get inside and parts of the surrounding area may be off-limits for some years to come while a massive redesign programme is underway. The plan is to turn the catastrophe of the storms of December 1999 – when ten thousand trees in the park were uprooted – into an opportunity to recreate the elaborate gardens as they must have looked under Marie-Antoinette.

The terraces between the château and the park form Le Nôtre's statue-studded **gardens**, for which you have to pay entry between April and October (€3). In the summer months, the **fountains** dance elaborately to the tune of classical music (July–Sept Sat & Sun 11am, 3.30pm & 5.20pm; April–June Sat only; €5.50).

Distances in the park are considerable. If you can't manage them on foot, a **petit train** shuttles between the terrace in front of the château and the Trianons (€3.50); it runs about every 15min in summer. There are **bikes** for hire at the Grille de la Reine, Porte St-Antoine and by the Grand Canal. Boats are for hire on the Grand Canal, next to a pair of **café-restaurants** – picnics are officially forbidden.

---

To **connect between St-Germain-en-Laye, Marly-le-Roi and Versailles**, take bus #1, which runs roughly every half-hour (more like every 90min on Sun) from Versailles' train and RER station, stopping at place Hoche, near the château gates. From there it continues to the Musée Promenade at Marly and on to the centre of St-Germain-en-Laye and its RER station. The trip takes roughly half an hour from Versailles through to St-Germain.

## The town

The **tourist office** is on the left of Versailles-Rive Gauche RER station, at 2bis av de Paris (daily May–Sept 9am–7pm, Oct–April 9am–6pm; ℡01.39.24.88.88, ⓦwww.versailles-tourisme.com), but there's little to drag you away from the château, unless you're desperate to see the **Salle du Jeu de Paume** on rue du Jeu de Paume (May–Sept Sat & Sun 12.30–6pm; free), the tennis court where the representatives of the Third Estate set the revolution in progress. More interesting is the **Potager du Roi**, the king's kitchen-garden, which lies five minutes' walk east of the château's main gate, with its entrance on rue Joffre (April–Oct daily 10am–6pm; weekdays €4.50, weekends €6.50). Nine hectares were under the care of the head-gardener, Jean-Baptiste La Quintinie, who managed to produce strawberries in January and asparagus in December; the best of the fruit and vegetables produced here was sent by the King to those in favour. A statue of La Quintinie stands on the raised terrace watching over his plot, a great sunken square of espaliered fruit trees and geometrically arranged vegetables. In summer, or on a fine day in late March or early April, when many fruit trees flower, it's a lovely spot to wander, the gardens seemingly surveyed by the stately church of St-Louis, on the other side of the western wall. Some of the 150 varieties of apples and pears, and 50 types of vegetables, are sold in the little farm shop (closed noon–2pm).

The dominant population of the town is aristocratic, those holding pre-revolutionary titles rather disdainful of those dating merely from Napoleon. On Bastille Day, local conservatives like to show their colours, donning black ribbons and ties to mourn the passing of the *ancien régime*. Near the park entrance at the end of boulevard de la Reine, there's a suitably posh place **to take tea**: the *Hôtel Palais Trianon*, where the final negotiations for the Treaty of Versailles took place in 1919. At the other end of the scale, Versailles' **markets** offer excellent bargains, both for food in the Marché Notre-Dame (Sun, Tues & Fri 8am–1pm), and for secondhand stuff (Fri, Sat & Sun 10am–7pm, Thurs 2–7pm) in the passage de la Geôle.

# Marly-le-Roi

Louis XIV's more intimate residence, **Marly-le-Roi**, 10km north at Marly, was destroyed during the revolution. However, the grounds retain their outlines and a small museum on site preserves paintings, etchings and some of the furniture of this second residence. Built between 1681 and 1684 according to plans drawn up by Hardouin-Mansart, the château at Marly was used for hunting escapades and games, with a few select guests only. A walk round the grounds coupled with the small museum of Marly memorabilia, makes for a pleasant stroll and a glimpse of a less public side of the Sun King.

The **Musée Promenade Marly-le-Roi**, on the east side of the park, by the Grille Royale (open Wed–Sun 2–6pm; €3.05) documents the history of Marly Château through paintings, etchings and architectural plans of the château. Given Louis' taste for grandeur at Versailles, the residence at Marly was surprisingly small; remains of the foundations can be seen on the terrace above the large pool in the park. The main feature was water, pumped up from the Seine by the innovative Marly water-machine and brought by aqueduct up to the hill behind, from where it sourced the pools and fountains of Marly as well as running south to feed the fountains at Versailles. Only two of the pools remain and they are devoid of the statuary features for which Marly was so renowned. Copies of two of the sculptor Coustou's large rearing horse sculptures (known as the Marly horses) do adorn their original position (at the north end, by the *abreuvoir*); the originals are on display in the Marly courtyard in the Louvre museum along with some of the other retrieved statues (see p.69).

To **get to the park** at Marly-le-Roi from the centre of Paris, take the train from St-Lazare (direction St-Nom-La-Bretèche) and get off at Marly-le-Roi, from whence it's a fifteen-minute walk up avenue Général-Leclerc (opposite the train station) through the pretty old part of Marly and left down Grande-Rue to the western edge of the park. The entrance is to the left of the tourist office. Crossing the park eastwards to reach the museum takes roughly fifteen minutes.

# St-Germain-en-Laye

Predating the châteaux of Versailles and Marly-le-Roi, the unattractively reno-vated château of **St-Germain-en-Laye**, 4km north of Marly and 20km out of Paris, was one of the main residences of the French court before the move to Versailles. It now houses the extraordinary **Musée des Antiquités Nationales** (daily except Tues 9am–5.15pm; €4, Sun €2.60) or national archeology museum.

The presentation and lighting make the visit a real pleasure, although modern panelling covers up many of the original features of the château. The extensive Stone Age section includes mock-ups of several cave drawings and carvings, as well as a beautiful collection of decorative objects and tools. All ages of prehis-tory are covered, as well as more recent history, with exhibitions on the Celts, Romans and Franks. There's a great section on the battle of Alésia when the Gallic chieftain Vercingétorix found himself and his armies besieged by the Romans. A model of Caesar's double fortifications that ringed the bottom of the hill of Alésia shows how, despite being attacked from the inside by Vercingétorix's army, as well as from the outside by the called-for reinforcements, the Romans, thanks to their ingenious fortifications, managed to win. The end piece is a room of **comparative archeology**, with objects from cultures across the globe.

From right outside the château, a **terrace** – Le Nôtre arranging the land-scape again – stretches for more than 2km above the Seine, with a view over the whole of Paris. Behind it is the **forest** of St-Germain, a sizeable expanse of woodland that's nowadays crisscrossed by too many roads to make it a con-vincing wilderness.

If you've got time to spare, the centre of St-Germain-en-Laye is pleasant for a wander, with a fair few pedestrianized streets and upmarket shops. To reach St-Germain-en-Laye take RER line A direct to the terminus at St-Germain-en-Laye; the journey takes roughly twenty minutes.

# Malmaison

The relatively small and enjoyable **Château of Malmaison** (April–Oct Mon & Wed–Fri 9.30am–12.30pm & 1.30–5.45pm, Sat & Sun 10am–6.30pm;

Nov–March Mon & Wed–Fri 9.30am–12.30pm & 1.30–5.15pm, Sat & Sun 10am–6pm) is set in the beautiful grounds of the **Bois-Préau**, about 15km west of central Paris.

This was the home of the Empress Josephine. During the 1800–1804 Consulate, Napoleon would drive out at weekends, though by all accounts his presence was hardly guaranteed to make the party go with a bang. Twenty minutes was all the time allowed for meals, and when called upon to sing in party games, the great man always gave a rendition of "Malbrouck s'en va-t'en guerre" (Malbrouck Goes to War), out of tune. A slightly odd choice, too, when you remember that it was Malbrouck, the Duke of Marlborough, who had given the French armies a couple of drubbings a hundred years earlier. According to his secretary, Malmaison was "the only place next to the battle-field where he was truly himself". After their divorce, Josephine stayed on here, building up her superb rose garden and occasionally receiving visits from the emperor until her death in 1814.

Visitors today can see the official apartments, which perfectly preserve the distinctive First Empire style, as well as Josephine's clothes, china, glass and personal possessions. During the Nazi occupation, the imperial chair in the library was rudely violated by the fat buttocks of Reichsmarschall Goering, dreaming perhaps of promotion or the conquest of Egypt. There are other Napoleonic bits in the nearby Bois-Préau museum, currently closed for renovation with no opening date in sight.

To reach Malmaison, take the métro to Grande-Arche-de-la-Défense, then bus #258 to Malmaison-Château. If you don't mind walking, take the RER to Rueil-Malmaison and walk from there, or to make a slightly longer feature of it, follow the GR11 footpath for about two kilometres from the Pont de Chatou along the left bank of the Seine and into the château park.

# Chatou

A long narrow island in the Seine, the **Île de Chatou**, between Rueil-Malmaison and St-Germain-en-Laye, was once a rustic spot where Parisians came on the newly opened train line to row on the river, and to dine, dance and flirt at the *guinguettes* – the classic Parisian dancehall-restaurants on the riverbank. A favourite haunt of artists was the **Maison Fournaise**, just below the Pont de Chatou road bridge, which is now once again an attractive restaurant (closed Sun evening in winter; ☎01.30.71.41.91; menu €25), with a small museum of memorabilia (Wed–Sun noon–6pm; €4). One of Renoir's best-known canvases, *Le Déjeuner des Canotiers*, shows his friends lunching on the balcony of Maison Fournaise, which is still shaded by a magnificent riverside plane tree. A copy of the painting pasted to a board next to the restaurant marks the spot where Renoir would have placed his easel. Habitués of the restaurant included Impressionist painters as well as de Vlaminck and his fellow Fauves, Derain and Matisse. The **Maison Levanneur**, opposite, was rented between 1900 and 1905 by Derain and de Vlaminck as a studio. It has since been renovated and now houses the **Centre National de l'Estampe et de l'Art Imprimé** (Wed–Sun noon–6pm; free; ☎01.39.52.45.35, ⓦwww .cneai.com), which puts on temporary exhibitions linked to the art of printing.

Heading south, under the Pont de Chatou, will bring you to the Parc des Impressionnistes, a fairly nondescript park with a few picnic tables. If you

For painters in search of visual inspiration, the countryside around Paris began to take a primary role in the late nineteenth century. Many a Paris-based artist left the city, either on a day jaunt or on a more permanent basis, in search of direct sunlight, clouds and the effect of light on water. The towns along the banks of the Seine read like a roll-call of the Musée d'Orsay's Impressionist paintings, and pockets of unchanged towns and scenery remain. Local museums, set up to record these pioneering artistic days, are well worth a visit, particularly in **Auvers-sur-Oise** (see below) and the island of **Chatou** (see p.225).

To explore further, around **Bougival**, **Louveciennes** and **Le Port-Marly**, contact the tourist office in Marly, 2 av des Combattants (℡01.30.61.61.35), which produces an **Impressionist trail** leaflet and map. If you're willing to roam a little further afield, excursions can also be made to **Barbizon** (see p.236), home to the influential Barbizon group, and to Monet's studio and Japanese-style garden at **Giverny**, in Normandy (see p.240), where he lived and painted his experimental waterlily sequences.

continue beyond the park, however, a narrow wooded path with the Seine running either side takes you as far as the **Grenouillère** (ten-minute walk), a popular spot in the early 1900s for riverside drinking, dancing, bathing and boating; it was much frequented and painted by the Impressionists. Nothing remains of the *café-bal* that existed, but there are a couple of reproduced paintings by Monet and Renoir that are part of an Impressionist trail and, aside from a wooden bench and steps down to the river, it's a surprisingly untouched part of the island in the Seine. A small **museum** (Tues, Thurs and Sun 2–6pm; closed mid-Dec to mid-Jan; €3.20) of memorabilia related to the Grenouillère is housed in the Maison Joséphine (so-called because Joséphine de Beauharnais lived there for two years before her marriage to Napoleon) on the other side of the river in Croissy, but you need to head back up the Pont de Chatou to cross over, and follow the river downstream on the Chatou/Croissy side to get there.

**Access** to the island is from the Rueil-Malmaison RER stop. Take the exit avenue Albert-1$^{er}$, go left out of the station and right along the dual carriageway onto the bridge – a ten-minute walk. Bizarrely, the island hosts a twice-yearly **ham and antiques** fair (March & Sept), which is fun to check out. **River cruises** round Chatou or as far as Auvers-sur-Oise (an all-day expedition) depart from the Capitainerie on the Rueil-Malmaison bank of the Seine, opposite the Maison Fournaise (May–Oct Sundays and public holidays; €40/58 depending on the cruise, with obligatory lunch; ℡01.47.16.72.66 for tickets and information).

# Auvers-Sur-Oise

On the banks of the River Oise, about 35km northwest of Paris, **AUVERS** makes an attractive rural excursion. It's the place where **Van Gogh** spent the last two months of his life, in a frenzy of painting activity, producing more canvases than the days of his stay. The church at Auvers, the portrait of Dr Gachet, black crows flapping across a wheat field – many of Van Gogh's best-known works belong to this period. He died in his brother's arms, after an incompetent attempt to shoot himself, in the tiny attic room he rented in the **Auberge Ravoux**. The *auberge* still stands, repaired and renovated, on the main street. A visit to Van Gogh's room (mid-Dec to mid-March daily 10am–6pm; €5) is movingly modest, and there's a short video about his time in Auvers.

The **Musée de l'Absinthe** (June–Sept Wed–Sun 11am–6pm; Oct, Nov & March–May Sat & Sun 11am–6pm; €4.50) is devoted to the cloudy aniseed-flavoured liqueur, banned in France since 1915, that was said to enhance creativity and was Van Gogh's favourite drink. Inside the museum, there's a mock-up of a typical bar of the era, along with the various implements – glasses, holed spoons – associated with the ritual of drinking it. You can't try the stuff on the spot, but the shop is allowed to sell various brands in sealed bottles, and they even have a few miniatures. It's as potent as they say.

At the entrance to the village is the handsome but undistinguished **Château d'Auvers**, which offers a technological tour of the world the Impressionists inhabited (Tues–Sun: April–Sept 10.30am–7.30pm; Oct–March 10.30am–6pm; Ⓦwww.chateau-auvers.fr; €10). As you wander through the various rooms mocked-up as cafés, period trains and so on, with cinema-style projections and special effects, an audiohelmet relays evocative music and a commentary. If you really want to conjure the Impressionists' world, however, simply take a walk through the old part of the village, past the church and the red lane into the famous wheat field and up the hill to the cemetery where, against the far left wall in a humble ivy-covered grave, the Van Gogh brothers lie side by side.

Auvers boasts further artistic connections – most notably with Van Gogh's predecessor **Daubigny**, a contemporary of Corot and Daumier. A small **museum** (Wed–Sun: March–Oct 2–6pm, Nov–Feb 2–5pm; €3.50), dedicated to him and his art, can be visited above the tourist office. His **studio-house** (April–Oct Tues–Sun 2–6.30pm; €4.50), built to his own requirements, can also be visited at 61 rue Daubigny. From here, Daubigny would go off for weeks at a time, in his boat, to paint, hence the boat sitting in the garden which is, in fact, a replica of a smaller boat once owned by Monet.

To reach Auvers **by road**, take the autoroute A15 towards Cergy-Pontoise, the exit for Saint-Ouen-L'Aumône, then turn off on the D928 to Auvers-sur-Oise. **Trains** depart from Gare du Nord or Gare St-Lazare, changing at Pontoise. For something **to eat**, try the *Hostellerie du Nord* and the *Auberge Ravoux*, both of which can provide an excellent lunch for around €20.

# St-Denis

For most of the twentieth century, **St-Denis**, 10km north of the centre of Paris and accessible by métro (M° St-Denis-Basilique), was one of the most heavily industrialized communities in France, and a bastion of the Communist party. Since those days, factories have closed, unemployment is rife and immigration has radically altered the ethnic mix. For bourgeois Parisians, the political threat of the *banlieue rouge* ("red suburbs") has become the social threat of the *banlieue chaude* ("hot suburbs"). Visitors, however, are likely to find a buoyant, youthful community – one in three of its residents are under 25, a far cry from the silver-haired centre of Paris – its pride buttressed by the town's twin attractions: the ancient **basilica of St-Denis** and the hyper-modern **Stade-de-France**, seat of the 1998 World Cup final.

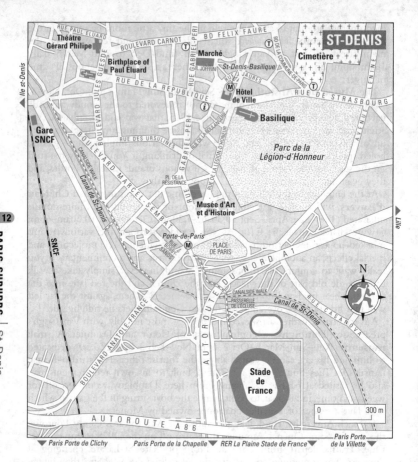

Map labels:

RUE PAUL ELUARD
Théâtre
Gérard Philipe
BOULEVARD CARNOT
BD FELIX FAURE
+ + + + + +
+ + + + + + +
ST-DENIS
Birthplace of
Paul Éluard
Marché
Cimetière
Île st-Denis
RUE DE LA RÉPUBLIQUE
JOFFRIN
St-Denis-Basilique
RUE GABRIEL-PÉRI
BD DE LA COMMUNE-DE-PARIS
RUE JAURÈS
Hôtel
de Ville
RUE DE STRASBOURG
AVENUE LÉNINE
Gare
SNCF
RUE DES URSULINES
Basilique
BOULEVARD JULES GUESDE
CANALSIDE WALK
Canal de St-Denis
BOULEVARD MARCEL SEMBAT
RUE GABRIEL-PÉRI
RUE DE LA LÉGION-D'HONNEUR
RUE DE LA BOULANGERIE
Parc de la
Légion-d'Honneur
SNCF
PL. DE LA
RÉSISTANCE
Musée d'Art
et d'Histoire
Porte-de-Paris
RUE
BOBBY
SANDS
PLACE
DE PARIS
AUTOROUTE DU NORD A 1
N
BOULEVARD ANATOLE-FRANCE
CANALSIDE WALK
PASSERELLE
DE L'ÉCLUSE
Canal de St-Denis
RUE CASANOVA
Stade
de
France
RUE CASANOVA
0        300 m
AUTOROUTE A 86
Lille
Paris Porte
de la Villette
Paris Porte de Clichy     Paris Porte de la Chapelle     RER La Plaine Stade de France     

# The basilica

Close by the St-Denis-Basilique métro station, the **Basilique St-Denis** (April–Sept Mon–Sat 10am–7pm, Sun noon–7pm; Oct–March Mon–Sat 10am–5pm, Sun noon–5pm) is generally regarded as the birthplace of the Gothic style in European architecture. The new basilica was built on the foundations of an earlier abbey church by Abbot Suger, friend and adviser to kings, in the first half of the twelfth century. With its two towers, three large sculpted portals and high rose window, the west front set the pattern of Gothic facades to come, but it was the choir that impressed contemporaries: the list of bishops attending the dedication service almost matches the list of great Gothic cathedrals that were to be raised in the next half century. Suger's innovations can still be seen in the lowest storey of the choir, but the upper storeys were rebuilt in the mid-thirteenth century, at the same time as the nave was constructed. The nave's extraordinary clerestory is almost entirely made of glass, a flat sheet of light soaring above the deep, opaque nave arcade, with the narrow triforium level holding the two styles in balance. It was a brilliant architectural idea, defining the mature Rayonnant style which dominated church architecture for

The first church at St-Denis was probably founded by an early (mid-third-century) Parisian bishop known by the name of Saint Denis, or St Dionysius in English. The legend goes that after he was decapitated for his beliefs at Montmartre – so called because it is the "Mount of the Martyr" – he picked up his own head and walked all the way to St-Denis, thereby establishing the abbey. It's not in fact all that far – just over five kilometres – though as a friend of Edward Gibbon's once remarked, "the distance is nothing, it's the first step that counts".

the next century and a half. The abbey's **royal history** began with the coronation of Pepin the Short, in 754, but it wasn't until Hugh Capet, in 996, that it became the burial place of the kings of France. Since then, all but three of France's kings have been interred here, and their very fine tombs and effigies are distributed about the transepts and **ambulatory** (€5.50; closed during services). Among the most interesting are the enormous Renaissance memorial to François 1er on the right just beyond the entrance, and the tombs of Louis XII, Henri II and Catherine de Médicis on the left side of the church. Also on the left, close to the altar steps, Philippe the Bold's is one of the earliest lookalike portrait statues, while to the right of the ambulatory steps you can see the stocky little general Bertrand du Guesclin, who gave the English the runaround after the death of the Black Prince. On the level above him – invariably graced by bouquets of flowers – are the undistinguished statues of Louis XVI and Marie-Antoinette. Around the corner on the far side of the ambulatory is Clovis himself, king of the Franks way back in 500, a canny little German who wiped out Roman Gaul and turned it into France, with Paris a capital.

A good way to appreciate the atmosphere in the basilica is during the **St-Denis Festival** (end of June; ☎01.48.13.06.07, ⊛www.festival-saint-denis.fr) when it plays host to various concerts.

## The town

The **tourist office** (daily 10am–1pm & 2–5pm; ☎01.55.87.08.70, ⊛www .ville-saint-denis.fr), opposite the basilica at 1 rue de la République, sells tickets for the St-Denis festival and can provide maps of the town.

Although the centre of St-Denis still retains traces of its small town origins, the area immediately abutting the basilica has been transformed into an extraordinary fortress-like housing and shopping complex, where local youths hang out on mopeds and skateboards, women shop for African groceries and men, fresh from the latest conflict zone, beg for a few cents. The thrice-weekly **market**, in the main place Victor Hugo (Tues, Fri & Sun mornings), peddles vegetables at half the price of Parisian markets, as well as cheap curios, clothes and fabrics. Adjacent, off rue Dupont, are the covered *halles*, a multi-ethnic affair where the quantity of offal on the butchers' stalls – ears, feet, tails and bladders – shows this is not rich folks' territory.

About five minutes' walk south of the basilica is the **Musée d'Art et d'Histoire de la Ville de St-Denis** (Mon, Wed & Fri 10am–5.30pm, Thurs 10am–8pm, Sat & Sun 2–6.30pm; €4), housed in a former Carmelite convent on rue Gabriel-Péri. The quickest route is along rue de la Légion-d'Honneur, then take the third right. The exhibits on display are not of spectacular interest, though the presentation is excellent. The **local archeology** collection is good, and there are some interesting paintings of nineteenth- and twentieth-century industrial landscapes, including the St-Denis canal. The one unique collection is of documents relating to **the Commune**: posters, cartoons, broadsheets, paintings, plus an audiovisual presentation. There's also an exhibition of manuscripts and rare editions of the Communist poet, **Paul Éluard**, native son of St-Denis.

About ten minutes' further down rue Gabriel-Péri you come to the métro stop St-Denis Porte-de-Paris. Just beyond it, a broad footbridge crosses the motorway and Canal St-Denis to the **Stade de France**, scene of France's World Cup victory in 1998. At least €430 million was spent on the construction of this stadium, whose elliptical structure is best appreciated at night when lit up. If there isn't a match or a mega-rock event on, you can visit its grounds, facilities and a small museum (daily 10am–6pm; €6).

From the northern side of the stadium's footbridge it's possible to **walk back to Paris** all the way along the canal towpath. Parts of the canalside are being rehabilitated and may necessitate a slight detour, and there are stretches where it may feel as if you're not supposed to be there, but press on regardless and you'll eventually fetch up at Porte de la Villette, after no more than two hours. On the way you pass peeling villas with unkempt gardens, patches of greenery, sand and gravel docks, and waste ground where larks rise above rusting bedsteads and old fridges. Decaying tenements and improvised shacks give way to lock-keepers' cottages with roses and vegetable gardens, then derelict factories and huge sheds where trundling gantries load bundles of steel rods onto Belgian barges.

# Le Bourget – Musée de l'Air et de l'Espace

Five kilometres east of St-Denis, a short hop up the A1 motorway, is **Le Bourget** airport. Until the development of Orly in the 1950s it was Paris's principal airport and is closely associated with the exploits of France's pioneering aviators – Lindbergh landed here after his epic first flight across the Atlantic.

Today Le Bourget is used only for internal flights, while some of the older buildings have been turned into a museum of flying machines, the **Musée de l'Air et de l'Espace** (Tues–Sun: May–Oct 10am–6pm; Nov–April 10am–5pm; €6). It consists of five adjacent hangars and a large exhibition space, the Grande Galerie, with displays ranging from early flying machines through to the latest spacecrafts. The first set of displays, dedicated to the Montgolfier brothers, inventors of the first successful hot-air balloon, shows society going balloon crazy. Displays of aeroplanes begin in the Grande Galerie: the first contraption to fly 1km, the first cross-channel flight, the first aerobatics . . . successes and failures are all on display here.

The Grande Galerie also showcases World War I planes, while highlights of World War II aircraft are housed along with the first Concorde prototype

At **Drancy**, near Le Bourget airport, the Germans and the French Vichy regime had a transit camp for Jews en route to Auschwitz – this was where the poet Max Jacob, among many others, died. A cattle wagon and a stone stele in the courtyard of a council estate commemorate the nearly 100,000 Jews who passed through here. Only 1518 returned.

in the Hall Concorde. **Hangars C and D** cover the years from 1945 to the present day with France's high-tech achievements represented by the super-sophisticated, best-selling Mirage fighters and two Ariane space-launchers, Ariane I and the latest, Ariane V (both parked on the tarmac outside). **Hangar E** contains light and sporty aircraft and **Hangar F**, nearest to the entrance, is devoted to **space**, with rockets, satellites, space capsules, and the like. Some are mock-ups, some the real thing. Among the latter are a Lunar Roving Vehicle, the Soyuz craft in which a French astronaut flew and France's own first successful space rocket. Everything is accompanied by extremely good explanatory panels – though in French only.

To get to the Musée de L'Air et de l'Espace **from Paris**, take RER line B from Gare du Nord to Gare du Bourget, then bus #152 to Le Bourget/Musée de l'Air. Alternatively, take bus #350 from Gare du Nord, Gare de l'Est and Porte de la Chapelle, or #152 from Porte de la Villette.

# Meudon and Sèvres

The tranquil suburb of **Meudon**, 10km southwest of Paris, was where **Rodin** spent the last years of his life. His house and studio, the **Villa des Brillants**, is at 19 av Rodin (May–Oct Fri–Sun 1–5.15pm; €2) and is worth a visit for its wealth of preparatory sketches, plaster casts and studies. The studies, figuring many of his most famous works, were donated to the state in 1916 by Rodin and have the distinction of being the primary material, in direct contact with Rodin's hand, something that can't be said of the finished product. It was in this house that he lived with his companion, Rose Beuret, and here that he married her, after fifty years together, just a fortnight before her death in February 1917. His own death followed in November, and they are buried together on the terrace below the house, beneath a bronze version of *The Thinker*. The classical facade behind masks an enormous pavilion which once housed a landmark Rodin retrospective at the Universal Exposition of 1901; today it contains plaster versions of his most famous works.

To get to Rodin's house at Meudon, take RER line C to Meudon-Val Fleury, then it's a fifteen-minute walk along avenues Barbusse and Rodin. Meudon and Sèvres are conveniently connected by bus #389 (from stop "Paul Besnard" to "Pont-de-Sèvres"; roughly twenty minutes' journey) making a combined afternoon or day-trip a possibility.

A couple of kilometres west, Meudon's neighbour, **Sèvres**, has been manufacturing fine **porcelain** since the eighteenth century, and, since the beginning of the nineteenth century, has been home to the **Musée National de la Céramique** (daily except Tues 10am–5pm; €4). A ceramics museum may possibly seem a bit too rarefied an attraction to justify a trip out of Paris, but if you do have the time, there is much to be savoured. Inevitably, displays centre on Sèvres ware, but there are also collections of Islamic, Chinese, Italian, German, Dutch and English pieces.

Right by the museum is the **Parc de St-Cloud**, good for fresh air and visual order, with a geometrical sequence of pools and fountains. You could, if you wanted, take a train from St-Lazare to St-Cloud and head south through the park to the museum. For a more direct route to the museum, take the métro to the Pont-de-Sèvres terminus, then cross the bridge and spaghetti junction; the museum is the massive building facing the river bank on your right.

# 13

# Further afield

I n the further reaches and beyond the boundaries of Île-de-France lie exceptional towns and sights that are still accessible as day-trips from Paris and
worth making the effort to visit. An excursion to **Chartres** can seem a long
way to go just to see one building; but then you'd have to go a very long
way indeed to find a building to beat it. Of the châteaux that abound in this
region, we detail only a select few: **Chantilly** with its wonderful art museum;
**Vaux-le-Vicomte**, the envy of Louis XIV; and **Fontainebleau** with its
Italianate decoration that influenced a whole school of art. For artistic attractions, the most satisfying, and consequently the most popular, experience is
undoubtedly **Monet's garden** at Giverny, the inspiration for all his waterlily
canvases in the Marmottan and Musée d'Orsay.

   **Travel details** are given under "practicalities", at the end of each account,
but to check times of specific trains, call ☎08.36.68.41.14 (in English) or visit
SNCF's website at ⓦ www.sncf-voyages.com.

## Chantilly

The main associations with **Chantilly**, a small town 40km north of Paris, are
horses and cream. Some three thousand thoroughbreds prance the forest rides
of a morning, and two of the season's classiest flat races are held here – the
Jockey Club and the Prix de Diane, held on the first and second Sundays in
June. The **château**, which rises romantically from the centre of a lake amid
gardens and a forested park, has stables almost as grand as the main building;
they are still in use today, as the **museum of the horse**. As for **cream**, the
Chantilly recipe is basically whipped and sugared and delicious, and you can
try it in the café in the Hameau, the rustic faux-village within the château
grounds.

### The château

The Chantilly estate used to belong to two of the most powerful clans in
France: first to the Montmorencys, then, through marriage, to the Condés. The
present **château** (July & Aug daily 10am–6pm; March–June, Sept & Oct daily
except Tues 10am–6pm; Nov–Feb Mon & Wed–Fri 10.30am–12.45pm &
2–5pm, Sat & Sun 10.30am–5pm; €7; park open daily same hours, €3) was
put up in the late nineteenth century. It replaced a palace, destroyed in the
Revolution, which had been built for the Grand Condé, who smashed Spanish
military power for Louis XIV in 1643. It's a beautiful structure, graceful and

romantic, surrounded by water and looking out in a haughty manner over a formal arrangement of pools and pathways designed by the busy Le Nôtre.

The entrance is across a moat, past two realistic bronzes of hunting hounds. The visitable parts mainly consist of an enormous collection of paintings and drawings owned by the Institut de France (see p.127), the **Musée Condé**. Stipulated to remain as organized by Henri d'Orléans, the son of France's last king and the donor of the château, the arrangement is haphazard by modern standards but immensely satisfying to eclectic appetites. Some highlights can be found in the Rotunda of the picture gallery – Piero di Cosimo's *Simonetta Vespucci* and Raphael's *La Vierge de Lorette* – and in the so-called Sanctuary, with Raphael's *Three Graces* displayed alongside Filippo Lippi's *Esther et Assuerius* and forty miniatures from a fifteenth-century Book of Hours attributed to the great French Renaissance artist Jean Fouquet. Pass through the Galerie de Psyche with its series of sepia stained glass illustrating Apuleius' Golden Ass, to the room known as the Tribune, where Italian art, including Botticelli's *Autumn*, takes up two walls, and Ingres and Delacroix have a wall each.

A free guided tour will take you round the apartments of the sixteenth-century wing known as the Petit Château. The first port of call is the well-stocked library, where a facsimile of the museum's single greatest treasure is on display, **Les Très Riches Heures du Duc de Berry**, the most celebrated of all the Books of Hours. The illuminated pages illustrating the months of the year with representative scenes from contemporary (early 1400s) rural life – like harvesting and ploughing, sheep-shearing and pruning – are richly coloured and drawn with a delicate naturalism. The remaining half-dozen rooms on the tour mostly show off superb furnishings, with exquisite *boiseries* panelling the walls of the **Singerie**, or Monkey Gallery, wittily painted with allegorical stories in a pseudo-Chinese style. A grand parade of canvases in the long gallery depicts the many battles won by the Grand Condé.

## The Musée Vivant du Cheval

Five minutes' walk back towards town along the château drive stands the colossal stable block, which has been transformed into a museum of horses and horsemanship, the **Musée Vivant du Cheval** (April–Oct Mon & Wed–Fri 10.30am–5.30pm, Sat & Sun 10.30am–6pm; May & June also open Tues 2–5.30pm; July & Aug also open Tues 10.30–5.30pm; Nov–March Mon–Fri 2–5pm, Sat & Sun 10.30am–5pm; €8, or €14 combined ticket with château and park; Ⓦwww.musee-vivant-du-cheval.fr). The building was erected at the beginning of the eighteenth century by the incumbent Condé prince, who believed he would be reincarnated as a horse and wished to provide fitting accommodation for 240 of his future relatives.

In the vast, barrel-vaulted main hall, horses of different breeds from around the world are stalled, with a central ring for equestrian **demonstrations** (April–Oct 11.30am, 3.30pm & 5.15pm; Nov–March weekends 11.30am, 3.30pm & 5.15pm, weekdays 3.30pm only) of the Spanish Riding School type. In the further wing, life-size model horses draw various chariots, carts and drays, and wear saddles and harnesses built for racing, polo, bullfighting and other activities for which horses are used. Off to the sides a handful of rooms are devoted to other horsey specialisms, the one for veterinary medicine proudly displaying a real horse's diseased intestine.

### Chantilly practicalities

**Trains** take about thirty minutes from Paris's Gare du Nord to Chantilly, with slightly fewer than one every hour. Occasional free buses run between the station to the château, though on foot it's a pleasant, two-kilometre stroll through the forest; turn right outside the station, then left at the major roundabout on the signposted **footpath**.

Various **restaurants** tout for custom in town, among which *La Belle Bio*, opposite the horse museum at 22 rue de Connétable (closed Sun eve & Mon), is a standout, serving high quality organic meals for around €25–40.

# Vaux-le-Vicomte

Of all the great mansions within reach of a day's outing from Paris, the classical château of **Vaux-le-Vicomte** (mid-March to mid-Nov daily 10am–6pm; €10), 46km southeast of Paris, is the most architecturally harmonious, the most aesthetically pleasing and the most human in scale. It stands isolated in the countryside amid fields and woods, and its gardens make a lovely place to picnic.

The château was built between 1656 and 1661 for **Nicolas Fouquet**, Louis XIV's finance minister, to the designs of three of the finest French artists of the day. The result was magnificence and precision in perfect proportion, and a bill that could only be paid by someone who occasionally confused the state's accounts with his own. Fouquet, however, had little chance to enjoy his magnificent residence. On August 17, 1661, he invited the king and his courtiers to a sumptuous housewarming party. Three weeks later he was arrested – by d'Artagnan of Musketeer fame – charged with embezzlement, of which he was certainly guilty, and clapped into jail for the rest of his life. Thereupon, the design team of Le Vau, Le Brun and Le Nôtre were carted off to build the king's own piece of one-upmanship, the palace of Versailles.

Stripped of much of its furnishings by the king, the château remained in the possession of Fouquet's widow until 1705, when it was sold to the Maréchal de Villars, an adversary of the Duke of Marlborough in the War of Spanish Succession. In 1764 it was sold, again, to the Duc de Choiseul-Praslin, Louis XV's navy minister. His family kept it until 1875, when, in a state of utter dereliction – the gardens had vanished completely – it was taken over by Alfred Sommier, a French industrialist, who made its restoration and refurbishment his life's work. It was finally opened to the public in 1968.

## The château and gardens

Seen from the entrance, the **château** is a rather austerely magnificent pile surrounded by an artificial moat. It is only when you go through to the south side, where the gardens decline in measured formal patterns of grass and water, clipped box and yew, fountains and statuary, that you can look back and appreciate the very harmonious and very French qualities of the building – the combination of steep, tall roof and central dome with classical pediment and pilasters.

As to the interior, the predominant impression is inevitably of opulence and monumental cost. The main artistic interest lies in the work of **Le Brun**. He was responsible for the two fine **tapestries** in the entrance, made in the local workshops set up by Fouquet specifically to adorn his house, and subsequently removed by Louis XIV to become the famous Gobelins works in Paris (see p.163). Le Brun also painted numerous **ceilings**, notably in Fouquet's bedroom, the Salon des Muses, his *Sleep* in the Cabinet des Jeux, and the so-called King's bedroom, whose decor is the first example of the style that became known as Louis Quatorze. Other points of interest are the **kitchens**, which have not been altered since construction, and a room displaying letters in the hand of Fouquet, Louis XIV and other notables. One, dated November 1794 (mid-Revolution), addresses the incumbent Duc de Choiseul-Praslin as *tu*. "Citizen," it says, "you've got a week to hand over one hundred thousand pounds . . .", and signs off with "Cheers and brotherhood". You can imagine the shock to the aristocratic system.

The **Musée des Équipages** in the stables comprises a collection of horse-drawn vehicles, including the method of transport used by Charles X fleeing Paris and the Duc de Rohan retreating from Moscow. Every fine Saturday evening from May to mid-October, between 8pm and midnight (€13 entrance), the **state rooms** are illuminated with a thousand candles, as they probably were on the occasion of Fouquet's fateful party. The **fountains** and other waterworks can be seen in action on the second and last Saturdays of each month between April and October, from 3pm until 6pm.

### Vaux-le-Vicomte practicalities

**By road**, Vaux-le-Vicomte is 7km east of Melun, which is itself 46km southeast of Paris by the A4 autoroute (exit Melun-Sénart) or a little further by the A6 (exit Melun). **By train** there are regular services from Gare de Lyon as far as Melun (40min), and a rather sparse bus service covers the journey to the château on weekends. Otherwise, short of walking, the only means of covering the last 7km is **by taxi** (around €20). There is a taxi rank on the forecourt of the train station, with telephone numbers to call if there are no taxis waiting.

# Fontainebleau

The **château of Fontainebleau**, 60km south of Paris, owes its existence to its situation in the middle of a magnificent forest, which made it the perfect base for royal hunting expeditions. A lodge was built here as early as the twelfth century, but its transformation into a luxurious palace only took place in the sixteenth century on the initiative of François 1$^{er}$, who imported a colony of Italian artists to carry out the decoration, most notably Rosso Fiorentino and Niccolò dell'Abate. The palace continued to enjoy royal favour well into the nineteenth century; Napoleon spent huge amounts of money on it, as did Louis-Philippe. And, after World War II, when it was liberated from the

Germans by General Patton, it served for a while as Allied military HQ in Europe. The town in the meantime has become the seat of INSEAD, a prestigious and elite multilingual business school.

The **buildings**, unpretentious and attractive despite their extent, have none of the architectural unity of a purpose-built residence like Vaux-le-Vicomte. Their distinction is the sumptuous interiors worked by the Italians, notably the celebrated **Galerie François-1<sup>er</sup>** – which had a seminal influence on the subsequent development of French aristocratic art and design – the Salle de Bal, the Salon Louis-XIII, and the Salle du Conseil with its eighteenth-century decoration.

The **gardens** are equally luscious. If you want to escape into the relative wilds, head for the surrounding **Forest of Fontainebleau**, which is full of walking and cycling trails, all marked on Michelin map #196 (*Environs de Paris*). Its rocks are a favourite training ground for Paris-based climbers.

### Fontainebleau practicalities

The château is **open** daily except Tuesdays (June–Sept 9.30am–6pm; Oct–May 9.30am–5pm; €5.50). The Musée Chinois is open when there's enough staff, and entry is included with ticket for the château. The Musée Napoleon offers guided tours mornings only, while guided tours of the Petits Appartements take place in the afternoon (both €3). Ring for further details (℡01.60.71.50.70). **Getting to Fontainebleau** from Paris is straightforward. By road it is 16km from the A6 autoroute (exit Fontainebleau). By train, it is 50 minutes from the Gare de Lyon to Fontainebleau-Avon station. Bus #A or #B from Fontainebleau-Avon station will take you to the château gates in fifteen minutes. You can buy a combined train/bus/château ticket at the Gare de Lyon (€9).

## Barbizon

Ten kilometres northwest of Fontainebleau on the other side of the forest, the country town of **Barbizon** is easily accessible from Fontainebleau by car. The landscape and country living around Barbizon, southeast of Paris, inspired painters such as Rousseau and Millet to set up camp here, initiating an artistic movement, the Barbizon group. More painters followed as well as writers and musicians, all attracted by the lifestyle and community. The *Auberge du Père Ganne*, on the main road, became the place to stay, not unrelated to the fact that the generous owner accepted the artists' decorations of his inn and furniture as payment. Now home to a **museum** (Mon & Wed–Fri 10am–12.30pm & 2–5.30pm; €4.50), the inn still contains the original painted furniture, as well as many Barbizon paintings.

**Buses** run to Barbizon from Fontainebleau only on a Wednesday and Saturday.

# Chartres

When King Philip-Auguste visited **Chartres** to mediate between church and townsfolk after the riots of October 1210, the cathedral chapter noted that "he did not wish to stay any longer in the city but, so as to avoid the blasphemous citizens, stayed here only for one hour and hastened to return." Chartres' modern visitors don't tend to stay much longer, but if you've come all the way from Paris, a journey of 80km, the modest charms of the little town at the cathedral's feet may persuade you to linger.

## The Cathédrale Notre-Dame

The **Cathédrale Notre-Dame** (May–Oct 8am–8pm; Jan–April & Nov–Dec 8am–7.15pm) is one of the finest examples of Gothic architecture in Europe and, built between 1194 and 1260, perhaps the quickest ever to be constructed. It's best experienced on a cloud-free winter's day when the low sun transmits the stained-glass colours to the interior stone, the quiet scattering of people leaves the acoustics unconfused, and the exterior is unmasked for miles around. Meditatively cloudy days are more typical, however, making the cathedral's spinily buttressed hulk and mismatched spires look like a scene from a Flemish landscape painting as they rise from the flat arable fields of the Beauce.

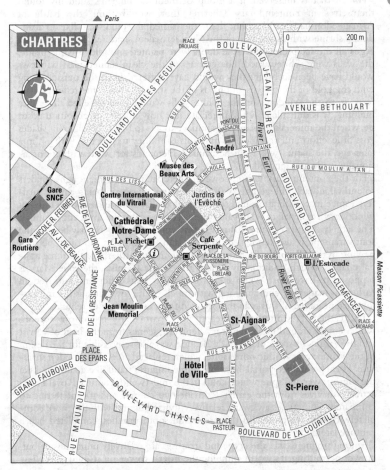

The best-preserved medieval cathedral in Europe is, for today's visitors, only flawed by changes in Roman Catholic worship. The immense distance from the door to the altar, which, through mists of incense and drawn-out harmonies, emphasized the distance that only priests could mediate between worshippers and worshipped, has been abandoned. The central altar undermines (from a secular point of view) the theatrical dogma of the building and puts cloth and boards where the coloured lights should play. Fortunately, the chairs no longer cover up the labyrinth on the floor of the nave – an original thirteenth-century arrangement and a great rarity, since the authorities at other cathedrals had them pulled up as distracting frivolities. The **Chartres labyrinth** traces a path over 200m long, enclosed within a diameter of 13m, the same size as the rose window above the main doors. The centre used to have a bronze relief of Theseus and the Minotaur and the pattern of the maze was copied from classical texts – the medieval Catholic idea of the path of life to eternity echoing Greek myth. Finding your own way round the labyrinth is permitted on Fridays in summer (April–Oct).

For all that is preserved, if a group of medieval pilgrims suddenly found themselves in contemporary Chartres they would think the battle of Armaggedon had been lost. For them, the cathedral would seem like an abandoned shrine with its promise of the New Jerusalem shattered. In **the Middle Ages** all the sculptures above the doors were painted and gilded while inside, the walls were whitewashed. The colours in the clean stained-glass windows would have been so bright they would have glittered from the outside along with the gold of the crowns and halos of the statuary. Inside, the reflected patterns from the windows on the white walls would have jewelled the entire building. It is difficult now to appreciate just how important **colour** used to be, when the minerals or plant and animal extracts to make the different shades cost time, effort and considerable amounts of money to procure. Perhaps, in a later age, the statues will again be painted. Demands for whitewash are occasionally made and ignored.

For the contemporary visitor, however, there are more than enough wonders to enthral, notably the geometry of the building, unique in being almost unaltered since its consecration, and the shining circular symmetries of the transept windows, virtually all of which are original, dating from the thirteenth century. The largely twelfth-century "**Blue Virgin**" window, in the first bay beyond the south transept, is also renowned. Pilgrims and worshippers can often be seen praying in the **Chapelle St-Sacrement**, the most northerly of the three apsidal chapels, which traditionally houses the Sancta Camisia, the robe Mary is supposed to have worn when she gave birth to Jesus. After fire destroyed an earlier Romanesque church, along with much of the town, it was the miraculous reappearance of this relic that spurred the townspeople to rebuild.

The cathedral's **stonework** is captivating, particularly the **choir screen**, which curves around the ambulatory, depicting scenes from the lives of Christ and the Virgin. Its sculptor, Jehan de Beauce, was also responsible for the design of the Flamboyant Gothic north spire, which replaced an earlier wooden structure. At each entrance portal, hosts of sculpted figures stand like guardians. Like the south tower and spire which abuts it, the mid-twelfth century Royal Portal actually survives from the earlier Romanesque church, and it's interesting to compare its sometimes awkward, relatively stylized figures with the more completely Gothic sculptures on the north and south porches, completed half a century later.

Among paying extras, the crypt and treasures are relatively unimpressive but, crowds permitting, it's worth climbing the **north tower** for its bird's-eye view

One of the best ways to appreciate the detail of the Cathédrale Notre-Dame is to join a **guided tour** given by the erudite Englishman Malcolm Miller. From April to November, he does two tours at noon and 2.45pm from Monday to Saturday, starting just inside the west door (days and times vary in winter: call ☎02.37.28.15.58; €10). The cost may seem extravagant, but this is no ordinary patter – it's a labour of love from someone who has studied, written and lectured about Chartres for decades. Mr Miller explains the cathedral as a library in which the windows and the statuary are the books, revealing their storylines with fascinating digressions into the significance of the building's symbols, shapes and numbers.

of the sculptures and structure of the cathedral (Mon–Sat 9am–12.30pm & 2–4.30pm, Sun 2–4.30pm; May–Aug open until 5.30pm; €4). There are **gardens** at the back from where you can contemplate at ease the complexity of stress factors balanced by the flying buttresses.

# The Town

Though the cathedral is the main attraction, a wander round the town of Chartres also has its rewards. Occasionally, stunning exhibitions of stained glass are displayed in a medieval wine and grain store, now the **Centre International du Vitrail**, at 5 rue du Cardinal-Pie on the north side of the cathedral (Mon–Fri 9.30am–12.30pm & 1.30–6pm, Sat & Sun 10am–12.30pm & 2.30–6pm; €4; ⓦwww.centre-vitrail.org). The **Musée des Beaux Arts** (May–Oct Wed–Sat 10am–noon & 2–6pm, Sun pm only; Nov–April Wed–Sat 10am–noon & 2–5pm, Sun pm only; €1.50), in the former episcopal palace just north of the cathedral, has some beautiful tapestries, a room full of Vlaminck, and Zurbaran's *Sainte Lucie*, as well as good temporary exhibitions. Behind it, rue Chantault leads past old town houses to the river Eure and Pont du Massacre. You can follow this reedy river lined with ancient wash-houses upstream via rue du Massacre on the right bank. The cathedral appears from time to time through the trees and, closer at hand, on the left bank, is the Romanesque church of **St-André**, now used for art exhibitions, jazz concerts and so on.

A left turn at the end of rue de la Tannerie, then third right, will bring you to one of Chartres' more eccentric tourist attractions. The **Maison Picassiette**, at 22 rue du Repos (April–Oct Mon & Wed–Sat 10am–noon & 2–6pm, Sun 2–6pm; €2.40), has been decorated with mosaics using bits of pottery and glass and is a fine example of Naïve art. Back at the end of rue de la Tannerie, the bridge over the river brings you back to the **medieval town**. At the top of rue du Bourg there's a turreted staircase attached to a house, and at the eastern end of place de la Poissonnerie, a carved salmon decorates a sixteenth-century house. The **food market** takes place on place Billard and rue des Changes (Sat morning), and there's a **flower market** on place du Cygne (Tues, Thurs & Sat).

At the edge of the old town, on the junction of boulevard de la Résistance and rue Collin-d'Arleville (to the right as you're coming up from the station), stands a memorial to **Jean Moulin**, Prefect of Chartres until he was sacked by the Vichy government in 1942. When the Germans occupied the town in 1940, Moulin refused to sign a document to the effect that Senegalese soldiers in the French army were responsible for Nazi atrocities. He later became de

Gaulle's number-one man on the ground, coordinating the Resistance, and died at the hands of Klaus Barbie in 1943.

## Chartres practicalities

**Trains** run from Gare du Montparnasse at least every hour on weekdays, but note that there are slightly fewer trains at weekends, especially on Sundays; the journey takes roughly one hour. From the **gare SNCF**, avenue J-de-Beauce leads straight up to place Châtelet. Diagonally opposite is rue Ste-Même, which leads to place Jean-Moulin; turn left at place Jean-Moulin and you'll find the cathedral and the **tourist office** (April–Sept Mon–Sat 9am–7pm, Sun 9.30am–5.30pm; Oct–March Mon–Sat 10am–6pm, Sun 10am–1pm & 2.30–4.30pm; ☎02.37.18.26.26). They can supply free maps and help with accommodation.

Cloître-Notre-Dame, along the south side of the cathedral, has a number of simple **eating** places. The friendly *Café Serpente*, at no. 2, may seem rather tatty, but the food is reliable, simple French fare and served all day. For something more substantial, try *Le Pichet*, 19 rue de Cheval Blanc, almost under the north-west spire (closed Mon & Wed, Tues & Sun eve; ☎02.37.21.08.35), or *L'Estocade*, 1 rue de la Porte Guillaume (May–Oct Tues–Sun; ☎02.37.34.27.17), which has a terrace overlooking the Eure.

# Giverny

**Claude Monet** considered his **gardens at Giverny** as his "greatest master-piece" (March–Oct Tues–Sun 9.30am–6pm; house and gardens €5.50, gardens only €4; ⓦwww.fondation-monet.com). They are a long way out from Paris (65km in the direction of Rouen), and you'll need to take a train and bus to reach them, but the rewards are great. Monet lived in Giverny from 1883 till his death in 1926, painting and repainting the effects of the changing seasonal light on the gardens he laid out between his house and the river. Each month is reflected in a dominant colour, as are each of the rooms in the house, pre-served exactly as he left them along with his wonderful collection of Japanese prints. May and June, when the rhododendrons flower round the lily pond and the wisteria bursts into colour over the famous Japanese bridge, are the best of all times to visit. But any month, from spring to autumn, is overwhelming in the beauty of this arrangement of living shades and shapes. Although you have to contend with crowds photographing the waterlilies and posing on the bridge, there's no place like it.

Just up rue Claude Monet from the gardens is the flashy **Musée d'Art Américain** (May & June Tues–Sun 9am–7pm; March, April & July–Oct Tues–Sun 10am–6pm; Nov Thurs–Sun 10am–6pm; €5; ⓦwww.maag.org). The display rotates pictures from the Terra Foundation for the Arts collection, which includes paintings by Sargent and lots of works by American Impressionists who lived in the small colony that grew up around Claude Monet. Temporary exhibitions, usually high quality, spin variations on Franco-American influences, Japanese art and Impressionism.

## Giverny practicalities

Without a car, the easiest **approach to Giverny** is by train to Vernon from

Paris-St-Lazare (Mon–Sat 5 daily; Sun 4 daily; 45min). **Buses** meet each train for the six-kilometre ride to the gardens or you can rent a **bike** or **walk** (1hr), in which case cross the river and turn right on the D5; take care as you enter Giverny to follow the left fork, otherwise you'll make a long detour to reach the garden entrance.

There are lots of indifferent tea shops in town, but it's worth walking up beyond the Musée d'Art Américain to the *Ancien Hôtel Baudy* at 81 rue Claude Monet (closed Sun eve, Mon & Nov–March); once a lodging house for international artists, it's now the best **eating** option in the village, with good salads for around €7–12, and a set lunch menu for €18.

# Disneyland Paris

Children will love **Disneyland Paris** – there are no two ways about it. What their minders will think of it is another matter, though a cartoon moment will still cadge a smile from most grown-ups, and you can ter-rify yourself on a roller coaster at any age. There is the question of whether it's worth it. Quite why American parents might bring their charges here is hard to fathom: even British parents might well decide that it would be better to buy a family package to Florida, where sunshine is assured, Disney World has better rides, and where the conflict between enchanted kingdom and enchanting city does not arise.

Carping aside, at just 25km distance east of the capital, it's easy to visit in a day-trip from Paris, and since the opening of Space Mountain and the Rock 'n' Roller Coaster, Disneyland Paris has a variety of good fear-and-thrill rides. There are a much wider variety of things to do than at a funfair or ordinary theme park too, and many of the sets are incredibly detailed. The complex is divided into three areas: **Disneyland Park**, the original Magic Kingdom, with most of the big rides; **Walt Disney Studios Park**, a more technology-based attempt to recreate the world of cartoon film-making, along with a few rides; and **Disney Village** and the hotels, where you can eat and sleep if you're determined to see both the other attractions. For all the omnipresent Americana, occasional French elements do creep through: science-fiction writer Jules Verne appears in a couple of Discoveryland rides; Sleeping Beauty's Castle is based on an illustration in the medieval manuscript *Les Très Riches Heures du Duc de Berry* (see p.233); and there's a faintly discernible French slant to some of the cinema-themed attractions in Walt Disney Studios. Otherwise, that's about it and the food throughout the resort is almost all Stateside fare. That said, the commentaries or scripts in the more theatrical attractions are almost always in French, though there are sometimes disappointing translated summaries displayed on a caption board, and, in the most audience-focused attractions, you'll always find an English-language headset to don.

The best **time to go** is on an off-season weekday (Mon & Thurs are the best), when you'll probably get round every ride you want, though queuing for and walking between rides can be purgatorial in wet or very cold weather. At other times, longish waits for the popular rides are common in the middle of the day, though the most popular attractions use the "Fastpass" booking scheme (see p.246).

## Getting there

**From London**, **Eurostar** runs trains straight to Disneyland, but it can some-times be quicker or cheaper to change onto the TGV at Lille; all these trains

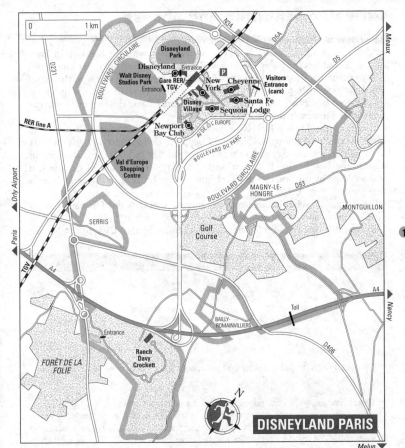

DISNEYLAND PARIS

arrive at Marne-la-Vallée/Chessy station, right outside the main entrance. If you're coming straight **from the airport**, there is a shuttle bus from Charles de Gaulle and Orly (roughly every 30min; 8.30am–7.45pm; for recorded information call ☎01.49.64.47.08). Tickets cost €14 one-way, but children under twelve pay €11.50, and under-3s go free.

**From Paris**, take RER line A (from Châtelet-Les Halles, Gare-de-Lyon, Nation) to Marne-la-Vallée/Chessy station, which is right next to the train terminal, and opposite the main park gates. The journey takes about forty minutes and costs €11.90 round-trip (children under twelve €5.94, under-3s free). For prices of Mobilis travel cards, including Disneyland Paris, see p.28.

**By car**, the park is 32km east of Paris along the A4, direction Metz/Nancy (exit 13 for Ranch Davy Crockett and exit 14 for the "Parc Disneyland" and the hotels); from Calais follow the A26 changing to the A1, the A104 and finally the A4. From Paris, take the "Porte de Bercy" exit off the Périphérique, then follow "Metz/Nancy" on the A4 motorway for 34km.

# Arrival, orientation and access

The layout is simple enough. If you've come by public transport, you step out of the train and RER stations onto a central plaza, with the bus stop in front of you. Ahead lies the glitzy **Disney Village**, a pedestrianized street lined with noisy restaurants, shops and cinemas. A hundred metres or so away to the right, stand the two main park gates. The first you come to leads through the landmark *Disneyland Hotel* to the original **Disneyland Park**; the farther one to the new **Walt Disney Studios Park**.

To get to the Disney **hotels**, you can stroll through Disney Village to the hotel area behind (though all except *Hotel New York* are too far away to walk to comfortably with luggage), or take one of the free yellow buses from the bus station; the hotel name is shown on the display on the front of each bus. If you've come by car, you can drive straight to your hotel or to the parking areas (car parking costs €8 per day).

For people in **wheelchairs** or with limited mobility, the Disabled Visitors Guide details accessibility of the rides. You can pick it up at City Hall in Disneyland Park, or Studio Services in Walt Disney Studios Park; to have it sent

## Admission fees and opening hours

### Admission fees

|          | Low season<br>(Oct–March excl Christmas hols) | High season<br>(April–Sept & 3rd week Dec–1st week Jan) |
|----------|------------|-------------|
| 1 day    | €29/25     | €39/29      |
| 3 days   | €79/69     | €107/80     |

Children aged 3–11 pay the reduced tariff shown above, while under-3s go free.

### Ticket passes

**Ticket passes**, known as "passports", can be purchased in advance – highly recommended in order to avoid long queues at the park itself – at the Paris Tourist Office and at all Disney shops, or you can buy admission passes and train tickets in Paris at all RER line A and B stations and in major métro stations. You can also buy tickets **online** at ⓦ www.disneylandparis.com.

The **one-day pass** allows you to visit either the main Disneyland Park or the Walt Disney Studios Park. You can't swap between both areas, but if you choose the Walt Disney Studio, you're entitled to move on to the Disneyland Park section (which stays open later) after the Studios close in the evening. Otherwise, you can come and go during the day – your wrist is stamped with invisible ink when you leave the park, allowing you to return. If you buy the **three-day pass** you can move freely between both park areas, and you don't have to use the ticket on three consecutive days.

### Opening hours

**Opening hours** vary depending on the season and whether it's a weekend, but they are roughly: low season daily 10am to 8pm; high season daily 9am to 11pm. Check when you buy your ticket.

### Special packages

Special **accommodation and entry packages** are available in advance. For details go online or call ☎00 33.1.60.30.60.81 from the US, ☎0870/606 6800 in the UK, and ☎01.60.30.60.53 in France, or from other countries.

to you in advance, call ☎01.60.30.60.30. Note that Disney staff aren't allowed to lend assistance in getting into and out of the less accessible rides, but all the loos, phones, shops and restaurants have wheelchair access.

# Disneyland Park

The introduction to Disneyland Paris is the same as in Florida, LA and Tokyo. **Main Street USA** is a mythical vision of a 1900s American town, and it leads up to **Central Plaza**, the hub of the park. Clockwise from Main Street are Frontierland, Adventureland, Fantasyland and Discoveryland. The **castle**, directly opposite Main Street across Central Plaza, belongs to Fantasyland. A steam train **Railroad** runs round the park with stations at each "land" and at the main entrance.

The listings on pp.247–250 are a selection of the best and worst rides, with some warnings about suitability. Apart from some height restrictions, Disney offers little guidance about suitability, and indeed it's surprisingly difficult to tell what one child will find exhilarating and another upsetting. For the youngest kids, **Fantasyland** is likely to hold the most thrills. There are no height restrictions here, and rides are mostly gentle. Each of the other three themed areas offers a landmark rollercoaster and a theme: **Adventureland** has the most outlandish, jungly sets, **Frontierland** is set in the Wild West, while **Discoveryland** emphasizes technology and the space age.

Though there are a few green patches, there is no lawn to loll on, a design flaw in a park designed for families. Opportunities for afternoon naps are limited, which shows by late afternoon in the general frayed tempers: renting a pushchair (see p.246) for even an older child might be a good idea.

## Information and practicalities

Passing underneath the wedding-cake *Disneyland Hotel*, you enter the park underneath Main Street Station, on the internal railroad system. **City Hall** is to the left, where you can get **information** about the day's programme of events, and retrieve **lost property**. You can enquire about lost children here, too, and there's a dedicated **Lost Children** area in the First Aid complex by the *Plaza Gardens Restaurant* on Central Plaza (in the block between Main Street and Discoveryland). Next door, you can change nappies, breastfeed and heat baby-food in the **Baby Care Centre**, sponsored by the ever-thoughtful Nestlé corporation. **Luggage** can be left in lockers in "Guest Storage" under

---

### Eating and drinking

As you'd expect, the **food** in Disneyland Paris is generally overpriced American junk. It's probably safest to avoid the swankier restaurants in Disney Village and go for hamburger-style snacks at the various themed eateries around the park. Thankfully, the former Disney policy of no alcohol has been abandoned, and adults can now sip wine or beer at any of the park's restaurants.

Officially, you're not allowed to bring any refreshments into the park, but, if you don't want to spend anything more than the entrance fee, you could eat a good Parisian breakfast and smuggle in some discreet snacks. Whether Goofy will turn nasty if he sees you eating a brand name not on the list of Disney sponsors is anyone's guess.

One-hour waits for the popular rides are not uncommon – don't be fooled by the length of the visible queues; they often snake for a further 100m or more inside. Bring sunhats or umbrellas, and make sure your kids have all been to the toilet recently before you begin to queue, as once you're in, it's very hard to get out; keep snacks and drinks handy, too. To avoid the worst of the queues, some of the most popular rides use the so-called **Fastpass** scheme, in which you insert your entry card into a ticket machine by the entrance to the ride; the machine then spews out a time at which you should come back, whereupon you are entitled to join the much shorter fastpass queue.

Main Street Station (€1.50). You can rent wheelchairs and **pushchairs** (€5) in the building opposite City Hall.

# Main Street USA

On the corner of **Main Street**, Town Square Photography rents out still and video cameras, and sells film, lenses, cameras and tripods amid a collection of museum pieces. Kodak is one of Disney's main sponsors, and kiosks throughout the park sell film and offer two-hour print developing.

If you succumb at this early stage to the idea of takeaway snapshots and the Disneyland Paris home movie, you'll be in serious financial trouble by the end of the day. As a practice run, see if you can get down Main Street without buying one of the following: a balloon, a hat with your name embroidered on it, an ice-cream, bag of sweets, silhouette portraits of your kids, the *Wall Street Journal* of 1902, a Disney version of a children's classic in hardback, an evening dress and suit and tie, a Donald Duck costume, a model rocket, a tea service and set of crystal glasses, some muffins, a Coke, a few cakes, a limited edition Disney lithograph, and a complete set of Disney characters in ceramics, metal, plastic, rubber or wool.

## The parades

The main "Wonderful World of Disney" **Parade** happens every day at 4pm and lasts for half an hour. This is not a bad time to make for the most popular rides, but if you have kids they will no doubt force you to press against the barriers for the ultimate Disney event. One of the best vantage spots is on the queuing ramp for *It's a Small World*, right by the gates through which the floats appear. From here, the parade progresses, very slowly, to Town Square. The best seating is in front of the Fantasyland Castle, one of the points where the floats stop and the characters put on a performance. The parade floats represent all the top box-office Disney movies – *Dumbo*, *Snow White*, *Cinderella*, *Pinocchio*, *The Jungle Book*, *Peter Pan, Mary Poppins*, *Beauty and the Beast*, *Aladdin* and *Hercules*, with Mickey and Minnie Mouse and Donald Duck making an appearance. Everyone waves and smiles, and characters on foot shake hands with the kids who've managed to get to the front.

Smaller events such as costumed Dixie bands and jungle-themed hoe-downs take place throughout the day, and every night at 7.30pm, the **Electrical Parade** follows the main parade route, with a procession of floats strung with light bulbs and adorned by dancing, costumed Disney characters, the whole thing accompanied by zany music.

**Firework displays** happen about twice a week during the summer. Check with the programme available at City Hall for dates and times.

Leaving Main Street is quickest on foot (crowds permitting), although omnibuses, trams, horse–drawn streetcars, fire trucks and police vans are always on hand, plus the Disney *pièce de résistance*, the Railroad, for which **Main Street Station** has the longest queues.

## Discoveryland

**Autopia** Miniature futuristic cars to drive on rails. Good fun, especially for little kids, but there's no possibility of any race-day strata-gems. Minimum height to drive is 1.32m.

**Honey, I Shrunk The Audience** Visitors enter the "Imagination Institute" wearing 3D glasses to meet Eric Idle, host of the "Inventor of the Year" Awards. The audi-ence is then dive-bombed by Rick Moranis and "shrunk" using his "shrinking machine", a process that involves loud music, clever 3D and film effects, and general mayhem. Not exactly scary, but overwhelming and therefore not recommended for young children.

**Les Mystères du Nautilus** A rather disap-pointing stroll through a mock-up of the *Nautilus* submarine – Captain Nemo's vessel in *20,000 Leagues Under the Sea*. What's supposed to impress you is the faithfulness of the decor to the original Disney set, though there is a fishy surprise inside.

**Orbitron** The "rockets" on this ride go round and round fairly slowly and go up (at your control) to a daring 30 degrees above the horizontal. Suitable for small kids and for those who hate more violent rides.

**Space Mountain** The star attraction and not for the faint-hearted. You're catapulted upwards, suspended weightless and then spun through an interstellar world at speeds of up to 40km, with a 360-degree sidewinder loop and corkscrew loop. Minimum height is 1.40m, and pregnant women and people with health problems are advised not to ride. Uses the Fastpass scheme.

**Star Tours** Giddy, simulated ride in a space-craft (with sixty other people all in neat rows) piloted by friendly incompetent C3PO of *Star Wars* fame. The projection of what you're supposed to be careering through is actually from the film, which pleases fans. Pregnant women and those with health problems are advised not to board. Using Fastpass skips the queues.

**Le Visionarium** 360-degree film presented by a robotic timekeeper host. The story involves travelling through time and picking

### Rollercoasters

Each of the park's areas, apart from the child-focused Fantasyland, centres on its rollercoaster. The runaway train on Frontierland's **Big Thunder Mountain** and the mine-carts of Adventureland's **Indiana Jones and the Temple of Peril: Backwards!** are fast and exciting, but the emphasis is on thrills rather than sheer terror – you can tell that things aren't going to be too bad because you're kept in your seat by a bar, rather than being fully strapped in. **Space Mountain**, in Discoveryland, and the **Rock 'n' Roller Coaster Starring Aerosmith**, over in the Walt Disney Studios sec-tion, are a different matter altogether. Their upside-down loops, corkscrews and ter-rifying acceleration require a lock-in padded brace to keep you in place, and you'll need a strong constitution to really enjoy it.

All four rides have different height restrictions, and as you queue for the latter two you'll be bombarded with warnings to discourage pregnant women or people with neck or back problems. You can avoid queues on all of them by using the Fastpass scheme (see opposite), and arriving early can also be a good strategy but be warned: the experience can be so intense that the park's gentler rides may seem disappointing. Children, in particular, may want to return again and again.

When you emerge from the exit gates, video screens show close-up images of ter-rified faces captured moments before. While it's fun to hang around until you spot your own twisted visage, buying a photographic copy is fairly expensive and the quality is poor.

up Jules Verne at the 1900 *Exposition Universelle* in Paris just as he and H G Wells, played by Jeremy Irons, are discussing time travel. They show Jules all the wonders of contemporary life – TGVs and Mirage jets mainly. Headphones for English translation provided.

# Fantasyland

**Alice's Curious Labyrinth** A maze with surprises. There are passages that only those under 1m can pass through and enough false turns and exits to make it an irritatingly good labyrinth. Takes fifteen to twenty minutes, though there is the option to exit at the halfway point.

**Blanche-Neige et les Sept Nains** This *Snow White and the Seven Dwarfs* ride takes you through lots of menacing moving trees, swinging doors and cackling witches, recreating scenes from the classic Disney film. Can frighten smaller kids.

**Le Carrousel de Lancelot** A stately merry-go-round, whose every horse has its own individual medieval equerry in glittering paint.

**Dumbo the Flying Elephant** Dumbo and his clones provide a safe, slow, aerial ride in which you can regulate the rise and fall of the revolving elephants yourself with a lever. One of the most popular rides in Fantasyland, though it only lasts a measly 25 seconds.

**It's a Small World** This is a quintessential Disney experience: there's one in every Disneyland, and Walt considered it to be the finest expression of his corporation's philosophy. Your boat rides through a polystyrene and glitter world, where animated dolls in national/ethnic/tribal costumes dance beside their most famous landmarks or landscapes, singing the song *It's a Small World*. Some children seem to enjoy the sugar-coated fantasy.

**Mad Hatter's Tea Cups** Great big whirling teacups slide past each other on a chequered floor. Again, not a whizzy ride, but fun for younger ones.

**Le Pays des Contes de Fées** A boat ride through fairytale scenes: *Alice in Wonderland*, *Pinocchio*, etc. Fine for little kids.

**Peter Pan's Flight** The very young seem to really enjoy this jerky ride above Big Ben and the lights of London to Never-Never Land. Uses Fastpass.

**Sleeping Beauty's Castle** The castle stands at the entrance to Fantasyland, just off the central plaza at the end of Main Street. There's little to see inside other than a few bits of plasticky vaulting, naff stained glass and cartoon tapestries, though a huge animated dragon lurks in the dungeon.

# Adventureland

**Adventureland Bazaar** A clever bit of shopping mall disguised as a *souk*, with traditional Arab latticed walls, desert pastel colours, and all sorts of genuine Hollywood details.

**Adventure Isle** Not a ride, but a sort of playground of caves, bouncy bridges, huge boulders, trees, tunnels and waterfalls built on two small islands in the middle of Adventureland. Parents of over-tired children and those who need a break from the queues should not underestimate the thrill of just being able to wander around unfettered.

**La Cabane des Robinson** The 27-metre mock banyan tree at the top of Adventure Isle is one of Disneyland Paris's most obsessively detailed creations, complete with hundreds of thousands of false leaves and blossoms. It's reached by walkways and a series of more than 170 steps, so it's best avoided by pram-pushers and toddler-haulers.

**Indiana Jones and the Temple of Peril: Backwards!** A fast and quite violent rollercoaster through a classic Indy landscape, made all the more frightening by the fact that it's done backwards. The minimum height for the ride is 1.40m. Children under about 8 years old, pregnant women and people with health problems should steer clear. Queues can be avoided by using Fastpass.

**Pirates of the Caribbean** This satisfyingly long ride is one of the finest, consisting of an underground ride on water and down waterfalls, past scenes of evil piracy. The animated automata are the best yet – be warned that they set small children whimpering and crying immediately. Battles are staged across the water, skeletons slide into the deep, parrots squawk, chains rattle and a treasure trove is revealed.

## Frontierland

**Big Thunder Mountain** A proper scream-out-loud funfair thrill, this is a rollercoaster mimicking a runaway mine train round a "mining mountain". There are wicked twists and turns, sudden tunnels and hairy moments looking down on the water, but no violent upside-down or corkscrew stuff. Minimum height 1.02m; not suitable for small children. Use Fastpass.

**The Chapparal Theater** Shows seasonal theatrical spectaculars featuring all the usual Disney suspects. Times are displayed outside, and on the back of the main park map.

**Phantom Manor** *Psycho*-style house on the outside and Hammer Horror Edwardian mansion within. Holographic ghosts appear before cobweb-covered mirrors and ancestral portraits, but nothing actually jumps out and screams at you. Probably too frightening for young children nevertheless.

**Rustler Roundup Shootin' Gallery** The only "attraction" for which there's a fee (€1), because, without some check, people stay for hours and hours shooting Infra-red beams at fake cacti.

**Thunder Mesa Riverboat Landing** A rather pointless cruise around the lake, but the paddleboat steamer is carefully built to offer lots of antique-style curiosities, and it's fun to watch the rollercoaster rattle around the rocks of Big Thunder Mountain.

# Walt Disney Studios Park

Other than the "Rock 'n' Roller Coaster Starring Aerosmith", a terrifyingly fast, corkscrew-looping, Metal-playing white-knuckler, the new **Walt Disney Studios Park** complex lacks the big rides offered by its older, larger neighbour. In some ways it's a more satisfying affair, focusing on what Disney was and is still renowned for – animation. You can try your hand at drawing, there are mock film and TV sets where you can be part of the audience, and the special-effects and stunt shows are impressive in their way, although probably not as impressive as just going to the movies.

## The Rides

**Animagique** Disney characters in full fluffy costumes act out classic scenes from Disney films.

**Armageddon Special Effects** Your group of fifty or so is ushered into a circular chamber decked out as a space station. As meteors rush towards the screens on all sides, the whole ship seems about to break up. Less cynical children may find the whole experience overwhelming.

**Art of Disney Animation** You progress through two mini-theatres, one showing famous moments from Disney cartoons, the next with a "cartoonist" having a conversation with an on-screen animated creation, explaining to the creature how it came to look as it did. In the lobby area, children are taught to draw identical Mickey Mouse faces.

**Cinémagique** A theatrical screening of a century of movie moments, with actors appearing to jump into and out of the on-screen action, helped by special effects.

**Flying Carpets over Agrabah** A good, solid fairground ride where the carpet-shaped cars wheel around the central lamp for a disappointingly short time. Very popular with smaller children, especially the lever which makes their carpet rise up and down. Using Fastpass can avoid the long queues.

**Moteurs ... Action! Stuntshow Spectacular**
Decked out like a Mediterranean village, a big arena is the scene for some spectacular stunts: jumping rally cars, sliding motorbikes, leaping jet skis, stuntmen falling from heights and so on. Various timed shows throughout the day.

**Rock 'n' Roller Coaster Starring Aerosmith**
A real heart-stopper. There are corkscrews, loops and violent lurches, and the whole thing takes place in a neon-lit and hard-rock-soundtracked darkness that makes it all the more alarming. The whole thing is over in less than two minutes. Uses Fastpass. Minimum height 1.2m; not suitable for small children.

**Studio 1** For "boulevard of dreams", read row of shops and restaurants. Not a ride, however it's listed on the map.

**Studio Tram Tour Featuring Catastrophe Canyon** An electric tram takes you on a sedate circuit of various bits and pieces of film set. The high point is the halt among the Wild West rocks of Catastrophe Canyon – sit on the left for the scariest ride.

**Walt Disney Television Studios** Television shows are produced here with the help of a ready-to-hand live audience. Moderately entertaining to watch how it's all done, with cameras, chatty compères and so on.

# Disney Village and the hotels

The **Disney Village** entertainment and restaurant complex, opposite the RER and train stations, is basically a street lined with expensive shops and restaurants. It's Frank O. Gehry's work, and looks like a circus-top tent that has had its top carried off by a bomb, with a pedestrian street driven through the middle of it. *Buffalo Bill's Wild West Show*, with real guns, horses, bulls and bison (nightly 6.30pm & 9.30pm; €50, children 3–11 €30), *Billy Bob's Country Western Saloon*, *Hurricanes* disco, the new multiplex cinema, *Annette's Diner*, *Rock 'n' Roll America* and a *Planet Hollywood Restaurant* await you, with live music on summer nights and various sideshows.

When you're nearing exhaustion from so much enchantment, you can return to your **hotel** and have a sauna, jacuzzi or whirlpool dip and be in bed in time to feel fresh and fit to meet Mickey and Minnie again over breakfast. In the hotel area of the resort, you can play golf, skate (in winter), sail (in summer) and jog on a special "health circuit". In reality, all these activities are secondary to the main attraction, and they're expensive.

## Disneyland Hotels

Disney's six themed **hotels** are a mixed bag of hideous eyesores and over-ambitious kitsch designed by some of the world's leading architects – Michael Graves, Antoine Predock, Robert Stern and Frank Gehry. For all the dramatically themed exteriors and lobbies, the rooms are much the same inside: comfortable, well-furnished and distressingly huge. The hotels are only worth staying in as part of a multi-day package including park entry, which you can book through Disney (see box on p.244) or major travel agents. If you book directly it can turn out much more expensive. Free bright yellow **shuttle buses** run between the hotels, the train station and the two theme parks.

**Prices** vary hugely according to season, and which package you book. Winter, obviously, is cheaper than summer, but even within these periods there are low and high seasons. Weekends or French holidays in winter, for example, tend to be more expensive than off-peak periods in early or late summer. Prices are highest throughout July and August. Most rooms are family rooms with two double beds; in winter, children aged 3–11 stay for free, while in summer there's usually a supplement of around €100 per child per night. In the two-star *Hotel Santa Fé*, you could pay around €150 per adult in low season, while prices rise to over €600 for a peak-season room in the *Disneyland Hotel*, inside the Magic Kingdom. The hotels below are listed in order of price, starting with the cheapest. The cheapest alternative, as long as you have a car, is the park's *Davey Crockett Ranch*, a fifteen-minute drive away, with self-catering log cabins. To really economize, you could camp at the nearby *Camping du Parc de la Colline*, Route de Lagny, 77200 Torcy (☎01.30.58.56.20), which is open all year and offers minibus shuttles to the park.

**Disneyland Hotel** Situated over the entrance to the park with wings to either side, the large, frilly, pastel-pink *Disneyland Hotel* is decked out in glitzy Hollywood style. It's the most upmarket and best located by far.

**Newport Bay Club** This "New England seaside resort circa 1900" spreads like a game of dominoes. Blue-and-white striped canopies over the balconies fail to give it that cosy guesthouse feel, but some rooms have the benefit of looking out over the lake.

**Hotel New York** Outside, the hotel is a plasticky, post-Modern attempt at conjuring up the New York skyline, while the furnishings within are pseudo Art Deco with lots of apples. Comfortable, but showing its age. In winter, the outdoor ice-rink makes it a good option for children.

**Sequoia Lodge** Built around the theme of the "mountain lodge" typically found in the National Parks of the western United States, but on a giant scale.

**Hotel Cheyenne** Along with *Sante Fe*, the *Cheyenne* is broken up into attractively small units: the film-set buildings of a Western frontier town, complete with wagons, cowboys, a hanging tree and scarecrows. With its Wild West theme and bunk beds in all the rooms, this is a good hotel for children.

**Hotel Santa Fe** Accommodation takes the form of smooth, mercifully unadorned, imitation sun-baked mud buildings in various shapes and sizes. Between them are tasteful car wrecks, a cactus in a glass case, strange geological formations and other products of the distinctly un-Disney imagination of New Mexican architect Antoine Predock. A scowling cheroot-chewing Clint Eastwood creates the drive-in movie entrance.

**Davy Crockett Ranch and camping** The *Davy Crockett Ranch* costs from €55 to €130 per person for a self-catering log cabin (4–6 people). The ranch is a fifteen-minute drive from the park, with no transport laid on.

# Listings

# Listings

# 15

# Accommodation

A ccommodation in Paris is often booked up well in advance, particularly in the spring and autumn. It's wise to reserve a place as early as you can, particularly if you fancy staying in one of the more characterful places. You can simply call – all receptionists speak some English – but it's also worth bearing in mind that more and more places offer **online booking** as well. If you book by phone, many hotels will ask for a credit card number, others for written or faxed confirmation, while a few inexpensive places may even ask for a deposit to be sent in the post. If you're stuck, the main **tourist office** at Champs-Élysées and the branches at Gare de Lyon and the Eiffel Tower will find you a room: all book accommodation for that day only, and you have to turn up at the office in person (€3–8 commission for a hotel room depending on the number of stars, €1.20 for a hostel). Alternatively, the student travel agency **OTU Voyages**, at 119 rue St-Martin, opposite the Pompidou Centre, 4ᵉ (Mon–Fri 9.30am–6.30pm, Sat 10am–5pm; ☎08.25.00.40.24, ⊛www.otu.fr; Mᵒ Châtelet-Les Halles) and at 39 av Georges Bernanos, 5ᵉ (☎08.25.00.40.27; Mᵒ Port Royal) can find inexpensive rooms for a fee of €12.

Bed and breakfasts, hostels and campsites are listed separately on pp. 266–270.

## Hotels

Paris is enormously well supplied with **hotels** in all price categories. Prices aren't exorbitant by European standards, but rooms can be surprisingly small for the money, as all but the most expensive establishments have been carved out of cramped nineteenth-century mansion blocks. The **star system** provides some clues as to the pretensions of a hotel, particularly its price, but little else – a two-star hotel might have lovely rooms but fail to be awarded a third star because its staff don't speak enough languages, or its foyer is small. Though many traditional family-run places have now been bought out by conglomerates, you can still find a double room in an old-fashioned two-star for between €55 and €85 (❹–❺), though don't expect much in the way of decor at the lower end of the scale. For something with a bit more class – whether that means a touch of character, smooth efficiency or a minibar – you'll pay upwards of €85 (❻); in swankier areas, expect to pay €100 or more (❼–❾). It is possible to find a double room in a central location, for around €40 (❸), sometimes even less, though at this level you will probably have to accept a room with just a sink (*lavabo*) and a shared bathroom on the landing – and a few such places still charge for use of the shower. Out of season, in smaller hotels, it's sometimes possible to negotiate a reduction of up to ten percent or more on the advertised rate, depending on your length of stay.

## Accommodation price codes

Each hotel and guesthouse in this book has been graded according to the following price codes, which indicate the price for the **cheapest double room available during the high season**.

| | | |
|---|---|---|
| ❶ Under €30 | ❹ €55–70 | ❼ €100–125 |
| ❷ €30–40 | ❺ €70–85 | ❽ €125–150 |
| ❸ €40–55 | ❻ €85–100 | ❾ Over €150 |

Even within one hotel, rooms can vary considerably, and it's worth asking what's available – almost all hoteliers speak at least enough English to get by. Rooms at the back, overlooking an internal courtyard (*côté cour/jardin*), can be dark; rooms on the street (*côté rue*) tend to be larger, but noise can be a problem if there isn't double-glazing. Certain standard terms recur: *douche/WC* and *bain/WC* mean that you have a shower or bath as well as toilet in the room. A room with a *grand lit* (double bed) is invariably cheaper than one with *deux lits* (two separate beds).

**Breakfast** (*petit déjeuner*, or PD) is sometimes included (*compris*) in the room price but is normally extra (*en sus*) – around €5–8 per person. Always make it clear whether you want breakfast or not when you take the room. Either way, it's usually an indifferent continental affair of croissant/baguette, orange juice and coffee.

The best **areas for budget-priced hotels** are the 11e and 10e, especially around place de la République and Bastille, though the latter can get pretty rowdy at night. Quieter areas, further out, where you can get some good deals are the 13e and 14e, south of Montparnasse, and the 17e and 20e, on the western and eastern sides of the city.

Our hotel recommendations are listed by area, following the same chapter divisions used in the guide. Price categories refer to the **cheapest double rooms** normally available in **high season** (see box above) – a tariff that, for the majority of Paris hotels, applies all year round. Most hotels have a selection of rooms at different prices; where there are only very few rooms in a hotel in the lower price categories, we show the complete price range on offer.

### The Islands

*The hotels in this section are marked on the map on pp.54–55.*
**Henri IV 25 place Dauphine** ⓣ01.43.54.44.53.
An ancient and well-known cheapie in a beautiful central location on the Île de la Cité. Some of the rooms have recently been renovated and have en-suite bathrooms. Most, though, come with nothing more luxurious than a cabinet de toilette and are now very run down. Essential to book well in advance. No credit cards. M° Pont-Neuf/Cité. ❷
**Hôtel de Lutèce 65 rue St-Louis-en-l'Île** ⓣ01.43.26.23.52, ⓕ01.43.29.60.25, ⓔlutece@hotel-ile-saintlouis.com. Small but exquisite rooms in an old town house on the most desirable island in France. Only

24 rooms, so book well in advance. M° Pont-Marie. ❽

### The Champs-Élysées and around

*The hotels in this section are marked on the map on pp.76–77.*

#### The Champs-Élysées, Arc de Triomphe and around

**Hôtel d'Artois 94 rue la Boétie, 8e** ⓣ01.43.59.84.12, ⓕ01.43.59.50.70. One of the cheapest in this, the smartest part of town, with unusually gracious and spacious rooms of the old-fashioned variety. Run by very obliging staff. M° St-Philippe-du-Roule. ❸–❺
**Le Bristol 112 rue du Faubourg St-Honoré, 8e** ⓣ01.53.43.43.00, ⓕ01.53.43.43.01,

@www.hotel-bristol.com. The city's most luxurious and spacious hotel manages to remain discreet and warm. Gobelins tapestries and private roof gardens with some of the rooms. A large colonnaded interior garden, as well as the expected swimming pool, health club and gourmet restaurant. Doubles start at €660. M° Miromesnil. **❾**

**Hôtel des Champs-Élysées** 2 rue d'Artois, 8<sup>e</sup> ☎01.43.59.11.42, ⊕01.45.61.00.61. The rooms have recently been redecorated in warm colours and all come with shower or bath, plus satellite TV, minibar, hairdryer and safe. Breakfast is served in a converted stone cellar. M° St-Philippe-du-Roule. **❺**

**Hôtel de l'Élysée** 12 rue des Saussaies, 8<sup>e</sup> ☎01.42.65.29.25, ⊕01.42.65.64.28, @www.paris-hotel.com/elysee. Chandeliers and four-posters – classic luxury. M° St-Philippe-du-Roule. **❽**

**Hôtel Keppler** 12 rue Keppler, 16<sup>e</sup> ☎01.47.20.65.05, ⊕01.47.23.02.29. Rooms are a little small, but spotless and quite comfortable. Located in a quiet street just a few steps from the Arc de Triomphe. M° George-V/Kléber. **❺**

**Hôtel Lancaster** 7 rue de Berri, 8<sup>e</sup> ☎01.40.76.40.76, ⊕01.40.76.40.00, @www.hotel-lancaster.fr. An elegantly restored nineteenth-century town-house with 58 rooms, each retaining original features and antiques, but with a touch of contemporary chic. A small interior zen-style garden and pleasant service make for a relaxing stay. Doubles start at €410. M° George V. **❾**

### The Tuileries

**Hôtel Brighton** 218 rue de Rivoli, 1<sup>er</sup> ☎01.47.03.61.61, ⊕01.42.60.41.78, ⊜hotel.brighton@wanadoo.fr. A smart hotel, with light, airy rooms. Its main asset, however, is the magnificent views of the Tuileries gardens from the front-facing rooms – if your budget stretches to it, go for one with a balcony right at the top. M° Tuileries. **❼–❾**

**Costes** 239 rue St-Honoré, 1<sup>er</sup> ☎01.42.44.50.00, ⊕01.42.44.50.01, @www.hotelcostes.com. Opened in the mid-1990s and an instant hit with media and fashion celebrities, this Costes brothers' hotel marries Second Empire style with all up-to-date amenities. Doubles from €300. M° Tuileries. **❾**

**Hôtel Lion d'Or** 5 rue de la Sourdière, 1<sup>er</sup> ☎01.42.60.79.04, ⊕01.42.60.09.14, @wwwhotelduliondor.com. A friendly and very central hotel, with twenty en-suite rooms – simple but clean and recently renovated. You can check your email in the attached cybercafé. M° Tuileries. **❹**

**Hôtel Meurice** 228 rue de Rivoli, 1<sup>er</sup> ☎01.44.58.10.10, ⊕01.44.58.10.15, @www.meuricehotel.com. Palatial opulence in the style of Louis XVI, with great views over Paris. You'll be so busy having tea in the winter garden or taking a Turkish bath that the delights of Paris just on your doorstep are likely to go ignored. Doubles start at €720. M° Tuileries. **❾**

## The Grands Boulevards, passages and Les Halles

### Grands Boulevards

*The hotels in this section are marked on the map on pp.86–87.*

**Hôtel Chopin** 46 passage Jouffroy, 9<sup>e</sup>; entrance on bd Montmartre, near rue du Faubourg-Montmartre ☎01.47.70.58.10, ⊕01.42.47.00.70. Charming, quiet hotel in a splendid period building hidden away at the end of an elegant 1850s *passage*. Rooms are pleasantly furnished, though the cheaper ones are on the small side and a little dark. M° Grands-Boulevards. **❺**

**Hôtel de Noailles** 9 rue Michodière, 2<sup>e</sup> ☎01.47.42.92.90, ⊕01.49.24.92.71. Although part of an international chain, the *Noailles* hasn't lost its own identity and offers contemporary styling with traditional pleasures of garden and *terrasse*. M° Opéra/4-Septembre. **❽**

**Hôtel Vivienne** 40 rue Vivienne, 2<sup>e</sup> ☎01.42.33.13.26, ⊕01.40.41.98.19, ⊜paris@hotel-vivienne.com. Ideally located for the Opéra Garnier and the Grands Boulevards, this is a friendly hotel, with good-sized, cheery rooms, some with Internet points. M° Grands-Boulevards. **❹**

### Les Halles and Châtelet

*The hotels in this section are marked on the map on p.94.*

**Agora** 7 rue de la Cossonnerie, 1<sup>er</sup> ☎01.42.33.46.02, ⊕01.42.33.80.99. Expensive for a two-star, but it's in a good location – on a pedestrianized street right in the heart

of Les Halles. Individually styled, old-fashioned rooms, all with bathroom. M°
Châtelet-Les-Halles. **❻**

**Hôtel du Palais** 2 Quai de la Mégisserie, 1er
☏01.42.36.98.25, ℱ01.42.21.41.67. The
rooms at the top are basic and cheap;
alternatively pay €10 more for a view over
the Seine and a shower in your room.
Location and views at this price are hard to
beat. M° Châtelet. **❸**

**Relais du Louvre** 19 rue des Prêtres St-
Germain l'Auxerrois, 1er ☏01.40.41.96.42,
ℱ01.40.41.96.44, ℮au-relais-du-louvre
@dial.deane.com. Small, discreet hotel done
out in Second Empire style. Its relaxed
atmosphere and charming service attract a
faithful clientele. M° Palais-Royal-Musée-
du-Louvre. **❺**

**Hôtel St-Honoré** 85 rue St-Honoré, 1er
☏01.42.36.20.38, ℱ01.42.21.44.08, ℮hotel-
st-honore@wanadoo.fr. Conveniently close to
the heart of things, this is a stylishly renovated old building with 29 rooms, all en-
suite. M° Châtelet/Les Halles/Louvre. **❺**

**Tiquetonne** 6 rue Tiquetonne, 2e
☏01.42.36.94.58. On a pedestrianized street,
close to the red-light stretch of St-Denis,
this old-fashioned budget hotel dates back
to the 1920s and looks as though it's
changed little since. Its 47 rooms are well-
maintained and clean though. M° Étienne-
Marcel. **❸**

**Vauvilliers** 6 rue Vauvilliers, 1er
☏01.42.36.89.08. Well-established, popular
budget option in a quiet street. Rooms are
spartan though acceptable at this price. M°
Châtelet-Les Halles/Louvre. **❶**

## Beaubourg, the Marais and the Bastille

*The hotels in this section are marked on the map on pp.98–99.*

### Beaubourg and the Marais

**Hôtel Acacias** 20 rue du Temple, 4e
☏01.48.87.07.70, ℱ01.48.87.17.20. Small, no-
frills hotel in a refurbished eighteenth-century mansion sandwiched between the
Pompidou, the Marais and bustling rue de
Rivoli. Provides all expected amenities and
is particularly gay-friendly. M° Hôtel-de-Ville.
**❻**

**Caron de Beaumarchais** 12 rue Vieille-du-
Temple ☏01.42.72.34.12, ℱ01.42.72.34.63.
Named after the eighteenth-century French

playwright Beaumarchais, who lived just up
the road, this gem of a hotel has only nineteen rooms. Everything in the hotel – down
to the original engravings and Louis XVI-
style furniture, not to mention the piano-
forte in the foyer – evokes the refined tastes
of high-society pre-Revolutionary Paris.
Rooms overlooking the courtyard are small
but cosy, while those on the street are more
spacious, some with balcony. Book well in
advance. M° Hôtel-de-Ville. **❽**

**Hôtel Central Marais** 33 rue Vieille-du-Temple,
4e ☏01.48.87.56.08, ℱ01.42.77.06.27,
℮www.hotelcentralmarais.com. The only self-
proclaimed gay hotel in Paris, with a relaxed
bar downstairs. Seven small rooms with
shared bathrooms. Also lets an apartment
that sleeps four (€100). The entrance is on
Rue Sainte-Croix-de-la-Bretonnerie. M°
Hôtel-de-Ville. **❻**

**Grand Hôtel Jeanne d'Arc** 3 rue de Jarente,
4e ☏01.48.87.62.11, ℱ01.48.87.37.31,
℮www.hoteljeannedarc.com. An attractive old
Marais building, just off place du Marché
Sainte-Catherine. The rooms are a decent
size, with nice individual touches, plus
cable TV. The triple at the top has good
views over the rooftops. Booking essential.
M° St-Paul. **❹**

**Grand Hôtel du Loiret** 8 rue des Mauvais-
Garçons, 4e ☏01.48.87.77.00, ℱ
01.48.04.96.56, ℮hotelloiret@aol.com. A
friendly, good-value hotel, recently renovated. The two triples on the top floor have
excellent views of the Sacré Coeur.
Cheaper rooms have washbasin only, but
all have TV and telephone, and there's also
an email access point in the lobby. M°
Hôtel-de-Ville. **❸**

**Grand Hôtel Malher** 5 rue Malher, 4e
☏01.42.72.60.92, ℱ01.42.72.25.37,
℮www.grandhotelhmalher.com. Family-run
hotel, situated right in the heart of the
Marais. Rooms are light and well decorated,
with gleaming-white bathrooms. Breakfast is
served in a renovated seventeenth-century
vaulted wine cellar. M° St-Paul. **❼**

**Hôtel de Nice** 42bis rue de Rivoli, 4e
☏01.42.78.55.29, ℱ01.42.78.36.07. Very
pretty rooms – some with french windows
and balconies; the rooms on the upper
floors have views of the towers of Notre-
Dame and the small square below. M°
Hôtel-de-Ville. **❻**

**Hôtel Pavillon de la Reine** 28 pl des Vosges
☏01.40.29.19.19, ℱ01.40.29.19.20,

@ www.pavillon-de-la-reine.com. A perfect honeymoon or romantic-weekend hotel in a beautiful ivy-covered mansion secreted away off the place des Vosges. Rooms are sumptuously decorated with rich fabrics, antique furnishings and four-poster beds and come with all the modern comforts of a four-star hotel. Doubles start at €300. M° Bastille. ❾

**Hôtel St-Louis Marais** 1 rue Charles-V, 4ᵉ ☏01.48.87.87.04, ℻01.48.87.33.26, @ www.hotelsaintlouismarais.com. Formerly part of the seventeenth-century Célestins Convent, this comfortable hotel offers taste-fully furnished, somewhat small, but cosy rooms. M° Sully-Morland. ❼

**Hôtel du Séjour** 36 rue du Grenier-St-Lazare, 3ᵉ ☏01.48.87.40.36. A very clean, no-frills establishment run by a nice couple, and only a short walk from the Pompidou Centre. Around half the rooms have showers; the others have access to a shower on the third floor, for which you pay €4. M° Rambuteau/Étienne-Marcel. ❸

**Hôtel du Septième Art** 20 rue St-Paul, 4ᵉ ☏01.44.54.85.00, ℻01.42.77.69.10, @ hotel7art@wanadoo.fr. Pleasant, comfort-able place decorated with posters and photos from old movies; a similarly themed *salon de thé* downstairs. The stairs and bathrooms live up to the black-and-white-movie style. Every room is equipped with a safe. M° St-Paul/Sully Morland. ❺

**Hôtel Sévigné** 2 rue Malher, 4ᵉ ☏01.42.72.76.17, ℻01.42.78.68.26, @ www.le-sevigne.com. A comfortable, pleasant hotel, just off rue de Rivoli. The rooms are small but well-maintained and double-glazed; the cheapest come with shower and toilet on the landing. M° St-Paul. ❹

## Quartier du Temple

**Hôtel du Cantal** 7 rue des Vertus, 3ᵉ ☏01.42.77.65.52, ℻01.42.77.64.95, @ hcantal.online.fr. Located near the Picasso Museum on a quiet, pedestrian-ized street, this small hotel with only four-teen rooms represents extremely good value for the area. The recently renovated rooms are attractively, if simply, decorated, with some period features, like exposed beams. There's also a small family suite on the top floor. Breakfast is available in the café-bar downstairs, as is dinner. Note that there's a midnight curfew. M° Arts-et-Métiers. ❹

**Hôtel du Marais** 16 rue de Beauce, 3ᵉ ☏01.42.72.30.26, @ hotelmarais@voila.fr. A prewar Paris budget hotel, untouched, with brown spiral stairs, tiled floors, squat loos and an old-fashioned bar on the ground floor. Primitive, certainly, and the beds are very saggy, but clean, quiet and with pleasant service. M° Arts-et-Métiers/Filles-du-Calvaire/Temple. ❷

**Paris France Hôtel** 72 rue de Turbigo, 3ᵉ ☏01.42.78.00.04, ℻01.42.71.99.43, @ www.paris-france-hotel.com. Near the noisy inter-section of rue de Turbigo and rue du Temple, but in an animated quartier off the beaten track. Rooms vary, so it's best to view before committing yourself. M° Temple/République. ❺

**Hôtel Picard** 26 rue de Picardie, 3ᵉ ☏01.48.87.53.82, ℻ 01.48.87.02.56, @ www.france-hotel-guide.com /h75003picard2.htm. A little frayed around the edges, but a clean and comfortable establishment with decent-sized rooms overlooking the Carreau du Temple and in the same block as Paris's best Internet café (see p.290). Ten percent reduction if you produce your *Rough Guide*. M° Temple/République. ❸

## The Bastille

**Citadines Bastille Marais** 37 bd Richard Lenoir, 11ᵉ ☏01.53.36.90.00, ℻01.53.36.90.22, @ www.citadines.com. An apartment-hotel with 108 studios sleeping two and 30 two-roomed apartments for four. Each comes with its own kitchen and bathroom and some have balconies. The excellent food market on Richard Lenoir (Thurs & Sun) is a good source of provisions if you plan on doing some self-catering. Rooms, deco-rated in attractive contemporary style, come with TV, CD player and Internet point. You also benefit from all the ameni-ties of a three-star hotel, plus parking, laundry services and the option of break-fast. Minimum stay 2 nights. ❻

**Méridional** 36 bd Richard-Lenoir, 11ᵉ ☏01.48.05.75.00, ℻01.43.57.42.85, @ www.hotel-meridional.com. A welcoming and attractive three-star on a fairly quiet road, handily located for the Marais and Bastille. Rooms are equipped with minibar, TV and Internet point and have recently been refurbished in light oak and pastel colours. M° Bréguet-Sabin/Bastille. ❼

**Pax Hotel** 12 rue de Charonne, 11<sup>e</sup> ☎01.47.00.40.98, ℱ01.42.28.57.81. A reasonable, no-frills establishment well placed for the Bastille's nightlife, but don't count on it living up to its name – quiet it isn't, and there's no double glazing either. M° Ledru-Rollin/Bastille. ❸

## The Left Bank

### Quartier Latin

*The hotels in this section are marked on the map on pp.116–117.*

**Agora St-Germain** 42 rue des Bernardins, 5<sup>e</sup> ☎01.46.34.13.00, ✉agorastg@club-internet.fr. Very pleasant hotel, with all the comfort you'd expect for the price, though rear-facing rooms are dark and not such good value. M° Maubert-Mutualité. ❻

**Hôtel des Alliés** 20 rue Berthollet, 5<sup>e</sup> ☎01.43.31.47.52, ℱ01.45.35.13.92. Plain, rather dull rooms, but the place is clean and well run, and the price is a bargain. Rooms with bathroom (❹) are very spacious. M° Censier-Daubenton. ❸

**Hôtel le Central** 6 rue Descartes, 5<sup>e</sup> ☎01.46.33.57.93. Decent but dowdy rooms in a typically Parisian house above a café-restaurant on the Montagne Ste-Geneviève; all rooms come with a shower. M° Maubert-Mutualité/Cardinal-Lemoine. ❷

**Hôtel du Commerce** 14 rue de la Montagne-Ste-Geneviève, 5<sup>e</sup> ☎01.43.54.89.69, ⓦwww.commerce-paris-hotel.com. Completely renovated budget hotel aimed at backpackers and families, in the heart of the Quartier Latin. Rooms come at a range of prices, from washbasin-only cheapies up to en-suite rooms, and there are singles and three- and four-bed rooms. Communal kitchen and dining area. M° Maubert-Mutualité. ❸

**Hôtel Esmeralda** 4 rue St-Julien-le-Pauvre, 5<sup>e</sup> ☎01.43.54.19.20, ℱ01.40.51.00.68. Nestling in an ancient house on square Viviani, this discreet old hotel has small, cosy rooms with an old-fashioned feel, some with superb views of Notre-Dame. A trio of singles come with washbasin only for €30. M° St-Michel/Maubert-Mutualité. ❺

**Familia Hôtel** 11 rue des Écoles, 5<sup>e</sup> ☎01.43.54.55.27, ⓦwww.hotel-paris-familia.com. Friendly, family-run hotel in the heart of the quartier. Rooms are small but characterful, with beams, elegant toile de Jouy wallpaper and pretty murals. Some top-floor rooms have views of nearby Notre-Dame, and others have their own balcony with table and chairs. The *Minerva*, an attractive three-star next door, has the same owners. M° Cardinal-Lemoine/Maubert-Mutualité/Jussieu. ❺

**Hôtel Gay-Lussac** 29 rue Gay-Lussac, 5<sup>e</sup> ☎01.43.54.23.96, ℱ01.40.51.79.49. Excellent value for the area – close to the Luxembourg gardens. The old-fashioned atmosphere kept up by the genteel lady owners is appealing, as long as you don't mind the no-frills aspect and slightly worn decor. No credit cards. RER Luxembourg. ❹

**Grand Hôtel St-Michel** 19 rue Cujas, 5<sup>e</sup> ☎01.46.33.33.02, ⓦwww.grand-hotel-st-michel.com. Extremely pleasant rooms overlooking the Sorbonne and a stone's throw from both the Panthéon and the Luxembourg gardens. The hotel itself has an atmosphere of cosseted luxury but the student nightlife in the area can get a little rowdy – light sleepers should ask for a room at the back. RER Luxembourg. ❾

**Hôtel des Grandes Écoles** 75 rue du Cardinal-Lemoine, 5<sup>e</sup> ☎01.43.26.79.23, ⓦwww.hotel-grandes-ecoles.com. Comfortable, pretty hotel in the heart of the Quartier Latin, set around a large and peaceful courtyard garden. M° Cardinal-Lemoine. ❼

**Libertel Quartier Latin** 9 rue des Écoles, 5<sup>e</sup> ☎01.44.27.06.45, ⓦwww.libertel-hotels.com. The cool, modern decor is straight out of a style mag, though it's mostly business clients who can afford to enjoy it – doubles cost upwards of €200. Rooms have air-conditioning and all the other chain-hotel touches, but the place is small enough not to feel impersonal. M° Cardinal-Lemoine/Maubert-Mutualité. ❾

**Hôtel Marignan** 13 rue du Sommerard, 5<sup>e</sup> ☎01.43.54.63.81, ⓦwww.hotel-marignan.com. One of the best bargains in town, with breakfast thrown in. Totally sympathetic to the needs of rucksack-toting foreigners, with free laundry and ironing facilities, plus a room to eat your own food in – plates, fridge and microwave provided – and rooms for up to five people. M° Maubert-Mutualité. ❹

**Hôtel Médicis** 214 rue St-Jacques, 5<sup>e</sup> ☎01.43.54.14.66. Basic hotel, but the low prices make it very popular with hard-up backpackers, and the owners are charming. RER Luxembourg. ❷

**Hôtel Port-Royal** 8 bd Port-Royal, 5ᵉ
☎01.43.31.70.06, ⌨www.portroyalhotel.fr.st. A
real bargain – immaculately clean, attractive
and friendly. It's located out at the southern
edge of the quarter, at the rue Mouffetard
end of the boulevard, but near the métro.
Fifteen inexpensive rooms (❸) are available
with shared bathroom facilities (be warned,
showers cost €2.50). M° Gobelins. ❹

**Hôtel St-Jacques** 35 rue des Écoles, 5ᵉ
☎01.44.07.45.45, ✉hotelsaintjacques
@wanadoo.fr. This pretty hotel in the heart of
the district combines original nineteenth-
century features, including a wrought-iron
staircase and decorative ceiling mouldings,
with modern comforts. Spacious rooms,
some with balconies offering great views of
the Panthéon. M° Maubert-
Mutualité/Odéon. ❺

**Hôtel de la Sorbonne** 6 rue Victor-Cousin, 5ᵉ
☎01.43.54.58.08, ⌨www.hotelsorbonne.com.
Housed in an attractive old building close to
the Luxembourg gardens and Panthéon,
the *Sorbonne* is a quiet, comfortable hotel
with some designer touches. RER
Luxembourg/M° Cluny-La Sorbonne. ❻

**Hôtel des Trois Collèges** 16 rue Cujas, 5ᵉ
☎01.43.54.67.30, ⌷01.46.34.02.99. Light, airy
rooms and young, helpful staff in this classy
modernized hotel. RER Luxembourg/M°
Cluny-La Sorbonne. ❻

## St-Germain

*The hotels in this section are marked on the
map on pp.128–129.*

**Hôtel de l'Angleterre** 44 rue Jacob, 6ᵉ
☎01.42.60.34.72, ✉anglotel@wanadoo.fr.
Classy and extremely elegant hotel in a
building that once housed the British
Embassy and, later, Ernest Hemingway,
although in those days he only paid three
francs a night. The more expensive rooms
(❾) are huge, and many have giant roof-
beams. M° St-Germain-des-Prés. ❽

**Hôtel Aviatic** 105 rue de Vaugirard, 6ᵉ
☎01.53.63.25.50, ⌨www.aviatic.fr. Charming,
unpretentious and extremely comfortable
three-star, with friendly staff. Conveniently
located for Montparnasse, with its station
and glitzy café-brasseries, and within
walking distance of the heart of St-
Germain's shopping area. M°
Montparnasse-Bienvenüe/St-Placide. ❽

**Hôtel de Beaune** 29 rue de Beaune, 7ᵉ
☎01.42.61.24.89, ⌷01.49.27.02.12. A very

pretty hotel with just nineteen rooms, in an
ideal location close to St-Germain and the
Musée d'Orsay, on a street lined with
antique and art dealers. M° Rue-du-Bac. ❼

**Hôtel Bersoly's St-Germain** 28 rue de Lille, 7ᵉ
☎01.42.60.73.79, ⌨www.bersolyshotel.com.
This attractive eighteenth-century building
houses small but exquisite rooms, each
named and themed after an artist.
Impeccable service. M° Rue-du-Bac. ❼

**Hôtel Delhy's** 22 rue de l'Hirondelle, 6ᵉ
☎01.43.26.58.25, ⌷01.43.26.51.06. An old
house in a tiny street just off place St-Michel.
Nothing special, but well maintained and in a
very central location. M° St-Michel. ❺

**Hôtel du Globe** 15 rue des Quatre-Vents, 6ᵉ
☎01.43.26.35.50, ⌷01.46.33.62.69. Extremely
welcoming hotel in a tall, narrow, seventeenth-century building decked out in a
rather eccentric medieval theme: four-
posters, stone walls, roof beams and even
a suit of armour. Breakfast (€8) is a more
interesting affair than the usual, with fancy
*viennoiseries*. M° Odéon. ❹–❻

**Grand Hôtel des Balcons** 3 rue Casimir-
Delavigne, 6ᵉ ☎01.46.34.78.50, ⌨www
.balcons.com. An attractive and comfortable
hotel with Art Deco touches and modern
rooms. It's good value and in a lovely location near the Odéon and Luxembourg gardens. The balconies are all small, decorative affairs, except on the fifth floor. M°
Odéon. ❻

**L'Hôtel** 13 rue des Beaux-Arts, 6ᵉ
☎01.44.41.99.00, ⌨www.l-hotel.com.
Extravagantly kitsch "destination" hotel –
Oscar Wilde died here, "fighting a duel"
with his wallpaper – with prices climbing
above the €300 mark. The twenty eccentrically individual rooms retain their original
1960s designer decor, and there's a small
pool underground. M° Mabillon/St-
Germain-des-Prés. ❾

**Hôtel des Marronniers** 21 rue Jacob, 6ᵉ
☎01.43.25.30.60, ⌷01.40.46.83.56. Relatively
pricey but romantic place, with small
rooms swathed in deep velvet curtains and
fabric wallcoverings. The dining room gives
onto a courtyard garden. M° St-Germain-
des-Prés. ❾

**Hôtel de Nesle** 7 rue de Nesle, 6ᵉ
☎01.43.54.62.41, ⌨www.hoteldenesle.com.
Friendly, offbeat hotel with historical or literary themed rooms, and decorated with
wacky cartoon murals you'll either love or
hate. M° St-Michel. ❺

**Hôtel de l'Odéon** 13 rue St-Sulpice, 6ᵉ ☎01.43.25.70.11, ⊛www.paris-hotel -odeon.com. Old-fashioned luxury – flowers, antique furniture, some four-poster beds, and great service. Mº St-Sulpice/Odéon. **❾**

**Hôtel Récamier** 3bis place St-Sulpice, 6ᵉ ☎01.43.26.04.89, ℻01.46.33.27.73. Comfortable, old-fashioned and solidly bourgeois hotel, superbly situated on a corner tucked away behind the grand church of St-Sulpice. Mº St-Sulpice/St-Germain-des-Prés. **❼**

**Relais Saint-Sulpice** 3 rue Garancière, 6ᵉ ☎01.46.33.99.00, ℮relaisstsulpice @wanadoo.fr. Set in a beautiful, aristocratic townhouse on a side street immediately behind St-Sulpice's apse, this is a discreetly classy hotel with well-furnished rooms painted in cheery Provençal colours. Mº St-Sulpice/St-Germain-des-Prés. **❾**

**Welcome Hotel** 66 rue de Seine, 6ᵉ ☎01.46.34.24.80, ⊛www.welcomehotel -paris.com. The bedrooms at this friendly, cosy hotel may be slightly small and dowdy, but the price is good and the location is great – on bustling rue de Seine (the rooms have double glazing), right by the rue de Buci street market and its speciality food shops. Mº Odéon. **❻**

## Trocadéro and the Septième

*The hotels in this section are marked on the map on pp.136–137.*

**Hôtel du Champs-de-Mars** 7 rue du Champs-de-Mars ☎01.45.51.52.30, ⊛www.hotel-du -champ-de-mars.com. Friendly and well-run hotel just off the rue Cler market. The rooms are decidedly cosy, with swathes of colourful fabrics adorning the bedheads, curtains and chairs. Excellent value. Mº École-Militaire. **❺**

**Hôtel Eiffel Rive-Gauche** 6 rue du Gros-Caillou, 7ᵉ ☎01.45.51.24.56, ⊛www.123france.com. A refurbishment has introduced rather cheap modern furnishings to this traditional two-star, but the wonderful top rooms have close-up views of the Eiffel Tower. Mº École-Militaire. **❺**

**Grand Hôtel Lévêque** 29 rue Cler ☎01.47.05.49.15, ⊛www.hotel-leveque.com. Located smack in the middle of the posh rue Cler market, this is a largish, decent, family-run place. Book a month ahead for the brighter front-facing rooms. Mº École-Militaire/La Tour-Maubourg. **❺**

**Hôtel d'Orsay** 93 rue de Lille, 7ᵉ ☎01.42.21.46.74, ℻01.45.55.51.16. An attractive and relaxing place to stay, with spacious rooms by Parisian standards. Mº Solférino/RER Musée-d'Orsay. **❻**

**Hôtel du Palais Bourbon** 49 rue de Bourgogne, 7ᵉ ☎01.44.11.30.70, ⊛www.hotel -palais-bourbon.com. A handsome old building in a sunny street by the Musée Rodin, with spacious and light rooms. Mº Varenne. **❼**

**Le Pavillon** 54 rue St-Dominique ☎01.45.51.42.87, ℮patrickpavillon@aol.com. A tiny former convent set back from the tempting shops of the rue St-Dominique. Rooms are small and very simple, but good value for this area. Mº Invalides/La Tour-Maubourg. **❺**

**Hôtel Saint Dominique** 62 rue Saint-Dominique, 7ᵉ ☎01.47.05.51.44, ℮hotel.saint.dominique@wanadoo.fr. Welcoming hotel in the heart of this upmarket, villagey neighbourhood, which sits in the shadow of the Eiffel Tower. The prettily wallpapered rooms are arranged around a bright little courtyard with tables and chairs amid the greenery. Mº Invalides/La Tour-Maubourg. **❼**

**Hôtel de la Tulipe** 33 rue Malar, 7ᵉ ☎01.45.51.67.21, ⊛www.hoteldelatulipe.com. Attractively chintzy and cottage-like two-star with exposed-stone walls and flagstones recalling its former life as a convent. There's a miniature patio for summer breakfast and drinks, but you pay for the location. Mº Invalides/La Tour-Maubourg. **❽**

## Montparnasse and southern Paris

### Montparnasse and the 14ᵉ

*The hotels in this section are marked on the map on pp.148–149.*

**Celtic Hôtel** 15 rue d'Odessa, 14ᵉ ☎01.43.20.93.53 ℻01.43.20.66.07. Attractively old-fashioned but well-maintained hotel almost in the shadow of the Tour Montparnasse. Mº Montparnasse-Bienvenüe/Edgar-Quinet. **❹**

**Hôtel Istria** 29 rue Campagne-Première, 14ᵉ ☎01.43.20.91.82, ℮hotel.istria@wanadoo.fr. Beautifully decorated hotel, with legendary artistic associations: Duchamp, Man Ray, Aragon, Mayakovsky and Rilke all stayed here. Mº Raspail. **❻**

**Hôtel du Parc Montsouris** 4 rue du Parc-Montsouris, 14e ☏01.45.89.09.72, ⊛www.hotel-parc-montsouris.com. Modern and a bit impersonal, but in a lovely, tiny street right by the park. M° Porte-d'Orléans/RER Cité-Universitaire. ➍

### The 15e

*The hotels in this section are marked on the map on pp.158–159.*

**Hôtel Fondary** 30 rue Fondary, 15e ☏01.45.75.14.75, ☏01.45.75.84.42. In a quiet street just off one of the more animated streets of the attractively bourgeois 15e. Homely, peaceful rooms, soft colours and a sunny breakfast room. M° Émile-Zola. ➍

**Hôtel Pasteur** 33 rue du Docteur-Roux, 15e ☏01.47.83.53.17, ☏01.45.66.62.39. Rooms are comfortable and well equipped for the price, and there's a small garden. Closed Aug. M° Pasteur. ➍

**Hôtel Printemps** 31 rue du Commerce, 15e ☏01.45.79.83.36, ☏01.45.79.84.88, ☺hotel.printemps.15e@yahoo.fr. Offers a friendly welcome and rooms that are sparsely furnished but clean. Popular with backpackers. M° La Motte-Picquet. ➋

### The 13e

*The hotels in this section are marked on the map on p.162.*

**Résidence Les Gobelins** 9 rue des Gobelins, 13e ☏01.47.07.26.90, ⊛www.hotelgobelins.com. A delightful establishment within walking distance of the Quartier Latin's rue Mouffetard. With its large, comfortable rooms, this is a well-known bargain, so book far in advance. M° Les Gobelins. ➍

**Hôtel Tolbiac** 122 rue de Tolbiac, 13e ☏01.44.24.25.54, ⊛www.hotel-tolbiac.com. Situated on a noisy junction, but all rooms are pleasant, with private or shared showers, and very inexpensive. In July and August you can rent small studios by the week. M° Tolbiac. ➋

**Le Vert-Galant** 41 rue Croulebarbe, 13e ☏01.44.08.83.50, ☏01.44.08.83.69. Set in a quiet, verdant backwater, this pleasant hotel sits above a renowned Basque restaurant, the *Auberge Etchegorry* (see p.301), with a vine climbing up the wall from the garden. Cosy rooms, some with kitchenette. M° Les-Gobelins. ➏

## Montmartre and northern Paris

### Montmartre

*The hotels in this section are marked on the map on p.167.*

**Hôtel André Gill** 4 rue André-Gill ☏01.42.62.48.48, ☏01.42.62.77.92. Quiet rooms in a great location on the slopes of Montmartre, in a dead-end alley off rue des Martyrs. No-smoking. M° Pigalle/Abbesses. ➎

**Hôtel Bonséjour** 11 rue Burq, 18e ☏01.42.54.22.53, ☏01.42.54.25.92. Set in a marvellous location on a quiet untouristy street on the slopes of Montmartre, this hotel is run by friendly and conscientious owners, and the rooms, which are basic, but clean and spacious, are Montmartre's best deal. Ask for the corner rooms 23, 33, 43 or 53, all of which have a balcony. M° Abbesses. ➋

**Hôtel le Bouquet de Montmartre** 1 rue Durantin, 18e ☏01.46.06.87.54, ⊛www.bouquetdemontmartre.com. The decor is rather overwhelmingly chintzy, but the rooms are comfortable and good value, and the location on the corner of lively place des Abbesses, directly underneath the Butte, is excellent. M° Jules-Joffrin. ➍

**Hôtel Caulaincourt** 2 sq Caulaincourt (by 63 rue Caulaincourt), 18e ☏01.46.06.42.99, ⊛www.caulaincourt.com. One of the nicest and friendliest of the cheaper hotels. The rooms are fairly well kept, and the more expensive ones are en suite. From the larger room of the brand new youth-hostel section (€23 a night), the lucky backpackers get a magnificent view. M° Lamarck-Caulaincourt. ➌

**Hôtel du Commerce** 34 rue des Trois-Frères, 18e ☏01.42.64.81.69. Cheerfully grotty hotel for the hardened traveller only. Arrive in the morning for a room that night. M° Abbesses/Anvers. ➊

**Ermitage** 24 rue Lamarck, 18e ☏01.42.64.79.22. This discreet, elegant hotel is characterfully decorated in deep colours. Only a stone's throw from the Sacré Coeur but it's best to approach via M° Anvers and the *funiculaire* to avoid the steep climb. M° Lamarck-Caulaincourt/Château-Rouge. ➎

**Hôtel du Puy de Dôme** 180 rue Ordener (av St-Ouen end) , 18e ☏01.46.27.78.55, ☏01.42.29.13.67. On the north side of Montmartre, close to a big street market and the métro. A pleasant, friendly and well-maintained budget hotel. M° Guy-Môquet. ③

**Timhotel Montmartre** pl Émile-Goudeau, 11 rue Ravignan, 18ᵉ ☎01.42.55.74.79, €montmartre@timhotel.fr. Rooms are modern, comfortable and freshly decorated in a nondescript chain-hotel way. The location, however, is unbeatable – on the beautiful shady square where Picasso had his studio in 1900, with views across the city from the more expensive (⑥) rooms. M° Abbesses/Blanche. ⑦

### Pigalle and South of Pigalle

*The hotels in this section are marked on the map on p.167.*

**Langlou/des Croisés** 63 rue St-Lazare, 9ᵉ ☎01.48.74.78.24, €hotel-des -croises@wanadoo.fr. Superbly genteel hotel that's hardly changed in half a century, with a beautiful old lift and unusually large rooms. M° Trinité. ⑥

**Perfect Hotel** 39 Rue Rodier, 9ᵉ ☎01.42.81.18.86, ⑤01.42.85.01.38. Popular hotel on a lively street populated with restaurants. Simple, clean rooms and a warm welcome. M° Anvers. ③

### The Stations and Faubourgs

*The hotels in this section are marked on the map on p.175.*

**Chabrol Opéra Hôtel** 46 rue de Chabrol, 10ᵉ ☎01.45.23.93.10, ⓦwww.hotelchabrol.com. A reliable, welcoming little hotel within walking distance of the stations. Exposed roof beams add a warm note to the otherwise completely modernized rooms. M° Poissonière/Gare-de-l'Est. ⑤

**Grand Hôtel d'Amiens** 88 rue du Faubourg-Poissonnière (nr junction with rue La-Fayette), 10ᵉ ☎01.48.78.71.18, ⑤01.48.74.89.41. Worn stairs and no frills, but the rooms are clean and reasonably spacious, and the more expensive ones (②) have bathrooms. M° Poissonnière. ②

**Hôtel Jarry** 4 rue de Jarry, 10ᵉ ☎01.47.70.70.38, ⑤01.42.46.34.45 (see colour map 3). Simple but welcoming hotel in a lively immigrant quarter. Distinctly fresher than the cheaper dives in the area. M° Gare-de-l'Est/Château-d'Eau. ②

**Marclau Hôtel** 78 rue du Faubourg Poissoniére ☎01.47.70.73.50, ⑤01.44.83.95.89. Efficient budget option

situated on a quiet corner at the posher end of the quartier. Some frayed edges, but the rooms are large, clean and good value. M° Poissoniére. ③

**Nord-Est Hôtel** 12 rue des Petits-Hôtels, 10ᵉ ☎01.47.70.07.18, €hotel.nord.est@wanadoo.fr. A safe option if you need to be close to the station. Rooms are clean and modern, though characterless. M° Poissonnière/Gare-du-Nord/Gare-de-l'Est. ⑤

**Hôtel Palace** 9 rue Bouchardon, 10ᵉ ☎01.40.40.09.45 or 01.42.06.59.32, ⑤01.42.06.16.90. Run by nice, helpful owners, this cheapie has acceptable rooms in a busy, colourful and central district near the Porte St-Martin. The non-en-suite rooms (single €17, double €25) have access to showers on a separate floor for a supplement of €3.50. An extra €11 gets you a room with a shower. M° Strasbourg-St-Denis. ①

**Hôtel du Savoy** 9 rue Jarry, 10ᵉ ☎01.47.70.03.72 (see colour map 3). Basic, shabby no-star in a very down-at-heel area but you'll be hard pushed to find a cheaper room anywhere, and there are other basic options on the same street if this one is full. M° Gare-de-l'Est/Château-d'Eau. ①

**Terminus Nord** 12 bd de Denain, 10ᵉ ☎01.42.80.20.00, ⑤01.42.80.63.89. A traditional-style luxury hotel right in front of the Gare du Nord. The restoration was undertaken when the hotel was bought by the Libertel group and bears a few signs of the chain-hotelier, but its aspirations and services are those of a four-star hotel and it's a very comfortable and convenient place to stay. Rooms start at around €170. M° Gare-du-Nord. ⑨

### Batignolles

*The hotels in this section are marked on the map on p.178.*

**Hôtel Avenir-Jonquière** 23 rue de la Jonquière, 17ᵉ ☎01.46.27.83.41, ⑤01.46.27.88.08. Clean, friendly establishment offering bargain accommodation. Close to the tempting food stores on av de St-Ouen. M° Guy-Môquet/Brochant. ③

**Hôtel des Batignolles** 26–28 rue des Batignolles, 17ᵉ ☎01.43.87.70.40, ⓦwww.batignolles.com. Quiet and very reasonable hotel, in a neighbourhood that prides itself on its village character. M° Rome/Place-de-Clichy. ④

**Hôtel Eldorado** **18 rue des Dames, 17e ⓣ01.45.22.35.21, ⓦwww.eldorado.cityvox.com.** You can't miss the bright yellow front of this hotel, which sets the tone for the sunny, sometimes idiosyncratic colour scheme within. A funky, trendy and reasonably priced place to stay. M° Rome/Place-de-Clichy. ❹

**Hôtel Savoy** **21 rue des Dames, 17e ⓣ01.42.93.13.47.** Typical unmodernized Paris cheapie offering a choice of rooms with shared bathrooms or private showers. M° Place-de-Clichy/Rome. ❶

**Style Hôtel** **8 rue Ganneron (av Clichy end), 18e ⓣ01.45.22.37.59, ⓕ01.45.22.81.03.** Wooden floors, marble fireplaces, a secluded internal courtyard, and nice people. Great value, especially in the rooms with shared bathrooms (❷). No lift. M° Place-Clichy. ❸

## Eastern Paris

### Place de la République and The Canala St-Martin

*The hotels in this section are marked on the map on pp.184–185.*

**Hôtel Beaumarchais** **3 rue Oberkampf, 11e ⓣ01.53.36.86.86, ⓕ01.43.38.32.86, ⓦwww.hotelbeaumarchais.com.** Fashionable, funky and gay-friendly hotel with personal service and colourful Fifties-inspired decor; all 31 rooms are en suite with air conditioning, safes and cable TV. M° Filles-du-Calvaire/Oberkampf. ❻

**Hôtel Gilden-Magenta** **35 rue Yves Toudic, 10e ⓣ01.42.40.17.72, ⓕ01.42.02.59.66, ⓦwww.multi-micro.com/hotel.gilden.magenta.** A friendly hotel, with fresh, colourful decor; rooms 61 and 62, up in the attic, are the best and have views of the Canal St Martin. Breakfast is served in a pleasant patio area. M° République/Jacques-Bonsergent. ❹

**Ibis Paris La Villette** **31–35 Quai de L'Oise, 19e ⓣ01.40.38.04.04, ⓕ01.40.38.48.90, ⓦwww.ibishotel.com (not on the map).** Situated right on the canal facing the Parc de la Villette, this good-value modern chain hotel is a great spot to stay if you want to spend a few days exploring the park or attending concerts at the Cité de la Musique. It's also convenient if you're bringing your own car, as it's easily reached from the boulevard périphérique exiting at the Porte de la Villette, with free parking included. M° Corentin Cariou/Ourcq. ❹

**Mary's Hôtel** **15 rue de Malte, 11e ⓣ01.47.00.81.70, ⓕ01.47.00.58.06, ⓦwww.maryshotel.com.** Comfortable and clean, if somewhat cramped, hotel on the edge of the Marais, run by courteous people. The cheaper rooms are good value for money, the en-suite rooms less so. M° Oberkampf/République. ❸

**Hôtel Moderne du Temple** **3 rue d'Aix, 10e ⓣ01.42.08.09.04, ⓕ01.42.41.72.17, ⓦhmt.chez.tiscali.fr.** A bargain hotel run by Czechs. The forty rooms are simple but clean, some en suite. M° République/Goncourt. ❷

**Hôtel de Nevers** **53 rue de Malte, 11e ⓣ01.47.00.56.18, ⓕ01.43.57.77.39, ⓦwww.hoteldenevers.com.** Three smoky-grey cats patrol the entrance to this friendly one-star. Rooms are small and vary in standard, but most are well-kept and cheerful. When it's working, a rickety 1930s lift rumbles its way between the floors. An Internet point in the foyer is available for checking email. M° Oberkampf/République. ❷

**Hôtel République** **30 rue Lucien Sampaix, 10e ⓣ01.42.08.19.74, ⓕ01.42.08.27.28, ⓦwww.hotelsjardinsdeparis.com.** In a pleasant street, close to the St-Martin canal. Reasonable value for money: all 39 rooms are en suite with TV and radio. M° Jacques-Bonsergent. ❺

**Hôtel Verlain** **97 rue Saint Maur, 11e; ⓣ01.43.57.44.88, ⓕ01.43.57.32.06, ⓦwww.3and1hotels.com.** Neat, clean, and cheerful rooms – some with balconies – in a lively neighbourhood. M° Rue St-Maur. ❼

### Belleville, Ménilmontant and Charonne

*The hotels in this section are marked on the map on pp.184–185.*

**Ermitage Hôtel** **42bis rue de l'Ermitage, 20e ⓣ01.46.36.23.44, ⓕ01.46.36.89.13.** A clean and decent cheapie, close to the leafy rue des Pyrénées with its provincial feel. M° Jourdain. ❶

**Hôtel Pyrénées-Gambetta** **12 av du Père-Lachaise, 20e ⓣ01.47.97.76.57, ⓕ01.47.97.17.61.** On a quiet road and luxurious for this part of town, yet unpretentious and very pleasant. All rooms with cable TV. M° Gambetta. ❸

**Hôtel Rhin et Danube** 3 pl Rhin-et-Danube, 19ᵉ ✆01.42.45.10.13, ℻01.42.06.88.82, ⊛www.gaf.tm.fr. Studio apartments with small kitchenettes geared to the self-catering and located northeast of the city centre, near the entrance to the Parc de la Villette on the airy heights of Belleville. Good value. Mᵒ Danube. ❹

### Down to the Faubourg St-Antoine & The 12ᵉ

*The hotels in this section are marked on the map on pp.200–201.*

**Hôtel de la Porte Dorée** 273 av Daumesnil, 12ᵉ ✆01.43.07.56.97, ℻01.49.28.08.18, ⊛www.paris-hotels-paris.com. A charming two-star, renovated with great care and taste by an American-French family. Traditional features such as ceiling mouldings, fireplaces and the elegant main staircase have been retained and many of the furnishings in the rooms are antique. Modern touches include Internet point, satellite TV and hairdryers in all the rooms. The Bastille is seven mintues away by metro or a pleasant twenty-minute walk along the Promenade Plantée. Mᵒ Porte-Dorée. ❹

**Hôtel des Pyrénées** 204 rue du Faubourg-St-Antoine, 11ᵉ ✆01.43.72.07.46, ℻01.43.72.98.45. A good-value hotel with thirty comfortable and spacious, if a little old-fashioned, rooms; those on the road are lighter and double-glazed. Mᵒ Faidherbe-Chaligny. ❹

**Hôtel Tamaris** 14 rue des Maraîchers, 20ᵉ ✆01.43.72.85.48 or toll free 0800.20.13.66, ℻01.43.56.81.75, ⊛www.hotel-tamaris.fr. An old-fashioned, well-maintained hotel run by nice people. Extremely good value and understandably popular. Only four metro stops from the Bastille and close to the terminus of bus route #26 from Gare du Nord. Mᵒ Porte-de-Vincennes. ❷

**Hôtel-Résidence Trousseau** 13 rue Trousseau, 11ᵉ ✆01.48.05.55.55, ℻01.48.05.83.97, ✉tr@hroy.com. Modern, serviced studio apartments, that sleep from two to six people, and come with fully equipped kitchens – perfectly positioned for food shopping in the nearby place d'Aligre market – plus satellite TV. Car parking available for €12.50 per day. Mᵒ Bastille/Ledru-Rollin. ❻

### Western Paris

*The hotels in this section are marked on the map on p.208.*

**Hameau de Passy** 48 rue Passy, 16ᵉ ✆01.42.88.47.55, ℻01.42.30.83.72, ⊛www.hameaudepassy.com. An utterly peaceful modern hotel, tucked away in a *villa*. Rooms are on the small side, but are pleasantly decorated in hues of green and look out onto a pretty tree-lined patio. Faultless service is assured by a charming, polyglot staff. Mᵒ Muette/Passy. ❼

**Queen's Hotel** 4 rue Bastien-Lepage, 16ᵉ ✆01.42.88.89.85, ℻01.40.50.67.52, ⊛www.queens-hotel.fr. A three-star hotel run by helpful staff and offering modern comfort on a lovely side street in the centre of old Auteuil. Located near the métro stop just off rue de la Fontaine. Mᵒ Michel-Ange Auteuil. ❻

## Apartments, apartment-hotels and bed and breakfast

Rented **apartments and apartment-hotels** – a hotel made up of mini apartments each with its own self-contained kitchen – are attractive alternatives for families with young children who want a bit more independence and the option to do their own catering, and also for visitors who are planning an extended stay. Staying on a **bed and breakfast** basis in a private house is also worth considering if you want to get away from the more impersonal set-up of a hotel and is a reasonably priced option. The following is a list of recommended organizations.

**Citadines** ⊛www.citadines.com. A European-wide chain of apartment-hotels. Most of its 17 Paris establishments are centrally located and offer high-standard, comfortable accommodation consisting of self-contained studios and apartments sleeping up to six, with well-equipped kitchen and bathroom. Offers all the usual amenities of a three-star hotel, plus parking, laundry facilities and the option of breakfast. A studio sleeping two starts from around €105, an apartment for four costs around €185 a night, though they sometimes have special offers and there are lower rates for long stays.

**France Lodge** 2 rue Meissonier, 17ᵉ ☎01.56.33.85.80, ℻01.56.33.85.89, ⓦwww.apartments-in-paris.com. Offers bed and breakfast rooms inside and outside Paris. Prices start at €23 single or €35 double, plus a €15 booking fee. They can usually find something last minute, but reserve well in advance to be sure of something more special. They can also organize accommodation in furnished apartments by the week (from €380) or month (from €1000). Mº Le-Peletier.

**Good Morning Paris** 43 rue Lacépède, 5ᵉ ☎01.47.07.28.29, ℮info@goodmorningparis.fr. Bed-and-breakfast doubles, all in central Paris, starting at around €60. You have to stay at least two nights but there's no reser- vation fee – payment in full confirms your booking.

**Lodgis** 16 rue de la Folie Méricourt, 11ᵉ ☎01.48.07.11.11, ℻01.48.07.11.15, ⓦwww.lodgis.com. A reputable agency with over a thousand furnished flats on its books. A studio flat in the 5ᵉ starts from around €515 a week.

**Paris B and B** ☎1-800 872 2632, ⓦwww.parisbandb.com. US-based online bed-and-breakfast booking service. The rooms offered are on the luxurious side and start from $90 for a double. Apartments from $120.

**Studio-in-paris.com** ⓦwww.studio-in-paris.com. Small, friendly Paris-based accommodation service, with nine pleasant flats in the Marais, Palais Royal and Montorgueil areas. Studios from €420 a week.

## Hostels, foyers and student accommodation

Hostels are an obvious choice when you're keeping to a tight budget, though it's worth bearing in mind that you can often find a double room in an inex- pensive hotel for very little more, especially in the outer arrondissements where many hostels are located. There's normally a **maximum length of stay**, mostly less than a week, and there is often a **curfew** at around 2am, though many hostels will loan you a key or give you a pass code that opens the main door.

Most places now take advance bookings, including all three main **hostel groups**, FUAJ (part of Hostelling International, or HI), UCRIF and MIJE. Paris only has two central HI hostels, both part of the Fédération Unie des Auberges de Jeunesse (**FUAJ**; ⓦwww.fuaj.fr), but they can put you in touch with two more HI hostels, *Cité des Sciences* and *Léo Lagrange*, both just outside the city limits. You need membership, but it's available on the spot. It's advis- able to book ahead in summer – this can be done anywhere in the world via their computerized International Booking Network (contact your nearest Hostelling International office before leaving home or look up details on the Internet). In Paris itself, the central FUAJ office is near the Pompidou Centre at 9 rue Brantôme, 3ᵉ (☎01.48.04.70.40). A second, larger hostel group is run by **UCRIF** (Union des Centres de Rencontres Internationaux de France; ⓦwww.ucrif.asso.fr), which caters largely to groups. Again, we've detailed only the most central hostels, but a complete list is available online, and individual hostels should help you find a room elsewhere if they're full. Alternatively, UCRIF's main office at 27 rue de Turbigo, 2ᵉ (Mon–Fri 9am–6pm; ☎01.40.26.57.64; Mº Étienne-Marcel) can tell you where there are free places. A third group, **MIJE** (Maison Internationale de la Jeunesse et des Étudiants; ⓦwww.mije.com), runs three hostels in historic buildings in the Marais dis- trict. All are very pleasant places to stay and need to be booked a long time in advance.

**Independent hostels** tend to be noisier, more party-oriented places, often with bars attached and mostly attracting young visitors from Europe and the United States. Several suburban hostels exist on the outskirts of Paris; the tourist office has a list of these and can provide directions. Finally, you can always stay in one of the church- , state- or charity-operated **foyers** – residential hostels aimed at students during term time and young workers new to Paris. For other foyer addresses visit the CIDJ (Centre d'Information de la Jeunesse) office at 101 quai Branly, 15ᵉ (℡01.44.49.12.00, ⒲www.cidj.com; Mᵒ Bir-Hakeim).

**Student accommodation** is let out during the summer vacation. Rooms are spartan, part of large modern university complexes, often complete with self-service kitchen facilities and shared bathrooms. Space tends to fill up quickly with international students, school groups and young travellers, so it's best to make plans well in advance. Expect to pay €15–30 per night for a room. The organization to contact for information and reservations is CROUS, Académie de Paris, 39 av Georges-Bernanos, 5ᵉ (Mon–Fri 9am–5pm; ℡01.40.51.55.55, ⒲www.crous-paris.fr; Mᵒ Port-Royal).

Except where indicated, there is no effective age limit at any of these places.

## Hostel groups

**D'Artagnan** 80 rue Vitruve, 20ᵉ ℡01.40.32.34.56, ⒲www.fuaj.fr (see map on pp.184–185). A colourful, funky, modern HI hostel, with a fun atmosphere and lots of facilities including a small cinema, restaurant and bar, and a local swimming pool nearby. Located on the eastern edge of the city near Charonne, which has some good bars. Huge, but very popular so try to get here early – reservations by fax or from other HI hostels only. Dorm beds cost €20.60 a night. No private rooms, but some dorms have three or four beds. Mᵒ Porte-de-Bagnolet.

**BVJ Paris Quartier Latin** 44 rue des Bernardins, 5ᵉ ℡01.43.29.34.80, ⒲www.bvjhotel.com (see map on pp.116–117). Typically institutional UCRIF hostel, but spick and span and in a good location. Dorm beds (€25), plus single or double rooms (€30/27 per person). Mᵒ Maubert-Mutualité.

**Le Fauconnier** 11 rue du Fauconnier, 4ᵉ ℡01.42.74.23.45, ⒡01.40.27.81.64 (see map on pp.98–99). MIJE hostel in a superbly renovated seventeenth-century building with a courtyard. Dorms (€24–26 per person) sleep three to eight, and there are some single (€30) and double rooms too (€40 with shower). Breakfast included. Mᵒ St-Paul/Pont-Marie.

**Le Fourcy** 6 rue de Fourcy, 4ᵉ ℡01.42.74.23.45 (see map on pp.98–99). Another MIJE hostel (same prices as *Le Fauconnier*, above) housed in a beautiful mansion, this one has a small garden and a restaurant with *menus* from €9.50. Dorms and some doubles and triples. Mᵒ St-Paul.

**Foyer International d'Accueil de Paris Jean Monnet** 30 rue Cabanis, 14ᵉ ℡01.43.13.17.00, ⒲www.fiap.asso.fr (see map on p.162). A huge, efficiently run UCRIF hostel in a fairly sedate area, with singles (€49.50), doubles (€32 per person) and dorms (€22.50–29, depending on number of beds). Facilities include meeting rooms and a disco; ideal for groups. Mᵒ Glacière.

**Jules Ferry** 8 bd Jules-Ferry, 11ᵉ ℡01.43.57.55.60, ⒲www.fuaj.fr (see map on pp.184–185). Fairly central HI hostel, in a lively area at the foot of the Belleville hill. Very difficult to get a place, but when full they will help you find a bed elsewhere. Only two to four people in each room; beds cost €19. Mᵒ République.

**Maison des Clubs UNESCO de Paris** 43 rue de la Glacière, 13ᵉ ℡01.43.36.00.63, ⒲www.clubs-unesco.asso.fr (see map on p.162). Bland UCRIF-linked place catering mostly to groups, some on UNESCO-funded exchange programmes. Beds cost €20 per person in a triple room, €23 in a double, and €28 in a single, though there are few of these. Bathroom facilities are shared between rooms. Open 24hr. Mᵒ Glacière.

**Maubuisson** 12 rue des Barres, 4ᵉ ℡01.42.74.23.45 (see map on pp.98–99). An MIJE hostel in a magnificent medieval building on a quiet street. Shared use of the restaurant at *Le Fourcy* (see above). Dorms only, sleeping four (€25 per person). Breakfast included. Mᵒ Pont-Marie/Hôtel-de-Ville.

**Maurice Ravel** 6 av Maurice-Ravel, 12ᵉ ℡01.44.75.60.00, ⒲www.cisp.asso.fr (see map on pp.200–201). This hostel, run by CISP (Centre International de Séjour de Paris), is some distance from central Paris, but close to the lovely Bois de Vincennes, and there's a swimming pool. Rooms come in a wide variety of sizes, from eight-bed dorms (€15.40 per person) to twins (€25) and singles (€30), but all share shower rooms. CISP have another hostel set in a park near the Porte-d'Italie, at the southern end of the 13ᵉ. M° Porte-de-Vincennes/Porte-Dorée.

## Independent hostels

**Aloha Hostel 1 rue Borromé, 15ᵉ** ☎01.42.73.03.03, ⓦwww.aloha.fr (see map on pp.158–159). American-dominated hostel with the same management as *Three Ducks Hostel*, below. Nov–March €17, April–Oct €21 for a bed in a four-bed dorm, which can be booked in advance by credit card. Turn up at 8am for one of the double rooms, which cost €25 per person, or €22 Nov–March. M° Volontaires.

**Auberge Internationale des Jeunes 10 rue Trousseau, 11ᵉ** ☎01.47.00.62.00, ⓦwww.aijparis.com (see map on pp.200–201). Despite the official-sounding name, a laid-back (but very noisy) independent hostel in a great location five minutes' walk from the Bastille. Clean and professionally run with 24hr reception, generous breakfast (included) and free luggage storage. Rooms for 2, 3 and 4. €13 Nov–Feb, €14 March–Oct. M° Bastille/Ledru-Rollin.

**The Blue Planet Hostel 5, rue Hector Malot, 12ᵉ** ☎01.43.42.06.18, ⓕ01.43.42.09.89, ⓦwww.hostelblueplanet.com (see map on pp.200–201). Popular with backpackers and less of a party scene than some of the others, this family-run hostel charges €21 per night including breakfast. No curfew. M° Gare de Lyon.

**Hôtel Caulaincourt 2 sq Caulaincourt (by 63 rue Caulaincourt), 18ᵉ** ☎01.46.06.42.99, ⓦwww.caulaincourt.com (see map on p.167). Friendly hotel with a new dormitory section (€23 a night) from which there's a fine view out over Paris. M° Lamarck-Caulaincourt.

**Centre International de Paris/Louvre 20 rue Jean-Jacques-Rousseau, 1ᵉʳ** ☎01.53.00.90.90 (see map on pp.76–77). A clean, modern and efficiently run hostel for 18- to 35-year-olds. Bookings can be made up to ten days prior to your stay. Accommodation ranges from single rooms to dorms sleeping eight. From €18.30 per person. M° Louvre/Châtelet-Les Halles.

**Maison Internationale des Jeunes 4 rue Titon, 11ᵉ** ☎01.43.71.99.21, ⓔmij.cp@wanadoo.fr (see map on pp.200–201). A clean, well-run establishment located between Bastille and Nation, geared to 18- to 30-year-olds for stays of between three and five days. Doors are open from 6am till 2am. Rooms range from doubles to dorms sleeping eight. €22.50 per person including shower, breakfast and sheets. Reservations should be made in advance and a fifty per cent deposit is required. M° Faidherbe-Chaligny.

**Peace and Love Hostel 245 rue La Fayette, 10ᵉ** ☎01.46.07.65.11, ⓦwww.paris-hostels.com (see colour map 3). Tucked away at the top end of the 10ᵉ, but offering some of the least expensive beds in town, from €16 per person in a four-bed room up to a dizzy €20 per person in a twin room. The bargain-priced bar that's open till 2am gives a clue to the style of the place. Open 24 hr. M° Jaurès.

**Three Ducks Hostel 6 place Étienne-Pernet, 15ᵉ** ☎01.48.42.04.05, ⓦwww.3ducks.fr (see map on pp.158–159). Private youth hostel with no age limit. In high season, beds cost €22 in dorm rooms (sleeping from four to ten people), €25 per person in a double; there are discounts in winter. Kitchen facilities as well as a bar with very cheap beer. Essential to book ahead between May and Oct: send the price of the first night or leave a credit card number online. Lockout 11am–5pm, curfew at 2am. M° Commerce/Félix-Faure.

**Le Village Hostel 20 rue d'Orsel, 18ᵉ** ☎01.42.64.22.02, ⓦwww.villagehostel.fr (see map on p.167). Attractive, brand-new hostel with a relatively old-fashioned feel, and good facilities such as phones in the rooms. There's a view of the Sacré-Coeur from the terrace. Dorms (€21.50) or twin rooms (€25); price includes breakfast. M° Anvers.

**Woodstock Hostel 48 rue Rodier, 9ᵉ** ☎01.48.78.87.76, ⓦwww.woodstock.fr (see map on p.167). A reliable hostel in the *Three Ducks* stable, with its own bar, and set in a great location on a pretty street, not far from Montmartre. Dorms €20/15, depending on season. Twin rooms available (€23/17); price includes breakfast. Book ahead. M° Anvers/St-Georges.

**Young and Happy Hostel 80 rue Mouffetard, 5ᵉ** ☎01.45.35.09.53, ⓦwww.youngandhappy.fr

(see map on pp.116–117). Noisy, basic and studenty independent hostel in a lively, if a tad touristy, position. Dorms, with shower, sleep four (€20 per person), and there are a few doubles (€25 per person). Curfew at 2am. M° Monge/Censier-Daubenton.

## Foyers

**Cité Universitaire**19 bd Jourdan, 14ᵉ ☎01.44.16.64.41, ⓦwww.ciup.fr; Mon–Fri 9am–5pm (off map). The student campus can provide a list of the different internationally-themed *maisons* or *fondations* (see p.156) that let out rooms during the summer holidays, some April–Sept. Costs are usually around €20 a night, with a minimum stay of three nights, but you have to be a student, and may also have to show that you need to be in Paris to study. RER Cité-Universitaire.

**Foyer Tolbiac** 234 rue Tolbiac, 13ᵉ ☎01.44.16.22.22, ⓦwww.foyer-tolbiac.com (see map on p.162). Caters to women aged 18–25 only, and lets private rooms either by the month (€399) or the day (€20). Excellent facilities. M° Glacière.

**Maison des Étudiants** 18 rue Jean-Jacques-Rousseau, 1ᵉʳ ☎01.45.08.02.10, ☎01.40.28.11.43 (see map on pp.76–77). Available to travellers July and August; minimum stay five nights. B&B in a double room costs €22 per person, €25 in a single. M° Palais-Royal.

# Camping

The least expensive option is of course **camping**. With the exception of the one in the Bois de Boulogne, most of Paris's **campsites** are some way out of town, although the ones listed here are linked by public transport. Below is a selected list: for other possibilities, contact the tourist office or look online at ⓦwww.camping-fr.com.

**Camping du Bois de Boulogne** Allée du Bord-de-l'Eau, 16ᵉ ☎01.45.24.30.00, ⓦwww .abccamping.com/boulogne.htm. Much the most central campsite, with space for 436 tents, next to the River Seine in the Bois de Boulogne, and usually booked out in summer. The ground is pebbly, but the site is well equipped and has a useful information office. Prices start at €11 for a tent with two people; there are also bungalows for four to six people starting at €48 for four per night, which works out very inexpensively per person. M° Porte-Maillot then bus #244 to Moulins Camping (bus runs 6am–9pm). An extra shuttle bus runs between the campsite and M° Porte-Maillot April–Oct from 8.30am to 12.30am.

**Camping la Colline** Route de Lagny, Torcy ☎01.60.05.42.32, ⓦwww.camping-de-la -colline.com. Pleasant wooded lakeside site to the east of the city near Disneyland (minibus shuttle to Disneyland costs €12 return), offering rental of anything from luxury tents to bungalows; erecting your own tent costs €15 per night for two people. RER line A4 to Torcy, then phone from the station and they will come and collect you or take bus #421 to stop Le Clos.

**Camping du Parc-Étang St-Quentin-en-Yvelines** Montigny-le-Bretonneux ☎01.30.58.56.20. Adequately equipped large campsite in a leisure complex southwest of Paris; costs €14.64 for two people and a tent. Open March–Oct. RER line C St-Quentin-en-Yvelines.

# 16

# Eating and drinking

A s in the rest of France, Parisian cooking has art status, the top chefs are stars, and dining out is a national pastime, whether it's at the *bistrot* on the corner or at a famed house of haute cuisine. In recent years, prices at the top end of the market have come down – with some superb-value midday set *menus* on offer – while the quality at the bottom end, particularly in the tourist hotspots, has sunk. Our advice to gourmets is to snack it out for a few days, then go for a blowout (but don't forget that wine with a €35 set *menu* can easily send the bill to €60 or more).

Paris is also renowned for its **foreign cuisine**. There are numerous excellent Thai, Chinese and Vietnamese establishments, and you'll find restaurants of Caribbean, Middle Eastern, North African, Central African, Latin American, and Western and Eastern European origin, along with Kurdish, Afghan, Japanese and even Tibetan.

Like other Latin Europeans, the French seldom separate the major pleasures of eating and drinking – **drinking** is never an end in itself, as it so often is for Anglo-Saxons. In consequence, there are thousands of establishments in Paris where you can both eat and drink. In order to simplify matters, we have divided them into two broad categories: **Restaurants** and **Cafés and bars**. Listings for the latter are places recommended for snacks and drinks – whether coffee, tea, beer, wine or cocktails – whereas the Restaurants listings are places you'd want to go for a full meal. For that reason you can find *brasseries* and *bistrots* in either section, depending on what we like about them.

## Snacks and picnics

For those occasions when you don't want – or can't face – a full meal, Paris offers numerous **street stalls** and stand-up **sandwich bars**. In addition to the indigenous *frites* (French fries), *crêpes*, *galettes* (wholewheat pancakes), *gaufres* (waffles) and fresh sandwiches, there are Tunisian snacks like *brik à l'œuf* (a fried pastry with an egg inside), *merguez* (spicy North African sausage), couscous, Greek *souvlaki* (kebabs), Middle Eastern *falafel* (deep-fried chickpea balls with salad), Japanese sushi, and all manner of good things from eastern European and Asian delis.

For **picnics** and takeaway food, head for either a **charcuterie** proper or the delicatessen counter in a good supermarket. Although specializing in pork-based preparations like salami and ham, most charcuteries also stock a wide range of cold cuts, pâtés, terrines, ready-made salads and fully prepared main courses. These are not exclusively meaty, either: artichokes *à la grecque*, stuffed tomatoes and paellas are common. You buy by weight, by the slice (*tranche*) or by the carton (*barquette*).

See pp.339–341 of the Shopping chapter for listings of charcuteries and other specialist food outlets.

The listings are arranged in alphabetical order and broadly correspond to the chapter headings in the guide chapters. Where you need to book for a restaurant we've given the phone number. By way of an introduction, we have included a description of the various kinds of establishment that you'll come across, as well as some indication of the conventions that surround eating and drinking in France.

You'll also find boxes on vegetarian (p.273), ethnic (pp.282–283) and late-night restaurants (pp.284–285), as well as bars good for an evening out (pp.284–285). For help with ordering and translating menus turn to the menu reader on pp.414–420 in the language section.

## Cafés and bars

Chilling out in **cafés and bars** is one of the chief pleasures of a trip to Paris and the best way to get your finger on the city's pulse. One of the mainstays of Parisian society, they're places where people come to debate and discuss, pose and people-watch, or simply read a book, knowing that once they've bought their drink, the waiter will leave them undisturbed for hours at a stretch. Some establishments have a chameleon existence, changing from traditional hangouts in the day to loud, buzzing venues in the evening.

### Choosing a café

The most enjoyable **cafés in Paris** are often ordinary, local places, but there are particular areas which café-lizards head for. Boulevards Montparnasse and St-Germain on the Left Bank are especially favoured. There you'll find the *Select*, *Coupole*, *Closerie des Lilas*, *Deux Magots* and *Flore* – the erstwhile hangouts of Apollinaire, Picasso, Hemingway, Sartre and de Beauvoir, and mostly still popular today with the Parisian intelligentsia.

The location of other lively Left Bank cafés is largely determined by the geography of the university. Science students gravitate towards the cafés in rue Linné, by the Jardin des Plantes. The humanities gather in the place de la Sorbonne and rue Soufflot. And the whole world – especially non-Parisians – finds its way to the place St-André-des-Arts and the downhill end of boulevard St-Michel.

The more contemporary, up-and-coming gay, arty and hip café culture is found on the Right Bank around the Marais, Bastille and eastern Paris, where the new concept of the culture café goes beyond the literary and intellectual scene into art exhibitions, live music and Internet access. The opening of the landmark Bastille Opéra in 1989 saw a growth in new cafés, art galleries, restaurants and bars in the immediate area and futher east in the traditional working-class quarters of Belleville, Ménilmontant and Charonne. As the young and the trendy have moved in, they've kept the old charm of premises like the *Café Charbon* (p.306), while giving them a contemporary energy. You can drink a leisurely cup of coffee in a plethora of gay bars in the Marais by day before they transform into spots for night-time revelry. Nearby, Les Halles, once fashionable, now finds its trade is principally transient out-of-towners up for the bright lights.

As to **cost**, obviously, addresses in the smarter or more touristy arrondissements set prices soaring. The Champs-Élysées and rue de Rivoli, for instance, are best avoided, at double or triple the price of a café in Belleville, La Villette or the lower 14e. As a rule of thumb, if you are watching your budget, avoid the main squares and boulevards. Cafés a little removed from the main thoroughfares are invariably cheaper.

In our "Cafés and bars" category, we've included cafés, café-bars, café-brasseries, *salons de thé*, *bistrots à vin*, cocktail-type bars, and beer cellars/pubs. Of these, the last two are the only ones where you may not find anything to eat.

Some **brasseries** are more restaurant than café (see p.276), and others have little to distinguish them from cafés and café-bars. The principal difference is that anything with "brasserie" in the title will serve proper meals in addition to the usual range of sandwiches, snacks, alcoholic and non-alcoholic drinks. **Salons de thé** and **bistrots à vin**, on the other hand, do have a distinctive identity, which is not adequately conveyed by the standard English translations, tearoom and wine bar; for details, see p.275.

Many bars and cafés advertise **les snacks** or *un casse-croûte* (a bite), but, even when they don't, they're usually able to make you up a baguette filled with cheese or meat (*une baguette/au beurre/au jambon*, etc) on request. This, or a croissant, with hot chocolate or coffee, is generally the best way to eat **breakfast** – and can work out cheaper than the rate charged by most hotels. Brasseries are also possibilities for cups of coffee, eggs, snacks and other breakfast- or brunch-type food.

If you **stand at the counter**, which is always cheaper than sitting down, you may see a **basket of croissants** or some **hard-boiled eggs** (they're usually gone by 9.30am or 10am). The drill is to help yourself – the waiter will keep an eye on how many you've eaten and bill you accordingly.

## Paris for vegetarians

France's reputation as a virtual buffet for the culinary epicure is, unfortunately, lost on **vegetarians**. In most restaurants, aside from the usual salads and cheeses, there is precious little choice for those who don't eat meat, as almost every dish, if not made entirely of beef, chicken, or fish, is almost always garnished with *lardons* (bacon), *anchois* (anchovies), or *jambon* (ham). That said, some of the newer, more innovative restaurants will often have one or two vegetarian dishes on offer. It's also possible to put together a vegetarian meal at even the most meat-oriented brasserie by choosing dishes from among the starters (*crudités*, for example, are nearly always available) and soups, or by asking for an omelette. Useful French phrases to help you along are *Je suis végétarien(ne)* ("I'm a vegetarian") and *Il y a quelques plats sans viande?* (Are there any non-meat dishes?).

A *salon de thé* is often a good bet, as they are more apt to offer lighter fare, such as soups and tarts *(tartes)*, which tend to be vegetarian. Also, ethnic restaurants – Middle Eastern or Indian – usually offer a few vegetarian dishes.

The few vegetarian restaurants that do exist tend to be based on a healthy diet principle rather than haute cuisine, but at least you get a choice. All the establishments listed below are reviewed in the pages that follow.

**Aquarius** 54 rue Ste-Croix-de-la-Bretonnerie, 4<sup>e</sup>; p.289; 40 rue Gergovie, 14<sup>e</sup>; p.299.

**Au Grain de Folie** 24 rue de La Vieuville, 18<sup>e</sup>; p.302.

**Grand Appétit** 9 rue de la Cerisaie, 4<sup>e</sup>; p.291.

**Le Grenier de Notre-Dame**, 18 rue de la Bûcherie, 5<sup>e</sup>; p.294.

**La Petite Légume** 36 rue Boulangers, 5<sup>e</sup>; p.294.

**Piccolo Teatro** 6 rue des Écouffes, 4<sup>e</sup>; p.290.

**Les Quatre et Une Saveurs** 72 rue du Cardinal-Lemoine, 5<sup>e</sup>; p.294.

**La Victoire Suprême du Cœur** 41 rue des Bourdonnais, 1<sup>er</sup>; p.287.

Many cafés also offer reasonably priced **lunches**. These usually consist of salads, the more substantial kind of snack such as *croque-monsieurs* or *croque-madames* (both variations on the grilled-cheese sandwich), a **plat du jour** (chef's daily special), or a **formule**, which is a limited or no-choice set menu, consisting of a main course and either a starter or dessert.

**Full price lists** have to be displayed in every bar or café by law, usually without the fifteen percent service charge added, but detailing separately the prices for consuming at the bar (*au comptoir*), sitting down (*la salle*), or on the terrace (*la terrasse*) – all progressively more expensive. You pay when you leave, unless your waiter is just going off shift.

## Alcoholic and soft drinks

All cafés and bars serve a full range of alcoholic and non-alcoholic drinks throughout the day. Although on the whole there is much less drunkenness than in Britain, it's still common to see people starting their day with a beer, cognac or *coup de rouge* (glass of red wine). A *café cognac* is the popular combination of a cup of espresso and a glass of cognac.

On the **soft drink** front, bottled fruit juices and the universal standard canned 7-Up-style lemonades (*limonade*), Cokes (*Coca*) and clones are widely available. You can also get freshly squeezed orange and lemon juice (*orange pressé/citron pressé*), the latter of which is a refreshing choice on a hot day – the lemon juice is served in the bottom of a long ice-filled glass, with a jug of water and a sugar bowl so you can sweeten it to your taste. Particularly French are the various **sirops**, diluted with water to make cool, eye-catching drinks with traffic-light colours, such as *menthe* (peppermint) and *grenadine* (pomegranate). Bottles of **mineral water** (*eau minérale*) are widely drunk, from the best-selling Badoit to the most obscure spa product. Ask for *gazeuse* for sparkling, *plate* for still. That said, there's not much wrong with the tap water (*l'eau du robinet*), which will always be brought free to your table if you ask for it.

### Wine

**Wine** – *vin* – is drunk at just about every meal or social occasion. Red is *rouge*, white *blanc*, or there's *rosé*. *Vin de table* or **vin ordinaire** – table wine – is always cheap and generally drinkable. AC – **Appellation d'Origine Contrôlée** – wines are another matter. They can be excellent value at the lower end of the price scale, where favourable French taxes keep prices down to around €4 a bottle, but move much above it and you're soon paying serious prices for serious bottles. This said, you can buy a very decent bottle of wine for €5; €10 and over will buy you something really nice.

**Restaurant mark-ups** of AC wines can be outrageous. Popular AC wines found on most restaurant lists include Côtes du Rhône (from the Rhône valley), St-Émilion and Médoc (from Bordeaux), Beaujolais (the release of the "new" Beaujolais – "le Beaujolais Nouveau est arrivé" – is a much-heralded event on November 15 of every year) and very upmarket Burgundy.

The **basic wine terms** are *brut*, very dry; *sec*, dry; *demi-sec*, sweet; *doux*, very sweet; *mousseux*, sparkling; *méthode champenoise*, mature and sparkling. There are grape varieties as well, but the complexities of the subject take up volumes.

A **glass of wine** at a bar is simply *un verre de rouge*, *de blanc* or *de rosé*. If it is an AC wine you may have the choice of *un ballon* (a large round glass). *Un pichet* (a pitcher) is normally a quarter-litre of the house wine if available, or you can simply ask for *un quart* or *un demi* – a quarter- or half-litre carafe.

Characteristically French **apéritifs** are the aniseed drinks – *pastis*, in French – Pernod and Ricard. Like Greek *ouzo*, they turn cloudy when diluted with water and ice cubes (*glaçons*) – very refreshing and inexpensive. Two other drinks designed to stimulate the appetite are *Pineau* (cognac and grape juice) and *kir* (white wine with a dash of *cassis* – blackcurrant syrup – or champagne instead of wine for a *kir royal*).

**Beers** are the familiar Belgian and German brands, plus homegrown ones from Alsace. Draught (*à la pression*, usually Kronenbourg) is the cheapest drink you can have next to coffee and wine. Ask for *un demi* (one-third of a litre). A light, summertime option is shandy (*un panaché*). For a wider choice of draughts and bottles you need to go to the special beer-drinking establishments, or English- and Irish-style pubs found in abundance in Paris. A small bottle at one of these places will cost at least twice as much as a *demi* in a café. In supermarkets, however, bottled or canned beer is exceptionally cheap.

As for the harder stuff, there are dozens of **eaux de vie** (brandies distilled from fruit) and **liqueurs**, in addition to the classic cognacs or Armagnac. Among less familiar names, you could try Poire William (pear brandy), Marc (a spirit distilled from grape pulp) or the grappa-like Basque Izarra. Measures are generous, but they don't come cheap: the same applies for imported spirits like whisky, often called *scotch*.

## Salons de thé

**Salons de thé** are a relatively new-fangled invention, cropping up characteristically in both established upper-class haunts and newly gentrified parts of town. As bars are still characteristically more popular with men, *salons de thé* tend to attract a female clientele. More refined than anything suggested by the translation "tea room", they serve everything from light midday meals, brunches, salads and quiches to rich confections of cake and ice cream. The oldest *salon de thé* is *Angélina's* (see p.280), with its marble cake-frosting exterior. More exotic and relaxed is *Café de la Mosquée* (p.292), in one of the least Parisian of the city's buildings.

## Bistrots à vins

**Bistrots à vins,** unlike *salons de thé*, are an ancient institution, traditionally working-class sawdust-on-the-floor drinking haunts. Some genuine *bistrots* still exist, such as *Le Rubis* (p.279) and *Le Baron Rouge* (p.308), unpretentious and catering for everyone. The newer generation, however, which ironically owe their existence in large part to the English influence, have a distinctly yuppified flavour, and are far from

## Coffee and tea

**Coffee** is invariably made with an espresso machine and is very strong. *Un café* or *un express* is black; *une noisette* has a touch of milk; *un crème* is milky; and *un grand café* or *un grand crème* is a large cup of milky coffee. In the morning you could also ask for *un café au lait* – espresso in a large cup or bowl filled up with hot milk. *Un déca*, decaffeinated coffee, is very widely available. **Hot chocolate** (*chocolat chaud*) can also be had in any café.

Drinkers of **tea** (*thé*), nine times out of ten, have to settle for Lipton's teabags. Tea is served black, and you can usually have a slice of lemon (*citron*) with it if you want; for some milk with it, ask for *un peu de lait frais* (some fresh milk). *Tisanes* or *infusions* are the generic terms for **herb teas** – every café serves them. The more common ones are *verveine* (verbena), *tilleul* (lime blossom), *menthe* (mint) and *camomille*.

cheap. Most serve at least a limited range of dishes or *plats*, often deriving from a particular regional cuisine, and specialize in the less usual and less commercial wines, again often from a particular region. Some, like *Le Baron Rouge*, sell good, inexpensive wine from the barrel if you bring your own containers. The basic idea is to enable you to try wines by the glass.

## Restaurants

In terms of both quality and price, there's nothing to choose between restaurants (*auberges* or *relais*, as they sometimes call themselves) and brasseries. The distinction is that **brasseries**, which often resemble cafés, serve quicker meals and at most hours of the day, while restaurants tend to stick to the **traditional mealtimes** of noon until 2pm, and 7pm until 9.30pm or 10.30pm.

The **latest time** at which you can walk into a restaurant and order is usually about 9.30pm or 10pm, although once ensconced you can often remain well into the night. (Hours – last orders – are stated in the listings below, and unusually or specifically **late-night places** are included in the box on pp.284–285.) After 9pm or so, some restaurants serve only *à la carte* meals, which invariably work out more expensive than eating the set *menu*. For the more upmarket places, it's wise to make **reservations** – easily done on the same day. When hunting, avoid places that are half-empty at peak time, and treat the business of sizing up different menus as an enjoyable appetizer in itself.

### Prices

You should find a display of **prices** and what you get for them posted outside every restaurant. There is often a choice between one or more fixed-price **menus** (simply called a *menu* in French – the French word for "menu" in the English sense is *carte*), where the number of courses for the stated price is fixed and the choice accordingly limited. It's possible to find bargain lunchtime three-course *menus* for €12 or under, while in the evenings they usually start at €15. For around €23 you'll have a choice of more interesting cuisine, including, probably, some regional

### Over the top: Paris's gourmet restaurants

Paris is the perfect place to blow out on the meal of a lifetime. Top rated is *Alain Ducasse* at the *Plaza Athénée* hotel, considered one of the best restaurants in Europe. The first-ever chef to have been awarded six Michelin stars (shared between two restaurants), Alain Ducasse swept like a tidal wave through the world of French cuisine in the early 1990s and hasn't looked back. Other greats include *L'Ambroisie* (see p.289); the splendid Art Nouveau restaurant *Lucas Carton*, 9 place de la Madeleine, 8e (☎01.42.65.22.90), directed by chef Alain Senderens; and *Taillevent*, 15 rue Lamennais, 8e (☎01.44.95.15.01), where Michel del Burgo's cuisine is rated as sublime and the wine list out of this world. Prices at most of these restaurants are often cheaper if you go at midday during the week, and some offer a set lunch *menu* for around €60. In the evening, prices average at about €150, and there's no limit on the amount you can pay for top wines.

Recently, some of the star chefs have made their fine cuisine more accessible to a wider range of customers by opening up less expensive, more casual, but still high-quality establishments. In addition to presiding over the *Plaza Athénée*, for example, Alain Ducasse also runs the cutting-edge *bistrot Spoon, Food & Wine* (see p.280) and is soon to open another.

and other specialities, and once over €30 you should be getting some gourmet satisfaction. If you just want a main course it's worth looking out for the *plat du jour* (chef's daily special), which may be a regional dish.

Eating *à la carte*, of course, gives you access to everything on offer, though you'll pay a fair bit more. The *à la carte* prices we give are for an average three-course meal with half a bottle of wine. One simple and perfectly legitimate ploy is to have just one course instead of the expected three or more. There is no minimum charge.

**Wine** (*vin*) or a drink (*boisson*) may be included in the *menu*, though it's unlikely on *menus* less than €16. When ordering house wine (*vin ordinaire*), ask for *un pichet* (a small jug); they come in quarter-litre (*un quart*) or half-litre (*un demi*) sizes. A bottle of wine can easily add €14 to the bill.

**Service** is legally included in your bill at all restaurants, bars and cafés, though it's considered polite to leave a **tip** of €1–2 at restaurants depending on the service and to round up your drinks bill at bars and cafés.

## Student restaurants

Students of any age are eligible to apply for tickets for the **university restaurants** under the direction of CROUS de Paris. We've listed some of the more central restaurants below; you can find a complete list on the CROUS website, Ⓦ www.crous-paris.fr, or from their offices at 39 av Georges-Bernanos, 5ᵉ (☎01.40.51 .36.00; Mon–Fri 9am–5pm; RER Port-Royal). The tickets have to be obtained from the particular restaurant of your choice: just turn up during opening hours

## Chain restaurants

There are a number of French **restaurant chains** with outlets all over the city. Service is usually quick, and there's no need to book, though they're not the best places in which to experience the ritual of a leisurely French meal.

**Le Bistrot Romain** This Italian *bistrot* (*formules* from €10) has gone somewhat downhill, but is trying to win back clientele with cheaper *menus*. Branches at 10 rue Coquillière, 1ᵉʳ; and 9 bd des Italiens, 2ᵉ, among others. Daily till midnight.

**Chez Clément** The most brasserie-like of the chains. Three courses cost around €28; oysters and shellfish are specialities or you can choose beef, duck or salmon from the *rôtisserie*. Central restaurants at 123 av des Champs-Élysées, 8ᵉ; 17 bd des Capucines, 2ᵉ; 19 rue Marbeuf, 8ᵉ; 106 bd du Montparnasse, 14ᵉ; 21 bd Beaumarchais, 4ᵉ. Open daily till 1am.

**La Criée** Specializes in seafood and fish and is dependable, offering three-course set meals for €27. Branches at 31 bd Bonne-Nouvelle, 2ᵉ; 15 rue Lagrange, 5ᵉ; 54 bd du Montparnasse, 15ᵉ. Open till midnight.

**Hippopotamus** Although it's not particularly good, this is one of the cheaper chains, with three-course *menus* for €21.30, and it does stay open more or less round-the-clock – some branches serve till 5am. Central addresses include: 29 rue Berger, Les Halles, 1ᵉʳ; and 1 bd des Capucines, 2ᵉ.

**Flunch** Three branches in Paris, at 5 rue Pierre Lescot, 1ᵉʳ, 1 rue Caulaincourt, 18ᵉ and right next to the Pompidou Centre. Although very canteen-like with overcooked food, it's a good place to fill an empty stomach on a tight budget; the dish of the day costs €5.90 and you can go back for as many vegetable dishes as you like. Open daily till 10pm.

**Léon de Bruxelles** Does various mussels-and-chips combinations; a three-course meal with drink will cost around €25. Main branches at 63 av des Champs-Élysées, 8ᵉ; 8 place de la République, 11ᵉ; 3 bd Beaumarchais, 4ᵉ; 131 bd St-Germain, 6ᵉ. Daily till 1am.

(generally 11.30am–2pm & 6–8pm), buy a ticket (cash only; bring your student ISIC card as proof of status) – and then get your meal. Not all serve both midday and evening meals, and most are closed on the weekend and during term time (details given on website). Though the food is less than wonderful, it's certainly filling, and you can't complain for the price: meals cost E4.40.

## Student Restaurants

3 rue Censier, 5e (Mo Censier-Daubenton); 10 rue Jean-Calvin, 5e (Mo Censier-Daubenton); 8 rue Cuvier, 5e (Mo Jussieu); 31 av G-Bernanos, 5e (RER Port-Royal; open weekends); 17 rue Santeuil, 5e (Mo Censier-Daubenton); 12 pl du Panthéon, 5e (RER Luxembourg); 3 rue Mabillon, 6e (Mo Mabillon); 45 rue des Saints-Pères, 6e (Mo St-Germain-des-Prés); 12 rue Clément, 6e (Mo St-Sulpice); and 21 rue d'Assas, 6e (RER Port-Royal/Mo Notre-Dame-des-Champs).

# The Islands

The listings in this section are marked on the map on pp.54–55.

## Cafés and Bars

**Berthillon 31 rue St-Louis-en-l'Île, Île St-Louis, 4e**. Long queues form for these excellent ice creams and sorbets (€3.65 a triple) which come in all sorts of unusual fruity flavours, such as rhubarb. They're also available at other island sites listed on the door. Mo Pont-Marie. Wed–Sun 10am–8pm.

**Taverne Henri IV 13 pl du Pont-Neuf, Île de la Cité, 1er**. Old-style wine bar with formica tables and net curtains that's probably changed little since Yves Montand used to come here with Simone Signoret. It's best to drop in at lunchtime when it's at its buzziest, usually full of lawyers from the nearby Palais de Justice. Wine by the glass starts at €3.50; generous plates of meats and cheeses for around €11, *tartines* (with a choice of cheeses, hams, pâté and *saucisson*) are €4.60. Mo Pont-Neuf. Mon–Fri 11.30am–3.30pm & 6–9pm, Sat noon–4pm; closed Sun & Aug.

## Restaurants

**Les Fous de l'Île 33 rue des Deux-Ponts, 4e**. Reminiscent of a slightly fusty Victorian pantry, with old china teapots and empty bottles in glass cabinets, this neighbourhood restaurant/*salon de thé* makes a refreshing change from the more touristy places on the main thoroughfare. It does light lunches, such as goat's cheese salad, for around €11, and from 3pm to 7pm serves tea and cakes, as well as Berthillon

ice creams. The *à la carte* dinner menu features dishes such as *pavé de foie de veau au caramel balsamique* (€14). The only drawback is the slightly offhand service. Mo Pont-Marie. Dinner until 11pm; closed Sat midday, Sun evening & Mon all day. Brunch on Sunday. Live jazz Tues & Wed from 10pm.

**Nos Ancêtres les Gaulois 39 rue Saint-Louis-en-l'Île, 4e ☎01.46.33.66.07, ⊛www.nosance-treslesgaulois.com**. A virtual Gaulois (Asterix and Obelix) theme park, with rustic tables and musty animal skins, this restaurant offers a copious all-you-can-eat-and-drink buffet, including grilled beef or lamb, a choice of vegetables, including excellent ratatouille, and a huge cheese platter, all for €35; a true feast. There's also a children's *menu* for €15. Mo Pont-Marie. Mon–Sat 7pm–2am, Sun noon–4pm & 7pm–2am.

**Le Relais de l'Île 37 rue St-Louis-en-l'Île, 4e ☎01.46.34.72.34**. Eight small tables are crammed into the ground floor of this cosy, candlelit jazz-restaurant with several more on a wooden mezzanine balcony. The food is reasonable (if not exceptional) – you'll pay around €45 for three courses with wine, with mains like rabbit in prune sauce or lemon chicken with honey – but it's the ambience that makes this place special: the convivial atmosphere, friendly service, the pianist tinkling away, and the chef occasionally popping out from the kitchen to join in. Mo Pont-Marie. Noon–2pm & 7.30–11pm; closed Tues.

# The Champs-Élysées and Tuileries

The listings in this section are marked on the map on pp.76–77.

## The Champs-Élysées and around

### Cafés and Bars

**Le Fouquet's 99 av des Champs-Élysées, 8ᵉ**
℡01.47.23.70.60. Dating from 1899, *Le Fouquet's* brasserie is such a well-established watering hole for the rich and famous, that it's now been classified a Monument Historique. You pay dearly to sit in the deep leather armchairs – the espresso at €4.60 must be the city's most expensive. The restaurant (last orders 11.30pm) isn't quite as pricey as you'd expect, however, with meals around €35, though there's little on the wine list for under €30. Mᵒ George-V. Daily till 1.30am.

**Musée Jacquemart-André 158 bd Haussmann, 8ᵉ.** Part of the Musée Jacquemart-André (see p.79) but with independent access, this is the most sumptuously appointed *salon de thé* in the city. Admire the ceiling frescoes by Tiepolo while savouring the fine pastries or salads (€8–13). Mᵒ St-Philippe-du-Roule/Miromesnil. Daily 11.30am–5.30pm.

**Le Rubis 10 rue du Marché-St-Honoré, 1ᵉʳ.** One of the oldest wine bars in Paris, known for its excellent wines – mostly from the Beaujolais and Loire regions – and home-made *rillettes* (a kind of pork paté). Very small and very crowded. Glasses of wine from €2.40 and *plats du jour* around €9. Mᵒ Pyramides. Mon–Fri 7.30am–10pm, Sat 9am–3pm; closed mid-Aug.

### Restaurants

**L'Appart' 9 rue du Colisée, 8ᵉ**
℡01.53.75.16.34. A stylish place popular with a young and trendy crowd. There's a bar downstairs and restaurant upstairs resembling an elegant living room, with wood panelling, fireplaces and deep red fabrics. Classic French dishes on a €30 *menu,* with wine starting at €22 a bottle. Mᵒ St-Philippe-du-Roule. Restaurant: daily noon–2.30pm & 7.30–11pm. Bar: daily noon to midnight (11pm on Sun & Mon).

**Dragons Élysées 11 rue de Berri, 8ᵉ**
℡01.42.89.85.10. The Chinese–Thai cuisine includes dim sum, curried seafood and baked mussels, but the overriding attraction is the extraordinary decor. Beneath the glass-tile floor water runs from pool to pool inhabited by exotic fish. Water even pours down part of one wall, and on the ceiling pinpoints of light imitate stars, all amid the standard chinoiserie of red lanterns and black furniture. Evening *menu* €33. Mᵒ George-V. Daily 11am–3pm & 7–11pm.

**La Fermette Marbeuf 1900 5 rue Marbeuf, 8ᵉ**
℡01.53.23.08.00. The main reason to come here is for the superb Art Nouveau decor: try to get a table in the tiled and domed inner room. The classic French cuisine isn't bad either, though not especially cheap; a set meal costs €29.30. Despite the rather well-heeled clientele, foreign as well as French, it's not stuffy. Mᵒ Franklin-D.Roosevelt. Daily noon–3pm & 7–11.30pm.

**Lasserre 17 av Franklin-D.Roosevelt, 8ᵉ**
℡01.43.59.53.43. Exquisite haute cuisine restaurant with a beautiful belle époque dining room, decorated with flower-draped balustrades and graced with an extraordinary roof, which can be rolled back on balmy summer days. The cuisine has reached new heights recently with the arrival of chef Jean-Louis Nomicos, trained by Alain Ducasse (see p.276); highlights include his lemon-crust seabass and sublime duck à l'orange, though you can't go wrong whatever you choose. As you'd expect, prices are high – à la carte you'll pay upwards of €120, not including wine, though you can eat more cheaply if you come at lunchtime and opt for the €55 prix fixe *menu*. *The* place to come for a special occasion. Mᵒ Franklin-D.Roosevelt. Mon–Fri noon–2pm & 7.30–10pm.

**Le Relais de l'Entrecôte 15 rue Marbeuf, 8ᵉ.** If you like steak, this is the place to come. There's no main-course menu, the only dish being steak and frites. This is no ordinary steak though – it's served with a delicious sauce, the ingredients of which are a closely kept secret. Count on €19.80 a head, including a salad first course, or €25 with dessert. There's a second branch at 20bis rue St-Benoit, 6ᵉ (Mᵒ St-Germain-des-Prés). Mᵒ Franklin-D.Roosevelt. Noon–2.30pm & 7.30–11pm.

**Rue Balzac 3–5 rue Balzac, 8ᵉ.**
℡01.53.89.90.91. This super-stylish, buzzing

restaurant is the enterprise of singer Johnny Hallyday and chef Michel Rostang. The low lighting and subdued reds and yellows of the decor provide an atmospheric backdrop to classy cuisine, available in small or large servings ("petit modèle" and "grand modèle"); most people find the former filling enough. Three courses with wine comes to around €60. M° George-V. Daily noon–2pm & 7.30–11pm.

**Spoon, Food and Wine 14 rue de Marignan, 8e** ☎01.40.76.34.44. An innovative world-food *bistrot* opened by star chef Alain Ducasse a few years ago and an instant success. The chic, minimalist decor and inventive cuisine, marrying unusual flavours and ingredients, attract a fashionable crowd. Expect to pay around €50 a head. M° Franklin-D.Roosevelt. Noon–2pm & 7.30–11pm; closed Sat, Sun & mid-July to mid-Aug.

**Le Tillsit 14 rue de Tilsitt, 8e.** A stone's throw away from the Arc de Triomphe and sporting a gaudy glass centrepiece, this otherwise unassuming little brasserie is a locals' favourite and fills up quickly at lunchtime. *Plats du jour* might include *turban de sole à la dieppoise* (€9.50) or *paupiette de veau à la bolognaise* (€11). Salads (€11) are mountainous and filling. Service is courteous and efficient. M° Charles-de-Gaulle-Etoile. Daily 7am–midnight.

**Yvan 1 bis rue J-Mermoz, 8e** ☎01.43.59.18.40.

A good place for a special meal out, this is a classy restaurant with plush interior and deep-red walls hung with paintings. The excellent cuisine is New French and includes dishes such as pigeon with polenta. Three courses and wine for around €60. M° Franklin-D.Roosevelt. Mon–Fri noon–2.30pm & 8pm–midnight, Sat eve only; closed Sat lunch & Sun.

### The Tuileries

#### Cafés

**Angélina 226 rue de Rivoli, 1er.** Long-established gilded cage, where the well-coiffed sip the best hot chocolate in town – a generous jugful with whipped cream on the side will set you back €6. Patisseries (around €5) and savouries are of the same high quality.

**Café Véry (also known as Dame Tartine) Jardin des Tuileries, 1er.** The best of a number of café-restaurants in the gardens, with tables outside under shady horse chestnuts. Snacks and more substantial meals available (€5–8). It's especially popular at lunch, so be sure to turn up in good time. M° Tuileries. Mon–Fri 9.15am–7pm, Sat & Sun 9.15am–7.30pm; closed Tues in July & Aug. M° Concorde. Daily noon–11pm.

# The Grands Boulevards, passages and Les Halles

### Grands Boulevards

The listings in this section are marked on the map on pp.86–87.

#### Cafés and Bars

**L'Arbre à Cannelle 57 passage des Panoramas, 2e.** Tucked away in an attractive *passage*, this *salon de thé* with its exquisite wood panelling, frescoes and painted ceilings makes an excellent spot to treat yourself to salads (from €10) and tarts both savoury and sweet (€4.55). M° Grands-Boulevards. Mon–Sat till 6pm.

**Fauchon 26 place de la Madeleine, 8e.** Swish *salon de thé* with *plats du jour*, sandwiches and mouthwatering pâtisseries – try the Darjeeling-tea tart – though at a price. M° Madeleine. Mon–Sat 8am–7pm.

**Kitty O'Shea's 10 rue des Capucines, 2e.** A favourite haunt of expats, with excellent Guinness and Smithwicks. Live music on Sun at 9pm. M° Opéra. Daily noon–1.30am.

#### Restaurants

**Chartier 7 rue du Faubourg-Montmartre, 9e,** ⊕www.bouillon-chartier.com. Brown linoleum floor, dark-stained woodwork, brass hat-racks, clusters of white globes suspended from the high ceiling, mirrors, waiters in long aprons – the original decor of an early twentieth-century soup kitchen. Worth seeing and, though crowded and rushed, the food is not bad at all. Three courses for €15, and a bottle of wine from €5.80. See box opposite. M° Grands-Boulevards. Daily 11.30am–3pm & 6–10pm.

**Le Grand Café Capucines 4 bd des Capucines, 9ᵉ.** A favourite post-cinema or -opera spot with over-the-top, belle époque decor and excellent seafood. Count on around €42 a head for three courses, not including wine. Mᵒ Opéra. Daily 24hr.

**Au Petit Riche 25 rue Le Peletier, 9ᵉ** ☎01.47.70.68.68, ⊛www.aupetitriche.com. Long-established restaurant with a mirrored, early-1900s interior, serving solid French cuisine such as *carré d'agneau roti aux épices* and *filet de sandre roti au Vouvray*. A favoured haunt of bankers, especially at lunchtime. *Menu* at €22.50, *menu enfant* €11. Mᵒ Richelieu-Drouot. Mon–Sat 12.15–2.30pm & 7pm–12.15am.

## Passages and Palais-Royal

The listings in this section are marked on the map on pp.86–87.

### Cafés and Bars

**Le Bar de l'Entracte on the corner of rue Montpensier and rue Beaujolais, 1ᵉʳ.** Theatre people, bankers and journalists come for quick snacks of *gratin de pomme de terre* and Auvergnat ham in this almost traffic-free spot. Fills up to bursting during the intervals at the Palais-Royal theatre just down the road. *Plats* from €9. Mᵒ Palais-Royal-Musée-du-Louvre. Daily 10am–2am, except Mon when closes at 9pm.

**Aux Bons Crus 7 rue des Petits-Champs, 1ᵉʳ.** A relaxed, workaday place that has been serving good wines and cheese, sausage and ham for more than eighty years. A carafe from €5; plate of cold meats from €9. Mᵒ Palais-Royal. Mon 9am–4pm, Tues–Sat 9am–11pm, closed Mon evening & Sun.

**Café de la Comédie 153 rue St-Honoré, 1ᵉʳ.** Small, traditional café opposite the Comédie Française, complete with a mirror painted with theatrical scenes at the back.

The *tartines* (open sandwiches) and *croque monsieur* are especially good. Mᵒ Palais-Royal-Musée-du-Louvre. Tues–Sun 10am–midnight.

**Juveniles 47 rue de Richelieu, 2ᵉ.** Very popular, tiny wine bar run by a Scot. Wine from €13 a bottle; *plats du jour* around €11. Mᵒ Palais-Royal. Mon–Sat noon–11pm.

**La Muscade 67 Galerie de Montpensier, 1ᵉʳ.** Smart but relaxed café-restaurant in the Palais Royal gardens serving excellent hot chocolate, a variety of teas and cakes (afternoon tea served 3–6.15pm), as well as more substantial *plats du jour* for €13.50. Seating in the gardens in summer. Mᵒ Palais-Royal-Musée-du-Louvre. Tues–Sat 9.30am–8.30pm, Sun 9.30am–7pm.

**A Priori Thé 35 Galerie-Vivienne, 2ᵉ.** Classy little *salon de thé* in a charming *passage*. Tea and cakes, but more substantial dishes also available. Mᵒ Pyramides/Sentier. Mon–Sat 9am–6pm, Sun 12.30–6.30pm.

### Restaurants

**Baan Boran 43 rue Montpensier, 1ᵉʳ** ☎01.40.15.90.45. Delicious, authentic Thai cuisine served in simple surroundings. Mains cost around €12. Mᵒ Palais-Royal/Musée-du-Louvre. Mon–Sat noon–3pm & 7–11.30pm.

**Le Dauphin 167 rue St-Honoré, 1ᵉʳ** ☎01.42.60.40.11. Just over the way from the Comédie Française, this old *bistrot* with its original Art Deco stained glass serves up inventive southwestern dishes. Specialities are the *parrilladas* (mixed grill) such as the rich and meaty *parillada du boucher* made up of steak, duck, chicken breast and sausage; veggies are catered for too with the *parillada de la terre* (tomatoes, courgette, aubergine, fenil, peppers and endives). Lunchtime *menu* (except Sun) €23, evening €34. Mᵒ Palais-Royal-Musée-du-Louvre. Daily noon–2pm & 7.30–11pm.

## Chartier

*Chartier* was first opened in 1896 by Camille and Frédéric Chartier to provide affordable meals for those who couldn't manage regular restaurant prices. It was a roaring success, coinciding as it did with the arrival in Paris of tens of thousands of people escaping the poverty and hardship of life in the hills of the Massif Central: the *bougnats*, as they were called, in imitation of their accents and the fact that so many of them were involved in the charcoal industry – *charbougna*. It spawned some thirty similar establishments, but the original *Chartier* is the only one to have survived. Little changes at *Chartier*: same staff and same customers year after year.

Our selection of Paris's **ethnic restaurants** can only scratch the surface of what's available. **North African** places can be found throughout the city; apart from rue Xavier-Privas in the Latin Quarter, where the trade is chiefly tourists, the heaviest concentration is the Little Maghreb district along boulevard de Belleville.
**Indo–Chinese** restaurants are also widely scattered, with notable concentrations around avenue de la Porte-de-Choisy in the 13ᵉ and in the Belleville Chinatown. At the south end of rue du Faubourg-St-Denis, there are numerous good snack bars and restaurants – mainly **Turkish and Kurdish** in rue d'Enghien and rue de l'Échiquier, **Indian and Pakistani** around passage Brady. **Greek** eateries are tightly corralled, in rue de la Huchette, rue Xavier-Privas and along rue Mouffetard, all in the 5ᵉ and, for the most part, a bit of a rip-off.

### Afghan
Kootchi 40 rue du Cardinal-Lemoine, 5ᵉ; p.294.

### African and North African
Au Bistrot de la Sorbonne 4 rue Toullier, 5ᵉ. North African and French; p.293.
Café de la Mosquée 39 rue Geoffroy-St-Hilaire, 5ᵉ. North African; p.292.
L'Homme Bleu 57 rue Jean-Pierre-Timbaud, 11ᵉ. Berber; p.305.
La Mansouria 11 rue Faidherbe-Chaligny, 11ᵉ. Moroccan; p.308.
N'Zadette M'Foua 152 rue du Château, 14ᵉ. Congolese; p.300.

### American/Cajun
Haynes 3 rue Clauzel, 9ᵉ; p.303.
Thanksgiving 20 rue St-Paul, cnr rue Charles-V, 4ᵉ; Cajun; p.290.

### East European and Jewish
Goldenberg's 7 rue des Rosiers, 4ᵉ. Jewish; p.289.
Pitchi-Poï 7 rue Caron, 4ᵉ. Central European/Jewish; p.290.
Le Ravaillac 10 rue du Roi-de-Sicile, 4ᵉ. Polish; p.290.

### Greek
Mavrommatis 42 rue Daubenton, 5ᵉ; p.294.
Orestias 4 rue Grégoire-de-Tours, 6ᵉ; p.296.

### Italian
L'Enoteca 25 rue Charles-V, 4ᵉ; p.289.
Au Jardin des Pâtes 4 rue Lacépède, 5ᵉ; p.294.

---

Foujita 41 rue St-Roche, 1ᵉʳ ☎01.42.61.42.93. Quick and crowded, this is one of the cheaper but better Japanese restaurants, as proved by the numbers of Japanese eating here. Soup, sushi, rice and tea for €11 at lunchtime; plate of sushi or sashimi from €7. Mº Tuileries/Pyramides. Mon–Sat noon–2.15pm & 7.30–10pm; closed mid-Aug.
Le Grand Colbert passage Colbert, rue Vivienne, 2ᵉ ☎01.42.86.87.88. An elegant belle époque brasserie with high ceilings and swirly drapes. Bankers and theatre-goers drop in for solid French cooking such as confit de canard and andouillette.

Their all-day menu costs €25, including coffee. Mº Bourse. Daily noon–3pm & 7.30pm–1am; closed mid-July to mid-Aug.
Le Grand Véfour 17 rue de Beaujolais, 1ᵉʳ ☎01.42.96.56.27, @www.grand-vefour@wanadoo.fr. The carved wooden ceilings, frescoes, velvet hangings and late eighteenth-century chairs haven't changed since Napoleon brought Josephine here. Considering the luxury of the cuisine, the lunchtime menu for €71 is a cinch. Go à la carte and the bill could easily top €200. Mº Pyramides/Bourse. Mon–Fri 12.30–2pm & 7.30–10pm.

Rital & Courts 1 rue des Envierges, 20e; p.307.

### Indian
Pooja 91 passage Brady, 10e; p.304.

### Indo–Chinese
Baan Boran 43 rue Montpensier, 1er. Thai; p.281.

Le Bambou 70 rue Baudricourt, 13e. Vietnamese; p.301.

Blue Elephant 43–45 rue de la Roquette, 11e. Thai; p.291.

Dragons Élysées 11 rue de Berri, 8e. Chinese-Thai; p.279.

Lao Siam 49 rue de Belleville, 19e. Thai and Laotian; p.307.

Lao-Thai 128 rue de Tolbiac, 13e. Thai and Laotian; p.301.

Le Pacifique 35 rue de Belleville, 20e. Chinese; p.307.

Pho-Dong-Huong 14 rue Louis-Bonnet, 11e. Vietnamese; p.307.

Pho 67 59 rue Galande, 5e. Vietnamese; p.294.

Phuong Hoang Terrasse des Olympiades, 52 rue du Javelot, 13e. Vietnamese, Thai and Singaporean; p.301.

Tricotin Kiosque de Choisy, 15 av de Choisy, 13e. Thai, Vietnamese, Chinese and Cambodian; p.301.

### Japanese
Foujita 41 rue St-Roch, 1er; p.282.

Higuma 32bis rue Ste-Anne. 1er; p.283.

### Kurdish
Dilan 13 rue Mandar, 2e; p.286.

### Lebanese
Baalbeck 16 rue Mazagran, l0e; p.304.

Byblos Café 6 rue Guichard, 16e; p.308.

Aux Saveurs du Liban 11 rue Eugène-Jumin, 19e; p.306.

### Spanish
Boca Chica 58 rue de Charonne, 11e. Tapas; p.291.

Au Pavillon Puebla Parc Des Buttes-Chaumont, 19e. Catalan; p.307.

### Tibetan
Tashi Delek 4 rue des Fossés-St-Jacques, 5e; p.295.

**Higuma 32bis rue Ste Anne, 1er**
℗01.47.03.38.59. Authentic Japanese canteen with cheap, filling ramen dishes and a variety of set *menus* starting at €10. M° Pyramides. Daily 11.30am–10pm.

**Le Vaudeville 29 rue Vivienne, 2e**
℗01.40.20.04.62. There's often a queue to get a table at this lively, late-night brasserie, attractively decorated with marble and mosaics. Dishes include grilled cod with truffle sauce and *belle tête de veau*. *À la carte* from €30; lunchtime *formule* €21.50. M° Bourse. Open daily 7am–2am.

### Sentier

The listings in this section are marked on the map on pp.86–87.

### Cafés and Bars

**Le Café 62 rue Tiquetonne, 2e.** A hip, buzzing café, full of old travel posters, yellowing maps and African sculptures. *Plats du jour* €8. M° Les Halles/Étienne-Marcel. Mon–Sat 10am–2am, Sun noon–midnight.
**Lina's Sandwiches 50 rue Étienne-Marcel, 2e (M° Étienne-Marcel); also at 8 rue Marbeuf, 8e (M° Alma-Marceau), 27 rue St-Sulpice, 6e**

**Late-opening bars and brasseries** are not unusual in Paris. The list below comprises cafés and bars open till 1.30am or later, and restaurants open until midnight and beyond. If you're looking for a night out, but don't necessarily want to go clubbing try one of the cafés /bars marked with an asterisk – they pack in the crowds and have plenty of buzz and atmosphere, some with DJs or live music.

### Cafés and bars

**Les Halles**

**Le Sous-Bock** 49 rue St-Honoré, 1er. Until 5am; p.286.
**Le Tambour** 41 rue Montmartre, 2e. 24 hours; p.286.
**Au Trappiste** 4 rue St-Denis, 1er. Fri–Sun till 4am; p.286.

**Marais**

**Café des Phares** 7 pl de la Bastille, west side, 4e. Daily 7am–4am; p.291.
**\*The Lizard Lounge** 18 rue du Bourg-Tibourg, 4e. Daily noon–2am; p.288.
**\*Le Quetzal** 10 rue de la Verrerie, 4e. Mon–Thurs 2pm–4am, Fri–Sun 5pm–5am; p.289.
**\*Web Bar** 32 rue Picardie, 3e. Mon–Fri 8.30am–2am, Sat 11am–2am, Sun 11am–midnight; p.290.

**Bastille and east**

**L'Atmosphère** 49 rue Lucien-Sampaix, 10e. Tues–Fri until 2am, Sat until 4am; p.304.
**Bar des Ferrailleurs** 18 rue de Lappe, 11e. Daily 5pm–2am; p.291.
**\*Café Charbon** 109 rue Oberkampf, 11e. Daily 9am–2am; p.306.
**\*Cithéa** 112 rue Oberkampf, 11e. Daily 5pm–5.30am; p.306.
**\*La Fleche d'Or** 102bis rue de Bagnolet, 20e; p.306.
**\*La Fontaine** 1 rue de Charonne, 11e. Daily 8.30am–2am; p.291.
**\*Havanita Café** 11 rue de Lappe, 11e. Daily 5pm–2am; p.291.
**\*Iguana** 15 rue de la Roquette, cnr rue Daval, 11e. Daily 10am–2am; p.291.
**Lou Pascalou** 14 rue des Panoyaux, 20e. Daily 9am–2am; p.306.
**\*L'Opus** 167 quai de Valmy, 10e. Daily until 4am; p.305.
**\*SanZSanS** 49 rue du Faubourg-St-Antoine, 11e. Daily 9am–2am; p.291.
**Le Viaduc Café** 43 av Daumesnil, 12e. Until 4am; p.308.

**Latin Quarter and Saint-Germain**

**Bar du Marché** 75 rue de Seine, 6e. Daily until 2am; p.295.
**\*Le Bateau Ivre** 40 rue Descartes, 5e. Daily until 2am; p.292.
**\*Café Mabillon** 164 bd St-Germain, 6e. Daily 7.30am–6.30am; p.295.
**\*Chez Georges** 11 rue des Canettes, 6e. Tues–Sat until 2am; p.295.
**\*Le 10** 10 rue de l'Odéon, 6e. Daily until 2am; p.295.
**\*Les Etages St-Germain** 5 rue de Buci, 6e. Daily until 2am; p.295.
**\*Le Piano Vache** 8 rue Laplace, 5e. Mon–Fri until 2am, Sat & Sun until 2am; p.293.
**La Pinte** 13 carrefour de l'Odéon, 6e. Mon–Thurs & Sun until 2am, Fri & Sat until 5am; p.296.
**Le Reflet** 6 rue Champollion, 5e. Daily until 2am; p.293.
**\*La Taverne de Nesle** 32 rue Dauphine, 6e. Mon–Thurs & Sun 6pm–4am, Fri & Sat until 5am; p.296.
**\*Le Violon Dingue** 46 rue de la Montagne-Ste-Geneviève, 5e. Daily until 2.30am; p.293.

**Monparnasse and around**

**La Closerie des Lilas** 171 bd du Montparnasse, 6e. Daily until 1.30am; p.298.
**L'Entrepôt** 7–9 rue Francis-de-Pressensé, 14e. Mon–Sat until 2am; p.299.

\*Mustang Café 84 bd du Montparnasse, 14ᵉ. Daily until 5am; p.299.
\*Le Rosebud 11bis rue Delambre, 14ᵉ. Daily until 2am; p.299.
Le Select 99 bd du Montparnasse, 6ᵉ. Mon–Thurs & Sun until 3am, Fri & Sat until 4.30am; p.299.

**Butte-aux-Cailles**
\*Le Diapason 15 rue Butte-aux-Cailles, 13ᵉ. Tues–Sat 5pm–2am; p.300.
\*La Folie en Tête 33 rue Butte-aux-Cailles, 13ᵉ. Mon–Sat until 2am; p.300.
\*Le Merle Moqueur 11 rue Butte-aux-Cailles, 13ᵉ. Daily until 2am; p.301.

**Montmartre and around**
\*Le Bar du Relais 12 rue Ravignan, 18ᵉ. Daily until 2am; p.302.
\*Le Dépanneur 27 rue Fontaine, 9ᵉ. Daily until 7am; p.303.
L'Endroit 67 place Félix-Lobligeois, 17ᵉ. Daily until 2am; p.302.
\*La Fourmi Café 74 rue des Martyrs, 18ᵉ. Mon–Thurs until 2am, Fri & Sat until 4am, Sun until 2am; p.302.
Le Grand Café Capucines 4 bd des Capucines, 9ᵉ. All-nighter; p.281.

## Restaurants
### Les Halles and around
Le Grand Colbert passage Colbert, rue Vivienne, 2ᵉ. Daily until 1am; p.282.
Au Pied de Cochon 6 rue Coquillière, 1ᵉʳ. 24 hours; p.286.
Le Vaudeville 29 rue Vivienne, 2ᵉ. Daily until 2am; p.283.

**Marais**
Chez Jenny 39 bd du Temple, 3ᵉ. Daily until 1am; p.290.
Les Fous d'en Face 3 rue du Bourg-Tibourg, 4ᵉ. Daily until midnight; p.287.
Goldenberg's 7 rue des Rosiers, 4ᵉ. Daily until midnight; p.289.

**Bastille and east**
Blue Elephant 43–45 rue de la Roquette, 11ᵉ. Until midnight; p.291.
Bofinger 7 rue de la Bastille, 3ᵉ. Until 1am; p.291.
Chez Paul 13 rue de Charonne, 11ᵉ. Daily until 12.30am; p.292.
Chez Prune 36 rue Beaurepaire, 10ᵉ. Daily until 1.45am; p.305.
Flo 7 cours des Petites-Écuries, I0ᵉ. Daily until 1.30am; p.304.
Julien 16 rue du Faubourg-St-Denis, I0ᵉ. Daily until 1am; p.304.
Le Pacifique 35 rue de Belleville, 20ᵉ. Daily until 1am; p.307.
Terminus Nord 23 rue de Dunkerque, 10ᵉ. Daily until 1am; p.304.

**Left Bank**
Brasserie Lipp 151 bd St-Germain, 6ᵉ. Daily until 1am; p.296.
Chez Gladines 30 rue des Cinq-Diamants, 13ᵉ. Daily until 1am; p.301.
La Coupole 102 bd du Montparnasse, 14ᵉ. Daily until 1am; p.299.
Natacha 17bis rue Campagne-Première, 14ᵉ. Mon–Sat until 1am; p.300.
N'Zadette M'Foua 152 rue du Château, 14ᵉ. Tues–Sun until 2am; p. 300.
Le Petit Prince 12 rue Lanneau, 5ᵉ. Fri & Sat until 12.30am; p.294.
Polidor 41 rue Monsieur-le-Prince, 6ᵉ. Mon–Sat until 12.30am; p.297.
Le Procope 13 rue de l'Ancienne-Comédie, 6ᵉ. Daily until 1am; p.296.
Vagenende 142 bd St-Germain, 6ᵉ. Daily until 1am; p.299.

**Montmartre and around**
Haynes 3 rue Clauzel, 9ᵉ. Tues–Sat till 12.30am; p.303.
Le Relais Gascon 6 rue des Abbesses, 18ᵉ. Daily until 2am; p.303.
Au Virage Lepic 61 rue Lepic, 18ᵉ. Daily except Tues till 2am; p.303.

(M° St-Sulpice), 7 av de l'Opéra, 1er (M° Pyramides), 30 bd des Italiens, 9e (M° Opéra), 105 rue du Faubourg-St-Honoré, 8e (M° St-Philippe-du-Roule). Excellent sandwiches, plus salads, soups, brownies and breakfasts – ideal for a window-shopping break. Mon–Sat 8.30am–4.30pm.

**Le Tambour 41 rue Montmartre, 2e.** A colourful local habitués' bar, eccentrically furnished with recycled street signs, old paving stones and the like. A *demi* costs €2.60; hearty salads and snacks available. M° Sentier. Open 24hr daily.

## Restaurants

**Dilan 13 rue Mandar, 2e ☎01.42.21.14.88.** An excellent-value Kurdish restaurant. Beautiful starters, stuffed aubergines (*babaqunuc*), fish with yoghurt and courgettes (*kanarya*). *Plats* around €10. M° Les Halles/Sentier. Mon–Sat noon–2pm & 7.30–10.30pm.

## Les Halles and Châtelet

The listings in this section are marked on the map on p.94.

### Cafés and Bars

**A la Cloche des Halles 28 rue Coquillière, 1er.** The bell hanging over this little wine bar is the one that used to mark the end of trading in the market halls. Today's noise is provided by the traffic on this busy corner, but you're assured of some very fine wines. M° Châtelet-Les Halles/Louvre. Open till 10pm; closed Sat eve & Sun.

**Le Cochon à l'Oreille 15 rue Montmartre, 1er.** This classic little café-bar, with its raffia chairs outside and scenes of the old market on ceramic tiles inside, dates from the market days; the only thing that's changed is the opening hours. M° Châtelet-Les Halles/Étienne-Marcel. Mon–Sat 8am–7pm.

**Self-Service de la Samaritaine Magasin 2, rue de la Monnaie, 1er.** On the tenth floor of their *magasin principal*. The view over the Seine is probably more of an attraction than the food, though that isn't bad for the price (€8.50 *plat du jour*). M° Pont-Neuf. Open May–Oct Mon–Sat 9.30am–7pm, Thurs 9.30am–9pm.

**Le Sous-Bock 49 rue St-Honoré, 1er.** Hundreds of beers – bottled and on tap (from €3.05) – and whiskies to sample, plus simple, inexpensive food. Mussels a speciality (from €8.90). Frequented by night owls. Prices go up after 7pm. M° Châtelet-Les Halles. Mon–Sat 11am–5am, Sun 3pm–5am.

**Au Trappiste 4 rue St-Denis, 1er.** Numerous draught beers include Jenlain, France's best-known *bière de garde*, Belgian Blanche Riva and Kriek from the Mort Subite (Sudden Death) brewery – plus *moules frites* for €11 and various *tartines*. M° Châtelet. Mon–Thurs noon–2am, Fri–Sun noon–4am.

## Restaurants

**Le Gros Minet 1 rue des Prouvaires, 1er ☎01.42.33.02.62.** Relaxed, small restaurant with distinct charm. The menu centres on duck, including *carpaccio de canard* (very thin slices of raw duck), but there are plenty of alternatives on offer. *Menu* at €15.50, *à la carte* around €30. M° Châtelet-Les Halles. Mon–Sat 7.30–11.30pm, Tues–Fri noon–2pm.

**L'Ostréa 4 rue Sauval, 1er.** First-class fish and seafood served in a simple, wooden-beamed room hung with fish hooks and model ships. Choose from herrings (€7) served in one of six different ways, mussels (€11) and fish mains (€19). M° Louvre-Rivoli/Châtelet. Noon–2pm & 7–11pm; closed Sat lunchtime, Sun & Aug.

**Au Pied de Cochon 6 rue Coquillière, 1er.** A Les Halles institution, this is the place to go for extravagant middle-of-the-night pork chops, oysters and of course pigs' trotters. Seafood platter €33. *Carte* around €42. M° Châtelet-Les Halles. Daily 24hr.

**La Robe et le Palais 13 rue des Lavandières St-Opportune, 1er ☎01.45.08.07.41.** Small, busy *restaurant à vins* serving traditional cuisine and an excellent selection of wines. Typical main courses include sea bream, *boudin noir* (black pudding), *andouillette* (tripe sausage), and steak. The two-course lunch *menu* is good value at €13.50, and large meat or cheese platters for €10 are also available. M° Châtelet. Mon–Sat noon–2pm & 7.30–11pm.

**La Tour de Montlhéry (Chez Denise) 5 rue des Prouvaires, 1er ☎01.42.36.21.82.** An old-style Les Halles *bistrot* serving substantial food; always crowded and smoky. *Carte* from €38. M° Louvre-Rivoli/Châtelet. Open 24hr Mon–Fri; closed mid-July to mid-Aug.

La Victoire Suprême du Cœur 41 rue des Bourdonnais, 1er ☎01.40.41.93.95. Vegetarian restaurant of the Sri Chinmoy variety – the Indian guru's photos and drawings cover the walls. The menu offers a wide range of tasty salads, quiches and *plats du jour* (€8.20), all very wholesome. M° Louvre-Rivoli/Châtelet. Mon–Fri 11.45am–2.45pm & 7–10pm, Sat noon–4pm & 7–10pm.

# Beaubourg, the Marais and the Bastille

Unless otherwise indicated, the listings below are marked on the map on pp.98–99.

## Beaubourg and Hôtel de Ville

### Cafés and Bars

**Café Beaubourg 43 rue St-Merri, 4e.** A seat under the expansive, not to say expensive (€5 for a *café crème*), awnings of this stylish café, bearing the trademark sweeping lines of designer Christian de Portzamparc, is one of the best places for people-watching on the Pompidou Centre's piazza. M° Rambuteau/Hôtel-de-Ville. Mon–Thurs & Sun 8am–1am, Sat 8am–2am.

**Dame Tartine 2 rue Brisemiche, 4e.** Overlooking the Stravinsky fountain, with pleasant outdoor seating under shady plane trees, this popular café serves particularly delicious open toasted sandwiches from €5, and does a *menu enfant* for €9.90. M° Rambuteau/Hôtel-de-Ville. Daily noon–11.30pm.

**Georges Centre Georges Pompidou, 4e.** On the top floor of the Pompidou Centre, this trendy, ultra-minimalist café commands stunning views over the rooftops of Paris (smoking seats have the best views) and makes a stylish place for lunch or dinner. The French–Asian fusion cuisine is passable, though somewhat overpriced (club sandwiches for €12, prawn risotto €26), but then that's not really why you come. M° Rambuteau/Hôtel-de-Ville. Daily except Tues noon–midnight.

**Le Petit Marcel 63 rue Rambuteau, 3e.** Speckled tabletops, mirrors and Art Nouveau tiles, a cracked and faded ceiling and about eight square metres of drinking space. Friendly bar staff and "local" atmosphere. M° Rambuteau. Mon–Sat till midnight.

### Restaurants

**Les Fous d'en Face 3 rue du Bourg-Tibourg, 4e** ☎01.48.87.03.75. Delightful little restaurant and wine bar serving wonderful marinated salmon and scallops. Midday *menu* €17, otherwise reckon on €27 upwards. M° Hôtel-de-Ville. Daily 11.30am–3pm & 7pm–midnight.

**Le Grizzli 7 rue St-Martin, 4e ☎01.48.87.77.56.** A characterful, bustling fin-de-siècle *bistrot* serving superb food with specialities from the Pyrenees such as cassoulet. Desserts include creamy apple tart with calvados. Figure on €44 *à la carte*, including half a bottle of wine. M° Châtelet. Mon–Sat till 11pm.

**Le Quincampe 78 rue Quincampoix, 3e** ☎01.40.27.01.45. Mediterranean/Moroccan restaurant and *salon de thé*, with a snug atmosphere, high-quality food and delicious mint tea. You can eat around a real fire in the room at the back in winter. Tagines, *pastilla* and *plat du jour* €11. M° Étienne-Marcel/Rambuteau/RER Châtelet. Noon–11pm, closed Mon, Sat lunch & Sun.

**Au Vieux Molière Passage Molière, 157 rue Saint-Martin, 3e ☎01.42.78.37.87, ⊛www.vieuxmoliere.com.** Hidden away down a characterful *passage*, this atmospheric restaurant has French chansons playing softly in the background. There's outdoor seating in summer, and the interior is elegant and comfortable, with deep-red velour seats and old photos and prints of literary figures. Fairly traditional food with some unusual twists – typical dishes are garlic-roasted chicken and mullet in saffron sauce. Lunchtime *formule* €15.25, in the evening *à la carte* from €35. M° Étienne-Marcel/Rambuteau/RER Châtelet. Closed Sun lunch & Mon.

## The Marais

### Cafés and Bars

**Amnésia Café 42 Vieille-du-Temple, 4e.** Forget your troubles over drinks and sandwiches in the alluring ambience of this low-lit, spacious café. Popular brunch served from noon to 5pm. Gets pretty wild at night; primarily gay, but straight-friendly. M° St-Paul. Daily 10am–2am.

**L'Apparement Café** 18 rue des Coutures-St-Gervais, 3ᵉ. Chic but cosy café resembling a series of comfortable sitting rooms, with quiet corners and deep sofas. Recommended are the "salades composées", which in this case you compose yourself by ticking off your chosen ingredients and handing your order to the waiter. Popular Sunday brunch until 4pm costs €14. M° St-Sébastien-Froissart. Mon–Fri noon–2am, Sat 4pm–2am, Sun 12.30pm–midnight.

**Bar Central** 33 rue Vieille-du-Temple, cnr rue Ste-Croix-de-la-Bretonnerie, 4ᵉ. One of the most enduring gay bars in the Marais, attracting a quieter, older, more laid-back clientele. M° St-Paul. Mon–Fri 4pm–2am, Sat & Sun 2pm–2am.

**Bar de Jarente** 5 rue de Jarente, 4ᵉ. Tiny, old-fashioned café-bar off the pretty place du Marché Ste-Catherine, which remains nonchalantly indifferent to the shifting trends around it. M° St-Paul. Closed Sun & Mon.

**Café Martini** 11 rue du Pas-de-la-Mule, 4ᵉ. Just off place des Vosges, this airy and relaxing little café offers low prices and taped jazz in the background. Panini from €3.05, good cappuccino, and a *demi* is only €2.29. Hard to squeeze into, but you can always take the sandwiches away and picnic on the grass of the nearby *place*. M° St-Paul. Daily 8.30am–2am.

**Café des Psaumes** 14–16 rue des Rosiers, 4ᵉ. This bustling little place in the heart of the Jewish quarter has a wonderful wood and marble interior and serves up kosher falafel for €6 and more substantial *plats* from €10. M° St-Paul. Mon–Thurs noon–3.30pm & 6.30–11.30pm, Fri noon–2pm & Sun noon–11.30pm; closed Sat.

**L'Ébouillanté** 6 rue des Barres, 4ᵉ. A two-floor café that spills onto a picturesque, cobbled street behind the church of St-Gervais in nice weather. An extensive choice of drinks, from homemade hot chocolate to iced fruit cocktails. Soup of the day for €6.50 and Tunisian crèpes from €7, or indulge in their excellent chocolate cakes and *tartes*. M° Hôtel-de-Ville. Tues–Sun noon–10pm, till 9pm in winter.

**Feria Café** 4 rue du Bourg Tibourg, 4ᵉ. Buzzing tapas bar with funky baroque decor. Tapas range from €5 to €12 and there's a good choice of cocktails, including caipirinha (€7.50), and sangria for €3.50. M° Hôtel-de-Ville. Daily 9am–midnight. Happy hour 6–8pm.

**The Lizard Lounge** 18 rue du Bourg-Tibourg, 4ᵉ. Loud and lively, attractive, stone-walled bar on two levels; American-run and popular with young expats. Especially busy for Sunday brunch (around €15), featuring Bloody Marys. M° Hôtel-de-Ville. Daily noon–2am.

**Le Loir dans la Théière** 3 rue des Rosiers, 4ᵉ. Characterful, long-established *salon de thé* that has remained resolutely itself in this otherwise trend-conscious area. Sink into a battered sofa, feast on enormous portions of scrummy homemade cakes (€6), and ponder the antique toys and Alice-in-Wonderland murals. If you're here for lunch, try the excellent vegetarian quiches. M° Saint-Paul. Mon–Fri 11am–7pm, Sat & Sun 10am–7pm.

**Page 35** 4 rue du Parc Royal, 3ᵉ ☎01.44.54.35.35. Just round the corner from the Picasso Museum, an arty café-restaurant run by friendly staff and specializing in savoury and sweet crèpes. Their €10.50 *formule* consisting of an entrée, crèpe and dessert is excellent value. The changing contemporary artworks on the wall are for sale. M° Saint-Paul/Chemin Vert. Open 11.30am–3pm & 7–9.30pm; closed Tues eve & only till 8pm on Sun.

**Le Pain Quotidien** 18 rue des Archives, 4ᵉ. Trendy café-bakery with air of a monks' refectory about it: plenty of natural wood, and diners have the option of sitting at a long, communal *table d'hôte*. It specializes in hearty breads, huge salads (around €10) and *tartines* (open sandwiches) and is especially popular for its delicious Saturday and Sunday brunch. Other branches at 18 pl du Marché-Saint-Honoré and 135 rue Mouffetard. M° Hôtel-de-Ville. Daily 8am–7pm.

**Le Petit Fer à Cheval** 30 rue Vieille-du-Temple, 4ᵉ. Very attractive small *bistrot*/bar with original fin-de siècle decor, including a marble-topped bar in the shape of a horseshoe (*fer à cheval*). It's a popular drinking spot, with agreeable wine, and you can snack on sandwiches or *plats* (around €11) in the little back room furnished with old wooden metro seats. M° St-Paul. Mon–Fri 9am–2am, Sat & Sun 11am–2am; food served noon–midnight.

**Le Quetzal 10 rue de la Verrerie, cnr rue Moussy, 4ᵉ.** This fashionable and stylish gay bar, with space for dancing, takes the art of cruising to new heights. M° St-Paul. Daily 5pm–5am.

**7 Lézards 10 rue des Rosiers, 4ᵉ.** Serves up tapas (€4.50) and pasta dishes (€7.50), along with an impressive line-up of international jazz musicians (schedule at ⓦwww.jazzvalley.com/7lézards; concerts begin 9.30pm Mon–Sat, 7.15pm Sun; around €10). No credit cards. M° St-Paul. Mon & Tues 6pm–midnight, Wed–Sun noon–midnight.

**La Tartine 24 rue de Rivoli, 4ᵉ.** This *bar à vins* is the genuine 1900s article, though pretty run down now and staffed by gruff barmen. It still cuts across class boundaries in its clientele, though, and has a good selection of affordable wines, plus excellent cheese and *saucisson* with *pain de campagne*. M° St-Paul. Mon & Wed–Sun till 10pm; closed Tues & Aug.

## Restaurants

**L'Ambroisie 9 pl des Vosges, 4ᵉ** ☎01.42.78.51.45. Scoring 19 out of 20 in the gourmet's bible *Gault et Millau* and run by celebrity chef Bernard Pacaud, *L'Ambroisie* offers exquisite food in a magnificent dining room hung with tapestries. It'll put a serious dent in your budget though, with a meal costing upwards of €200. Book well in advance. M° Chemin-Vert/St-Paul. Till 10.15pm; closed Sun, Mon and Aug.

**Aquarius 54 rue Ste-Croix-de-la-Bretonnerie, 4ᵉ** ☎01.48.87.48.71. Long-established vegetarian restaurant which also functions as a health-food store, New Age bookshop and *salon de thé* between lunch and dinner, when it serves some fine fruit tarts and cakes. Its lunch and dinner specialities are galettes, omelettes and *assiette paysanne* – sautéed potatoes, mushrooms, warm goats' cheese and garlic croutons. It's not quite as austere as it once was – alcohol is now on the menu, albeit mostly organic wines – but it's still strictly no-smoking, and the decor is quite spare. Lunch and dinner *menus* around €10. M° St-Paul/Rambuteau. Mon–Sat noon–10pm; closed last fortnight in Aug.

**Auberge de Jarente 7 rue Jarente, 4ᵉ** ☎01.42.77.49.35. This hospitable and friendly Basque restaurant serves up first-class food at moderate prices: *cassoulet*, hare stew, *magret de canard*, and *piperade* – ratatouille. *Menus* from €18. M° St-Paul. Tues–Sat noon–2.30pm & 7.30–10.30pm; closed Aug.

**Au Bourgignon du Marais 52 rue François Miron, 4ᵉ** ☎01.48.87.15.40. A warm, relaxed restaurant and *cave à vins* with tables outside in summer, serving excellent Burgundian cuisine with carefully selected wines to match. Reckon on €30 a head for three courses, excluding wine. Booking strongly advised. M° St-Paul. Mon–Fri noon–3pm & 8–11pm; closed two weeks in Aug.

**Le Coude Fou 12 rue du Bourg-Tibourg, 4ᵉ** ☎01.42.77.15.16. A popular, relaxed wine *bistrot*, with wooden beams and brightly painted murals. The menu offers some unusual wines from all over France to accompany traditional and more adventurous dishes, like *filet de cannette aux kumcoats* and *entrecôte au bleu d'Auvergne*. Lunchtime *formule* €16, including a glass of wine; dinner set *menu* for €23. Booking advisable on weekends. M° Hôtel-de-Ville. Daily noon–2.45pm & 7.30–midnight.

**L'Enoteca 25 rue Charles-V, 4ᵉ** ☎01.42.78.91.44. A fashionable Italian *bistrot à vins* in an old Marais building. If you take your Italian wine seriously this is the place to come: the list runs to 22 pages and features over 400 varieties, with an ever-changing selection available by the glass. Food doesn't take a back seat either: choose from an array of *antipasti*, fresh pasta (€11) or more substantial dishes like stuffed courgettes (€15). Two-course lunchtime *menu* for €12 including a glass of wine. M° St-Paul. Open daily noon–11.30pm; closed one week in Aug.

**L'Excuse 14 rue Charles-V, 4ᵉ** ☎01.42.77.98.97. The cuisine is *nouvelle*-ish, as refined and elegant as the very pretty decor. A good place for a quiet but stylish date. *Menus* €24–29. M° St-Paul. Open noon–2pm & 7.30–10.30pm; closed Sun & first three weeks of Aug.

**Jo Goldenberg's 7 rue des Rosiers, 4ᵉ.** Dating back to the 1920s, this is the best-known Jewish restaurant in the capital. Some say standards have declined over the years, but it can still pull off decent *borscht, blinis, zakouski* and *apfel strudel*. Occasional live music, often violin and guitar playing jazz favourites, lends atmosphere. Daily changing *plat du jour* €13, *carte* around €35. M° St-Paul. Daily until 1.30am.

**Piccolo Teatro** 6 rue des Écouffes, 4e ☎01.42.72.17.79. Great vegetarian restaurant with low lighting, stone walls and wooden beams. The speciality is *gratin*: try for example the *douceur et tendresse* made of spinach, mint, mozzarella and gruyere. Midday *menu* at €8.20, evening €14.50. Best to book on weekends. M° St-Paul. Tues–Sun noon–3pm & 7.15–11pm; closed Aug.

**Pitchi-Poï** 7 rue Caron, cnr place du Marché-Ste-Catherine, 4e ☎01.42.77.46.15. A warm and homely restaurant with outdoor seating on one of the Marais' most attractive squares. The cuisine revolves around central European/Jewish dishes like *tchoulent* and salmon coulibiac. Don't leave without sampling one of the Polish flavoured vodkas – the honey one goes down a treat. €21 lunch and dinner *menu*, childrens' *menu* €11.50. M° St-Paul. Daily 10am–midnight.

**Le Ravaillac** 10 rue du Roi-de-Sicile, 4e. Long-established Polish restaurant with warm, wood-beamed interior. Specialities include meat *perushkis*, beef stroganoff, and *choucroute,* plus a long list of vodkas. Excellent quality for the price – €20 *à la carte*. M° St-Paul. Open noon–3pm & 7.15–11pm; closed Sun & Aug.

**Le Rouge Gorge** 8 rue St-Paul, 4e. Small, friendly *restaurant à vins* with bare stone walls and jazz or classical music playing in the background. Devoted to exploring a wide range of wines: one week it might be Corsica, the next Spain or the Loire, and the theme is taken up in the frequently changing menu. For three courses at lunchtime count on paying €22 and at dinner €28. Wine by the glass starts at €2.80; if you're taken by a particular vintage you can buy a bottle to take home. M° St-Paul. Open Mon–Sat; closed last fortnight in Aug.

**Thanksgiving** 20 rue St-Paul, cnr rue Charles-V, 4e. Highly regarded restaurant serving Cajun and Louisiana cuisine, plus some regular American favourites. You can get it all here: gumbo, jambalaya, crabcakes, even spare ribs and bagels and lox. €35 *menu*. M° St-Paul. Open for dinner Tues–Sat 7.30–10.30pm; Cajun brunch Sat noon–3pm; traditional brunch Sun 11am–4pm. Closed Aug.

## Quartier du Temple

### Cafés and Bars

**Le Taxi Jaune** 13 rue Chapon, 3e. An ordinary café made special by the odd poster, good taped rock and new-wave music, as well as interesting food. Daily changing *plats* for around €14. Offers the occasional concert. M° Arts-et-Métiers; see colour map 2. Mon–Sat until 11pm; closed Sat lunch & Sun.

**Web Bar** 32 rue de Picardie, 3e, ⊛www.webbar.fr. Paris's best cybercafé, on three levels in a converted industrial space, with around twenty terminals on a gallery level. A real culture zone: pick up a printed programme of the art exhibitions, short film screenings and other arty events or consult their website. Comfy couches to loll on and a resident DJ make it a good place to chill, and simple healthy food comes in generous portions (€9 for quiche with mountains of salad). M° République/Filles-du-Calvaire. Mon–Fri 8.30am–2am, Sat 11am–2am, Sun 11am–midnight.

### Restaurants

**Chez Jenny** 39 bd du Temple, 3e ☎01.44.54.39.00. Thirties Alsatian brasserie serving superb *choucroute*. Menu at €24, children's *menu* €11.50, *carte* around €35. M° République. Daily 11.30am–1am.

**Chez Nénesse** 17 rue Saintonge, 3e ☎01.42.78.46.49. Steak in bilberry sauce and figs stuffed with cream of almonds are two of the unique delights on offer at this restaurant, along with homemade chips on Thursday lunchtimes. *À la carte* around €30. M° Filles-du-Calvaire; see colour map 2. Mon–Fri noon–2pm & 8–10.30pm; closed Aug.

**Chez Omar** 47 Rue de Bretagne, 3e ☎01.42.72.36.26. Very popular North African couscous (€11–20) restaurant in a nice old brasserie set with mirrors. Attracts a young crowd. No credit cards. M° Arts-et-Métiers; see colour map 2. Daily except Sun lunch noon–2.30pm & 7–11.30pm.

## Bastille

### Cafés and Bars

**Bar des Ferrailleurs 18 rue de Lappe, 11ᵉ.**
Dark and stylishly sinister, with rusting metal decor, an eccentric owner, fun wig-wearing bar staff and a relaxed and friendly crowd. Mº Bastille. Daily 5pm–2am.

**Café de l'Industrie 16 rue St-Sabin, 11ᵉ.** One of the best Bastille cafés, packed out every evening. Rugs on the floor around solid old wooden tables, mounted rhinoceros heads, old black-and-white photos on the walls and a young, unpretentious crowd enjoying the comfortable absence of minimalism. *Plats du jour* around €12. Mº Bastille. Daily 10am–2am.

**Café des Phares 7 place de la Bastille (west side), 4ᵉ.** Every Sunday at 11am a public philosophy debate is held in the back room here. The debates were pioneered by Nietsche specialist, Marc Sautet, and although he's no longer here, the sessions continue to attract large gatherings and have spawned a number of other *café philos* in the city. At other times the *terrasse* is a good spot for people-watching on the place de la Bastille. Mº Bastille. Daily 7am–4am.

**La Fontaine 1 rue de Charonne, 11ᵉ.** Don't be fooled by its "just another neighbourhood bar on the corner" look; this place is as trendy as the others even if it is a tad less self-conscious and expensive. Mº Bastille. Daily 8.30am–2am.

**Grand Appétit 9 rue de la Cerisaie, 4ᵉ.** Vegetarian meals for around €15 served by dedicated eco-veggies at the back of this unassuming shop. Mº Bastille. Mon–Fri noon–2.30pm.

**Havanita Café 11 rue de Lappe, 11ᵉ.** Large, comfortable Cuban-style bar with battered old leather sofa. Cocktails from €7.50; happy hour till 8pm. Mº Bastille. Daily 5pm–2am.

**Iguana 15 rue de la Roquette, cnr rue Daval, 11ᵉ.** A place to be seen in. Decor of trellises, colonial fans, and a brushed bronze bar. The clientele studies *recherché* art reviews, and the coffee is excellent. Mº Bastille. Daily 10am–2am.

**Pause Café 41 rue de Charonne, cnr rue Keller, 11ᵉ.** More like "Pose Café" – given its popularity with the *quartier*'s young and fashionable who pack the pavement tables

at lunch and aperitif time. *Plats du jour* around €10. Mº Ledru-Rollin. Tues–Sat 8am–2am, Sun till 9pm.

**SanZSanS 49 rue du Faubourg-St-Antoine, 11ᵉ.** Gothic decor of red velvet, oil paintings and chandeliers, and a young crowd in the evening. Drinks reasonably priced; main courses for around €9. DJ every evening. Mº Bastille. Daily 9am–2am.

**Le Temps des Cerises 31 rue de la Cerisaie, 4ᵉ.** It's hard to say what's so appealing about this café, with its dirty yellow decor, old posters and prints of *vieux Paris*, save that the *patronne* knows most of the young, relaxed clientele. €11.50 *menu*. Not to be confused with the socialist worker's co-op of the same name in the 13ᵉ. Mº Bastille. Mon–Fri until 8pm; food at midday only; closed Aug.

### Restaurants

**Le Bar à Soupes 33 rue de Charonne, 11ᵉ.** The exceedingly upbeat owner creates seven different soups each day, which run the gamut from Portugese haddock to a chilled tomato consommé laced with ginger. A good alternative to an excess of rich and heavy three-course meals. Mº Bastille. Mon–Sat noon–3pm & 6.30–11pm.

**Blue Elephant 43–45 rue de la Roquette, 11ᵉ** ☎01.47.00.42.00. Superb Thai restaurant with dishes featuring liberal amounts of papaya, coconut milk and seafood. Figure on at least €40 per head. Booking essential. Mº Bastille/Richard-Lenoir. Daily till midnight; closed Sat midday.

**Boca Chica 58 rue de Charonne, 11ᵉ** ☎01.43.57.93.13. Popular tapas bar, with a colourful, arty decor. Two floors of indoor seating as well as an awning-covered alley. Fresh tapas (from €4.60), including tortillas, gratins, and sampler platters, and half-price beer and sangria during happy hour 4–7pm. Mº Ledru-Rollin. Daily 8am–2am.

**Bofinger 7 rue de la Bastille, 3ᵉ** ☎01.42.72.87.82. This popular fin-de-siècle brasserie, with its splendid, perfectly preserved, original decor, is frequented by Bastille Opera-goers and tourists. Specialities are sauerkraut and seafood. You'll get a better chance of sitting in the main dining room under the splendid glass coupole if you go for smoking rather than non-smoking. Three courses plus wine around €45. **Le Petit Bofinger** (☎01.42.72.05.23; noon–3pm & 7pm–midnight), opposite at no. 6, is under the same management, and serves lighter dishes, with *plats du jour* from €12. M° Bastille. Daily noon–3pm, 6.30pm–1am.

**Le Capricorne 3 bd Richard Lenoir, 11ᵉ** ☎01.47.00.25.00. A friendly, neighbourhood restaurant with a loyal following. The chef gets his ingredients direct from the market, so you can be sure everything is fresh and varied. The evening set *menu* at €16 is hard to beat for this area and features traditional dishes like *pavé de boeuf*, while *plats du jour* might include *gratin de filet de dorade*. There's an extensive wine list too. M° Bastille. Tues–Sat noon–2pm & 7.15–11pm.

**Chez Paul 13 rue de Charonne, cnr rue de Lappe, 11ᵉ** ☎01.47.00.34.57. Wonky corner building housing a small restaurant which preserves the faded colours and furnishings of an older Bastille, right down to the black-and-white tiles on the floor. The young customers who pack the place out, however, have a distinctly contemporary style. Food is traditional and affordable, the ambience very congenial. Mains from €10. Booking advised. M° Bastille. Daily noon–2.30pm & 7.30pm–12.30am.

**Dame Jeanne 60 rue de Charonne, 11ᵉ** ☎01.47.00.37.40, ⊛www.damejeanne.fr. Not

long opened and already a firm local favourite, this relaxed restaurant takes its food seriously – it even offers cookery classes. The high-quality cuisine is built around well-prepared vegetables and delicately flavoured sauces. Mains are around €15 for the likes of *parmentier de canard* or skate with onion compote. The vegetarian set *menu* for €20 is especially recommended. *Menu enfant* €12. M° Ledru-Rollin. Mon–Sat noon–2pm & 7.30–11pm. Closed three weeks in Aug.

**Le Petit Keller 13 rue Keller, 11ᵉ** ☎01.47.00.12.97. Colourful restaurant, with decorative tiled floor and art exhibitions on the walls, serving surprisingly affordable food. The decor may be modern but the food is traditional home-cooking – dishes like rabbit with prunes, and very fresh vegetable-oriented starters. *Menu* €14. M° Ledru-Rollin. Open 8am–2.30pm & 7.30–11pm; closed Sat lunchtime & all day Sun.

**Wok Restaurant 23 rue des Taillandiers, 11ᵉ**. Part of the neighbourhood-wide wave of new restaurants with highly creative cuisine. Walk in, receive a bowl with rice or noodles, choose ultra-fresh vegetables, meat and fish from the buffet and head up to the open kitchen to let the chefs know what spices to add. Served in a pleasant, almost zen-like dining area. €14. M° Bastille. Mon–Sat 7.30pm–midnight.

# The Left Bank

## The Quartier Latin

The listings below are marked on the map on pp.116–117.

### Cafés and Bars

**Le Bateau Ivre 40 rue Descartes, 5ᵉ**. Small, studenty bar just clear of the Mouffetard tourist hotspot, though it attracts a fair number of Anglos in the evenings. M° Cardinal-Lemoine. Happy hour 5–9pm. Daily 6pm–2am.

**Café des Arts cnr place Contrescarpe and rue Lacépède, 5ᵉ**. Prettier cups, cheaper coffee and a younger crowd than its touristy neighbour *La Chope* in this café-packed square. M° Monge. Daily 7.30am–midnight.

**Café de la Mosquée 39 rue Geoffroy-St-**

Hilaire, 5ᵉ. Drink mint tea and eat sweet cakes beside a fountain and assorted fig trees in the courtyard of this Paris mosque – a delightful haven of calm. The salon has a beautiful Arabic interior. Meals are served in the adjoining restaurant for around €15 and up. M° Monge. Daily 9am–11pm.

**Café de la Nouvelle Mairie 19 rue des Fossés-St-Jacques, 5ᵉ**. Sleek café-wine bar with a relaxed feel generated by its largely university-based clientele. Serves good food like curry d'agneau, linguine and salads (around €10), and you can drink at the outside tables on sunny days. M° Cluny-La Sorbonne/RER Luxembourg. Mon, Wed & Fri 9am–10pm, Tues & Thurs 9am–11pm.

**Café Notre-Dame cnr quai St-Michel and rue St-Jacques, 5ᵉ**. This café is fairly ordinary in all ways but one: the view straight across the river to the cathedral. Oh, and Lenin used to drink here. M° St-Michel. Daily 7am–11.30pm.

**L'Ecritoire** 3 pl de la Sorbonne, 5ᵉ. Classic university café right opposite the Sorbonne, with outside tables by the fountain and little booths concealed at the back. Don't expect polite, unhurried service; do expect a lot of black polonecks. M° Cluny-La Sorbonne/RER Luxembourg. Daily 7am–midnight.

**La Fourmi Ailée** 8 rue du Fouarre, 5ᵉ. Simple, light fare is served in this former feminist bookshop which has been transformed into a relaxed *salon de thé*. A high ceiling painted with a lovely mural and a book-filled wall contribute to the atmosphere. Around €8–10 for a *plat*. M° Maubert-Mutualité. Daily noon–midnight.

**Le Piano Vache** 8 rue Laplace, 5ᵉ. Venerable bar crammed with students drinking at little tables. Cool music and a laid-back, grungey atmosphere. A *pression* costs just over €3. M° Cardinal-Lemoine. Mon–Fri noon–2am, Sat & Sun 9pm–2am.

**Les Pipos** 2 rue de l'École-Polytechnique, 5ᵉ. Old carved wooden bar in a long-established position opposite the gates of the former grande école. Serves wines from €2.50 a glass along with simple plates of Auvergnat charcuterie, cheese and the like. M° Maubert-Mutualité/Cardinal-Lemoine. Mon–Sat 8am–1am; closed two weeks in Aug.

**Le Reflet** 6 rue Champollion, 5ᵉ. This artsy cinema café has a strong flavour of the nouvelle vague, with its scruffy black paint scheme, lights rigged up on a gantry and rickety tables packed with intellectual-looking film-goers and chess players. Perfect for a drink either side of a film at one of the arts cinemas on rue Champollion, perhaps accompanied by a good steak, quiche or salad from the short list of blackboard specials. M° Cluny-La Sorbonne. Daily 10am–2am.

**Le Verre à Pied** 118bis rue Mouffetard, 5ᵉ. Deeply old-fashioned market bar where traders take their morning glass of wine at the bar, or sit down to eat the €10 lunchtime *formule*. M° Monge. Closed Sun afternoon & Mon.

**Le Violon Dingue** 46 rue de la Montagne-Ste-Geneviève, 5ᵉ. Long, dark student pub that's also popular with young travellers. Noisy

and friendly, with English-speaking bar staff and cheap drinks. The cellar bar stays open until 4.30am on busy nights. M° Maubert-Mutualité. Daily 6pm–2.30am; happy hour 8–10pm.

## Restaurants

**Au Bistrot de la Sorbonne** 4 rue Toullier, 5ᵉ ☏01.43.54.41.49. Traditional French and delicious North African food served at reasonable prices to a crowd of locals and students in a nice, bright, muralled interior. €11.50 lunch *menu*; evening *menus* from €15.10. RER Luxembourg. Daily noon–2.30pm & 7–11pm.

**Brasserie Balzar** 49 rue des Écoles, 5ᵉ ☏01.43.54.13.67. Classic high-ceilinged brasserie much frequented by the literary intelligentsia of the Quartier Latin. Almost intimidatingly Parisian – some diners feel as if they're on a film set – though if you're unlucky, or choose to eat early, the tourist clientele can spoil the Left Bank mood. *À la carte* around €30. M° Maubert-Mutualité. Daily 8am–11.30pm.

**Au Buisson Ardent** 25 rue Jussieu, 5ᵉ ☏01.43.54.93.02. Copious helpings of inventive, first-class cooking served in a warm-coloured, pleasantly traditional dining room. Lunch *menu* €15, evenings €28. Reservations recommended. M° Jussieu. Closed Sat lunch & Sun, and two weeks in Aug.

**Chez Léna et Mimile** 32 rue Tournefort, 5ᵉ t01.47.07.72.47. The south-facing *terrasse*, perched above a shady little square, is the main attraction, and the €35 *menu* with wine and coffee included is excellent. Serves a €18 *menu* at lunchtime on weekdays. M° Censier-Daubenton. Closed Sun and Mon & Sat lunch.

**Chez René** 14 bd St-Germain, cnr rue du Cardinal-Lemoine, 5ᵉ ☏01.43.54.30.23. A grand old *bistrot* serving the humble old favourites – coq au vin and bœuf bourguignon – in the grand old style. Expect to pay €40 and up, except at lunchtime, when the €28 *menu* includes wine. M° Maubert-Mutualité. Tues–Sat noon–2.30pm & 7.30–11pm; closed Aug.

**Les Degrés de Notre-Dame** 10 rue des Grands Degrés, 5ᵉ ☏01.55.42.88.88. Reliable, inexpensive and substantial French food, with a good-value lunch *menu* at €11.50. M° Maubert-Mutualité. Closed Sun.

**L'Ecurie** 58 rue de la Montagne Ste-Geneviève, cnr rue Laplace, 5ᵉ ☏01.46.33.68.49.

Shoe-horned into a former stables on a particularly lovely corner of the Montagne Ste-Geneviève, this family-run restaurant is cramped, bustling and very lovable. Outside tables and the cave-like cellar below provide a few extra seats, but not many, so book ahead. Expect well-cooked meat dishes served without flourishes – grilled with chips, mostly – for less than €15, and simple starters and desserts for around €5. Mº Maubert-Mutualité/Cardinal-Lemoine. Mon–Sat noon–3pm & 7pm–midnight, Sun 7pm–midnight.

**Les Fontaines** 9 rue Soufflot, 5ᵉ. The dated brasserie decor looks unpromising from the outside, but the welcome inside this family-run place is warm and genuine, and the cooking is in the same spirit, with honest French meat and fish dishes, or game in season. Main courses €12–16. RER Luxembourg. Mon–Sat noon–3pm & 7.30–10.30pm.

**Le Grenier de Notre-Dame** 18 rue de la Bûcherie, 5ᵉ ☎01.43.29.98.29. See for yourself: some veggies love this tiny place; others hate its posh candle-lit atmosphere, cramped tables and cheesy music. Substantial fare, including traditional French dishes made with tofu and unreconstructed vegetarian classics like cauliflower cheese. *Menu* at €12, otherwise around €20. Mº Maubert-Mutualité. Mon–Sat noon–11.30pm, Sun noon–3pm.

**Au Jardin des Pâtes** 4 rue Lacépède, 5ᵉ ☎01.43.31.50.71. Delicious homemade pasta only, but made with all manner of freshly ground organic grains, and served with wonderful flourishes and garnishes. Up to €20 for a full meal. There's another branch at 33 bd Arago, 13ᵉ (Mº Gobelins; closed Sun). Mº Jussieu. Daily noon–2.30pm & 7–11pm.

**Kootchi** 40 rue du Cardinal-Lemoine, 5ᵉ ☎01.44.07.20.56. Shabby but well-regarded Afghan restaurant. A traditional *qhaboli pulawo* of meat cooked with vegetables and raisins can be had for €11.50, and there are *menus* at €9.20 and €12.20 (lunchtime) and €15.50 (evening). Mº Cardinal-Lemoine. Mon–Sat noon–2.30pm & 7.30–10pm.

**Mavrommatis** 42 rue Daubenton, 5ᵉ ☎01.43.31.17.17. A sophisticated Greek restaurant, whose cooking has been favourably influenced by French attention to detail. Quite expensive – even the lunchtime

*menu* is €19 – but you are definitely tasting Greek food at its best. Mº Censier-Daubenton. Tues–Sun noon–2.30pm & 7.30–10pm.

**Pho 67** 59 rue Galande, 5ᵉ ☎01.45.25.56.69. Authentic Vietnamese place just off the touristy Greek-taverna madness around rue de la Huchette. There's a good range of dishes for around €5, but try the famous pho soup, in this case made with tender French steak. Mº Maubert-Mutualité. Daily noon–3pm & 7–11pm.

**Perraudin** 157 rue St-Jacques, 5ᵉ. One of the classic *bistrots* of the Left Bank.The atmosphere is thick with Parisian chatter floating above the brightly lit, packed-in tables. Solid home cooking, with midday *menus* at €13 and €20, evening *menu* at €16 or *carte* at around €13–20 for a main course. No reservations, but you can wait at the bar for a place. RER Luxembourg. Service until 10.15pm; closed Sat & Sun, last fortnight in Aug.

**Le Petit Prince** 12 rue Lanneau, 5ᵉ ☎01.43.54.77.26. Classic French food with occasionally inventive combinations that can be hit and miss. Most of the tables are hidden away at the cosy end of the restaurant, where there's a camp and happy atmosphere. *Menus* at €15 and €21.15. Mº Maubert-Mutualité. Mon–Thurs & Sun 7.30pm–midnight, Fri & Sat 7.30pm–12.30am.

**La Petite Légume** 36 rue des Boulangers, 5ᵉ ☎01.40.46.06.85. This health-food grocery doubles as a vegetarian restaurant and tea room, serving homely, organic *plats* for €8–12, along with fresh-tasting organic Loire wines. Mº Jussieu. Mon–Sat noon–2.30pm & 7.30–10pm.

**Les Quatre et Une Saveurs** 72 rue du Cardinal-Lemoine, 5ᵉ ☎01.43.26.88.80. Inventive, high-class, organic vegetarian food. *Plats* around 11–15, with a *menu* at €25. Mº Cardinal-Lemoine. Daily noon–2.30pm & 7.30–10.30pm. Closed Fri eve.

**Le Reminet** 3 rue des Grands Degrés, 5ᵉ ☎01.44.07.04.24. This artful little *bistrot*-restaurant shows its class through small touches: snowy-white tablecloths and fancy chandeliers liven up the simple dining room, while imaginative sauces grace high-quality traditional French ingredients. Gastronomic *menu* at €50, but you can get away with two courses *à la carte* for about half that.

M° Maubert-Mutualité. Mon & Thurs–Sun noon–2.30pm &7.30–11pm; closed two weeks in Aug.

**Le Refuge du Passé 32 rue du Fer-à-Moulin, 5e ☎01.47.07.29.91.** Stuffed full of bric-a-brac and musical instruments, this welcoming restaurant serves up good dishes from southwest France, with *menus* in the low twenties. M° Les Gobelins. Daily noon–2.30pm &7.30pm–11pm.

**Tashi Delek 4 rue des Fossés-St-Jacques, 5e ☎01.43.26.55.55.** Elegantly styled Tibetan restaurant serving Himalayan regional dishes ranging from hearty, warming noodle soups to the addictive, ravioli-like *momok*. There's even yak butter tea, a salty, soupy concoction that's an acquired taste. You can eat well for under €10. If you prefer a more monastic, Tibetan-style decor, head round the corner and across the street to **Kokonor**, 206 rue St-Jacques, which serves many of the same specialities. RER Luxembourg. Mon–Sat noon–2.30pm & 7.30–10pm; closed two weeks in Aug.

## St-Germain

The listings below are marked on the map on pp.128–129.

### Cafés and Bars

**L'Assignat 7 rue Guénégaud, 6e.** Zinc counter, bar stools, bar football and young regulars from the nearby art school in an untouristy café close to quai des Augustins. Homely *plats du jour* for around €7. M° Pont-Neuf. Mon–Sat 7.30am–8.30pm, food noon–3pm; closed three weeks in July.

**Bar du Marché 75 rue de Seine, 6e.** Thrumming café where the *serveurs* are cutely kitted out in flat caps and aprons. Admittedly, you pay a little extra for the colours and smells of the rue Buci market on the doorstep. M° Mabillon. Daily 7am–2am.

**Bistrot des Augustins 39 quai de Grands Augustins, 6e.** Small, traditional *bistrot* on the riverbank between the Pont Neuf and Place St-Michel. Serves homely hot dishes for around €12, and lighter *plats* – charcuterie and salads – for around €8. M° St-Michel. Daily 9am–midnight.

**Le Bonaparte cnr rue Bonaparte and pl St-Germain, 6e.** Quieter and less touristy than the nearby *Deux Magots* or *Flore*, and situated at the quieter, sunnier end of the

square. Hot and cold snacks served at reasonable prices. M° St-Germain-des-Prés. Daily 7.30am–2am.

**Café de la Mairie pl St-Sulpice, 6e.** A peaceful, pleasant café on the sunny north side of the square, opposite the church of St-Sulpice. M° St-Sulpice. Mon–Sat 7am–2am.

**Café Mabillon 164 bd St-Germain, 6e.** Hyper-trendy, hyper-modern café/bar/club (depending on what time you turn up) that pulls in modish Parisians and international types. Best for a posey night of cocktails (around €10), chatter and cool vinyl. M° Mabillon. Daily 7.30am–6.30am.

**Chez Georges 11 rue des Canettes, 6e.** Deeply old-fashioned, tobacco-stained wine bar with its old shop-front still in place, though sadly Georges himself is not. The downstairs bar attracts a younger, beery crowd that stays lively well into the small hours. M° Mabillon. Tues–Sat noon–2am; closed Aug.

**Cosi 54 rue de Seine, 6e.** Fantastic sandwiches (€5–8) made on homemade focaccia bread, using wonderful Italian deli ingredients. You can eat in, with a glass of wine (€3), and the opera-loving owner plays a different opera on the CD player each day. M° St-Germain-des-Prés. Daily noon–midnight.

**À la Cour de Rohan cour du Commerce, off rues St-André-des-Arts and Ancienne-Comédie, 6e.** A genteel, chintzy drawing-room atmosphere down a picturesque eighteenth-century alleyway close to bd St-Germain. Cakes, tartes, poached eggs, etc, and *plats du jour* from around €10. No smoking. M° Odéon. Daily noon–7.30pm; closed mid-July–mid-Aug.

**Les Deux Magots 170 bd St-Germain, 6e.** Right on the corner of place St-Germain-des-Prés, this expensive café is the victim of its own reputation as the historic hangout of Left Bank intellectuals, but it's great for people-watching. Worth arriving early for the €13.70 breakfast. M° St-Germain-des-Prés. Daily 7.30am–1am; closed one week in Jan.

**Le 10 10 rue de l'Odéon, 6e.** Classic Art Deco-era posters line the walls of this small dark bar, and the theme is continued in the atmospherically vaulted cellar bar, where there's a lot of chatting-up among the studenty clientele. M° Odéon. Daily 6pm–2am.

**Les Etages St-Germain 5 rue de Buci, 6e.** Outpost of boho trendiness at the edge of the rue de Buci street market, with a certain trashy glamour. The downstairs café-bar is open to the street, with overhead heaters on colder days. Upstairs and later on, you can lounge around on dogeared armchairs, chilling out with a cocktail. M° Mabillon. Daily 11am–2am.

**Le Flore 172 bd St-Germain, 6ᵉ.** The great rival and immediate neighbour of *Les Deux Magots*, with a trendier and more local clientele. Sartre, De Beauvoir, Camus and Marcel Carné used to hang out here. Best enjoyed during a late-afternoon coffee or after-dinner drink. M° St-Germain-des-Prés. Daily 7am–1.30am.

**La Palette 43 rue de Seine, 6ᵉ.** Once-famous Beaux-Arts student hangout, now frequented by art dealers and their customers. The decor of this relaxed bar is superb, including, of course, a large selection of colourful, used palettes hung about the walls. There's a a fairly roomy *terrasse* outside. M° Odéon. Mon–Sat 8am–2am.

**Le Procope 13 rue de l'Ancienne-Comédie, 6ᵉ** ☎01.40.46.79.00. Opened in 1686 as the first establishment to serve coffee in Paris, this is still a great place to enjoy a cup and bask in the knowledge that over the years, Voltaire, Benjamin Franklin, Rousseau, Marat and Robespierre, among others, have done the very same thing. At lunchtimes and evenings it turns into a restaurant, with a decent, if rather over-priced, evening *menu* at €30. M° Odéon. Daily noon–1am.

**La Pinte 13 carrefour de l'Odéon, 6ᵉ.** Boozy, crowded beer cellar, with a horde of exotic beers. M° Odéon. Mon–Thurs & Sun 6pm–2am, Fri & Sat 6pm–5am; closed Aug.

**La Taverne de Nesle 32 rue Dauphine, 6ᵉ.** Full of local night owls fuelled up by happy hour cocktails (around €7) and beers (just over €3). Gets busier during student terms, especially at weekends when DJs take to the decks. M° Odéon. Mon–Thurs & Sun 6pm–4am, Fri & Sat till 5am.

**Veggie 38 rue de Verneuil, 7ᵉ.** Organic take-away from a healthfood shop near the Musée d'Orsay. M° Solférino. Mon–Fri 10.30am–2.30pm & 4.30–7.30pm.

**Au Vieux Colombier 65 rue de Rennes, 6ᵉ.** An attractive Art Deco café on the corner of rue du Vieux-Colombier, with enamelled dove medallions, ice-cream-cone lights and stained green wooden window frames.

Good for a coffee break while shopping. M° St-Sulpice. Daily 7am–midnight.

## Restaurants

**Brasserie Lipp 151 bd St-Germain, 6ᵉ.** One of the most celebrated of all the classic Paris brasseries, the haunt of the very successful and very famous, with a wonderful 1900s wood-and-glass interior. Decent *plats du jour*, including the famous sauerkraut, for under €20, but the full *menu* is very expensive. No reservations, so be prepared to wait. M° St-Germain-des-Prés. Daily noon–1am.

**Aux Charpentiers 10 rue Mabillon, 6ᵉ** ☎01.43.26.30.05. A friendly, old-fashioned place – though the atmosphere can suffer due to over-exposure in guidebooks – belonging to the Compagnons des Charpentiers (Carpenters' Guild), with appropriate decor of model roof-trees and tie beams. Traditional *plats du jour* are their forte – tripe sausage, calf's head and the like – for about €15. Lunch *menu* at €19. M° Mabillon. Daily until 11.30pm; closed hols.

**Jacques Cagna 14 rue des Grands-Augustins, 6ᵉ** ☎01.43.26.49.39, ⊛www.jacques-cagna.com. Classy surroundings for very classy food – beef with Périgord truffles and the like will set you back €80 for the evening *menu*, or rather more *à la carte*, and then there's wine on top. The midday *menu* at €40 is excellent value. Chef Cagna also runs the kitchen of the nearby **L'Espadon Bleu**, 25 rue des Grands Augustins, 6ᵉ (☎01.46.33.00.85), specializing in fish, and **La Rôtisserie d'en Face**, 2 rue Christine, 6ᵉ (☎01.43.26.40.98), specializing in grilled meats; both offer relatively inexpensive lunchtime *menus*. M° Odéon/St-Michel. Mon & Sat 7.30–10.30pm, Tues–Fri noon–2.30pm & 7.30–10pm.

**Orestias 4 rue Grégoire-de-Tours, 6ᵉ** ☎01.43.54.62.01. Large helpings of honest, inexpensive Greek and French food, with *menus* from €8. M° Odéon. Mon–Sat noon–2.30pm & 7.30–10pm; closed two weeks in Aug.

**Le Petit St-Benoît 4 rue St-Benoît, 6ᵉ** ☎01.42.60.27.92. A simple, genuine and very appealing local for the neighbourhood's chattering classes. Another of the tobacco-stained St-Germain institutions, where aproned *serveurs* deliver hearty and, at times, heavy traditional fare such as *hachis parmentier* (a version of shepherd's pie). Count on €20 *à la carte*, including house wine. M° St-Germain-des-Prés. Mon–Sat noon–2.30pm & 7.30–10.30pm.

**Le Petit Vatel 5 rue Lobineau, 6ᵉ** ☏01.43.54.28.49. A tiny, matey, atmospheric place nicely done out with bright yellow walls, old train and film posters and quirky colourful cutlery. Popular with students. Good, plain home cooking, including a vegetarian *plat*. Lunch *formule* for €11; a three-course meal will set you back around €16. M° Mabillon. Tues–Sat noon–2.30pm & 7.30–10pm.

**Le Petit Zinc 11 rue St-Benoit, 6ᵉ** ☏01.42.61.20.60. Excellent traditional dishes, especially seafood, in stunning Art-Nouveau-style premises (actually built thirty years ago). It's not cheap – the *menu* costs €32, and a lavish seafood platter will set you back €82 for two – but the quality is reliable. M° St-Germain-des-Prés. Daily noon–midnight.

**À la Petite Chaise 36 rue de Grenelle, 6ᵉ** ☏01.42.22.13.35. The refined, upmarket atmosphere at this elegant, ancient *bistrot* is matched by the attentive service and the decor – a modernized version of eighteenth-century formality. The simple formula – two courses for €24, three courses for €29 – gives centre stage to the food: classic, carefully cooked French dishes, with lots of duck and foie gras. M° Sèvres-Babylone/Rue de Bac. Daily noon–2.30pm & 7.30–10.30pm.

**Polidor 41 rue Monsieur-le-Prince, 6ᵉ** ☏01.43.26.95.34. A traditional *bistrot*, open since 1845, whose visitors' book, they say, boasts more of history's big names than all the glittering palaces put together. Packed with noisy regulars until late in the evening, when the *menu* costs €18. Bargain lunch *menu* for €9. M° Odéon. Mon–Sat noon–2.30pm & 7–12.30pm, Sun noon–2.30 & 7–11pm.

**Vagenende 142 bd St-Germain, 6ᵉ** ☏01.43.26.68.18. An Art Nouveau marvel that is registered as an historic monument and brings to life the Parisian brasserie that is fast fading to memory. Touristy, but worthwhile if you go for the ambience rather than the food – primarily solid brasserie fare. *Menu* at €23, or upwards of €30 *à la carte*. M° Mabillon. Daily noon–1am.

## Trocadéro and the Septième

The listings below are marked on the map on pp.136–137

### Cafés and Bars

**Café du Marché 38 rue Cler, 7ᵉ**. Big, busy café-brasserie serving excellent-value meals, with a *plat du jour* for €8 that's as fresh tasting as you'd expect, given the position in the middle of the rue Cler market. M° La Tour-Maubourg. Mon–Sat noon–11pm.

**Café du Musée d'Orsay 1 rue Bellechasse, 7ᵉ**. The Musée d'Orsay's rooftop café offers one of the city's quirkier views – over the Seine and towards Montmartre – seen through the giant clockface dominating the room. Serves snacks and drinks. RER Musée-d'Orsay/M° Solférino. Tues–Sun 11am–5pm.

**Le Poch'tron 25 rue de Bellechasse, 7ᵉ**. With a fine selection of snacks and wines by the glass, this is an excellent place to revive yourself after visiting the museums in the arrondissement. Also serves lunch and dinner; main dishes at around €12. M°

Solférino. Mon–Fri 9am–10.30pm.

**Sancerre 22 av Rapp, 7ᵉ**. Welcoming wine shop and bar serving glasses of Sancerre from around €4, including the rarer red variety. Accompanying snacks include little *crottins de Chavignol* – goat's cheese "droppings" – and good omelettes and charcuterie. M° Alma-Marceau. Mon–Fri 8am–10pm, Sat 8am–2pm.

**Totem southern wing of the Palais de Chaillot, pl du Trocadéro, 16ᵉ**. Walk nonchalantly past the full-on native-American-themed restaurant to the terrace at the back, which offers magnificent views of the Eiffel Tower and a chance to enjoy it with a coffee or something stronger. M° Trocadéro. Daily noon–2am.

### Restaurants

**L'Affriolé 17 rue Malar, 7ᵉ** ☏01.44.18.31.33. Don't be put off by the chilly pseudo-Athenian decor, the welcome is warm here and the food superb. This chef-led *bistrot* is traditionally French, but Mediterranean flavours and some brilliant combinations really bring the fresh produce to life. At lunch, two courses with wine costs €19, or there's an €30 *menu* in the evening. M° Invalides. Tues–Sat noon–2.30pm & 7.30–10pm.

**L'Ami Jean 27 rue Malar, 7ᵉ** ℡01.47.05.86.89. Good, robust Basque food (paella, *pipérade*, *poulet basquaise*) for around €15 for a main course. The ambience is cosy, but gets as robust as the food on rugby nights – the owner is a fan. M° La Tour-Maubourg. Mon–Sat noon–2.30pm & 7.30–10pm; closed Aug.

**Au Babylone 13 rue de Babylone, 7ᵉ** ℡01.45.48.72.13. Lots of old-fashioned charm and culinary basics like *rôti de veau* and steak, plus wine on the €17 *menu*. M° Sèvres-Babylone. Mon–Sat lunch only; closed Aug.

**Le Basilic 2 rue Casimir-Périer, 7ᵉ** ℡01.44.18.94.64. A very classy restaurant with lots of polished brass and a terrace overlooking the apse of Ste-Clotilde church. Specialities such as *gigot d'agneau* will set you back €15, but count on €40 for a full meal. M° Solférino. Daily noon–2.30pm & 7.30–10.30pm.

**Le Bourdonnais 113 av La Bourdonnais, 7ᵉ** ℡01.47.05.47.96. A gem of a restaurant and a high-class one at that, if you'll forgive the claustrophobic, hotel-like decor. You can ruin yourself *à la carte*, but memorable *menus* can be had for €42 at lunch; €64 or €80 in the evening. M° École-Militaire. Daily noon–2.30pm & 8–11pm.

**Chez Germaine 30 rue Pierre-Leroux, 7ᵉ** ℡01.42.73.28.34. A simple and tiny restaurant packing them in for the excellent-value *menu* at €12, or €9 at lunch. M° Duroc/Vaneau. Closed Sat evening, Sun & Aug.

**Au Petit Tonneau 20 rue Surcouf, 7ᵉ** ℡01.47.05.09.01. A small *bistrot*-style restaurant serving refined traditional French cuisine; wild mushrooms are a speciality. All prices are *à la carte*: under €10 for starters, anything from €15–30 for mains. M° Invalides. Daily noon–3.30pm & 7–11.30pm.

**Au Pied de Fouet 45 rue de Babylone, 7ᵉ** ℡01.47.05.12.27. An atmospheric, little – just four tables and no reservations – place, perfect for dining on simple French classics. Under €15 for a full meal. M° St-François-Xavier/Sèvres-Babylone. Mon–Fri noon–2.30pm & 7–9.30pm, Sat noon–2.30pm; closed Sun & Aug.

**Le P'tit Troquet 28 rue de l'Exposition, 7ᵉ** ℡01.47.05.80.39. Tiny, discreet family restaurant decked out like a quirkily elegant antiques shop. Serves exquisite traditional cuisine to the diplomats and politicians of the *quartier*. *Menu* at €27. M° École Militaire. Tues–Sat noon–2.30pm & 7.30–10pm; Mon 7.30–10pm.

**Thoumieux 79 rue St-Dominique, 7ᵉ** ℡01.47.05.49.75. Cavernous, traditional brasserie replete with mirrors, carved wood, hatstands and bustling, black-and-white clad waiters. Popular with a smart local clientele for carefully prepared classics, many with a southwestern emphasis. Basic lunch *menu* at €14, or €31 in the evening. M° La Tour-Maubourg. Daily noon–3.30pm & 6.30pm–midnight.

**La Varangue 27 rue Augereau, 7ᵉ** ℡01.47.05.51.22. Also known as Philippe's restaurant, after the proprietor, who presides over the tiny, homely dining room from his minuscule open kitchen, dishing up salads, desserts and simple *plats* – many of them vegetarian – straight over the counter. Lots of *formules*, with a good three-course deal for €11.50. M° École-Militaire. Mon–Sat noon–3pm & 6–9pm.

# Montparnasse and southern Paris

## Montparnasse

Unless otherwise stated, the listings below are marked on the map on pp.148–149.

### Cafés and Bars

**La Closerie des Lilas 171 bd du Montparnasse, 6ᵉ.** The smartest and most ancient Montparnasse café of them all, with excellent cocktails for around €12 and a resident pianist. The tables are name-plated after celebrated former habitués (Verlaine, Mallarmé, Lenin, Modigliani, Léger, Strindberg). The restaurant is very expensive, but brasserie main courses can be

had for under €20. RER Port-Royal. Daily
noon–1.30am.

**Mustang Café 84 bd du Montparnasse, 14ᵉ.**
Open long after other bars close, *Mustang*
draws a happily drunken international
crowd for dancing, cocktails and beers. Mº
Montparnasse-Bienvenue. Daily
10am–5am.

**Le Rosebud 11bis rue Delambre, 14ᵉ.** A faintly
exclusive bar just off the boulevard
Montparnasse where the clientele tries
bravely to maintain the arty traditions of the
area. The barmen, who seem to date from
the same era as the decor, serve up wonderful, traditional cocktails – think Martinis
rather than Sex on the Beach – for around
€10. Mº Vavin. Daily 7pm–2am.

**La Rotonde 105 bd du Montparnasse, 6ᵉ.**
Another of the grand old Montparnasse
establishments, frequented by Lenin and
Trotsky in their time. Decent *menu* at lunch
for €12.50 with wine and coffee. Mº Vavin.
Daily till 1am.

**Le Select  99 bd du Montparnasse, 6ᵉ.** The
least spoilt and most traditional of the
Montparnasse cafés. Mº Vavin. Mon–Thurs
& Sun till 3am, Fri & Sat till 4.30am.

**Tea and Tattered Pages 24 rue Mayet, 6ᵉ.**
This secondhand English-language bookshop is rather a long way from anywhere,
but inside you can have tea and cakes,
speak English and browse through a very
good selection of English books. Mº Duroc.
Daily 11am–7pm.

## Restaurants

**Chez Maria 16 rue du Maine, 14ᵉ**
℡01.43.20.84.61. Zinc bar and candlelight,
posters and paper tablecloths – an intimate
gloom that appeals to arty theatre creatures
after hours. Tasty traditional French food in
the evening for around €25; inexpensive
quiches and salads only at lunchtime. Mº
Montparnasse. Mon–Sat noon–2pm &
8pm–midnight.

**La Coupole 102 bd du Montparnasse, 14ᵉ**
℡01.43.20.14.20. The largest and perhaps
the most famous and enduring arty-chic
Parisian hangout for dining, dancing and
debate. Although lavishly renovated by the
prince of Paris's turn-of-the-century
brasseries, Jean-Paul Bucher of *Flo* and
*Julien* fame, *La Coupole* remains a genuine
institution, buzzing with conversation and
clatter from the diners packed in tightly
under the high, chandeliered roof. Lunch

*menus* at €16.50 and €29, evening *menu*
at €30.50, with a €21.50 *menu* served
after 10.30pm. Montparnasse traditions –
of a sort – are even kept up with a downstairs nightclub (see p.311). Mº Vavin. Daily
8.30am–1am.

**Le Dôme 108 bd du Montparnasse, 6ᵉ.** Three
doors down from *La Coupole* (see above),
and another of Sartre's haunts. Wonderful
but expensive (upwards of €50) seafood at
the *bistrot*, but you can soak up the atmosphere in the café section, where cinema
pics decorate each alcove. Mº Vavin. Daily
noon–3pm & 7pm–12.30am; café
8am–1.30am.

**Le Parc aux Cerfs 50 rue Vavin, 14ᵉ**
℡01.43.54.87.83. Once an artists' hangout,
this is now a restrained but not overly
formal little restaurant with some modern
touches – a touch of chorizo here, crayons
to draw on your paper place mat there.
Delicate, occasionally exquisite French
dishes feature on all the €20–30 lunch and
evening *menus*, and there's a brilliant wine
list and a small garden. Mº Vavin. Daily
noon–2.30pm & 7.30–10.30pm.

## The 14ᵉ

Unless otherwise indicated, the listings below are marked on the map on
pp.148–149.

### Cafés and Bars

**L'Entrepôt 7–9 rue Francis-de-Pressensé.** Arty
cinema with a spacious, relaxed café and
outside seating in the courtyard. *Plats* for
€10–15. Mº Pernety. Mon–Sat noon–2am.

**Le Rallye 6 rue Daguerre.** A good place to
recover from the catacombs or
Montparnasse cemetery. The patron offers
a bottle for tasting; gulping the lot would be
considered bad form. Good cheese and
*saucisson*. Mº Denfert-Rochereau.
Tues–Sat until 8pm; closed Aug.

### Restaurants

**Aquarius 40 rue de Gergovie** ℡01.45.41.36.88.
Hearty, homely vegetarian restaurant
serving wholesome if not spectacular meals
to a friendly, noisy crowd, with main
courses for around €10. A sister restaurant
is located in the 4ᵉ (see p.289). Mº
Pernety/Plaisance. Mon–Sat noon–2.30pm
& 7.30–10.30pm; closed Sun and three
weeks in Aug/Sept.

**Natacha** 17bis rue Campagne-Première
℡01.43.20.79.27. Cool, spacious *bistrot* that
attracts a celebrity crowd. In the kitchen,
they introduce warm Mediterranean flavours
to traditional dishes, and there's even a
pasta course. You could scrimp by for
around €25, but double that figure for a full
meal with wine. Mº Raspail. Mon–Sat
8.30pm–1am.

**Pavillon Montsouris** 20 rue Gazan
℡01.45.88.38.52. A special treat for
summer days. Sit on the terrace overlooking the park, and choose from a
menu featuring truffles, *foie gras* and the
divine *pêche blanche rôtie à la glace
vanille*. Single *menu* at €44. RER Cité-
Universitaire; off map. Mon–Sat
noon–2.30pm & 7.30–10pm; Sun
noon–3pm.

**La Régalade** 49 av Jean-Moulin
℡01.45.45.68.58. You need to book several
days in advance for this very high-class and
good-value restaurant. The standard €30
*prix fixe* delivers a memorable meal, and for
once the wines aren't marked up with the
cooking. Mº Alésia. Tues–Fri noon–2.30pm
& 7pm–midnight, Sat 7pm–midnight; closed
Aug.

**Au Rendez-Vous des Camionneurs** 34 rue
des Plantes ℡01.45.40.43.36. No lorry drivers
any more, but you'll get a warm welcome
and a really good meal with a small *pichet*
of wine for around €15. It's wise to book.
Mº Alésia. Mon–Fri noon–2pm &
7.30–10pm; closed Aug.

**Restaurant Bleu** 46 rue Didot
℡01.45.43.70.56. Excellent high-class
cooking in a small and well-tended restaurant. The three-course *menu du marché* is
€19, or else you can choose the speciality
*truffade* (mashed potato and sausage)
amongst others from the *à la carte* menu
for €23. Mº Plaisance. Tues–Fri
noon–2.30pm & 7.30–10pm; Mon & Sat
7.30–10pm.

**N'Zadette M'Foua** 152 rue du Château
℡01.43.22.00.16. A small, cheerily tacky
Congolese restaurant serving tasty dishes
such as *maboké* (meat or fish baked in
banana leaves). *Menu* at €14. Mº Pernety.
Tues–Sun 7pm–2am.

## The 15e

The listings below are marked on the
map on pp.158–159.

## Cafés and Bars

**Au Roi du Café** 59 rue Lecourbe, 15e.
Traditional café with a decor that didn't
change much during the twentieth century
and a pleasant terrace, albeit on a busy
road. Mº Volontaires/Sèvres-Lecourbe.
Daily 7am–2am.

## Restaurants

**Le Bistrot d'André** 232 rue St-Charles, 15e
℡01.45.57.89.14. A reminder of the old
Citroën works before the Parc André-
Citroën was created, with pictures and
models of the classic French car. Homely
dishes and great puds. Midday *menu* €11,
otherwise up to €25. Mº Balard. Mon–Sat
noon–2.30pm & 7.30–10pm.

**Le Café du Commerce** 51 rue du Commerce,
15e ℡01.45.75.03.27. A two-storey restaurant
that's been catering for *le petit peuple* for
over a hundred years. Serves varied, nour-
ishing and inexpensive fare. Lunch *menus*
from €10.60, evening menus around €20–25.
Mº Émile-Zola. Daily noon–midnight.

**Sampieru Corsu** 12 rue de l'Amiral-Roussin,
15e. Decorated with the posters and passionate declarations of international
socialism, this restaurant provides good
meals for the homeless or unemployed. As
a visitor, you pay what your conscience dic-
tates – at least €8, though most will think a
three-course meal is worth more. The
restaurant only survives on the generosity of
its supporters, and it's a wonderful place.
Mº Cambronne. Mon–Fri noon–1pm &
6.30–9.30pm.

## The 13e

The listings below are marked on the
map on p.162.

## Cafés and Bars

**Le Diapason** 15 rue Butte-aux-Cailles. Classic
narrow, shopfront-style Butte-aux-Cailles
bar, this time with a noisy reggae flavour.
Mº Place d'Italie/Corvisart. Tues–Sat
5pm–2am; happy hour till 8pm.

**La Folie en Tête** 33 rue Butte-aux-Cailles.
Alternative-spirited bar with friendly
Saturday-night World music dance sessions. Cheap drinks and snacks in the daytime. A very warm and laid-back place. Mº
Place-d'Italie/Corvisart. Mon–Sat
5pm–2am.

**Le Merle Moqueur** 11 rue Butte-aux-Cailles. Tiny bar with a distressed chic ambience, serving up laid-back music and homemade flavoured rums to young Parisians. Mº Place-d'Italie/Corvisart. Daily 5pm–2am.

## Restaurants

**Auberge Etchegorry** 41 rue Croulebarbe ☎01.44.08.83.51. A former *guinguette* on the banks of the Bièvre, this Basque restaurant has an old-fashioned atmosphere of relaxed conviviality, and the food's good too. *Menus* at €18.30 at lunchtime and €24 in the evening. Mº Gobelins. Tues–Sat noon–2.30pm & 7.30–10pm.

**L'Avant Goût** 37 rue Bobillot ☎01.45.81.14.06. Small neighbourhood restaurant with a big reputation for excitingly good modern French cuisine, and wines to match. Cool contemporary decor and presentation. Superb value lunch *menu* at €11 and evening *menu* at €26. Mº Place d'Italie. Tues–Sat noon–2.30pm & 7.30–11pm; closed three weeks in Aug.

**Le Bambou** 70 rue Baudricourt ☎01.45.70.91.75. Tiny Asian-quarter restaurant crammed with punters, French and Vietnamese alike, tucking into sublimely fresh-tasting Vietnamese food. Serves giant, powerfully flavoured pho soups, packed with beef and noodles (only choose the large version if you really mean it), a full menu of specialities, and the addictive Vietnamese tea and coffee that's made with condensed milk. Mº Tolbiac. Tues–Sun noon–3.30pm & 7–10.30pm.

**Chez Gladines** 30 rue des Cinq-Diamants ☎01.45.80.70.10. This tiny corner *bistrot* is always warm and welcoming, and packed with a young clientele. Excellent wines and hearty Basque and southwest dishes; the mashed/fried potato is a must and goes best with *magret de canard*. Less than €20 for a (very) full meal. Mº Corvisart. Daily 9am–1am.

**Chez Grand-Mère** 92 rue Broca ☎01.47.07.13.65. The name says it all: you could almost be in your French grandmother's parlour, though you'd be lucky if she cooked this well. Excellent terrines, rabbit in mustard sauce and stuffed trout on the *menus*, both of which are under €20. Mº Gobelins. Open Mon–Sat noon–2.15pm & 7.15–10.15pm.

**Chez Paul** 22 rue Butte-aux-Cailles ☎01.45.89.22.11. This *bistrot* successfully treads a fine line between upmarket and relaxed. Warm wood is matched with designer cutlery, and the traditional French country food gets an elegant finish – expect lots of offal, superbly cooked. Such finesse doesn't come cheap: expect to pay around €40. Mº Place-d'Italie/Corvisart. Daily noon–2.30pm & 7.30pm–midnight.

**Le Jean-Baptiste-Clément** 11 rue Butte-aux-Cailles ☎01.45.80.27.22. Specializes in filling, tasty *charbonnades* – meats chargrilled at your table, served with gratin Dauphinois and three house sauces. *Menus* at €14.95 and €18.15. Mº Place-d'Italie/Corvisart. Daily noon–3pm & 7.30pm–midnight.

**Le Languedoc** 64 bd Port-Royal, 5ᵉ ☎01.47.07.24.47. Actually, just in the 5ᵉ, but closer to the Gobelins than the Latin Quarter. An utterly traditional check-table-cloth *bistrot* with an illegible menu on which you might decipher cassoulet, confit duck and other southwestern classics. Good value €19 *menu*. Mº Gobelins. Thurs–Mon noon–2pm & 7–10pm; closed Aug.

**Lao-Thai** 128 rue de Tolbiac ☎01.44.24.28.10. Big, glass-fronted resto on a busy interchange, serving fine Thai and Laotian food. Midday *menu* at €7.95, otherwise from around €21.50 for two. Mº Tolbiac. Mon, Tues & Thurs–Sun noon–2.30pm & 7.30–11pm.

**Phuong Hoang** Terrasse des Olympiades, 52 rue du Javelot ☎01.45.84.75.07. Take the escalator up from rue Tolbiac to this large, well-known restaurant serving Vietnamese, Thai and Singaporean specialities on a variety of *menus* from €8 and up. Not the most authentic of restaurants, but the food is reliable, and the skyscrapers around the *terrasse* loom overhead like a Modernist architectural fantasy. Mº Tolbiac. Daily until 11pm.

**Le Temps des Cerises** 18–20 rue Butte-aux-Cailles ☎01.45.89.69.48. Truly welcoming restaurant – it's run as a workers' co-op – with elbow-to-elbow seating and a different daily choice of imaginative dishes. Lunch *menu* at €10 and evening *menus* at €12.50 and €22. Mº Place-d'Italie/Corvisart. Mon–Fri noon–2pm & 7.30–11.45pm, Sat 7.30pm–midnight.

**Tricotin** Kiosque de Choisy, 15 av de Choisy ☎01.45.85.51.52 & 01.45.84.74.44. *Tricotin's* "kiosque", glazed in like a pair of overgrown fish tanks, is just set back from the broad avenue de Choisy, next to the Chinese-signed McDonalds. The two restaurants cover much the same ground, and cover it well, but no. 1 (closed Tues) specializes in Thai and grilled dishes, while no. 2 has a longer list of Vietnamese, Cambodian and steamed foods. *Plats complets* cost under €10, but you could multiply dishes and spend around €18. M° Porte-de-Choisy. Daily 9.15am–11pm.

# Montmartre and northern Paris

## Montmartre

The listings are marked on the map on p.167.

### Cafés and Bars

**Le Bar du Relais 12 rue Ravignan, 18e.** A quaint building in a beautiful spot just under the Butte, with tables out on the little square where Picasso's Beateau-Lavoir studio used to be, and good music inside. M° Abbesses. Daily 5pm–2am.

**L'Été en Pente Douce 23 rue Muller, 18e (cnr rue Paul-Albert)** ☎01.42.64.02.67. The food's reasonable enough here – traditional French with *plats* around €13 – but the main reason for coming is to soak up the pure Montmartre atmosphere. Chairs and tables are set out alongside the steps leading up to Sacré-Cœur from the eastern side, just off the beaten track. M° Château-Rouge. Daily noon–midnight.

**La Fourmi Café 74 rue des Martyrs, 18e.** Trendy, high-ceilinged café-bar full of con-scientiously beautiful young Parisians drinking coffee by day and cocktails at night. M° Pigalle/Abbesses. Mon–Thurs 8am–2am, Fri & Sat 8am–4am, Sun 10am–2am.

**Aux Négociants 27 rue Lambert (cnr rue Custine), 18e** ☎01.46.06.15.11. An intimate and friendly *bistrot à vins* with a selection of well-cooked *plats*, homemade charcuterie and excellent wines by the glass. It's wise to book if you plan to eat – count on around €25 for a full meal. The clientele is resolutely local, with a smattering of arty-intellectual types. M° Château-Rouge. Mon–Fri noon–2.30pm & 8–10pm; closed Aug.

**Au Petit Café de Montmartre 7 rue Joseph de Maistre, 18e.** A small, traditional bar where the prices and atmosphere are unaffected by tourism, though weekend occasional jazz duos pull in the punters. M° Château-Rouge. Tues–Thurs & Sun 3pm–11pm; Fri & Sat 11am–midnight; closed two weeks in Aug.

**Le Sancerre 35 rue des Abbesses, 18e.** A fashionable hangout for the young and trendy of all nationalities under the southern slope of Montmartre, with a row of outside tables perfect for watching the world go by. The food can be disappointing though. M° Abbesses. Daily 7am–2am.

### Restaurants

**L'Assiette 78 rue Labat, 18e** ☎01.42.59.06.63. A bit out of the way, but a very friendly place, serving delicious southwestern food as well as surprising Ukrainian specialties like the beetroot sorbet starter. Good-value €15 *menu*. M° Château-Rouge. Mon, Tues, Thurs & Fri noon–2.30pm & 8–10.30pm, Wed noon–2.30pm, Sat 8–10.30pm.

**La Casserole 17 rue Boinod, 18e** ☎01.42.54.50.97. Good and copious help-ings, a wide variety of game in season, and a jolly atmosphere helped along by the curious knick-knacks that festoon the walls. *À la carte* will set you back around €30, but there's a lunchtime *menu* at €13 during the week. M° Simplon/Marcadet-Poissonniers. Tues–Sat noon–2.30pm & 7.30–10pm; closed mid-July to mid-Aug. (Not on map).

**Au Grain de Folie 24 rue La Vieuville, 18e** ☎01.42.58.15.57. Tiny, simple and colourfully dilapidated vegetarian place with a short, wholesome and inexpensive menu. M° Abbesses. Mon–Sat 12.30–2.30pm & 7–11.30pm, Sun 12.30–11.30pm.

**L'Homme Tranquille 81 rue des Martyrs, 18e** ☎01.42.54.56.28. Simple and pleasant *bistrot* ambience, with posters and nicotine-coloured paint. Imaginative French dishes on the €21 *menu* include chicken in honey, coriander and lemon. M° Abbesses. Mon–Sat 7.30–11.30pm; closed Aug.

**Le Moulin à Vins 6 rue Burq, 18e** ☎01.42.52.81.27. Cheery, intimate wine bar and *bistrot* with a really interesting selection of wines to accompany the excellent cheese and charcuterie. *Plats* such as coq au vin change every day and cost around

€22. M° Abbesses. Tues–Sat 7pm–midnight; bar till 2am; closed three weeks in Aug.

**A la Pomponnette** 42 rue Lepic, 18ᵉ ☏01.46.06.08.36. A genuine old Montmartre *bistrot*, with posters, drawings, zinc-top bar, etc. The food is excellent, with a *menu* at €28.50; otherwise it will cost you €35–50 *à la carte*. M° Blanche/Abbesses. Tues–Thurs noon–2.30pm & 7–11pm, Fri & Sat noon–2.30pm & 7pm–midnight.

**Le Relais Gascon** 6 rue des Abbesses, 18ᵉ ☏01.42.58.58.22. Serving hearty, filling meals all day, this two-storey restaurant (upstairs is cosier but smoky) provides a welcome blast of straightforward Gascon heartiness in this alternately trendy, run-down and touristy part of town. The enormous hot salads cost €9, and there are equally tasty *plats* for around €10–12. M° Abbesses. Daily 10am–2am.

**Le Rendez-vous des Chauffeurs** 11 rue des Portes-Blanches, 18ᵉ ☏01.42.64.04.17. The €12 *menu*, including wine, offers a large range of excellent quality French fare. Of course, that means this traditional little restaurant is always packed – you'll usually have to share a table. Arrive early or reserve. M° Marcadet-Poissonniers. Daily except Wed noon–2.30pm & 7.30–11pm. (Not on map).

**Le Restaurant** 32 rue Véron, 18ᵉ ☏01.42.23.06.22. Fashionable but welcoming corner restaurant with some contemporary twists to classic French ingredients. M° Abbesses. Mon–Fri 12.30–2.30pm & 7.30pm–midnight, Sat 7.30–11.30pm.

**Au Virage Lepic** 61 rue Lepic, 18ᵉ ☏01.42.52.46.79. Simple, good-quality meaty fare served in a noisy, friendly, old-fashioned *bistrot*. Small, smoky and very enjoyable. Two-course *menu* at €16. M° Blanche/Abbesses. Daily except Tues 7pm–2am.

## Pigalle and south of Pigalle

The listings below are marked on the map on p.167.

### Cafés and Bars

**Le Dépanneur** 27 rue Fontaine, 9ᵉ ☏01.40.16.40.20. Relaxed all-night bar just off place Pigalle. One to know about for winding down after clubbing. M° Pigalle. Daily 11am–7am.

## Restaurants

**L'Alsaco** 10 rue Condorcet (at the extreme eastern end), 9ᵉ ☏01.45.26.44.31. A real Alsatian *winstub* serving the traditional dishes and wines of Alsace. The two *menus* (at €19 & €30) come with carefully chosen beers and lots of cheese. M° Poissonnière. Mon & Sat 7pm–midnight, Tues–Fri noon–2.15pm & 7pm–midnight; closed mid-July through Aug.

**Aux Deux-Théâtres** 18 rue Blanche, cnr rue Pigalle, 9ᵉ ☏01.45.26.41.43. Classic luvvie hangout serving particularly good food in a long, plush dining room decorated with actors' photos. Single all-in *menu* at €29. M° Trinité. Daily 11.30am–2.30pm & 7pm–midnight.

**Haynes** 3 rue Clauzel (cnr rue des Martyrs), 9ᵉ ☏01.48.78.40.63. There's a long tradition of black Americans in Paris, ever since jazz and Josephine Baker and ever since black GIs found themselves more welcome here than at home. This restaurant has been going since the 1940s, serving generous quantities of rich and heavy soul food. Despite the grotto-like decor, the atmosphere is warm, and there's blues or jazz most nights from around 8pm. It's certainly something different in Paris. *À la carte* only, at around €35, with wine. M° St-Georges. Tues–Sat 7.30pm–12.30am.

**Le Relais Savoyard** 13 rue Rodier, cnr rue Agent-Bailly, 9ᵉ ☏01.45.26.17.18. Generous helpings of hearty Savoyard cuisine in a little dining room at the back of a local bar. Two courses for €16, three for €23. M° Notre-Dame-de-Lorette/Anvers/Cadet. Mon 7.30–10pm, Tues–Sat noon–2.30pm & 7–10pm; closed two weeks in Aug.

**La Table d'Anvers** 2 pl d'Anvers, 9ᵉ ☏01.48.78.35.21. This is one of the city's best restaurants, despite the ugly business-beige decor. The *menu* at €39 gives a good taste of the chef's skills, but the full experience on the menu gastronomique will set you back €85. M° Anvers. Noon–2pm & 7–11pm; closed Mon & Sat lunchtime & Sun.

**Velly** 52 rue Lamartine, 9ᵉ ☏01.48.78.60.05. Excellent modern French cooking in an intimate *bistrot* setting. You can choose from any of the dishes on the blackboard, which change daily. The sole *menu* costs €21 at lunchtime and €28 in the evening, and there are good wines for less than €20. M°

Notre-Dame-de-Lorette. Mon–Fri noon–2.30pm & 7.30–10.45pm, Sat 7.30–11pm; closed three weeks in Aug.

## The stations and faubourgs

The listings below are marked on the map on p.175.

### Cafés and Bars

**L'Atmosphère 49 rue Lucien-Sampaix, 10ᵉ.** Lively café-bar with decent evening *plats*, on a pleasant corner beside the canal St-Martin. Tables on the towpath on sunny days, and occasional live music on Sundays, with an alternative flavour. Mº Gare-de-l'Est. Tues–Fri 11am–2am, Sat 3pm–4am, Sun 3pm–8pm.

**China Express Nord 3 bd Denain, 10ᵉ.** Friendly Chinese deli and café a few steps south of the Gare du Nord. Good for something hot and inexpensive while you wait for your train. Mº Gare-du-Nord. Mon–Sat 10.30am–10.30pm.

**L'Enchotte 11 rue de Chabrol, 10ᵉ** ℡01.48.00.05.25. A pleasantly ramshackle wine bar opposite the St-Quentin market, with tobacco-stained paintwork and a simple tiled floor. Cheese and charcuterie at around €10, as well as more substantial dishes. Mº Gare-de-l'Est. Mon–Fri 12.30–2.30pm & 7.30–10.30pm; closed last two weeks of Aug.

**Le Réveil du Dixième 35 rue du Château-d'Eau, 10ᵉ** ℡01.42.41.77.59. A welcoming, unpretentious wine bar serving glasses of wine and regional *plats* at around €10. Mº Château-d'Eau. Mon–Sat 7.15am–9pm.

### Restaurants

**Baalbeck 16 rue de Mazagran, 10ᵉ** ℡01.47.70.70.02. Much liked by the moneyed refugees, this Lebanese restaurant has dozens of appetizers. For €50 you can have a representative selection for two, with *arak* to drink. Belly-dancing and sticky Levantine/Turkish cakes, too. Very busy, so reserve or go early. Mº Bonne-Nouvelle. Mon–Sat noon–2.30pm & 7.30pm–midnight.

**Chez Arthur 25 rue du Faubourg-St-Martin, 10ᵉ** ℡01.42.08.34.33. An easygoing, attractive restaurant, popular with theatregoers and actors, especially for post-theatre dining – it actually stays open beyond the official serving hours. The cuisine can be interesting, too, with appealing variations on the usual suspects on the €20 *menu*. Mº Strasbourg-St-Denis. Mon 7–11.30pm, Tues–Sat noon–2.30pm & 7–11.30pm.

**La Consigne 2 bd de Denain, 10ᵉ** ℡01.48.78.22.94. Bog-standard Parisian brasserie, but it's right opposite the Gare du Nord. The waiters are understandably jaded by the constant flow of out-of-towners, but the €10 *plats du jour* are reliable classics like *moules frites* and steak, and there's pleasant seating in the window and on the pavement. Food served till 11pm. Mº Gare-du-Nord. Daily 6am–1am.

**Flo 7 cours des Petites-Écuries, 10ᵉ** ℡01.47.70.13.59. Dark, extremely handsome old-time brasserie where you eat elbow to elbow at long tables, served by waiters in ankle-length aprons. Fish and seafood are the specialities, but generally it's all excellent, as is the atmosphere. Good-value *menu* at €30.50, including wine, or €21.50 on weekday lunchtimes. Mº Château-d'Eau. Daily until 1.30am.

**Julien 16 rue du Faubourg-St-Denis, 10ᵉ** ℡01.47.70.12.06. Part of the same enterprise as *Flo* (see above), with an even more splendid decor – all globe lamps, hatstands, white linen, brass and polished wood. Serves the same good traditional French cuisine as *Flo*, at the same prices, and it's just as crowded. Mº Strasbourg-St-Denis. Daily until 1am.

**Pooja 91 passage Brady, 10ᵉ** ℡01.48.24.00.83. Located in a glazed *passage* that is Paris's own slice of the Indian subcontinent, *Pooja* is slightly pricier and sometimes slightly more elaborate than its many neighbours. Lunch *formules* for under €10; evening *menu* for just short of €20. Mº Strasbourg-St-Denis/Château-d'Eau. Daily noon–3pm & 6–11pm; closed Mon lunchtime.

**Terminus Nord 23 rue de Dunkerque, 10ᵉ** ℡01.42.85.05.15. 1920s brasserie with brusque staff and high prices, but the decor is magnificent, the food is usually good, unless you're eating at an odd time of day, and it's right opposite the Gare du Nord. Mº Gare-du-Nord. Daily 11am–1am.

## Batignolles

The listings below are marked on the map on p.178.

### Cafés and Bars

**L'Endroit 67 pl Félix-Lobligeois, 17ᵉ.** A

smartish neighbourhood café and late-night bar, with a *terrasse* overlooking the attractive square. Youngish locals drop in for great cocktails (around €8), but it's also a great place for a copious Sunday brunch (€15). M° Rome/La Fourche. Daily noon–2am.

# Eastern Paris

## The Canal St-Martin and around

Unless otherwise indicated, the listings below are marked on the map on pp.184–185.

### Cafés and Bars

**Chez Imogène** cnr rue Jean-Pierre-Timbaud and rue du Grand-Prieuré, 11ᵉ. Cheap and cheerful crêperie with €8.50 midday *menu* including drink. The €13.60 dinner *menu* includes a kir breton (cassis with cider instead of champagne) and three courses. M° Oberkampf. Open till 10.30pm; closed all day Sun & lunchtime on Mon.

**L'Opus** 167 quai de Valmy, 10ᵉ ☎01.40.34.70.00, ⊛www.opus-club.com. A stylish modern-chintzy atmosphere in a barn-like space used as a British officers' mess during World War I. Live music every evening: *chansons*, gospel, blues, salsa, African. Drinks €9–12 average, plus €10 entry for the music. There's also a dining area on the mezzanine floor overlooking the action (three-course *menu* €40). M° Louis-Blanc. Mon–Sat 8pm–4am.

### Restaurants

**Astier** 44 rue Jean-Pierre-Timbaud, 11ᵉ ☎01.43.57.16.35. Very successful and popular restaurant with simple decor, unstuffy atmosphere, and food renowned for its freshness and refinement. Outstanding selection of perfectly ripe cheeses. Essential to book; lunch is often less crowded (€20.50 *menu*) and just as enjoyable. Evening *menu* at €25. M° Parmentier. Mon–Fri noon–2pm & 8–11pm; closed Aug, fortnight each in May & at Christmas.

**Chez Prune** 36 rue Beaurepaire, 10ᵉ ☎01.42.41.30.47. One of the most popular hangouts in the 10ᵉ, this is a very friendly

### Restaurants

**Le Morosophe** 83 rue Legendre ☎01.53.06.82.82. Relaxed contemporary *bistrot* serving unpretentious, well-cooked seasonal dishes. Lunchtime *menu* at €12, evenings at €25. M° Brochant. Mon–Sat noon–12.30pm & 7–11pm.

and laid-back café-restaurant with pleasant outdoor seating overlooking the canal. Creative *assiettes* (around €7) are guaranteed to tempt both meat-eaters and vegetarians, and it's a romantic place to sip a glass of wine or indulge in a dessert. *Plats* around €11. M° Jacques-Bonsergent. Mon–Sat 7.30am–1.45am & Sun 10am–1.45am.

**Le Clown Bar** 114 rue Amelot, 11ᵉ ☎01.43.55.87.35. An attractive and increasingly popular wine *bistrot* near the Cirque d'Hiver with a circus clientele come the colder months; the beautifully tiled interior shows the antics of clowns, of course. *Plats du jour* from €10.50, such as *sauté de boeuf minute au paprika*. No credit cards. M° Filles-du-Calvaire. Daily except Sun lunch noon–3pm & 7pm–1am.

**L'Homme Bleu** 57 rue Jean-Pierre-Timbaud, 11ᵉ ☎01.48.07.05.63. Very affordable and pleasant Berber restaurant that's popular with students. M° Parmentier. Mon–Sat 5pm–2am.

**Au Rendez-Vous de la Marine** 14 quai de la Loire, 19ᵉ ☎01.42.49.33.40. Busy, successful old-time restaurant on the east bank of the Bassin de la Villette – but no water view – renowned for its meats and desserts. A really good meal for around €25. Booking advised. M° Jaurès. Lunchtime & eves until 10pm; closed Sun & Mon.

**Le Rendez-Vous des Quais** 10 quai de la Seine, 19ᵉ ☎01.40.37.02.81. Part of the MK2 cinema complex on the west bank of the Bassin de la Villette, this is a great spot for a coffee before taking a canal cruise (the office is opposite; see p.350). Contemporary *bistrot* fare and tables overlooking the water. *Plats* for around €12. M° Stalingrad. Daily 10am–midnight.

**Restaurant de Bourgogne** 26 rue des Vinaigriers, 10ᵉ ☎01.46.07.07.91. Homely old-fashioned restaurant with midday *menu* at €9 and evening *menu* at €10, including a drink. Still has a strong local character despite the changing nature of the area. M° Jacques-Bonsergent. Lunchtime & eve until 11pm; closed Sat eve, Sun & last week July to third week Aug.

**Au Trou Normand 9 rue Jean-Pierre-Timbaud, 11ᵉ ⊕01.48.05.80.23.** Small, totally unpretentious local *bistrot* serving good traditional food at knock-down prices. *Plat du jour* from €4.90. Mon–Fri lunchtime & eve until 9.30pm, Sat eve only; closed Aug. M° Filles-du-Calvaire/Oberkampf/République.

## La Villette

Unless otherwise indicated, the listings below are marked on the map on pp.184–185.

### Cafés and Bars

**Café de la Musique 213 av Jean-Jaurès, 19ᵉ.** Part of the Cité de la Musique, this café, with a popular terrace just inside the La Villette complex, was designed by the Cité architect Portzamparc and exudes sophistication, discretion and comfort, but be prepared to pay over the odds for a coffee. M° Porte-de-Pantin. Daily till 2am.

### Restaurants

**Aux Saveurs du Liban 11 rue Eugène-Jumin, 19ᵉ ⊕01.42.00.17.01.** Excellent, authentic Lebanese food at this tiny restaurant in a lively local street not far from the Parc de la Villette. Very good value, with *plats* for €5.35; sandwiches from €3.35 to take away; €7.10 lunchtime *formule*. M° Porte-de-Pantin. Mon–Sat 11.30am–4pm & 7–11pm.

## Belleville, Ménilmontant, Charonne and Père-Lachaise

### Cafés and Bars

**Le Baratin 3 rue Jouye-Rouve, 20ᵉ.** Friendly, down-to-earth *bistrot à vins* in a run-down area with a good mix of people. Fine selection of lesser-known wines and whiskies. Midday *menu* €11.13, around €20 in the evenings. M° Pyrénées.
Tues–Fri 11am–1am, Sat 6pm–1am; closed first week Jan & two weeksAug.
**Le Blue Billard 111–13 rue St-Maur, 11ᵉ.** Young and arty, featuring blue-carpeted bar and billiard tables, in a glass-roofed ex-

factory. *Menu* is €15. M° St-Maur/Parmentier. Daily 11am–2am; closed Sun eve.

**Café Charbon 109 rue Oberkampf, 11ᵉ.** A very successful and attractive resuscitation of an early twentieth-century café. Particularly popular with the younger, fashionable crowd who are moving into these old working-class districts. Snacks around €5; beer €2.50. DJ Thurs, Fri & Sat eves 10pm–2am and live music on Sun from 8.30pm. M° St-Maur/Parmentier. Daily 9am–2am.

**Cithéa 112 rue Oberkampf, 11ᵉ ⊛www .kollectiveone.com/cithea/.** Popular bar and music venue for Afro funk, funk reggae, world beat, jazz fusion, etc on Thurs, Fri & Sat nights. Cocktails €7. No admission charge for the music. M° St-Maur/Parmentier. Daily 5pm–5.30am.

**La Flèche d'Or 102bis rue de Bagnolet, cnr rue des Pyrénées, 20ᵉ ⊕01.43.72.04.23, ⊛www.flechedor.com.** A large, lively café attracting the biker, arty, punkish Parisian youth. The decor is *très destroy* – railway sleepers and a sawn-off bus front hanging from the ceiling – and the building itself is the old Bagnolet station on the *petite ceinture* railway that encircled the city until around thirty years ago. It's a nightly venue for live world music, pop, punk, ska, fusion and *chanson*, and the reasonably priced food also has a multicultural slant. Extra €5 or €6 for music. M° Porte-de-Bagnolet/Alexandre-Dumas – a fifteen-minute walk in either case. Daily 10am–2am.

**Lou Pascalou 14 rue des Panoyaux, 20ᵉ.** Trendy but friendly bar with burnt-umber walls and a zinc bar. Wide range of beers bottled and on tap from €2, cocktails from €5. M° Ménilmontant. Daily 9am–2am.

**Le Vieux Belleville 12 rue des Envierges, 20ᵉ.** Simple and attractive old-fashioned café. Lunchtime *menu* €10. M° Pyrénées. Open 7am–11pm; closed Sat lunchtime, all day Sun & Mon eve.

### Restaurants

**Les Allobroges 71 rue des Grands-Champs, 20ᵉ ⊕01.43.73.40.00.** A charming neighbourhood restaurant, serving traditional French cuisine to consistently high standards. The *menu* at €15 is excellent value, though the wines are a bit pricey. Booking essential. M° Maraîchers. Tues–Fri noon–2pm & 7–9.30.

**Chez Jean** 38 rue Boyer (near cnr with rue de Ménilmontant), 20ᵉ ☎01.47.97.44.58. A charming, friendly, intimate place, with a small but carefully chosen *menu*. Around €30 *à la carte*. Mᵒ Gambetta/Ménilmontant. Mon–Fri lunchtime & eves till 11pm; closed Sat midday, Sun & first half of Aug.

**Lao Siam** 49 rue de Belleville, 19ᵉ ☎01.40.40.09.68. The surroundings are nothing special, but the excellent Thai and Lao food, popular with locals, makes up for it. Dishes €6.50–9.50. Best to book in advance. Mᵒ Belleville. Daily till 11pm.

**Le Pacifique** 35 rue de Belleville, 20ᵉ. A huge Chinese eating house with variable culinary standards, but low prices and open late. €13 *menu*. Mᵒ Belleville. Daily 11am–2am.

**Au Pavillon Puebla** Parc des Buttes-Chaumont, 19ᵉ ☎01.42.08.92.62. Luxury cuisine in an old hunting lodge (enter by the rue Botzaris/av Bolivar gate to the park). Poached lobster, stuffed baby squid, duck with *foie gras*, and spicy oyster raviolis are some of the *à la carte* delights. *Menus* for €30–40, around €70 *à la carte*. Mᵒ Buttes-Chaumont. Tues–Sat noon–10pm. Closed Sun, Mon & two weeks in August.

**Pho-Dong-Huong** 14 rue Louis-Bonnet, 11ᵉ ☎01.43.57.18.88. Spotlessly clean Vietnamese resto, where all dishes are around €7 and come with piles of fresh green leaves. Spicy soups, crispy pancakes, but service can be slow. Mᵒ Belleville. Daily except Tues noon–10.30pm.

**Aux Rendez-Vous des Amis** 10 av Père-Lachaise, 20ᵉ. A handy lunch stop a stone's throw from Père-Lachaise. Simple surroundings for very good, satisfying family cooking. *Menu* at €10.21. Mᵒ Gambetta. Mon–Sat noon–3pm; closed last week July to mid-Aug.

**Rital & Courts** 1 rue des Envierges, 20ᵉ ☎01.47.97.08.40. Café, wine bar and trattoria (food served noon–2.30pm & 8–11.30pm) in contemporary surroundings in an unbeatable situation overlooking the delightful Parc de Belleville. Get a pavement table on a summer evening, and you'll have the best restaurant view in Paris. The Italian food is tasty and affordable, with a large pasta selection, including loads of vegetarian options, from €8. Short films (*courts métrages*) are shown daily 6–7pm & midnight–1am. Mᵒ Pyrénées. Daily 11am–midnight.

**Le Zéphyr** 1 rue Jourdain, 20ᵉ ☎01.46.36.65.81. Trendy but relaxed 1930s-style *bistrot* with a lunch *menu* for €11, and €26 in the evenings. Mᵒ Jourdain. Open till 11.30pm; closed Sat lunch and all day Sun.

## To the Faubourg St-Antoine

Unless otherwise indicated, the listings below are marked on the map on pp.200–201.

### Cafés and Bars

**L'Armagnac** 104 rue de Charonne, 11ᵉ ☎01.43.71.49.43. This unpretentious café-bar makes a great spot for coffee in the afternoon or drinks well into the night. Mᵒ Charonne. Daily till 2am.

**Jacques-Mélac** 42 rue Léon-Frot, 11ᵉ ☎01.43.70.59.27. Some way off the beaten track (between Père-Lachaise and place Léon-Blum) but a highly respected and very popular *bistrot à vins*, whose patron even makes his own wine – the solitary vine winds round the front of the shop. The food (*plats* around €11), wines and atmosphere are great; no bookings. Mᵒ Charonne. Tues–Sat 9am–10.30pm; closed Aug.

### Restaurants

**Les Amognes** 243 rue du Faubourg-St-Antoine, 11ᵉ ☎01.43.72.73.05. Attractive surroundings of stone walls and exposed beams form the backdrop to this smart *bistrot*, which puts a creative spin on traditional dishes. Mains might include *lapin de garenne*, *chou rouge et figues* and *cabillaud rôti au citron et thym*. Booking essential. *Menu* at €33, otherwise around €45. Mᵒ Faidherbe-Chaligny. Noon–2.30pm & 7.30–10.30pm; closed Sat & Mon lunch, Sun & two weeks in Aug.

**Le Bistrot du Peintre** 116 av Ledru-Rollin, 11ᵉ ☎01.47.00.34.39. A charming, traditional *bistrot*, where small tables are jammed together beneath faded Art Nouveau frescoes and wood panelling. The emphasis is on hearty Auvergne cuisine, with *plats* for around €12. Mᵒ Ledru-Rollin. Mon–Sat 7am–2am, Sun 10am–8pm.

**Chardenoux** 1 rue Jules-Vallès, 11ᵉ ☎01.43.71.49.52. An authentic oldie, with engraved mirrors dating to 1900. Still serving solid meaty fare like calves' kidneys grilled in mustard. Upwards of €30 *à la carte*. M° Faidherbe-Chaligny. Noon–2pm & 8–10.30pm; closed Sat lunch, Sun & Aug.

**La Mansouria 11 rue Faidherbe-Chaligny, 11ᵉ** ☎01.43.71.00.16. An excellent and elegant Moroccan restaurant dishing up superb couscous and tagines. *Menu* €29, *carte* around €38. M° Faidherbe-Chaligny. Open until 11.30pm; closed Sun and lunchtime on Mon & Tues, and a fortnight in Aug.

## The 12ᵉ

The listings below are marked on the map on pp.200–201.

### Cafés and Bars

**Le Baron Rouge 1 rue Théophile-Roussel, cnr pl d'Aligre market.** A popular *bar à vins*, as close as you'll find to the spit-on-the-floor stereotype of the old movies. Many locals and shoppers repair here for a light lunch or aperitif after visiting the place d'Aligre market, especially on Sundays. If it's crowded inside you can join the locals on the pavement and stand around the wine barrels lunching on *saucisson* or mussels washed down with a glass of wine. M° Ledru-Rollin. Tues–Sat 10am–2pm & 5–9.30pm, Sun 10am–2pm only.

**T pour 2 Bercy Village, 23 Cour Saint Émilion.** The old stone walls of this coolly converted wine warehouse in Bercy combine with contemporary furnishings to create an attractive and relaxed interior. The lunchtime *formule* for €10 gets you a bagel – French-style, homemade dessert (eg pear mousse with chocolate coulis) and a glass of wine. M° Cour Saint-Émilion. Daily 9am–9pm.

**Le Viaduc Café 43 av Daumesnil** ☎01.44.74.70.70. In one of the Viaduc des Arts' converted railway arches, with seating outside in nice weather. Makes a good spot for a drink if you've been walking, rollerblading, or perusing the nearby galleries. The three-course (€21) Sunday jazz brunch from noon to 4pm is popular. M° Gare-de-Lyon. Daily 8am–4am (food served till 3am).

### Restaurants

**L'Ébauchoir 43–45 rue de Cîteaux** ☎01.43.42.49.31. Good *bistrot* fare in a relaxed and convivial atmosphere; midday *menu* for €12; *carte* €25 upwards. It's advisable to book for the evening. M° Faidherbe-Chaligny. Mon–Sat until 11pm.

**Le Square Trousseau 1 rue Antoine Vollon** ☎01.43.43.06.00. A handsome belle-époque brasserie with a regularly changing menu featuring excellent New French cuisine. Lunch *menu* for €21, evening is *à la carte* – reckon on €38 excluding wine. You can also eat at midday in their little annexe next door, hung with haunches of ham and lined with wine bottles; here you get a *plat du jour* for €13 and wine by the glass from €3. In fact, wine is what it's all about: there's a well-stocked cellar from which you can sample any number of wines and take a bottle of what you like home with you. Booking recommended for the evening. M° Ledru-Rollin. Tues–Sat noon–2pm & 7.30–midnight; closed in Aug.

# Western Paris

## Auteuil and Passy

The listings below are marked on the map on p.208.

### Restaurants

**Byblos Café 6 rue Guichard, 16ᵉ** ☎01.42.30.99.99. An excellent Lebanese restaurant, serving traditional mezzes, moussaka and the like in relaxed and convivial surroundings. Prices are very reason-able for the area – for around €7 you get mezzes, falafel and Lebanese sausage. M° Muette. Daily 11am–3pm & 5–11pm.

**La Gare 19 Chaussée de la Muette, 16ᵉ** ☎01.42.15.15.31. This renovated train station is now an elegant restaurant-bar serving, among other things, a very popular €23 lunch *menu*. You can sit out on the attractive terrace on sunny days. M° Muette. Daily noon–3pm & 7pm–midnight. Bar open noon–2am.

# Music and nightlife

The strength of the Paris **music scene** is its diversity – a reputation gained mainly from its absorption of immigrant and exile populations. The city has no rivals in Europe for the variety of **world music** to be discovered: Algerian, West and Central African, Caribbean and Latin American sounds are represented in force. Hip-hop remains fashionable, both imported and home-grown, though it's scarcely visible in the city's **bars and clubs**, where **house** and **techno** still rule, mixed in with good-time Mediterranean, Latin and African flavours. For a relaxed flavour of the nightlife of the past, head for one of the old suburban eating-and-drinking venues known as **guinguettes** (see p.351).

**Jazz** fans are in for a treat, with all styles from New Orleans to current experimental to be heard. Then there's French **chanson**, a tradition long associated with the city of Paris, particularly during the war years through cabaret artists like Edith Piaf, Maurice Chevalier and Charles Trenet, and in the 1960s with poet-musicians as diverse as Georges Brassens, Jacques Brel and Serge Gainsbourg. *Chanson* is currently undergoing something of a revival, with nostalgic releases by artists like Patrick Bruel, and excellent *chanson* evenings in restaurants and bars.

**Classical music**, as you might expect in this Neoclassical city, is alive and well and takes up twice the space of "jazz-pop-folk-rock" in the listings magazines. The **Paris Opéra**, with its two homes – the Opéra-Garnier and Opéra-Bastille – puts on a fine selection of **opera and ballet**. The need for advance reservations (except sometimes for the concerts held in churches) rather than the price is the major inhibiting factor here. If you're interested in the **contemporary** scene of Systems composition and the like, check out the Cité de la Musique at La Villette or IRCAM near the Pompidou Centre.

At the end of the chapter are details of all the **big performance halls** for major events from heavy metal to opera. On June 21 the **Fête de la Musique** sees live bands and free concerts of every kind of music throughout the city.

## Tickets and information

To find out **what's on** you need to get hold of one of the city's listings magazines; see "Basics" p.22 for a run-down. If you want more in-depth coverage, try the *Hot Guide* pull-out section (in French) of the monthly magazine *Nova* (Ⓦ www.novaplanet.com), which also runs its own radio station (see box on p.310). The best way to find out about the latest club nights is to head to a specialist music shop (see p.343), or pick up flyers in the trendy shops and cafés of the Marais and Bastille.

The private **TV channel** Canal Plus broadcasts big European concerts, while M6 has some late-night music programmes, as well as numerous video clips during the day, and Arte, the fifth channel (after 7pm), shows contemporary opera productions and documentaries on all types of music.

Of the **local radio stations**, Radio Nova (101.5 MHz) plays the best cross-section of what's new, from house to hip-hop, and broadcasts updates on the latest and coolest club nights, or *soirées*. Radio France-Mahgreb (99.5 MHz) does raï; FIP (105.1 MHz) has plenty of jazz; Africa Numero 1 (107.5 MHz) has African music; Radio Latina (99.0 MHz) is the Latin American music station; Oui FM (102.3 MHz) is the all-day rock radio; and techno and house can be heard on the station Radio FG (98.2 MHz). The **national station** Europe 1 (104.7 MHz) has some imaginative music programming, and France-Musiques (91.7 MHz) carries classical, contemporary, jazz, opera and anything really big. Under strict language laws, forty percent of pop music played by any radio station has to be French, and there's a dire Parisian radio station playing nothing but French music, Chante France (90.9 MHz).

The easiest places to get **tickets** for concerts, whether rock, jazz, *chansons* or classical, are at FNAC, whose main branch is in the Forum des Halles, 1–5 rue Pierre-Lescot, 1$^{er}$ (Mon–Sat 10am–7.30pm; ☎01.40.41.40.00, ⓦwww.fnac.fr; M° Chatelet-Les Halles). Alternatively, you can use one of the FNAC Musique branches (see p.343), or Virgin Megastore, at 56–60 av des Champs-Élysées, 8$^{e}$ (daily 10am–midnight; ☎01.49.53.50.00, ⓦwww.virginmega.fr; M° Franklin-D.Roosevelt), and at the Carrousel du Louvre, beneath the Louvre, 1$^{er}$ (Sun–Tues 10am–8pm, Wed 10am–9pm, Thurs–Sat 10am–10pm; M° Palais-Royal/Musée-du-Louvre).

## Clubbing

Musically, Paris is at its most cutting-edge with hip-hop, techno and drum and bass, but most **clubs** play a more mainstream mix of house or techno. The clubs listed below are dedicated and usually dependable dance venues, but note that the style of music and the general vibe really depends on who's running the "soirée" on a particular night. Some showcase occasional live acts, too, especially when there's a Latin theme, and equally, many rock and world music venues (see p.313) hold DJ-led sessions after hours. Check out the list of **gay and lesbian** venues (see pp.372–373), too, many of which attract mixed crowds from the trendy end of the nightlife spectrum. And note that several of the bars and "pubs" listed in Chapter 16 (see p.271) bring in DJs for weekend nights.

Bear in mind that some clubs operate very snooty and sometimes outright racist door policies. Most **entry prices** include one free drink. The barges moored to the banks of the Seine (see *Batofar*, opposite, and *La Guinguette Pirate*, on p.313) are your best bets for a relatively inexpensive good night out.

Given the difficulty of finding a **taxi after hours** (see p.29), many Parisian clubbers aim to keep going until the métro starts up at around 5.30am, or even later, dancing away the morning hours at an *after* event. You can do the same in even grander style on Eurostar: the "Night Clubber" deal offers £35 fares from London if you leave after 4pm on a Saturday and return before 10.30pm on Sunday.

## Nightclubs

**Les Bains** 7 rue du Bourg-l'Abbé, 3e
℡01.48.87.01.80. As posey as they come,
set in an old Turkish bathhouse with a
plunge pool. The music is mostly house,
hip-hop and garage. Fussy bouncers and
expensive drinks. Admission €16 weekdays, €20 at the weekend. M° Étienne-
Marcel. Daily midnight–dawn.

**Balajo** 9 rue de Lappe, 11e ℡01.47.00.07.87.
This old-style music hall of *gai Paris* gets a
mention for its extravagant 1930s decor
and large dance floor, but the famous old-
fashioned *bal musette* nights have died a
death, and the club now draws a cheesy,
aggressively flirty out-of-town crowd.
Admission price is around €15, including
first drink. M° Bastille. Wed 9pm–3am,
Thurs–Sat 11pm–dawn, Sun 3–7pm.

**Batofar** quai de la Gare, 13e ℡01.56.29.10.00.
An old lighthouse boat moored at the foot
of the Bibliothèque Nationale. Brilliant line-
up of DJs from all over the world spinning
techno for the most part. Your best bet for
a not-too-expensive club night out.
Admission under €10. M° Quai-de-la
Gare/Bibliothèque-Tolbiac. Daily
9pm–3am.

**Chapelle des Lombards** 19 rue de Lappe, 11e
℡01.43.57.24.24. This erstwhile *bal musette*
still plays the occasional waltz and tango,
but for the most part the music is Afro-
Latin: salsa, reggae, steel drums, zouk, raï
and the rest. Its renown as a pick-up joint
means unabashed advances. Entry and first
drink Thurs €13, Fri & Sat €18. M° Bastille.
Thurs–Sat 11pm–dawn.

**La Coupole** 100 bd du Montparnasse, 14e
℡01.43.27.56.00. *La Coupole*'s formula has
survived through most of the twentieth century – gorgeous, historic brasserie upstairs,
cool nightclub downstairs – though the
music has changed. Latino nights on
Tuesdays, house music at weekends. Entry
€16–18. M° Vavin. Tues–Sat
11.30pm–3am.

**Élysée Montmartre** 72 bd de Rochechouart,
18e ℡01.55.07.06.00, ⓦwww
.elyseemontmartre.com. Historic Montmartre
nightspot that pulls in a young, excitable
crowd with its up-tempo club nights, held
under the huge, arching roof. Every other
Saturday there's a school-disco style party
night called *Le Bal* (€14), with live
rock/dance acts and DJs playing all those

Eighties French pop tunes you never sang
along to, but everyone around you clearly
did. Frequent gigs midweek. M° Anvers.

**La Fabrique** 53 rue du Faubourg-St-Antoine,
11e ℡01.43.07.67.07. Uber-trendy club-bar
heaving with Bastille trendies partying well
into the morning. Mon–Thurs free admission; Fri & Sat under €10. M° Bastille.

**Folies Pigalle** 11 place Pigalle, 9e
℡01.48.78.25.26. Famed for its sleazy past,
and only slightly less sleazy present, trans-
sexual clientele and all, the *Folies* is a landmark on the club scene for its house nights
and "*after*" events early on Saturday
morning and right through Sunday. M°
Pigalle. Tues–Sat midnight–dawn; Sun
dawn–midnight.

**La Java** 105 rue du Faubourg-du-Temple, 10e
℡01.42.02.20.52. Fast-moving salsa-tropical
club, with regular live bands and a seriously
good-time vibe. Admission Thurs €8, Fri &
Sat €15, Sun €5. M° Belleville. Thurs–Sat
11pm–5am, Sun 2–7pm.

**La Locomotive** 90 bd de Clichy, 18e
℡08.36.69.69.28, ⓦwww.laloco.com. High-
tech monster club with three dance floors,
all playing variations on house. Admission
€10 weekdays, €20 weekends. M°
Blanche. Tues–Sun 11pm–dawn.

**Nouveau Casino** 109 rue Oberkampf, 11e
℡01.43.57.57.40, ⓦwww.nouveaucasino.net.
Eclectic, innovative mix of musical styles
played at this large, trendy club – anything
from electro to house and funk. Concerts
earlier in the evening are even wider-ranging
– from post-rock to hip-hop. Club admission €10. M° Parmentier. Thurs–Sun
11pm–dawn.

**Le Queen** 102 Champs-Élysées, 8e
℡01.53.89.08.89, ⓦwww.queen.fr. Legendary
club whose success has far transcended its
gay origins, though Saturdays and Sundays
are strictly gay and only the best-dressed
women get past the door. The crowd
includes drag queens and model types; the
music is house except on Sunday (dance)
and Monday (disco). Admission €10 Mon,
Wed & Thurs; €20 Fri & Sat; €12 Sun. M°
George-V. Daily 11pm–dawn.

**Rex Club** 5 bd Poissonnière, 2e
℡01.42.36.28.83. The clubbers' club: spacious and serious about its music, which is
strictly electronic, notably techno. Attracts
big-name DJs. Admission €11. M° Grands-
Boulevards. Thurs–Sat 11.30pm–6am;
closed Aug.

# Rock and world music

In the last few years Paris clubs and rock venues have begun to concentrate on international sounds, mostly **Latin** and **African** music, or French takes on those sounds, leaving the big rock bands to play the major arenas. Most of the **venues** listed below are primarily concert venues, though some double up as clubs on certain nights, or after hours. A few of them will have live music all week, but the majority host bands on just a couple of nights. Admission prices vary depending on who's playing.

## From yé-yé to Daft Punk

Although a lot of commercial French **pop** is best avoided, the French rock, pop and techno scene is now taken seriously. Internationally, it's **electronic music** that's proved the most successful, with the techno group Daft Punk, DJ Laurent Garnier and the mellower sounds produced and mixed by artists such as Alex Gopher and Étienne de Crécy. French rock and pop haven't quite established themselves internationally, but on a national level confidence has risen dramatically and there are some exciting new sounds drawing on the mix of cultures in French society.

Big names in **world music** are almost always in town, in particular **zouk** musicians from the French Caribbean, and musicians from **West Africa**. Algerian **raï** continues to flourish, with singers like Khaled and Cheb Mami enjoying megastar status.

As the divisions between world sounds blur, more and more bands have produced their own rewarding hybrids: **Les Négresses Vertes**, still going strong, were perhaps the first group to experiment on this level and be recognized internationally. The Parisian-based **Orchestre National de Barbès** has a distinctly African flavour and is made up of ten members, each bringing something of their own musical heritage with them. **Manu Chao**, former member of Mano Negra, combines Latin American, rap, reggae and rock influences to create his own inimitable style. The Toulouse-based group **Zebda** parades a strong Maghrebi influence and has an admirable social conscience – profits from some of their records have been donated to suburban regeneration projects.

The "marginale" culture of the *banlieue*, the dispossessed immigrant suburbs, has found musical expression in **hip-hop**, appreciation of which has become more mainstream. Names to look out for are NTM, IAM and MC Solaar, who has had considerable commercial success with his lyrical style.

As for rock, the so-called **yé-yé** bands, pale imitations of US acts, have thankfully died a death, though France's rock'n'roll megastar still rocks on: now in his sixties, **Johnny Halliday** is still packing out stadiums and churning out endless soft-rock albums. Fortunately, he does not represent contemporary **French rock**. More representative of the quality and innovation are the soloists Miossec and Jean-Louis Murat, and the groups Les Rita Mitsouko, Louise Attaque, Noir Désir and La Tordue, whose styles combine rock and distinctively gallic elements.

French **chanson** (see p.313) still exerts a powerful influence on contemporary music. Ever since the great Serge Gainsbourg blended it with jazz, pop and rock in the 1960s and 70s, French *auteurs* (singer-songwriters) have had serious credibility both at home and abroad. **Dominique A** has emerged as one of the most interesting singer-songwriters of the moment, while **Patrick Bruel**'s album *Entre-Deux* shot to the top of the charts in 2002, with new angles on old classics.

The rage, however, is increasingly for professionally produced **techno** and **electro**, staples of the Parisian club scene. There's even a yearly Techno Parade (see p.42). Daft Punk has made a name for itself internationally as well as in France, whilst groups such as Air and St-Germain create a mellower sound, mixing electronic sounds with jazz and pop.

See also under "Nightclubs" (p.311), many of which also host gigs; "Major concert venues" (p.318) for concerts that attract big international names in all fields of music; and "Mainly Jazz" (p.314) for venues which programme jazz concerts but branch into other genres, such as world music and folk.

## Rock and world music venues

**Le Bataclan 50 bd Voltaire, 11ᵉ**
℡01.43.13.35.35, ⊛www.bataclan.fr. Classic ex-theatre venue with one of the best and most eclectic line-ups covering anything from international and local dance and rock musicians – Francis Cabrel, Chemical Brothers, Khaled, Moby – to opera, comedy and techno nights. Mº Oberkampf.

**Café de la Danse 5 passage Louis-Philippe, 11ᵉ** ℡01.47.00.57.59. Rock, pop, world and folk music played in an intimate and attractive space. Open nights of concerts only. Mº Bastille.

**La Cigale 120 bd de Rochechouart, 18ᵉ** ℡01.49.25.89.99. An eclectic programming policy in an old-fashioned converted theatre, long a fixture on the Pigalle scene. Mº Pigalle.

**Le Divan du Monde 75 rue des Martyrs, 18ᵉ** ℡01.44.92.77.66. A youthful venue in a café whose regulars once included Toulouse-Lautrec. One of the city's most diverse and exciting programmes, ranging from techno to Congolese rumba, with dancing till dawn on weekend nights. Mº Pigalle.

**Élysée Montmartre 72 bd de Rochechouart, 18ᵉ** ℡01.55.07.06.00, ⊛www .elyseemontmartre.com. A historic Montmartre nightspot that pulls in a young, excitable crowd with its rock and dance acts. Also hosts up-tempo Latin and club nights. Mº Anvers.

**La Flèche d'Or 102bis rue de Bagnolet 20ᵉ** ℡01.43.72.42.44, ⊛www.flechedor.com. Friendly alternative venue set in a converted train station. Most nights from around 9pm

there's a cutting-edge programme of inexpensive electro, dub, world music concerts and club nights, while political and arty events take place in the daytime, and there's a *bal salsa* from 5pm on Sunday afternoons. Mº Porte-de-Bagnolet.

**La Guinguette Pirate quai François Mauriac, 13ᵉ** ℡01.52.61.08.49. Beautiful Chinese barge, moored alongside the quay in front of the Bibliothèque Nationale, hosting relaxed but upbeat world music nights from Tuesday to Sunday. Your best bet for an inexpensive (€6) good night out. Mº Quai-de-la-Gare.

**Maison des Cultures du Monde 101 bd Raspail, 6ᵉ** ℡01.45.44.72.30, ⊛www.mcm.asso.fr. All the arts from all over the world, for once not dominated by Europeans. Runs its own world music label, Inedit, and holds a festival of world theatre and music in March. Mº Rennes.

**Maroquinerie 23 rue Boyer, 20ᵉ** ℡01.40.33.30.60. The smallish concert venue is the downstairs part of a trendy arts centre. The line-up is rock, folk and jazz, with a particularly good selection of French musicians. Mº Gambetta.

**Péniche Makara quai François Mauriac, 13ᵉ** ℡01.44.24.09.00. Another barge moored to the banks of the Seine, this time with a chilled-out reggae and world flavour. Mº Quai-de-la-Gare. Tues–Sun 6pm–2am.

**Trabendo Parc de la Villette, 19ᵉ** ℡01.49.25.81.75. The ex-Hot Brass revamped and with a wider range of programming – world, jazz and rock, as well as big name French and international acts. Open nights of concerts only. Mº Porte-de-Pantin.

# Jazz, blues and chansons

**Jazz** has long enjoyed an appreciative audience in France, most especially since the end of World War II, when the intellectual rigour and agonized musings of bebop struck an immediate chord of sympathy in the existentialist hearts of the *après-guerre*. Charlie Parker, Dizzy Gillespie, Miles Davis – all were being listened to in the 1950s, when in Britain their names were known only to a tiny coterie of fans.

Gypsy guitarist Django Reinhardt and his partner, violinist Stéphane Grappelli, whose work represents the distinctive and undisputed French contribution to the jazz canon, had much to do with the music's popularity. But it was also greatly enhanced by the presence of many front-rank black American musicians, for whom Paris was a haven of freedom and culture after the racial prejudice and philistinism of the States. Among them were the soprano sax player Sidney Bechet, who set up in legendary partnership with French clarinettist Claude Luther, and Bud Powell, whose turbulent exile partly inspired the tenor man played by Dexter Gordon (himself a veteran of the Montana club) in the film *Round Midnight*.

Jazz is still alive and well in the city, with a good selection of clubs plying all styles from New Orleans to current experimental. Frequent **festivals** are also a good source of concerts, particularly in the summer (see "Festivals", p.41). Some names to look out for are saxophonist Didier Malherbe; violinist Didier Lockwood; British-born but long resident in Paris, guitarist John McLaughlin; pianist Alain JeanMarie; clarinettist Louis Sclavis; and accordionist Richard Galliano, who updates the French *musette* style. All of them can be found playing small gigs, regardless of the size of their reputations. Bistrots and bars are a good place to catch musicians carrying on the tradition of Django Reinhardt – Romane and the Ferré brothers are just some of musicians doing the rounds – as well as French traditional *chansons*. Gigs aren't usually advertised in the press, but you'll see handmade posters in the bistrots themselves, or you could check out the sites ⓦwww.zingueurs.com and ⓦwww.jazzfrance.com.

## Mainly jazz

**Le Baiser Salé 58 rue des Lombards, 1er** ☏01.42.33.37.71. A bar downstairs and a small, crowded upstairs room with live music every night from 10pm – usually jazz, rhythm & blues, Latino-rock, reggae or Brazilian. Admission €8–15. Mº Châtelet. Mon–Sat 8pm–5am.

**Le Bilboquet 13 rue St-Benoît, 6e** ☏01.45.48.81.84. A smart, comfortable bar/restaurant with live jazz every night, featuring local and international stars. The music starts at 10.45pm and food is served until 1am. No admission fee, but pricey drinks (€18.50). Mº St-Germain. Mon–Sat 9pm–dawn.

**Caveau de la Huchette 5 rue de la Huchette, 5e** ☏01.43.26.65.05. A wonderful slice of old Parisian life in an otherwise touristy area. Both Sidney Bechet and Lionel Hampton played here. Live jazz, usually trad and big band, to dance to on a floor surrounded by tiers of benches, and a bar decorated with caricatures of the barman drawn on any material to hand. Mº St-Michel. Daily 9.30pm–2am or later. Sun–Thurs €9; Fri & Sat €13; drinks from €4. Fri–Sun 5–9pm, happy hour with swing, free entrance.

**Au Duc des Lombards 42 rue des Lombards, 1er** ☏01.42.33.22.88, ⓦwww.jazzvalley.com/duc. Small, unpretentious bar with performances every night from 9pm. This is the place to hear gypsy jazz, as well as jazz piano, blues, ballads and fusion. Sometimes has big names. Admission €16–19; drinks from €4.50. Mº Châtelet/Les-Halles. Daily until 3am.

**L'Eustache 37 rue Berger, 1er** ☏01.40.26.23.20. Young and friendly Les Halles café, the cheapest place to hear good jazz in the capital. Live jazz 9.30pm–2am on Thurs. Mº Châtelet/Les-Halles. Daily 11am–4am.

**Instants Chavirés 7 rue Richard-Lenoir, Montreuil** ☏01.42.87.25.91, ⓦwww.instantschavires.fr.st. Avant-garde jazz joint – no comforts – on the eastern

## A note on prices

For virtually all the jazz clubs listed, expense is a real drawback to enjoyment – *Utopia* and *L'Eustache* are the cheaper ones. Admission charges are generally high, and, when they're not levied, there's usually a whacking charge for your first drink. Subsequent drinks, too, are absurdly priced – about twice what you'd pay in a similar club in London, and more than double what you'd pay in New York.

edge of the city, close to the Porte de Montreuil. A place where musicians go to hear each other play; its reputation has attracted subsidies from both state and local authorities. Admission €11. M° Robespierre. Tues–Sat 8pm–1am; concerts at 9pm.

**Lionel Hampton Bar** Hôtel Méridien, 81 bd Gouvion-St-Cyr, 17ᵉ ☎01.40.68.30.42. First-rate jazz venue with big-name musicians. Inaugurated by Himself, but otherwise the great man is only an irregular visitor. Admission €23–25. M° Porte-Maillot. Mon–Sat 10pm–2am.

**Quai du Blues** 17 bd Vital-Bouhot, Île de la Jatte, Neuilly ☎01.46.24.22.00, ⊛www.quaidublues.com. Not the most central of places to get to, but worth the hike if you're a blues fan. Mainly blues, R&B, gospel by American musicians. There's also a restaurant (set menu from €24). Admission €15. M° Pont-de-Levallois, then down the steps from the bridge. Thurs–Sat, 8.30pm onwards.

**New Morning** 7–9 rue des Petites-Écuries, 10ᵉ ☎01.45.23.51.41, ⊛www.newmorning.com. The decor's somewhat spartan, resembling an underground garage, but this is the place to catch the big international names in jazz. Get here early or it's likely to be standing room only. Admission around €19. M° Château-d'Eau. Usually Mon–Sat 9pm–1.30am (concerts start around 9.30pm).

**Le Petit Journal** 71 bd St-Michel, 5ᵉ ☎01.43.26.28.59. Small, smoky bar, long frequented by Left-Bank student-types, though these days it's rather middle-aged and touristy. Plays good, mainly French, traditional and mainstream sounds. Admission €15; €31–40 including meal. RER Luxembourg. Mon–Sat 9pm–2am; closed Aug.

**Le Petit Journal Montparnasse** 13 rue du Commandant-Mouchotte, 14ᵉ ☎01.43.21.56.70. Under the Hôtel Montparnasse, and sister establishment to the above, with bigger visiting names, both French and international. Admission free; first drink €16.77. M° Montparnasse-Bienvenüe. Mon–Sat 9pm–2am.

**Le Petit Opportun** 15 rue des Lavandières-Ste-Opportune, 1ᵉʳ ☎01.42.36.01.36. It's worth arriving early to get a seat for the live music in the dungeon-like cellar, where the acoustics play strange tricks and you can't

always see the musicians. Fairly eclectic policy and a crowd of genuine connoisseurs. The first set starts at 10.30pm. Admission €13–16. M° Châtelet-Les Halles. Tues–Sat 9pm–dawn; closed Aug.

**Les 7 Lézards** 10 rue des Rosiers, 4ᵉ ☎01.48.87.08.97, ⊛www.7lezards.com. A recently established jazz club, with a cosy, intimate atmosphere, that has already made a name for itself, attracting local and international acts alike. There's also a restaurant. Admission €10–16. M° St-Paul. Wed–Sat 7.15pm–2am.

**Slow Club** 130 rue de Rivoli, 1ᵉʳ ☎01.42.33.84.30. Jazz club where you can bop the night away to the sounds of Claude Luther's quintet and visiting New Orleans musicians. Admission €9–13 (students €9). M° Châtelet/Pont-Neuf. Tues & Thurs–Sat 9.30pm–4am.

**Le Sunset/Le Sunside** 60 rue des Lombards, 1ᵉʳ ☎01.40.26.46.20. Two clubs in one: Le Sunside on the ground floor features mostly traditional jazz, whereas the downstairs Sunset is a venue for electric and fusion jazz. The Sunside concert usually starts at 9pm, the Sunset at 10pm, so you can sample a bit of both. Attracts some of the best musicians – the likes of pianist Alain JeanMarie and Turk Mauro. Admission €12–20. M° Châtelet/Les-Halles. Mon–Sat 9.30pm–2.30am.

**Utopia** 1 rue de l'Ouest, 14ᵉ ☎01.43.22.79.66. No genius here, but good atmosphere and good French blues singers interspersed with jazz and blues tapes, and a mostly young and studenty crowd. Admission free. M° Pernety. Mon–Sat 10pm–dawn; closed Aug.

## Mainly chansons

**Casino de Paris** 19 rue de Clichy, 9ᵉ ☎01.49.95.99.99, ⊛www.casinodeparis.fr. This decaying, once-plush casino in one of the seediest streets in Paris is a venue for all sorts of performances – chansons, poetry combined with flamenco guitar, cabaret. Check the listings magazines under "Variétés" and "Chansons". Tickets from €17 upwards. M° Trinité.

**Le Lapin Agile** 22 rue des Saules, 18ᵉ ☎01.46.06.85.87, ⊛www.au-lapin-agile.com. Old haunt of Apollinaire, Utrillo and other Montmartre artists, some of whose pictures adorn the walls. Cabaret, poetry and

*chansons.* You may be lucky enough to catch singer-composer Arlette Denis, who carries Jacques Brel's flame. €24 including first drink, students €17 (except Sat); subsequent drinks €7. M° Lamarck-Caulaincourt. Tues–Sun 9pm–2am.
**Le Magique 42 rue de Gergovie, 14ᵉ** ℡**01.45.42.26.10.** Bar and "*chanson*

cellar" with traditional French *chanson* performances by lesser-known stars during the week – at weekends the owner takes to the piano. Admission is free, payment for the show is at your own discretion, and drinks are very reasonably priced. M° Pernety. Wed–Sat 10pm–2am.

# Classical music

Paris is a stimulating environment for **classical** music, both established and contemporary. The former is well represented with a choice of ten to twenty concerts every day of the week, with numerous performances making the most of churches' fine acoustics, often for free or relatively little. Excellent chamber music can be heard in the fine settings of the Musée du Louvre and Musée d'Orsay. The main **orchestras** to look out for are the Orchestre de Paris, which has built up a formidable reputation under Christopher Eschenbach, and the Orchestre National de France, which has just come under the baton of Kurt Masur.

**Early music** has a dedicated following in Paris. The capital's most respected baroque ensemble is William Christie's Les Arts Florissants, known for their exciting renditions of Rameau's operas and choral pieces, and works by Lully and Charpentier. The highly regarded Marc Minkowski, another champion of French baroque music, also conducts regularly in the capital.

**Contemporary** and experimental computer-based work flourishes, too; leading exponents are Paul Mefano and Pierre Boulez, a pupil of Olivier Messiaen, the grand old man of modern French music, who died in 1992. Boulez's experiments have for many years received massive public funding in the form of a vast laboratory of acoustics and "digital signal processing" – a complex known as **IRCAM** (see opposite & p.102), housed next to the Pompidou Centre. Boulez no longer conducts IRCAM's acclaimed Ensemble InterContemporain (ⓦwww.ensembleinter.com) – it's currently under the direction of Jonathan Nott – but it still bears its creator's stamp and is committed to performing new work. Other Paris-based practitioners of contemporary and experimental music include Philippe Manoury, Jean-Claude Eloy, Pascal Dusapin and Luc Ferrarie. Among the younger generation of less sectarian composers, some names to look out for are Nicos Papadimitriou, Thierry Pécourt, François Leclere, Marc Dalbavie, Yan Mharesz, and Georges Aperghis, whose speciality is musical theatre.

The city hosts a good number of **music festivals**, which vary from year to year; the major ones are listed on pp.41–43. For more details, pick up the current year's festival schedule from any of the tourist offices or the Hôtel de Ville, 29 rue du Rivoli, 4ᵉ (M° Hôtel-de-Ville).

Two **periodicals** devoted to the music scene are the monthly *Le Monde de la Musique* and *Diapason*. Two free monthlies – *Cadences* and *La Terrasse* – are distributed outside concert venues. Good, general **websites** include ⓦwww.arpeggione.fr and ⓦwww.concertclassic.com.

## Regular concert venues

**Tickets** for classical concerts are best bought at the box offices, though for big names you may find overnight queues, and a large number of seats are always booked by subscribers. The price range is very reasonable. The listings magazines and daily newspapers will have details of concerts in the following venues, in the churches and in the suburbs. Look out for posters as well.

## Auditoriums and Theatres

**Cité de la Musique** 221 av Jean-Jaurès, 19ᵉ ☎01.44.84.44.84 for the Salle des Concerts, ⊛www.cite-musique.fr. Adjustable concert hall with seating for 800–1200 listeners depending on the programme, which can cover anything from traditional Korean music to the contemporary sounds of the Ensemble InterContemporain. Performances also in the museum amphitheatre with the occasional airing of instruments from the museum. Ticket prices range from €6.50 to €25. Mᵒ Jaurès.

**Conservatoire National Supérieur de Musique et de Danse de Paris** 209 av Jean Jaurès, 19ᵉ ☎01.40.40.46.46, ⊛www.cnsmdp.fr. Debates, master-classes and free performances from the conservatoire's students. Mᵒ Porte-de-Pantin.

**IRCAM (Institut de Recherche et Coordination Acoustique/Musique)** 1 pl Igor Stravinsky, 4ᵉ ☎01.44.78.48.16, ⊛www.ircam.fr. IRCAM, the experimental music laboratory set up by Pierre Boulez, has begun opening its doors for regular concerts and also performs in the main hall of the nearby Pompidou Centre. Ticket prices vary. Mᵒ Hôtel-de-Ville.

**Maison de Radio France** 116 av du Président-Kennedy, 16ᵉ ☎01.56.40.15.16, ⊛radio-france.fr. Radio station France Musique programmes an excellent range of classical music, operas, jazz and world music and sometimes puts on free concerts – just turn up half an hour in advance to claim your *carton d'invitation*. Tickets €7.50–55. Mᵒ Passy.

**Salle Gaveau** 45 rue de la Boétie, 8ᵉ ☎01.49.53.05.07. This atmospheric concert hall has recently been renovated and can now host full orchestral concerts as well as chamber music. Ticket prices from €12–30. Mᵒ Saint-Augustin.

**Salle Pleyel** 252 rue du Faubourg-St-Honoré, 8ᵉ ☎01.45.61.53.00, ⊛www.salle-pleyel.fr. Closed for renovation until spring 2004.

The Orchestre de Paris, the city's top orchestra, performs here most frequently along with visiting international performers. Ticket prices €14–84. Mᵒ Concorde.

**Théâtre des Champs-Élysées** 15 av Montaigne, 8ᵉ ☎01.49.52.50.50, ⊛www.theatrechampselysees.fr. Two-thousand-seat capacity in this historic theatre built in 1913. Home to the Orchestre National de France under Kurt Masur and the Orchestre Lamoureux, but also hosts international superstar conductors, ballet troupes and operas. Ticket prices €5–110. Mᵒ Alma-Marceau.

**Theatre Mogador** 25 rue Mogador, 9ᵉ ☎01.453.32.32.00, ⊛www.mogador.net. This old music hall is currently enjoying a new lease of life as a serious venue for classical music while the Salle Pleyel (see above) undergoes renovation. Ticket prices vary. Mᵒ Lazare.

**Théâtre Musical de Paris** Théâtre du Châtelet, 1 pl du Châtelet, 1ᵉʳ ☎01.40.28.28.00, ⊛www.chatelet-theatre.com. Puts on operas, ballets, concerts and solo recitals. Ticket prices range from €11 to €106. Mᵒ Châtelet.

## Churches and Museums

**La Madeleine** pl de la Madeleine, 8ᵉ ☎01.42.50.96.18. Organ recitals and choral concerts. €15–23. Mᵒ Madeleine.

**Musée du Louvre** palais du Louvre, 1ᵉʳ ☎01.40.20.84.00, ⊛www.louvre.fr. Midday and evening concerts of chamber music in the auditorium. €10–23. Mᵒ Louvre-Rivoli/Palais-Royal-Musée-du-Louvre.

**Musée d'Orsay** 1 rue de Bellechasse, 7ᵉ ☎01.40.49.47.57, ⊛www.musee-orsay.fr. Varied programme of midday and evening recitals of chamber music in the auditorium. €15–25. Mᵒ Solférino/RER Musée d'Orsay.

**St-Julien-le-Pauvre** 23 quai de Montebello, 5ᵉ ☎01.42.26.00.00. Varied programmes. €13–23. Mᵒ St-Michel.

**St-Séverin** 5 rue des Prêtres St-Séverin, 5ᵉ, ☎01.48.24.16.97. Varied programmes. €15–23. Mᵒ St-Michel.

**Ste-Chapelle** 4 bd du Palais, 1ᵉʳ ☎01.42.77.65.65. A fabulous setting for mainly early-music chamber and choral concerts. €15–23. Mᵒ Cité.

# Opera

The Opéra National de Paris has two homes, the original **Palais Garnier** (see p.85), place de l'Opéra, 9$^e$ (M° Opéra), and the **Opéra Bastille** (see pp.113 & 328), 120 rue de Lyon, 12$^e$ (M° Bastille), Mitterrand's most extravagant legacy to the city, which opened, with all due pomp, in 1989. Its first years however were far from easy; it was beset from the start by politico-musical wranglings resulting in a series of resignations, including that of Daniel Barenboim as musical director, followed soon after by the dismissal of Rudolph Nureyev from the same post. His successor, the relatively unknown South Korean, Myung Whun Chung (now successfully directing the Orchestre Philharmonique de Radio France), proved to be a controversial though popular musical director, but was sacked by the new chief, Hughes Gall. Things do at last seem to be settling down and there's been a period of stability under the current musical director James Conlon.

It's taken Parisians a while to warm to their new opera house, a rather bloated construction that completely dominates the place de la Bastille. The building hasn't worn particularly well either: the facade has started to crumble in places and unsightly netting holds bits of it in place. Opinions differ over the acoustics, but the stage is certainly well designed and allows the auditorium uninterrupted views. Under the baton of James Conlon, productions have been critically acclaimed and very popular – booking well in advance is recommended. Whether the new opera house has succeeded in bringing "opera to the masses", as was Mitterrand's vision, is debatable, but tickets are certainly reasonably priced.

The restored, lavish **Palais Garnier** is generally used for smaller-scale productions and ballets. It may not enjoy the high-tech facilities of the Bastille and views from some of the side seats can be very poor, but an evening in this glittering palace is unforgettable.

**Tickets** (€10–109) for operas at both venues can be booked Monday to Saturday 9am to 7pm on ℡08.36.69.78.68 at least four weeks in advance, via the Internet (⊛www.opera-de-paris.fr) from three months to three days in advance, or at the ticket office (Mon–Sat 11am–6.30pm) within two weeks of the performance – the number of tickets available by this stage however is limited and people start queuing at 9am, if not earlier. Unfilled seats are sold at a discount to students five minutes before the curtain goes up. For programme details, have a look at their website or call the above number.

The Bastille opera house enjoys a friendly rivalry with the **Théâtre Musical de Paris**, part of the Théâtre du Châtelet (see above), which also stages large-scale opera productions. In addition, occasional operas and concerts by solo singers are hosted by the **Théâtre des Champs-Élysées** (see p.75). Solo singers are guests at the **Salle Favart** (Opéra Comique), which also puts on daring classic and modern operas and musicals (see p.326). Both opera and recitals are sometimes staged at the multipurpose performance halls (see opposite).

# Major concert venues

Events at any of the performance spaces listed below will be well advertised on billboards and posters throughout the city. Tickets can be obtained at the halls themselves, though it's easier to get them through agents like FNAC or Virgin Megastore (see pp.332, 342 & 343).

**Olympia** 28 bd des Capucines, 9ᵉ
☎01.47.42.25.49, ⊚www.olympiahall.com.
Recently renovated old-style music hall
hosting well-known international rock and
pop acts, with a good programme of
domestic stars as well. Mᵒ
Madeleine/Opéra.

**Palais des Congrès** pl de la Porte-Maillot, 17ᵉ
☎01.40.68.00.05, ⊚www
.palaisdescongres-paris.com. Opera, ballet,
orchestral music, trade fairs, and middle-of-
the-road superstars. Mᵒ Porte-Maillot.

**Palais Omnisports de Bercy** 8 bd de Bercy,
12ᵉ ☎08.92.69.23.00, ⊚www.bercy.fr. Opera,
cycle racing, Bruce Springsteen, ice
hockey, and Citroën launches – a multipurpose stadium, with seats that give vertigo
to the most level-headed. Mᵒ Bercy.

**Palais des Sports** Porte de Versailles, 15ᵉ
☎01.48.28.40.10, ⊚www.palaisdessports.com.

Another vast auditorium, ideal for stadium
rock and giant French musicals. Mᵒ Porte-
de-Versailles.

**Stade de France** St-Denis ☎08.92.70.09.00,
⊚www.stadefrance.fr. One-hundred-thou-
sand capacity stadium, purpose-built for
France's hosting of the 1998 Football
World Cup and doubling up for use by
stadium-rockers. RER B La-Plaine-Stade-
de-France/RER D Stade-de-France-St-
Denis.

**Zenith** Parc de la Villette, 211 av Jean-Jaurès,
20ᵉ ☎01.42.08.60.00, ⊚www.le-zenith
.com/paris. Seating for 6000 in a giant tent
designed exclusively for rock and pop concerts, with a good programme including relatively forward-looking acts like Coldplay
and Morcheeba. Head for the concrete
column with a descending red aeroplane.
Mᵒ Porte-de-Pantin.

# 18

# Film, theatre and dance

Moviegoers have a choice of around three hundred **films** showing in any one week. The scene isn't limited to contemporary French films and Hollywood budget-busters, though there are plenty of these, but takes in classics from all eras and a diverse spread of films from all over the world. In Paris, you can walk into a beautiful old cinema and watch a film that you'd struggle to find on video in another city.

The city also has a vibrant **theatre** scene. Several superstar directors are based here, such as Peter Brook and Ariane Mnouchkine, renowned for their highly innovative, cutting-edge performances. As an obvious stop-off point for touring troupes, Paris is also a great place to catch the pick of the season's festivals. More space is slowly being given over to the exciting developments in **dance** and multi-genre stage performances, some of it incorporating mime, which, alas, is rarely performed in its own right these days.

As for **cabarets**, with names that conjure up the classic connotations of the sinful city – the *Lido* or the *Moulin Rouge* – they thrive off group bookings for a dinner-and-show formula that is extortionately priced, and retains none of the populist, bawdy atmosphere depicted in Toulouse-Lautrec's sketches. For details, see box on p.173.

**Listings** for all films and stage productions are detailed in *Pariscope* (see p.22) and other weeklies, with brief résumés or reviews. Venues with wheelchair access will say "accessible aux handicapés". Note that it's common practice in Parisian theatres and occasionally in independent cinemas for the ushers to expect a small **tip** from each customer (€1 or so).

## Film

Paris remains one of the few cities in the world in which it's possible to get not only serious entertainment but a serious film education from the programmes of regular – never mind specialist – **cinemas**. A few of the more obscure movie houses may have closed in recent years, but plenty of others remain and continue to resist the popcorn-touting clout of the big chains, UGC and Gaumont, by screening classic and contemporary films.

If your French is up to it, you can watch your way through the entire careers of individual directors in the **mini-festivals** held at many independent cinemas, notably the Action chain, the Escurial, the Entrepôt and Le Studio 28. And if you can read French subtitles, you can go and see a Senegalese, Brazilian or Finnish film that might never be screened in Britain or the US. Even if you have no French at all, it's easy to find **v.o.** (*version originale*) films, both modern and classic. The alternative, to be avoided where possible, is **v.f.** (*version française*), which means the film has been dubbed into French. You may also see v.a. (*version anglaise*), which means the film is the English version of an international co-production. Listings for all films are detailed in **Pariscope** (see p.22).

The **Quartier Latin**, around the Sorbonne, has a particularly high concentration of arts cinemas showing an almost incredible repertoire of classic films, while the area around the Gare Montparnasse is chock-full with big-screen movie-houses offering the latest glossy releases. For the biggest screen of all, check-out the Gaumont cinema on Place de l'Italie. Some of the **foreign institutes** in the city have occasional screenings, so if your favourite director is a Hungarian, a Swede or a Korean, check what's on at those countries' cultural centres. These will be listed along with other cinema-clubs and museum screenings under "Séances exceptionnelles" or "Ciné-clubs", and are usually cheaper than ordinary cinemas.

*Séances* (programmes) start between 1 and 3pm at many places, sometimes as early as 11am, and usually continue through to the early hours. **Tickets** rarely need to be purchased in advance, and they're cheap by European standards. An average price is €8, though prices are a couple of euros lower at many independent cinemas, and almost all venues have reductions for students and the unemployed, at least from Monday to Thursday. Some matinée *séances* also carry discounts. For long-termers, UGC, MK2 and Gaumont sell various booklets of tickets and subscriptions, and some independents offer a *carte de fidélité*, giving you a free sixth entry. All Paris's cinemas are non-smoking.

## Cinemas

**L'Arlequin 76 rue de Rennes, 6ᵉ.** Owned by Jacques Tati in the 1950s, then by the Soviet Union as the Cosmos cinema until 1990, L'Arlequin has now been renovated and is once again *the* cinephile's palace in the Latin Quarter. There are special screenings of classics every Sunday at 11am, followed by debates in the café opposite. M° St-Sulpice.

**L'Entrepôt 7–9 rue Francis-de-Pressensé, 14ᵉ** @www.lentrepot.fr. One of the best alternative Paris cinemas, which has been keeping ciné-addicts happy for years with its three screens dedicated to the obscure, the subversive and the brilliant, as well as its bookshop and bar-restaurant. M° Pernety.

**L'Escurial Panorama 11 bd de Port-Royal, 13ᵉ.** Combining plush seats, big screen, and more art than commerce in its programming policy, this cinema is likely to be showing a French classic on the small screen and the latest offering from a big-name director – French, Japanese or American – on the panoramic screen (never dubbed). M° Gobelins.

**Forum des Images 2 Grande Galerie, Porte St-Eustache, Forum des Halles, 1ᵉʳ** @www.forumdesimages.net. This venue screens several films or videos daily, but also has a large library of newsreel footage, film clips, adverts, documentaries, etc – all connected with Paris – that you can access yourself from a computer terminal. You can make your choice via a Paris place name, an actor, a director, a date, and so on; there are instructions in English at the desk, and a friendly librarian to help you out. €5.50 for two hours research, plus any films shown that day. RER Châtelet-Les Halles. Tues–Sun 1–9pm, Thurs till 10pm.

**Gaumont Grand Écran Italie 30 pl d'Italie, 13ᵉ.** Three screens, including the 24-metrewide *grand écran*. Big-draw movies inevitably, with all foreign titles dubbed. M° Place-d'Italie.

**Grand Action and Action Écoles 5 & 23 rue des Écoles, 5ᵉ (M° Cardinal-Lemoine/Maubert-Mutualité); Action Christine Odéon, 4 rue Christine, 6ᵉ (M° Odéon/St-Michel).** The Action chain specializes in new prints of old classics and screens contemporary films from

Parisians have treated **cinema** as an art form ever since the first projection by the **Lumière** brothers "Cinematograph" at the Parisian *Grand Café du Boulevard des Capucines* in 1895. The 1930s were the golden age of French cinema, as stars of musicals and theatres invaded the cinemas, many of them on liberally censored film vehicles that helped create the French reputation for naughtiness. Meanwhile, more artistically minded *auteurs* were scripting, directing and producing moody, often melodramatic films. The key figure was **Jean Renoir**, son of the Impressionist painter Auguste Renoir. For Parisian scenes, check out his left-wing **Le Crime de Monsieur Lange** (1935), set in a printshop in the then-crumbling Marais. The movement known as Poetic Realism grew up around Renoir and the director Marcel Carné, who made the Canal St-Martin area of Paris famous in **Hôtel du Nord** (1938), a film that starred Arletty, the great populist actress of the 30s and 40s. Arletty and Poetic Realism reached their apogee in Carné's wonderful **Les Enfants du Paradis** (1945), set in the theatrical world of nineteenth-century Paris, with a script by the poet Jacques Prévert.

After the war, the state stepped in to boost French cinema, levying taxes on box-office sales, and subsidizing art cinema (as it still does today). Renoir continued to make great films: his **French CanCan** (1955) is *the* film about the Moulin Rouge and the heyday of Montmartre, though it was all shot in the studio. In 1959, the **Nouvelle Vague** ("New Wave") set about changing all that. Among the seminal works of the movement, **Les Quatre Cents Coups** (1959), by François Truffaut, and **A Bout de Souffle** (1959), by Jean-Luc Godard, both have contemporary Paris as the real star, their directors daring to take their new, lightweight cameras out onto the streets. Perhaps the best collaboration between the city and the directors of the Nouvelle Vague is **Paris Vu Par** (*Six in Paris*; 1965), a collection of six shorts by the key figures of the genre, including the prolific Claude Chabrol and Eric Rohmer. Other directors associated with the Nouvelle Vague have turned out to be less wedded to its values: the career of the director Louis Malle encompasses an underwater film with Jacques Cousteau, the quirky **Zazie dans le Métro** (1961) – a real Paris spectacular – and the moving international hit, *Aux Revoir Les Enfants* (1987). For Parisian settings, few films do better than Agnès Varda's **Cléo de 5 à 7** (1962), which depicts two hours in the life of a singer as she moves through the city.

Since Claude Berri's *Jean de Florette* (1986), which launched the international career of Gérard Depardieu, the French film industry has increasingly concentrated on glossier, more exportable "heritage" movies, which do the city few favours. Balancing the historical spectaculars, but equally exportable, has been the movement known as the **Cinéma du Look**, producing cool, image-conscious films such as Jean-Pierre Jeunet's outright cranky *Delicatessen* (1991), Jean-Jacques Beineix's *Diva* (1981) and *Betty Blue* (1986), and Luc Besson's *Nikita* (1990) and **Subway** (1985), set in the RER stations at La Défense and Les Halles. Much edgier was Mathieu Kassovitz's **La Haine** (1996), an original portrayal of exclusion and racism in the Paris *banlieue*. More recently, Kassovitz had a massive international hit as an actor with the Jeunet-directed *Le Fabuleux destin d'Amélie Poulain* (2001), better known in Anglophone markets as **Amélie**.

For more information on cinema in France, the **website** Ⓦ www.filmsdefrance .com has excellent listings of French films, searchable by year or by name, as well as directors' and actors' biographies. The best Parisian source of information on films is the Les Halles *videothèque* (see p.353).

around the world. A *carnet* of ten tickets costs €40.

**Le Grand Rex 1 bd Poissonnière, 2ᵉ.** Just as outrageous as La Pagode (see opposite),

but in the kitsch line, with a *Metropolis*-style tower blazing its neon name, 2750 seats and a ceiling of stars and Moorish city sky-line. The ultimate Thirties public movie-seeing experience, though you're most likely to be watching a blockbuster and, if foreign, it'll be dubbed. Mº Bonne-Nouvelle.

**Le Latina 20 rue du Temple, 4ᵉ.** Specializes in Latin American, Portuguese, Italian and Spanish films, as well as food, art and tango, salsa and flamenco sessions in its restaurant and gallery spaces. Mº Hôtel-de-Ville.

**Lucernaire Forum 53 rue Notre-Dame-des-Champs, 6ᵉ.** An art complex with three screening rooms, two theatres, an art gallery, bar and restaurant. Shows old arty movies and undubbed current films from around the world. Mº Notre-Dame-des-Champs/Vavin.

**Max Linder Panorama 24 bd Poissonnière, 9ᵉ.** Opposite Le Grand Rex, this Art Deco cinema always big a screen, this Art Deco cinema always shows films in the original and has state-of-the-art sound. Mº Bonne-Nouvelle.

**MK2 Quai de la Seine 14 quai de la Seine, 19ᵉ.** On the banks of the Bassin de la Villette. Part of the MK2 chain but distinctive in style – it's covered in famous cinematic quotes and has a varied art-house repertoire. Mº Jaurès/Stalingrad.

**La Pagode 57bis rue de Babylone, 7ᵉ.** The most beautiful of the city's cinemas, transplanted from Japan at the turn of the last century to be a rich Parisienne's party place. The wall panels of the Grande Salle auditorium are embroidered in silk; golden dragons and elephants hold up the candelabra; and a battle between Japanese and Chinese warriors rages on the ceiling. Financial problems have made its future uncertain but at the time of writing it was due to keep going; check *Pariscope* for details. Mº François-Xavier.

**Reflet Medicis Logos, Quartier Latin and Le Champo 3 rue Champollion, 9 rue Champollion and 51 rue des Écoles, 5ᵉ.** A cluster of inventive, scruffy little cinemas, tirelessly offering up rare screenings and classics, including frequent retrospective cycles covering great directors, both French and international (always in *v.o*). The small cinema café *Le Reflet*, on the other side of the street, is a little-known cult classic in itself. Mº Cluny-La-Sorbonne/Odéon.

**Le Studio 28 10 rue de Tholozé, 18ᵉ.** In its early days, after one of the first showings of Buñuel's *L'Age d'Or*, this was done over by extreme right-wing Catholics who destroyed the screen and the paintings by Dalí and Ernst in the foyer. The cinema still hosts avant-garde premières, followed occasionally by discussions with the director, as well as regular festivals. Mº Blanche/Abbesses.

**Le Studio des Cinéastes – Les Ursulines 10 rue des Ursulines, 5ᵉ.** *The Blue Angel* had its world première here and avant-garde movies are still premièred here, often followed by in-house debates with the directors and actors. Mº Censier-Daubenton.

## Cinémathèques

For the seriously committed film-freak, the best movie venues in Paris are the **cinémathèques**. The **Cinémathèque Française** (Ⓦ www .cinemathequefrancaise.com) is currently housed in two separate locations: the Salle du Palais Chaillot, 7 av Albert–de–Mun, 16ᵉ (Mº Trocadéro; Ⓣ01.56.26.01.01), and the Salle Grands Boulevards, 42 bd Bonne Nouvelle, 10ᵉ (Mº Bonne-Nouvelle; closed Mon; Ⓣ01.56.26.01.01). By 2005 the whole thing should be reunited, along with the museum of cinema, at 51 rue de Bercy. It gives you a choice of more than fifty different films a week, many of which would never be shown commercially, and tickets are only €5 (€3 for students and members). The **Forum des Images** (Ⓣ01.44.76.62.00, Ⓦ www .forumdesimages.net), in the Forum des Halles (see p.93), is another excellent-value venue for the bizarre or obscure on screen. Their repertoires are always based around a particular theme, often with some connection to Paris. The €5.50 entrance fee (€4.50 for anyone under 30 or over 60) allows you access all day to as many screenings as you can stomach, as well as private video viewings in the archive, or *vidéothèque* (see p.353).

Cultural institutions also have their own cinemathèques, notably the Auditorium du Louvre, Palais du Louvre, 1ᵉʳ (Mº Palais-Royal-Louvre; Ⓣ01.40.20.84.00, Ⓦ www.louvre.fr), and the Pompidou Centre, place Georges-Pompidou, 4ᵉ (Mº Rambuteau; Ⓣ01.44.78.12.33).

While it doesn't sink quite as low as its Mediterranean neighbours, **French TV** is hardly a beacon of French culture – though media "intellectuals" get a surprising amount of airtime, pontificating about politics, culture or other talk shows. Programming is dominated by such celebrity-led talking shops, as well as game shows, bought-in Transatlantic soaps and, increasingly, reality TV – notably the titillating *Loft Story*, France's take on Big Brother.

There are six channels (see "Basics" p.39 for details). Arte and La Cinq are two different channels sharing the same frequency. La Cinq, an educational channel, broadcasts during the day, then at 7pm, Arte, a joint Franco–German cultural venture, takes over. Its highbrow programmes, daily documentaries, art criticism, serious French and German movies and complete operas are transmitted simultaneously in French and German. Canal Plus is the main movie channel (and financer of the French film industry), with repeats of foreign films usually shown at least once in the original language. F3 screens a fair selection of serious movies, with its Cinéma de Minuit slot late on Sunday nights good for foreign, undubbed films.

### Film festivals

The **International Festival of Women's Films**, held in the last week in March, is organized by the Maison des Arts in Créteil (℡01.49.80.38.98, Ⓦwww.filmsdefemmes.com; M° Créteil-Préfecture). At the same time of year (from mid-March to the end of the month) and also in the suburbs, in Bobigny to the northeast of the city, the Magic Cinéma (rue du Chemin-Vert, 93000 Bobigny; ℡01.41.60.12 .34, Ⓦhttp://perso.wanadoo.fr/magic .cinema/) runs the festival **Théâtres au Cinéma**, which concentrates on the links between literature and the cinema. More mainstream films are

previewed at the end of March at the **Festival du Film de Paris**, which takes place at the Cinéma Gaumont Marignan at 27–33 av des Champs-Élysées, 8e (℡01.45.72.96.40, Ⓦwww .festivaldufilmdeparis.com).

During the summer, the Parc de la Villette (M° Porte-de-Pantin) organizes the **Festival du Cinéma en Plein Air** (℡01.40.03.75.75, Ⓦwww.la-villette.com; free). Films based on changing themes are shown every night at sunset (usually from the second week in July to mid-August at around 10pm) to an audience of picnickers on the grass. Deckchairs (€6.10) are available for hire, too.

## Theatre

Certain directors in France do extraordinary things with the medium of **theatre**. Classic texts are shuffled into theatrical moments, where spectacular and dazzling sensation takes precedence over speech. Their shows are overwhelming: huge casts, vast sets (sometimes real buildings never before used for theatre), exotic lighting effects, original music scores. It adds up to a unique experience, even if you haven't understood a word. The director par excellence of this form is **Ariane Mnouchkine**, whose **Théâtre du Soleil** is based at the Cartoucherie in Vincennes. **Peter Brook**, the English director based at the Bouffes du Nord theatre, is another great magician of the all-embracing several-day show. His most recent offering is an acclaimed production of *Hamlet*. Also a big name, though often involved in films rather than the theatre, is **Patrice Chéreau**. Any show by these three should not be missed, and there are likely to be other weird and wonderful productions by younger directors, such as **Jérôme Savary**, who produces an exciting programme of events at the Opéra Comique.

At the same time, bourgeois farces, postwar classics, Shakespeare, Racine and the like, are staged with the same range of talent, or lack of it, that you'd find in London or New York. What you'll rarely find are the homegrown, socially concerned and realist dramas of the sort that have in the past kept theatre alive in Britain. Edward Bond plays (scarcely performed now in the UK), in translation, are currently a regular feature on Parisian theatre programmes and productions of Sarah Kane's hard-hitting plays are proving quite successful – the French equivalents hardly exist.

The great generation of French or Francophone dramatists, which included Anouilh, Genet, Camus, Sartre, Adamov, Ionesco and Cocteau, came to an end with the death of **Samuel Beckett** in 1990 and **Ionesco** in 1994. Their plays, however, are still frequently performed. The Huchette has been playing Ionesco's *La Cantatrice Chauve* every night since October 1952, and the **Comédie Française**, the national theatre for the classics, is as likely to put on Genet's *Les Paravents*, which set off riots on its opening night, as Corneille and Racine.

One of the encouraging things about France and its public authorities is that they take their culture, including the theatre, seriously. Numerous theatres and theatre companies in Paris are subsidized, either wholly or in part, by the government or the Ville de Paris. And the suburbs are not left out, thanks to the ubiquitous **Maisons de la Culture**, which were the brainchild of man of letters André Malraux, de Gaulle's wartime aide, and eventually, in the 1960s, his Minister of Culture. Ironically, however, although they were designed to bring culture to the masses, their productions are often among the most "difficult" and intellectually inaccessible.

Another plus is the Parisian theatre's openness to **foreign influence** and foreign work. The troupe at the Théâtre du Soleil is made up of around twenty different nationalities, and foreign artists and directors are frequent visitors. In any month there might be an Italian, Mexican, German or Brazilian production playing in the original language, or offerings by radical groups from Turkey or China, who are denied a venue at home.

The best time of all for theatre lovers to come to Paris is for the **Festival d'Automne** from mid-September to mid-December (see p.42), an international celebration of all the performing arts, which attracts stage directors of the calibre of the American Bob Wilson, Canadian Robert Lepage and Polish director Tadeusz Kantor.

## Buying theatre tickets

The easiest place to get **tickets** to see a stage performance in Paris is from one of the **FNAC** shops or Virgin Megastore (see pp.332, 343 & 344). In addition, same-day tickets at half-price and €2.50 commission are available from the ticket kiosks on **place de la Madeleine**, 8ᵉ, opposite no. 15, and on the *parvis* of the **Gare du Montparnasse**, 14ᵉ (Tues–Sat 12.30–8pm, Sun 12.30–4pm), but queues can be very long. You can also book tickets **online** at ⓦ www.theatreonline.com.

**Booking** well in advance is essential for new productions and all shows by the superstar directors. **Prices** vary between around €8 and €30. Previews at half price are advertised in *Pariscope*, etc, and there are weekday discounts for students. Most theatres are closed on Sunday and Monday, and during August.

## Noteworthy venues

**Bouffes du Nord** 37bis bd de la Chapelle, 10ᵉ ☎01.46.07.34.50, ⊛www.bouffesdunord.com. Peter Brook's long-time Paris base, where he occasionally mounts epic productions. The rest of the time the theatre invites renowned international directors and hosts top-notch chamber music recitals. Mᵒ La Chapelle.

**Cartoucherie** rte du Champ-de-Manœuvre, 12ᵉ. This ex-army munitions dump is home to several cutting-edge theatre companies: the Théâtre du Soleil (see above; ☎01.43.74.24.08, ⊛www.theatre-du -soleil.fr); the French–Spanish troupe, Théâtre de l'Épée de Bois (☎01.43.08.39.74); the Théâtre de la Tempête (☎01.43.28.36.36); the Théâtre du Chaudron (☎01.43.28.97.04); and the Théâtre de l'Aquarium (☎01.43.74.99.61). Mᵒ Château-de-Vincennes.

**Comédie Française** 2 rue de Richelieu, 1ᵉʳ ☎01.44.58.15.15, ⊛www.comedie -francaise.fr. This venerable national theatre is a longstanding venue for the classics – Molière, Racine, Corneille – as well as Anouilh, Genet and the like. Mᵒ Palais-Royal.

**Maison des Arts de Créteil** pl Salvador-Allende, Créteil ☎01.45.13.19.19, ⊛www .maccreteil.com. As well as hosting the International Festival of Women's Films (see p.324), the Maison des Arts de Créteil also serves as a lively suburban theatre, with a festival of multicultural performances near the beginning of May, known as Festival Exit. Mᵒ Créteil-Préfecture.

**MC93** 1 bd Lénine, Bobigny ☎01.41.60.72.72, ⊛www.mc93.com. MC93 succeeds with highly challenging productions, and regularly invites in foreign directors. Mᵒ Pablo-Picasso.

**Odéon Théâtre de l'Europe** (national theatre), 1 pl Paul-Claudel, 6ᵉ ☎01.44.41.36.36, ⊛www.theatre-odeon.fr. Closed until autumn 2004 for renovation, this splendid Neoclassical theatre puts on contemporary plays by top directors such as Patrice Chéreau, as well as *version originale* productions by well-known foreign companies. During May 1968, the theatre was occupied by students and became an open parliament with the backing of its directors,

Jean-Louis Barrault (of Baptiste fame in *Les Enfants du Paradis*) and Madeleine Renaud, one of the great French stage actresses. Promptly sacked by de Gaulle's Minister for Culture, they formed a new company and moved to the disused Gare d'Orsay. Their final years in the Théâtre du Rond-Point gave Paris its best performances of Beckett. Mᵒ Odéon.

**Opéra Comique** pl Boïeldieu, rue Favart ☎01.42.44.45.46. Director Jérôme Savary's diverse and exciting programme blends all forms of stage arts: modern and classical opera, musicals, comedy, dance and pop music. Mᵒ Richelieu-Drouot.

**Théâtre des Amandiers** 7 av Pablo-Picasso, Nanterre, 92 ☎01.46.14.70.00. Renowned as the suburban base for Jean-Paul Vincent's innovative productions. RER Nanterre-Préfecture and theatre shuttle bus.

**Théâtre des Artistic-Athévains** 45bis rue Richard-Lenoir, 11ᵉ ☎01.43.56.38.32. Small company heavily involved in community and educational theatre. Mᵒ Voltaire.

**Théâtre de la Bastille** 76 rue de la Roquette, 11ᵉ ☎01.43.57.42.14. One of the best places for new work and fringe productions. Mᵒ Bastille.

**Théâtre de la Colline** (national theatre) 15 rue Malte-Brun, 20ᵉ ☎01.44.62.52.52, ⊛www.colline.fr. Known for its modern and cutting-edge productions under director Alain Françon. Mᵒ Gambetta.

**Théâtre de l'Est Parisien** 159 av Gambetta, 20ᵉ ☎01.43.64.80.80. Well respected for its experimental work. Mᵒ Gambetta.

**Théâtre de Gennevilliers** Centre Dramatique National, 41 av des Grésillons, Gennevilliers ☎01.41.32.26.26. Several stimulating productions by Bernard Sobel have brought acclaim – and audiences – to this suburban venue in recent years. Mᵒ Gabriel-Péri.

**Théâtre National de Chaillot** (national theatre), Palais de Chaillot, pl du Trocadéro, 16ᵉ ☎01.53.65.30.00, ⊛www.theatre-chaillot.fr. Puts on an exciting programme of contemporary dance and theatre, and regularly hosts foreign productions; Deborah Warner was here recently directing Fiona Shaw in *Medea*. Mᵒ Trocadéro.

**Théâtre de Nesle** 8 rue de Nesle, 6ᵉ ☎01.46.34.61.04. New French work and reworkings of old texts, as well as English and American in the original. Mᵒ Odéon.

# Dance and mime

Paris has few homegrown dance companies itself: government subsidies go to regional companies expressly to decentralize the arts. It makes up for this however by regularly hosting all the best contemporary practitioners. As well as big international names like Merce Cunningham, other frequent visitors worth looking out for are Régine Chopinot's troupe from La Rochelle, Maguy Marin's from Rillieux-la-Pape, Jean-Claude Gallotta's from Grenoble, Catherine Diverrès' from Rennes, and Angelin Preljocaj's from Aix-en-Provence. Creative choreographers based in or around Paris include François Verret and the Californian Carolyn Carlson.

Some of the most **innovative French dance companies** combine different media and genres to create dazzling, unclassifiable spectacles. One such is the Compagnie Montalvo-Hervieu, based in Créteil, just outside Paris and founded in 1988 by Spanish dancer and choreographer José Montalvo, and Dominique Hervieu; their hugely entertaining shows combine every dance genre going: hip-hop, ballet, contemporary dance, acrobatic dance, all set against a background of giant video images, with which the dancers interact, and accompanied by a soundtrack of music ranging from Vivaldi to Fat Boy Slim.

Other cutting-edge performers to look out for are Joëlle Bouvier and Régis Obadia, who trained at dance school and at the Lecoq school of mime. Their company, L'Esquisse, combining both disciplines, takes inspiration from paintings, and portrays a dark, hallucinatory world. Pure **mime** is not so widely seen these days, and its most famous practitioner, Marcel Marceau, now in his 70s and still performing, remains the only mime artist in France of any standing. Mime skills, however, have been incorporated into theatre (by Peter Brook, for example) and dance, greatly enriching both.

Many of the **theatres** listed opposite include both mime and dance in their programmes: the Théâtre de la Bastille shows works by young dancers and choreographers; a prestigious competition for young choreographers is held in March at the Maison de la Culture in Bobigny; and the Théâtre des Amandiers in Nanterre hosts major contemporary works.

Plenty of space and critical attention are also given to **tap**, **tango**, **folk** and **jazz dancing**, and to visiting traditional dance troupes from all over the world. There are also a dozen or so black African companies in Paris and the fashionable Japanese *butoh*, as well as several Indian dance troupes, the Ballet Classique Khmer, and many more from exiled cultures.

As for **ballet**, the principal stage is at the restored Opéra Garnier, home to the Ballet de l'Opéra National de Paris. After a troubled period under the directorship of the late, great Rudolf Nureyev, many of the best French classical dancers have returned to the company, with the exception, however, of the ravishing superstar Sylvie Guillem, who is now with the Royal Ballet. But ballet fans can still be sure of masterly performances – at the Opéra Garnier, the Opéra Bastille, the Théâtre des Champs-Élysées and the Théâtre Musical de Paris.

The highlight of the dance year is the **Concours International de Danse de Paris** in October and November, which involves contemporary, classical and different national traditions (☎01.45.22.28.74). Other **festivals** combining theatre, dance, mime, classical music and its descendants include the Festival Exit in February/March in Créteil (ⓦwww.maccreteil.com), the Paris Quartier d'Été from mid-July to mid-August (☎01.44.94.98.00, ⓦwww.quartierdete.com), the Festival Agora at the Pompidou Centre's IRCAM in

June (Wwww.ircam.fr), and the Festival d'Automne from mid–September to mid–December (T01.53.45.17.00, Wwww.festival–automne.com), where Trisha Brown usually makes an appearance.

## Venues

**Centre Mandapa 6 rue Wurtz, 13e**
T01.45.89.01.60. Hosts mainly classical Indian dance and also gives lessons. M° Glacière.

**Opéra de la Bastille pl de la Bastille, 12e**
T08.36.69.78.68, Wwww.opera-de-paris.fr. Stages some productions by the Ballet de l'Opéra National de Paris, but in general its programme moves away from the classics. M° Bastille.

**Opéra de Paris Garnier pl de l'Opéra, 9e**
T08.36.69.78.68, Wwww.opera-de-paris.fr. Main home of the Ballet de l'Opéra National de Paris and the place to see ballet classics. M° Opéra.

**Pompidou Centre rue Beaubourg, 4e**
T01.44.78.16.25. The Grande Salle in the basement is used for dance performances by visiting companies. M° Rambuteau/RER Châtelet-Les Halles.

**Regard du Cygne 210 rue de Belleville, 20e**
T01.43.58.55.93, Wwww.redcygne.free.fr. Innovative and exciting new work. One of the centre's best-known events is its series of Spectacles Sauvages (see website for dates), in which virtually anyone can perform a ten-minute piece to the public. M° Place-des-Fêtes.

**Théâtre des Abbesses 31 rue des Abbesses, 18e** T01.42.74.22.77, Wwww.theatredelaville-paris.com. Sister company to the Théâtre de la Ville, with slightly more off-beat and daring performances. M° Abbesses.

**Théâtre de la Bastille 76 rue de la Roquette,**
11e T01.43.57.42.14. As well as more traditional theatre, there are also dance and mime performances. M° Bastille.

**Théâtre des Champs-Élysées 15 av Montaigne, 8e** T01.49.52.50.50, Wwww.theatrechampselysees.fr. This prestigious venue, where Stravinsky's premiere of the *Rite of Spring* caused a riot in 1913, tries to outdo the Opéra with even grander and more expensive ballet productions. M° Alma-Marceau.

**Théâtre de la Cité Internationale 21 bd Jourdan, 14** T01.43.13.50.50, Wwww.theatredelacite.ciup.fr. An exciting dance venue that hosts the Presqu'ils de la Danse contemporary dance festival in March and performances from the Festival d'Automne later in the year. RER Cité Universitaire.

**Théâtre Musical de Paris pl du Châtelet, 4e**
T01.40.28.28.40, Wwww.chatelet-theatre.com. It was here, in 1910, that Diaghilev put on the first season of Russian ballet, assisted by Cocteau. Though mainly used for classical concerts and opera, it also hosts top-notch visiting ballet companies like the Mariinsky. M° Châtelet.

**Théâtre de la Ville 2 pl du Châtelet, 4e**
T01.42.74.22.77, Wwww.theatredelaville-paris.com. The height of success for contemporary dance productions is to end up here. Karine Saporta's work is regularly featured, as is Maguy Marin, Carolyn Carlson and Pina Bausch, together with modern theatre classics, comedy and concerts. M° Châtelet.

# Shops and markets

When it comes to shopping, Paris is an epicurean wonderland. As if the quality, style and variety weren't stunning enough, the attention to the tiniest detail – a ribbon on a package from the bakery, for instance – makes shopping an absolute delight.

Despite pressures to concentrate consumption in gargantuan underground and multi-storey complexes, Parisians, for the most part, remain fiercely loyal to their small local traders and independently-owned shops. Whether you can afford to buy or not, some of the most entertaining and memorable experiences of a trip to Paris are to be had for free just browsing in small shops, their owners proudly displaying their cache of offbeat items, particular passions, one-of-a-kind oddities and mouthwatering treats, carefully created according to instructions handed down from generation to generation.

The most distinctive and unusual shopping possibilities are in the nineteenth-century arcades of the *passages* in the **2ᵉ and 9ᵉ arrondissements**, almost all now smartly renovated and harbouring the kind of outlets that make shopping an exciting expedition rather than a chore. On the streets proper, the square kilometre around **place St-Germain-des-Prés** is hard to beat. To the north of the square, the narrow streets are lined with antiques shops and arts and interior design boutiques, while to the south you'll find every designer clothing brand you can think of, Parisian or otherwise.

**Les Halles** is another well-shopped district, good for everything from records through to designer clothes: pedestrianized rue Tiquetonne is especially worth a wander for its young and trendy fashion boutiques. The aristocratic **Marais**, the hip quartier of the **Bastille** and northeastern Paris (**Oberkampf** and the **Canal Saint Martin**) have filled up with dinky little boutiques, interior design, arty and specialist shops and galleries. For Parisian **haute couture** – Hermès and the like – the traditional bastions are avenue Montaigne, rue François-1ᵉʳ and the upper end of **rue du Faubourg-St-Honoré** in the 8ᵉ. In recent years, newer, cutting-edge, designers have begun colonizing the lower reaches of rue du Faubourg-St-Honoré, between rue Cambon and rue des Pyramides – a trend that started with the opening of the ultra-cool *Hotel Costes*, near the corner of rue de Castiglione, in the late Nineties, followed by the concept store, *Colette* (see p.330).

**Place de la Madeleine** is the place to head for luxury **food** stores, such as Fauchon and Hédiard. For essential foodstuffs, the cheapest supermarket chain is Ed l'Épicier. Other last-minute or convenience shopping is probably best done at FNAC shops (for books and records), the big department stores (for high-quality merchandise) and Monoprix (for basics). **Toy shops**, and shops selling children's clothes and books, are detailed in Chapter 21. Information on **VAT reimbursement** for non-EU citizens is given on p.376.

**Markets**, too, are a grand spectacle. A cornucopia of food from half the countries of the globe, intoxicating in their colour, shape and smell, assail the senses in even the drabbest parts of town. In Belleville and the Goutte d'Or, North Africa predominates; Southeast Asia in the 13$^e$ arrondissement. Though the food is perhaps the best offering of the Paris markets, there are also street markets dedicated to secondhand goods (the *marchés aux puces*), clothes and textiles, flowers, birds, books and stamps. See pp.345–348 for a full run down on Paris's markets.

# Art and design

The **commercial art galleries** are concentrated in **the 8$^e$**, especially in and around avenue Matignon; in **the Marais**; on **rue Quincampoix**, near the Pompidou Centre; around **the Bastille**; and in **St-Germain**. A new crop of next-generation conceptual art galleries are located in **rue Louise-Weiss** in the 13$^e$, just west of the new Bibliothèque Nationale de France-Mitterrand.

There are literally hundreds of galleries, and for an idea of who is being exhibited where, look up details in *Pariscope* under "Expositions", or *L'Officiel des Spectacles* under "Galeries". Entry to commercial galleries is free to all.

## Artist materials

**Comptoire des Écritures** 35 rue Quincampoix, 4$^e$ ⓦ www.comptoirdesecritures.com. A delightful shop entirely devoted to the art of calligraphy, with an extensive collection of paper, pens, brushes and inks. Also runs lessons and mounts exhibitions. M° Rambuteau. Tues–Sat 11am–7pm.

**Papier Plus** 9 rue du Pont-Loius-Philippe, 4$^e$ ⓦ www.papierplus.com. Fine-quality, colourful stationery, including notebooks, photo albums and artists' portfolios. M° St-Paul. Mon–Sat noon–7pm.

**Paris American Art** 2 & 4 rue Bonaparte, 6$^e$. Local art suppliers for the Beaux-Arts students residing around the corner. M° St-Germain-des-Prés. Tues–Sat 10am–1pm & 2–6.30pm.

**Sennelier** 3 quai Voltaire, 7$^e$. Upmarket art supplies, with some beautiful sets of oils. Mon 2–6.30pm, Tues–Sat 9.30am–12.30pm & 2–6.30pm. M° St-Germain-des-Prés.

## Design

A small selection of places where contemporary and the best of twentieth-century **design** can be seen is listed below. Also worth checking out are the shops of the art and design museums, and the streets around the Bastille, with a high concentration of shops specializing in particular periods.

**Colette** 213 rue Saint-Honoré, 1$^{er}$ ⓦ www.colette.fr. This cutting-edge concept store, combining high fashion and design, complete with photo gallery and exhibition space, is as cool as it comes. When you've finished sizing up the Pucci underwear, Stella McCartney womenswear and Sonia Rykiel handbags, head for the *Water Bar*, with its 80 different kinds of the precious stuff – agonize between the Brazilian Petropolis Paulista, the Corsican Orezza and the limited-edition Evian. M° Tuileries. Mon–Sat 10.30am–7.30pm.

**Prisunic supermarket** 109 rue de la Boétie, 8ᵉ (Mᵒ Franklin-D.Roosevelt). Open till midnight Mon–Sat.

**Boulangerie de l'Ancienne-Comédie** 10 rue de l'Ancienne-Comédie, 6ᵉ (Mᵒ Odéon). Open 24hr daily.

**Drugstore** 133 av des Champs-Élysées, 8ᵉ (Mᵒ Charles-de-Gaulle/Étoile). Books, newspapers, tobacco and all kinds of gift gadgetry. Daily 10am till 2am.

**Kiosque** pl Charles-de-Gaulle, 8ᵉ (Mᵒ Charles-de-Gaulle/Étoile). Newsagents open 24hr daily.

### Tabacs

**La Favourite** 3 bd St-Michel, 5ᵉ (Mᵒ St-Michel). Daily till 2am.

**Old Navy** 150 bd St-Germain, 6ᵉ (Mᵒ St-Germain-des-Prés). Open till 5am.

**Shell Garage** 6 bd Raspail, 7ᵉ (Mᵒ Rue-du-Bac). 24hr food shop and garage.

---

**CSAO (Compagnie du Sénégal et de l'Afrique de l'Ouest)** 1 & 3 rue Elzévir, 3ᵉ ⓦ www.csao.fr. Fairly traded crafts and artwork from West Africa, including Malian cotton scarves in rich, earthy tones and painted glass from Senegal. Mᵒ St-Paul. Mon–Sat 11am–7pm, Sun 2–7pm.

**Eugénie Seigneur** 16 rue Charlot, 3ᵉ. The place to take your print or original for a highly unique frame. Also sells one-off beautiful old floral tiles, mirrors and interesting brooches. Mᵒ Republique. Mon–Fri 10am–7pm, Sat 10am–1pm & 3–7pm.

**Fiesta Galerie** 45 rue Vieille-du-Temple, 4ᵉ. A big selection of twentieth-century kitsch objects. Mᵒ Hôtel-de-Ville. Tues–Sat noon–7pm, Sun & Mon 2–7pm.

**Galerie Documents** 53 rue de Seine, 6ᵉ. The place to come for vintage posters all well displayed in this upscale gallery. Mᵒ Odéon. Mon 2.30–7pm, Tues–Sat 10.30am–7pm.

**Galerie Maeght** 42 rue du Bac, 7ᵉ. Famous gallery that makes its own beautifully printed art books. Mᵒ Rue-du-Bac. Mon 10am–6pm, Tues–Sat 9.30am–7pm.

**Galerie Patrick Séguin** 34 rue de Charonne, 11ᵉ. A fine collection of furniture and objects from the 1950s, including pieces by Le Corbusier and Jean Prouvé. There's another showroom nearby in rue des Taillandiers. Mᵒ Bastille. Tues–Sat noon–7pm.

**Louvre des Antiquaires** 2 pl du Palais-Royal ⓦ www.louvre-antiquaires.com. An enormous antiques and furniture hypermarket where you can pick up anything from a Mycenaean seal ring to an Art Nouveau vase – for a price. Mᵒ Palais-Royal/Musée-du-Louvre. Tues–Sun 11am–7pm; closed Sun in July and Aug.

**Lulu Berlu** 27 rue Oberkampf, 11ᵉ ⓦ www .luluberlu.com. Crammed with twentieth-century toys and curios, most with their original packaging. Mᵒ Oberkampf. Mon–Sat noon–8pm.

**Résonsances** 9 cour St-Émilion, 12ᵉ ⓦ www.resonances.fr. Stylish kitchen and bathroom accessories, with an emphasis on French design. Covetable items include elegant wine decanters and a white porcelain hot-chocolate maker. Mᵒ Cour St-Émilion. Daily 11am–9pm.

**Le Viaduc des Arts** 9–129 av Daumesnil, 12ᵉ. Practically the entire north side of the street is dedicated to an extremely high standard of skilled workmanship and craft. Each arch of this old railway viaduct houses a shop front and workspace for the artists within, who produce contemporary metalwork, ceramics, tapestry, sculpture and much more. Mᵒ Bastille/Gare de Lyon. Most shops open Mon–Sat 10.30am–7.30pm. See also p.202.

## Bookshops

The best areas for book shopping are the Seine **quais**, with their rows of new and secondhand bookstalls perched against the river parapet, and the narrow streets of the **Quartier Latin**.

## English-Language

English-language bookshops operate as home-away-from-home for expats, often with readings from visiting writers, and sometimes handy notice-boards for flat-shares, language lessons and work. The Australian Bookshop and Abbey's in particular operate as cultural ambassadors for Australia and Canada respectively, with a large range of the national literature available in French translation.

**Abbey Bookshop** 29 rue de la Parcheminerie, 5e. A Canadian bookshop round the corner from Shakespeare & Co (see below), with lots of secondhand British and North American fiction; good social science sections; knowledgeable and helpful staff – and free coffee. M° St-Michel. Mon–Sat 10am–7pm.

**Brentano's** 37 av de l'Opéra, 2e ⊛www.brentanos.fr. English and American books. Good section for kids, with storytelling on Wednesday afternoons and Saturday mornings. M° Opéra. Mon–Sat 10am–7pm.

**Galignani** 224 rue de Rivoli, 1er. Claims to be the first English bookshop established on the Continent way back in 1802. Stocks a good range, including fine art and children's books. M° Concorde. Mon–Sat 10am–7pm.

**Red Wheelbarrow** 13 rue Charles V, 4e. Newly opened, a Canadian-run bookshop with regular book readings. M° St-Paul. Mon–Sat 10am–7pm.

**San Francisco Bookshop** 17 rue Monsieur le Prince, 6e. American-run secondhand bookshop with a selection of contemporary literature that would be impressive anywhere. Quite a collection of books on jazz, and sections for everything from gay and lesbian to Latin American studies. Well-organized and calm – not a social hangout. M° Odéon. Mon–Sat 11am–9pm, Sun 2–7.30pm.

**Shakespeare & Co** 37 rue de la Bûcherie, 5e. A cosy, famous literary haunt, American-run (see p.119), with the biggest selection of secondhand English books in town. Also poetry readings and the like. M° Maubert-Mutualité. Daily noon–midnight.

**Tea and Tattered Pages** 24 rue Mayet, 6e. Secondhand bookshop with more than 15,000 titles in English, mostly tatty fiction. You can munch on cheesecake, bagels and the like in the small attached *salon de thé*. M° Duroc. Mon–Sat 11am–7pm, Sun noon–6pm.

**Village Voice** 6 rue Princesse, 6e ⊛www .villagevoicebookshop.com. A welcoming recreation of a neighbourhood bookstore, with a good selection of contemporary fiction and non-fiction, and a decent list of British and American poetry and classics. M° Mabillon. Mon 2–8pm, Tues–Sat 10am–8pm, Sun 2–7pm.

**W. H. Smith** 248 rue de Rivoli, 1er. Parisian outlet of the British chain. Wide range of new books, newspapers and magazines. M° Concorde. Daily 9.30am–7pm.

## General French

For general **French titles**, the biggest and most convenient shop has to be the FNAC in the Forum des Halles, though it's hardly the most congenial of places. If you fancy a prolonged session of browsing, the other general bookshops below are probably more suitable.

**FNAC** at the Forum des Halles, niveau 2, Porte Pierre-Lescot (M°/RER Châtelet-Les Halles). Other branches include 136 rue de Rennes, 6e (M° Saint-Placide); 26 av des Ternes, 17e (M° Ternes); and CNIT, 2 pl de la Défense (M° La Défense); ⊛www.fnac.com. Lots of *bandes dessinées*, guidebooks and maps, among everything else. Mon–Sat 10am–7.30pm.

**Gallimard** 15 bd Raspail, 7e. Most French publishers operate their own flagship bookshops, and Gallimard's boulevard Raspail store is one of the greats. M° Sèvres-Babylone. Daily 10am–7pm.

**Gibert Jeune** 10 pl St-Michel & 27 Quai St-Michel, 5e. The biggest of the Quartier Latin student/academic bookshops with a vast selection of French books. There's a fair English-language and discounted selection at Gibert Joseph, 26 bd St-Michel. An institution. M° St-Michel. Mon–Sat 10am–7pm.

**La Hune** 170 bd St-Germain, 6e. One of the biggest and best, with a strong art section. M° St-Germain-des-Prés. Mon–Sat 10am–midnight.

**Librairie Culture** 17 bis rue Pavée, 4e. A real Aladdin's cave, spread over three floors, with books piled up everywhere you look – mostly secondhand and returns, with some good deals on art books. M° Saint-Paul. Mon–Sat 10.30am–7pm.

## Ethnic French

**L'Harmattan** 16 rue des Écoles, 5ᵉ ⓦ www .editions-harmattan.fr. Excellent, very knowledgeable bookshop, especially good for Arab/North African literature in French, with a few titles in English. Publishes its own books, too. Mᵒ Maubert-Mutualité. Mon–Sat 10am–12.30pm & 1.30–7pm.

**Librairie de l'Institut du Monde Arabe** 1 rue des Fossés-St-Bernard. Good range of books on Arab culture, mostly in French and mostly quite serious, though the shop also stocks an excellent CD collection and various souvenir items. Mᵒ Cardinal-Lemoine/Jussieu. Tues–Sun 10am–6pm.

**Présence Africaine** 25bis rue des Écoles, 5ᵉ. Specialist black African bookshop, with titles ranging from literature to economics and philosophy by Caribbean and North American as well as African writers. Mᵒ Maubert-Mutualité. Mon–Fri 10am–7pm, Sat 10.30am–1pm & 2–7pm.

## Art and architecture

**Artcurial** 7 Rond-Point des Champs-Elysées, 8ᵉ ⓦ www.artcurial.com. The art bookshop in Paris – French and foreign editions. There is also a gallery, which puts on interesting exhibitions. Mᵒ Franklin-D.Roosevelt. Mon–Fri 10.30am–7pm; closed two weeks in Aug.

**Librairie de l'École Supérieure des Beaux-Arts** 17 quai Malaquais, 6ᵉ. The bookshop of the national Fine Art school: own publications, posters, reproductions, postcards, etc. Mᵒ St-Germain-des-Prés. Mon–Fri 10am–6pm; closed Aug.

**Librairie du Musée d'Art Moderne de la Ville de Paris** Palais de Tokyo, 11 av du Président-Wilson, 16ᵉ. Specialist publications on modern art, including foreign works. Mᵒ Iéna. Tues–Fri 10am–5.30pm, Sat & Sun 10am–6.30pm.

**Librairie du Musée des Arts Décoratifs** 107 rue de Rivoli, 1ᵉʳ. Design, posters, architecture, graphics, etc. Mᵒ Palais-Royal. Daily 10am–7pm.

## Film and photography

**Ciné Reflet** 14 rue Serpente, 6ᵉ. Just round the corner from the rue Champollion cluster of independent cinemas, this little shop has an interesting, if dusty, collection of books on cinema, most but not all in French, as well as pieces of film memorabilia. Mᵒ Cluny-La Sorbonne. Mon–Sat 1–8pm.

**La Chambre Claire** 14 rue St-Sulpice, 6. Photography specialist, with a good number of English-text titles. Sells photographs too. Mᵒ Odéon. Tues–Sat 10am–7pm.

## Comics (*Bandes Dessinées*)

**Album** 60 rue Monsieur-le-Prince, 6ᵉ (Mᵒ Odéon). Also at 6–8 rue Dante, 5ᵉ (Mᵒ Maubert-Mutualité). Serious collection of French BDs, some of them rare editions with original artwork. Tues–Sat 10am–8pm.

**Boulinier** 20 bd St-Michel, 6ᵉ. Renowned for its selection of new and secondhand comics, including many that are difficult to obtain. Good collection of secondhand CDs as well. Mᵒ St-Michel. Mon–Sat 10am–11pm, Sun 2–11pm.

**Librairie d'Images** 84 bd St-Germain, cnr rue St-Jaques, 6ᵉ. Big range of new comic books and luxury editions, but the best thing about this place is the comic-related paraphernalia: posters, t-shirts and models. Mᵒ Cluny-La-Sorbonne/Maubert-Mutualité. Mon–Sat 10am–8pm, Sun noon–7pm.

**Thé-Troc** 52 rue Jean-Pierre-Timbaud, 11ᵉ. The friendly owner publishes *The Fabulous Furry Freak Brothers* in French (*Les Fabuleux Freak Brothers*) and English; he is a friend of the author of the famous Seventies comics, Gilbert Shelton, who lives nearby. There are other comic books on sale, too, among Freak Bros books, t-shirts and posters, as well as a wide selection of teas and teapots, secondhand records, jewellery and assorted junk. The attached *salon de thé* (until 7pm) is comfy, colourful and restful, with board-games. Mᵒ Parmentier. Mon–Fri 9am–8pm, Sat 11am–8pm.

## Cookery, Gardening, Crafts

**Librairie Gourmande** 4 rue Dante 5ᵉ ⓦ www.librairie-gourmande.fr. The very last word in books about cooking. Mᵒ Maubert-Mutualité. Daily 10am–7pm.

**La Maison Rustique** 26 rue Jacob, 6ᵉ. Satisfying range of gardening and interior decoration books, many in English and many beautifully produced. Mᵒ St-Germain-des-Prés. Mon–Sat 10am–7pm.

### Gay and Lesbian

**Les Mots à la Bouche 6 rue Ste-Croix-de-la-Bretonnerie, 4ᵉ.** Selling mainly gay-interest books, guides and magazines, plus some lesbian titles. There's a section with English-language literature, and the staff speak good English. A handy place for contacts, with a good notice board and a stack of free listings magazines. Mᵒ Hôtel-de-Ville. Mon–Sat 11am–11pm, Sun 2–8pm.

### Performing Arts

**Librairie Bonaparte 31 rue Bonaparte, 6ᵉ.** Exhaustive stock of books on ballet, theatre, opera, puppets, music hall, *chan-sonniers* and the like, and some prints. Mᵒ St-Germain-des-Prés. Tues–Sat 10am–7pm.

### Travel

**Institut Géographique National (IGN) 107 rue La-Boétie, 8ᵉ ⊛ www.ign.fr.** The French Ordnance Survey: the best for maps of France and the entire world, plus guide-books, satellite photos, day packs, map holders, etc. Mᵒ St-Philippe-Roule. Mon–Fri 9.30am–7pm, Sat 11–12.30 & 2–6.30pm.
**Librairie Ulysse 26 rue St-Louis-en-L'Île, 4ᵉ.** An antiquarian travel bookshop in a charming location. Mᵒ Pont-Marie/Sully-Morland. Tues–Sat 2–8pm.

## Clothes

There may be no way you can get to see the haute couture shows (see the box below), but there's nothing to prevent you trying on fabulously expensive

### Haute couture

Paris, the capital of **haute couture**, is represented nowhere more extravagantly than in the January and July fashion shows. Invitations go out exclusively to the élite of the world's fashion editors and to the two thousand or so clients who don't flinch at price tags between £10,000 and £100,000 for a dress. The world's press have a field day as the top hotels, restaurants and palace venues disgorge famous bodies cloaked in famous names, and every arbiter of taste and style maintains the myth that fashion is the height of human attainment. The truth, of course, is that the catwalks and the clientele are there to promote more mass-consumed luxuries, *prêt-à-porter* (ready-to-wear) lines and perfumes.

A growing disillusionment with these big-business realities and the loss of the client-couturier relationship were partly behind the decision of Yves Saint Laurent, Paris's greatest designer, to retire in 2002, though ironically he himself was one of the pioneers of the process. It's said that YSL had also became disenchanted with the theatrical excess of the younger generation. Certainly the trend over the last few years has been for lavish shows, sometimes staged in unconventional places, such as sports stadiums and even train stations. Enfants terribles John Galliano and Alexander McQueen are known in particular for their wild extravaganzas; in 2002 McQueen chose the medieval setting of the Conciergerie for a show with a sinister edge, in which wolf-like dogs accompanied leather-clad models down the catwalk.

Whatever you think about the theatricality and the gap between what the models are wearing and what most people actually want to wear, the Paris catwalk certainly places no constraints on the designer's creativity. Indeed, it makes the other fashion shows look decidedly dull: Milan is too much of a commercial affair to allow for much imagination, New York's shows have, understandably, been more subdued in the last year or two, and London designers can barely scrape enough money together to hire models (these days, models command about forty percent of the budget). London may have produced some of the trend-setting designers of tomorrow – Galliano, McQueen, Stella McCartney, Phoebe Philo, Julien McDonald – but Paris is where they all head for.

creations in rue du Faubourg-St-Honoré, avenue François-1$^{er}$ and avenue Montaigne – apart from the intimidating air of the assistants and the awesome chill of the marble portals. Likewise, you can treat the **younger designers** on the eastern stretch of rue du Faubourg-St-Honoré, around the Bastille and Marais, and the designer-led chains in the area south of place St-Germain, as stops on your sightseeing itinerary. For **smart clothes** without the fancy labels the best areas are rue St-Placide and rue St-Dominique in the 6$^e$ and 7$^e$. The **department stores** Galeries Lafayette and Printemps have good selections of designer prêt-à-porter; and the **Forum des Halles** and surrounding streets are chock-a-block with high-street fashion.

The **sales** take place in January and July, with reductions of up to forty percent on designer clothes. Ends of lines and old stock of the couturiers are sold year round in **discount shops** concentrated in rue d'Alésia in the 14$^e$ and rue St-Placide in the 6$^e$. For **shoes**, take a wander down rue du Cherche-Midi in the 6$^e$, rue de Grenelle in the 7$^e$ and rue Meslay in the 3$^e$. For **jewellery** – gems and plastic – try rue du Temple and adjoining rue de Montmorency.

## Discount

The best areas to wander for shops selling end-of-line and last year's models at thirty- to fifty-percent reductions are in rue d'Alésia in the 14$^{e,}$ west of place Victor-Blasch; boulevard Victor in the 15$^e$ between rue Lecourbe and rue Desnouettes (M° Balard). Before you get too excited, however, remember that twenty percent off €750 still leaves a hefty bill – not that all items are this expensive. The best times of year to join the scrums are after the new collections have come out in January and October.

**Cacharel Stock 114 rue d'Alésia, 14$^e$.** One of many factory shops on this stretch of rue d'Alésia, with an excellent range of Cacharel seconds, end-of-line and last season's clothes. M° Alésia. Mon–Sat 10am–7pm.

**La Clef des Marques 124 bd Raspail, 7$^e$.** Huge store with a wide choice of inexpensive brand-name clothes for men and women – also lots of lingerie and children's clothes. M° Vavin. Mon 2–7pm, Tues–Sat 10.30am–7pm.

**Défilé de Marques 171 rue de Grenelle, 7$^e$.** *Dépôt-vente* shop selling a wide choice of designer clothes for women – as returned unsold from the big-name boutiques. Labels from Prada to Paco Rabanne discounted for around €200–300. M° La Tour-Maubourg. Tues–Sat 10am–2pm & 3–7.30pm.

**Kookai Stock 82 rue Réamur, 2$^e$.** Trendy young women's clothes, up to seventy percent off end-of-line and old stock. M° Réamur-Sebastopol. Tues–Sat 10am–7pm.

**Le Mouton à Cinq Pattes 8 rue St-Placide, 6$^e$.** Names such as Helmut Lang and Gaultier can be found among the racks of smart but discounted end-of-line and last-season's clothes. M° Sèvres-Babylone. Men have their own separate store at 138 bd St-Germain. M° Mabillon. Mon–Sat 10.30am–7.30pm.

**Passez Devant 62 rue d'Orsel, 18$^e$.** Big-name labels such as Yamamoto hang alongside smaller designers' work, most of it ex-sale-or-return stock at heavily discounted prices. M° Abbesses. Tues–Sat 10.30am–1pm & 2–7pm, Sun 2–7pm.

## Secondhand and rétro

**Rétro** means "period clothes", mostly unsold factory stock from the 1950s and 1960s, though some shops specialize in expensive high-fashion articles from as far back as the 1920s. Plain secondhand stuff is referred to as *fripe* – not especially interesting compared with London or New York, and dominated by the US combat-jacket style. The best place to look is probably the Porte de Montreuil flea market (see p.345).

**Ding Dong Bazaar 24 rue Mouffetard, 5$^e$.** Tiny store stocking attractive oddments of

## Designer fashion

The addresses below are those of the main or most conveniently located outlets of Paris's top designers. For a more complete list, including branch boutiques and websites, get online at ⓦ www.modeaparis.com.

**Agnès B** 6 rue du Jour, 1$^{er}$ (M° Châtelet-Les Halles), 6 & 10 rue du Vieux Colombier, 6$^e$ (M° St-Sulpice).

**Azzedine Alaïa** 7 rue de Moussy, 4$^e$ (M° Hôtel-de-Ville).

**Balenciaga** 10 av George V, 8$^e$ (M° George-V).

**Balmain** 44 rue François-1$^{er}$, 8$^e$ (M° George-V).

**Cacharel** 64 rue Bonaparte, 6$^e$ (M° St-Germain-des-Prés).

**Carven** 6 rond-point des Champs-Élysées-M-Daussault, 8$^e$ (M° Franklin-D.Roosevelt).

**Cerruti** 9 pl de la Madeleine, 8$^e$ (M° Madeleine).

**Chanel** 31 rue Cambon, 1$^{er}$ (M° Madeleine).

**Chloë** 54 rue du Faubourg-St-Honoré, 8$^e$ (M° Madeleine).

**Christian Lacroix** 73 rue du Faubourg-St-Honoré, 8$^e$ (M° Concorde).

**Comme des Garçons** 54 rue du Faubourg-St-Honoré, 8$^e$ (M° Concorde).

**Courrèges** 40 rue François-1$^{er}$, 8$^e$ (M° George-V).

**Dior** 30 av Montaigne, 8$^e$ (M° Franklin-D.Roosevelt).

**Dolce e Gabbana** 22 av Montaigne, 8$^e$ (M° Alma-Marceau).

**Emmanuelle Khanh** 36 rue du Faubourg-St-Honoré, 8$^e$ (M° Concorde).

**Gianni Versace** 62 rue du Faubourg-St-Honoré, 8$^e$ (M° Concorde).

**Giorgio Armani** 6 pl Vendôme, 1$^{er}$ (M° Opéra).

**Givenchy** 8 av George-V, 8$^e$ (M° Alma-Marceau).

**Gucci** 23 rue Royale, 8$^e$ (M° Madeleine).

**Inès de la Fressange** 14 av Montaigne, 8$^e$ (M° Alma-Marceau).

**Issey Miyake** 3 pl des Vosges, 4$^e$ (M° St-Paul).

**Jean-Louis Scherrer** 51 av Montaigne, 8$^e$ (M° Franklin-D.Roosevelt).

**Jean-Paul Gaultier** 30 rue du Faubourg-St-Antoine, 12$^e$ (M° Bastille) & 6 rue Vivienne, 2$^e$ (M° Bourse).

**Jil Sander** 52 av Montaigne, 8$^e$ (M° Franklin-D.Roosevelt).

**José Lévy** 70 rue Vieille-du-Temple, 3$^e$ (M° Hôtel-de-Ville).

**Junko Shimada** 54 rue Étienne-Marcel, 2$^e$ (M° Les Halles/RER Châtelet-Les-Halles).

**Kenzo** 3 pl des Victoires, 1$^{er}$ (M° Bourse).

**Lagerfeld Gallery** 40 rue de Seine, 6$^e$ (M° St-Germain-des-Prés).

**Lanvin** 15 rue du Faubourg-St-Honoré, 8$^e$ (M° Concorde).

**Nina Ricci** 19 rue François-1$^{er}$, 8$^e$ (M° George-V).

**Paco Rabanne** 7 rue du Cherche-Midi, 6$^e$ (M° Sèvres-Babylone).

**Pierre Cardin** 27 av Marigny, 8$^e$ (M° Place-Clemenceau).

**Prada** 10 av Montaigne, 8$^e$ (M° Alma-Marceau).

**Sonia Rykiel** 175 bd St-Germain, 6$^e$ (M° St-Germain-des-Prés).

**Thierry Mugler** 49 av Montaigne, 8$^e$ (M° Alma-Marceau).

**Ungaro** 2 av Montaigne, 8$^e$ (M° Alma-Marceau).

**Valentino** 17 av Montaigne, 8$^e$ (M° Alma-Marceau).

**YSL Rive Gauche** 6 pl St-Sulpice, 6$^e$ (M° St-Sulpice/Mabillon).

clothes and paste jewellery dating from the prewar years. M° Place Monge. Noon–2pm & 4–8pm, closed Tues.

**L'Occaserie 30 rue de la Pompe, 16ᵉ** ⓦwww.occaserie.com. Specialists in second-hand haute couture – Dior, Prada, Cartier and the like. "Secondhand" doesn't mean cheap though: Chanel suits are around €720, Louis Vuitton handbags €300. M° Muette/Passy. Mon–Sat 11am–7pm. Several smaller boutiques nearby: 16 & 21 rue de l'Annonciation, 14 rue Jean Bologne and 19 rue de la Pompe.

**Réciproque 89, 92, 93–97, 101 & 123 rue de la Pompe, 16ᵉ.** A similar series of shops to *L'Occaserie*'s. Women's design at no. 93–95; accessories and coats for men at no. 101; more accessories and coats for women at no. 123. M° Pompe. Tues–Sat 11am–7.30pm.

## Trendy

**APC 3 & 4 rue de Fleurus, 6ᵉ.** The clothes here are young and urban, but still effort-lessly classic in that Parisian way. The men's and women's shops face each other across the road. M° St-Placide. Mon–Thurs 10.30am–7pm, Fri & Sat 11am–7pm. The same gear, but discounted over-stock fare, can be found at Surplus APC, 45 rue Madame, 6ᵉ (M° St-Sulpice).

**Bonnie Cox 38 rue des Abbesses, 18ᵉ.** Young fashion names such as Michiko and Custo have their sartorial creations on show here, at relatively uninflated prices – think €150 for a dress. Also stocks its own very afford-able label, with some cool hats and shoes. M° Abbesses. Daily 11am–8pm.

**Comptoir des Cotonniers 59ter rue Bonaparte, 63.** Utterly reliable little chain stocking comfortable, well-cut women's basics that nod to contemporary fashions without being out-modish. Trousers, shirts and dresses for around €100. M° St-Germain-des-Prés. Mon 11am–7pm, Tues–Sat 10am–7.30pm.

**Isabel Marant 16 rue de Charonne, 11ᵉ.** Marant has established an international rep-utation for her feminine and flattering clothes in quality fabrics such as silk and cashmere. Prices are €90 upwards for skirts, around €250 for coats. M° Bastille. Mon–Sat 10.30am–7.30pm.

**Kabuki 25 rue Étienne-Marcel, 1ᵉʳ.** A one-stop store for all your Prada, Issey Miyake and Calvin Klein needs. M° Étienne-Marcel. Mon–Sat 10.30am–7.30pm.

**Kiliwatch 64 rue Tiquetonne, 2ᵉ.** No problems coming up with an original clubbing outfit here: a clubbers' mecca, where rails of new cheap 'n' chic youth streetwear and a slew of trainers meet the best range of unusual secondhand clothes and accessories in Paris. M° Étienne-Marcel. Mon 2–7pm, Tues–Sat 11am–7.30pm.

**Vanessa Bruno 25 rue St-Sulpice, 6ᵉ.** Bright, breezy and effortlessly beautiful women's fashions, with a hint of updated hippy chic. M° Odéon. Mon–Sat 10.30am–7pm.

**Zadig & Voltaire 1 & 3 rue du Vieux Colombier, 6ᵉ.** The women's clothes at this small Parisian chain are pretty and trendy in a relaxed way. In style it's not a million miles from Agnès B – and her shop's just oppo-site too – only with a more wayward flair. M° St-Sulpice. Mon–Sat 10am–7pm. Branches at 15 rue du Jour, 1ᵉʳ; 9 rue du 29 Juillet, 1ᵉʳ; 11 rue Montmartre, 1ᵉʳ; 36 rue de Sévigné, 4ᵉ.

## Shoes

**Freelance 30 rue du Four, 6ᵉ.** From leather to feathers, this very popular free-spirited shoe store attracts the young and extremely funky. M° Mabillon. Mon–Sat 10am–7pm.

**Patrick Cox 62 rue Tiquetonne, 2ᵉ.** The chic and friendly Paris outlet of the London-based shoe designer. Clothes to match. M° Étienne-Marcel. Mon–Sat 10am–7pm.

**Swingtap 21 rue Keller, 11ᵉ** ⓦwww .swingtap.com. The hoofers' mecca: tap shoes, CDs to dance along to, and details on tap-dancing classes and shows around town. M° Ledru-Rollin. Tues–Sat 2–7pm.

## Accessories and jewellery

**Cécile et Jeanne 49 av Daumesnil, 12ᵉ.** Innovative jewellery design in one of the Viaduc des Arts showrooms. Many pieces under €100. M° Gare-de-Lyon. Mon–Fri 10am–7pm, Sat & Sun 2–7pm.

**Décalage 33 rue des Francs-Bourgeois, 4ᵉ.** Beautiful handcrafted jewellery – in classic and contemporary designs. Prices are rea-sonable: earrings, for example, start at €50. M° St-Paul. Tues–Sat 11am–7pm, Sun & Mon 2–7pm.

**Divine 39 rue Daguerre, 14ᵉ.** With a huge selection of both new and secondhand hats, this is a fun place to try out a few of your fantasy Parisian looks with a rakishly angled beret or a coquettish cloche. M° Denfert-Rochereau. Tues–Sat 10.30am–1pm & 3–7pm.

**Hermès 24 rue du Faubourg-St-Honoré, 8ᵉ.** Luxury clothing and accessory store. Come here for the ultimate silk scarf – at a price. M° Concorde. Mon–Sat 10am–6.30pm.

**Jamin-Puech 61 rue d'Hauteville, 10ᵉ** Ⓦ www.jamin-puech.com. An exquisite range of beautifully crafted bags in brightly coloured leather, crepe silk and other luxury fabrics, plus fetching footwear to match. Handbags cost around €200. M° Poissonière. Tues–Sat 10.30am–7pm.

**Tati Or 19 rue de la Paix, 1ᵉʳ (M° Opéra) & 42 av Général-Leclerc, 14ᵉ (M° Denfert-Rochereau).** The well-known cheap clothing chain, Tati, also sells gold jewellery, priced well below other Parisian jewellers. Mon–Sat 10am–7pm.

**Ursule Beaugeste 15 rue Oberkampf, 11ᵉ.** Handbag designer Ann Grand-Clement's delicious trademark crocheted handbags, some made on old looms, as well as beautifully engraved leather bags and cloth hats (and raffia bags in summer), all presented in a simple industrial-chic decor. Although Ann's designs have been featured in all the top international fashion magazines, the shop is not the least bit snobby. M° Oberkampf. Mon–Fri 11am–7.30pm, Sat 3–7pm.

**Virginie Monroe 30 rue de Charonne, 11ᵉ.** Delicate and unusual jewellery made from stones, glass, feathers and other non-precious materials. Earrings from €60, rings €50. M° Ledru-Rollin. Tues–Sat 10.30am–7pm.

## Department stores and hypermarkets

Paris's two largest **department stores**, Printemps and Galeries Lafayette, are right next door to each other near the St-Lazare station, and between them there's not much they don't have. Catching up with them is La Samaritaine, which is moving steadily upmarket and set for expansion. Best for food is Au Bon Marché.

In addition, Paris has its share of **hypermarkets** – giant shopping complexes – of which the Forum des Halles, in the 1ᵉʳ; the Centre Maine-Montparnasse, in the 14ᵉ; and the

Quatre-Saisons, in La Défense, are the biggest.

**Bazar de l'Hôtel de Ville (BHV) 52–64 rue de Rivoli, 4ᵉ.** Only two years younger than the Bon Marché and noted in particular for its DIY department, artists' materials and cheap self-service restaurant overlooking the Seine. For lighter refreshment, check out the *Bricolo Café* in the DIY section, done out like an old-fashioned workshop complete with workbenches and lamps. The store is less elegant in appearance than some of its rivals, perhaps, but the value for money is pretty good. M° Hôtel-de-Ville. Mon–Sat 9.30am–7pm, except Wed & Thurs till 8.30pm.

**Au Bon Marché 38 rue de Sèvres, 7ᵉ.** Paris's oldest department store, founded in 1852. Prices are lower on average than at the more chic Galeries Lafayette and Printemps. Excellent kids' department and a legendary food hall. M° Sèvres-Babylone. Mon–Sat 9.30am–7pm, Sat till 8pm.

**Galeries Lafayette 40 bd Haussmann, 9ᵉ** Ⓦ www.galerieslafayette.com. The store's forte is high fashion with two floors given over to the latest creations by leading designers, plus a large section devoted to clothes for children on the fourth floor. Then there's household stuff, a host of big names in men's and women's accessories, a sizeable lingerie department, a huge *parfumerie*, not to mention a branch of the *Angélina salon de thé*, full of lunching ladies – all under a superb 1900 dome. M° Havre-Caumartin. Mon–Sat 9.30am–7pm, Thurs till 9pm.

**Printemps 64 bd Haussmann, 9ᵉ** Ⓦ www .printemps.fr. Books, records, a *parfumerie* even bigger than the rival Galeries Lafayette's. Excellent fashion department for women spread over five floors. The sixth-floor restaurant is right underneath the beautiful Art Nouveau glass dome. M° Havre-Caumartin. Mon–Sat 9.30am–7pm, Thurs till 10pm.

**La Samaritaine 75 rue de Rivoli, 1ᵉʳ.** This venerable belle époque building used to aim downmarket of the previous two, but recently it was taken over by the luxury goods group LVMH and has undergone something of a makeover. What hasn't changed however are the superb views of Paris from the tenth-floor terrace café (closed Oct–March). M° Pont-Neuf. Mon–Sat 9.30am–7pm, Thurs till 10pm.

**Tati** 4 bd Rochechouart, 18e ⊛ www.tati.fr.
Hugely succesful budget department store
chain with a distinctive pink gingham logo.
Sells reliable and utterly cheap clothing,
among a host of other items. Branches at
Galerie Gaîté Montparnasse, 68 av du
Maine, 14e; M° Gaîté); 172 rue du Temple,
3e; M° République; 11 bis rue Scribe, 9e; M°
Opéra); 106 rue du Fbg du Temple, 11e; M°
Belleville). M° Barbès. Mon–Sat 10am–7pm.

# Food and drink

The general standard of **food shops** throughout the capital is remarkably high,
both in quality and presentation: a feast for the eyes quite as much as the palate.
These listings are for the **specialist places**, many of which are veritable palaces
of gluttony and fairly expensive. Markets are detailed in a separate section at
the end of this chapter.

  **Food halls** to equal that of Harrods are to be found at Fauchon's, on place
de la Madeleine, and the Grande Épicerie, in the Bon Marché department
store – each with exhibits to rival the best of the capital's museums. In addition, there are **one-product specialists** for whom gourmets will cross the
city: Poilâne's or Ganachaud's for bread, Barthélémy for cheese, La Maison de
l'Escargot for snails.

  As for buying food with a view to **economic eating**, you will be best off
shopping at the street markets or supermarkets – though save your bread-
buying at least for the local boulangerie and let yourself be tempted once in a
while by the apple *chaussons, pains aux raisins, pains au chocolat, tartes aux fraises*
and countless other goodies. Useful **supermarkets** with branches throughout
the city are Félix Potin, Prisunic and Monoprix. The cheapest supermarket
chain is Ed l'Épicier; choice, inevitably, is limited, but they do some things very
well – jams, for instance.

  Next door to the Tang Frères emporium in Chinatown (see pp.183 & 343)
is the Supermarché Paris Store, 44 av d'Ivry, 13e (M° Porte-d'Italie). Open
daily 9.30am–7pm, this is one of the best **Chinese supermarkets**, selling
everything from teacups to ampoules of royal jelly and ginseng. There's another
branch at 10 bd de la Villette, 19e (M° Belleville).

## Bread

**Ganachaud** 226 rue des Pyrénées, 20e.
Although father Ganachaud has left the
business, his three daughters continue his
recipes, and the bread is still out of this
world. Start the day with a *pain biologique*
and you'll live a hundred years, guaranteed. M° Gambetta. Tues–Sat
7.30am–8pm.

---

Any list of food shops in Paris has to have at its head the two **palaces**:
**Fauchon** 24–30 pl de la Madeleine, 8e. An amazing range of extravagantly
beautiful groceries, fruit and veg, charcuterie, wines both French and foreign –
almost anything you can think of, all at exorbitant prices. The quality is assured
by blind testing, which all suppliers have to submit to. Just the place for
presents of tea, jam, truffles, chocolates, exotic vinegars, mustards and so
forth. A self-service counter for pâtisseries and *plats du jour*, and a *traiteur*
which stays open a little later, until 8.30pm. M° Madeleine. Mon–Sat
9.30am–7pm.

**Hédiard** 21 pl de la Madeleine, 8e. Since the 1850s, the aristocrat's grocer, with
sales staff as deferential as servants, as long as you don't try to reach for items
for yourself. Superlative quality. Among the other branches are those at 126 rue
du Bac, 7e; 106 bd de Courcelles, 17e; and Forum des Halles, level-1, 1er. M°
Madeleine. Mon–Sat 8am–10pm.

**Legay Choc 45 rue Sainte-Croix-de-la-Bretonnerie, 4ᵉ.** The two brothers who opened this bakery a year or two ago have already built up a formidable reputation for excellent bread and pastries. Mº Hôtel-de-Ville. Daily 7.30am–8pm except Wed.

**Poilâne 8 rue du Cherche-Midi, 6ᵉ ⊛www .poilane.fr.** The source of the famous "Pain Poilâne" – a bread baked using traditional methods (albeit ramped up on an industrial scale) as conceived by the late, legendary Monsieur Poilâne himself. Mº Sèvres-Babylone. Mon–Sat 7.15am–8.15pm.

**Poujauran 20 rue Jean-Nicot, 7ᵉ.** The shop is exquisite, with its original painted glass panels and tiles, the bread is excellent and so too are the pâtisseries. Mº Latour-Maubourg. Tues–Sat 8am–8.30pm.

## Charcuterie

**Aux Ducs de Gascogne 111 rue St-Antoine, 4ᵉ.** Excellent range of high-quality charcuterie, as well as enticing – and expensive – deli goods ranging from little salads to caviar. Mº St-Paul. Mon–Sat 10am–8pm. Branches at 112 bd Haussman, 8ᵉ (Mº St-Augustin) and 4 rue du Marché-St-Honoré, 1ᵉʳ (Mº Tuileries).

**Flo Prestige 42 pl du Marché-St-Honoré, 1ᵉʳ.** All sorts of super delicacies, plus wines, champagne and exquisite ready-made dishes. Mº Pyramides. Daily 8am–11pm.

**Labeyrie 6 rue Montmartre, 1ᵉʳ.** Specialist in products from the Landes region, pâtés in particular: Bayonne hams, goose and duck pâtés, conserves, etc. Mº Châtelet-Les Halles. Tues–Sat 10.30am–2pm & 3–6pm.

**Maison de la Truffe 19 pl de la Madeleine, 8ᵉ.** Truffles, of course, including Piedmontese white truffles for around £1500 a pound, and more from the Dordogne and Landes. Mº Madeleine. Mon 9am–8pm, Tues–Sat 9am–9pm.

**Sacha Finkelsztajn 27 rue des Rosiers, 4ᵉ.** Marvellous Jewish deli for takeaway snacks and goodies: gorgeous East European breads, apple strudel, *gefilte* fish, aubergine purée, tarama, *blinis* and *borscht*. Mº St-Paul. Wed–Mon 10am–2pm & 3–7pm; closed Aug.

## Cheese

**Barthélémy 51 rue de Grenelle, 7ᵉ.** Purveyors of cheeses to the rich and powerful. Can arrange home delivery. Mº Bac. Tues–Sat 8.30am–1pm & 4–7.30pm; closed Aug.

**Fromagerie Alléosse 13 rue Poncelet, 17ᵉ.** A connoisseur's selection of high-quality cheeses, including Brie from Champagne, creamy Brillat-Savarin and nutty-flavoured Mont d'Or. Mº Ternes. Tues–Sat 9am–1pm & 4–7pm, Sun 9am–1pm.

**La Maison du Fromage 118 rue Mouffetard.** Offers a wonderful selection, beautifully displayed. Specializes in goat, sheep and mountain cheeses. Mº Censier-Daubenton. Tues–Sat 8.30am–1pm & 3–7.45pm, Sun 8.30am–1pm. Another branch at 62 rue de Sèvres, 6ᵉ (Mº Sèvres-Babylone).

## Chocolates and pâtisseries

**Cacao et Chocolat 29 rue de Buci, 6ᵉ.** The aroma alone makes it worth stopping in at this chocolate shop, which crafts confections of cacao from around the world and offers its own version of liquid chocolate in the small *salon* area. Mº Mabillon. Also at 63 rue Saint-Louis-en-l'Isle, 4ᵉ (Mº Pont-Marie). Both open Tues–Sat 10.30am–7.30pm.

**Debauve and Gallais 30 rue des Sts-Pères, 7ᵉ.** A beautiful shop specializing in chocolate and elaborate sweets that's been around since chocolate was taken as a medicine – and an aphrodisiac. Mº St-Germain-des-Prés/Sèvres-Babylone. Mon–Sat 9.30am–7pm; closed Aug.

**Ladurée 16 rue Royale, 8ᵉ.** Justly famous for their melt-in-your-mouth macaroons which are crispy, gooey, and worth every cent. Slightly more substantial fare in the chic *salon de thé*. Mº Madeleine. Mon–Sat 8.30am–7pm.

**Pâtisserie Stohrer 51 rue Montorgueil, 2ᵉ.** Bread, pâtisseries, chocolate and charcuterie baked here for more than 250 years. Discover what standard-fare *pain aux raisins* should really taste like. Mº Sentier. Daily 7.30am–8pm; closed first two weeks Aug.

## Herbs, spices and oils

**Allicante 26 bd Beaumarchais, 11ᵉ.** An impressive array of exotic oils for bath and kitchen, including almond and pistachio varieties, oils extracted from peach and apricot and rare olive oils from Greece and Italy. Mº Bastille. Tues–Sat 10.30am–1pm & 2.30–7pm.

**Izraël 30 rue François-Miron, 4ᵉ.** A cosmopolitan emporium of goodies from all round the globe: vinegars, oils, spices and mustards. M° St-Paul. Tues–Fri 9.30am–1pm & 2.30–7pm, Sat 9.30am–7pm.

**Shah et Cie 33 rue Notre-Dame-de-Lorette, 9ᵉ.** The oldest Indian grocer in Paris. M° St-Georges.

## Health food

**Naturalia 52 rue St-Antoine, 4ᵉ.** Feel you need a vitamin boost? Or, after too many rich meals, some rice cakes and seaweed? This is where to come. Several other branches. M° St-Paul/Bastille. Mon–Sat 10am–7.30pm.

**Rendez-Vous de la Nature 96 rue Mouffetard, 5ᵉ.** One of the city's largest and most comprehensive healthfood stores, with everything from organic produce to herbal teas. M° Cardinal-Lemoine. Tues–Sat 9.30am–7.30pm, Sun 9.30am–1pm.

## Honey

**Les Abeilles 21 rue Butte-aux-Cailles, 13ᵉ.** Honey from all over France and further afield, sold by an experienced beekeeper. Around €5 for a 250g pot. M° Corvisart/Place-d'Italie. Tues–Sat 11am–7pm.

## Kitchen equipment

**E Dehillerin 18–20 rue Coquillière, 1ᵉʳ.** Laid out like a traditional ironmonger's: no fancy displays, prices buried in catalogues, but good-quality stock at reasonable prices. In business since 1820. M° Châtelet-Les-Halles. Mon 8am–12.30pm & 2–6pm, Tues–Sat 8am–6pm.

**MORA 13 rue Montmartre, 1ᵉʳ.** An exhaustive collection of tools of the trade for the top professionals. M° Châtelet-Les-Halles. Mon–Fri 9am–6.15pm, Sat 8.30am–5pm.

**La Vaissellerie 80 bd Haussmann, 8ᵉ.** Simple, inexpensive French crockery, mostly in white, but they also stock the cheerful bright-yellow Chocolat Menier and Banania ranges. M° Havre-Caumartin. Also branches at 85 rue de Rennes, 6ᵉ; 79 rue St-Lazare, 9ᵉ; 332 rue St-Honoré, 1ᵉʳ; and 92 rue St-Antoine, 4ᵉ. Mon–Sat 9.30am–7pm.

## Salmon, caviar and other seafood

In addition to the establishments below, more caviar, along with truffles, *foie gras*, etc, is to be found at the lower end of rue Montmartre by the Forum des Halles in the 1ᵉʳ.

**Caviar Kaspia 17 pl de la Madeleine, 8ᵉ.** Blinis, smoked salmon and Beluga caviar. M° Madeleine. Mon–Sat 10am–1am.

**Comptoir du Saumon 60 rue François-Miron, 4ᵉ and several other addresses.** Salmon especially, but eels, trout and all things fishy as well. Plus a delightful little restaurant in which to taste the fare. M° St-Paul. Mon–Sat 10am–10pm.

**Petrossian 18 bd de Latour-Maubourg, 7ᵉ.** Not just gilt-edged fish eggs, but other Russian and French delicacies too. You can try delights such as smoked salmon sorbet at the restaurant next door. M° Latour-Maubourg. Mon–Sat 9.30am–8pm.

## Snails

**La Maison de l'Escargot 79 rue Fondary, 15ᵉ.** As the name suggests, this place specializes in snails: they even sauce them and re-shell them while you wait. M° Dupleix. Tues–Sat 9am–7.30pm, Sun 9am–1pm; closed mid-July to Sept. There is a restaurant for *dégustation* opposite at no. 70 (around €10, with a glass of wine).

## Tea

**Mariage Frères 30 rue du Bourg-Tibourg, 4ᵉ.** Hundreds of teas, neatly packed in tins, line the floor-to-ceiling shelves of this 100-year-old tea emporium. There's also a classy *salon de thé* (daily noon–7pm) on the ground floor, decorated in Neocolonial style with rattan chairs, and offering exquisite pastries as well as tea of course. The tiny museum upstairs has oddities such as the nineteenth-century *tasses à moustaches*, china teacups with a lip that the drinker could rest his moustache on and so avoid any unseemly wet bristles. M° Hôtel-de-Ville. Daily 10.30am–7.30pm.

## Vegetarian

**Diététique D J Fayer 45 rue St-Paul, 4ᵉ.** Tiny shop, one of the city's oldest specialists, selling dietary, macrobiotic and vegetarian products. M° St-Paul. Mon–Sat 9.30am–1.30pm & 2.30–8.45pm.

## Wine

**Les Caves Augé 116 bd Haussmann, 8ᵉ.** The

oldest *cave* in Paris. M° St-Augustin. Mon 1–7.30pm, Tues–Sat 9am–7.30pm.

**Le Baron Rouge 1 rue Théophile-Roussel, 12<sup>e</sup>.** A good selection of dependable lower-range French wines; €2 for a small tasting glass. Very drinkable Merlot at €2.50 a litre, if you bring your own containers. M° Ledru-Rollin. Tues–Fri 10am–2pm & 5–9.30pm, Sat 10am–9.30pm, Sun 10.30am–1pm.

**Caves Michel Renaud 12 pl de la Nation, 12<sup>e</sup>.** Established in 1890 and purveying superb-value French and Spanish wines, champagnes and Armagnac. M° Nation. Daily 9.30am–1pm & 2–8.30pm; closed Sun pm and Mon am.

**Les Caves St-Antoine 95 rue St-Antoine, 4<sup>e</sup>.** A small, amicable outfit. M° St-Paul. Tues–Fri 9am–1pm & 3–8pm, Sat 9am–8pm, Sun 9am–1pm.

**Nicolas 31 pl de la Madeleine, 8<sup>e</sup>.** A reliable merchant, with dozens of shops across the city. A good general selection. M° Madeleine. Mon–Sat 9am–8pm.

**Le Repaire de Bacchus 112 rue Mouffetard, 5<sup>e</sup>.** A good chain to look out for, with branches in every arrondissement. Sells many lesser-known and cheaper wines. M° Censier-Daubenton.

## A miscellany

**Abdon 6 bd Beaumarchais, 11<sup>e</sup>.** New and secondhand photographic equipment. If they don't have what you're looking for, try the half-dozen other camera shops on the same street. M° Chemin-Vert. Tues–Sat 9.30am–12.30pm & 1.30–6.30pm.

**Archives de la Presse 51 rue des Archives, 3<sup>e</sup>.** A fascinating shop for a browse, trading in old French newspapers and magazines. The window always has a display of out-dated newspapers corresponding to the current month, and there are piles upon piles of old magazines inside, with vintage *Vogues* giving a good insight into the changing fashion scene. M° Rambuteau. Mon–Sat 10.30am–7pm.

**Attica 64 rue de la Folie Méricourt, 11<sup>e</sup>** @www.attica-langues.com. All the books, CD-ROMS, dictionaries, videos, and audio cassettes one could possibly need to learn any number of the two hundred languages represented at this language-learning mecca. Online ordering enables you to hit the books before hitting the road. M° Oberkampf. Tues–Sat 10am–7pm.

**Boîte à Musique Anna Joliet Jardin du Palais Royal, 9 rue de Beaujolais, 1<sup>er</sup>.** Swiss-owned shop selling every style of music box, from inexpensive self-winding toy models to grand cabinets costing thousands of euros. Parisians have long loved mechanical instruments, and many of these play old favourites such as La Vie en Rose. The shop itself is a delightful, minuscule boutique squeezed behind glass at the northern end of the Palais Royal garden. M° Palais Royal-Musée du Louvre. Mon–Sat 10am–7pm.

**Diptyque 34 bd St-Germain, 5<sup>e</sup>.** Luxurious scented candles and other fragrant products. M° Maubert-Mutualité. Tues–Sat 10am–7pm.

**Editions de Parfums Frédéric Malle 37 rue de Grenelle, 7<sup>e</sup>** @www.editionsdeparfums.com. This boutique analyses your taste in perfumes before offering you a selection. All the perfumes have been created by "authors", which means professional *parfumeurs* working under their own name through this "publishing house". A 50ml bottle costs upwards of €50. M° Rue du Bac. Mon–Sat 11am–7pm; closed two weeks in Aug.

**Le Laguiole du Marais 6 rue du Pas de la Mule, 3<sup>e</sup>.** Tiny shop selling a large range of the celebrated knives from Laguiole in the Massif Central. M° Chemin-Vert. Mon–Sat 10am–12.30pm & 1.30–7pm, Sun 2–7pm.

**La Maison du Collectionneur 137 av Émile-Zola, 15<sup>e</sup>.** Old books, hats, newspapers of the wartime liberation, and assorted junk. M° Émile-Zola.

**La Maison de la Fausse Fourrure 34 bd Beaumarchais, 11<sup>e</sup>.** Sumptuous lengths of fake fur draped and pinned over every surface imaginable. M° Chemin-Vert. Mon–Sat 10am–7pm.

**Marché St-Pierre 2 rue Charles-Nodier, 18<sup>e</sup>.** Five floors of very inexpensive fabrics well worth a visit. M° Anvers. Mon 2–7pm, Tues–Sat 10am–7pm.

**Le Petit Bleu 21 rue Jean-Pierre Timbaud, 11<sup>e</sup>.** An excellent place for a last-minute present-buying expedition, this unclassifiable shop sells all things fragrant and delicious – wines, oils, teas, soaps, candles – and other gifts for the home. M° Oberkampf. Mon noon–8pm, Tues–Sat 10.30am–8pm, closed two weeks Aug.

**Pierre Frey 1 & 2 rue de Fürstenberg, 6<sup>e</sup>.** Stocks a huge range of stunning fabrics for furnishings and curtains. If you don't find what you're after here, try the handful of rival shops in the same street. M° Mabillon/St-Germain-des-Prés. Daily 10am–6.30pm.

**Pylones 57 rue St-Louis-en-l'île, 4ᵉ (M° Sully-Morland), and many other branches.** Playful and silly things, including inflatable fruit bowls, grasshopper can crushers, hand-puppet face-washers and sparkly resin jewellery. Daily 11am–7.30pm.

**Séphora 70 av des Champs-Élysées, 8ᵉ** ⓦ www.sephora.com. Huge perfumery with related books, an exhibition and a sampling area, and a big range of cosmetics. M° Franklin-D.Roosevelt. Mon–Sat 10am–midnight, Sun 11am–midnight. Also branches at Forum des Halles, level 3, 1ᵉʳ; 1 rue Pierre Lescot, 1ᵉʳ; and 30 av d'Italie, 13ᵉ (Mon–Sat 10am–7.30pm).

**Tang Frères 48 av d'Ivry, 13ᵉ.** A vast emporium of all things oriental, pungent with exotic smells. M° Porte-d'Ivry. Tues–Sun 9am–7.30pm.

**Trousselier 73 bd Haussmann, 8ᵉ** ⓦ www.trousselier.com. Described in French *Vogue* as the artificial flower shop. Every conceivable species of flora fashioned from manmade fibre. Decadent and pricey, but fun. M° St-Augustin. Mon–Sat 10am–7pm.

## Music

**Records**, **cassettes** and **CDs** are not particularly cheap in Paris, but there are plenty of secondhand bargains, and you may come across selections that are novel enough to tempt you. Brazilian, Caribbean, Antillais, African and Arab albums that would be **specialist rarities** in London or the States, as well as every kind of jazz, abound in Paris. **Rue Keller** and **rue des Taillandiers**, in the 11ᵉ (M° Bastille), have a wide range of offbeat record shops selling current trends. Secondhand traders offer up scratchy treats – anything from the Red Army choir singing the *Marseillaise* to African drummers on skins made from spider ovaries. The **flea markets** (St-Ouen especially), and the *bouquinistes* along the Seine, are good places to look for old records.

In the **classical** department, the choice of interpretations is generous and multinational. For all new and mainstream records, FNAC Musique (see below) usually has the best prices.

Also listed below are a couple of **bookshops** selling sheet music, scores and music literature, and some that sell instruments. Victor-Massé, Douai, Houdon, boulevard Clichy and other streets in the **Pigalle** area are full of instrument and sound-system shops. Guitarists especially will enjoy a look in at 16 rue V-Massé, 9ᵉ – afternoons only – where François Guidon builds jazz guitars for the greats and amateurs. For instruments and scores, head for Paul Beuscher, at the Bastille, which has amazing sales in spring.

**Afric' Music 3 rue des Plantes, 14ᵉ.** A small shop with an original selection of African, Caribbean and reggae discs. M° Mouton-Duvernet. Mon–Sat 10am–7pm.

**Arts Sonores 8 rue des Taillandiers, 14ᵉ.** Sells secondhand vinyl and is particularly strong on French *chanson*. M° Bastille. Tues–Sun 1.30–7.30pm.

**Camara 45 rue Marcadet, 18ᵉ.** Paris's best selection of West African music on cassette and video. M° Marcadet-Poissonnière. Mon–Sat noon–8pm.

**La Chaumière 5 rue de Vaugirard, 6ᵉ.** Classical music and some jazz, with more than 15,000 CD recordings to choose from, many discounted. You can listen before you buy, and the staff are happy to give advice. M° Odéon. Mon–Fri 11am–8pm, Sat 10am–8pm, Sun 2–8pm.

**Crocodisc 40–42 rue des Écoles, 5ᵉ.** Folk, Oriental, Afro-Antillais, raï, funk, reggae, salsa, hip-hop, soul, country. New and secondhand, at some of the best prices in town. M° Maubert-Mutualité. Tues–Sat 11am–7pm.

**Crocojazz 64 rue de la Montagne-Ste-Geneviève, 5ᵉ.** Mainly new imports of jazz and blues. M° Maubert-Mutualité. Tues–Sat 11am–7pm.

**Disc' Inter 2 rue des Rasselins, 20ᵉ.** Wide-ranging stock of Afro-Caribbean music on CD, cassette, video and vinyl. M° Porte-de-Montreuil. Mon–Sat 10am–7pm.

**Dream Store 4 pl St-Michel, 6ᵉ.** Good discounts on classical in particular but also some jazz, rock and French *chanson*. M° St-Michel. Mon 1.30pm–7.15pm, Mon–Sat 9.30am–7.30pm.

**FNAC Musique 4 pl de la Bastille, 12ᵉ, next to**

the opera house ⓦ www.fnac.fr. Extremely stylish shop in black, grey and chrome with computerized catalogues, every variety of music, books, and a concert booking agency. M° Bastille. Mon–Sat 10am–8pm, Wed & Fri till 10pm. The other FNAC shops (see under "Bookshops") sell music and hi-fi. Try FNAC-Étoile, at 26 av des Ternes, 17ᵉ (M° Ternes), Mon–Sat 10am–7pm, for jazz.

**Hamm 55bis rue de Rennes, 6ᵉ.** The biggest general music shop in Paris, selling instruments new and old, sheet music, scores, manuals, librettos etc. M° St-Placide. Tues–Sat 10.15am–7pm. Branches at 17 & 21 rue Monge (M° Place Monge).

**Librairie Musicale de Paris 68bis rue Réaumur, 3ᵉ.** Huge selection of books on music and of music, from Baroque oratorios to heavy metal. M° Réaumur-Sébastopol. Tues–Sat 10.15am–7pm.

**Maison Sauviat 124 bd de la Chapelle, 18ᵉ.** Wonderful shop that's been going strong since the 1920s. Now specializing in North and West African and Middle Eastern music. M° Barbès-Rochechouart. Mon–Sat 9am–7.30pm.

**Moby Disques 28 rue Monge, 5ᵉ.** Passionate jazz fans will like this small shop; jazz on vinyl – many collectors' items and Japanese imports – bought, sold and exchanged at reasonable prices. M° Cardinal-Lemoine. Mon–Sat 1.30–6pm.

**Parallèles 47 rue St-Honoré, 1ᵉʳ.** Principally an alternative bookshop, but with a good selection of pop and rock and secondhand CDs. M° Châtelet-Les Halles. Mon–Sat 10am–7pm.

**Paris Jazz Corner 5 & 7 rue Navarre, 5ᵉ.** Worth it just for the dustily dedicated atmosphere of the shop, which faces the Arènes de Lutèce. Great collection of jazz and blues, with lots of secondhand vinyl. M° Monge. Mon–Sat noon–8pm.

**Paul Beuscher 15–27 bd Beaumarchais, 4ᵉ** ⓦ www.paul-beuscher.com. A music department store that's been going strong for more than a hundred years. Instruments, scores, books, recording equipment, etc. M° Bastille. Mon 2–7pm, Tues–Sat 10.15am–7pm.

**Virgin Megastore 52 av des Champs-Élysées, 8ᵉ (M° Franklin-D.Roosevelt); and Carrousel du Louvre, under the Louvre, 1ᵉʳ (M° Palais-Royal-Musée-du-Louvre).** One of the biggest music stores, but lacks the wax rock heroes of the London store. Concert-booking agency and expensive Internet connection. Mon–Sat

10am–midnight, Sun noon–midnight.

**Voltage 23 rue Roi de Sicile, 4ᵉ.** An extensive collection of good-condition vinyl – mostly heavy metal and thrash rock. M° St-Paul Mon–Sat 10am–7pm.

## Sport

**Bicloune 7 rue Froment, 11ᵉ** ⓦ www.bicloune.fr. A bike shop with some bizarre models on show. Repairs carried out. M° Bréguet-Sabin. Tues–Sat 10.30am–1.30pm & 2–7pm, Sun 10am–1pm & 2–6.30pm.

**Le Ciel Est à Tout le Monde 10 rue Gay-Lussac, 5ᵉ** ⓦ www.lecielestatoutlemonde.com. Wonderful kites and other flying toys, plus frisbees, boomerangs, books and traditional wooden toys. RER Luxembourg. Mon–Sat 10am–7pm.

**Décathlon 26 av de Wagram, 17ᵉ.** A brilliant selection of sports gear and swimming costumes. M° Charles-de-Gaulle-Étoile. Mon–Sat 10am–8pm.

**La Haute Route 33 bd Henri-IV, 4ᵉ** ⓦ www.lahauteroute.com. Mainly skiing and mountaineering equipment: to rent or to buy – new and secondhand. M° Bastille. Mon 2–7pm, Tues–Sat 9.30am–1pm & 2–7pm.

**La Maison du Vélo 11 rue Fénelon, 10ᵉ.** Classic models, mountain bikes, tourers and racers; also does bike rental. M° Poissonnière. Tues–Sat 10am–7pm.

**Marathon 26 rue Léon Jost, 17ᵉ.** Specialists in running shoes. The shop is owned by an experienced marathon runner. M° Courcelles. Tues–Sat 10am–7pm.

**Nomades 37 bd Bourdon, 4ᵉ** ⓦ www.nomadeshop.com. The place to buy and hire rollerblades and equipment, with its own bar out back where you can find out about the scene. See also "Rollerblading" p.356. M° Bastille. Mon–Fri 11am–7pm, Sat & Sun 10am–7pm.

**Au Vieux Campeur 48 rue des Écoles, 5ᵉ.** This giant outdoor activities group has colonized an entire couple of blocks immediately north of rue des Écoles and east of rue St-Jacques with a dozen well-stocked shops – there's even a small climbing wall. You'll be directed to the right branch for maps, guides, boots, climbing, hiking, camping and ski gear, tents, sleeping bags and so on. M° Maubert-Mutualité. Mon–Fri 11am–7.30pm, Wed till 9pm, Sat 9.30am–7.30pm.

**SHOPS AND MARKETS** | Food and drink

# Markets

Several of the **markets** listed below are described in the text of the Guide. These, however, are the details – and the highlights. The map on pp.346–347 shows their locations.

## Books, stamps and art

As well as the specialized **book markets** listed below, you should of course remember the wide array of books and all forms of printed material on sale from the **bouquinistes**, who hook their green padlocked boxes onto the riverside quais of the Left Bank.

**Marché du Livre Ancien et d'Occasion Pavillon Baltard, Parc Georges-Brassens, rue Brancion, 15e.** Secondhand and antiquarian books. M° Porte-de-Vanves. Sat & Sun 8am–1pm.

**Marché aux Timbres junction of avs Marigny & Gabriel, on the north side of place Clemenceau in the 8e.** The stamp market. M° Champs-Élysées–Clemenceau. Thurs, Sat, Sun & hols 10am–7pm.

## Clothes and flea markets

Paris has three main **flea markets** (*marchés aux puces*) of ancient descent gathered about the old gates of the city. No longer the haunts of the flamboyant gypsies and petty crooks of literary tradition, they are nonetheless good entertainment, and if you go early enough you might just find something special. Some of the food markets have spawned secondhand clothes and junk stalls, notably the place d'Aligre, in the 12e, and the place des Fêtes, in the 20e.

**Porte de Montreuil 20e.** Cheap new clothes have begun to dominate what was the best of flea markets for secondhand clothes – still cheapest on Mon when leftovers from the weekend are sold off. Also old furniture, household goods and assorted junk. M° Porte-de-Montreuil. Sat, Sun & Mon 7.30am–5pm.

**Porte de Vanves av Georges-Lafenestre/av Marc-Sangnier, 14e.** The best choice for bric-a-brac little Parisian knick-knacks. Professionals deal alongside weekend amateurs. M° Porte-de-Vanves. Sat & Sun 7am–1.30pm.

**St-Ouen/Porte de Clignancourt 18e.** The biggest and most touristy flea market, with stalls selling new and secondhand clothes, shoes, records, books and junk of all sorts. The majority of the covered market, however, is now given over to expensive antiques. For a full description, see pp.179–180. M° Porte-de-Clignancourt. Mon, Sat & Sun 7.30am–7pm.

## Flower markets

Paris used to have innumerable **flower markets** around the streets, but today just the three listed below remain. Throughout the week, however, there's also the heavy concentration of **plant and pet shops** along the quai de la Mégisserie, between Pont-Neuf and Pont-au-Change.

**Place Lépine Île de la Cité, 1er.** On Sunday, the flower market is augmented with birds and pets. M° Cité. Daily 8am–7pm.

**Place de la Madeleine 8e.** Flowers and plants. M° Madeleine. Tues–Sun 8am–7.30pm.

**Place des Ternes 8e.** Flowers and plants. M° Ternes. Tues–Sun 8am–7.30pm.

## Food

The street **food markets** provide one of the capital's more exacting tests of willpower. At the top end of the scale, there are the lavish arrays in rue de Lévis in the 17e and rue Cler in the 7e, both of which are more market street than street market, with their stalls mostly metamorphosed into permanent shops. The **real street markets** include a tempting scattering in the Left Bank – in rue de Buci (the most photographed), near St-Germain-des-Prés, rue Mouffetard, place Maubert and place Monge. Bigger ones are at Montparnasse, in boulevard Edgar-Quinet, and opposite Val-de-Grâce

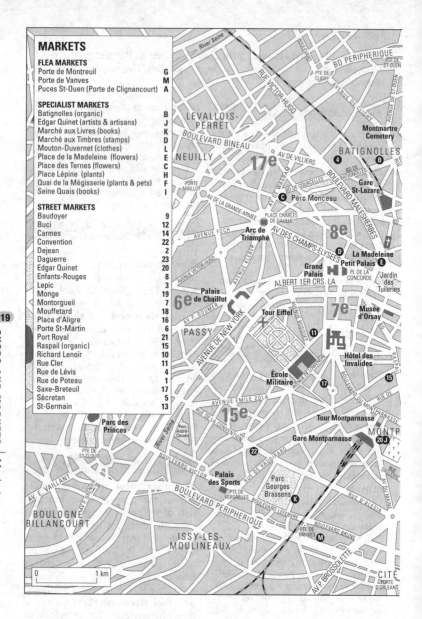

in boulevard Port-Royal. The largest is in rue de la Convention, in the 15e.

For a different feel and more exotic foreign produce, take a look at the **Mediterranean/Oriental** displays in boulevard de Belleville and rue d'Aligre.

Markets are traditionally morning affairs, usually starting between 7am and 8am and tailing off around 1pm. However, 2002 saw the opening of

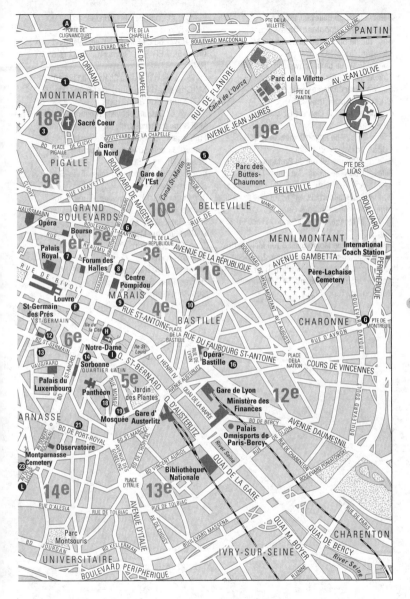

the city's first afternoon market, on place Baudoyer in the 4ᵉ; if it proves popular there are plans to open more. The covered markets have specific **opening hours**, which are given below, along with details of locations and days of operation.

**Baudoyer pl Baudoyer, 4ᵉ.** Mº Hôtel-de-Ville. Wed 4–8pm & Sat 7.30am–2.30pm.

**Batignolles rue de Turin and rue des Batignolles, 8ᵉ.** Organic produce. Mº Rome. Sat 8.30am–1pm.

**Belleville** bd de Belleville, 20ᵉ. M°
Belleville/Ménilmontant. Tues & Fri.
**Buci** rue de Buci & rue de Seine, 6ᵉ. M°
Mabillon. Tues–Sun.
**Convention** rue de la Convention, 15ᵉ. M°
Convention. Tues, Thurs & Sun.
**Dejean** pl du Château-Rouge, 18ᵉ. M°
Château-Rouge. Tues–Sun.
**Daguerre** 14ᵉ. M° Denfert-Rochereau.
Tues–Sun.
**Edgar-Quinet** bd Edgar-Quinet, 14ᵉ. M°
Edgar-Quinet. Wed & Sat.
**Enfants-Rouges** 39 rue de Bretagne, 3ᵉ. M°
**Filles-du-Calvaire.** Tues–Sat 8am–1pm &
4–7.30pm, Sun 9am–1pm.
**Maubert** pl Maubert, 5ᵉ. M° Maubert-
Mutualité. Tues, Thurs & Sat.
**Monge** pl Monge, 5ᵉ. M° Monge. Wed, Fri &
Sun.
**Montorgueil** rue Montorgueil & rue Montmartre,
1ᵉʳ. M° Châtelet-Les Halles/Sentier. Tues–Sat
8am–1pm & 4–7pm, Sun 9am–1pm.
**Mouffetard** rue Mouffetard, 5ᵉ. M° Censier-
Daubenton. Tues–Sun.

**Place d'Aligre** 12ᵉ. M° Ledru-Rollin.
Tues–Sun until 1pm.
**Port-Royal** bd de Port-Royal, near Val-de-
**Grâce, 5ᵉ.** RER Port-Royal. Tues, Thurs &
Sat.
**Porte-St-Martin** rue du Château-d'Eau, 10ᵉ .
M° Château-d'Eau. Tues–Sat 8am–1pm &
4–7.30pm, Sun 8am–1pm.
**Raspail** bd Raspail, between rue du Cherche-
**Midi & rue de Rennes, 6ᵉ.** M° Rennes. Tues &
Fri. Organic on Sun.
**Richard Lenoir** bd Richard Lenoir, 11ᵉ. M°
Bastille. Thurs & Sun.
**Rue Cler** 7ᵉ. M° École-Militaire. Tues–Sun
8.30am–noon.
**Rue Lepic** 18ᵉ. M° Abbesses. Tues–Sat.
**Rue du Poteau** 18ᵉ. M° Jules-Joffrin.
Tues–Sat.
**St-Germain** rue Mabillon, 6ᵉ. M° Mabillon.
Tues–Sat 8am–1pm & 4–7.30pm, Sun
8.30am–1pm.
**Secrétan** av Secrétan/rue Riquet, 19ᵉ. M°
Bolivar. Tues–Sat 8am–1pm & 4–7.30pm,
Sun 8am–2pm.

# Activities and sports

I f you've had enough of following crowds through museums or wandering through the city in the blazing sun or pouring rain, then it may just be time to do like the Parisians do. There are saunas to soak in, ice-skating rinks to fall on, vintage wines to taste, dance halls to tango in, libraries to peruse, and swimming pools to dive into. You can rent a bike, go on a boat trip or view the city from a helicopter. If you're feeling especially bold, try your hand at learning the tricks of the gourmet chef at a cookery school or toss a few rounds of boules and bring home the souvenir of a new skill.

*Pariscope* has useful listings of **sports** facilities, pools, *hammams* and so on (under "Sport et bien-être"). Information on municipal facilities is available from the town hall, the Mairie de Paris; you can pick up their free 500-page tome *Parisports* at the Hôtel de Ville and at any individual arrondissement's Mairie; alternatively, call ☎08.20.00.75.75, or check the comprehensive website Ⓦ www.paris.fr

For details of current **sporting events**, try the daily sports paper *L'Équipe*. A major venue for all sports, including athletics, cycling, show jumping, ice hockey, ballroom dancing, judo and motorcross, is the Palais Omnisport Paris-Bercy (POPB), 8 bd Bercy, 12ᵉ (☎01.40.02.60.60, Ⓦ www.bercy.fr; Mᵒ Bercy). The highlight of the calendar is, of course, the triumphal arrival of cycling's Tour de France in July.

## Boat trips, balloon and heli rides

Seeing Paris by boat is one of the city's most popular and durable tourist experiences – and a lot of fun. Seeing it from the air is even better.

### Bateaux-Mouches

Many a romantic evening walk along the quais has been rudely interrupted by the sudden appearance of a bulging **Bateau-Mouche**, with its dazzling floodlights and blaring commentaries. One way of avoiding the ugly sight of these hulking hulls is to get on one yourself. You may not be able to escape the trite narration, but the rides certainly give a glamorous close-up view of the classic buildings along the Seine.

Bateaux-Mouches **boat trips** start from the Embarcadère du Pont de l'Alma, on the Right Bank in the 8ᵉ (information ☎01.40.76.99.99, reservations ☎01.42.25.96.10; Mᵒ Alma-Marceau). The rides, which usually last an hour, run roughly hourly to every half hour, depending on the season. Summer departures are 10am–10.30pm, winter 11am–9pm. Tickets cost €7, or €4 for under-12s and over-60s. Avoid the outrageously priced lunch and

## Great views of the city

Few cities present such a uniform skyscape as Paris. Looking down on the ranks of seven-storey apartment buildings from above, it's easy to imagine the city as a lead-roofed plateau split by the leafy canyons of the boulevards and avenues. Spires, towers, and parks – not to mention multicoloured art museums and glass pyramids – stand out all the more against the solemn grey backdrop. Fortunately, many of Paris's tall buildings provide access to wonderful **rooftop views**. Here are a dozen of the best vistas in town:

**Arc de Triomphe** (see p.74): look out on an ocean of traffic.

**Centre Pompidou** (see p.97): a stunning backdrop to modern art.

**Grande Arche de la Défense** (see p.214): take the long view.

**Eiffel Tower** (see p.139): the classic, best at night.

**Institut du Monde Arabe** (see p.121): sip mint tea on the rooftop overlooking the Seine.

**Musée d'Orsay** (see p.146): look through the old station clock towards Montmartre.

**Notre-Dame** (see p.58): perch among the gargoyles.

**Parc André-Citroën** (see p.157): a tethered balloon rises 150m above this quirky park.

**Parc de Belleville** (see p.192): watch the sunset over the city.

**Sacré-Coeur** (see p.171): this puffball dome soars over Montmartre.

**La Samaritaine** (see p.95): posh department store with a seriously central rooftop.

**Tour Montparnasse** (see p.150): stand eye to eye with the Eiffel Tower.

dinner trips, for which "correct" dress is mandatory.

The main **competitors** to the Bateaux-Mouches are: Bateaux Parisiens Notre-Dame, Quai de Montebello, 5ᵉ (☎01.43.26.92.55; Mᵒ St-Michel); Bateaux Parisiens Tour Eiffel, Port de la Bourdonnais, 7ᵉ (☎01.44.11.33.44; Mᵒ Trocadero); Bateaux-Vedettes de Paris, Port de Suffren, 7ᵉ (☎01.47.05.71.29; Mᵒ Bir-Hakeim); and Bateaux-Vedettes du Pont Neuf, Square du Vert-Galant, 1ᵉʳ (☎01.46.33.98.38; Mᵒ Pont-Neuf). They're all much the same, and can be found detailed in *Pariscope* under "Croisières" in the "Visites-Promenades" section and in *L'Officiel des Spectacles* under "Promenades" in the "À Travers Paris" section.

An alternative way of riding on the Seine – one in which you are mercifully spared the commentary – is the **Batobus** (☎01.44.11.33.99), a river transport system operating from May to September. See "Basics" (p.29) for more details.

### Canal trips

Less overtly touristy than the Bateaux-Mouches and their clones are the **canal-boat trips**. Canauxrama (reservations ☎01.42.39.15.00, ⊛www .canauxrama.com) chugs up and down between the Port de l'Arsenal (opposite 50 bd de la Bastille, 12ᵉ; Mᵒ Bastille) and the Bassin de la Villette (13 quai de la Loire, 19ᵉ; Mᵒ Jaurès) on the Canal St-Martin. There are daily departures at 9.45am and 2.45pm from La Villette and at 9.45am and 2.30pm from the Pont de l'Arsenal. At the Bastille end is a long tunnel from which you don't surface till the 10ᵉ arrondissement. The ride lasts almost three hours – not bad for €13 (students €10, under-12s €8, under-6s free; no reductions weekends or holiday afternoons).

A more stylish vessel for exploring the canal is the **catamaran** of Paris-Canal, with trips between the Musée d'Orsay (quai Anatole-France by the Pont Solférino, 7ᵉ; Mᵒ Solférino) and the Parc de la Villette (La Folie des Visites Guidées, on the canal by the bridge between the Grande Salle and the Cité des Sciences, 19e; M° Porte-de-Pantin), which also last three hours. The catamaran departs from the Musée d'Orsay at 9.30am daily. Parc de la Villette departures are at 2.30pm. Trips cost €16, 12–25s and over-60s €12 (except Sun and holiday afternoons), 4–11s €9; reservations ☎01.42.40.96.97.

### Paris by helicopter or balloon

After Paris from the water, the next step up is Paris from the air. Don't imagine yourself looping the Eiffel Tower, however, as overflying Paris is restricted to the military. A **helicopter tour** is somewhat pricey, but if whirligig rides turn you on more than a four-star meal or a stalls seat at the theatre, then a quick spin around Versailles and Disneyland is on. Contact Mont Blanc Hélicoptères at the Héliport de Paris, 4 av de la Porte-de-Sèvres, 15e (☎01.40.60.10.14, ⓦwww.montblanc-helicopteres.fr; M° Balard). A 45-minute trip will set you back €150 for each passenger, and a minimum of four is required, though the agency can match you up with other would-be pilots.

For a more leisurely lofty overview, you can opt to go up in a **hot-air balloon**. France Montgolfières (☎01.60.95.15.86, ⓦwww.france balloons.com) can oblige. Cost is approximately €150–300, depending on the length of the trip and whether it's midweek or a weekend.

# Tea dances and guinguettes

For many years, a less obvious but very Parisian way to fill the afternoon hours was at a **bal musette** – a traditional knees-up, usually to the tune of an accordion (*musette*) band. The dance halls where they took place were the between-the-wars solution in the down-and-out parts of the city to depression, the dole and the demise of the Popular Front. Since the end of Balajo (see p.311), the nearest equivalent has been a **tea dance**, or *thé dansant* – a much more genteel or camp experience, often held by different promoters on a monthly or occasional basis (check the listings in magazines like *Zurban* or *Nova*, see pp.22 and 309). Absolutely free and more casual are the open-air dances held on Sunday afternoons throughout the summer at the **Kiosque de Musique** at the Parc de la Villette. The music is live, loud and international and the atmosphere is particularly conducive to kicking off your shoes and dancing on the grass. See p.186 for details of the park.

For the ultimate Parisian retro experience, head for a traditional riverbank **guinguette**. You can usually eat good, homely French food, but the real draw is the orchestra. Families, older couples and trendy young things from the city sway with varying degrees of skill to foxtrots, tangos and lots of well-loved accordion numbers – especially good for a Sunday afternoon.

**Chalet du Lac** facing the lac de St-Mandé, Bois de Vincennes, 11e ☎01.43.28.09.89. Afternoon dancing on Monday, Thursday and Friday, but it's best to save yourself for the elegant Sunday specials (3–9pm; €10), when a live band helps smooth out your footwork, and you can segue into the evening's Grand Bal, which continues until 2am. The restaurant serves good brasserie classics, with a menu at €30. M° St-Mandé-Tourelles.

**Chez Gégène** 162bis quai de Polangis, Joinville-le-Pont ☎01.48.83.29.43. Just the other side of the Bois de Vincennes, this is a genuine *guinguette* established in the 1900s, though the band mixes in pop anthems with the accordion classics. There's a decent restaurant, but the time to come is on Saturday nights (9pm–2am) and Sunday afternoons (3–7pm), when a live band plays ballroom classics and traditional

French numbers. Admission €17 for non-diners. RER Joinville-le-Pont. Open April–Dec.

**Divan du Monde 75 rue des Martyrs, 18ᵉ**
℡01.44.92.77.66 A venue to keep an eye on, with occasional afternoon events such as gay tea dances or the monthly kids' ball. Mᵒ Pigalle.

**La Flèche d'Or 102 bis rue de Bagnolet, 20ᵉ**
℡01.43.72.98.18. A relaxed soirée called "Je hais les dimanches" ("I hate Sundays") takes place roughly one Sunday a month (5pm–2am; €6), attracting families with children and clubbers winding down from the night before. On other Sundays, things get a bit more upbeat, with Afro-Latin and salsa sessions. Mᵒ Alexandre Dumas.

**Guinguette de l'île du Martin-Pêcheur 41 quai Victor-Hugo, Champigny-sur-Marne**
℡01.49.83.03.02. Traditional and charming *guinguette* situated on an island in the River Marne. You don't have to dine – or pay – to dance. RER A2 to Champigny-sur-Marne. Dancing April–Dec Wed–Sat 10pm–2am, Sun 4–7pm.

**Le Petit Robinson 164 quai de Polangis, Joinville-le-Pont** ℡01.48.89.04.39. Fifty metres along from *Chez Gégène* and a bit more upmarket, this is the place where serious dancers go to show off their immaculate waltzes, foxtrots and tangos. Like its neighbour, it has a huge dance floor, but it also boasts a live orchestra and is open year-round. Dancing Fri–Sat 8pm–2am, Sun 3–7pm. Admission and drink €10–15. RER Joinville-le-Pont.

**Le Tango 13 rue Au-Maire, 3ᵉ**
℡01.42.72.17.78. Tea dances, mostly gay- and lesbian-oriented, take place most Sunday afternoons from 5pm or 6pm, with entry price at €5–7, depending on the event. Mᵒ Arts-et-Métiers.

# Libraries

The city's **libraries** naturally provide the perfect environment for a quiet moment with a book or a newspaper, and some have beautiful interiors. For English-language books, the collection of the American library is unrivalled. Paris also has a library of films, the **vidéothèque** (see listing below), where getting out a movie and watching it on the spot is as easy as taking out a book. Some of the collections below require non-residents without a library card to buy day passes (around €3).

**American Library in Paris 10 rue du Général-Camou, 7ᵉ** ℡01.53.59.12.60, ⊛www .americanlibraryinparis.org. Hundreds of American magazines and newspapers and a vast range of books, plus readings and other events. Day pass €11, annual €87. Free internet access in 30-min increments. Mᵒ École-Militaire. Tues–Sat 10am–7pm.

**Bibliothèque des Femmes Marguerite Durand 79 rue Nationale, 13ᵉ.** A feminist library with books, journals, photos, posters and original manuscripts and letters. Mᵒ Nationale/Tolbiac.Tues–Sat 2–6pm.

**BIFI 100 rue du Faubourg-St-Antoine, 12ᵉ.** The Bibliothèque du Film encompasses magazines, books, stills, posters, videos and DVDs. €3 day pass. Mᵒ Ledru-Rollin. Mon–Fri 10am–7pm.

**Bibliothèque Forney Hôtel de Sens, 1 rue du Figuier, 4ᵉ.** Medieval building filled with volumes on fine and applied arts. Mᵒ Pont-Marie. Tues–Fri 1.30–8.15pm, Sat 10am–8.15pm.

**Bibliothèque Historique de la Ville de Paris Hôtel Lamoignon, 24 rue Pavée, 4e.** Sixteenth-century mansion housing centuries of texts and picture books on the city. Mᵒ St-Paul. Mon–Sat 9.30am–6pm.

**Bibliothèque Mazarine Institut de France, 23 quai de Conti, 6ᵉ.** History of France and of religion; genealogy. The setting, in a magnificent seventeenth-century building, with fine views across the Seine to the Louvre, is the real lure here. Some identification is required. Mᵒ St-Michel. Mon–Fri 10am–6pm.

**Bibliothèque Nationale François Mitterrand quai François-Mauriac, 13ᵉ.** The elephantine new national library, with two levels, one for the public, the other for accredited researchers. For a fuller description, see p.165. Mᵒ Quai-de-la-Gare/Bibliothèque-François Mitterrand station. €3 day pass.Tues–Sat 10am–7pm, Sun noon–6pm.

**Bibliothèque Ste-Geneviève 10 pl du Panthéon, 5ᵉ.** Reference library with beautiful murals in the foyer and a gorgeous reading room built around an iron skeleton. You need to be keen to get in: you have to register, bringing identification and a photo. RER Luxembourg. Mon–Sat 10am–10pm.

**BPI Centre Georges Pompidou, 3ᵉ.** The vast Bibliothèque Publique d'Information collection includes the foreign press, videos and a language lab to brush up on your French. Free. Mᵒ Rambuteau. Mon & Wed–Fri noon–10pm, Sat, Sun & public hols 11am–10pm; closed Tues & 1 May.

**Vidéothèque Forum des Images, 2 Grande Galerie, Porte St-Eustache, Forum des Halles, 1ᵉʳ ☎01.44.76.62.00, ☜www .forumdesimages.net.** For €5.50 (€4.50 for under-30s or over-60s), you can watch any of the four videos or films screened each day, and in the Salle Pierre

Emmanuel, make your own selection from thousands of film clips, newsreel footage, commercials, documentaries, soaps and the like, from 1896 to the present day. All the material is connected to Paris in some way, and you can make your choice – on your individual screen and keyboard – via a Paris place name, actor, director, date, and so on. Don't be put off by the laboratory atmosphere. All are welcome, and there are instructions in English at the desk and a friendly "librarian" to help you out. Once you're in the complex you can go back and forth between the projection rooms, the Salle Pierre Emmanuel and a Cyber Café, where the entrance fee gives you half an hour's free Internet access. RER Châtelet-Les Halles/Mᵒ Châtelet). Tues–Sun 1–9pm, Thurs till 10pm.

## Cookery and wine courses

Paris is, of course, the perfect place to try to get to grips with French gastronomy and wines. There are a large number of places offering courses to extend your knowledge, a handful of which are listed below.

**CIDD 30 rue de la Sablière, 14ᵉ** ☎01.45.45.44.20. The Centre d'Information, de Documentation et de Dégustation runs free "Porte-Ouvertes" days with tastings, and wine-tasting courses in English (a three-hour session costs around €70). Mᵒ Pernéty.

**Cordon Bleu 8 rue Léon-Delhomme, 15ᵉ** ☎01.53.68.22.50, ☜www.cordonbleu.net. Offers cookery demonstrations followed by tastings (morning or afternoon sessions, some in English; 48-hr advance booking; €38), or day-long hands-on sessions (again some in English, two weeks' advance booking required; €125). Mᵒ Vaugirard/Convention.

**Écoles Grégoire Ferrandi 28 rue de l'Abbé-Grégoire, 6ᵉ** ☎01.49.54.28.03. Christiane Andres runs friendly sessions for amateurs

on Wednesday evenings. Along with a dozen-odd Parisians, you help prepare a demonstration three-course meal, then sit down to eat and discuss it. You'll need good French however, as there's no translation. €60 for the evening; longer courses also available. Mᵒ St-Placide/Montparnasse-Bienvenüe.

**Promenades Gourmandes 187 rue du Temple, 3ᵉ ☎01.48.04.56.84, ☜www .theinternationalkitchen.com.** At the other end of the scale from the Cordon Bleu school is this a one-woman show. Run by Paulle Caillat, who speaks English fluently, you take a trip to the market then back to the kitchen for a three-course demonstration, with lots of hands-on work. This level of personal attention doesn't come cheap: the full day costs €290. Mᵒ Temple.

## Gyms, fitness clubs and dance classes

The body beautiful is big business in Paris. You'll find any number of aerobics classes, dance workouts and anti-stress fitness programmes offered, along with yoga, t'ai chi and martial arts. For shops selling sporting gear and equipment, see p.344. Many **fitness clubs** organize their activities in courses or require a minimum month's or year's subscription (big gym chains like Garden Gym and Gymnase Club are financially prohibitive), but if your last meal has left you feeling you need it, here are some options.

**Aquaboulevard** **4 rue Louis-Armand, 15e ⓣ01.40.60.10.00, ⓦwww.aquaboulevard.com.** The biggest in town, with a state-of-the-art fitness centre, squash and tennis courts, a climbing wall, golf tees, aquatic diversions, *hammams*, dance floors, shops and restaurants. To gain access to the full range of facilities, most importantly the gym, you're supposed to be accompanied by a member, but exceptions are sometimes made. €25 for a day pass. M° Balard/Porte de Versailles/RER Bd-Victor.

**Centre de Danse du Marais** **41 rue du Temple, 4e ⓣ01.42.72.15.42, ⓦwww.parisdanse.com.** Try out rock'n'roll, folkloric dance classes from the East, tap dancing, modern dance, physical expression or flamenco. You'll find a board advertising all the workshops in the alleyway. Each 90-minute session costs €15. Daily 9am–9pm. M° Hôtel-de-Ville.

**Centre de Yoga Sivananda** **123 bd de Sébastopol, 2e ⓣ01.40.26.77.49, ⓦwww.sivananda.org.** A first trial lesson is free, and while speaking French helps, it's not essential. M° Strasbourg-St-Denis.

**Club Quartier Latin** **19 rue de Pontoise, 5e ⓣ01.55.42.77.88, ⓦwww.clubquartierlatin.com.** Dance, gym, swimming and squash; €14 day pass for the pool and gym. M° Maubert-Mutualité. Mon–Fri 9am–10pm, Sat & Sun 9.30am–7pm.

**Espace Vit'Halles** **pl Beaubourg, 48 rue Rambuteau, 3e ⓣ01.42.77.21.71.** One of the flashiest fitness clubs in the city, with endless classes of every kind, weight rooms, various gyms, a sauna and *hammam*, and everything else you'd expect. For €20, the day pass gives access to all of the above. Mon–Fri 8am–10.30pm, Sat 10am–7pm, Sun 10–6pm. M° Rambuteau.

## Swimming pools

For €2.40, you can go swimming in most of Paris's **municipal pools** and, if you plan to go swimming a lot, the carnet of ten tickets (each good for one entrance) works out to be even cheaper. **Privately run pools**, whether owned by the city or not, are usually much more expensive.

### Municipal pools

At weekends, all the pools listed below, except the Butte-aux-Cailles pool, are open Sat 7am–5.30pm, Sun 8am–5.30pm. On weekdays during school hours, opening hours in municipally owned pools (whether publicly or privately run), are complicated. A general rule is that they open for an hour in the early morning and at lunch, then close for the morning and afternoon school sessions, then reopen in the early evening until about 6–8pm. It's best to ring in advance, check the Mairie's website (ⓦwww.paris.fr) or choose a pool nearby and consult their timetable. Many are closed on Monday in school terms. The following are among the best.

**Les Amiraux** **6 rue Hermann-Lachapelle, 18e ⓣ01.46.06.46.47.** Pool where Juliette Binoche memorably swam in the Kieslowski film *Three Colours Blue*. M° Simplon.

**Armand-Massard** **66 bd Montparnasse, 15e ⓣ01.45.38.65.19.** Three underground pools – 33-metre, 25-metre and a 12.5-metre kiddies pool – with lots of space to lounge about in between. M° Vavin.

**Butte aux Cailles** **5 pl Paul-Verlaine, 13e ⓣ01.45.89.60.05.** Housed in a spruced-up 1920s brick building with an Art Deco ceiling, this is one of the most pleasant swims in the city. There's a children's pool inside, and a 25-metre outside pool. M° Place-d'Italie. Sat 7–8am & 10am–6pm, Sun 8am–5.30pm.

**Château-Landon** **31 rue du Château-Landon, 10e ⓣ01.55.26.90.35.** Two pools, including one for children. M° Louis-Blanc.

**Henry-de-Montherlant** **32 bd Lannes, 16e ⓣ01.40.72.28.30.** Two pools, one 25-metre and one 15-metre, plus a terrace for sunbathing, a solarium – and the Bois de Boulogne close by. M° Porte-Dauphine.

**Jean Taris** **16 rue Thouin, 5e ⓣ01.55.42.81.90.** A 25-metre unchlorinated pool in the centre of the Latin Quarter and a student favourite. There's a small pool for children and swim groups for those with disabilities. M° Cardinal-Lemoine.

## Privately run pools

**Aquaboulevard 4 rue Louis-Armand, 15<sup>e</sup>** ☎01.40.60.10.00, ⊛www.aquaboulevard.com. The pool has wave machines and some incredible water slides, and there are jacuzzis and a grassy outdoor sunning area. €20 (€10 for children aged 3–11). M° Balard/Porte de Versailles/RER Bd-Victor.

**Georges-Vallerey Tourelles 148 av Gambetta, 20<sup>e</sup>.** Two pools – one 37-metre – and a solarium. €3.80. M° Porte-des-Lilas.

**Les Halles Susanne Berlioux 10 pl de la Rotonde, niveau 3, Porte du Jour, Forum des Halles, 1<sup>er</sup>** ☎01.42.36.98.44. A 50-metre pool with a vaulted concrete ceiling and a glass wall looking through to a tropical garden. €3.80. RER Châtelet-Les Halles/M° Châtelet.

**Pontoise-Quartier Latin 19 rue de Pontoise, 5<sup>e</sup>** ☎01.55.42.77.88. Art Deco architecture, beautiful blue mosaic interior and a 33-metre pool. On weekdays outside school terms, features night sessions until 11.45pm. Pool €4.25. There are squash courts too – see Club Quartier Latin opposite and on p.358. M° Maubert-Mutualité.

**Roger-Le Gall 34 bd Carnot, 12<sup>e</sup>** ☎01.44.73.81.12. Most of the extras are reserved for club members, but anyone can swim in the 50-metre pool (open in summer; covered in winter). €4.10. M° Porte-de-Vincennes.

# Hammams

**Hammams**, or Turkish baths, are one of the unexpected delights of Paris. Much more luxurious than the standard Swedish sauna, these are places to linger and chat, and you can usually pay extra for a massage and a *gommage* – a rub down with a rubber glove – followed by mint tea to recover. Don't let modesty get the better of you, all are quite restrained in terms of nudity and the staff are consummate professionals. You're provided with a strip of linen, but swimsuits are almost always required for mixed men-and-women sessions.

**Les Bains du Marais 31–33 rue des Blancs-Manteaux, 4<sup>e</sup>** ☎01.44.61.02.02, ⊛www .lesbainsdumarais.com. As much a posh health club as a *hammam*, with a rather chi-chi clientele. Offers facials, massage and haircuts, and you can lounge about in a robe with mint tea and a newspaper. Sauna and steam room entry costs €30, massage is €30 extra; there are mixed sessions on Wednesday evenings (7–11pm) and Sundays (11am–11pm) for which you have to bring a partner and a swimsuit. M° Rambuteau/St-Paul.

**Cléopatra Club 53 bd de Belleville, 11<sup>e</sup>** ☎01.43.57.34.32. Women only. €15 for the *hammam*, €8 for *gommage*; €40 for *hammam*, *gommage* and massage. Very relaxed with beautiful tiling; mint tea served. M° Belleville. Tues–Sun 10am–6pm; closed July & Aug.

**Hammams des Grands Boulevards 28 bd Bonne Nouvelle, 10<sup>e</sup>** ☎01.48.24.33.65. Fashionable new *hammam* with a good central location and a range of massage styles on offer, as well as a number of mixed sessions that are ideal for couples. Women: Sat 1–5pm; mixed (swimsuit obligatory): Mon 3–10pm, Wed 1–5pm, Sat 5–9pm, Sun 1–9pm; Men: Tues 1–10pm & Fri 1–8pm; nude sessions: Thurs 1–10pm (mixed; female partner obligatory for men), Wed 5–10pm (women only). Mon–Fri €21, Sat & Sun €23; massage, *gommage* and towels €52. M° Bonne Nouvelle.

**Hammam Med 43–45 rue Petit, 19<sup>e</sup>** ☎01.42.02.31.05. A bit far away from the centre, but it's one of the nicer *hammams* in the city, offering great mud treatments. Women: Mon–Fri & Sun 11am–10pm; mixed (bring a swimsuit): Sat 11am–10pm. €34 *hammam* and *gommage*; €49 with massage. M° Laumière.

**Hammam de la Mosquée 39 rue Geoffroy-St-Hilaire, 5<sup>e</sup>** ☎01.43.31.38.20. One of the most atmospheric baths in the city, with its vaulted cooling-off room and marble-lined steam chamber, and it's not intimidating if you've never taken a public bath before. It's very good value for €15, though towels are extra, and you can also have a reasonably priced massage and *gommage*. After your bath you can order mint tea and honey cakes around a fountain in the little courtyard café. Times may change, so check first, but generally women: Mon, Wed, Thurs & Sat 10am–9pm, Fri 2–9pm; men: Tues 2–9pm, Sun 10am–9pm. M° Censier-Daubenton.

## Participatory sports

Ice-skating, skateboarding, jogging, billiards, boules – it's all here to be enjoyed. Recently, cycling and rollerblading have become popular. **Soccer**-players may be able to shoulder their way in to a pick-up game in the Jardin des Tuileries. One sport that is not really worth trying in Paris is horse riding (*équitation*). You need to have all the gear with you and a licence, the Carte Nationale de Cavalier, before you can mount. For shops selling sporting gear and equipment, see p.344.

### Rollerblading and skateboarding

**In-line skating** has become so popular in Paris that it takes over the streets most Friday nights from 9.45pm, when expert skaters – up to 25,000 on fine evenings – meet on the esplanade of the Gare Montparnasse in the 14e (M° Montparnasse) for a demanding three-hour circuit of the city; check out Ⓦwww.pari-roller.com for details. A more sedate outing – and a better choice for kids – takes place on Sundays, departing at 2.30pm from the Place de la Bastille (Ⓦwww.rollers-coquillages.org).

Three good places to find more information and hire blades (around €10 for a half day) are: Vertical Line, 60bis, av Raymond Poincarré, 16e (☎01.47.27.21.21, Ⓦwww.vertical-line.com; M°Victor Hugo); Nomades, 37 bd Bourdon, 4e (☎01 .44.54.07.44, Ⓦwww .nomadeshop .com; M° Bastille); and Bike 'N Roller, 38 rue Fabert, 7e (Mon–Sat 10am–7.30pm, Sun 10am–7pm; ☎01.45.50.38.27, Ⓦwww .bikenroller.fr; M° Invalides); all hold their own roller events. The main outdoor **in-line skating and skateboarding arenas** are on the concourses of the Palais Omnisport, Bercy (M° Bercy) and the Palais de Chaillot (M° Trocadéro). The flat areas just beside the place de la Bastille and place du Palais-Royal are also very popular, as well as the central quais of the Seine on Sundays (see Cycling, opposite).

### Ice skating

You can get on the ice year round at the **Patinoire de Bercy**, at the Palais Omnisports, 8 bd de Bercy, 12e ☎01.40.02.60.60 (Fri 9.30pm–12.30am, Sat 3–6pm & 9.30pm–12.30am, Wed & Sun 3–6pm; M° Bercy). From early December to February, a big **outdoor rink** is set up on Place de l'Hôtel de Ville, 3e (M° Hôtel de Ville; Mon–Thurs noon–10pm, Fri noon–midnight, Sat 9am–midnight, Sun 9am–10pm). Two further seasonal rinks can be found on Place Raoul Dautry, 15e (M° Montparnasse-Bienvenüe), and on Place de la Bataille de Stalingrad, 19e (M° Stalingrad). Entrance is free, though skate (*patins*) hire is €5.

### Jogging – and the Marathon

For running or **jogging**, the Jardin du Luxembourg, Tuileries and Champs de Mars are particularly popular with Parisians: all provide decent, varied runs, and are more or less flat. If you want to run hills, head for the Parc des Buttes-Chaumont in the 19e or Parc Montsouris in the 14e for plenty of suitably punishing gradients. If you have easy access to them, the Bois de Boulogne and the Bois de Vincennes are the largest open spaces, though both are cut through by a number of roads.

The **Paris Marathon** is held in April over a route from place de la

Concorde to Vincennes. If you want to join in and need details and equipment, check out ⓦwww.paris-marathon.com, where you can register to run. A half-marathon is held in early March, and "Les 20km de Paris", takes place in mid-October, beginning and ending at the Eiffel Tower.

## Cycling

Since 1996 the Mairie de Paris has made great efforts to introduce dedicated **cycle lanes** in the city, which now add up to some 250km. You can pick up a free leaflet, *Paris à Vélo*, outlining the routes, from town halls, the tourist office, or bike rental outlets (see below). You can also download it from the web at ⓦwww.paris.fr – click on the "Sport" link. If you prefer cycling in a more natural environment, the Bois de Boulogne and the Bois de Vincennes have extensive bike tracks. A town hall-sponsored scheme closes off the following roads on Sundays and public holidays between May and September, making them popular places for cyclists and in-line skaters to meet up: the right bank of the Seine in the 8$^e$ and 12$^e$ arrondissements, along voie Georges Pompidou (10am–6pm); the left bank from quai Anatole France to quai Branly, in the 7$^e$ (10am–6pm); around rue Mouffetard, rue Descartes and rue de l'Ecole Polytechnique in the 5$^e$ (10am–6pm); on quai Valmy and quai de Jemmapes, in the 10$^e$ (2–6pm).

Several outlets detailed below **rent bikes**, by the hour, day, weekend or week. Prices depend on the type of bike, but usually range from about €15–20 a day, or upwards of €50 for a week; you have to leave a variable *caution* (deposit) or your credit-card details. If you want a bike for Sunday, when all of Paris takes to the quais, you'll need to book in advance. Some companies also offer **bike tours**.

**Bike 'n' Roller** 38 rue Fabert, 7$^e$ ☎01.45.50.38.27, ⓦwww.bikenroller.fr. Also rents out rollerblades. M° Invalides. Daily 10am–7pm.

**Bois de Boulogne** near the Porte de Sablons entrance. For rides through the wood. M° Les Sablons.

**Mike's Bike Tours** 24 rue Edgar Faure, 15$^e$ ☎01.56.58.10.54, ⓦwww.mikesbike-toursparis.com. Bike rental and four-hour guided bicycle trips in English, with a choice of day (€24) and night (€28) tours. Groups meet and leave from the base of the Eiffel Tower, March to mid-Nov only. Good exercise and cheerful camaraderie for those looking to cruise the streets of Paris, but don't want to go it alone. Reservations required. M° Dupleix. Daily 9am–7pm.

**Paris À Vélo C'est Sympa/Vélo Bastille** 37 bd Bourdon, 4$^e$ ☎01.48.87.60.01, ⓦwww.parisvelosympa.com. One of the least expensive (from €24 for the weekend) and most helpful for bike rental. Their excellent three-hour tours of Paris – including one at night and another at dawn – all cost €30, under-26s €26. M° Bastille. Daily 9am–7pm, closed weekdays 1–2pm.

**Paris-Vélo** 2 rue du Fer-à-Moulin, 5$^e$ ☎01.43.37.59.22. 21-speed and mountain bikes. M° Censier-Daubenton. Mon–Sat 10am–12.30pm & 2–7pm.

## Billiards and pool

Unlike bowling, **billiards** (*billard*) is an original and ancient French game played with three balls and no pockets. If you want to watch or try your hand (for around €10 per hour, plus around €15 deposit), head for one of the following:

**Académie de Billard Clichy-Montmartre** 84 rue de Clichy, 9$^e$ ☎01.48.78.32.85. The classiest billiard hall in Europe, where the players look like they've stepped out of a 1940s movie (or a *Men in Vogue* ad) and the decor is all ancient gilded mirrors, high ceilings and panelled walls. Pool tables too. €11 per hour. M° Place-de-Clichy. Daily 11am–4am.

**Blue-Billard** 111 rue St-Maur, 11$^e$ ☎01.43.55.87.21. Cocktails, chess and backgammon as well as billiards, in an arty-intellectual café–bar close to Belleville. If you arrive between 2pm and 4pm, you can have the *plat du jour* and an hour's billiards for €8.50. €11 per hour. M° Parmentier. Daily 11am–2am.

**Salle de Billard des Halles niveau 2, 14 rue Porte-du-Jour, Forum des Halles, 1er.** Two French billiard tables among the half-dozen pool tables. RER Châtelet-Les Halles. Tues & Thurs–Sun 9am–10pm, Mon 10am–9pm, Wed 10am–10pm.

## Boules

The classic French game involving balls, **boules** (or *pétanque)*, is best performed or watched at the Arènes de Lutèce (see p.126) and the Bois de Vincennes (see p.203). The principle is the same as British bowls but the terrain is always rough – usually gravel or sand and never grass – and the area much smaller. The metal ball is usually thrown upwards from a distance of about 10m, with a strong backspin that stuns it in order to stop it skidding away from the wooden marker (*cochonnet)*. It's very male-dominated, and socially the equivalent of darts or perhaps pool: there are café or neighbourhood teams and endless championships. On balmy summer evenings it's a common sight in many of the city's parks and gardens.

## Tennis, squash and table tennis

One of the nicest places to play **tennis** is on one of the six asphalt courts at the Jardins du Luxembourg (daily 8am–9pm; €5.75 per hour; M° Notre-Dame-des-Champs). Officially, you need to possess a municipal sports card (Carte Paris Sports) to play, and if you want to book in advance, you need to have access to French minitel system (3615 Paris, code RTEN). In practice, it's usually OK to just turn up with your kit and wait on the spot – usually no more than an hour.

Other municipal courts are listed on the website Ⓦ www.paris.fr and in *Parisports*. Private clubs demand steep membership fees.

There are several dedicated **squash** centres, including Squash Montmartre, 14 rue Achille-Martinet, 18e ☎ 01.42 .55.38.30 (Mon–Fri 10am–10.30pm, Sat & Sun 10am–8pm; M° Lamarck-Caulaincourt), which charges €14 for 45min. Alternatively, the Club Quartier Latin (see p.354) has squash courts for €11.50 for 45min.

The Mairie provides outdoor **table-tennis** tables in many of the smaller parks and outdoor spaces in Paris. It's up to you to bring a racket and balls. Some good locations include: Jardin Marco-Polo (6e), Square de la Trinité (9e), Parc Floral (12e), Parc Georges-Brassens (15e), Jardin des Batignolles (17e), and Place des Abbesses (18e).

# Spectator sports

Paris St-Germain (PSG) is one of France's richest and most powerful **football** teams, owned by the French cable station Canal-Plus. That said, it hardly enjoys a local following. The capital's teams retain a special status, too, in the **rugby, cycling** and **tennis** worlds. **Horse racing** is as serious a pursuit as in Britain, Australia or North America.

## Football and rugby

The Parc des Princes, 24 rue du Commandant-Guilbaud, 16e (M° Porte-de-St-Cloud) is the capital's main stadium for both **rugby union** and domestic **football** events (*le foot)*, and home ground to the first-division Paris football team PSG (Paris St-

Germain) and the rugby team, Le Racing. For PSG tickets, contact the club directly on ☎ 08.25.07.50.78 or online at Ⓦ www.psg.fr. The **Stade de France**, on rue Francis de Pressensé in St-Denis (☎ 08.92.70.09.00, Ⓦ www.stadefrance.com; RER Stade-de-France-St-Denis), specially built to host the 1998 World Cup, is now the venue for international football matches and rugby Six Nations' Cup matches.

## Cycling

The sport the French are truly mad about is **cycling**, and the biggest event of the French sporting year is the grand finale of the **Tour de France**, which ends in a sweep along the Champs-Élysées in the third week of July with the French president himself presenting the *maillot jaune* (the winner's yellow jersey).

It was, after all, in Paris's Palais Royal gardens in 1791 that the precursor of the modern bicycle, the *célérifère*, was presented, and seventy years later that the Parisian father-and-son team of Pierre and Ernest Michaux constructed the *vélocipède* (hence the modern French term *vélo* for bicycle), the first really efficient bicycle. The French can also legitimately claim the sport of cycle racing as their own, with the first event, a 1200-metre sprint, held in Paris's Parc St Cloud in 1868 – sadly for national pride, however, the first champion was an Englishman.

The Tour de France was inaugurated in 1903; France, though, hasn't had a victory since Bernard Hinault in 1985. In theory, the last day of the 4000-odd-kilometre, 25-stage, three-week race is a competitive time trial, but most years this amounts to a triumphal procession, the overall winner of the Tour having long since been determined. Only very rarely does Paris witness memorable scenes such as those of 1989, when American Greg Lemond snatched the coveted *maillot jaune* on the final day. Requiring what seems like superhuman endurance – and there are persistent drug scandals – around two hundred riders usually start the race, but sometimes less than 150 finish.

Other classic long-distance bike races that begin or end in Paris include the 600-kilometre **Bordeaux–Paris**, the world's longest single-stage race, first held in 1891; the **Paris–Roubaix**, instigated in 1896, which is reputed to be the most exacting one-day race in the world; the **Paris–Brussels** held since 1893; and the rugged six-day **Paris–Nice** event, covering more than 1100km.

The Palais Omnisports de Bercy (see below) holds cycling events including time trials.

## Tennis

The French equivalent of Britain's Wimbledon complex, **Roland-Garros**, lies between the Parc des Princes and the Bois de Boulogne, with the excellent address of 2 av Gordon-Bennett, 16e (☎01.47.43 .48.00; Ⓦwww.frenchopen.org; M° Porte-d'Auteuil). The **French Tennis Open**, one of the four major events which together comprise the Grand Slam, takes place in the last week of May and first week of June. Tickets need to be reserved months in advance using the postal booking system (check the website above for details), and tennis club members are heavily favoured. However, you can sometimes pick up tickets for unseeded matches online at Ⓦwww.ticketnet.fr, or at Roland Garros itself on the day of the tournament – if you're lucky.

## Athletics and other sports

The Palais Omnisports Paris-Bercy (POPB) at 8 bd Bercy, 12e (☎01.46 .91.57.57, Ⓦwww.bercy.com; M° Bercy) hosts all manner of sporting events – athletics, cycling, handball, dressage and show-jumping, ice hockey, ballroom dancing, judo and motocross – as well as stadium rockers like Iron Maiden and Lord of the Dance. Keep an eye on the sports pages of the newspapers (except *Le Monde*, which has no sports coverage at all), and you might find something that interests you. The complex holds 17,000 people, so you've a fair chance of getting a ticket at the door, championships excepted. Otherwise, tickets are sold through the usual outlets: FNAC and Virgin Megastore (see pp.332, 343 & 344), and online at Ⓦ www.ticketnet.fr/bercy.

## Horse racing

The **biggest races** are the Grand Prix de L'Arc de Triomphe and the Prix de la République, held on the first and last Sundays in October respectively at Auteuil and Longchamp. The week starting the last Sunday in June sees nine big events, at Auteuil, Longchamp, St-Cloud and Chantilly (see p.232). If you want to try your luck with **bet-ting**, any bar or café with the letters PMU will take your money on a three-horse bet, known as *le tiercé*.

St-Cloud Champ de Courses is in the Parc de St-Cloud off Allée de Chamillard. Auteuil is off the route d'Auteuil ((M° Porte-d'Auteuil), and Longchamp off the route des Tribunes (M° Porte-Maillot and then bus 244), both in the Bois de Boulogne. *L'Humanité* and *Paris-Turf* carry details, and admission charges are less than €5.

**Trotting races**, with the jockeys in chariots, run from August to September on the Route de la Ferme in the Bois de Vincennes.

ACTIVITIES AND SPORTS | Spectator sports

# Kids' Paris

The French are extremely welcoming to children on the whole and Paris's vibrant atmosphere, with its street performers and musicians, lively pavement cafés and brightly lit carousels is certainly family-friendly. The obvious pull of Disneyland aside (covered in Chapter 14), there's plenty of other attractions and activities to keep kids happy from circuses to rollerblading. As you'd expect, museum-hopping with youngsters in Paris can be as tedious as any other big city, but remember that while the Louvre and Musée d'Orsay cater to more acquired tastes, the Musée des Arts et Métiers, the Pompidou Centre, Parc de la Villette and some of the other attractions listed below will interest the young and old alike. Travelling with a child also provides the perfect excuse to enjoy some of the simpler pleasures of city life – the playgrounds, ice-cream cones, toy shops and pastries that Paris seems to offer in endless abundance.

In terms of **practicalities**, many cafés, bars or restaurants offer *menus enfants* or are often willing to cook simpler food on request, and hotels tack only a small supplement for an additional bed or cot on to the regular room rate. You should have no difficulty finding disposable nappies, baby foods and milk powders (see box overleaf) for infants. Throughout the city the RATP (Paris Transport) charges half-fares for 4–10s; under-4s travel free.

The most useful **sources of information** for current shows, exhibitions and events, are the special sections in the listings magazines: "Enfants" in *Pariscope* and "Pour les jeunes" in *L'Officiel des Spectacles*. The best place for **details of organized activities**, whether sports, courses or local youth clubs, is the Centre d'Information et de Documentation de la Jeunesse (CIDJ), 101 quai Branly, 15e; ☏01.43.06.15.38, ⊛www.cidj.com (M° Bir-Hakeim; Mon–Fri 9.30am–6pm & Sat 9.30am–1pm). The Mairie of Paris provides information about sports and special events at the Kiosque Paris-Jeunes, 25 bd Bourdon, 4e ☏01.42.76.22.60 (M° Bastille; Mon–Fri noon–7pm). The tourist office also publishes a free booklet in French, *Paris-Île-de-France avec des Yeux d'Enfants*,

## Babysitting

Reliable **babysitting** agencies include Kid Services, 17 rue Molière, 1er (☏08.20.00.02.30, ⊛www.kidservices.fr; €6 per hour plus €12 fees) and Baby Sitting Services, 4 rue Nationale, Boulogne Billancourt 92100 (☏01.46.21.33.16, ⊛www.babysittingservices.com; €5.90–6.60 per hour – minimum of three consecutive hours – plus €9.90–15.90 fees). Otherwise, try individual notices at the American Church, 65 quai d'Orsay, 6e (M° Invalides; ⊛www.acparis.org), the Alliance Française, 101 bd Raspail, 6e (M° St-Placide; ⊛www.alliancefr.org), or CIDJ, 101 quai Branly, 15e (M° Bir-Hakeim; ☏01.44.49.12.00, ⊛www.cidj.com).

with lots of ideas and contacts, or you can check out the children section on its website ⓦ www.paris-touristoffice.com.

It's worth remembering that **Wednesday afternoons**, when primary school children have free time, and **Saturdays** are the peak times for children's activities and entertainment; Wednesdays continue to be child-centred even during the school holidays.

## Parks, gardens and zoos

Younger kids in particular are well catered for by the **parks and gardens** within the city. The most standard forms of entertainment are puppet shows and **Guignol**, the French equivalent of Punch and Judy; these usually last about 45 minutes, cost around €2.50 and are most common on Wednesday, Saturday and Sunday afternoons. Children under about eight seem to appreciate these shows most, with the puppeteers eliciting an enthusiastic verbal response from them; even though it's all in French, the excitement is contagious and the stories are easy enough to follow.

Although there aren't, on the whole, any open spaces for spontaneous games of football, baseball or cricket, most parks have an enclosed playground with swings, climbing frames and a sandpit, while there's usually a netted enclosure where older children play casual **ballgames**. Otherwise, French sport tends to be thoroughly organized (see Chapter 20, "Activities and sports").

The real star attractions for young children have to be the **Jardin d'Acclimatation** and the **Parc de la Villette**, though you can also let your kids off the leash at the **Jardin des Plantes**, 57 rue Cuvier, 5ᵉ (Mᵒ Jussieu/Monge). Open from 7.30/8am until dusk, it contains a small **zoo**, the **Ménagerie** (summer Mon–Sat 9am–6pm, Sun till 6.30pm; winter Mon–Sat 9am–5pm, Sun till 6.30pm; €6/€3.50, under-4s free), a playground, hothouses and plenty of greenery; for more details see p.126. Paris's top zoo is at the **Bois de Vincennes** (see p.203), the **Parc Zoologique**, at 53 av de

### Paris with babies

You will have little problem in getting hold of essentials for **babies**. Familiar brands of baby food are available in the supermarkets, as well as disposable nappies (*couches à jeter*), etc. After hours, you can get most goods from late-night pharmacies, though they are slightly more expensive.

Getting around with a pushchair poses the same problems as in most big cities. The métro is especially bad, with its constant flights of stairs (and few escalators), difficult turnstiles and very stiff doors. Some stations, however, have a disabled access door: you'll need to ask at the ticket desk for them to open it and you'll be expected to pass your ticket through the turnstile first.

Unfortunately, many of the lawns in Parisian parks are often out of bounds ("*pelouse interdite*"), so sprawling on the grass with toddlers and napping babies is often out of the question. That said, more and more parks are now opening the odd grassy area to the public. Just be sure to spot others indulging before you do.

Finding a place to change and nurse a baby is especially challenging. While most of the major museums and some department stores have areas within the women's toilets equipped with a shelf and sink for changing a baby, most restaurants do not. Breastfeeding in public, though not especially common among French women, is, for the most part, tolerated if done discreetly.

For emergency medical care, see under "Health".

St-Maurice, 12ᵉ (Mᵒ Porte-Dorée; April–Sept daily 9am–6pm or 6.30pm; Oct–March daily 9am–5pm or 5.30pm; €8/€5, under-4s free). This zoo was one of the first in the world to get rid of cages and use landscaping to simulate a more natural habitat and give the animals more room to exercise. The most exciting part of the day for the animals and, hence, their most animated moments, are at feeding times, scheduled throughout the afternoon.

## The Jardin d'Acclimatation

In the Bois de Boulogne, by Porte des Sablons (Mᵒ Les Sablons/Porte-Maillot), ⓦ www.jardindacclimatation.fr. Adults and children €2.30, under-3s free; rides around €2, or buy a carnet of 20 tickets for €35. Daily: June–Sept 10am–7pm; Oct–May 10am–6pm, with special attractions Wed, Sat, Sun & all week during school hols, including a little train to take you there from Mᵒ Porte-Maillot (behind L'Orée du Bois restaurant; every 15min, 11am–6pm; €4.60 return, includes admission). The garden is a cross between a funfair, zoo and amusement park, with temptations ranging from bumper cars, go-karts, pony and camel rides, sea lions, birds, bears and monkeys, to a magical mini-canal ride (la rivière enchantée), distorting mirrors, a huge trampoline, scaled-down farm buildings, and a puppet theatre. Astérix and friends may be explaining life in their Gaulish village, or Babar the world of the elephants in the created-for-children Musée en Herbe (Mon–Fri & Sun 10am–6pm, Sat 2–6pm). The museum also has a permanent interactive exhibition aimed at 4- to 12-year-olds, introducing them to the history of European art. There'll be game sheets (also available in English), workshops and demonstrations of traditional crafts. The newest attraction is the high-tech Exploradôme, designed to help children discover science, the five human senses and art through interactive computer-based exhibits and the usual array of hands-on activities. Children who are after more passive participation can just watch and listen at the Théâtre du Jardin pour l'Enfance et la Jeunesse, which puts on musicals, ballets and poetry readings. Outside the jardin, in the Bois de Boulogne, older children can amuse themselves with mini-golf and bowling, or boating on the Lac Inférieur. By the entrance to the jardin there's bike rental (bring your passport) for roaming the wood's 14km of cycle trails. See p.212 for more on the Bois de Boulogne.

## Parc de la Villette

In the 19ᵉ between avs Jean-Jaurès and Corentin-Cariou; ☎01.40.03.75.75, ⓦwww.la-villette.com. Mᵒ Porte-de-Pantin/Porte-de-la-Villette. Daily 6am–1am; entry to park free. As well as the Cité des Sciences, various satellite attractions (see p.186), and wide-open spaces to run around or picnic in, the Parc de la Villette has a series of ten

## Food for kids

Restaurants in Paris are usually good at providing small portions or allowing children to share dishes. Dame Tartine, 2 rue Brisemiche, 4ᵉ (Mᵒ Rambuteau/Hôtel-de-Ville; daily noon–11.30pm), is family-friendly, relaxed and affordable in a great spot overlooking the Stravinsky Fountain, right beside the Pompidou Centre. Kids can share things from the menu like the delicious open toasted sandwiches (from €4.50), or there's a special kids' menu at €7.50. Several other eating places listed in our Eating & Drinking section (see pp.271–308) offer a menu enfant, including Chez Jenny (see p.290) and Chez Imogène (see p.305). One thing to remember when ordering a steak, hamburger, etc, is that the French will serve it rare unless you ask for it "bien cuit".

Junk-food addicts no longer have any problems in Paris. McDonald's, Quick Hamburger and their clones are to be found all over the city. The French-style "fast foude" chain, Hippopotamus, is slightly healthier (branches throughout the centre of the city, including 1 bd des Capucines, 2ᵉ ☎01.47.42.75.70; Mᵒ Opéra; daily 11am–5am; €7.50 menu enfant).

themed gardens, some specially designed for kids.

Polished steel monoliths hidden amongst the trees and scrub cast strange reflections in the Jardin des Miroirs, while Le Jardin des Brouillards has jets and curtains of water at different heights and angles. Formalized shapes of dunes and sails, windmills and inflated mattresses make up the Jardin des Vents et des Dunes (under-12s only and their accompanying adults). Strange music creates a fairytale or horror-story ambience in the imaginary forests of the Jardin des Frayeurs Enfantines. The Jardin des Voltiges has an obstacle course with trampolines and rigging. Small bronze figures lead you through the vines and other climbing plants of the Jardin de la Treille; and the Jardin des Bambous is filled with the sound of running water. On the north side of the canal de l'Ourcq is the extremely popular eighty-metre-long **Dragon Slide**.

Some of the park's "follies" have activities for kids: video editing in the Folie Vidéo and a game-filled crèche for 2- to 5-year-olds in the Petite Folie, both on the south bank of the canal de l'Ourcq. There are also arts activities for 7- to 10-year-olds in the Folie des Arts Plastiques, by the northeast corner of the Grande Halle (details on ☎01.40.03.75.03 or see website).

## Parc Floral

**In the Bois de Vincennes, on rte de la Pyramide (M° Château-de-Vincennes, then bus #112 or a ten-minute walk past the Château de Vincennes), ⊛www.parcfloraldeparis.com. April–Sept 9.30am–8pm; Oct–March 9.30am–5/6pm; admission €1.50, children aged 6–17 €0.75 plus supplements for some activities, under-6s free.**

There's always fun and games to be had at the **Parc Floral**, on the other side of the Bois de Vincennes towards the zoo. The excellent playground has slides, swings, ping-pong (racket and ball €6) and pedal carts (from 2pm; €7–10 per half-hour), mini-golf modelled on Paris monuments (from 2pm; €5, children under 12 €3), an electric car circuit, and a little train touring all the gardens (April–Oct daily 1–5pm; €1). Tickets for the paying activities are sold at the playground between 2pm and 5.30pm weekdays and until 7pm on weekends;

activities stop fifteen minutes afterwards. Note that many of these activities are available from March/April to August only and on Wednesdays and weekends only in September and October. On Wednesdays at 2.30pm (May–Sept) there are free performances by clowns, puppets and magicians. Also in the park is a children's theatre, the **Théâtre Astral**, which has mime, clowns or other not-too-verbal shows for small children aged 3 to 8 (Wed & school hols 3pm, Sat 3.30pm, Sun & public hols April–Oct 4.30pm, Nov–March 3.30pm; €5.50; ☎01.43.71.31.10). There is also a series of pavilions with child-friendly educational exhibitions (free entry), which look at nature in Paris; the best is the **butterfly garden** (mid-May to mid-Oct Mon–Fri 1.30–5.15pm, Sat & Sun 1.30–6pm).

## Jardin des Enfants aux Halles

**105 rue Rambuteau, 1er ☎01.45.08.07.18 (M°/RER Châtelet-Les Halles). Tues, Thurs & Fri 9am–noon & 2–6pm, Sat & Wed 10am–6pm, Sun & holidays 1–6pm; Nov–March till 4pm; closed Mon & during bad weather; €0.35 for a one-hour slot; 7–15s only except Sat am).**

Right in the centre of town, just west of the Forum des Halles, the **Jardin des Enfants aux Halles** is great if you want to lose your charges for the odd hour. A whole series of fantasy landscapes fill this small but cleverly designed space. On Wednesdays, animators organize adventure games; and at all times the children are supervised by professional child-carers. You may have to reserve a place an hour or so in advance. On Saturday mornings (10am–2pm) adults too can go in and play while they take charge of their under-seven-year-olds – the only time the little ones have access. Several languages are spoken, including English. Opening times vary a bit in the middle of the day, so it might be best to phone ahead.

## Other parks, squares and public gardens

All of these assorted **open spaces** can offer play areas, puppets or, at the very least, a bit of room to run around in, and are open from 7.30 or 8am till dusk. **Guignol and puppet shows** take place on Wednesday and weekend afternoons (more frequently in the summer holidays) and cost around €2.50.

**Buttes-Chaumont** 19e ☏01.42.40.88.66. *Guignol* and grassy slopes to roll down (see p.190). M° Buttes-Chaumont/Botzaris.

**Champs-de-Mars** 7e ☏01.48.56.01.44. Puppet shows. M° École-Militaire.

**Jardin du Luxembourg** 6e ☏01.43.26.46.47. A large playground, pony rides, toy boat rental, bicycle track, rollerblading rink, and puppets (see p.132). M° St-Placide/Notre-Dame-des-Champs/RER Luxembourg.

**Jardins du Ranelagh** av Ingres, 16e. Marionettes, cycle track, rollerblading rink and playground. M° Muette.

**Jardins du Trocadéro** pl du Trocadéro, 16e. Rollerblading, skateboarding and aquarium. M° Trocadéro.

**Jardin des Tuileries** pl de la Concorde/rue de Rivoli, 1er. Pony rides, marionettes, toy sailing boats, ice rink (in winter), funfair in July. See p.81. M° Place-de-la-Concorde/Palais-Royal–Musée-du-Louvre.

**Parc Georges-Brassens** rue des Morillons, 15e ☏01.48.42.51.80. Climbing rocks, puppets, artificial river, playground and scented herb gardens (see p.160). Enter the park at the entrance across from 86 rue Brancion. M° Convention/Porte-de-Vanves.

**Parc de Monceau** bd de Courcelles, 17e ☏01.42.67.04.63. Rollerblading rink (see p.79). M° Monceau.

**Parc Montsouris** bd Jourdan, 14e. Puppet shows by the lake (see p.156). M° Glacière/RER Cité-Universitaire.

**Place des Vosges** Marais, 4e. Has a popular sand pit and plenty of space to run around (see p.107). M° Bastille.

# Funfairs

There are three big **funfairs** (*fêtes foraines*) held in Paris each year. The season kicks off in late March with the Fête du Trône in the Bois de Vincennes (running until late May), followed by the funfair in the Tuileries gardens in mid-June to late August, with more than forty rides, including a giant ferris wheel, and ending up with the Fête à Neu Neu, held near the Bois de Boulogne from early September to the beginning of October. Look up "Fêtes Populaires" under "Agendas" in *Pariscope* for details if you're in town at these times. Very occasionally, rue de Rivoli around M° St-Paul hosts a mini-fairground.

There's usually a **merry-go-round** at the Forum des Halles and beneath Tour St-Jacques at Châtelet, with carousels for smaller children on place de la République, at the Rond-Point des Champs-Élysées by avenue Matignon, at place de la Nation, and at the base of the Montmartre funicular in place St-Pierre.

## Swimming, rollerblading and other family activities

One of the most fun things a child can do in Paris – and as enjoyable for the minders – is to have a wet and wild day at **Aquaboulevard**, a giant leisure complex with a landscaped wave pool, slides and a grassy outdoor park. In addition, many municipal **swimming pools** in Paris have dedicated children's pools. See "Activities and sports", p.354 for more details.

**Cycling** and **rollerblading** are other fun undertakings for the whole family. Sunday is now the favoured day to be *en famille* on wheels in Paris, when the central quais of the Seine and the Canal St-Martin are closed to traffic. One of the most thrilling wheelie experiences is the **mass rollerblading** that takes place on Friday nights and Sunday afternoons (the Sunday outings are more family affairs). See p.356 for more details and a list of bike and rollerblade hire places. Paris à Vélo C'est Sympa (see p.357) has a good range of kid-sized bikes as well as baby carriers and tandems, and they also offer bicycle tours of Paris.

**Bowling** and **billiards** are both popular in Paris and might amuse your teenagers (see p.357 and p.358).

There is also a funfair museum, the privately owned **Musée des Arts Forains**, on the edge of the Parc de Bercy at 53 av des Terroirs de France, 12ᵉ. Located within one of the old Bercy wine warehouses, the museum has working merry-go-rounds as well as fascinating relics from nineteenth-century fairs. Visits are by arrangement only on ☎01.43.40.16.15; M° Bercy then bus #24.

# Theme parks

Disneyland Paris (see Chapter 14) has put all Paris's other fantasy worlds and **theme parks** into the shade. And unfortunately it's the only one with direct transport links. But, if you're prepared to make the effort, **Parc Astérix** is better mind-fodder and cheaper than Disney.

### Parc Astérix

Ⓦ www.parcasterix.fr
In Plailly, 38km north of Paris off the A1 autoroute, most easily reached by half-hourly shuttle bus (9.30am–1.30pm & 4.30–6/7pm) from RER Roissy-Charles-de-Gaulle (line B). April–June Mon–Fri 10am–6pm, Sat & Sun 9.30am–7pm; July & Aug daily 9.30am–7pm; Sept & Oct Wed, Sat & Sun only 10am–6pm. Also closed for several days in May and June – it's best to check the website (in English and French) or phone ☎03.44.62.34.34. Admission is €31, 3–12s €23, under-3s free; at most RER and métro stations you can buy an inclusive transport (including shuttle bus) and admission fee ticket for €36.85 and under-12s €26.60.
A Via Antiqua shopping street, with buildings from every country in the Roman Empire, leads to a Roman town where gladiators play comic battles and dodgem chariots line up for races. There's a legionaries' camp where incompetent soldiers attempt to keep watch, and a wave-manipulated lake which you cross on galleys and longships. In the Gaulish village, Panoramix mixes his potions, Obélix slavers over boars, Astérix plots further sorties against the occupiers, and the dreadful bard is exiled up a tree. In another area, street scenes of Paris show the city changing from Roman Lutetia to the present-day capital. All sorts of rides are on offer (with long queues for the best ones); dolphins and sea lions perform tricks for the crowds; there are parades and jugglers; restaurants for every budget; and most of the actors speak English (even if they occasionally get confused with the variations on the names).

# Circus, theatre and cinema

Language being less of a barrier for smaller children, the younger your kids, the more likely they are to appreciate Paris's many special theatre shows and films. There's also mime and the circus, which need no translation.

### Circus (Cirque)

**Circuses**, unlike funfairs, are taken seriously in France. They come under the heading of culture as performance art (and there are no qualms about performing animals). Some circuses have permanent venues, of which the most beautiful in Paris is the nineteenth-century Cirque d'Hiver Bouglione (see below). You'll find details of the seasonal ones under "Cirques" in the "Pour les Jeunes" section of *L'Officiel des Spectacles* and under the same heading in the "Enfants" section of *Pariscope,* and there may well be visiting circuses from Warsaw or Moscow.
**Cirque Diana Moreno Bormann 9 bd du Bois Lepretre, 17ᵉ** ☎01.47.39.44.71. A traditional circus, with lion tamers, elephants, zebras, acrobats, jugglers, trapeze artists – the lot. Performances on Wed, Sat and Sun at 3pm throughout the year. From €10, chil-

dren under 4 free. M° Porte de Saint-Ouen.

**Cirque d'Hiver Bouglione** 110 rue Amelot, 11ᵉ ☎01.47.00.12.25, ⊛www.cirquedhiver.com. Strolling players and fairy lights beneath the dome welcome circus-goers from Oct to Jan (and TV and fashion shows the rest of the year). M° Filles-du-Calvaire.

**Cirque de Paris** Parc des Chantereines, 115 bd Charles-de-Gaulle, Villeneuve-La Garenne ☎01.47.99.40.40. This dream day out allows you to spend an entire day at the circus (Oct–June Wed, Sun & school hols 10am–5pm; €36.50–41, under-12s €29–34.50). In the morning you are initiated into the arts of juggling, walking the tightrope, clowning and make-up. You have lunch in the ring with your artist tutors, then join the spectators for the show, after which, if you're lucky, you might be taken round to meet the animals. You can, if you prefer, just attend the show at 3pm (€18–24, under-12s €12.50–14.50), but you'd better not let the kids know what they missed. RER Gennevilliers/St-Denis.

### Theatre and magic

Several **theatres**, apart from the ones in the Parc Floral and the Jardin d'Acclimatation, specialize in shows for children.

Au Bec Fin, 6 rue Thérèse, 1ᵉʳ (☎01.42.96.29.35; M° Palais-Royal), Blancs-Manteaux, 15 rue des Blancs-Manteaux, 4ᵉ (☎01.48.87.15.84, ⊛www.blancsmanteaux.fr; M° Hôtel-de-Ville) and Point Virgule, 7 rue Sainte-Croix-de-la-Bretonnerie, 4ᵉ (☎01.42.78.67.03; M° Hôtel-de-Ville) in the Marais have excellent reputations for occasional programming for kids, while the Théâtre des Jeunes

Spectateurs in Montreuil (26 pl Jean-Jaurès; ☎01.48.70.48.91; M° Mairie-de-Montreuil) specializes in children's theatre, but it's doubtful how much pleasure your children will get unless they're bilingual. Magic, mime, dance or music shows are probably more promising and it's worth checking under "Spectacles" in the "Enfants" section of *Pariscope*.

The magicians' venue, **Le Double-Fond**, 1 pl du marché Ste-Catherine, 4ᵉ (☎01.42.71.40.20), has a special children's magic show every Saturday and Wednesday at 3.30pm, but it's pricey at €9 for a child or adult, and there's a lot of chat in French along with the sleight of hand. If your kids are really into magic they should visit the **Musée de la Curiosité** (see p.112), where a magician performs throughout the day.

### Cinema

There are many **cinemas** showing cartoons and children's films, but if they're foreign they are inevitably dubbed into French. Listings of the main Parisian cinemas are given in Chapter 18. The pleasure of an Omnimax projection at La Géode in La Villette or Dôme-Imax at La Défense, however, is greatly enhanced by not understanding the commentary. The Cinaxe projection at La Villette simulates motion to accompany high-definition film (see p.189). Films at the Louis-Lumière cinema (also in the Cité des Sciences – see overleaf) may be less accessible, but you can ask at the inquiry desk for advice.

## Museums and sights

The best treat for children of every age from 3 upwards is the **Cité des Sciences** in the Parc de la Villette. All the other museums, despite entertaining collections and special activities and workshops for children, pale into insignificance. So beware that, if you visit the Cité on your first day, your offspring may decide that's where they want to stay.

Given kids' particular and sometimes peculiar tastes, the choice of other museums and monuments is best left to them, though the Musée des Enfants itself, purveying sentimental images of childhood, is certainly one to avoid. On the other hand, don't forget the gargoyles of Notre-Dame, the tropical fish- and crocodile-filled **aquarium** at the former Musée des Arts Africains et Océaniens (see p.205), the inventions at the **Musée des Arts et Métiers** (p.111) and the **Grande Galerie de l'Évolution** (see p.126), which also has a children's discovery room on the first floor with child-level microscopes, glass cases with live caterpillars and moths and a burrow of Mongolian rodents. The **Musée de la Poupée** (see p.102) should please children who like dolls; and the bizarre nature of the **Musée de la Curiosité** (see p.112) should appeal to most kids. The revamped **Pompidou Centre** (pp.96–101) has a children's *espace*, consisting of a room filled with hands-on exhibits designed to encourage experimentation and exploration and worth a few minutes of entertainment for young children. The collections of cutting-edge furniture and gadgets at the **Musée de l'Art Moderne** (p.138) may well appeal to some teenagers. Excursions to the **catacombs** or even the **sewers** (see opposite) will also delight some children.

If outer space is the kids' prime interest, then bear in mind the two **planetariums**, in the Palais de la Découverte (see p.78) and the Cité des Sciences.

Certain museums have **children's workshops**. For a current programme, look under "Animations" in the "Pour les Jeunes" section of *L'Officiel des Spectacles*. The **Musée d'Art Moderne de la Ville de Paris** has special exhibitions and workshops in its children's section (Wed, Sat & Sun; entrance 14 av de New-York; €7.50). The **Musée d'Orsay** provides worksheets (English promised) for 8- to 12-year-olds that make them explore every aspect of the building. Other museums with sessions for kids include the **Musée Carnavalet**, **Musée de la Mode et du Costume**, **Musée des Arts Décoratifs**, **Institut du Monde Arabe**, the **Louvre** and the **Petit Palais**; costs are around €4.

Full details of all the state museums' activities for children, which are all included in the admission charge, are published in *Objectif Musée*, a booklet available from the museums or from the Direction des Musées de France (34 quai du Louvre, 1er; closed Tues).

Two fun ways for children to find out about Paris itself and its history are the **Paris-Story** (see p.88), an enjoyable and informative 45-minute, wide-screen film on the history of Paris, and the **Musée Grévin** (see p.85), with its mockups of key events in French history.

---

### Cité des Enfants

@www.cite-sciences.fr Cité des Sciences, Parc de la Villette, 30 av Corentin-Cariou, 19e (M° Porte-de-la-Villette); see p.186 for detailed information on La Villette and the Cité des Sciences.

The **Cité des Enfants** (90min sessions; Tues, Thurs & Fri 9.45am, 11.30am, 1.30pm & 3.30pm; Wed, Sat, Sun & public hols 10.30am, 12.30pm, 2.30pm & 4.30pm; €5; advance reservations at the Cité des Sciences ticket office on ℡08.92.69.70.72 are advised to avoid disappointment), the Cité's special section for children, divided between 3–5s and 6–12s, is totally engaging. The kids can touch and smell and feel inside things, play about with water, construct buildings on a miniature construction site (complete with cranes, hard hats and barrows), experiment with sound and light, manipulate robots, race their own shadows, and superimpose their image on a landscape. They can listen to different languages by inserting telephones into the appropriate country on a globe, and put together their own television news. Everything, including the butterfly park, is on an appropriate scale, and the whole area is beautifully organized and managed. If you haven't got a child, it's worth borrowing one to get in here.

The rest of the museum is also pretty good for kids, particularly the planetarium, the various film shows, the *Argonaute* submarine, children's *médiathèque* (noon–8pm; free) and the frequent temporary exhibitions designed for the young. In the Parc de la Villette, there's lots of wide open green space, the dragon slide and seven themed gardens featuring mirrors, trampolines, water jets and spooky music.

## The catacombs and the sewers

**Catacombs:** 1 pl Denfert-Rochereau, 14ᵉ. Tues 11am–4pm, Wed–Sun 9–4pm; closed Mon & hols; €5/€2.60; Mᵒ Denfert-Rochereau.
**Sewers:** place de la Résistance, on the corner of quai d'Orsay and the Pont de l'Alma, 7ᵉ. May–Sept Mon–Wed, Sat & Sun 11am–5pm; Oct–April same days 11am–4pm; closed the last three weeks in Jan; €4/€2.30; Mᵒ Alma-Marceau.

Horror fanatics and ghouls should get a really satisfying shudder from the **catacombs**, though perhaps you should read p.154 first.

The archetypal pre-teen fixation, on the other hand, can be indulged in the sewers – **les égouts**. They are dank, damp, dripping, claustrophobic and filled with echoes: just the sort of place kids love. For further details, see p.140.

# Shops

The fact that Paris is filled with beautiful, enticing, delicious and expensive things all artfully displayed is not lost on most modern youngsters. Toys, gadgets and clothing are all bright, colourful and very appealing while the sheer amount of ice cream, chocolate, biscuits and sweets of all shapes and sizes is almost overwhelming. The only goodies you are safe from are high-tech toys, of which France seems to offer a particularly poor selection. Below is a small selection of shops to seek out, be dragged into or to avoid at all costs.

## Books

The following stock a good selection of English books:
**Brentano's** 37 av de l'Opéra, 2ᵉ ⓦ www.brentanos.fr. Storytelling sessions, singing and crafts on Wednesday afternoons and Saturday mornings. Call first to check. Mᵒ Opéra. Mon–Sat 10am–7pm.
**Chantelivre** 13 rue de Sèvres, 6ᵉ. A huge selection of everything to do with and for children, including good picture books for the younger ones, an English section, and a play area. Mᵒ Sèvres-Babylone. Mon 1–6.50pm, Tues–Sat 10am–6.50pm; closed mid–Aug.
**Galignani** 224 rue de Rivoli, 1ᵉʳ. Mᵒ Tuileries. Mon–Sat 10am–7pm.
**W H Smith** 248 rue de Rivoli, 1ᵉʳ. Mᵒ Concorde. Mon–Sat 9.30am–7pm.

## Toys and games

**Le Ciel Est à Tout le Monde** 10 rue Gay-Lussac, 5ᵉ (RER Luxembourg); 7 av Trudaine, 9ᵉ (Mᵒ Anvers). The best kite shop in Europe also sells frisbees, boomerangs, etc, and, next door, books, slippers, mobiles and traditional wooden toys. Mon–Sat 10am–7pm; closed Sun.
**Cité des Sciences** (see above). The museum shop has a wonderful selection of books, models, games, scientific instruments and toys covering a wide price range.
**Au Cotillon Moderne** 13 bd Voltaire, 11ᵉ. Celluloid and supple plastic masks of animals and fictional and political characters, plus trinkets, festoons and other party paraphernalia. Mᵒ Oberkampf. Mon–Fri 9.30am–6.30pm, Sat 10am–12.30pm & 2–6pm; closed Aug.
**Les Cousins d'Alice** 36 rue Daguerre, 14ᵉ. *Alice in Wonderland* decorations, toys, games, puzzles and mobiles, plus a general range of books and records. Mᵒ Gaîté/Edgar-Quinet. Tues–Sat 10am–1pm & 3–5pm, Sun 11am–1pm; closed Mon & Aug.
**Galeries Lafayette** 40 bd Haussmann, 9ᵉ ⓦ www.galerieslafayette.com. A virtual toy emporium filled with Lego sets, dolls, stuffed animals, building toys, and all sorts of little shiny things that kids just love. Mᵒ Havre-Caumartin. Mon–Sat 9.30am–7pm, Thurs till 9pm.
**Mayette Magie Moderne** 8 rue des Carmes, 5ᵉ ⓦ www.mayette.com. The oldest French

magic shop, founded in 1808 and a magician's paradise. There's usually someone here who speaks English. M° Maubert-Mutualité. Mon–Sat 1.30–8pm.

**Le Monde En Marche 34 rue Dauphine, 6ᵉ.**
Small, friendly toy shop with a nice selection of wooden toys (some hand-crafted in France) for toddlers; marionettes, doll-house furniture and games for primary school-aged children. M° Odéon. Mon–Sat 10.30am–7.30pm.

**Au Nain Bleu 406–410 rue St-Honoré, 8ᵉ.**
Since opening in the 1830s, this shop has become expert at delighting children with wooden toys, dolls, and faux china tea sets galore. M° Madeleine. Mon–Sat 9.45am–6.30pm; closed Mon in Aug.

**Pains d'Épices 29 passage Jouffroy, 9ᵉ.**
Fabulous doll's house necessities from furniture to wine glasses, and puppets. M° Grands-Boulevards. Mon 12.30–7pm, Tues–Sat 10am–7pm, Thurs till 9pm.

**Puzzles Michèle Wilson 116 rue du Château, 14ᵉ ⓦ www.pmw.fr.** Puzzles galore, with workshop on the premises. M° Pernéty. Tues–Fri 10am–8pm, Sat 10am–7pm.

**Si Tu Veux 68 galerie Vivienne, 2ᵉ.** Well-made traditional toys plus do-it-yourself and ready-made costumes. M° Bourse. Mon–Sat 10.30am–7pm.

**Virgin Megastore 56–60 av des Champs-Élysées, 8ᵉ (M° George-V), & Carrousel du Louvre, 1ᵉʳ (M° Louvre–Rivoli).** As well as all the cassettes and CDs to listen to, there's a Nintendo Gameboy to play with. Mon–Sat 10am–midnight, Sun noon–midnight.

## Clothes

Besides the specialist shops listed here, most of the big department stores and discount stores have children's sections (see Chapter 19). Of the latter, Tati is the cheapest place to go. Surprisingly, Monoprix has decent prices and matching quality.

**ABC Carnaval et Fêtes 22 av Ledru-Rollin, 12ᵉ.** Need something a little different? Fancy dress galore, gimmicks, masks, accessories and stage make-up, all for hire or purchase. M° Gare-de-Lyon. Tues–Sat 10am–7pm.

**Agnès B 2 rue du Jour, 1ᵉʳ.** Very fashionable and desirable clothes as you'd expect from this chic Parisian designer. Just opposite is Le Petit B for babies selling lots of very French-looking outfits in navy blue and white. M°/RER Châtelet-Les Halles. Mon–Sat 10am–7pm.

**Baby Dior 252 bd Saint-Germain, 7ᵉ.** Unaffordable, but entertaining – especially the prices. M° Solférino. Mon–Sat 10am–6.30pm.

**Bain – Plus Enfants 23 rue des Blancs Manteaux, 4ᵉ.** Aimed at 0–12 year-olds, this stylish shop has an irresistible range of bed and bath items: chic pyjamas, hooded robes, fluffy towels and cuddly bears. M° Hôtel de Ville. Tues–Sat 11am–7.30pm.

**Menkes 12 rue de Rambuteau, 3ᵉ.** A vibrant selection of Spanish flamenco outfits, sombreros, fans and footwear for boys and girls. Classes also on offer. M° Rambuteau. Tues–Sat 10am–12.30pm & 2–7pm.

**Du Pareil au Même 122 rue du Faubourg-St-Antoine, 12ᵉ.** Beautiful kids' clothing at very good prices. Gorgeous floral dresses, cute jogging suits, and bright coloured basics. Branches all over Paris. M° Ledru-Rollin. Mon–Sat 10am–7pm.

**Petit Bateau 116 av des Champs-Élysées, 8ᵉ.** Stylish and comfortable cotton t-shirts and vests. M° Charles-de-Gaulles-Etoile. Mon–Sat 10am–7.30pm.

**Pom d'Api 13 rue du Jour, 1ᵉʳ.** The most colourful, imaginative and well-made shoes for kids in Paris (up to size 40/UK7, and from €40), plus exquisite chairs in the shapes of swans and dogs for the little ones to sit on. M°/RER Châtelet-Les Halles. Mon–Sat 10.30am–7pm. Also at 28 rue du Four, 6ᵉ (M° St-Germain-des-Prés; Mon–Sat 10am–7pm).

**Unishop 4 rue Rambuteau, 3ᵉ & 42 rue de Rivoli, 4ᵉ.** Very cheap and cheerful kids' clothes: vibrant selection of zebra leggings, teeny hooded sweatshirts and floral dresses. M° Hôtel-de-Ville. Both Tues–Sat 10.15am–7pm.

**Au Vieux Campeur 48 rue des Écoles, 5ᵉ ⓦ www.au-vieux-campeur.fr.** The best camping and sporting equipment range in Paris, spread over several shops in the quartier. The special attraction for kids is a climbing wall. M° Cluny-La Sorbonne. Mon 2–7pm, Tues, Thurs & Fri 10.30am–7.30pm, Wed 10.30am–9pm, Sat 10am–7.30pm.

# 22

# Gay and lesbian Paris

P aris is one of Europe's major centres for **gay men**, with numerous bars, clubs, restaurants, saunas and shops catering for a gay clientele. Its focal point is the **Marais**, whose central street, rue Ste-Croix-de-la-Bretonnerie, has visibly gay-oriented businesses at almost every other address. **Lesbians** are less well catered for commercially, but there are networks of feminist groups and specific publications that cater for the lesbian community.

The high spots on the calendar are the huge annual **Marche des Fiertés LGBT**, or gay pride march, which normally takes place on the last Saturday in June, and the **Bastille Day Ball** (July 13, 10pm–dawn), a wild open-air dance on the quai de la Tournelle, 5<sup>e</sup> (M° Pont-Marie), which is free for all to join in. See Festivals and Events, pp.41–43 for further details.

For a long time, the emphasis of the gay community in Paris tended towards providing the requisites for a hedonistic lifestyle – with the legal age of consent set at 16 and discrimination and harassment non-routine, campaigning was not a high priority. Matters changed somewhat with the advent of AIDS ("SIDA" in French), which caused a moderate surge in homophobia in the 1980s, though homophobic violence has always been very uncommon. A recent, positive development is the **PACS** law, passed in 1999, which allows couples over 18 of the same or different sex to sign a civil pact (*se pacser*), acknowledging their unity. In general, Parisians consider sexuality to be a private matter – no one seems any more bothered by the sexuality of Paris's gay mayor, Bertrand Delanoë, than they are by the sexual antics of straight politicians. On the whole, Paris is one of the world's great cities in which to be gay, though gays tend to be discreet outside specific venues, parades and the pink triangle between the Hôtel de Ville, the Bastille and Arts et Métiers.

## Information and contacts

The gay and lesbian community is well catered for by the **media**, the best source of information being *Têtu* (Ⓦ www.tetu.com), France's main gay monthly magazine – the name means "headstrong". The pull-out section, "Agenda", is full of contact details, addresses and reviews. The most widely available lesbian publication is *Lesbia*, available from most newsagents. Listed below are a handful of the most useful contacts.

## Useful contacts and organizations

**Association des Médecins Gais (AMG) 48 rue Damrémont, 11ᵉ** ☏01.48.05.81.71, ⊛www.medecins-gays.org. Gay doctors' association, offering help with all health concerns relative to the gay community. Telephone lines open Wed 6–8pm, Sat 2–4pm. M° Lamarck-Caulaincourt.

**Centre Gai et Lesbien de Paris** ☏01.43.57.21.47, ⊛www.cglparis.org. Paris's main information centre was closed and searching for newer, better premises at the time of writing; updates are available online.

**Inter-LGBT 127 rue Amelot, 11ᵉ** ☏01.53.01.47.01, ⊛www.inter-lgbt.org. Actively fights for gay rights and organizes the annual pride march. M° St-Sébastien-Froissart.

**Maison des Femmes 163 rue de Charenton, 12ᵉ** ☏01.43.43.41.13, ⊛www .maisondesfemmes.free.fr. The main women's centre in Paris and home to a number of lesbian groups, who organise workshops and hold frequent meetings. On Friday night there's a party in the café from 10pm until dawn. M° Reuilly-Diderot. Mon 1–6pm, Tues noon–5pm, Thurs 1–4pm, Fri 10am–5pm.

**Pharmacie du Village 26 rue du Temple, 4ᵉ** ☏01.42.72.60.71. Gay-run pharmacy. M° Hôtel-de-Ville. Open Mon 8.30am–8.30pm, Tues–Sat 8.30am–9.30pm, Sun 9am–8pm.

**SOS Homophobie** ☏01.48.06.42.41, ⊛www.sos-homophobie.org. First-stop helpline for victims of homophobia. Open Mon–Fri 8pm–10pm.

## The media and websites

⊛**www.attirentdelles.org** Magazine-style internet site in French with information and articles on all aspects of lesbian life.

⊛http://citegay.fr One of the best internet sites, with lots of links, features and contacts.

**e.m@le magazine** Free gay and lesbian paper with small ads, lonely hearts, services, etc.

**MAG 106 rue de Montreuil, 11ᵉ** ☏01.43.73.31.63, ⊛www.mag-paris.org. Useful online magazine from the Mouvement d'Affirmation des Jeunes Gais et Lesbiennes, a group aimed at young people that organizes occasional "tea dances" and gay cinema nights. M° Nation.

**Les Mots à la Bouche 6 rue Ste-Croix-de-la-Bretonnerie, 4ᵉ** ☏01.42.78.88.30, ⊛www .motsbouche.com. The main gay and lesbian bookshop, with exhibition space and meeting rooms; a selection of literature in English, too. Lots of free listings maps and club flyers to pick up, and one of the helpful assistants usually speaks English. M° Hôtel-de-Ville. Mon–Sat 11am–11pm, Sun 2–8pm.

# Nightlife

In terms of **nightlife**, Paris is a great place to be gay. The Marais area, especially, has a wide range of **gay venues** – the selection below only scratches the surface – and although lesbians don't enjoy a similarly wide selection of women-only places, they are welcome in some of the predominantly male clubs. The reputation of wild hedonism in gay clubs has spread outside the gay community and attracted heterosexuals in search of a good time. Consequently, straights are welcome in some gay establishments, especially when in gay company. In fact, some gay clubs have all but abandoned a gay policy – the legendary *Le Queen*, for instance, is gay only on weekends now – whilst many of the more mainstream clubs have started doing gay nights. For a complete rundown, consult *Têtu* magazine's Agenda section.

## Mainly women

**Boobsburg 26 rue de Montmorency, 3ᵉ** ☏01.42.74.04.82. Fashionable mainly lesbian bar, with good food, classy decor and a chic young clientele. M° Rambuteau. Tues–Sun 5pm–2am.

**Le Pulp 25 bd Poissonnière, 2ᵉ** ☏01.40.26.01.93. Paris's lesbian club par excellence, playing music from techno to Madonna. So cool that it pulls in a DJ-led, straight crowd on midweek nights. M° Bonne Nouvelle. Thurs–Sun from midnight.

**Les Scandaleuses 8 rue des Ecouffes, 4ᵉ**

@01.48.87.39.26. Trendy and high-profile lesbian bar in the Marais – men are welcome if accompanied. Lively atmosphere guaranteed, with DJs at weekends. M° Hôtel-de-Ville. Daily 5pm–5am.

**Le Tagada Bar** 40 rue des Trois-Frères, 18e
@01.42.55.95.56. Upbeat, camp and furiously trendy Montmartre bar, with a relaxed attitude and playlist. M° Anvers. Tues–Sun 5.30pm–2am.

**L'Utopia** 15 rue Michel le Comte, 3e. Bar on two levels, with themed karaoke and DJ nights, varied music and friendly atmosphere. Predominantly women. Mon–Sat 5pm–2am. M° Rambuteau.

## Mainly men

**Amnesia Café** 42 rue Vieille-du-Temple, 4e
@01.42.72.16.94. Fashionably dressed young things pack into this classic, relaxed gay bar, with its sofas and basement club. M° St-Paul. Daily 11am–2am.

**Banana Café** 13 rue de la Ferronnerie, 1er
@01.42.33.35.31. Seriously hedonistic clubbar, packing in the punters with up-tempo clubby tunes. M° Châtelet. Daily 6pm–5am.

**Le Central** 33 rue Vieille-du-Temple, 4e
@01.48.87.99.33. The oldest gay local in the Marais. Small, friendly and always crowded with tourists and locals. M° Hôtel-de-Ville. Mon–Thurs 4pm–2am, Fri–Sun 2pm–2am.

**Café Cox** 15 rue des Archives, 3e
@01.42.72.08.00. Muscly, body-beautiful clientele up for a seriously good time. A good pre-club place, with DJs on weekend nights. M° Hôtel-de-Ville. Daily noon–2am.

**Le Duplex** 25 rue Michel-le-Comte, 3e
@01.42.72.80.86. Popular with trendily intel-lectual media types for its relatively sophisticated atmosphere, but still relaxed and friendly. M° Rambuteau. Sun–Thurs 8pm–2am, Fri & Sat 8pm–4am.

**Folies Pigalle** 11 pl Pigalle, 9e
@01.48.78.25.26. See p.311. M° Pigalle.

**Le Mixer** 23 rue Ste-Croix de la Bretonnerie, 4e
@01.42.78.26.20. Another popular and crowded Marais bar, raising the pulse of gay and straight pre-clubbers with its pounding techno and house soundtrack. M° Hôtel-de-Ville. Daily 5pm–2am.

**Open Café** 17 rue des Archives, 4e
@01.48.87.80.25. The first gay bar/café to have tables out on the pavement. Hugely popular as a "look-at-me" pre-club venue, but more relaxed during the day. M° Hôtel-de-Ville. Daily 11am–2am.

**La Petite Vertu** 15 rue des Vertus, 3e
@01.48.04.77.09. Welcoming, inventive Marais address pulling in gay, lesbian and straight punters alike. Debates every other Wednesday on changing themes. M° Arts-et Métiers. Tues–Sun 5pm–2am.

**Le Piano Zinc** 49 rue des Blancs-Manteaux, 4e
@01.40.27.97.42. On Thurs, Fri and Sat, when the piano-playing starts at around 10pm, this bar becomes a happy riot of *chanson* music, music-hall acts and dance. M° Rambuteau/Hôtel-de-Ville. Daily 5pm–2am, Fri & Sat till dawn.

**Le Queen** 102 Champs-Élysées, 8e @01.53.89 .08.89, @www.fr. M° George-V. See p.311.

**Le Tango** 13 rue au-Maire, 3e
@01.42.72.17.78. Gay and lesbian dancehall with a traditional *bal* until midnight, then house and mainstream dance later on. Tea dances Sun 6–11pm. M° Arts-et-Métiers. Fri, Sat & public hols 10.30pm–dawn.

# Accommodation and eating

Although gays and lesbians aren't likely to come across any anti-social behaviour in restaurants and hotels, there is a choice of gay-oriented places to stay and eat in should you wish. You don't need to look any further than the Marais: hotels and restaurants are plentiful, and even if they aren't exclusively gay, the location can almost guarantee a gay-friendly atmosphere.

## Hotels

**Hôtel Acacias** 20 rue du Temple, 4e
@01.48.87.07.70. M° Hôtel-de-Ville. See p.258.

**Hôtel Central Marais** 33 rue Vieille-du-Temple, 4e @01.48.87.56.08, @www.hotelcentralmarais.com. M° Hôtel-de-Ville. See p.258.

**Hôtel St-Louis Marais** 1 rue Charles-V, 4e
@01.48.87.87.04, @www.hotelsaintlouis-marais.com. M° Sully-Morland. See p.259.

## Restaurants

**La Coupe Gorge** 2 rue de la Coutellerie, 4e
℡01.48.04.79.24. Traditional in cuisine and decor, with its old-style *zinc* bar counter, rustic upstairs room and great dishes such as *magret de canard*. Closed Sun and Sat & Mon lunch. M° Hôtel-de-Ville.

**Food Unlimited** 168 rue St-Martin, 3e
℡01.42.77.06.06. All-white designer restaurant with a fashionable thirty-something clientele and good, light fusion food. Lunch *menu* at €12, or around €25 *à la carte*. M° Rambuteau. Mon & Tues noon–4pm, Wed–Sun noon–4pm & 6.30–11pm.

**Le Loup Blanc** 42 rue Tiquetonne, 2e
℡01.40.13.08.35. Bustling, trendy restaurant with changing artwork on the walls. Serves great-value *assiettes* of grilled and marinated meats and fish, with a selection of delicious sauces on the side. M° Etienne Marcel. Daily 7.30pm–midnight.

**Le Petit Prince** 12 rue Lanneau, 5e
℡01.43.54.77.26. M° Maubert-Mutualité. See p.294.

# Directory

**AIDS/HIV** Information in English from FACTS-LINE (℡01.44.93.16.69 Mon, Wed & Fri 6–10pm). FACTS (Free AIDS Counselling Treatment Support) offers support groups and free counselling at 190 bd de Charonne, 20ᵉ (℡01.44.93.16.32; Mᵒ Alexandre-Dumas). SIDA info service ℡08.00.84.08.00 (toll-free, 24 hours).

**Airlines** Aer Lingus ℡01.48.62.99.88; Air Canada ℡08.25.88.08.81; Air France ℡01.42.99.21.01; British Airways ℡08.25.82.54.00; British Midland ℡01.53.43.25.27; Delta ℡08.00.35.40.80; Qantas ℡08.20.82.05.00.

**American Express** 11 rue Scribe, 9ᵉ ℡01.47.14.50.00; Mᵒ Opéra. Bureau de change open Mon–Fri 9am–6pm, Sat 9am–5pm, Sun 10am–4pm, public hols 9am–5pm. In a pinch, there is Chequepoint, 150 Champs-Élysées, 8ᵉ ℡01.42.56.48.63, Mᵒ Charles-de-Gaulle–Étoile, open daily 24hr.

**Banks** Barclays, 6 Rond-Point-des-Champs-Élysées, 8ᵉ ℡01.44.95.13.80; Mᵒ Franklin-D-Roosevelt; Mon–Fri 9.15am–4.30pm; branches throughout the city (info on ℡01.42.92.39.08).

**Car rental** Budget ℡08.00.10.00.01, ⓦwww.budgettrentacar.com; Europcar ℡08.25.35.23.52, ⓦwww.europcar.com; Hertz ℡01.55.31.93.21, ⓦwww.hertz.com. Or some good local firms are: Buchard, 99 bd Auguste-Blanqui, 13ᵉ (℡01.45.88.28.38; Mᵒ Place-d'Italie); Locabest, 3 rue Abel, 12ᵉ (℡01.43.46.05.05; Mᵒ Gare-de-Lyon), and at 104 bd Magenta, 10ᵉ (℡01.44.72.08.05; Mᵒ Gare-du-Nord). Look up "location" in the yellow pages for others.

**Electricity** 220V out of double, round-pin wall sockets. If you haven't bought the appropriate converter (*adapteur*) or trans-former (*transformateur* – for US appliances) before leaving home, head for the electrical section of a department store (try BHV, for example; see p.338), where someone is also more likely to speak English. If you are using an appliance larger than an electric razor or a radio – a laptop computer for example – you will need an adapter capable of transforming a large electrical load.

**Emergencies** Fire brigade (Sapeurs-Pompiers) ℡18; Ambulance (Service d'Aide Médicale Urgente – SAMU) ℡15; Police ℡17; Doctor call-out (SOS Médecins) ℡01.47.07.77.77 or 43.37.77.77; Rape crisis (SOS Viol; Mon–Fri 10am–6pm) ℡08.00.05.95.95; SOS Help (crisis line/any problem: 3–11pm) in English ℡01.47.23.80.80. English-speaking (private) hospitals: The American Hospital in Paris, 63 bd Victor-Hugo, Neuilly-sur-Seine (Mᵒ Porte-Maillot, then bus #82 to terminus; ℡01.46.41.25.25) and The Hertford British Hospital, 3 rue Barbès, Levallois-Perret (Mᵒ Anatole-France; ℡01.46.39.22.22). In the event of a car breakdown, call SOS Dépannage (℡01.47.07.99.99) for round-the-clock assistance; they can also send out locksmiths and plumbers.

**Exchange** Some of the more conveniently located bureaux de change are at Charles-de-Gaulle airport (daily 7am–10pm) and Orly airport (daily 6.30am–11pm); at Gare d'Austerlitz (Mon–Fri 7am–9pm), Gare de l'Est (summer 6.45am–10pm; winter 6.45am–7pm), Gare de Lyon (Mon–Sat 8am–8pm), Gare du Nord (8am–8pm), Gare St–Lazare (summer 8am–8pm; winter 8am–6.45pm); at the Office de Tourisme de Paris (127 av des Champs-Élysées, 8ᵉ; 9am–7.30pm; Mᵒ Charles-de-Gaulle–Étoile); and at CCF (127 av Champs-Élysées, 8ᵉ;

8.30am–8pm; M° George-V). Try also the main banks, American Express (see overleaf) or branches of Thomas Cook, eg at 4 bd St Michel, 6e (daily 8am–9pm; ☎01.42.34.70.00; M° St Michel).

**Laundry** You shouldn't have any trouble finding a laundry in Paris. If you can't immediately spot one near your hotel, look in the phone book under "Laveries Automatiques". They're often unattended, so come pre-armed with small change. The smallest machines cost around €3.50 for a load, though some laundries only have bigger machines and charge around €6.50. Generally, self-service laundry facilities open at 7am and close between 7pm and 9pm. The alternative *blanchisserie*, or pressing services, are likely to be expensive, and hotels in particular charge very high rates. If you're doing your own washing in hotels, keep quantities small, as most forbid doing any laundry in your room.

**Left luggage** Located at Gare Saint Lazare, Gare de L'Est, Gare du Nord, Gare de Lyon, Gare d'Austerlitz, and Montparnasse.

**Lost baggage** Airports: Orly ☎01.49.75.04.53; Charles de Gaulle ☎01.48.62.10.86.

**Lost property** Bureau des Objets Trouvés, Préfecture de Police, 36 rue des Morillons, 15e; ☎01.55.76.20.00 (M° Convention). Mon & Wed 8.30am–5pm, Thurs 8.30am–8pm, Fri 8.30am–5.30pm. For property lost on public transport, phone the RATP on ☎01.40.30.52.00. If you lose your passport, report it to a police station and then your embassy.

**Pedestrians** French drivers pay no heed to pedestrian/zebra crossings, marked with horizontal white stripes on the road. It's very dangerous to step out onto one and assume drivers will stop as is usually the case at home. Take just as great care as you would crossing at any other point, even at traffic lights.

**Pharmacies** see "Basics" p.20.

**Public transport RATP** information on ☎08.36.68.77.14 (6am–9pm; premium rate) or ☎08.36.68.41.14 (in English, premium rate) or online at ⊛www.ratp.fr.

**SNCF** information on ☎08.36.35.35.35 or online at ⊛www.sncf.com.

**Safer sex** A warning: Paris has the highest incidence of AIDS of any city in Europe; people who are HIV positive are just as likely to be heterosexual as homosexual.

Condoms (*préservatifs*) are readily available in supermarkets, and from dispensers in clubs, on the street – often outside pharmacies – and in the métro. From pharmacies you can also get spermicidal cream and jelly (*dose contraceptive*), suppositories (*ovules, suppositoires*), and (with a prescription) the pill (*la pilule*), a diaphragm or IUD (*le stérilet*). Pregnancy test kits (*tests de grossesse*) are sold at pharmacies; the morning-after pill (*la pilule du lendemain*) is available from pharmacies without prescription.

**Sales tax** VAT (Value Added Tax) is referred to as TVA in France (*taxe sur la valeur ajoutée*). The standard rate in France is 20.6 percent; it's higher for luxury items and lower for essentials, but there are no exemptions (children's clothes for example are a lot more expensive than in the UK). However, non-EU residents who have been in the country for less than six months are entitled to a refund (*détaxe*) of some or all of this amount (but usually around fourteen percent) if you spend at least €180 in a single trip to one shop. Not all stores participate in this scheme, though, so you'll need to ask first. The procedure is rather complicated: present your passport to the shop when you pay and ask for the three-page *bordereau de vente à l'exportation* form. They should help you fill it in and provide you with a self-addressed envelope. When you leave the EU, get customs to stamp the filled-in form (look for the *douane de détaxe* counter); you will then need to send two of the pages back to the shop in the envelope within six months; the shop will then transfer the refund through your credit card or bank. Some shops deduct the VAT there and then, but you still have to go through the above procedure. The Centre de Renseignements des Douanes (☎01.53.24.68.24, ⊛www.douane.gouv.fr) can answer any customs-related questions.

**Smoking** Laws requiring restaurants to have separate smokers' (*fumeurs*) and non-smokers' (*non-fumeurs*) areas are widely ignored. Non-smokers may well find themselves eating elbow-to-elbow alongside smokers, and waiters are not that likely to be sympathetic; even if there are clearly defined non-smoking areas they tend to be in the least desirable part of the restaurant, tucked away in a back room, for example. Smoking is not allowed on public transport, including surburban trains, or in cinemas. Most office reception areas are non-smoking. Smoking, however, is still a socially acceptable habit in France, and cigarettes are cheap in comparison with Britain, for example. Note that you can only buy tobacco in *tabacs*: a list of late-night *tabacs* is given on p.331.

**Student information CROUS** 39 av Georges-Bernanos, 5ᵉ ☎01.40.51.36.00, ⓦwww.crous.fr; RER Port-Royal.

**Taxis** Try Taxis Bleus (☎08.25.16.10.10, ⓦwww.taxis-bleus.com), Alpha Taxis (☎01.45.85.85.85), Artaxi (☎08.91.70.25.50, ⓦwww.artaxi.fr) or G7 (☎01.41.27.66.99; in English). Aéro Taxis (☎01.47.39.01.47) specialize in trips to the airports.

**Time** France is one hour ahead of Britain (Greenwich Mean Time), six hours ahead of Eastern Standard Time (eg New York), and nine hours ahead of Pacific Standard Time (eg Los Angeles). Australia is eight–ten hours ahead of France, depending on which part of the continent you're in. Remember also that France uses a 24hr clock, with, for example, 2am written as 2h and 2.30pm written as 14h30. The most confusing are noon and midnight – respectively 12h and 24h. For the talking clock phone ☎36.99. You can get an alarm call on ☎36.88, or with a digital phone dial *55* then the time in four figures (eg 0715 for 7.15am) then #. To annul, dial #55* then the time, then # (costs around €0.60).

**Toilets** Ask for *les toilettes* or look for signs for the WC (pronounced "vay say"); when reading the details of facilities outside hotels, don't confuse *lavabo*, which means washbasin, with lavatory. French toilets in bars are still often of the hole-in-the-ground squatting variety, and tend to lack toilet paper. Standards of cleanliness aren't always high. Toilets in railway stations and department stores are commonly staffed by attendants who will expect a bit of spare change. Some have coin-operated locks, as do the tardis-like automatic public toilets on the streets, so always keep some lose change to hand.

**Tours** The best walking tours of Paris in English are those offered by Paris Walks (☎01.48.09.21.40; 1hr 30min; €10, children €5), with subjects ranging from "Hemingway's Paris" to "Historic Marais". A full list of times, meeting points and prices can be found in *Pariscope* in the *Time Out Paris* English-language section. The Paris transport authority, RATP, also runs numerous excursions, some to quite far-flung places, and they cost much less than those offered by commercial operators. Details are available from RATP's Bureau de Tourisme, place de la Madeleine, 1ᵉʳ (☎01.40.06.71.45, ⓦwww.ratp.fr; Mº Madeleine).

**Traffic and road conditions** For Paris's traffic jams listen to 105.1 FM (FIP) on the radio; for the boulevard périphérique and main routes in and out of the city, ring ☎01.48.99.33.33.

**Weather** Paris and Île-de-France ☎08.36.68.02.75; rest of France ☎01.36.68.01.01. On the Internet at ⓦwww.meteo.fr and ⓦwww.weather.com.

**Youth information CIDJ** (Centre d'Information et de Documentation de la Jeunesse), 101 quai Branly, 15ᵉ (Mon–Fri 9.30am–6pm & Sat 9.30am–1pm; ☎01.43.06.15.38, ⓦwww.cidj.com; Mº Bir-Hakeim).

# Contexts

# Contexts

# The historical framework

Two thousand years of compressed history – featuring riots and revolutions, shantytowns, palaces, new street plans, sanitation and the Parisian people.

## Beginnings

It was **Rome** that put Paris on the map, as it did the rest of western Europe. When Julius Caesar's armies arrived in 52 BC, they found a Celtic settlement confined to an island in the Seine – the Île de la Cité. It must already have been fairly populous, as it had sent a contingent of eight thousand men to stiffen the Gallic chieftain Vercingétorix's doomed resistance to the invaders.

Under the name of **Lutetia**, it remained **a Roman colony** for the next three hundred years, prosperous commercially because of its commanding position on the Seine trade route, but insignificant politically. The Romans established their administrative centre on the Île de la Cité, and their town on the Left Bank on the slopes of the Montagne Ste-Geneviève. Though no monuments of their presence remain today, except the baths by the *Hôtel de Cluny* and the amphitheatre in rue Monge, their **street plan**, still visible in the north–south axis of rue St-Martin and rue St-Jacques, determined the future growth of the city.

When Roman rule disintegrated under the impact of **Germanic invasions** around 275 AD, Paris held out until it fell to **Clovis the Frank** in 486. In 511 Clovis' son commissioned the cathedral of St-Étienne, whose foundations can be seen in the *crypte archéologique* under the square in front of Notre-Dame. Clovis' own conversion to Christianity hastened the **Christianization** of the whole country, and under his successors Paris saw the foundation of several rich and influential monasteries, especially on the Left Bank.

With the election of **Hugues Capet**, Comte de Paris, as king in 987, the fate of the city was inextricably identified with that of the **monarchy**. The presence of the kings, however, prevented the development of the middle-class, republican institutions that the rich merchants of Flanders and Italy were able to obtain for their cities. The result was recurrent political tension, which led to open **rebellion**, for instance in 1356, when Étienne Marcel, a wealthy cloth merchant, demanded greater autonomy for the city. Further rebellions, fuelled by the hopeless poverty of the lower classes, led to the king and court abandoning the capital in 1418, not to return for more than a hundred years.

## The Right Bank, Latin Quarter and Louvre

As the city's livelihood depended from the first on its river-borne trade, commercial activity naturally centred round the place where the goods were landed. This was the **place de Grève** on the **Right Bank**, where the Hôtel de Ville now stands. Marshy ground originally, it was gradually drained to accommodate the business quarter. Whence the continuing association of the Right Bank with commerce and banking today.

The **Left Bank**'s intellectual associations are similarly ancient, dating from the growth of schools and student accommodation round the two great **monasteries** of Ste-Geneviève and St-Germain-des-Prés. The first, dedicated to the city's patron saint who had saved it from destruction by Attila's raiders, occupied the site of the present Lycée Henri-IV on top of the hill behind the Panthéon. In 1215 a papal licence allowed the formation of what gradually became the renowned **University of Paris**, eventually to be known as **the Sorbonne**, after Robert de Sorbon, founder of a college for poor scholars. It was the fact that Latin was the language of the schools both inside and outside the classroom that gave the district its name of Latin Quarter.

To protect this burgeoning city, **Philippe Auguste** (king from 1180 to 1223) built the Louvre fortress (whose excavated remains are now on display beneath the Louvre museum) and a wall, which swung south to enclose the Montagne Ste-Geneviève and north and east to encompass the Marais. The administration of the city remained in the hands of the king until 1260, when St Louis ceded a measure of responsibility to the leaders of the Paris watermen's guild, whose power was based on their monopoly control of all river traffic and taxes thereon. The city's government, when it has been allowed one, has been conducted ever since from the place de Grève/place de l'Hôtel-de-Ville.

# Civil wars and foreign occupation

From the mid-thirteenth to mid-fourteenth centuries Paris shared the same unhappy fate as the rest of France, embroiled in the long and destructive **Hundred Years War** with the English. Étienne Marcel let the enemy into the city in 1357, the Burgundians did the same in 1422, when the Duke of Bedford set up his government of northern France here. Joan of Arc made an unsuccessful attempt to drive them out in 1429 and was wounded in the process at the Porte St-Honoré. The following year the English king, Henry VI, had the cheek to have himself crowned king of France in Notre-Dame.

It was only when the English were expelled – from Paris in 1437 and from France in 1453 – that the economy had the chance to recover from so many decades of devastation. It received a further boost when **François 1er** decided to re-establish the royal court in Paris in 1528. Work began on reconstructing the Louvre and building the Tuileries palace for Catherine de Médicis, and on transforming Fontainebleau and other country residences into sumptuous Renaissance palaces.

But before these projects reached completion, war intervened, this time **civil war** between Catholics and Protestants, in the course of which Paris witnessed one of the worst atrocities ever committed against French Protestants. Some three thousand of them were gathered in Paris for the wedding of Henri III's daughter, Marguerite, to Henri, the Protestant king of Navarre. On August 25, 1572, **St Bartholomew's Day**, they were massacred at the instigation of the Catholic Guise family. When, through this marriage, Henri of Navarre became heir to the French throne in 1584, the Guises drove his father-in-law, Henri III, out of Paris. Forced into alliance, the two Henris laid siege to the city. Five years later, Henri III having been assassinated in the meantime, Henri of Navarre entered the city as king **Henri IV**. "Paris is worth a Mass", he is reputed to have said to justify renouncing his Protestantism in order to soothe Catholic susceptibilities.

The Paris he inherited was not a very salubrious place. It was overcrowded. No domestic building had been permitted beyond the limits of

Philippe-Auguste's twelfth-century walls because of the guilds' resentment of the unfair advantage enjoyed by craftsmen living outside the jurisdiction of the city's tax regulations. The population had doubled to around 400,000, causing an acute housing shortage and a terrible strain on the rudimentary water supply and drainage system. It is said that the first workmen who went to clean out the city's cesspools in 1633 fell dead from the fumes. It took seven months to clean out 6420 cartloads of filth that had been accumulating for two centuries. The overflow ran into the Seine, whence Parisians drew their drinking water.

# Planning and expansion

The first systematic attempts at **planning** were introduced by Henri IV at the beginning of the seventeenth century: regulating street lines and uniformity of facade, and laying out the first geometric squares. The **place des Vosges** dates from this period, as does the **Pont Neuf**, the first of the Paris bridges not to be cluttered with medieval houses. Henri thus inaugurated a tradition of grandiose public building, which was to continue to the Revolution and beyond, that perfectly symbolized the bureaucratic, centralized power of the newly self-confident state concentrated in the person of its absolute monarch.

The process reached its apogee under **Louis XIV**, with the construction of the **boulevards** from the Madeleine to the Bastille, the places Vendôme and Victoire, the Porte St-Martin and St-Denis gateways, the Invalides, Observatoire and the Cour Carrée of the Louvre – not to mention the vast palace at **Versailles**, whither he repaired with the court in 1671. The aristocratic *hôtels* or mansions of the Marais were also erected during this period, to be superseded early in the eighteenth century by the Faubourg St-Germain as the fashionable quarter of the rich and powerful.

The underside of all this bricks and mortar self-aggrandizement was the general neglect of the living conditions of the ordinary citizenry of Paris. The centre of the city remained a densely packed and unsanitary warren of medieval lanes and tenements. And it was only in the years immediately preceding the 1789 Revolution that any attempt was made to clean it up. The buildings crowding the bridges were dismantled as late as 1786. Pavements were introduced for the first time and attempts were made to improve the drainage. A further source of pestilential infection was removed with the emptying of the overcrowded cemeteries into the catacombs. One gravedigger alone claimed to have buried more than ninety thousand people in thirty years, stacked "like slices of bacon" in the charnel house of the innocents, which had been receiving the dead of 22 parishes for 800 years.

In 1786 Paris also received its penultimate ring of fortifications, the so-called wall of the Fermiers Généraux, with 57 *barrières* or toll gates (one of which survives in the middle of place Stalingrad), where a tax was levied on all goods entering the city.

# The 1789 Revolution

The immediate cause of the **Revolution of 1789** was a campaign by the privileged classes of the clergy and nobility to protect their status, especially exemption from taxation, against erosion by the royal government. The revolutionary movement, however, was quickly taken over by the middle classes, relatively well off but politically underprivileged. In the initial phases this meant essentially the provincial bourgeoisie. It was they who comprised the majority of the representatives of the **Third Estate**, the "order" that encompassed the whole of French society after the clergy, who formed the First Estate, and the nobility who formed the Second. It was they who took the initiative in setting up the **National Assembly** on June 17, 1789. The majority of them would probably have been content with constitutional reforms that checked monarchical power on the English model. But their power depended largely on their ability to wield the threat of a Parisian popular explosion.

Although the effects of the Revolution were felt all over France and indeed Europe, it was in Paris that the most profound changes took place. Being as it were on the spot, the people of Paris discovered themselves in the Revolution. They formed the revolutionary shock troops, the driving force at the crucial stages of the Revolution. They marched on Versailles and forced the king to return to Paris with them. They stormed and destroyed the Bastille on July 14, 1789. They occupied the Hôtel de Ville, set up an insurrectionary Commune and captured the Tuileries palace on August 10, 1792. They invaded the Convention in May 1793 and secured the arrest of the more conservative Girondin faction of deputies.

Where the bourgeois deputies of the Convention were concerned principally with political reform, the sans-culottes – literally, the people without breeches – expressed their demands in economic terms: price controls, regulation of the city's food supplies, and so on. By their practice of taking to the streets and occupying the Hôtel de Ville, they also established a tradition of revolutionary action that continued through to the 1871 Commune.

# Napoleon – and the barricades

Apart from some spectacular bloodletting, and yet another occupation of the city by foreign powers in 1814, Napoleon's chief legacy to France was a very centralized, authoritarian and efficient **bureaucracy** that put Paris in firm control of the rest of the country. In Paris itself, he left his share of pompous architecture – in the **Arcs de Triomphe** and **Carrousel**, rue de Rivoli and rue de la Paix, the Madeleine and facade of the Palais-Bourbon, plus a further extension for the Louvre and a revived tradition of court flummery and extravagant living among the well-to-do. For the rest of the nineteenth century after his demise, France was left to fight out the contradictions and unfinished business left behind by the Revolution of 1789. And the arena in which these conflicts were resolved was, literally, the streets of the capital.

On the one hand, there was a tussle between the class that had risen to wealth and power as a direct result of the destruction of the monarchy and the old order, and the survivors of the old order, who sought to make a comeback in the 1820s under the restored monarchy of **Louis XVIII** and **Charles X**. This conflict was finally resolved in favour of the new bourgeoisie. When Charles X refused to accept the result of the 1830 National Assembly elections, Adolphe Thiers – who was to become the veteran conservative politician of the nineteenth century – led the opposition in revolt. Barricades were erected in Paris and there followed three days of bitter street fighting, known as **les trois** glorieuses, in which 1800 people were killed (they are commemorated by the column on place de la Bastille). The outcome was the election of **Louis-Philippe** as constitutional monarch, and the introduction of a few liberalizing reforms, most either cosmetic or serving merely to consolidate the power of the wealthiest stratum of the population.

As the demands of the disenfranchised poor continued to go unheeded, so their radicalism increased, exacerbated by deteriorating living and working conditions in the large towns, especially Paris, as the Industrial Revolution got underway. There were, for example, twenty thousand deaths from cholera in Paris in 1832, and 65 percent of the population in 1848 were too poor to be liable for tax. Eruptions of discontent invariably occurred in the capital, with insurrections in 1832 and 1834. When the lid blew off the pot in **1848** and the **Second Republic** was proclaimed in Paris, it looked for a time as if working-class demands might be at least partly met. The provisional government included Louis Blanc and a Parisian manual worker. But in the face of demands for the control of industry, the setting up of co-operatives and so on, backed by agitation in the streets, the more conservative Republicans lost their nerve. The nation showed its feelings by returning a spanking reactionary majority in the April elections.

Revolution began to appear the only possible defence for the radical left. On June 23, 1848, **working-class Paris** – Poissonnière, Temple, St-Antoine, the Marais, Quartier Latin, Montmartre – rose in **revolt**. Men, women and children fought side by side against fifty thousand troops. In three days of fighting, nine hundred soldiers were killed. No one knows how many of the *insurgés* – the insurgents – died. Fifteen thousand people were arrested and four thousand sentenced to prison terms.

Despite the shock and devastation of civil war in the streets of the capital, the ruling classes failed to heed the warning in the events of June 1848. Far from redressing the injustices which had provoked them, they proceeded to exacerbate them – by, for example, reducing the representation of what Adolphe Thiers called "the vile multitude". The Republic was brought to an end in a coup d'état by **Louis Napoleon**, who within twelve months had himself crowned Emperor Napoléon III.

# Expansion and the changing face of the city

There followed a period of **foreign acquisitions** on every continent and of **laissez-faire capitalism** at home, both of which greatly increased the economic wealth of France, then lagging far behind Britain in the industrialization stakes. Foreign trade trebled, a huge expansion of the rail network was carried out, investment banks were set up, and so forth. The rewards, however, were very unevenly distributed, and the regime relied unashamedly on repressive measures – press censorship, police harassment and the forcible suppression of strikes – to hold the underdogs in check.

The response was entirely predictable. Opposition became steadily more organized and determined. In 1864, under the influence of Karl Marx in London, a French branch of the International was established in Paris and the youthful trade union movement gathered its forces in a federation. In 1869 the far from socialist Gambetta, briefly deputy for Belleville, declared, "Our generation's mission is to complete the French Revolution."

During these nearly twenty years of the **Second Empire**, while conditions were ripening for the most terrible of all Parisian revolutions, the 1871 Commune, the city itself suffered the greatest ever shock to its system. **Baron Haussmann**, appointed Prefect of the Seine department with responsibility for Paris by Napoléon III, undertook the total transformation of the city. In love with the straight line and grand vista, he drove 135km of broad new streets through the cramped quarters of the medieval city, linking the interior and exterior boulevards, and creating north–south, east–west cross-routes. His taste dictated the uniform grey stone facades, mansard roofs and six to seven storeys that are still the architectural hallmark of the Paris street today. In fact, such was the logic of his planning that construction of his projected streets continued long after his death, boulevard Haussmann itself being completed only in 1927.

While it is difficult to imagine how Paris could have survived without some Haussmann-like intervention, the scale of demolitions entailed by such massive redevelopment brought the direst social consequences. The city boundaries were extended to the 1840 fortifications where the boulevard périphérique now runs. The prosperous classes moved into the new western arrondissements, leaving the decaying older properties to the poor. These were divided and sub-divided into ever-smaller units as landlords sought to maximize their rents. Sanitation was nonexistent. Water standpipes were available only in the street. Migrant workers from the provinces, sucked into the city to supply the vast labour requirements, crammed into the old villages of Belleville and Ménilmontant. Many, too poor to buy furniture, lived in barely furnished digs or *demi-lits*, where the same bed was shared by several tenants on a shift basis. Cholera and TB were rife. Attempts to impose sanitary regulations were resisted by landlords as covert socialism. Many considered even connection to Haussmann's water mains an unnecessary luxury. Until 1870 refuse was thrown into the streets at night to be collected the following morning. When in 1884 the Prefect of the day required landlords to provide proper containers, they retorted by calling the containers by his name, *poubelle* – and the name has stuck as the French word for "dustbin".

Far from being concerned with Parisians' welfare, Haussmann's scheme was at least in part designed to keep the workers under control. Barracks were located at strategic points like the place du Château-d'Eau, now République, controlling the turbulent eastern districts, and the broad boulevards were intended to facilitate troop movements and artillery fire. A section of the Canal St-Martin north of the Bastille was covered over for the same reason.

# The Siege of Paris and the Commune

In September 1870, Napoléon III surrendered to Bismarck at the border town of Sedan, less than two months after France had declared war on the well-prepared and superior forces of the **Prussian** state. The humiliation was enough for a Republican government to be instantly proclaimed in Paris. The Prussians advanced and by September 19 were laying **siege** to the capital. Gambetta was flown out by hot-air balloon to rally the provincial troops but the country was defeated and liaison with Paris almost impossible. Further balloon messengers ended up in Norway or the Atlantic; the few attempts at military sorties from Paris turned into yet more blundering failures. Meanwhile, the city's restaurants were forced to change menus to fried dog, roast rat or peculiar delicacies from the zoos. For those without savings, death from disease or starvation became an ever more common fate. At the same time, the peculiar conditions of a city besieged gave a greater freedom to collective discussion and dissent.

The government's half-hearted defence of the city – more afraid of revolution within than of the Prussians – angered Parisians, who clamoured for the creation of a 1789-style Commune. The Prussians meanwhile were demanding a proper government to negotiate with. In January 1871, those in power agreed to hold elections for a new national assembly with the authority to surrender officially to the Prussians. A large monarchist majority, with Thiers at its head, was returned, again demonstrating the isolation from the countryside of the Parisian leftists, among whom many prominent old-timers, veterans of 1848 and the empire's jails like Blanqui and Delescluze, were still active.

On March 1, Prussian troops marched down the Champs-Élysées and garrisoned the city for three days while the populace remained behind closed doors in silent protest. On March 18, amid growing resentment from all classes of Parisians, Thiers' attempt to take possession of the National Guard's artillery in Montmartre (see p.170) set the barrel alight. The Commune was proclaimed from the Hôtel de Ville and Paris was promptly subjected to a second siege by Thiers' government, which had fled to Versailles, followed by all the remaining Parisian bourgeoisie.

The **Commune** lasted 72 days – a festival of the oppressed, Lenin called it. Socialist in inspiration, it had no time to implement lasting reforms. Wholly occupied with defence against Thiers' army, it succumbed finally on May 28, 1871, after a week of street-by-street warfare, in which three thousand Parisians died on the barricades and another twenty to twenty-five thousand men, women and children were killed in random revenge shootings by government troops. Among the non-human casualties were several of the city's landmark buildings, including the Tuileries palace, Hôtel de Ville, Cours des Comptes (where the Musée d'Orsay now stands) and a large chunk of the rue Royale.

# The Belle Époque

Physical recovery was remarkably quick. Within six or seven years few signs of the fighting remained. Visitors remarked admiringly on the teeming streets, the expensive shops and energetic nightlife. Charles Garnier's Opéra was opened in 1875. Aptly described as the "triumph of moulded pastry", it was a suitable image of the frivolity and materialism of the so-called naughty Eighties and Nineties. In 1889 the **Eiffel Tower** stole the show at the great Exposition. For the 1900 repeat, the **Métropolitain** (métro) – or Nécropolitain, as it was dubbed by one wit – was unveiled.

The years up to World War I were marked by the unstable but thoroughly conservative governments of the Third Republic. The trade union movement unified in 1895 to form the **Confédération Générale du Travail** (CGT), and in 1905 Jean Jaurès and Jules Guesde founded the **Parti Socialiste** (also known as the SFIO). On the extreme right, fascism began to make its ugly appearance with Maurras' proto-Brownshirt organization, the Camelots du

Roi, which inaugurated another French tradition, of violence and thuggery on the far Right.

Yet despite – or maybe in some way because of – these tensions and contradictions, Paris provided the supremely inspiring environment for a concentration of **artists and writers** – the so-called **Bohemians**, both French and foreign – such as Western culture has rarely seen. Impressionism, Fauvism and Cubism were all born in Paris in this period, while French poets like Apollinaire, Laforgue, Max Jacob, Blaise Cendrars and André Breton were preparing the way for Surrealism, concrete poetry and symbolism. Film, too, saw its first developments. After World War I, Paris remained the world's art centre, with an injection of foreign blood and a shift of venue from Montmartre to Montparnasse.

As **Depression** deepened in the 1930s and Nazi power across the Rhine became more menacing, politicized thuggery grew rife in Paris, culminating in a pitched battle outside the Chamber of Deputies in February 1934. (Socialist leader Léon Blum was only saved from being lynched by a funeral cortege through the intervention of some building workers who happened to notice what was going on in the street below.) The effect of this fascist activism was to unite the Left, including the Communists, led by the Stalinist Maurice Thorez, in the **Popular Front**. When they won the 1936 elections with a handsome majority in the Chamber, there followed a wave of strikes and factory sit-ins. Frightened by the apparently revolutionary situation, the major employers signed the Matignon Agreement with Blum – now Prime Minister – which provided for wage increases, nationalization of the armaments industry and partial nationalization of the Bank of France, a forty-hour week, paid annual leave and collective bargaining on wages. These reforms were pushed through parliament, but when Blum tried to introduce exchange controls to check the flight of capital the Senate threw the proposal out and he resigned. The Left returned to opposition, where it remained, with the exception of coalition governments, until 1981. Most of the Popular Front's reforms were promptly undone.

# The German Occupation

During the **occupation of Paris** in World War II, the Germans found some sections of Parisian society, as well as the minions of the Vichy government, only too happy to hobnob with them. For four years the city suffered fascist rule with curfews, German garrisons and a Gestapo HQ. Parisian Jews were forced to wear the star of David and in 1942 were rounded up – by other Frenchmen – and shipped off to Auschwitz (see p.157).

The **Resistance** was very active in the city, gathering people of all political persuasions into its ranks, but with communists and socialists, especially of East European Jewish origin, well to the fore. The job of torturing them when they fell into Nazi hands – often as a result of betrayals – was left to their fellow citizens in the fascist militia. Those who were condemned to death – rather than the concentration camps – were shot against the wall below the old fort of Mont Valérien above St-Cloud.

As Allied forces drew near to the city in 1944, the FFI (armed Resistance units), determined to play their part in driving the Germans out, called their troops onto the streets – some said, in a Leftist attempt to seize political power. To their credit, the Paris police also joined in, holding their Île de la Cité HQ for three days against German attacks. On 23 August, Hitler famously gave orders that Paris should be physically destroyed, but the city's commander, Von Cholitz, delayed just long enough. Liberation arrived on August 25 in the shape of General Leclerc's tanks, motoring up the Champs-Élysées to the roar of a vast crowd.

# Postwar Paris

Postwar Paris has remained no stranger to **political battles** in its streets. Violent demonstrations accompanied the Communist withdrawal from the coalition government in 1947. In the Fifties the Left took to the streets again in protest against the colonial wars in Indochina and Algeria. And, in 1961, in one of the most shameful episodes in modern French history, some two hundred Algerians were killed by the police during a civil rights demonstration.

This "secret massacre", which remained covered by a veil of total official silence until the 1990s, took place during the **Algerian war**. It began with a peaceful demonstration against a curfew on North Africans imposed by de Gaulle's government in an attempt to inhibit FLN (National liberation front) resistance activity in the French capital. Whether the police were acting on higher orders or merely on the authority of their own commanders is not clear. What is clear from hundreds of eyewitness accounts, including some from horrified policemen, is that the police went berserk. They opened fire, clubbed people and threw them in the Seine to drown. Several dozen Algerians were killed in the courtyard of the police HQ on the Île de la Cité. For weeks afterwards, corpses were recovered from the Seine, but the French media remained silent, in part through censorship, in part perhaps unable to comprehend that such events had happened in their own capital. Maurice Papon, the police chief at the time, was subsequently decorated by de Gaulle. He later came under scrutiny for his role in deporting Jews to camps in Germany during World War II and was later sentenced to ten years in prison "for complicity in crimes against humanity".

In the extraordinary month of **May 1968**, a radical, libertarian, Leftist movement began in the Paris universities. Students began by occupying university buildings in protest against old-fashioned and hierarchical university structures (see p.123), but the extreme reaction of the police and government helped the movement to spread until it represented a mass revolt against institutional stagnation that ended up with the occupation of hundreds of factories across the country and a general strike by nine million workers.

Yet this was no revolution. The vicious battles with the paramilitary CRS police on the streets of Paris shook large sectors of the population – France's silent majority – to the core. Right-wing and "nationalist" demonstrations – orchestrated by de Gaulle – left public opinion craving stability and peace; and a great many workers were satisfied with a new system for wage agreements. Elections called in June returned the Right to power, the occupied buildings emptied and the barricades in the Latin Quarter came down. For those who thought they were experiencing The Revolution, the defeat was catastrophic.

But French institutions and French society had changed – De Gaulle didn't survive a referendum in 1969. His successor, **Georges Pompidou**, only survived long enough to begin the construction of the giant Les Halles development, and the expressways along the quais of the Seine. In 1974, he was succeeded by the conservative Valéry Giscard d'Estaing, who appointed one Jacques

Chirac as his prime minister. In 1976, Chirac resigned, but made a speedy recovery as Mayor of Paris, less than a year later.

# The Mitterrand era

When **François Mitterrand** won the presidential elections over Giscard in 1981, thus inaugurating the first Socialist government for 23 years, the mood of euphoria on the left was akin to that felt when Tony Blair was elected prime minister of Britain in 1997. Even in conservative Paris, hopes and expectations were initially high, though the prospects for real change in the city were often to be thwarted by power struggles between right-wing mayor **Jacques Chirac** and the left-wing national government. The government pledged to increase state control over industry, introduce higher taxes for the rich, devolve more power to local government, raise the living standards of the least well-off and pursue European integration. By 1984, however, the flight of capital, inflation and budget deficits had forced a complete volte-face, and the Right won parliamentary elections in 1986, with Chirac as the new prime minister – while continuing as Paris's mayor. This was France's first period of "**cohabitation**": the head of state and head of government belonging to opposite sides of the political fence. For Parisians, clashes between Chirac and Mitterrand were nothing new.

While Mitterrand won a second mandate in 1988, Paris remained in the grip of the right – indeed, the town halls of all 20 of the city's arrondissements stayed under right-wing control through much of the 1980s. Nationally, Mitterrand's party failed to win an absolute majority in the parliamentary elections soon after the presidential vote, and although Mitterrand's new prime minister **Michel Rocard** halted Chirac's programmes, he did not reverse them. The Socialists also reneged on their electoral promise to tackle the social and economic deprivation of France's immigrant ghettos. Polls showed over two-thirds of the adult French population to be in favour of deporting legal immigrants for any criminal offence or for being unemployed for over a year. The leader of the far right Front National party, Jean-Marie **Le Pen**, proposed that immigrants should have second-class citizenship, segregated education and separate social security. He received widespread support.

In 1991, Mitterrand sacked Michel Rocard and appointed **Édith Cresson** as France's first woman prime minister. Her brand of left-wing nationalist rhetoric combined with centrist pragmatism made her highly unpopular at home and abroad. Furthermore, she jumped on the rampant racism bandwagon and said that special planes should be chartered to deport illegal immigrants. Shortly afterwards the International Federation of Human Rights published a highly critical report on racism in the **French police** force and said France "was not the home of human rights".

In 1992, Mitterrand staked his reputation on the important **Maastricht referendum**. Parisians, on the whole, voted "yes", but the referendum was passed by a very narrow margin. Meanwhile, **tent cities** were erected by homeless Africans in the 13$^e$ arrondissement and in the Bois de Vincennes to protest against discrimination in housing allocation. There was some public sympathy, but the issue was used as a political football between Mitterrand as president and Chirac as mayor of Paris. In the same year, following fresh scandals over cover-ups and corruption, Cresson was replaced with **Pierre Bérégovoy**. He survived a wave of strikes, but then news broke of a private loan from a friend of Mitterrand accused of insider dealing. Mitterrand distanced himself from his prime minister, the Socialists were routed in the 1993 parliamentary elections, and Bérégovoy shot himself two months later, on May Day, leaving no note of explanation.

Ushering in another period of cohabitation, **Edouard Balladur**, a fresh and fatherly face from the Right, was appointed prime minister. His government carried out a new privatization programme and relied more than ever on **market forces**. Balladur, however, soon lost the respect of his natural supporters after a series of U-turns following demonstrations by Air France workers, teachers, farmers, fishermen and school pupils, and the state's rescue of the Crédit Lyonnais bank after spectacular losses.

Mitterrand tottered on to the end of his presidential term, looking less and less like the nation's favourite uncle. Two months after Bérégovoy's suicide, Réné Bousquet, head of police in the Vichy government and responsible for the rounding up of Jews in 1942, was murdered. A personal friend of Mitterrand's, he was thought to have carried shady secrets about the president to his grave. A biography of Mitterrand, *Le Grand Secret*, stirred up further controversy, casting shadow on the president's war record as an official in the Vichy regime before he joined the Resistance. The book was banned in France but avidly read on the internet.

By now, allegations of **corruption** against mayors, members of parliament, ministers and leading figures in industry were becoming an almost weekly occurrence. Several mayors ended up in jail, but it seemed as if the Paris establishment was above the law. The Socialist Party needed a strong leader to take them into the forthcoming presidential elections and were disappointed when the popular **Jacques Delors**, chair of the European

## The Grands Projets

Mitterrand's most visible legacy is the fabulous collection of public buildings erected as part of his presidential **Grands Projets** – "big projects". Predictably enough, these buildings, most of them architecturally radical, were at first extremely controversial. Most shocking of all to conservative Paris was I.M. Pei's **glass pyramid**, erected in the very heart of the historic Louvre palace. It is a testament to a new spirit in the city that most Parisians have now taken this symbol of thrusting modernity to their hearts, along with the beautiful **Institut du Monde Arabe** (see p.119) in the Quartier Latin. Another *grand projet*, however, has proved less successful: the **Opéra Bastille** (see p.113), which Paris-based novelist Edmund White has described as resembling "a cow palace in Fort Worth". When architects originally submitted their designs for the opera house, the models were publicly presented to the president. The story goes that Mitterrand was briefed to choose the one on the far left, by Richard Meier, but somehow got confused and picked out the one on the far right, by Carlos Ott. Two equally bombastic projects were the **Grande Arche de la Défense** (see p.214) and the **Bibliothèque Nationale** (see p.165), the latter only completed after Mitterrand's death in 1996. It opened to praise from architects and howls of derision from librarians, who pointed out that you can't store fragile books in glass towers, exposed to all the worst that sunlight can do to ink and paper.

At least the *grands projets* could be said to have lasting value. The **bicentennial celebrations of the French Revolution**, on the other hand, were the most absurd blow-out of public funds ever, symbolizing a culture industry spinning mindlessly around the vacuum at the centre of the French vision for the future. Furthermore, they highlighted the contrast between the unemployed and homeless begging on the streets and the limitless cash available for prestige projects.

Commission, was unwilling to stand. Instead they had to make do with **Lionel Jospin**, the rather uncharismatic former education minister, who performed remarkably well in the first round, but lost out to **Chirac** by a small margin in the second.

By the time Mitterrand finally stepped down, he had been the French head of state for fourteen years, presiding over two Socialist and two Gaullist governments. During the period of his presidency, crime rose and increasing numbers of people found themselves excluded from society by racism, poverty and homelessness. Corruption scandals touched the president, politicians of all parties and business chiefs; terrorist bombs went off in Paris; and, as faith in old left-wing certainties foundered, support for extreme Right policies propelled the Front National from a minority faction to a serious electoral force. Despite this, when he died in January 1996, Mitterrand was genuinely mourned as a man of culture and vision, a supreme political operator, and for his unwavering commitment to the vision of a united Europe.

In the last few years, however, a number of further **scandals** have surfaced, badly tarnishing Mitterrand's reputation. These included the arrest in 2000 of his son Jean-Christophe, formerly his senior adviser on Africa, on suspicion of selling arms to Angola, and the jailing of his ex-foreign minister and close friend Roland Dumas for his part in a huge corruption scandal involving the Elf oil company. One of the most damaging accusations to come to light, however, is that Mitterrand ordered his anti-terrorist unit, formed in 1982, to secretly tap the phones of anyone he considered a potential threat to his public image. It is alleged that the phones of 150 people, including lawyers, journalists and rival politicians, were tapped between 1983 and 1986, and at the time of writing, twelve men, including Louis Schweitzer, current head of Renault, are standing trial.

# Chirac's first presidency

When **Jacques Chirac** was elected president in May 1995, Paris was once more running counter to the national trend. In the city elections of the same year, the left tripled its number of councillors and won the 3$^e$, 10$^e$, 11$^e$, 18$^e$, 19$^e$ and 20$^e$ arrondissments, and several ecologists, communists and members of the "Citizens Movement" were also elected. Chirac's Gaullists remained the largest party in the city, but lost their absolute majority in the Mairie de Paris, where the real power resides.

In the summer following the elections, a series of shocks hit Paris and the new regime, as **bombs** exploded in the RER stations of St-Michel and Port Royal. Planted by an extremist Algerian Islamic group, the deadly attacks played into the hands of the far right and diminished public confidence in the government as guardians of law and order. By November, public confidence in Alain Juppé's government had collapsed, and over a period of three weeks some five million people took to the streets of Paris in **protest** against arrogant, elitist politicians and economic austerity measures targeting state employees. There were typical scenes of Parisian revolt: railway sleepers being burnt at the Arc de Triomphe; tear-gas canisters, petrol bombs and stones flying between students and riot police; jazz bands, balloons and food stalls in place de la République. Despite the cold and the stress, the majority of Parisians – and even the police – showed sympathy to the strikers. Public transport was almost entirely shut down, and people walked, cycled, roller-bladed and hitched to work. Many commented on the feeling of public elation and the sense of solidarity on the streets. They felt truly Parisian.

The government's standing in the popularity stakes tumbled further as it was hit by a succession of **corruption scandals**. It was revealed that Prime Minister **Alain Juppé** was renting a luxury flat in Paris at below-market rates. Accusations of cover-ups and perversion of the course of justice followed, punctuated by revelations of illegal funding of election campaigns, politicians taking bribes and dirty money changing hands during privatizations. In the past, politicians feathering their own nests never roused much public anger, but ordinary people, faced with job insecurity and falling living standards, were now becoming disgusted by the behaviour of the "elites". Even the normally obsequious right-wing press asked questions about the judiciary's independence, something Chirac had promised to uphold in his election manifesto. The consequences were twofold: a widening of the gulf between the governors and the governed and a boost to the **Front National**, who played up their corrupt-free image.

The home affairs minister, **Charles Pasqua**, tapped into the general feelings of insecurity and stepped up anti-immigration measures. As a result, around 250,000 people living and working in France had their legal status removed. In March 1996 three hundred **Malian immigrants**, many of them failed asylum-seekers, sought refuge in the Paris church of St-Ambroise, in the 11$^e$ arrondissement, only to be forcibly evicted by riot police. A wave of protest marches ensued, but the government only tightened anti-immigration restrictions further. Fury and frustration at discrimination, assault, abuse and economic deprivation erupted into battles on the street, and several young blacks died at the hands of the police, while the right-wing media revelled in images of violent Arab youths. Racist assaults became more common, and xenophobic opinions became accepted platitudes.

For many young blacks or Arabs seeking work, particularly young men, the ring road dividing the city from its suburbs might as well be a wall of steel. **Unemployment** in some suburbs runs as high as fifty percent. In July 1996, Juppé announced yet another package of measures to create jobs in the most deprived suburban estates, but tax incentives used to lure in businesses have tended to attract fast food companies employing outsiders. Relatively, the city centre is often caricatured as a rich ghetto, yet the number of **SDF** – Sans Domicile Fixe, or homeless – has been estimated at as many as 50,000. In 1998, the minister of employment and solidarity, Martine Aubry, committed 21 billion francs to combat social exclusion. Some 350,000 new jobs were created in the public sector, but whether this addressed the root causes of unemployment and social exclusion is doubtful.

Feeling increasingly beleaguered and unable to deliver on the economy, Chirac called a snap parliamentary election in May 1997. His gamble failed spectacularly as he saw the Right trounced by the Socialists. Chirac lost much of his authority and was dubbed by one journalist as the "resident of the Republic". He was forced into a *cohabitation* with the Socialists, headed by **Lionel Jospin**, who promised new jobs and economic growth, as well as a greater commitment to Europe. Jospin got off to a good start with the introduction of a 35-hour working week, but his government was soon hit by a series of scandals. Nor was the Socialists' popularity aided by the trial in March 1999 of the Mitterrand-era cabinet ministers involved in the tragic **tainted blood scandal** of the mid-1980s. Through alleged stalling the government at the time had failed to implement blood-screening, with the result that by the time of the trial four thousand transfusion recipients had contracted AIDS. The court doled out acquittals and suspended sentences for the three main defendants, including former prime minister Laurent Fabius; needless to say the verdict was greeted with outrage by the victims and their families and a wave of public cynicism.

The Right was not exempt from scandal either. In 1998, **Jean Tiberi** – conservative Paris mayor since Chirac's move to the presidency in 1995 – was implicated in a scandal involving subsidized real-estate and salaries for fake jobs. This reflected badly on **Chirac**, recalling the string of town hall scandals that had taken place while he was mayor of Paris, including accusations that contracts were awarded in return for kickbacks. As if this wasn't bad enough, Chirac himself was also accused of using some £300,000 in cash from illegal sources to pay for luxury holidays for himself, his family and friends between 1992 and 1995. When investigating magistrates tried to question him, he claimed presidential immunity, a position upheld by France's highest court, though only as long as he remained in office: the prospect of having to stand trial if he failed to win a second mandate may well have had a galvanizing effect on Chirac's campaign for president in 2002.

If the mainstream parties weren't faring too well, neither were the extremists. In April 1998 **Le Pen** temporarily alienated himself from the political scene by assaulting and punching a woman Socialist candidate who was standing against his daughter in the National Assembly elections while the camera was still rolling. The party was split, and it seemed for a time that the far right was finished. They certainly didn't have much to say when France won the **World Cup** in July 1998 with a multi-ethnic team. The victory at the new Stade de France, in the multi-ethnic Paris suburb of St-Denis, prompted a wave of popular patriotism that ran across the colour barrier. That night, the Champs-Élysées became a river of a million cheering fans, and "une France tricolore et multicolore" was celebrated all over the country.

# Paris since 2000

In the first years of the new millennium, two seismic events shook Parisian politics. The first was the election of the quiet, unassuming Socialist candidate, **Bertrand Delanoë**, as Mayor of Paris in March 2001. The fact that this was the first time the left had won control of the capital since the bloody uprising of the Paris Commune in 1871 was far more of a shock to most Parisians than the fact that he was openly gay – in Paris, a politician's private life has almost always been seen as exactly that. His brief was to end town-hall corruption, tackle crime and instill new pride and energy into the city. Shortly after the election, Delanoë attempted to show he meant business as a reformer. During the summer, when many Parisians turn the city over to tourists, he shut off the riverside quais to traffic, causing apoplexy among Paris's fiercely independent car-users and huge tailbacks on neighbouring roads. The introduction of the **euro** on 1 January 2002 went relatively smoothly, though price hikes were standard as canny retailers took the opportunity to round up the old prices.

France's second cataclysm of the new millennium was the **presidential election** of spring 2002 and the shock success of the far-right candidate Jean-Marie Le Pen in the first round. Although both the Socialist candidate Lionel Jospin and the right-wing Chirac were seen as rather tired candidates with nothing new to offer, that both would emerge as winners of the first round seemed a foregone conclusion – so much so that many people didn't bother to vote. And so, it was with utter shock and disbelief that the country heard the announcement on April 21 that Jospin had been beaten into third place by Jean-Marie Le Pen, who gained 17 percent of the national vote. Many Parisians were startled to learn that almost ten percent of their supposedly relatively urbane and moderate fellow citizens had also voted for Le Pen. Chirac and Le Pen were now to stand against each other in the final run-off in May.

Much media space was devoted to analyzing what had led to such an unexpected result. The left were criticized for putting up too many candidates, thus splitting the vote and depriving Jospin of adequate backing. Many potential voters had abstained – nearly 30 percent – or voted for marginal candidates as a way of protesting against the mainstream parties: Paris's so-called *banlieue rouge*, the "red suburbs" like St-Denis, have a long history of voting for Communist candidates, but the national success of the **Trotskyist Arlette Laguiller**, with almost 6 percent of the vote, was unprecedented. It was also felt that Chirac unwittingly helped **Le Pen** by campaigning on issues of law and order, the very issues that, after immigration, formed the core of Le Pen's manifesto, effectively lending it some legitimacy.

The shock result acted like a **wake-up call** to the nation. There was a sudden renewed interest in politics and large numbers of people took to the streets to protest against Le Pen and his anti-immigration policies. On May 1, 800,000 people packed the boulevards of Paris in the biggest **demonstration** the capital had seen since the student protests of 1968. Le Pen held his own rally on the same day, but Chirac's victory in the next round was assured, with the Socialists calling on its supporters to vote for Chirac in order to keep Le Pen out. Two weeks later in the **run-off**, Chirac duly swept the board, winning 82 percent – 90 percent in Paris – by far the biggest majority ever won by a French president.

With the parliamentary elections still to come, Chirac's supporters rallied round to create an umbrella grouping of right-wing parties, called the **Union for a Presidential Majority**, to try and win for Chirac the majority in parliament that he'd failed to secure in 1997. The Socialists, severely shaken by Jospin's earlier defeat, were no match and the Right swept to power with 369 of the 577 seats in the National Assembly. They promptly formalized their coalition group as an official political party, called the **UMP** (Union pour un Mouvement Populaire), with former prime minister **Alain Juppé** as its leader.

The drama wasn't over yet though. During Paris's Bastille Day parade on July 14, a neo-Nazi sympathizer attempted to **assassinate** President Chirac. The incident drew attention to the bitterness felt by the far right at having failed to gain any seats in parliament despite winning 13 percent of the vote – in effect six million voters had been disenfranchised. This, together with Le Pen's score of 18 percent in the second round of the presidential poll and the high absention rate, forced the French elite to recognize the anger felt by a sizeable proportion of the electorate, not just against immigration and crime, but also at the remoteness of government and the unaccountability of bureaucrats in Paris.

## New beginnings

Two high-profile events in 2002 launched Paris's new image. Despite **mayor Bertrand Delanoë**'s vilification following the closure of the riverside quais in the previous year, a three-kilometre length of the riverbank was boldly turned into a public beach between 21 July and 18 August. Dubbed **Paris Plage** ("Paris beach"), the scene was complete right down to palm trees, deckchairs and 150 tonnes of sand – the only thing missing was the chance to take a dip in the river. With over half a million people visiting on the first day it is set to become an annual event.

The next landmark event was October's **Nuit Blanche** ("sleepless night"), in which hundreds of galleries, museums, bars, restaurants and public buildings remained open for a citywide all-night party of poetry readings, live music and performance art. The event was an enormous success for everyone except Delanoë himself: while attending the town hall's own champagne party, he was stabbed in the stomach by a man in the crowd, putting him in Paris's Pitié-Salpetrière hospital for a week.

Less glamorous and more important measures have run into trouble. In summer 2001, **bus and cycle lanes** were successfully installed along the central boulevards Rivoli and Sebastopol. Since then, however, some 40km of planned routes have been delayed by arguments with right-wing neighbourhood associations, police, lawyers and even with the planning commission, which judged the lane separators as "unaesthetic". Conservative opposition to traffic control is a given, but Delanoë is now being attacked by the green groups that initially supported him. Faced with the apparent success of London's congestion charge, he has been accused of taking the soft option. Major schemes such as the ring-road **tramway**, due to be started in 2006, and the creation of a residents-only traffic zone in central Paris, are looking increasingly unlikely. On the bright side for visitors, it does seem that Paris's **taxi** system will get a much-needed revamp. Since World War II, the total number of taxis has remained almost stable at just under 15,000, and many taxi drivers insist on their union-regulated working hours – which means three-hour lunch breaks and not working after 7pm. If it can be forced past the union, 1500 new taxi licences will be issued, and the sacred lunch hour will become a thing of the past.

Transport may be an irritation, but high rents are to blame for the flight of residents from Paris "intra-muros" to the suburbs. Intent on preventing the "museumification" of Paris, the mairie has started to buy up private apartment buildings in central Paris, to be rented out as social housing. However, at a rate of 3500 apartments a year, it's unlikely that this can turn around Paris's major trend of falling population. While Paris remains one of the developed world's most densely populated cities – double the density of Tokyo – the number of people living in the central arrondissements halved over the course of the twentieth century. The population is still dropping, though the rate of change has slowed in the last twenty years.

On the national level, one of Chirac's first measures was a **devolution** bill, giving more power to 26 regional assemblies and ending the domination of central government from Paris dating from the time of the 1789 revolution. The measure represents a major U-turn for the Gaullists, who have always been staunchly against any devolution of power. In addition, Chirac has responded to popular fears over rising crime by increasing the number of police officers – a move matched by Delanoë, who has promised 1000 new police officers on Paris's streets. Chirac has also pledged more prison places for young offenders and subsidies to help the unemployed find work – all this while promising to cut income tax. With economic growth down, finding the extra cash to pay for these measures won't be easy.

With such a large majority, the national government seemed to have a real chance to enact much needed unpopular reforms, such as reviewing the creaky pension system and health care provision. But whether Chirac will grasp the nettle remains to be seen. His prime minister, the unassuming **Jean-Pierre**

**Raffarin**, is from the provinces, unconnected with the Parisian elite, but his low-key, softly softly approach may not be effective. State pension reform has been predictably unpopular, with 100,000 state workers marching on the streets of Paris in April 2003 – much the same reaction as forced the government to drop similar plans last time round in 1995.

In the first half of 2003, the domestic political agenda was overshadowed by **economic problems** – growth targets have been halved, and France's budget deficit has shot past the 3 percent ceiling imposed on euro-zone countries – and international diplomacy over the **war on Iraq**. Chirac's threat to use France's UN Security Council veto proved as popular at home as it was derided in the US. It was even argued that France's almost five million-strong **Muslim** population, the largest in Western Europe, influenced the French government's position – though Muslim feelings didn't seem to prevent the government banning headscarves on ID photos, provoking yet another row on the subject. Throughout France, Chirac was feted for "standing up to the Americans", and the actions of the US government were widely caricatured as bullying, aggressive and imperialist. But as recession looms ever larger in France, Paris's vital tourist industry now faces the prospect of many Americans choosing to holiday at home – or at least not in France. Perhaps the prospect of a bid to host the 2012 **olympic games** will provide the city with a new focus and source of energy.

# Books

An extraordinary number of **books** have been written about Paris and all things Parisian. In the selected listing of books below, the abbreviation "o/p" means "out of print", and the book symbol marks titles that are particularly recommended.

## History and politics

**Richard Cobb** *The French and their Revolution.* A selection of expert essays on the French Revolution, with a personal touch.

**Robert Cole** *A Traveller's History of Paris.* This brief history of the city from the first Celtic settlement to the present day is an ideal starting point for those wishing to delve into the historical archives.

★ **Duc de Saint-Simon** *Memoirs.* Written by a true insider, this memoir of life at Versailles under Louis XIV is packed with fascinating, gossipy anecdotes. Be warned: even the five-hundred-page tome currently in print is a mere abbreviation of the duke's massive original journal.

**Christopher Flood & Laurence Bell** (eds) *Political Ideologies in Contemporary France.* Beginners' guide to the current political trends in France.

**Norman Hampson** *A Social History of the French Revolution.* An analysis that concentrates on the personalities involved. Its particular interest lies in the attention it gives to the sans-culottes, the ordinary poor of Paris.

**Christopher Hibbert** *The French Revolution.* Good, concise popular history of the period and events. *The Days of the French Revolution.* Compelling account of the details, complexities, personalities, and events surrounding the French Revolution.

★ **Alistair Horne** *The Fall of Paris* and *Seven Ages of Paris.* Highly regarded historian Alistair Horne's *The Fall of Paris* is a very readable and humane account of the extraordinary period of the Prussian siege of Paris in 1870 and the ensuing struggles of the Commune. The *Seven Ages of Paris* is a wonderfully compelling account of significant episodes in the city's history.

**Colin Jones** *The Cambridge Illustrated History of France.* A political and social history of France from prehistoric times to the mid-1990s, concentrating on issues of regionalism, gender, race and class. Good illustrations and a friendly, non-academic writing style.

**Peter Lennon** *Foreign Correspondents: Paris in the Sixties.* Irish journalist Peter Lennon went to Paris in the early 1960s unable to speak a word of French. He became a close friend of Samuel Beckett and was a witness to the May 1968 events.

**Lissagaray** *Paris Commune* (o/p). A highly personal and partisan account of the politics and fighting by a participant. Although Lissagaray himself is reticent about it, history has it that the last solitary Communard on the last barricade – in the rue Ramponneau in Belleville – was in fact himself.

★ **Philip Mansel** *Paris Between Empires.* Serious but gripping tale of an often-ignored patch of Paris's history: the turbulent years of revolutions and restorations that followed in the wake of Napoleon. Brilliantly conjures up the events of the streets and the salons.

**Karl Marx** *Surveys from Exile; On the Paris Commune*. *Surveys* includes Marx's speeches and articles at the time of the 1848 Revolution and after, including an analysis, riddled with jokes, of Napoléon III's rise to power. *Paris Commune* – more rousing prose – has a history of the Commune by Engels.

**Robert Rowell Palmer** *Twelve Who Ruled*. Another account of the French Revolution, so readable it is almost entertaining.

**Angelo Quattrocchi** *Beginning of the End: France, May 1968* (o/p). First-hand account of the disobedience of students that sparked the riots of factory workers and finally revolution, from the pen of an Italian journalist stationed in Paris to cover the events as they unfolded.

**Orest A. Ranum** *Paris in the Age of Absolutism*. A truly great work of city biography, revealing how and why seventeenth-century Paris rose from medieval obscurity to become the foremost city in Europe under Louis XIV.

**Paul Webster** *Pétain's Crime: The Full Story of French Collaboration in the Holocaust*. The fascinating and alarming story of the Vichy regime's more than willing collaboration with the German authorities' campaign to implement the "final solution" in occupied France, and the bravery of those, especially the Communist resistance, who attempted to prevent it. A mass of hitherto unpublished evidence.

★ **Theodore Zeldin** *A History of French Passions, 1848–1945*. French history tackled by theme, such as intellect and taste – a good read.

# Society and culture

★ **John Ardagh** *France Today*. Comprehensive journalistic overview, covering food, film, education and holidays as well as politics and education. Good on detail about the urban suburbs (and the shift there from the centre) of Paris.

**Roland Barthes** *Mythologies* and *Selected Writings*. The first, though dated, is the classic: a brilliant description of how the ideas, prejudices and contradictions of French thought and behaviour manifest themselves, in food, wine, cars, travel guides and other cultural offerings. Barthes' piece on the Eiffel Tower doesn't appear, but it's included in the *Selected Writings*, published in the US as *A Barthes Reader* (ed Susan Sontag).

**Simone de Beauvoir** *The Second Sex*. One of the prime texts of Western feminism, written in 1949,

covering women's inferior status in history, literature, mythology, psychoanalysis, philosophy and everyday life.

**Denis Belloc** *Slow Death in Paris*. A harrowing account of a heroin addict in Paris. Not recommended holiday reading, but if you want to know about the seamy underbelly of the city, this is the book.

★ **Walter Benjamin** *The Arcades Project*. An all-encompassing portrait of Paris from 1830–70, in which the *passages* are used as a lens through which to view Parisian society. Never completed, Benjamin's magnum opus is a kaleidoscopic assemblage of essays, notes and quotations, gathered under such headings as "Baudelaire", "Prostitution", "Mirrors" and "Idleness".

**James Campbell** *Paris Interzone*. The feuds, passions and destructive lifestyles of Left Bank writers in

1946–60 are evoked here. The cast includes Richard Wright, James Baldwin, Samuel Beckett, Boris Vian, Alexander Trocchi, Eugène Ionesco, Sartre, de Beauvoir, Nabokov and Allan Ginsberg.

**Richard Cobb** *Paris and Elsewhere.* Selected writings by the acclaimed historian of the Revolution reveal his unique encounter with the French.

**Adam Gopnik** *Paris to the Moon.* Intimately observed essays from the Paris correspondent of the *New Yorker* on society, politics, family life and shopping.

**Gisèle Halimi** *Milk for the Orange Tree* (o/p). Born in Tunisia, daughter of an Orthodox Jewish family; ran away to Paris to become a lawyer; defender of women's rights, Algerian FLN fighters and all unpopular causes. A gutsy autobiographical story.

**Patrice Higonnet** *Paris, Capital of the World.* An original cultural portrait of Paris, in which Higonnet, professor of French history at Harvard, examines the myths that have grown up around the city – the way it has been conceived, perceived and dreamed of by its inhabitants and visitors. He explores Paris as the capital of revolution, art and science, as well as crime and illicit pleasure. A scholarly read full of perceptive insights.

**Tahar Ben Jelloun** *Racism Explained to my Daughter.* An honest and straightforward account of the racial tensions in France as seen through the eyes of its Moroccan-born author. An international bestseller.

**François Maspero** *Roissy Express*; photographs Anaïk Frantz. A "travel book" along the RER line B from Roissy to St-Rémy-lès-Chevreuse (excluding the Paris stops). Brilliant insights into the life of the Paris suburbs, and fascinating digressions into French history and politics.

**Andrea Kupfer Schneider** *Creating the Musée d'Orsay: The Politics of Culture in France.* Interesting and sometimes amusing account of the struggles involved in transforming the Gare d'Orsay into one of Paris's most visited museums. An original insight, revealing French attitudes towards such grand cultural projects.

★ **Jean-Jacques Sempé** *Un peu de Paris.* The cartoonist Jean-Jacques Sempé has long been known in France for his lovingly drawn cartoons and gently satirical take on the passions and follies of ordinary people. The subject of his latest collection, published by Gallimard, is contemporary Paris, peopled by nosy *concierges*, rollerblading youths, feisty old ladies and mini Napoleons.

**Tyler Stovall** *Paris Noir: African Americans in the City of Light.* A well-researched and vivid account of the flight of African-American artists in the 1920's from a segregated and racist America to a welcoming Paris.

**Tad Szulc** *Chopin in Paris: The Life and Times of the Romantic Composer.* While musicologists may be disappointed by the lack of discussion of the works that made Chopin famous, others will revel in this exploration of his relationship with his friends – Balzac, Hugo, Liszt among them – and his lover, George Sand, and their shared life in Paris.

**Edmund White** *The Flâneur.* An American expat novelist muses over Parisian themes and places as diverse as the Moreau museum, gay cruising and the history of immigration, as well as the art of being a good *flâneur* – a loiterer or stroller.

**William Wiser** *The Twilight Years: Paris in the 1930s.* Breathless account of the crazy decade before the war, all jazz nights, scandals and the social lives of expat poets and painters.

**Theodore Zeldin** *The French.* A wise and original book that attempts to describe a country through the thoughts and feelings of its people. Draws on the author's conversations with a fascinating range of French people, about money, sex, phobias, parents and everything else.

# Art, architecture and photography

**Brassaï** *Le Paris Secret des Années 30.* Extraordinary photos of the capital's nightlife in the 1930s – brothels, music halls, street cleaners, transvestites and the underworld – each one a work of art and a familiar world (now long since gone) to Brassaï and his mate, Henry Miller, who accompanied him on his nocturnal expeditions. This friendship with Miller is captured in his book *Henry Miller: the Paris Years.*

★ **Henri Cartier-Bresson** *A Propos de Paris.* Some of the greatest photos ever taken: a brilliant blend of the ordinary and the surreal, of photojournalism and art photography.

**Robert Doisneau** *Three Seconds of Eternity.* The famous *Kiss in front of the Hôtel de Ville* takes the front cover, but there's more to Doisneau than this. A collection chosen by the man himself of photographs taken in France, but mainly Paris, in the 1940s and 1950s. Beautifully nostalgic.

**Norma Evenson** *Paris: A Century of Change, 1878–1978* (o/p). A large illustrated volume that makes the development of urban planning and the fabric of Paris an enthralling subject, mainly because the author's concern is always with people, not panoramas.

**Dan Franck** *The Bohemians – the Birth of Modern Art: Paris 1900–1930.* Anecdotes and encounters from within the bohemian *demi-monde* that gave birth to modern art. Encompasses the Montmartre years, when Picasso hung out with Apollinaire, and the Montparnasse era of André Derain, Man Ray and the Surrealists.

**Matthew Gale** *Dada and Surrealism.* Part of Phaidon's acclaimed Art and Ideas series, this stimulating account makes sense of these two revolutionary (and sometimes baffling) art movements. The author looks at works by a wide range of artists, including Duchamp, Ernst, Magritte and Dali – all amply illustrated with quality colour photographs.

**John James** *Chartres.* The story of Chartres cathedral, with insights into the medieval context, the character and attitudes of the masons, the symbolism, and the advanced mathematics of the building's geometry.

**Edward Lucie-Smith** *Concise History of French Painting* (o/p). If you're after an art reference book, then this will do as well as any, though there are of course dozens of other books available on particular French artists and art movements.

**William Mahder** (ed) *Paris Arts: The '80s Renaissance* (o/p), *Paris Creation: Une Renaissance* (o/p). Illustrated, magazine-style survey of French arts. The design and photos are reason enough in themselves to look it up.

★ **John Richardson** *The Life of Picasso: Vol 1 1881–1906* and *Vol 2 1907–17.* No twentieth-century artist has ever been subjected to scrutiny as close as that which Picasso receives in Richardson's exhaustive and brilliantly illustrated biography. The author has taken many years to complete the first two volumes, and there's a risk he'll never reach the end, but the mould-breaking years have now been covered, and it's impossible to imagine how anyone could surpass Richardson's treatment of them. Volumes 3 and 4 are in the pipeline.

**Willy Ronis** *Belleville Ménilmontant* (o/p). Misty black-and-white photographs of people and streets in the two "villages" of eastern Paris in the 1940s and 1950s.

**Judy Rudoe** *Cartier: 1900–1939*. Marvellous photos of the world-renowned Paris-based jeweller's creations including Art Deco necklaces, rings, bracelets, and brooches among other objets d'art.

**Vivian Russell** *Monet's Garden*. An exceptional book illustrated with sumptuous colour photographs by the author, old photographs of the artist and reproductions of his paintings. Superb opening chapter on Monet as "poet of nature", plus a detailed description of the garden's evolution, seasonal cycle and current maintenance, which will delight serious gardeners.

**Yves St-Laurent** *Forty Years of Creation*. Glossy pages of the best of YSL's stylish fashion photography and creations.

**Gertrude Stein** *The Autobiography of Alice B. Toklas*. The goings-on at Stein's famous salon in Paris. The most accessible of her works, written from the point of view of Stein's long-time lover, gives an amusing account of the artistic and literary scene of Paris in the 1910s and 1920s.

**Anthony Sutcliffe** *Paris – An Architectural History*. Excellent overview of Paris's changing cityscape, as dictated by fashion, social structure and political power.

**Heinfried Wischermann** *Paris: an Architectural Guide*. User-friendly guide to over two hundred Parisian landmark buildings. Each comes with a small black-and-white photo and a brief, pithy description.

## Cookery

**Linda Dannenberg** *Paris Bistro Cooking*. Poule au Pot and Rum Baba among other delicious French traditional dishes as cooked by some of Paris' best *bistrots*.

**Alain Ducasse** *Flavours of France* and *L'Atelier of Alain Ducasse: The Artistry of a Master Chef and His Proteges*. The charismatic culinary entrepreneur offers a tour of the gastronomy of France and some of the secrets of his successful kitchen, combining breezy prose with inspirational photos.

**Nicolle Meyer & Amanda Smith** *Paris in a Basket: Markets: The Food and The People*. Would be little more than a glossy coffee table book if it didn't capture the sights, smells, anecdotes and recipes of Paris's open-air markets with so much aplomb.

**Patricia Wells** *The Paris Cookbook*. American journalist and long-time resident of the capital, Patricia Wells takes her inspiration for these sophisticated recipes from her favourite Parisian restaurants, shops and markets.

## Paris in literature

### British/American

**Shari Benstock** *Women of the Left Bank: Paris, 1900–1940*. Follows the lives and creativity of two dozen American, British and French women who moved to Paris and dared to be different.

**Charles Dickens** *A Tale of Two Cities*. Paris and London during the 1789 Revolution and before. The plot's pure Hollywood, but the streets and at least some of the social backdrop are for real.

**Robert Ferguson** *Henry Miller* (o/p). Very readable biography of the old rogue and his rumbustious doings, including his long stint in Paris and affair with Anaïs Nin.

**Noel Riley Fitch** *Sylvia Beach and the Lost Generation: A history of literary Paris in the Twenties and Thirties.* Founder of the original Shakespeare & Co. bookstore and publisher of James Joyce's *Ulysses*, Beach was the lightning rod of literary Paris. The work also follows her relationship with her companion, Adrienne Monnier, the documentation of which helps to place homosexuality in a larger historical context.

**Brion Gysin** *The Last Museum* (o/p). The setting is the *Hôtel Bardo*, the Beat hotel: the co-residents are Kerouac, Ginsberg and Burroughs. Published posthumously, this is 1960s Paris in its most manic mode.

★ **Ernest Hemingway** *A Moveable Feast.* Hemingway's memoirs of his life as a young man in Paris in the 1920s. Includes fascinating accounts of meetings with literary celebrities Ezra Pound, F. Scott Fitzgerald, Gertrude Stein, etc.

**Jack Kerouac** *Satori in Paris* . . . and in Brittany, too. Uniquely inconsequential Kerouac experiences.

**Ian Littlewood** *Paris: A Literary Companion* (o/p). A thorough account of which literary figures went where, and what they had to say about it.

**Herbert Lottman** *Colette: A Life.* An interesting if somewhat dry account of this enigmatic Parisian writer's life.

**Barry Miles** *The Beat Hotel: Ginsberg, Burroughs, and Corso in Paris, 1958–1963.* Follows the self-indulgent exploits of the residents of The Beat Hotel at 9 rue Gît-le-Coeur on the Left Bank.

**Christopher Miller** *Nationalists and Nomads: Essays on Francophone African Literature and Culture.* An exploration of the intermingling issues of nationalism, colonialism and post-colonialism in Paris's ever-evolving literary landscape. Interesting topic if somewhat overly academic prose.

**Henry Miller** *Tropic of Cancer; Quiet Days in Clichy.* Again 1930s Paris, though from a more focused angle – sex, essentially. Erratic, wild, self-obsessed writing, but with definite flights of genius.

★ **Anaïs Nin** *Delta of Venus.* Written in the early 1940s for a dollar a page, these short stories make up what is probably the most inventive, literate and sexy pornography ever written.

★ **George Orwell** *Down and Out in Paris and London.* Documentary account of breadline living in the 1930s – Orwell at his best.

**Paul Rambali** *French Blues* (o/p). Movies, sex, down-and-outs, politics, fast food, bikers – a cynical, streetwise look at modern urban France.

**Jean Rhys** *Quartet.* A beautiful and evocative story of a lonely young woman's existence on the fringes of 1920s Montparnasse society.

## French (in translation)

**Paul Auster** (ed) *The Random House Book of Twentieth Century French Poetry.* Bilingual anthology containing the major French poets of the twentieth century, most of whom were based in Paris: includes Apollinaire, Cendrars, Aragon, Éluard and Prévert.

★ **Honoré de Balzac** *Le Père Goriot.* Biting exposé of cruelty and selfishness in the contrasting worlds of the fashionable faubourg St-Germain and a down-at-heel but genteel boarding house in the Quartier Latin. Like Dickens, but with a harder heart. Balzac's equally brilliant *Wild Asses Skin* is a strange moralistic tale of an ambitious young man's fall from grace in early nineteenth-century Paris.

**Baudelaire's Paris** translated by Laurence Kitchen. Gloom and doom by Baudelaire, Gérard de Nerval, Verlaine and Jiménez – in bilingual edition.

**Calixthe Beyala** *The Little Prince of Belleville*, translated by Marjolijn De Jager. The tale of 7-year-old Loukoum and his efforts to reconcile the hypocrisies and hard truths about his family and his adopted city. The harsh realities facing Paris's African immigrant communities are recounted with honest clarity.

☆ **André Breton** *Nadja*. First published in 1928, *Nadja* is widely considered the most important and influential novel to spring from the Surrealist movement. Largely autobiographical, it portrays the complex relationship between the narrator and a young woman in Paris.

**Louis-Ferdinand Céline** *Death on Credit*. A landmark in twentieth-century French literature, along with his earlier *Voyage to the End of the Night*, Céline recounts the delirium of the world as seen through the eyes of an adolescent in working-class Paris at the beginning of the twentieth century.

**Blaise Cendrars** *To the End of the World*. An outrageous bawdy tale of a randy septuagenarian Parisian actress, having an affair with a deserter from the Foreign Legion.

**Colette** *Chéri*. Considered Colette's finest novel, *Chéri* brilliantly evokes the world of a demi-monde Parisian courtesan who has a doomed love affair with a man at least half her age.

**Didier Daeninckx** *Murder in Memoriam*. A thriller involving two murders: one of a Frenchman during the massacre of the Algerians in Paris in 1961, the other of his son twenty years later. The investigation by an honest detective lays bare dirty tricks, corruption, racism and the cover-up of the massacre.

**Agnès Desarthe** *Good Intentions*. Shortlisted in Britain for the *Jewish Quarterly* prize and the *Independent* Foreign Fiction prize in 2002, Desarthe's unsettling novella describes with black humour a young woman's attempts to deal with difficult neighbours in a Belleville apartment block. The book came out in France around the same time as the feel-good film *Amélie* and couldn't be a better antidote.

**Alexandre Dumas** *The Count of Monte Cristo*. One hell of a good yarn, with Paris and Marseilles locations.

☆ **Gustave Flaubert** *Sentimental Education*. A lively, detailed 1869 reconstruction of the life, manners, characters and politics of Parisians in the 1840s, including the 1848 Revolution.

☆ **Victor Hugo** *Les Misérables*. A racy, eminently readable novel by the French equivalent of Dickens, about the Parisian poor and low-life in the first half of the nineteenth century. Book Four contains an account of the barricade fighting during the 1832 insurrection.

**François Maspero** *Le Sourire du Chat* (translated as *Cat's Grin*). Semi-autobiographical novel of the young teenager Luc in Paris during World War II, with his adored elder brother in the Resistance, his parents taken to concentration camps as Paris is liberated, and everyone else busily collaborating. An intensely moving and revealing account of the war period.

☆ **Guy de Maupassant** *Bel-Ami*. Maupassant's chef-d'oeuvre reveals the double standards of Paris during the Belle Époque with a keen observer's eye.

**Daniel Pennac** *The Scapegoat and The Fairy Gunmother*. Finally two of the series of four have been translated into English. Pennac has long been Paris's favourite contemporary writer, with his hilarious crime stories set among the chaos and colour of multi-ethnic Belleville.

**Georges Pérec** *Life: A User's Manual*. An extraordinary literary jigsaw puzzle of life, past and present, human, animal and mineral, extracted from the residents of an imaginary apartment block in the 17$^e$ arrondissement of Paris.

**Édith Piaf** *My Life*. Piaf's dramatic story told pretty much in her words.

★ **Marcel Proust** *Remembrance of Things Past*. Proust's 3000-page novel, much of it set in Paris, is one of the twentieth century's greatest works of fiction. Its fascination with memory, love and loss, and its stylistic innovation have had a huge influence on the modern novel.

**Jacques Réda** *The Ruins of Paris*. Impressionistic, meditative wanderings around the city written by a Parisian poet in the late 1970s. Either brilliantly avant-garde or deeply pretentious, depending on how well you can stomach Réda's self-conscious prose.

**Jean-Paul Sartre** *Roads to Freedom*

*Trilogy*. Metaphysics and gloom, despite the title.

★ **Georges Simenon** *Maigret at the Crossroads*, or any other of the Maigret novels. Literary crime thrillers; the Montmartre and seedy criminal locations are unbeatable. Those who don't like crime fiction should go for *The Little Saint*, the story of a little boy growing up in the rue Mouffetard when it was a down-at-heel market street.

**Michel Tournier** *The Golden Droplet*. A magical tale of a Saharan boy coming to Paris, where strange adventures, against the backdrop of immigrant life in the slums, overtake him because he never drops his desert oasis view of the world.

★ **Émile Zola** *Nana*. The rise and fall of a courtesan in the decadent times of the Second Empire. Not bad on sex, but confused on sexual politics. A great story nevertheless, which brings mid-nineteenth-century Paris alive, direct, to present-day senses. Paris is also the setting for Zola's *L'Assommoir*, *L'Argent* and *Thérèse Raquin*.

# Language

# Language

# Language

T here's probably nowhere harder to speak or learn French than Paris. Like people from most capital cities, many Parisians speak a kind of hurried slang. Worse still, many speak fairly good English – which they may assume is better than your French. Generations of keen visitors have been offended by being replied to in English after they've carefully enunciated a well-honed question or menu order. Then there are the complex codes of politeness and formality – knowing when to add Madame/Monsieur is only the start of it. Despite this, the essentials are not difficult to master and can make all the difference. Even just saying "Bonjour Madame/Monsieur" and then gesticulating will usually get you a smile and helpful service, even if your efforts to speak French come to nothing.

## French pronunciation

One easy rule to remember is that consonants at the end of words are usually silent. Pas plus tard (not later) is thus pronounced "pa-plu-tarr". But when the following word begins with a vowel, you run the two together: pas après (not after) becomes "pazapray".

Vowels are the hardest sounds to get right. Roughly:

| | | | |
|---|---|---|---|
| a | as in hat | o | as in hot |
| e | as in get | o/au | as in over |
| é | between get and gate | ou | as in food |
| è | like the ai in pair | u | as in a pursed-lip, clipped version of toot |
| eu | like the u in hurt | | |
| i | as in machine | | |

More awkward are the combinations in/im, en/em, on/om, un/um at the end of words, or followed by consonants other than n or m. Again, roughly:

| | | | |
|---|---|---|---|
| in/im | like the "an" in anxious | on/om | like "on" said by someone with a heavy cold |
| an/am, en/em | like "on" said with a nasal accent | un/um | like the "u" in understand |

Consonants are much as in English, except that ch is always sh, h is silent, th is the same as t, ll is like the y in "yes" when preceded by the letter "i", w is v, and r is growled (or rolled).

# Words and phrases

## Basics

| | | | |
|---|---|---|---|
| yes | oui | good evening | bonsoir |
| no | non | good night | bonne nuit |
| please | s'il vous plaît | OK/agreed | d'accord |
| thank you | merci | I understand | Je comprends |
| excuse me | pardon/excusez-moi | I don't understand | Je ne comprends pas |
| sorry | pardon, Madame/ Monsieur | Leave me alone | Laissez-moi tranquille |
| hello | bonjour | Please help me | Aidez-moi, s'il vous plaît |
| hello (phone) | allô | | |
| goodbye | au revoir | help! | au secours! |
| good morning/ afternoon | bonjour | | |

## Key words and phrases

French nouns are divided into masculine and feminine. This causes difficulties with adjectives, whose endings have to change to suit the gender of the nouns they qualify. If you know some grammar, you will know what to do. If not, stick to the masculine form, which is the simplest – it's what we have done in this glossary below.

| | | | |
|---|---|---|---|
| today | aujourd'hui | open | ouvert |
| yesterday | hier | closed | fermé |
| tomorrow | demain | big | grand |
| in the morning | le matin | small | petit |
| in the afternoon | l'après-midi | more | plus |
| in the evening | le soir | less | moins |
| now | maintenant | a little | un peu |
| later | plus tard | a lot | beaucoup |
| at one o'clock | à une heure | half | la moitié |
| at three o'clock | à trois heures | cheap | bon marché/ |
| at ten-thirty | à dix heures et demie | | pas cher |
| at midday | à midi | expensive | cher |
| man | un homme | good | bon |
| woman | une femme | bad | mauvais |
| here | ici | hot | chaud |
| there | là | cold | froid |
| this one | ceci | with | avec |
| that one | cela | without | sans |

## Talking to people

When addressing people you should always use Monsieur for a man, Madame for a woman, Mademoiselle for a girl. Plain bonjour by itself is not enough. This isn't as formal as it seems, and it has its uses when you've forgotten someone's name or want to attract someone's attention. Bonjour can be used well into the afternoon, and people may start saying bonsoir surprisingly early in the evening, or as a way of saying goodbye.

| | | | |
|---|---|---|---|
| How are you? | Comment allez-vous?/Ça va? | I'm English/ Irish/ | Je suis anglais(e)/ irlandais(e)/ |
| Fine, thanks | Très bien, merci | Scottish/ | écossais(e)/ |
| I don't know | Je ne sais pas | Welsh/ | gallois(e)/ |
| I see! | Ah bon! | American/ | américain(e)/ |
| Do you speak ? English | Vous parlez anglais? | Australian/ Canadian/ | australien(ne)/ canadien(ne)/ |
| How do you say… in French? | Comment ça se dit…en français? | a New Zealander | néo-zélandais(e) |
| What's your name? | Comment vous appelez-vous? | Can you speak slower? | S'il vous plaît, parlez moins vite |
| | | Let's go | Allons-y |
| My name is . . . | Je m'appelle . . . | See you tomorrow | À demain |
| | | See you soon | À bientôt |

## Questions and requests

The simplest way of asking a question is to start with s'il vous plaît (please), then name the thing you want in an interrrogative tone of voice. For example:

| | | | |
|---|---|---|---|
| Where is there a bakery? | S'il vous plaît, la boulangerie? | ticket office | vente de billets |
| Which way is it to the Eiffel Tower? | S'il vous plaît, pour aller à la Tour Eiffel? | how many kilometres? | combien de kilomètres? |
| | | how many hours? | combien d'heures? |
| We'd like a room for two | S'il vous plaît, une chambre pour deux. | on foot | à pied |
| | | Where are you going? | Vous allez où? |
| Can I have a kilo of oranges? | S'il vous plaît, un kilo d'oranges. | I'm going to . . . | Je vais à . . . |
| | | I want to get off at.... | Je voudrais descendre à . . . |
| where? | où? | | |
| how? | comment? | the road to . . . | la route pour . . . |
| how many | combien? | near | près/pas loin |
| how much is it? | c'est combien? | far | loin |
| when? | quand? | left | à gauche |
| why? | pourquoi? | right | à droite |
| at what time? | à quelle heure? | straight on | tout droit |
| what is/which is? | quel est? | on the other side of | de l'autre côté de |
| | | on the corner of | à l'angle de |
| | | next to | à côté de |

### Getting around and directions

| | | behind | derrière |
|---|---|---|---|
| metro/subway station | métro | in front of | devant |
| Where is the nearest metro? | Où est le métro le plus proche? | before | avant |
| | | after | après |
| bus | bus | under | sous |
| bus (coach) | car | to cross | traverser |
| bus station | gare routière | bridge | pont |
| bus stop | arrêt | to park the car | garer la voiture |
| car | voiture | car park | un parking |
| train/taxi/ferry | train/taxi/ferry | no parking | défense de stationner/ stationnement interdit |
| boat | bâteau | | |
| plane | avion | | |
| railway station | gare | petrol station | poste d'essence |
| platform | quai | | |
| What time does it leave? | Il part à quelle heure? | | |

### Accommodation

| | | | |
|---|---|---|---|
| What time does it arrive? | Il arrive à quelle heure? | a room for one/two people | une chambre pour une/deux personnes |
| a ticket to . . . | un billet pour . . . | | |
| single ticket | aller simple | with a double bed | avec un grand lit |
| return ticket | aller retour | a room with a shower | une chambre avec douche |
| validate your ticket | compostez votre billet | a room with a bath | une chambre avec salle de bain |
| valid for | valable pour | for one/two/three | Pour une/deux/ |

| | | | |
|---|---|---|---|
| nights | trois nuit(s) | quiet | calme |
| Can I see it? | Je peux la voir? | noisy | bruyant |
| a room in the courtyard | une chambre sur la cour | hot water | eau chaude |
| a room over the street | une chambre sur la rue | cold water | eau froide |
| first floor | premier étage | Is breakfast included? | Est-ce que le petit déjeuner est compris? |
| second floor | deuxième étage | I would like breakfast | Je voudrais prendre le petit déjeuner |
| with a view | avec vue | I don't want breakfast | Je ne veux pas le petit déjeuner |
| key | clef | campsite | un camping/ terrain de camping |
| to iron | repasser | | |
| do laundry | faire la lessive | | |
| sheets | draps | youth hostel | auberge de jeunesse |
| blankets | couvertures | | |

## Months, days, dates and numbers

| | | | |
|---|---|---|---|
| January | janvier | 3 | trois |
| February | février | 4 | quatre |
| March | mars | 5 | cinq |
| April | avril | 6 | six |
| May | mai | 7 | sept |
| June | juin | 8 | huit |
| July | juillet | 9 | neuf |
| August | août | 10 | dix |
| September | septembre | 11 | onze |
| October | octobre | 12 | douze |
| November | novembre | 13 | treize |
| December | décembre | 14 | quatorze |
| Monday | lundi | 15 | quinze |
| Tuesday | mardi | 16 | seize |
| Wednesday | mercredi | 17 | dix-sept |
| Thursday | jeudi | 18 | dix-huit |
| Friday | vendredi | 19 | dix-neuf |
| Saturday | samedi | 20 | vingt |
| Sunday | dimanche | 21 | vingt-et-un |
| August 1 | le premier août | 22 | vingt-deux |
| March 2 | le deux mars | 30 | trente |
| July 14 | le quatorze juillet | 40 | quarante |
| November 23, 2004 | le vingt-trois novembre, deux mille quatre | 50 | cinquante |
| | | 60 | soixante |
| | | 70 | soixante-dix |
| | | 75 | soixante-quinze |
| **Numbers** | | 80 | quatre-vingts |
| 1 | un | 90 | quatre-vingt-dix |
| 2 | deux | 95 | quatre-vingt-quinze |

| 100 | cent | 1000 | mille |
| 101 | cent un | 2000 | deux mille |
| 200 | deux cents | 1,000,000 | un million |

# Food and drink terms

## Basic words and phrases

| | | | |
|---|---|---|---|
| lunch | déjeuner | I'd like to reserve a table | Je voudrais réserver une table |
| dinner | dîner | for two people, at eight thirty | pour deux personnes, à vingt heures et demie |
| set menu | menu | | |
| individually priced dishes | à la carte | | |
| starters | entrées | I'm having the €15 menu | Je prendrai le menu à quinze euros |
| main courses | les plats | Waiter! | Monsieur/madame! (never say "garçon") |
| a carafe of tap water/wine | une carafe d'eau/ de vin | | |
| mineral water | eau minérale | the bill, please | l'addition, s'il vous plait |
| fizzy water | eau gazeuse | | |
| still water | eau plate | a glass of beer | une pression |
| wine list | carte des vins | coffee (espresso) | un café |
| a quarter/half-litre of red/white house wine | un quart/demi de rouge/blanc | white coffee | un crème |
| | | big bowl of milky breakfast coffee | un café au lait |
| a glass of white/ red wine | un (verre de) rouge/blanc | cappuccino | un cappuccino |

## Cooking terms

| | | | |
|---|---|---|---|
| Chauffé | Heated | à emporter | Takeaway |
| Cuit | Cooked | Fumé | Smoked |
| Cru | Raw | Salé | Salted/savoury |
| Emballé | Wrapped | Sucré | Sweet |

## Essentials

| | | | |
|---|---|---|---|
| Pain | Bread | Vinaigre | Vinegar |
| Beurre | Butter | Bouteille | Bottle |
| Oeufs | Eggs | Verre | Glass |
| Lait | Milk | Fourchette | Fork |
| Huile | Oil | Couteau | Knife |
| Poivre | Pepper | Cuillère | Spoon |
| Sel | Salt | Bio | Organic |
| Sucre | Sugar | | |

## Snacks

| | | | |
|---|---|---|---|
| **Crêpe** | Pancake (sweet) | **au plat** | fried |
| au sucre | with sugar | à la coque | boiled |
| au citron | with lemon | durs | hard-boiled |
| au miel | with honey | brouillés | scrambled |
| à la confiture | with jam | **Omelette** | Omelette |
| aux œufs | with eggs | nature | plain |
| à la crème | with chestnut | aux fines herbes | with herbs |
| de marrons | purée | au fromage | with cheese |
| **Galette** | Buckwheat | **Salade de** | Salad of |
| | (savoury) pancake | tomates | tomatoes |
| **Un sandwich/** | A sandwich . . . | betteraves | beetroot |
| une baguette | | concombres | cucumber |
| jambon | with ham | carottes rapées | grated carrots |
| fromage | with cheese | | |

### Other fillings/salads

| | | | |
|---|---|---|---|
| saucisson | with sausage | **Anchois** | Anchovy |
| rillettes | with coarse pâté | **Andouillette** | Tripe sausage |
| pâté(de campagne) | with pâté | **Boudin** | Black pudding |
| | (country-style) | **Cœurs de palmiers** | Palm hearts |
| croque-monsieur | Grilled cheese & | **Fonds d'artichauts** | Artichoke hearts |
| | ham sandwich | **Hareng** | Herring |
| croque-madame | croque-monsieur | **Langue** | Tongue |
| | with an egg on top | **Poulet** | Chicken |
| panini | Flat toasted | **Thon** | Tuna |
| | Italian sandwich | | |
| **Oeufs** | Eggs | | |

## Soups (soupes)

| | | | |
|---|---|---|---|
| **Bisque** | Shellfish soup | **Potage** | Thick vegetable soup |
| **Bouillabaisse** | Marseillais fish soup | **Rouille** | Red pepper, garlic & |
| **Bouillon** | Broth or stock | | saffron mayonnaise |
| **Bourride** | Thick fish soup | | with fish soup |
| **Consommé** | Clear soup | **Velouté** | Thick soup, usually |
| **Pistou** | Parmesan, basil & garlic | | made with fish or |
| | paste added to soup | | poultry |

## Starters (hors d'œuvres)

| | | | |
|---|---|---|---|
| **Assiette anglaise** | Plate of cold meats | **Hors d'œuvres** | Combination of the |
| **Crudités** | Raw vegetables | **variés** | above |
| | with dressings | | |

# Fish (poisson), seafood (fruits de mer) and shellfish (crustacés or coquillages)

| | | | |
|---|---|---|---|
| Anchois | Anchovies | Moules (marinière) | Mussels (with shallots in white wine sauce) |
| Anguilles | Eels | Oursin | Sea urchin |
| Barbue | Brill | Palourdes | Clams |
| Bigorneau | Periwinkle | Praires | Small clams |
| Brème | Bream | Raie | Skate |
| Brochet | Pike | Rouget | Red mullet |
| Cabillaud | Cod | Saumon | Salmon |
| Calmar | Squid | Sole | Sole |
| Carrelet | Plaice | Thon | Tuna |
| Claire | Type of oyster | Truite | Trout |
| Colin | Hake | Turbot | Turbot |
| Congre | Conger eel | | |
| Coques | Cockles | | |
| Coquilles St-Jacques | Scallops | | |
| Crabe | Crab | | |

## Fish: dishes and related terms

| | |
|---|---|
| Crevettes grises | Shrimps |
| Crevettes roses | Prawns |
| Daurade | Sea bream |
| Éperlan | Smelt or whitebait |
| Escargots | Snails |
| Flétan | Halibut |
| Friture | Whitebait |
| Gambas | King prawns |
| Hareng | Herring |
| Homard | Lobster |
| Huîtres | Oysters |
| Langouste | Spiny lobster |
| Langoustines | Saltwater crayfish (scampi) |
| Limande | Lemon sole |
| Lotte de mer | Monkfish |
| Loup de mer | Sea bass |
| Louvine, loubine | Similar to sea bass |
| Maquereau | Mackerel |
| Merlan | Whiting |
| Morue | dried, salted cod |

| | |
|---|---|
| Aïoli | Garlic mayonnaise served with salt cod other fish |
| Béarnaise | Sauce made with egg yolks, white wine, shallots & vinegar |
| Beignets | Fritters |
| Darne | Fillet or steak |
| La douzaine | A dozen |
| Frit | Fried |
| Fumé | Smoked |
| Fumet | Fish stock |
| Gigot de mer | Large fish baked whole |
| Grillé | Grilled |
| Hollandaise | Butter & vinegar sauce |
| A la meunière | In a butter, lemon & parsley sauce |
| Mousse/mousseline | Mousse |
| Quenelles | Light dumplings |

## Meat (viande) and poultry (volaille)

| | | | |
|---|---|---|---|
| Agneau (de pré-salé) | Lamb (grazed on salt marshes) | Bœuf | Beef |
| Andouille, andouillette | Tripe sausage | Bifteck | Steak |
| | Bavette beef flank steak | Boudin blanc | Sausage of white meats |

| | |
|---|---|
| Boudin noir | Black pudding |
| Caille | Quail |
| Canard | Duck |
| Caneton | Duckling |
| Contrefilet | Sirloin roast |
| Coquelet | Cockerel |
| Dinde | Turkey |
| Entrecôte | Ribsteak |
| Faux filet | Sirloin steak |
| Foie | Liver |
| Foie gras | Fattened (duck/goose) liver |
| Gigot (d'agneau) | Leg (of lamb) |
| Grillade | Grilled meat |
| Hachis | Chopped meat or mince hamburger |
| Langue | Tongue |
| Lapin, lapereau | Rabbit, young rabbit |
| Lard, lardons | Bacon, diced bacon |
| Lièvre | Hare |
| Merguez | Spicy, red sausage |
| Mouton | Mutton |
| Museau de veau | Calf's muzzle |
| Oie | Goose |
| Onglet | Cut of beef |
| Os | Bone |
| Porc | Pork |
| Poulet | Chicken |
| Poussin | Baby chicken |
| Ris | Sweetbreads |
| Rognons | Kidneys |
| Rognons blancs | Testicles |
| Sanglier | Wild boar |
| Tête de veau | Calf's head (in jelly) |
| Tournedos | Thick slices of fillet |
| Tripes | Tripe |
| Veau | Veal |
| Venaison | Venison |

## Meat and poultry: dishes and related terms

| | |
|---|---|
| Aile | Wing |
| Blanquette de veau | Veal in cream & mushroom sauce |
| Bœuf bourguignon | Beef stew with red wine, onions & mushrooms |
| Canard à l'orange | Roast duck with an orange-and-wine sauce |
| Carré | Best end of neck, chop or cutlet |
| Cassoulet | A casserole of beans & meat |
| Choucroute garnie | Sauerkraut served with sausages or cured ham |
| Civet | Game stew |
| Confit | Meat preserve |
| Coq au vin | Chicken with wine, onions & mushrooms, cooked till it falls off the bone |
| Côte | Chop, cutlet or rib |
| Cou | Neck |
| Cuisse | Thigh or leg |
| Daube, estouffade, hochepot, navarin and ragoût | All are types of stew |
| En croûte | In pastry |
| Épaule | Shoulder |
| Farci | Stuffed |
| Au feu de bois | Cooked over wood fire |
| Au four | Baked |
| Garni | With vegetables |
| Gésier | Gizzard |
| Grillé | Grilled |
| Magret de canard | Duck breast |
| Marmite | Casserole |
| Médaillon | Round piece |
| Mijoté | Stewed |
| Museau | Muzzle |
| Pavé | Thick slice |
| Rôti | Roast |
| Sauté | Lightly cooked in butter |
| Steak au poivre(vert/rouge) | Steak in a black (green/red) peppercorn sauce |
| Steak tartare | Raw chopped beef, topped with a raw egg yolk |

## For steaks

| | |
|---|---|
| Bleu | Almost raw |
| Saignant | Rare |
| A point | Medium |
| Bien cuit | Well done |
| Très bien cuit | Very well cooked |
| Brochette | Kebab |

## Garnishes and sauces

| | |
|---|---|
| Beurre blanc | Sauce of white wine & shallots, with butter |
| Chasseur | White wine, mushrooms & shallots |
| Diable | Strong mustard seasoning |
| Forestière | With bacon & mushroom |
| Fricassée | Rich, creamy sauce |
| Mornay | Cheese sauce |
| Pays d'Auge | Cream & cider |
| Piquante | Gherkins or capers, vinegar & shallots |
| Provençale | Tomatoes, garlic, olive oil & herbs |

# Vegetables (légumes), herbs (herbes) and spices (épices)

| | |
|---|---|
| Ail | Garlic |
| Algue | Seaweed |
| Anis | Aniseed |
| Artichaut | Artichoke |
| Asperges | Asparagus |
| Avocat | Avocado |
| Basilic | Basil |
| Betterave | Beetroot |
| Carotte | Carrot |
| Céleri | Celery |
| Champignons, cèpes, chanterelles | Mushrooms of various kinds |
| Chou (rouge) | (Red) cabbage |
| Chou-fleur | Cauliflower |
| Ciboulette | Chives |
| Concombre | Cucumber |
| Cornichon | Gherkin |
| Échalotes | Shallots |
| Endive | Chicory |
| Épinards | Spinach |
| Estragon | Tarragon |
| Fenouil | Fennel |
| Flageolets | White beans |
| Gingembre | Ginger |
| Haricots verts rouges beurres | Beans string (French) kidney butter |
| Laurier | Bay leaf |
| Lentilles | Lentils |
| Maïs | Corn |
| Menthe | Mint |
| Moutarde | Mustard |
| Oignon | Onion |
| Pâtes | Pasta |
| Persil | Parsley |
| Petits pois | Peas |
| Piment | Pimento |
| Pois chiche | Chickpeas |
| Pois mange-tout | Snow peas |
| Pignons | Pine nuts |
| Poireau | Leek |
| Poivron (vert, rouge) | Sweet pepper (green, red) |
| Pommes (de terre) | Potatoes |
| Primeurs | Spring vegetables |
| Radis | Radishes |
| Riz | Rice |
| Safran | Saffron |
| Salade verte | Green salad |
| Sarrasin | Buckwheat |
| Tomate | Tomato |
| Truffes | Truffles |

## Vegetables: dishes and related terms

| | |
|---|---|
| Beignet | Fritter |
| Farci | Stuffed |
| Gratiné/au gratin/ gratin de | Browned with cheese or butter |

| Jardinière | With mixed diced vegetables | | white wine sauce & shallots |
| Forestière | With mushrooms | Parmentier | With potatoes |
| À la parisienne | Sautéed in butter (potatoes); with | Sauté | Lightly fried in butter |
| | | À la vapeur | Steamed |

## Fruits (fruits) and nuts (noix)

| Abricot | Apricot | Myrtilles | Bilberries |
| Amandes | Almonds | Noisette | Hazelnut |
| Ananas | Pineapple | Noix | Nuts |
| Banane | Banana | Orange | Orange |
| Brugnon, nectarine | Nectarine | Pamplemousse | Grapefruit |
| Cacahouète | Peanut | Pêche (blanche) | (White) peach |
| Cassis | Blackcurrants | Pistache | Pistachio |
| Cerises | Cherries | Poire | Pear |
| Citron | Lemon | Pomme | Apple |
| Citron vert | Lime | Prune | Plum |
| Figues | Figs | Pruneau | Prune |
| Fraises (des bois) | Strawberries (wild) | Raisins | Grapes |
| Framboises | Raspberries | | |
| Fruit de la passion | Passion fruit | **Fruit: related terms** | |
| Groseilles | Redcurrants & gooseberries | Beignets | Fritters |
| | | Compote de . . . | Stewed . . . |
| Mangue | Mango | Coulis | Sauce |
| Marrons | Chestnuts | Flambé | Set aflame in alcohol |
| Melon | Melon | Frappé | Iced |

## Desserts (desserts or entremets) and pastries (pâtisserie)

| Barquette | Small boat-shaped flan | | cream |
| | | Crème fraîche | Sour cream |
| Bavarois | Refers to the mould, could be mousse or custard | Crème pâtissière | Thick eggy pastry-filling |
| | | Crêpe | Pancake |
| Bombe | A moulded ice cream dessert | Crêpe suzette | Thin pancake with orange juice & liqueur |
| Brioche | Sweet, high yeast breakfast roll | Fromage blanc | Cream cheese |
| Charlotte | Custard & fruit in lining of almond fingers | Galette | Buckwheat pancake |
| | | Génoise | Rich sponge cake |
| | | Glace | Ice cream |
| Coupe | A serving of ice cream | Île flottante/ œufs à la neige | Soft meringues floating on custard |
| Crème Chantilly | Vanilla-flavoured & sweetened whipped | Macarons | Macaroons |

| | | | |
|---|---|---|---|
| Madeleine | Small sponge cake | Petits fours | Bite-sized cakes/pastries |
| Marrons Mont Blanc | Chestnut purée & cream on a rum-soaked sponge cake | Poires Belle Hélène | Pears & ice cream in chocolate sauce |
| Mousse au chocolat | Chocolate mousse | Sablé | Shortbread biscuit |
| Palmiers | Caramelized puff pastries | Savarin | A filled, ring-shaped cake |
| Parfait | Frozen mousse, sometimes ice cream | Tarte | Tart |
| | | Tartelette | Small tart |
| | | Truffes | Truffles, chocolate or liqueur variety |
| Petit suisse | A smooth mixture of cream & curds | Yaourt, yogourt | Yoghurt |

## Cheese (fromage)

There are over 400 types of French cheese, most of them named after their place of origin. *Chèvre* is goat's cheese and *brebis* is cheese made from sheep's milk. *Le plateau de fromages* is the cheeseboard, and bread – but not butter – is served with it.

# French and architectural terms: a glossary

These are either terms you'll come across in this book, or come up against on signs, maps, etc, while travelling around.

**Abbaye** abbey

**Ambulatory** covered passage around the outer edge of a choir of a church

**Apse** semicircular termination at the east end of a church

**Arrondissement** district of the city

**Assemblée Nationale** the French parliament

**Auberge de Jeunesse (AJ)** youth hostel

**Baroque** High Renaissance period of art and architecture, distinguished by extreme ornateness

**Beaux-Arts** fine arts

**Car** bus

**Carolingian** dynasty (and art, sculpture, etc) founded by Charlemagne, late eighth to early tenth centuries

**CFDT** Socialist trade union

**Carrefour** intersection

**CGT** Communist trade union

**Chasse, Chasse Gardée** hunting grounds

**Château** mansion, country house, castle

**Château Fort** castle

**Chemin** path

**Chevet** end wall of a church

**CIDJ (Centre d'Informations Jeunesse)** youth information centre

**Classical** architectural style incorporating Greek and Roman elements – pillars, domes, colonnades, etc – at its height in France in the seventeenth century and revived in the nineteenth century as **Neoclassical**

**Clerestory** upper storey of a church, incorporating the windows

**Codene** French CND

**Consigne** luggage consignment

**Cours** combination of main square and main street

**Couvent** convent, monastery

**Défense de . . .** It is forbidden to . . .

**Dégustation** tasting (wine or food)

**Département** county – more or less

**Église** church

**En Panne** out of order

**Entrée** entrance

**Fermeture** closing period

**Flamboyant** florid form of Gothic

**FN (Front National)** far-right party led by Jean-Marie Le Pen

**FO** Catholic trade union

**Fresco** wall painting – durable through application to wet plaster

**Gallo-Romain** period of Roman occupation of Gaul (first to fourth centuries AD)

**Gare** station; **– Routière** bus station; **– SNCF** train station

**Gobelins** famous tapestry manufacturers, based in Paris; its most renowned period was in the reign of Louis XIV (seventeenth century)

**Grande Randonnée (GR)** long-distance footpath

**Halles** covered market

**HLM** public housing development

**Hôtel** a hotel, but also an aristocratic townhouse or mansion

**Hôtel de ville** town hall

**Jours fériés** public holidays

**Mairie** town hall

**Marché** market

**Merovingian** dynasty (and art, etc) ruling France and parts of Germany from the sixth to mid-eighth centuries

**Narthex** entrance hall of church

**Nave** main body of a church

**PCF** Communist Party of France

**Place** square

**Porte** gateway or door

**PS** Socialist party

**Poste** post office

**Quartier** district of a town

**Renaissance** art/architectural style developed in fifteenth-century Italy and imported to France in the early sixteenth century by François 1ᵉʳ

**Retable** altarpiece

**Rez-de-chaussée (RC)** ground floor

**RN (Route Nationale)** main road

**Romanesque** early medieval architecture distinguished by squat, rounded forms and naive sculpture

**RPR** Gaullist party

**SI (Syndicat d'Initiative)** tourist information office; also known as OT, OTSI and Maison du Tourisme

**SNCF (Société Nationale des Chemins de Fer)** French railways

**Soldes** sales

**Sortie** exit

**Stucco** plaster used to embellish ceilings, etc

**Tabac** bar or shop selling stamps, cigarettes, télécartes, etc

**Tour** tower

**Transept** cross arms of a church

**Triforium** narrow, middle storey of a church

**Tympanum** sculpted panel above a church door

**UDF** centre-right party

**UMP** new umbrella party grouping parties of the right and centre-right

**Vauban** seventeenth-century military architect – his fortresses still stand all over France

**Villa** a mews or a series of small residential streets, built as a unity

**Voussoir** sculpted rings in an arch over church door

**Zone Bleue** restricted parking zone

**Zone Piétonne** pedestrian zone

# Index
## and small print

# Index

Entries in colour indicate a map

# E

eating, see "restaurants"
École Militaire ...............140
École Normale
  Supérieure...............124
École Polytéchnique .....125
Édith Piaf, musée..........194
Église du Dôme ............142
Église St-Merri .............101
Égouts, musée des
  ...........................140, 369
Eiffel Tower .................139
Eiffel, Gustave..............157
electricity......................375
Élysée Palace.................77
email ..............................37
embassies, French..........19
emergencies .................375
Enfants-Rouges,
  Marché des ...............110
Erotisme, musée de l'...173
Étoile.............................74
euro...............................33
Eurostar ...................11, 26
Eurotunnel......................14
Éventail, musée de l' ....176
exchange .......................34
exchange, currency
  ...........................34, 375

# F

Fauchon.................89, 339
ferries
  from Ireland.......................13
  from the UK ........................13
festivals ...................41–43
**film**....................320–324
film festivals ................324
films set in Paris ..........322
fitness clubs..........353–354
Flea market, Porte-de-
  Vanves.....................156
Flea market, St-
  Ouen/Clignancourt.....179
flea markets ................345
flights ............................9
  from Australia.....................17
  from Canada.......................15
  from Ireland.......................10
  from New Zealand ..............17
  from the UK ......................10
  from the US ......................15
FNAC...........................332
Fondation Cartier pour
  l'Art Contemporain.....153

Fondation Cartier-
  Bresson.....................155
Fontaine de Médicis .....132
Fontaine des
  Innocents ...................95
Fontainebleau ..............235
football .........................358
Force (prison), la ...........104
Foucault's
  Pendulum...................124
François I .............142, 235
**French
  language** ..........409–420
French Revolution
  ...........................104, 113
funfairs .........................365

# G

Galerie Colbert...............91
Galerie de Valois.............90
Galerie des Glaces .......222
Galerie Véro-Dodat........91
Galerie Vivienne .............91
Galeries Lafayette..........88
Gare de l'Est ................176
Gare du Nord................176
gay and lesbian
  nightlife .....................372
gay hotels ....................374
**gay Paris** ..............371–377
gay restaurants .............373
Gehry, Frank O..............203
Géode, la ......................189
German
  Occupation ................388
Giverny.........................240
Gobelins tapestry
  workshops .................163
Goutte d'Or and
  the northern
  stations......................175
Goutte d'Or, la ......174–176
Grand Palais ...................77
Grand Trianon ..............222
Grande Arche (de la
  Défense), la ...............214
Grande Galerie de
  l'Évolution.................126
Grands Boulevards ........83
Grands Boulevards
  and passages ........86–87
Grands Projets..............391
Grenouillère, La............226
Grévin, musée................85
Guimard, Hector ...........206
Guimet, musée

Nationale des Arts
  Asiatiques ..................135
guinguettes ..................351
Gustave Moreau,
  musée .......................174
gyms ....................353–354

# H

Hall of Mirrors ...............222
Halle St-Pierre...............172
Halles St–Germain .......131
Halles, Forum des...........93
**Halles, Les** ...............93–95
Halles, Les and
  Châtelet ......................94
Hameau de la Reine .....222
Hameau des Artistes ....170
hammams .....................355
Haussmann, Baron ............
  52, 53, 85, 118, 166, 386
haute couture...............334
health ............................20
Hédiard ...................89, 339
helicopter rides .............351
Héloïse...................59, 195
Hemingway, Ernest
  ...................115, 150, 153
Henri IV ...............54,107
Histoire de France,
  musée de l' ................103
Histoire Naturelle,
  muséum national d' ...126
**history of Paris** ....381–397
holidays, public..............40
Homme, musée de l' ....135
Hôpital St-Louis............183
horse-racing..................359
Hôtel Carnavalet...........104
Hôtel d'Albret................103
Hôtel de Cluny
  ...................121, 140, 153
Hôtel de Sens ..............112
Hôtel de Sully ..............108
Hôtel de Ville................102
Hôtel des Invalides .......142
Hôtel des Monnaies......127
Hôtel Drouot ..................92
Hôtel Lamoignon ..........104
Hôtel Lauzun .................60
Hôtel Matignon ............144
Hôtel Salé ....................105
Hugo, maison
  de Victor....................108
Hugo, Victor
  .............58, 108, 124, 141
Hundred Years War.......382

INDEX

426

# W

# Y

# Z

INDEX

# A rough guide to Rough Guides

In the summer of 1981, Mark Ellingham, a recent graduate from Bristol University, was travelling round Greece and couldn't find a guidebook that really met his needs. On the one hand there were the student guides, insistent on saving every last cent, and on the other the heavyweight cultural tomes whose authors seemed to have spent more time in a research library than lounging away the afternoon at a taverna or on the beach.

In a bid to avoid getting a job, Mark and a small group of writers set about creating their own guidebook. It was a guide to Greece that aimed to combine a journalistic approach to description with a thoroughly practical approach to travellers' needs – a guide that would incorporate culture, history and contemporary insights with a critical edge, together with up-to-date, value-for-money listings. Back in London, Mark and the team finished their Rough Guide, as they called it, and talked Routledge into publishing the book.

That first *Rough Guide to Greece*, published in 1982, was a student scheme that became a publishing phenomenon. The immediate success of the book – with numerous reprints and a Thomas Cook Prize shortlisting – spawned a series that rapidly covered dozens of destinations. Rough Guides had a ready market among low-budget backpackers, but soon also acquired a much broader and older readership that relished Rough Guides' wit and inquisitiveness as much as their enthusiastic, critical approach. Everyone wants value for money, but not at any price.

Rough Guides soon began supplementing the "rougher" information about hostels and low-budget listings with the kind of detail on restaurants and quality hotels that independent-minded visitors on any budget might expect, whether on business in New York or trekking in Thailand.

These days the guides – distributed worldwide by the Penguin Group – offer recommendations from shoestring to luxury and cover more than 200 destinations around the globe, including almost every country in the Americas and Europe, more than half of Africa, and most of Asia and Australasia. Our ever-growing team of authors and photographers is spread all over the world, particularly in Europe, the USA and Australia.

In 1994, we published the *Rough Guide to World Music* and *Rough Guide to Classical Music*, and a year later the *Rough Guide to the Internet*. All three books have become benchmark titles in their fields – which encouraged us to expand into other areas of publishing, mainly around popular culture. Rough Guides now publish:

- Travel guides to more than 200 destinations worldwide
- Dictionary phrasebooks to 22 major languages
- History guides ranging from Ireland to Islam
- Maps printed on rip-proof and waterproof Polyart™ paper
- Music guides running the gamut from Opera to Elvis
- Restaurant guides to London, New York and San Francisco
- Reference books on topics as diverse as the Weather and Shakespeare
- Sports guides from Formula 1 to Man Utd
- Pop culture books from Lord of the Rings to Cult TV
- World Music CDs in association with World Music Network.

Visit **www.roughguides.com** to see our latest publications.

## Rough Guide credits

**Text editor**: Caroline Osborne
**Managing director**: Kevin Fitzgerald
**Series editor**: Mark Ellingham
**Editorial**: Martin Dunford, Jonathan Buckley, Kate Berens, Ann-Marie Shaw, Helena Smith, Olivia Swift, Ruth Blackmore, Geoff Howard, Claire Saunders, Gavin Thomas, Clifton Wilkinson, Alexander Mark Rogers, Polly Thomas, Joe Staines, Richard Lim, Duncan Clark, Peter Buckley, Lucy Ratcliffe, Alison Murchie, Matthew Teller, Andrew Dickson, Fran Sandham, Sally Schafer, Matthew Milton, Karoline Densley (UK); Andrew Rosenberg, Yuki Takagaki, Richard Koss, Hunter Slaton (US)
**Design & Layout**: Link Hall, Helen Prior, Julia Bovis, Katie Pringle, Rachel Holmes, Andy Turner, Dan May, Tanya Hall, John McKay, Sophie Hewat (UK); Madhulita Mohapatra,

Umesh Aggarwal, Sunil Sharma (India)
**Cartography**: Maxine Repath, Ed Wright, Katie Lloyd-Jones (UK); Manish Chandra, Rajesh Chhibber, Jai Prakash Mishra (India)
**Cover art direction**: Louise Boulton
**Picture research**: Sharon Martins, Mark Thomas
**Online**: Kelly Martinez, Anja Mutic-Blessing, Jennifer Gold, Audra Epstein, Suzanne Welles, Cree Lawson (US); Manik Chauhan, Amarjyoti Dutta, Narender Kumar (India)
**Finance**: Gary Singh
**Marketing & Publicity**: Richard Trillo, Niki Smith, David Wearn, Chloë Roberts, Demelza Dallow, Claire Southern (UK); Geoff Colquitt, David Wechsler, Megan Kennedy (US)
**Administration**: Julie Sanderson
RG India: Punita Singh

## Publishing information

This ninth edition published October 2003 by **Rough Guides Ltd**,
80 Strand, London WC2R 0RL
345 Hudson St, 4th Floor,
New York, NY 10014, USA.
**Distributed by the Penguin Group**
Penguin Books Ltd,
80 Strand, London WC2R 0RL
Penguin Putnam, Inc.
375 Hudson St, NY 10014, USA
Penguin Books Australia Ltd,
487 Maroondah Highway, PO Box 257,
Ringwood, Victoria 3134, Australia
Penguin Books Canada Ltd,
10 Alcorn Avenue, Toronto ON,
M4V 1E4 Canada
Penguin Books (NZ) Ltd,
182–190 Wairau Road, Auckland 10,
New Zealand
Typeset in Bembo and Helvetica to an original design by Henry Iles.
Printed in Italy by LegoPrint S.p.A.

448 pp includes index.
A catalogue record for this book is available from the British Library.

ISBN 1843530783

The publishers and authors have done their best to ensure the accuracy and currency of all the information in **The Rough Guide to Paris**; however, they can accept no responsibility for any loss, injury or inconvenience sustained by any traveller as a result of information or advice contained in the guide.

1   3   5   7   9   8   6   4   2

## Help us update

We've gone to a lot of effort to ensure that the ninth edition of **The Rough Guide to Paris** is accurate and up-to-date. However, things change – places get "discovered", opening hours are notoriously fickle, restaurants and rooms raise prices or lower standards. If you feel we've got it wrong or left something out, we'd like to know, and if you can remember the address, the price, the time, the phone number, so much the better.

We'll credit all contributions, and send a copy of the next edition (or any other Rough

Guide if you prefer) for the best letters. Everyone who writes to us and isn't already a subscriber will receive a copy of our full-colour thrice-yearly newsletter. Please mark letters: **"Rough Guide Paris Update"** and send to: Rough Guides, 80 Strand, London WC2R 0RL, or Rough Guides, 4th Floor, 345 Hudson St, New York, NY 10014. Or send an email to **mail@roughguides.com**.

Have your questions answered and tell others about your trip at **www.roughguides.atinfopop.com**.

# Acknowledgements

At Rough Guides, thanks to Caroline Osborne, Claire Saunders and Ann-Marie Shaw; Umesh Aggarwal and Sunil Sharma for picture layout and typesetting; Madhulita Mohapatra for proofreading; Louise Boulton and Mark Thomas for picture research; and Maxine Repath and The Map Studio, Romsey, Hants for the maps.

**Individually the authors would like to thank:**

**Ruth:** Véronique Potelet at the Paris tourist board; Damien Hall, Christine Bokobza, Christine Larson Greveldinger, Sam Mountford, Jean de Cherisey, Sarah Barnes; James, Carole, Loic and Hilary Ratcliff; Gavin Thomas for *une idée géniale*; Fenella Fairbairn for helping me research bookshops and pastries; Susan and Robert Blackmore for being excellent companions on some long walks; and Dylan Reisenberger for cups of tea, helpful criticism and fantastic support.

**James:** Ann-Sophie Ascher, Sarah Barnes, Marjorie Belleguic, Philippe Bourgeois, Brigitte Camus, Marie-Ange Courbel-Foucaut, Claire Fine, Alice Hunt, Christian Hyde, Federica, the Kolev family, Eva Loechner, Niko Melissano, Christopher Miller, Fabrice Petit, César Pigeard de Gurbert, Guillaume Pigeard de Gurbert, Jean-Etienne Rousseau, Richard Scholar, Julia, Otto and Josh Shillingford, Xavier Héraud, and Theodore Zeldin.

# Readers' letters

Thanks to all those readers of the eighth edition who took the trouble to write in with amendments and additions. Apologies for any misspellings or omissions.

Sophie Ariss, Kate Armstrong, Beryl Bâ, Jill Cameron, Jennifer Carter, Mike Clarkson, Darren Cooper, Jane and Lona Duckett, Don Eyres, Ann Feltham, Angela Fidgeon, M. Gill, Louis Hemmings, Robert Hill, Martin H. Hillman, Charlie Hore, Cecile Horkan, Dag Houdmont, John W. Jackson, Vicky Jones, Philip J. Keyte, Heeyun Kim, Drew Landsborough, Matthew Lockley, Jenny Lunnon, John MacClancy, Roberto Manzano, Athalinda McIntosh, Megan McBride, Thad Michael, Julian Shea, Irena Sibrijns, Niki Smith, Jacalyn Soo, Carol Spero, Fay Stevens, Eira Stoner, Tom Veldman, Sue Sun Yom.

# Photo credits

## Cover

Main front Notre Dame © Alamy
Small front top picture © Robert Harding
Small front lower picture, Pompidou Centre
  © Robert Harding
Back top picture, Place de la Concorde
  © Getty
Back lower picture, La Défense © Robert
  Harding

## Colour introduction

Eiffel Tower from Pont Alexandre III
  © James McConnachie
Metro sign © Mark Thomas
Bridges over the Seine
  © Steve J. Benbow/Axiom
The Eiffel Tower at dusk
  © Ian Cumming/Axiom
Busker on the Paris Metro system
  © Mark Thomas
Galerie Véro-Dodat © Dylan Reisenberger
Couple on the banks of the Seine
  © Ian Cumming/Axiom
La Palette © James McConnachie
Art stall, Montmartre © Mark Thomas
Les Invalides © James McConnachie

## Things not to miss

01 Place des Vosges © Dylan Reisenberger
02 The Lady and the Unicorn tapestry
   © James McConnachie
03 Le Champo © James McConnachie
04 Musée Rodin © James McConnachie
05 Musée d'Orsay © James McConnachie
06 Japanese garden, Giverny © James
   McConnachie
07 The Louvre © James McConnachie
08 Disneyland Paris © James McConnachie
09 Palais Royal © Steve J. Benbow/Axiom
10 St-Denis market © James McConnachie
11 Musée Jacquemart-André © Culture
   Espaces

12 The Catacombs © James McConnachie
13 Musée Picasso © James McConnachie
14 Sainte Chapelle © James McConnachie
15 Paris mosque © James McConnachie
16 Galerie du Grand-Cerf © Dylan
   Reisenberger
17 Blue Virgin window, Chartres © James
   McConnachie
18 The Eiffel Tower © Chris Coe/Axiom
19 Men playing chess in Jardin du
   Luxembourg © James McConnachie
20 Bastille Day © Owen Franken/Corbis
21 Marais bars © James McConnachie
22 Versailles © James McConnachie
23 Père-Lachaise Cemetery
   © E. Rowe/Axiom
24 Rollerbladers © Mark Thomas
25 Shopping © C. Bowman/Axiom
26 Brasserie © James McConnachie
27 Pompidou Centre © Ian Cumming/Axiom

## Black and white photos

Looking through Métro window onto station
  platform © Mark Thomas (p.30)
Notre-Dame Cathedral © Mark Thomas
  (p.57)
Statue, Jardin des Tuileries © Dylan
  Reisenberger (p.76)
Rollerskater on Paris boulevard © Mark
  Thomas (p.84)
Musée Picasso © James McConnachie
  (p.106)
Institut du Monde Arabe © James
  McConnachie (p.120)
The Eiffel Tower © James McConnachie
  (p.134)
Montparnasse Cemetery © James
  McConnachie (p.151)
Paris Metro station © James McConnachie
  (p.164)
Sacré Cœur © James McConnachie (p.169)
Versailles © James McConnachie (p.221)

SMALL PRINT

| Key: | 🌐 map | 🄱 phrasebook | ⊙ cd |
|---|---|---|---|

Rough Guides publishes new books every month.

Rough Guides music & reference

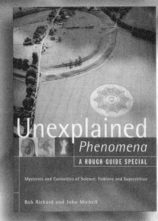

# Rough Guides To A World Of Music

'stick to the reliable Rough Guide series' *The Guardian (UK)*

The music of France is incredibly diverse, with a plethora of styles such as *chanson* and *bal musette* being popular nationwide. Local regions within the country, some with their own languages, are preserving and developing their own musical traditions. The arrival of migrants from all over the former French Empire, and elsewhere, during the last 100 years or so has added new sounds to this mix. *The Rough Guide To The Music Of France* gives you a glimpse of the variety of instruments, vocal styles, influences and dialects, taking you on a musical Tour de France.

THE ROUGH GUIDE TO THE MUSIC OF FRANCE

France

MUSIC ROUGH GUIDE

accordion to Occitan rap: a musical Tour de France

THE ROUGH GUIDE TO PARIS CAFE MUSIC

TAXI PARISIEN

Paris Café Music

MUSIC ROUGH GUIDE

French accordion: bal musette to rock-musette

Take a stroll through the streets of Paris and the music that drifts from the bars and cafés will most likely be *bal musette*, an accordion-based music developed in Paris at the turn of the century. Its more recent incarnation as *rock-musette*, a clever and dynamic mix with *chanson*, gypsy, *manouche* music and rock'n'roll, brings *bal musette* into the twenty-first century. *The Rough Guide To Paris Café Music* traces the history of this music, from its early beginnings to the exciting sound of the emerging Parisian bands.

Hear sound samples at WWW.WORLDMUSIC.NET

Available from book and record shops worldwide or order direct from
World Music Network, 6 Abbeville Mews, 88 Clapham Park Road, London SW4 7BX, U
T. 020 7498 5252  F. 020 7498 5353  E. post@worldmusic.net

# **B**ed *and* **B**reakfast
## in **P**aris

*We offer Bed and Breakfast accommodation in Paris,*
*in prime locations easily accessible by public transport.*

## Price per room, including breakfast

| Room | ☺ ☺ | ☺ ☺ ☺ |
|------|-----|-------|
| 1 person | 46 € | 54 € |
| 2 persons | 59 € | 69 € |
| 3 persons | 77 € | 87 € |

**Apartments (2 - 4 persons) : from 104 €**

\* The number of ☺ depends whether the bathroom is private or not.

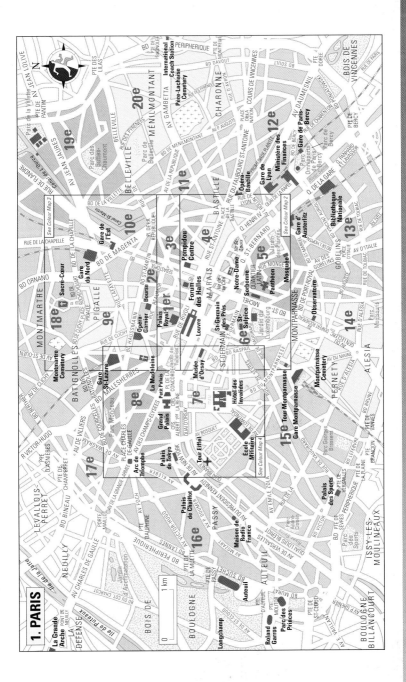

# 1. PARIS

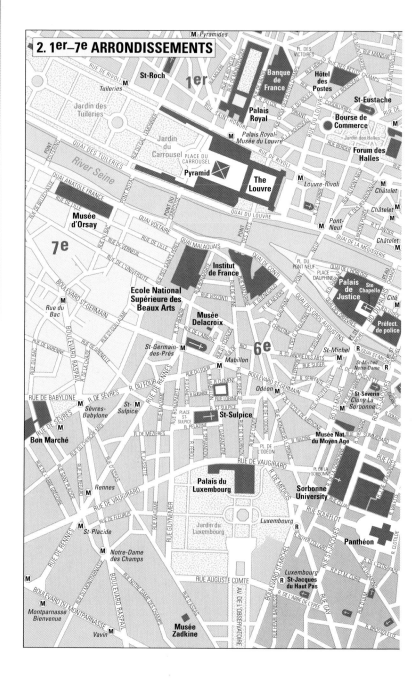

# 2. 1er–7e ARRONDISSEMENTS

**M** Pyramides

St-Roch
**M** Tuileries

**1er**

Jardin des Tuileries

Banque de France

Hôtel des Postes

St-Eustache

Palais Royal

Bourse de Commerce

Jardin des Halles

**M** Palais Royal–Musée du Louvre

Jardin du Carrousel

PLACE DU CARROUSEL

Forum des Halles

**Pyramid**

The Louvre

**M** Louvre-Rivoli

**M** Châtelet

River Seine

**M** Châtelet

QUAI DES TUILERIES

QUAI DU LOUVRE

Pont-Neuf **M**

Châtelet **M**

Musée d'Orsay

**7e**

QUAI DE LA MÉGISSERIE

Institut de France

PL. DU PONT NEUF

PLACE DAUPHINE

Palais de Justice

Ste Chapelle

Cité **M**

Ecole National Supérieure des Beaux Arts

Préfect. de police

**M** Rue du Bac

Musée Delacroix

**6e**

St-Germain-des-Prés **M**

St-Michel **M**

St-Michel/Notre-Dame **R**

Mabillon **M**

St-Séverin Cluny La Sorbonne

**M** Sèvres-Babylone

Odéon **M**

St-Sulpice **M**

PLACE ST-SULPICE

**St-Sulpice**

**Bon Marché**

Musée Nat. du Moyen Age

Rennes **M**

Palais du Luxembourg

Sorbonne University

**M** St-Placide

Jardin du Luxembourg

Luxembourg **R**

Panthéon

Notre-Dame des Champs **M**

Luxembourg **R**

St-Jacques du Haut Pas

RUE AUGUSTE COMTE

Montparnasse Bienvenue **M**

Vavin **M**

Musée Zadkine

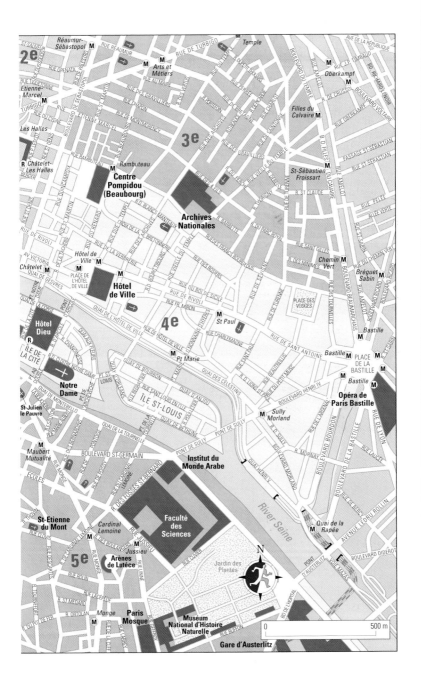

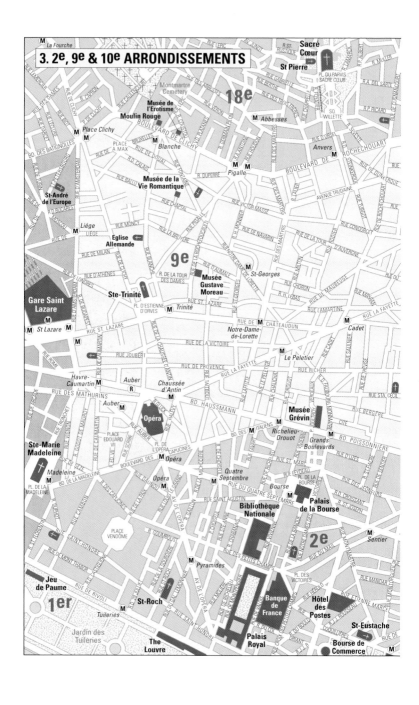
# 3. 2e, 9e & 10e ARRONDISSEMENTS

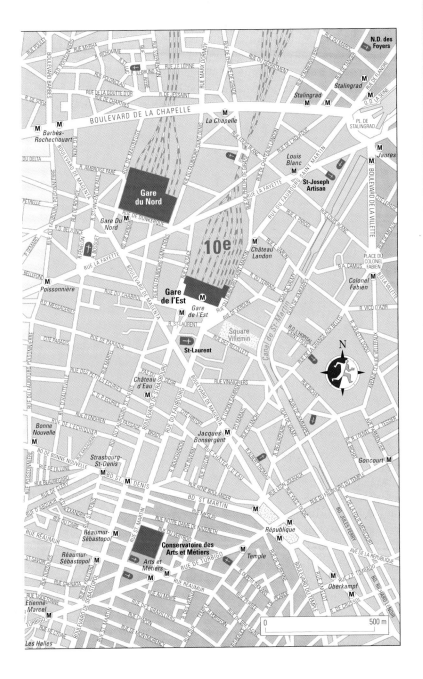

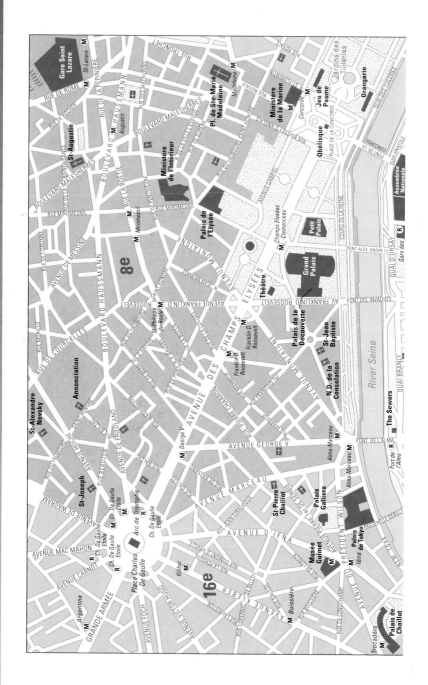

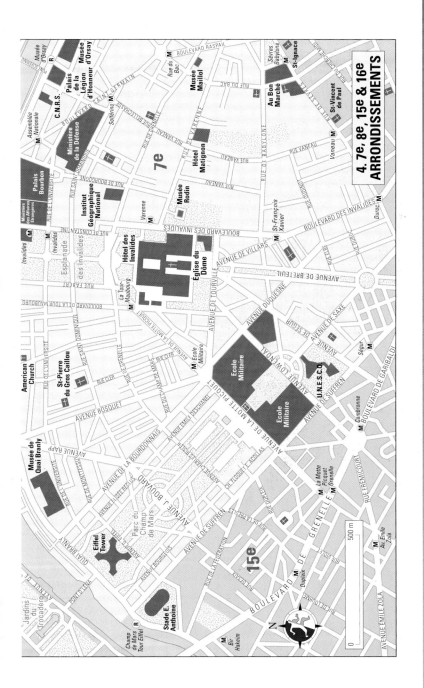

**4. 7e, 8e, 15e & 16e ARRONDISSEMENTS**

# 5. PARIS MÉTRO & RER

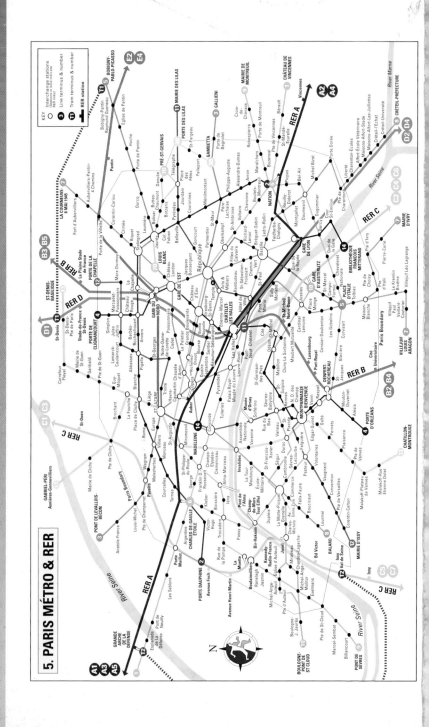